D0555424

Ruby

Developer's Guide

Robert Feldt

Lyle Johnson

Michael Neumann Technical Editor

KEY	SERIAL NUMBER
001	UJG4TFR2T5
002	AKJ7T4MAS4
003	VMERF3854N
004	SGD34BK9HN
005	85DFMU6N7H
006	NFG438GEM4
007	BAQ2HTR46T
008	CV5TR56KMR
009	83N5M4BT6Y
010	GT67FRWFEC

PUBLISHED BY
Syngress Publishing, Inc.
800 Hingham Street
Rockland, MA 02370

The Ruby Developer's Guide

Printed in the United States of America

1 2 3 4 5 6 7 8 9 0

ISBN: 1-928994-64-4

Technical Editor: Michael Neumann
Acquisitions Editor: Catherine B. Nolan
Developmental Editor: Kate Glennon
Cover Designer: Michael Kavish
Page Layout and Art by: Reuben Kantor and Shannon Tozier
Copy Editor: Jesse Corbeil
Indexer: Robert Saigh

Distributed by Publishers Group West in the United States and Jaguar Book Group in Canada.

Acknowledgments

We would like to acknowledge the following people for their kindness and support in making this book possible.

Richard Kristof and Duncan Anderson of Global Knowledge, for their generous access to the IT industry's best courses, instructors, and training facilities.

Ralph Troupe, Rhonda St. John, and the team at Callisma for their invaluable insight into the challenges of designing, deploying and supporting world-class enterprise networks.

Karen Cross, Lance Tilford, Meaghan Cunningham, Kim Wylie, Harry Kirchner, Kevin Votel, Kent Anderson, and Frida Yara of Publishers Group West for sharing their incredible marketing experience and expertise.

Mary Ging, Caroline Hird, Simon Beale, Caroline Wheeler, Victoria Fuller, Jonathan Bunkell, and Klaus Beran of Harcourt International for making certain that our vision remains worldwide in scope.

Annabel Dent of Harcourt Australia for all her help.

David Buckland, Wendi Wong, Marie Chieng, Lucy Chong, Leslie Lim, Audrey Gan, and Joseph Chan of Transquest Publishers for the enthusiasm with which they receive our books.

Kwon Sung June at Acorn Publishing for his support.

Ethan Atkin at Cranbury International for his help in expanding the Syngress program.

Jackie Gross, Gayle Vocey, Alexia Penny, Anik Robitaille, Craig Siddall, Darlene Morrow, Iolanda Miller, Jane Mackay, and Marie Skelly at Jackie Gross & Associates for all their help and enthusiasm representing our product in Canada.

Lois Fraser, Connie McMenemy, and the rest of the great folks at Jaguar Book Group for their help with distribution of Syngress books in Canada.

Technical Editor's Acknowledgements

I'd like to thank the Syngress staff for their support, and John Small, who encouraged me in overseeing the writing of this book. I'd like to thank Matz for creating such a wonderful language; Dave and Andy for two really great books about programming in general, and Ruby; Kentaro Goto for his tutorial that directed me three years ago to Ruby; and Hiroshi Nakamura for many valuable comments and explanations about SOAP4R. Finally, thank you to the team of Merlin.zwo for being patient with me, as well as to the whole Ruby community for letting me participate in such a great development.

Contributors

Jason Wong is the Chief Executive Officer of ionami design, a Web development and design firm headquartered in Berkeley, CA. His responsibilities include developing and maintaining client relationships, project management, application development and support, and operations management. Previously, he managed all aspects of 3dfxgamers.com, the 3dfx interactive community Web site. Jason holds a bachelor's degree from the University of California at Berkeley. He would like to thank Joyce, Ted and Tim, and his parents for all their support.

Lyle Johnson is a Software Team Leader at ResGen, Invitrogen Corporation in Huntsville, AL. Prior to his employment at ResGen, Lyle served as Group Leader for Graphical User Interface Development at CFD Research Corporation. Lyle has worked primarily in commercial software development for computational fluid dynamics and bioinformatics applications, but has also managed and contributed to a number of open-source software projects.

Lyle holds a bachelor's degree in Aerospace Engineering from Auburn University and a master's of Science degree in Aerospace Engineering from the Georgia Institute of Technology. He currently lives in Madison, AL with his wife, Denise.

Jonothon Ortiz is Vice President of Xnext, Inc. in Winter Haven, FL. Xnext, Inc. is a small, privately owned company that develops Web sites and applications for prestigious companies such as the New York Times Company. Jonothon is the head of the programming department and works together with the CEO on all company projects to ensure the best possible solution. Jonothon lives with his wife, Carla, in Lakeland, FL.

Robert Feldt is a Software Engineering Researcher at Chalmers University of Technology in Gothenburg, Sweden. His professional interest is in how to produce robust, reliable software. Robert's research focuses on what can be learned from applying the complex but robust systems found in nature to tools and methods for developing and testing software. Robert also teaches courses on software engineering to students in the Computer Science and Computer Engineering programs at Chalmers University.

Robert holds a master's degree from Chalmers University and is a member of the IEEE. He has previously worked as a consultant software engineer. He programs mostly in C, Haskell, and Ruby and uses Ruby frequently in his research since its dynamic nature allows him to easily test new ideas. He is working on a number of larger Ruby projects, including the Rockit compiler construction toolkit and the RubyVM project, to build a set of plug-and-play components for assembling Ruby virtual machines.

Robert currently resides in Gothenburg, Sweden with his wife, Mirjana, and daughter, Ebba. He wants to acknowledge them for their support and love.

Stephen Legrand (Ph.D.) has both an academic and commercial background. He was a post-doctoral fellow at MIT and has lectured both mathematical and computer science related subjects at the university level. He has taught graduate and undergraduate courses in such diverse areas as assembly language, automata theory, computability, discrete mathematics, computer graphics, and in mathematical subjects such as differential equations, advanced calculus, financial mathematics, and model theory. In addition, Stephen has over 10 years of software development expertise in such areas as fixed income derivatives, interest rate modeling, artificial intelligence, and telecommunications. He has authored computer graphics engines, computer chess games, option pricing engines, cellular propagation models, and workflow management systems. He is currently consulting on the IRROS project and on J2EE-related technologies in the Washington, DC area.

Technical Editor and Contributor

Michael Neumann is a Database and Software Developer for Merlin.zwo InfoDesign GmbH in Germany (near Stuttgart). He is also studying computer science at the University of Karlsruhe. Merlin.zwo develops large-scale database applications based on Oracle products. With more than 10 years of experience in software development, Michael has specialized in many different domains, from system–near programming, administration of Unix systems, and database development with several RDBMSs, to OOA/OOD techniques, and design and implementation of distributed and parallel applications. One of his greatest interests lies is the design principles of programming languages. Before he was employed at Merlin.zwo, he was a Database/Web Developer and Principal of Page-Store.

Contents

Ruby's design philosophy is known as the Principle of Least Surprise. That means that Ruby works the way that you expect it to work. The more you develop with Ruby, the more you're going to realize that you're spending time producing code—real code which works, is readable, and solves the problems at hand.

Chapter 2
GUI Toolkits for Ruby   43

Master the Grid Layout Manager

**Answers to Your Ruby
Database Questions**

Q: Using Ruby/DBI, I
have set the tracing
level to *2* and
output to standard
error, but nothing
happened. What's
wrong?

A: You may have
forgotten to require
the *dbi/trace* file at
the top of your
program.

Chapter 4
XML and Ruby   **211**

REXML has the following advantages:

1. It is written 100 percent in Ruby.
2. It can be used for both SAX and DOM parsing.
3. It is small—approximately 1845 lines of code.
4. Methods and classes are in easy-to-understand English.

Chapter 5
Web Services and Distributed Ruby   261

Monitoring TCP/IP Based Services

We can monitor Web services, or any TCP/IP-based client and server, by using a very simple monitor application that comes with XML-RPC for Ruby or TCPSocketPipe (available from the Ruby Application Archive [RAA]).

Chapter 7
Miscellaneous Libraries and Tools   **423**

**Dynamically Generating
XML with eruby**

You can also generate
XML with eruby and
mod_ruby. This is useful,
for example, if you want
to deliver XML to the
browser, which then (on
the client-side) invokes an
XSLT script to transform it
to HTML. Not many
browsers support this; in
fact only Microsoft's
Internet Explorer can do
this for certain.

NOTE

There are basically two types of libraries, those written in pure Ruby, and those that are C extensions to Ruby. Generally, pure Ruby extensions only require being on the search path. The C extensions to Ruby are usually installed by unzipping or untarring, and then at the command line typing **ruby extconf.rb**, which builds a Makefile.

Chapter 8
Profiling and Performance Tuning   515

A Process for Program Optimization

1. Question the need!
2. Look at the big picture!
3. Find the hot-spots!
4. Check structure and data!
5. Dig deep!
6. Know your Ruby environment and use it wisely.

Writing C/C++ Extensions

- Ruby alone may not provide the speed or functionality required for your Ruby applications. When this is true, you can write extension modules in C or C++ that look like regular modules to the Ruby interpreter.
- Ruby's C API provides a wide variety of functions that assist extension writers in defining modules, classes, and constants, and converting back and forth between C and Ruby datatypes.

Foreword

If you define efficiency as the ruler for the success of a language, Ruby should be one of the very first languages to come to mind. The introduction of Ruby to the programming world has astounded developers with its ability to simply make programming fun again. Ruby frees programmers to concentrate on the problem at hand, creating fewer obstacles than other languages. In Ruby, ideas flow directly into the code.

Even though Ruby is very effective, there's still a deficit of written documentation and tutorials about deploying it for real world applications. Deployment usually requires knowledge in one or more of these fields:

- Graphical User Interfaces (GUIs)
- Distributed Computing and Networking
- Accessing Databases
- Processing and Transforming XML
- Text-Processing and Parsing
- WWW-based Applications
- Profiling and Performance Tuning
- Connecting with other Languages, Extending, and Embedding

This is why we wrote this book. We hope it helps you become more a more productive programmer with Ruby—and that you have fun reading it and performing the examples.

Why Ruby?

With its clean object-oriented (OO) programming model (*everything is an object*) and its solid foundation, it is one of the simplest-to-use and most powerful OO languages. Ruby unifies many positive features of other languages, for instance :

- Strong dynamic typing; no need to declare variables

- Exceptions

- Closures, code-blocks, and iterators as found in Smalltalk, Sather, or CLU

- A powerful yet easy-to-use object-oriented class library, designed with the "principle of least surprise" in mind, and with several design patterns included (for example, Delegator, Observer, Visitor, and Singleton)

- A comfortable, familiar syntax, which is a mixture of elements from C++, Eiffel, Perl, and Python.

- Arbitrary precise integers with automatic conversion to and from fixed-sized integers

- Mark-and-sweep Garbage Collectors and a simple C-API for extending and embedding Ruby

- Lightweight threads and continuations

- Built-in regular expressions

Sweetened with a healthy amount of syntax, Ruby applications have the potential of being more concise and condensed than (or at least the same length as) an equivalent application written in Perl (or Python), as well as being easier to read, maintain, and learn—not to mention that it's much more fun to program!.

Who Should Read This Book?

This book will not serve as an introduction to Ruby, but more as an extension of existing books about Ruby programming, so we expect that the reader has gathered a certain degree of knowledge and experience with Ruby before reading this. Nevertheless, newcomers to Ruby who have even a basic understanding of the language may find it very useful to fortify their knowledge by studying many of the examples. Learning by doing is the best way to *really* learn a language. In addition, of course, readers of any level will be aided in exercising their natural interests in discovering new ideas and entertaining different and creative ways to solve existing problems!

Content of this Book

Ruby is a rapidly evolving language. Every few months, new projects are started and existing ones are being shaped and improved; we have accepted this challenge by providing a snapshot of the current state of development and encouraging you to look into the continuing evolution.

Chapter 1: *Booting Ruby* provides the basics of getting started by explaining Ruby syntax, and about working with applications and editors.

Chapter 2: *GUI Toolkits for Ruby* develops a sample application (a XML viewer) with four different GUI toolkits available for Ruby: Tk, Gtk, Fox, and VRuby.

Chapter 3: *Accessing Databases with Ruby* introduces you to programming with Ruby/DBI, a unique database-independent interface for accessing many relational databases; it covers Ruby/ODBC as well as other data storage solutions like CSV or Berkeley DBM-like file databases.

Chapter 4: *XML and Ruby* takes a look at some of the more popular parsing options available for Ruby and XML, including SAX and DOM, and open source parsers XMLParser, NQXML, and REXML.

Chapter 5: *Web Services and Distributed Ruby* describes and explains how to use the two XML-based communication protocols (XML-RPC and SOAP) from Ruby as well as how to connect two or more Ruby applications across a network using Distributed Ruby (DRb).

Chapter 6: *WWW and Networking with Ruby* develops a Web-based, database-driven online-shop application, comparing a CGI/FastCGI approach with the utilization of mod_ruby and eruby, and using Interpreted Objects for Web Applications (IOWA), Ruby's powerful application server.

Chapter 7: *Miscellaneous Libraries and Tools* explores Ruby extensions, which are either written in pure Ruby or are Ruby wrappers around C code, and compares them for ease of install, easy to read, and easy to customization and development.

Chapter 8: *Profiling and Performance Tuning* examines how to improve performance by looking at your overall algorithm, and how to analyze its complexity by using the ordo notation as a tool or by using a profiler such as RbProf; other solutions include result caching.

Chapter 9: *Parser Generators* looks at the options and benefits in producing a parser by writing it manually versus using a parser generator that will generate a parser from the grammar.

Chapter 10: *Extending and Embedding Ruby* explains how and why you might write a Ruby extension module in C/C++.

About the Web Site

The Syngress Solutions Web Site contains the code files that are used in specific chapters of this book. The code files for each chapter are located in a "chXX" directory. For example, the files for Chapter 6 are in ch06. Any further directory structure depends on the projects that are presented within the chapter.

It will be extremely useful for you to have the applications and tools included in these files on hand, however, because many of them are still evolving, within the chapters you will be able to find mention of other online sources, such as the Ruby Application Archive, from which you can obtain updates to the very latest versions.

 Look for this icon to locate the code files that will be included on our Web site.

## Chapter 1

Booting Ruby

Solutions in this chapter:

- **An Overview of Ruby**
- **Installing Ruby and its Tools**
- **A Short Syntax Style Guide**
- **Dangerous Ruby**
- **Comparing Ruby**
- **Convincing Management to Use Ruby**

☑ **Summary**

☑ **Solutions Fast Track**

☑ **Frequently Asked Questions**

Introduction

Programming should be like driving a good car: Buttons are clearly labeled and easy to reach; you're comfortable as soon as you get inside; there are always a couple of nuances, but soon, the machine becomes an extension of yourself; you zig, you zag, and you always get where you're going. Welcome to the Porsche of programming languages. Perhaps you come from the world of C++ or Java, but would like something easier on the eyes and the fingers. Perhaps you program in Perl, and would like to avoid bending over backwards for re-usability. Congratulations, you've found Ruby, an object-oriented language that's easy to write and easy to read.

Ruby usage is growing daily. For instance, Ruby is spreading like wildfire in Japan, ever since Yukihiro 'Matz' Matsumoto's posting of version 0.95 on Japanese domestic newsgroups. There, Ruby surpasses Python in popularity. In 2000, technical references began introducing and championing Ruby to the English-speaking markets as an alternative programming language, and Ruby growth became an international phenomenon. By adding Ruby to your language repository, you join a burgeoning rank of developers that know an easier, faster, and more enjoyable way to get the job done.

An Overview of Ruby

Ruby's design philosophy is known as the Principle of Least Surprise. That means that Ruby works the way that you expect it to work. The more you develop with Ruby, the more you're going to realize that you're spending time producing code. Real code, which works, is readable, and solves the problems at hand. Less time in the debugger, less time spent in setup—hence, the Principle of Least Surprise. Ruby, the vast majority of the time, works intuitively.

From this design philosophy comes a pure, powerful and simple object-oriented programming language. We like to believe that Ruby takes many of the best features from other languages and blends them together very, very well.

Ruby derives much of its object-oriented system from Smalltalk: All data structures are objects, allowing you to perform methods on them. Furthermore, you can add methods to a class or instance during runtime. Like Java or Smalltalk, Ruby features *single inheritance*. Because multiple inheritance sometimes leads to an almost mystic inheritance determination, single-inheritance reduces the chance for pilot error. If you miss multiple inheritance, you can import methods from multiple classes using modules, also known as *mixins*.

The open source nature of Ruby makes it free for anyone's use. Because of this, you are free to modify it. Many people have taken license to make Ruby a cross-platform language, so while primary development occurs on Unix, Ruby ports exist for a number of different platforms, including BeOS, DOS, MacOS, Win32, and many flavors of Unix, including Solaris and FreeBSD. Furthermore, Ruby's Application Programming Interface (API) is written in C. This enables straightforward extension writing with C.

Ruby's *dynamic typing* saves time and creates a more flexible design structure. In a static language, such as Java or C++, you must declare your variable types, which requires setup time. Ruby is smart enough to know "hello" is a string, 2.0 could be a double, and 2 is an integer. Furthermore, Ruby doesn't require explicit declaration of its internal representation. Fixnum, which is an integer type for small numbers, automatically converts to Bignum when it gets sufficiently large. Furthermore, dynamic typing allows for design changes without changing types across the program, as the interpreter makes type decisions during runtime.

An automatic mark-and-sweep garbage collector cleans all Ruby objects without needing to maintain a reference count; you won't have memory leaks, and this results in fewer crashes. With languages such as C++, you have to release allocated memory. However, Ruby flushes dynamically-allocated storage through program execution, and has periods set to reclaim memory.

Installing Ruby and its Tools

Your first step into Ruby starts with its home on the Web, which is at www.ruby-lang.org (Figure 1.1). You'll find the source tarball for stable and development versions, various links to documentation, commentary, the Ruby Application Archive (RAA), and more. You can download and install Ruby in less than 15 minutes. Some tools will be more or less complex, depending on size and their individual dependencies on other files. MySQL and PostgreSQL interfaces will require their respective databases, for instance.

Andrew Hunt and Dave Thomas (known as the *Pragmatic Programmers*) maintain www.rubycentral.com (Figure 1.2). This site contains the binary installation of Ruby, various articles, links, an FAQ and an online version of their book, *Programming Ruby: A Pragmatic Programmer's Guide*.

Figure 1.1 The Ruby Language Home Page

Figure 1.2 The RubyCentral Home Page

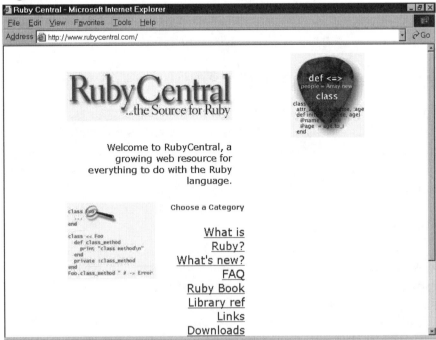

Installing Ruby on Unix

Adding Ruby to your Unix development toolbox is a snap. In the following sections, we'll show you how to download Ruby through various distribution mechanisms, and take you through the installation procedure. If you install anything through source, this is about as easy as it gets.

Installing Ruby from Source Code

For those of you that like to play with the latest stable and development versions, get the latest code drop using the Concurrent Versioning System (CVS), File Transfer Protocol (FTP), or by downloading it from Ruby's homepage. As the source uses less than 1 megabyte of hard drive space, you can get the Ruby source in less than five minutes over a 56k modem.

FTP Installation

FTP requires a client application. Standard distributions come with an FTP client installed. The commands used in a Unix FTP installation can be seen in Figure 1.3.

Figure 1.3 Unix FTP (or Windows DOS-based FTP) Commands

```
ftp ftp.ruby-lang.org
User: anonymous
Password: youremail@yourdomainname
binary
cd pub/ruby
ls
get ruby-x.tar.gz (latest version)
```

While some versions of Windows come with an FTP client, we suggest downloading Bullet Proof FTP (shareware) or LeechFTP (freeware) from www.download.com.

1. Set up your FTP client to log into ftp.ruby-lang.org, User: *anonymous*, Password: *youremail@yourdomainname*.

2. Change to directory pub/ruby.

3. Choose the latest version of Ruby for download: *ruby-x.tar.gz* (make sure you download it as binary).

After having downloaded the Ruby archive, unpack it and change into the newly created directory:

```
tar -xvzf ruby-1.6.6.tgz
cd ruby-1.6.6
```

Then configure and compile it:

```
./configure
make
```

Finally, install it with:

```
su -l root            # become a root user
make install
exit                  # become the original user again
```

After installation, see if you can start Ruby by issuing the following command on the command-line:

```
ruby --version
```

This should output the version of the installed Ruby interpreter; on my system this is revealed as a Unix version.

```
ruby 1.6.4 (2001-06-04) [i386-netbsd]
```

If you have problems with the Ruby interpreter or one of its libraries, write an e-mail to Ruby's mailing list and include this version output.

CVS Installation

By using CVS, you can get the latest and greatest version of Ruby. Be forewarned that this version is usually *not* stable, as it is a development version.

You can use either the Web or a CVS client. To access CVS via the Web, go to www.ruby-lang.org/cgi-bin/cvsweb.cgi/ruby. At the bottom of the page, there is a link to download the directory as a tarball or Zip archive. Download that directory, as well as the *doc, ext, lib, misc, sample,* and *win32* directories. Proceed with the downloaded tarballs in the same way as for the FTP installation except that you have to execute **autoconf** just before executing **./configure**.

To use a CVS client, check out the development version using the following two commands:

```
cvs -d :pserver:anonymous@cvs.ruby-lang.org:/src login
```

```
(Logging in to anonymous@cvs.ruby-lang.org)
CVS password: anonymous
cvs -z4 -d :pserver:anonymous@cvs.ruby-lang.org:/src co ruby
```

After that, change into the *ruby* directory in which CVS downloaded all files, and issue the **autoconf** command. Then proceed the same way as for the FTP installation.

Installing from Packages

Some prefer to do source installations, as that offers access to the latest source; and occasionally, packages get a little sticky with where directories are placed and such. That being said, there's no easier way to get Ruby onto your system than through a ready-made package.

Red Hat 7.2 currently ships with Ruby 1.6.4. You can download a Red Hat distribution from ftp.redhat.com. The **rpm –i rubyx.x.** command installs without a hitch.

FreeBSD and NetBSD ports (OpenBSD currently has only Ruby 1.4.6 in its port collection) of the newest Ruby interpreter are available through their port collections, as well as many other Ruby related packages.

The current stable branch of Debian Linux contains an older version of Ruby (currently 1.4.3), and will install and configure that version for you. Testing branches currently contain 1.6.3, and unstable versions will offer you the latest installation.

Installing Ruby on a Windows System

On Windows, the easiest possible installation option is to use the Pragmatic Programmer's binary release.

Grab the latest ruby-x.exe file at www.rubycentral.com/downloads/ruby-install.html. This double-click installation includes the Ruby interpreter, a required Cygwin DLL, documentation, and Tk and FOX support. If you run Windows 9x or above, we highly recommend using this package. It makes installation as simple as clicking the **Next** button a few times and you will be up and running with Ruby in minutes.

If you use Windows and absolutely, positively must have the latest version, the install process requires a few extra steps. You must first download Cygwin, which is a Unix environment for Windows.

1. Download Cygwin: Go to http://sources.redhat.com/cygwin and click **Install Cygwin Now**. The setup process will give you a number of files

to download. You should install everything, just in case. For this installation you should have copious amounts of hard disk space, but if you don't, you can remove files at your discretion (you *must* keep bash, GCC, and the basic Cygwin files).

2. Download the Ruby source via FTP or CVS.

3. Create an instance of Cygwin.

4. Change to the Ruby source directory where you've unpacked the Ruby sources.

5. Use standard Unix compile, configure, and install commands:

```
./configure
make
make install
```

If you use Windows 9x, add the following lines to your c:\autoexec.bat:

```
set PATH="D:\(ruby install directory)\bin;%PATH%"
```

Windows NT/2000 users need to modify their registries.

1. Click **Control Panel** | **System Properties** | **Environment Variables**.

2. Under **System Variables**, select **Path** and click **EDIT**.

3. Add your Ruby directory to the end of the Variable Value list and click **OK**.

4. Under System Variables, select **PATHEXT** and click **EDIT**.

5. Add **.RB** and **.RBW** to the Variable Value list and click **OK**.

Installing Applications and Libraries from RAA

If you program in Ruby for any length of time, you will need to know about the Ruby Application Archive (RAA), which is at www.ruby-lang.org/en/raa.html (see Figure 1.4). As fun as it is to write everything from scratch, save yourself some time by using libraries and applications written by other Ruby developers. The RAA contains a comprehensive list of links to Ruby applications in various stages of development. After you develop and find a place to host your application, you can add your Ruby application to the RAA by submitting your entry at www.ruby-lang.org/en/raa-entry.rhtml.

1. The RAA gives easy access to a wealth of applications and libraries. Many applications install painlessly, and attached README files provide

detailed instructions. For this example, we're going to use RubyUnit, which is a testing framework. If you use Extreme Programming, RubyUnit provides similar functionality to JUnit or SUnit (For more information on Extreme Programming, visit www.xprogramming.com). Download RubyUnit from the RAA in the Library section under *devel*.

2. Extract the file to your hard drive

```
tar -xvzf rubyunit-x.x.x.tar.gz
```

3. Install the application, in this case, the following:

```
cd rubyunit-x.x.x
ruby install.rb
```

Other Ruby packages may use a Ruby configuration script to grab parameters before installing. The *extconf.rb* installation procedure is fairly straightforward. After untarring your package, do the following:

```
ruby extconf.rb
make
make install
```

Figure 1.4 The Ruby Application Archive

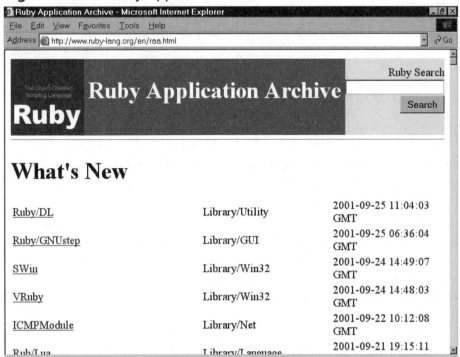

Getting Help

The Ruby community quickly responds to questions from both the uninitiated and advanced. If you pore through this text and the README file associated with the library or module you're using, and still encounter problems, Ruby users from around the world will answer your questions quickly.

First, perform a quick search through newsgroups to see if your question has already been asked and answered. www.ruby-talk.org contains a complete archive of posts to the English-based comp.lang.ruby and Ruby's mailing-list. Google also provides an easy-to-use archive of the Ruby newsgroup (although it contains about 5,000 fewer of the early messages) at http://groups.google.com/groups?hl=en&group=comp.lang.ruby. Polite questions draw a response within hours, if not minutes. As an alternative, the #ruby-lang channel on DALnet provides immediate satisfaction. You receive near-immediate responses to your questions. However, an order of magnitude fewer users exist at any one time in IRC than those that chat through the newsgroups/mailing-list.

IDE and Editor Support in Ruby

Your choice of editor has a direct effect on productivity, as there are strengths and weaknesses to every editor. While some developers stick with Windows' Notepad for its speed and simplicity, it doesn't support syntax highlighting, macros, and a host of other modern editor features. Invest time early to find a powerful editor that you like, get familiar with it, and learn to take advantage of the shortcuts. Build macros to save yourself time. This advice remains true regardless of what language you use for development.

Editor support for Ruby depends on the capabilities of the editor. At a minimum, your editor should support Ruby syntax highlighting, a way for your editor to help you differentiate between keywords in your program and increase its readability. Some editors, such as Emacs, allow "shells" to run Ruby, or Ruby applications on code within your editor.

Emacs

Configurability often comes at the cost of simplicity. Such is the case with
Emacs, an editor with a steep learning curve, but great opportunities to extend,
customize, and optimize to your development style.

Grab the latest version at ftp.gnu.org/gnu/emacs, or the Windows version at
ftp.gnu.org/gnu/windows/emacs/latest. With a little elbow grease, you can set up
Emacs for Ruby support:

1. Drop the elisp files (inf-ruby.el ruby-mode.el) into the emacs\lisp directory of your choice. For this example, I drop them into d:\emacs\lisp.

2. Add the code in Figure 1.5 to your .emacs file (located in your home
   directory).

Figure 1.5 Emacs Code to Add Ruby Support

```
(autoload 'ruby-mode "ruby-mode"
  "Mode for editing ruby source files")
(setq auto-mode-alist
   (append '(("\\.rb$" . ruby-mode)) auto-mode-alist))
(setq interpreter-mode-alist (append '(("ruby" . ruby-mode))
          interpreter-mode-alist))


(autoload 'run-ruby "inf-ruby"
  "Run an inferior Ruby process")
(autoload 'inf-ruby-keys "inf-ruby"
  "Set local key defs for inf-ruby in ruby-mode")
(add-hook 'ruby-mode-hook
   '(lambda ()
    (inf-ruby-keys)
))
```

If you enjoy tweaking Emacs, other Ruby developers have listed extensions
that they have written at www.rubygarden.org/ruby?EmacsExtensions. The page
is in Wiki format, so if you tweak Emacs, you can add your own extensions to
the list.

VIM

VIM (Vi IMproved) is straightforward and loads quickly, and its little brother, vi, is available on almost all Unix machines. If you're a Windows user, or you just haven't grown up on vi, you may not appreciate VIM's edit and command mode structures.

Download VIM at www.vim.org. VIM 5.7 and above support Ruby syntax highlighting.

Other Editors

For those budding Ruby enthusiasts who want more "Windows-like" editors, there are a number of alternatives. If you've grown up on Notepad, you may want to try TextPad. For a commercial editor, Visual SlickEdit is another powerful alternative that receives rave reviews in the press.

Other editors that support Ruby include NEdit, JEdit, CodeWright, Kate, and JED. There is a list of Ruby editors with extensions at the RAA. Perform a find on *Editor*, and the various Ruby extensions for editors will be listed.

TextPad

A low priced and powerful Notepad replacement for Windows, TextPad loads quickly and has a simple and straightforward interface. TextPad is shareware; there is a 30-day trial available at www.textpad.com, and you can purchase a single-user license online for $16.50.

You add Ruby support through the Ruby syntax file at www.textpad.com/add-ons/ntsyn.html.

Visual SlickEdit

If you prefer commercial packages, Visual SlickEdit (www.slickedit.com) wins high marks and comes with excellent documentation and, of course, commercial support. The primary disadvantage to using SlickEdit is its high price tag ($295 US), especially when compared to the free Emacs and VIM.

To add Ruby Syntax highlighting, use the code found at www.rubygarden.com/ruby?VisualSlickEditExtensions.

RubyWin

RubyWin is a Ruby Integrated Development Environment (IDE) for Windows. The Ruby binary installation, by Andy Hunt, supplies a version of RubyWin. You can also grab the latest version at the RAA in the Aplication section under *IDE*. This application provides syntax highlighting, buffer evaluation, the Interactive Ruby (discussed later), multiple window displays, line counts, and more. As RubyWin comes fully configured to take advantage of Ruby tools, it's a pretty decent place to start.

Ruby Development Environment (RDE)

Another Windows IDE is the Ruby Development Environment (RDE), by Sakazuki (see Figure 1.6). Features include file tabs, syntax highlighting, debugger support, and more. You can get RDE at the RAA in the Application section under *IDE*.

Figure 1.6 The RDE IDE

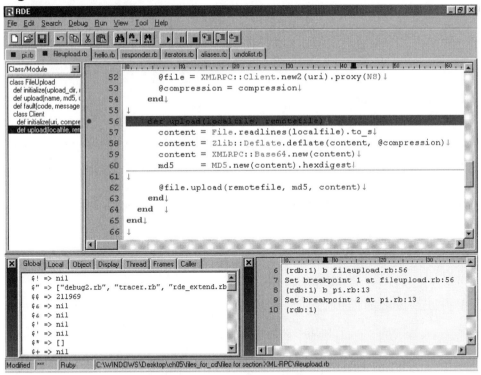

Additional Tools a Rubyist Must Have

While the RAA contains every known Ruby tool available, there are a couple with which you should get familiar immediately: Ri, IRb, and debug.rb.

Ruby Interactive (Ri)

The Ruby Interactive reference (or *Ri*) gives quick access to definitions, and method names. Download Ri at www.pragmaticprogrammer.com/ruby/downloads/ri.html. This proves invaluable when looking at other people's source code, when you need to view certain libraries, or when you are writing your own application and you can't remember a method name or usage.

Adding a macro that allows use of Ri from within your text editor provides an additional level of convenience. For VIM, add the following code (Figure 1.7) to your .vimrc:

Figure 1.7 .vimrc File Modifications

```
function Ri()
let b:x = system("ri '" . input("ri: ") . "' > /tmp/ri_output")
sp /tmp/ri_output
endfunction


map <F2> :call Ri()<CR>
```

Pressing **F2** lets you input a class name, method, etc. and shows Ri's output in a new window.

For information on a class or method, just call *ri* with it as argument:

```
ri Array
```

This results in the following output:

```
----------------------------------------------------------------------
    class: Array
----------------------------------------------------------------------
    Arrays are ordered, integer-indexed collections of any object.
    Array indexing starts at 0, as in C or Java. A negative index is
    assumed relative to the end of the array—that is, an index of -1
    indicates the last element of the array, -2 is the next to last
    element in the array, and so on.
----------------------------------------------------------------------
    &, *, +, —, <<, <=>, ==, ===, [], [], []=, assoc, at, clear,
```

```
collect, collect!, compact, compact!, concat, delete, delete_at,
delete_if, each, each_index, empty?, eql?, fill, first, flatten,
flatten!, include?, index, indexes, indices, join, last, length,
map!, new, nitems, pack, pop, push, rassoc, reject!, replace,
reverse, reverse!, reverse_each, rindex, shift, size, slice,
slice!, sort, sort!, to_a, to_ary, to_s, uniq, uniq!, unshift, |
------------------------------------------------------------------
```

If you see a method that about which you need more information, you can enter its class followed by a # and the method name, as done below:

ri "Array#collect"

This results in the following:

```
------------------------------------------------------ Array#collect
    arr.collect {| obj | block } -> anArray
------------------------------------------------------------------

    Returns a new array by invoking block once for every element,
    passing each element as a parameter to block. The result of block
    is used as the given element in the new array. See also
    Array#collect!.
      a = [ "a", "b", "c", "d" ]
      a.collect {|x| x + "!" }   #=> ["a!", "b!", "c!", "d!"]
      a                #=> ["a", "b", "c", "d"]
```

To add Emacs support, follow the directions within Ri's /contrib/csteele or /contrib./dblack/emacs directory.

GtkRi (Figure 1.8) is a graphical version of Ri, available at http://bocks.dhs.org/~pizman/myri. GtkRi offers extra browsing functionality, such as hyperlinks, tree view, and navigation buttons. This application (for Unix systems running X) requires Ruby/Gtk, Ri, and Gtk.

Interactive Ruby (IRb)

Interactive Ruby (IRb) provides a shell for experimentation (see Figure 1.9). Within the IRb shell, you can immediately view expression results, line by line. Grab the latest version at www.ruby-lang.org/en/raa-list.rhtml?name=irb+-+interactive+ruby or use the version that comes by default with Ruby.

Figure 1.8 GtkRi

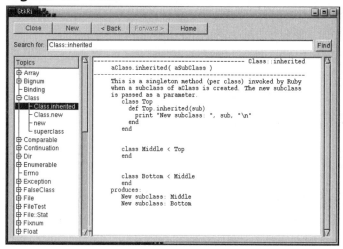

Figure 1.9 An Interactive Ruby Session

```
irb 0.6.1(99/09/16)
irb(main):001:0> 1+1
2
irb(main):002:0> def hello
irb(main):003:1>    out = "Hello World"
irb(main):004:1>    puts out
irb(main):005:1> end
nil
irb(main):006:0> hello
Hello World
nil
irb(main):007:0>
```

The latest versions of IRb include tab completion, a feature that allows you to save even more time. The following:

```
irb(main):001:0> al<tab>
```

completes the word as:

```
alias
```

Even better, pressing the **Tab** key in the following situation:

```
irb(main):001:0> a = "aString"
irb(main):002:0> a.u<tab>
```

outputs all applicable methods for the object referred by variable *a*:

```
a.unpack   a.untaint   a.upcase   a.upcase!   a.upto
```

To activate the tab completion module, start IRb with:

```
irb -r irb/completion
```

Debugging Ruby Applications with debug.rb

Ruby comes with a debugger included. To debug a Ruby program, simply start it with the **–r debug** option:

```
ruby -r debug applicationToDebug.rb
```

Suppose we have two files: test.rb (Figure 1.10) and pi.rb (Figure 1.11) that we want to debug (not really *debug*, because there are no errors in them, but we want to have a look at how they work).

Figure 1.10 File test.rb

```
require "pi"


arr = []


pi { |d|
  arr << d
  break if arr.size > 10
}
```

Figure 1.11 File pi.rb

```
def pi
  k, a, b, a1, b1 = 2, 4, 1, 12, 4
  loop do
    # Next approximation
```

Continued

Figure 1.11 Continued

```
    p, q, k = k*k, 2*k+1, k+1
    a, b, a1, b1 = a1, b1, p*a+q*a1, p*b+q*b1
    # Print common digits
    d = a / b
    d1 = a1 / b1
    while d == d1
      yield d
      a, a1 = 10*(a%b), 10*(a1%b1)
      d, d1 = a/b, a1/b1
    end
  end
end
```

Let's start by invoking the debugger:

ruby -r debug test.rb

Debug.rb

Emacs support available.

test.rb:1:require "pi"

At first, we display the debugger's help by typing **h** (or **help**) followed by a carriage return. This gives us the following output:

(rdb:1) **h**

Debugger help v.-0.002b

Commands

```
  b[reak] [file|method:]<line|method>
                              set breakpoint to some position
  wat[ch] <expression>        set watchpoint to some expression
  cat[ch] <an Exception>      set catchpoint to an exception
  b[reak]                     list breakpoints
  cat[ch]                     show catchpoint
  del[ele][ nnn]              delete some or all breakpoints
  disp[lay] <expression>      add expression into display expression list
```

```
undisp[lay][ nnn]              delete one particular or all display
                                   expressions
c[ont]                         run until program ends or hit breakpoint
s[tep][ nnn]                   step (into methods) one line or till
                                   line nnn
n[ext][ nnn]                   go over one line or till line nnn
w[here]                        display frames
f[rame]                        alias for where
l[ist][ (-|nn-mm)]             list program, - lists backwards
                                   nn-mm lists given lines
up[ nn]                        move to higher frame
down[ nn]                      move to lower frame
fin[ish]                       return to outer frame
tr[ace] (on|off)               set trace mode of current thread
tr[ace] (on|off) all           set trace mode of all threads
q[uit]                         exit from debugger
v[ar] g[lobal]                 show global variables
v[ar] l[ocal]                  show local variables
v[ar] i[nstance] <object>      show instance variables of object
v[ar] c[onst] <object>         show constants of object
m[ethod] i[nstance] <obj>      show methods of object
m[ethod] <class|module>        show instance methods of class or module
th[read] l[ist]                list all threads
th[read] c[ur[rent]]           show current thread
th[read] [sw[itch]] <nnn>      switch thread context to nnn
th[read] stop <nnn>            stop thread nnn
th[read] resume <nnn>          resume thread nnn
p expression                   evaluate expression and print its value
h[elp]                         print this help
<everything else>              evaluate
```

Then we type **l** (or **list**) to show the current executed line (preceded by =>) together with the 5 lines before and after it.

```
(rdb:1) 1
[-4, 5] in test.rb
```

```
=> 1   require "pi"

   2

   3   arr = []

   4

   5   pi { |d|
```

But we want to see the whole program, so we specify the range of numbers to be shown:

```
(rdb:1) 1 (1-10)
[0, 10] in test.rb
=> 1   require "pi"

   2

   3   arr = []

   4

   5   pi { |d|
   6      arr << d
   7      break if arr.size > 10
   8   }
```

Okay, now let's add a break point at the *pi* method of file pi.rb, and let the program run until a break or watch-point is reached, or until it exits:

```
(rdb:1) b pi.rb:pi
Set breakpoint 1 at pi.rb:pi
(rdb:1) c
Breakpoint 1, pi at pi.rb:pi
./pi.rb:1:def pi
```

As you see, the program has reached our defined breakpoint. Once again we type **l** to see where we are:

```
(rdb:1) l
[-4, 5] in ./pi.rb
=> 1   def pi
   2      k, a, b, a1, b1 = 2, 4, 1, 12, 4
   3      loop do
   4         # Next approximation
   5         p, q, k = k*k, 2*k+1, k+1
```

We manually execute the next few lines:

```
(rdb:1) n
./pi.rb:2:   k, a, b, a1, b1 = 2, 4, 1, 12, 4
(rdb:1) n
./pi.rb:5:      p, q, k = k*k, 2*k+1, k+1
(rdb:1) n 5
./pi.rb:10:      while d == d1
(rdb:1) s
./pi.rb:11:        yield d
```

and list the local variables by typing **v1** (or **var local**):

```
(rdb:1) v 1
  a => 12
  a1 => 76
  b => 4
  b1 => 24
  d => 3
  d1 => 3
  k => 3
  p => 4
  q => 5
```

Next, we move one line forward to list where we are in the program again:

```
(rdb:1) n
test.rb:6:  arr << d
(rdb:1) l
[1, 10] in test.rb
    1  require "pi"
    2
    3  arr = []
    4
    5  pi { |d|
=>  6    arr << d
    7    break if arr.size > 10
    8  }
```

At this position, we add a watchpoint that interrupts the execution if its expression evaluates as *true*. In our case this is the last iteration of the code block. After that, we continue to run the program.

```
(rdb:1) watch arr.size > 10
Set watchpoint 2
(rdb:1) c
Watchpoint 2, toplevel at test.rb:7
test.rb:7:  break if arr.size > 10
```

As you can see, our watchpoint caused the program to halt. We output the local variables and print the length of the variable *arr*:

```
(rdb:1) v l
  arr => [3, 1, 4, 1, 5, 9, 2, 6, 5, 3, 5]
  d => 5
(rdb:1) arr.size
11
```

That's all for now, so we leave the debugger by typing **q** (or **quit**).

```
(rdb:1) q
Really quit? (y/n) y
```

A Short Syntax Style Guide

Ruby style, with a few exceptions, follows standard guidelines for readability. This style guide is derived from Ruby code from numerous libraries. By following this guide, your code will be more readable, and allow other engineers to learn from your work more quickly. For additional style tips, consult www.rubygarden.com/ruby?RubyStyleGuide.

Using Comments

Source files should begin with comments that list class name, copyright, author name, filename, version number, date and time of last change, and license terms.

```
# StringReplace
# $Id: stringreplace.rb, v 1.0 10/15/01 20:05:17$
# Copyright © 2001, Jason Wong
# You can redistribute and/or modify it under the same term as Ruby
```

You may also use

```
=begin
Block of comments here
=end
```

Make sure trailing comments are far enough from the code that it is easily distinguished. If more than one trailing comment exists in a block, align them:

```
@counter      # keeps track times page has been hit
@siteCounter # keeps track of times all pages have been hit
```

should be:

```
@counter     # keeps track times page has been hit
@siteCounter # keeps track of times all pages have been hit
```

Naming

Classes and modules begin with an upper case letter. This is actually enforced by Ruby's interpreter. Each word in a class name begins with an upper case (unless it's part of an acronym):

```
module Observable
module ParseDate
class StringInputMethod
class StringReplace
class XMP
```

Method names start with a lower case letter

```
def sqrt
def abs
def puts
def getValue
```

Core Ruby library methods generally separate their names' parts with an underscore rather than upper case letter on the second word:

```
get_value
```

versus:

```
getValue
```

Iterators

For one line code blocks, use braces ({...}):

```
5.times {|i| puts i}
```

For iterators that use multiple lines, use *do...end*:

```
5.times do |i|
  puts i
  puts Math.sqrt(i)
end
```

Optionally, you may want to place a space between the pipes (|) and the variable names:

```
5.times do | i |
  puts i
end
```

Indentation, Spacing, Parentheses

Code begins at the far left with no indents. Sub–indents are usually two spaces.

Put parentheses (**()**) around all complex expressions or expressions that start with parentheses. This saves later confusion so the Ruby parser won't act in a manner different than what you expect. Look at the following two lines of code:

```
puts ((2+5) * 4))
puts (2+5) * 4
```

The former command results in *28* (the expected answer), while the latter yields an undefined method for *nil* (*NameError*).

Ruby takes the numbers between the parentheses as part of a parameter list. However, ** 4* is not part of the parameter list, and is applied on the return value of *puts*, which is *nil*, yielding the undefined method error.

Don't create white space ( ) where it may throw you off. For instance, don't put white space between a method and the parentheses enclosing its parameters.

```
Math.sqrt (6+3) * 9
```

The above results in *27*, where you may have been expecting *9*.

For clarity, it is better to rewrite the code as follows:

```
Math.sqrt(6+3) * 9
```

For the results of the square root of 6 + 3 ★ 9, place a parenthesis around the entire equation.

Dangerous Ruby

Ruby makes it easy to create a lot of functional code in a short period of time. However, there are some instances where you must be explicit and take care to avoid errors.

Local Variables versus Methods

If a local variable exists with the same name as a method, the local variable will be used unless you put parentheses behind the method or use *self.methodName*.

```
def colors(arg1="blue", arg2="red")
    "#{arg1}, #{arg2}"
end


colors = 6
print colors
```

The above outputs *6*. If you were expecting to use the *color* method, you might have been surprised. Using parentheses, in this case, would yield the desired result:

```
def colors(arg1="blue", arg2="red")
    "#{arg1}, #{arg2}"
end


colors = 6
print colors("purple", "chartreuse")
```

This outputs:

```
purple, chartreuse
```

More Whitespace Issues

You need to ensure that you use whitespace properly when using methods, as extra whitespace can result in errors.

```
def countdownLength= length
def countdownLength=(length)
def countdownLength= (length)
def countdownLength= ( length )
```

The above works fine, while this:

```
def countdownLength = (length)
```

results in a parse error, because the whitespace before the equal sign makes it part of the method name.

Block Local Variables

Be careful to keep variables in the scope for which they are intended. Not doing so will yield in unexpected results. Here's a particularly nasty one:

```
i = 0
while i < 10
  ...
  [1,2,3].each {|i| ... } # i gets overwritten here
  i += 1
end
```

While we intended the *i* within the *each* iterator to stay in its own scope, it actually overwrote the *i* in the *while* loop, resulting in an endless loop.

Comparing Ruby

Ruby has its roots in several different languages, including Smalltalk, Perl, and Eiffel. It puts together some of the best features of each, and along with Matz's ingenuity, forms a cohesive unit. By looking at Ruby in relation to Java and Perl, we will showcase these features and ease your transition into this wonderful language.

Java

Java makes all the programming headlines these days. Sun brought its brainchild to prominence in a flurry of public relations and marketing, and if you don't see Microsoft Visual Tools in an enterprise deployment, you'll probably see Java. Today, in many computer science curriculums, Java replaces C and C++ for first year introductory courses.

Java simplifies development for enterprise computing. Basic language features, object-orientation, single inheritance, garbage collection, (somewhat) cross platform development, and especially Sun's heavy marketing gives Java an edge in terms of sheer usage; if you use Java, you're going to find a lot of commercial and open source support, especially with regards to networking and Web development.

There are quite a few similarities between Java and Ruby: they're both cross-platform, meaning they'll run across MacOS, Windows, and the various Unices (FreeBSD, Unix, and Solaris, for instance). However, because Java is a closed system that requires a native interpreter, it doesn't exist on many platforms, and even on some more popular OSes (like FreeBSD), the Java environment is non-native (it uses a Unix emulation layer) and is also over a year old. With an open source platform like Ruby, people are free to port to their hearts' desire. The latest versions compile straight away on many flavors of Unix, and even less popular platforms, such as BeOS, have versions of Ruby running on them.

They both have strong support for error handling. They're both multi-threaded. However, Ruby features light-weight threads that are built into the interpreter, while Java uses native threads. Lightweight threads are far more portable than native (Ruby features threads even on plain DOS), and are superior in some situations.

Here's the Ruby code for creating 1000 threads that sleep:

```
print "Create 1000 Threads..."
1000.times do
  Thread.new { sleep }
End
puts "done"


# do some calculations
```

And here is the same in Java:

```
public class Test implements Runnable {

  public static void main(String[] args) {
    System.out.print("Create 1000 Threads...");
    for (int i=0; i<=1000; i++) {
      Thread th = new Thread(new Test());
      th.start();
```

```
    }
    System.out.println("done");

    // do some calculations
  }

  public void run() {
    try {
      Thread.currentThread().sleep(100000);
    } catch (InterruptedException e) {}
  }
}
```

If you are coming from the world of Java, picking up Ruby will be easy. The following example is a simple *string replace* application in Java. Ruby has strong string processing, which is derived from Perl. Because of this, the same application can be as small as half a dozen lines, depending on how you write it in Ruby.

You will, however, notice a few major differences. Java code requires a byte code compilation. The Java byte code is parsed by an interpreter before being run on the computer. Ruby, on the other hand, is a so-called *scripting language*, so the interpreter reads the Ruby script directly to run on the computer, or more precisely, Ruby creates an abstract syntax tree that it then executes.

Java is object oriented. However, unlike Ruby, it is not fully object oriented. As stated earlier, data is an object in Ruby, whereas in Java, this is not true. For example, strings are objects with methods (see Figure 1.12).

Figure 1.12 Performing an Operation on a String in Ruby

```
puts "Hello".length   # => 5
```

Finally, Java is *statically typed*. This means that all variables must be declared with a known type at the compile time. Ruby, on the other hand, uses *dynamic typing*. You won't have to declare whether a variable is an Array, String, or Integer before you start using it.

Let's take a simple example in which Ruby beats Java hands-down. Being strongly influenced by Perl, Ruby excels at regular expressions. The

StringReplace program (Figure 1.13) takes a search word, a replacement word, and the document for replacement.

Figure 1.13 The Java Version of StringReplace

```java
import java.io.*;

public class StringReplace {

  static void searchAndReplace( Reader in, Writer out, String search,
                                    String replace ) throws IOException
  {
    int si = 0;

    for ( int c = in.read(); c >= 0; c = in.read() ) {
      if ( c == search.charAt( si ) ) {
        si++;
        if ( si >= search.length() ) {
          out.write( replace );
          si = 0;
        }
      } else {
        if ( si > 0 ) {
          for ( int i = 0; i < si; i++ ) {
            out.write( search.charAt( i ) );
          }
          si = 0;
        }

        out.write( (char) c );
      }
    }
  }

  public static void main( String[] args ) {
```

Continued

Figure 1.13 Continued

```java
int     ai = 0;
String search = args[ ai++ ];
String replace = args[ ai++ ];

for ( ; ai < args.length; ai++ ) {
  try {
    String          fileName = args[ ai ];
    FileReader      in = new FileReader( fileName );
    StringWriter    buf = new StringWriter();

    try {
      searchAndReplace( in, buf, search, replace );
    } finally {
      in.close();
    }

    FileWriter out = null ;
    try {
      out = new FileWriter( fileName );
      out.write( buf.toString() );
    } finally {
      if ( out != null )
        out.close();
    }
  } catch ( Exception e ) {
    e.printStackTrace();
  }
}
}
}
```

Invoke the Java StringReplace by compiling it into bytecode and then running it through the JRE.

```
javac StringReplace.java
java StringReplace blue red blue.txt
```

The Java version of StringReplace requires 50 lines of code. There are a couple ways to write the Ruby version (see Figure 1.14).

Figure 1.14 Ruby Version of String Replace

```
def stringReplace(searchString, replaceString, fileName)
  # read the file content
  aFile = File.open(fileName, "r")
  aString = aFile.read
  aFile.close

  # replace/substitute ...
  aString.gsub!(searchString, replaceString)

  # write string back to file
  File.open(fileName, "w") { |file| file << aString }
end


stringReplace(*ARGV)
```

You may compact this even further:

```
def stringReplace(searchString, replaceString, fileName)
  # read file content
  aString = File.readlines(fileName).to_s

  # replace/substitute ...
  aString.gsub!(searchString, replaceString)

  # write string back to file
  File.open(fileName, "w") { |file| file << aString }
end


stringReplace(*ARGV)
```

Invoke the Ruby version with:

```
ruby stringreplace.rb blue red blue.txt
```

That's 6 lines, for starters. While we crushed the Java version in both length and readability, you can do this all on the command line if you don't mind a little verbosity:

```
ruby -pi -e "gsub('blue', 'red')" blue.txt
```

Perl

In Perl, Larry Wall created a great language to make simple projects easy. Perl is great for creating short scripts and getting the job done quickly. However, on larger projects, with multiple developers, it can quickly become a tangled mess, and the syntax quickly becomes confusing.

Ruby derives many concepts from Perl. Both are interpreted languages, and they share similar syntax. Regular expressions are a mainstay of both Perl and Ruby, and this makes both strong text processors.

The Perl version of the StringReplace program (see Figure 1.15) maintains Ruby's brevity, but you'll notice that while the syntax is similar, it's a bit more confusing.

Figure 1.15 Perl Version of StringReplace

```
foreach $file (glob($ARGV[2])) {
    open (FILE, "+<$file"), @contents = <FILE>, seek(FILE, 0, 0);
    foreach $line (@contents) {
        $line =~ s/\Q$ARGV[0]\E/$ARGV[1]/g, print FILE $line;
    }
}
```

Perl has a similar one-liner for command line use. Note that the command line options **–pi** and **–e** are the same in both Ruby and Perl.

```
perl -pi -e 's/blue/red/g'
```

Language Constructs

If you're coming from the land of Java or Perl, you'll notice significant differences in the way that the languages are structured. The following is a brief overview of their differences from Ruby in terms of major features.

Object-Oriented Programming

Java and Ruby were designed from the ground up for object-oriented programming (OOP), whereas Perl was a procedural language up until Perl 5, when OO features were added. Let's start by looking at how Ruby, Java, and Perl inherit from other classes.

Inheritance

There are some major differences in the way the three languages inherit objects. Java and Ruby were built from the ground up to support object-oriented programming, and as such, simplify development substantially.

Perl directly supports multiple inheritance. Packages that act as classes inherit methods of the inherited class. To resolve namespace clashes or determine which method to use , the package first inherits from the *blessed* class. If it doesn't exist, the package then inherits the first method in a left to right order.

```
package Square;

@ISA = qw( Shape Geometry )
```

Java uses single inheritance. This is meant to reduce the chances of programmer error by simplifying the development process. In the case where an object should inherit from two or more super classes (*ball* is both a *RoundObject* and *SportsItem*), there are interfaces, but no real way to implement methods from multiple classes.

```
class Square extends Shape
```

At first glance, Ruby supports single inheritance.

```
class Square < Shape
```

Ruby's modules provide a method for mixing in (*mixins*) methods from multiple classes, giving Ruby the functional equivalent of multiple inheritance without the namespace clashing, which saves us from many potential problems.

```
class Shape
  def randomMethod

  ...

  end
end


module Geometry
```

```
  def randomMethod
    ...
  end
end


class Square < Shape
  include Geometry

    ...

end
```

The Java equivalent of a module (or namespace) is a *package*. Packages allow the creation of class collections and access to the associated functionality.

```
package Shapes;

public class Square
{
//definition
}
```

To utilize the package, you would do this:

```
import Shapes.Square;
public class SquareUsage {
    Square firstSquare = new Square(5.0);
}
```

Access Control

Ruby access control keywords are the same as in Java, however, the meanings are slightly different. Additionally, unlike Java, access control in Ruby is determined dynamically at run time.

In both Ruby and Java, *public* methods are open for use from anywhere by default. In Ruby and Java, *private* methods cannot be called from outside the object. *Private* is the strictest form of access control in Ruby. Protected methods are only accessed by objects that are defined by the class and subclasses in Ruby, while Java's protected methods are accessible from classes within the same package and sub-classes from anywhere. The following example shows how private, protected, and public methods are declared in Ruby and Java.

In Ruby:

```
class RubyAccessControl
# methods are public by default
     def default()end
# private, protected, and public keywords declare the access control of
# the methods following them
     private
     def privateMethod()end
     protected
     def protectedMethod()end
     def secondProtectedMethod()end
     public
     def publicMethod()end
```

In Java

```
class JavaAccessControl {
# Method access control is declared immediately preceding each method
    public void publicMethod() {…}
    private void privateMethod() {…}
    protected void protectedMethod() {…}
```

Arrays and Hashes

The construct for Arrays and Hashes in each of the three languages are fairly similar. The main differences among the three languages are syntactical. With Java, type declaration is required, while variable type is declared in front of the array's name in Perl and Ruby (see Table 1.1).

Table 1.1 Array Constructs

Language	Array Construct
Java	int[] odds = {1, 3, 5, 7};
Perl	@odds= (1, 3, 5, 7);
Ruby	odds = [1, 3, 5, 7]

Hashes

Hash tables are a collection of key-value pairs. Hashes in Perl and Ruby are con-structed similarly to Arrays (see Table 1.2). A mapping is indicated by the use of =>.

Table 1.2 Hash Constructs

Language	Hash Construct
| Java | ```
Hashtable antonyms = new Hashtable();
antonyms.put("clean", "dirty"));
antonyms.put("black", "white");
numbers.put("fall", "fly");
System.out.println(antonyms.get("clean"));   #=> dirty
``` |
| Perl | ```
%antonyms = ( 'clean' => 'dirty', 'black' => 'white', 'fall' =>
      'fly', 'evil' => 'good' );

print antonyms{'clean'};   # => dirty
``` |
| Ruby | ```
antonyms = { 'clean' => 'dirty', 'black' => 'white', 'fall' =>
      'fly', 'evil'=> 'good' }

print antonyms['black']      # => white

antonyms.type                # => Hash
``` |

Iterators

In Ruby, an iterator is a method that yields control to a passed code block using *yield* or *Proc#call*.
```

```
antonyms = { 'clean' => 'dirty', 'black' => 'white', 'fall' => 'fly',
            'evil' => 'good' }


antonyms.each { |i| print i }
```

The closest Perl equivalent to this is a *foreach* loop or function *map*.

```
%antonyms = ( 'clean' => 'dirty', 'black' => 'white', 'fall' => 'fly',
            'evil' => 'good' );


# using foreach loop...


foreach $i (keys %antonyms) {
  print $i;
}


# or using function map...


map {print} keys %antonyms;
```

Java iterators work over collections. While Perl and Ruby can iterate over arrays, arrays are not collections in the way a hash table would be.

```
Hashtable h;
Iterator i = h.iterator();
while (i.hasNext()) {
  System.out.println(i.next());
}
```

Convincing Management to Use Ruby

Convincing the boss to use Ruby might not be an easy task. You'll hear all of the old excuses: Ruby is too new, why learn another language, we've built all this code on *x*, and so forth. Of course, at some point, most of the world was on Fortran—then C, and then Java. Same excuses, different eras. Ruby doesn't spend money to evangelize its effectiveness, relying instead on the passion of its development community. Unfortunately, passion doesn't buy analyst reports or public relations. That being said, your boss's job is to make you productive, and passion begets productivity. Present the benefits and convince him of the large efficiency gains, and you should be able to use Ruby at work, perhaps even creating a few converts along the way!

In a Perl shop, convincing management to use Ruby is a bit easier. You're probably running a Unix variant, and management is already using an open-source language. On the other hand, Perl is a language with a fairly long history and a large library (www.cpan.org). When taking your case up to the top, don't forget to mention the rapidly-growing RAA. Because of the similarities between the two languages, you, and anyone else on board, can get pretty familiar within a couple of days. Selling aspects should definitely include re-usability through object-oriented development and the readability of Ruby syntax.

Your boss needs real-world examples of Ruby? There's a page dedicated to it: See www.rubygarden.com/ruby?RealWorldRuby. Companies like Lucent use Ruby for their third generation wireless telephony products; a research group within Motorola uses Ruby to post and generate data for a simulator. For more public Web sites, the newsgroup gateway at www.ruby-talk.org is based on 200 lines of Ruby code! That is a testament to the ease of developing Ruby applications.

Many programming "thought leaders" are involved with Ruby. Extreme Programming gurus, such as Kent Beck and Ron Jeffries, have been spotted in the comp.lang.ruby newsgroups. The Pragmatic Programmers, Andrew Hunt and Dave Thomas, are regulars on the newsgroups and in the #ruby-lang IRC channel. Also, they have written the popular introduction, *Programming Ruby*.

To encourage a transition, you are going to need buy-in from your boss. Start small. This project shouldn't entail a lot of risk, and if possible, can be leveraged into larger projects. Look first at the Ruby Application Archive. As easy as writing Ruby code is, it's even easier if the code is written for you. If you need to re-use legacy code, there are extensions for Perl, Python and Java. Next, develop Ruby tools that aid development on your company's base language. The Lucent project created over 150,000 lines of C++ source code! Template generators, maintenance scripts, and the like can get you into the Ruby groove, and give you a taste of what's possible.

Summary

Ruby's beauty stems from its basis on the Principle of Least Surprise. With this guiding principle, Yukihiro 'Matz' Matsumoto created an easy to use, open source, object-oriented programming language.

Ruby, and every known Ruby application, is posted at www.ruby-lang.org and www.ruby-lang.org/en/raa.html. You can install most applications by decompressing them and following the instructions provided in the README file. Make sure that you grab Ri, and become familiar with IRb.

There are many editors to choose from. Make sure that you choose an editor with which you feel comfortable and can be efficient. It should cover all basic editor commands (cut, copy), and language-specific features (syntax highlighting, etc).

You can experience frustrating troubles for quite a while if you don't know what problems to look for. Some areas prone to error are due to extra whitespace, blocking, and forgetting to specify the use of a method when a local variable with the same name exists.

Ruby is a lot closer to Perl than Java in terms of syntax. Ruby code tends to be more terse than Java code, and much more readable than Perl. While all three languages are object-oriented, their implementations vary widely, from inheritance to the exact definition of an object.

Solutions Fast Track

An Overview of Ruby

- ☑ Everything in Ruby is an object. If you can see something (such as a variable), you can perform an operation on it.

- ☑ Ruby is an open source programming language. If you're interested in making changes to the language or porting it to another operating system, the source is openly available to you.

- ☑ There are many features designed to make programming easier, including garbage collection and dynamic typing.

Installing Ruby and its Tools

- ☑ Read the README. It will get you through most installations without a hitch.

- ☑ If all else fails, go online. Search the comp.lang.ruby newsgroup first, and then either post there, or ask on #ruby-lang (on IRC) for helpful advice.

- ☑ Get an editor and spend time to make yourself an expert at it. Make sure that it supports syntax highlighting, and from there, build macros that make your life easier.

A Short Syntax Style Guide

- ☑ Classes and modules begin with upper case letters.

- ☑ For one line iterators use {…}; for multiple-line iterators, use *do…end*.

- ☑ Code begins with no indents; sub-indent, 2 spaces. Place parentheses around all complex expressions or expressions that start with parentheses.

Dangerous Ruby

- ☑ If a local variable exists with the same name as a method, the local variable will be used by default unless you put parentheses behind the method or use *self.methodName*. Make sure you specify whether you intend to use the method or local variable if both share the same name.

- ☑ Block local variables. This keeps variables from operating out of their intended scope.

Comparing Ruby

- ☑ Java code tends to spend a lot of time in setup, which is part of the reason Java programs tend to be much larger than Ruby programs.

- ☑ Ruby and Perl share some syntax similarities, and both have strong regular expression support. Ruby code tends to be cleaner, and therefore more maintainable.

Convincing Management to Use Ruby

- ☑ Bring Ruby into the workplace slowly. Start with smaller projects.

- ☑ There are a number of examples where companies such as Motorola and Lucent are using Ruby. Have a look at www.rubygarden.com/ruby?RealWorldRuby.

Frequently Asked Questions

The following Frequently Asked Questions, answered by the authors of this book, are designed to both measure your understanding of the concepts presented in this chapter and to assist you with real-life implementation of these concepts. To have your questions about this chapter answered by the author, browse to **www.syngress.com/solutions** and click on the **"Ask the Author"** form.

Q: Where are the increment/decrement (**++** and **--**) operators?

A: Matz left out pre-post increment/decrement operators due to the lack of object-oriented semantics (see newsgroup: 2001-08-01 02:51:12 PST [ruby-talk:18951]).

Q: I'm a Windows developer, and I'm not particularly fond of being tied to Cygwin. What are my alternatives?

A: You can compile Ruby with mingw or Visual C++. For mingw, make sure you *./configure –enable-shared i386-mingw*.

Q: I love this language, and I want to get more involved in the Ruby Community! What's the next step I can take?

A: There are a number of ways to contribute. Starting user groups, evangelism, and writing a book are good ways. For those who are a little bit less extroverted, take a look at CPAN (Comprehensive Perl Archive Network). You'll notice that it's much larger than the RAA. Try working with someone on a Ruby module (you might want e-mail someone on the newsgroups or someone who's developed a module on the RAA), or start a module completely on your own. As Ruby's application base grows, so grows the community.

Chapter 2

GUI Toolkits for Ruby

Solutions in this chapter:

- Using the Standard Ruby GUI: Tk

- Using the GTK+ Toolkit

- Using the FOX Toolkit

- Using the SWin/VRuby Extensions

- Other GUI Toolkits

- Choosing a GUI Toolkit

☑ Summary

☑ Solutions Fast Track

☑ Frequently Asked Questions

Introduction

Although Ruby is an excellent tool for writing low-level scripts for system administration tasks, it is equally useful for writing end-user applications. And because graphical user interfaces (GUIs) are a must for modern end-user applications, you need to learn how to develop GUIs for Ruby. One of the benefits of Ruby programming that you've no doubt come to appreciate is that it enables rapid application development. In contrast to the time-consuming *code-compile-test* cycle of traditional programming languages, you can quickly make changes to your Ruby scripts to try out new ideas. This benefit becomes all the more evident when you start developing GUI applications with Ruby; it's both instructive and rewarding to build up the user interface incrementally, adding new elements and then re-running the program to see how the user interface has changed as a result.

You may already know that the standard Ruby source code distribution includes an interface to Tk, which is an established cross-platform GUI toolkit. If you peruse the Ruby Application Archive (RAA) however, you'll quickly discover that there is a large number of other GUI toolkit choices for use with Ruby (www.ruby-lang.org/en/raa.html). Why wouldn't you want to stick with Tk if it's the standard? Well, as you work through this chapter you'll learn about some of the considerations that might prompt you to look at alternatives. Like all software, these packages are in various stages of development: some are new and unstable, while others are older and quite robust, but most fall somewhere in-between. Most of the GUI toolkits for Ruby are cross-platform, meaning that applications built around them will work on multiple operating systems, while others are targeted towards a single operating system.

Every GUI toolkit has its own unique feel and feature-set, but there are some things that are true of almost any GUI toolkit with which you may work:

- GUI applications are event-driven. Many programs you'll write proceed from start to finish in a very predictable path, and for a given set of inputs they'll produce the same outputs with little or no user intervention. For example, consider a Ruby script written to process a large number of text files in batch mode, perhaps updating selected text in those files. Such a program will always produce the same results for a given set of input files, and it does so without any user intervention.

In contrast, event-driven programs spend most of their time waiting for user inputs (events) that drive the program's flow.

- Every toolkit has its own way of communicating these user interface events to your application code, which boils down at some point to your registering certain functions with the toolkit to "handle" the event.

- GUI toolkits consist of a large number of basic user interface objects (called *widgets*), like buttons, labels and text fields, as well as more complex widgets, like spreadsheets, calendars or text editors.

- User interface windows are constructed using a "parent-child" composition; the top-level main window contains one or more child windows; each child window may in turn contain child windows; and so on. This is an application of the *Composite* pattern, in that operations applied to parent windows (such as hiding it) usually affect the window's children as well (they are hidden as well).

- GUI toolkits offer one or more geometry (or layout) management options for arranging child windows (or widgets) inside other container windows.

The purposes of this chapter are to introduce some of the most popular GUI toolkits for Ruby, demonstrate how some of the common GUI programming idioms discussed above are implemented, and help you decide which might be the best choice for your applications. To do this, we'll first describe a simple application that has a lot of features and functionality that you would use in any GUI application. Then we'll take a look at how you would develop this application in each of the GUI toolkits. Along the way, we'll discuss other related topics, such as how to download, compile and install the toolkit on your system, and auxiliary tools (such as GUI builders) that can make application development with that GUI toolkit easier. Sources for additional information and resources can be found in the discussion of each respective toolkit.

Using this Book's Sample Applications

For each of the four major toolkits covered (Tk, GTK+, FOX and SWin/VRuby) we'll develop a similar sample application so that you can easily identify the similarities and differences among the toolkits while learning how to use them. The application is a simple XML viewer that uses Jim Menard's NQXML module as its document model, so you'll need to obtain and install that extension before you can actually run the sample applications on your system. For your convenience, this book provides the source code for each of the four sample applications at www.syngress.com/solutions:

- **tk-xmlviewer.rb** is the Ruby/Tk version of the sample application;

- **gtk-xmlviewer.rb** is the Ruby/GTK version of the sample application;

- **fxruby-xmlviewer.rb** is the FXRuby version of the sample application;

- **vruby-xmlviewer.rb** is the VRuby version of the sample application.

To give you a head start on developing your own GUI applications, the user interface for this application will demonstrate the following common features:

- Displaying a menu bar, with several pull-down menus and choices for opening XML files or quitting the application.

- Using common dialog boxes, like a file-open dialog, to request information from the user.

- Using geometry-layout managers to automatically arrange widgets.

- Using various widgets to display the XML document nodes (or entities) and their attributes.

Using the Standard Ruby GUI: Tk

The standard graphical user interface (GUI) for Ruby is Tk. Tk started out as the GUI for the Tcl scripting language developed by John Ousterhout in the mid-eighties, but has since been adopted as a cross-platform GUI by all of the popular scripting languages (including Perl and Python). Although Tk's widget set is a bit limited as compared to some of the more modern GUIs, it has the unique distinction of being the only cross-platform GUI with a strong Mac OS port.

Obtaining Tk

One of the primary advantages of using Tk with Ruby is that, because it is the standard, it's very easy to get started. Developing GUI applications with Ruby/Tk requires both a working installation of Tk itself as well as the Ruby/Tk extension module.

You're welcome to download the source code for Tk from the Tcl/Tk home page at www.tcltk.org and build it yourself, but precompiled binaries for Tk are available for most operating systems (including Linux and Microsoft Windows). To make life even easier, if you're running the standard Ruby for Windows distribution from the Pragmatic Programmers' site (www.pragmaticprogrammer.com/ruby/downloads/ruby-install.html), you already have a working Tk installation.

Similarly, most Linux distributions include Tcl/Tk as a standard installation option.

The other piece of the puzzle, the extension module that allows Ruby to access Tk, is included in the Ruby source code distribution. If you built Ruby from its source code, the Ruby/Tk extension was automatically built as well and should be installed along with the rest of the Ruby library on your system. The standard Ruby installer for Windows also includes the Ruby/Tk extension.

Ruby/Tk Basics

Ruby/Tk provides a number of classes to represent the different Tk widgets. It uses a consistent naming scheme and in general you can count on the class name for a widget being *Tk* followed by the Tk widget name. For example, Tk's Entry widget is represented by the *TkEntry* class in Ruby/Tk.

A typical structure for Ruby/Tk programs is to create the main or "root" window (an instance of *TkRoot*), add widgets to it to build up the user interface, and then start the main event loop by calling *Tk.mainloop*. The traditional "Hello, World!" example for Ruby/Tk looks something like this:

```
require 'tk'


root = TkRoot.new
button = TkButton.new(root) {
  text "Hello, World!"
  command proc { puts "I said, Hello!" }
}
button.pack
Tk.mainloop
```

The first line just loads the Ruby/Tk extension into the interpreter and the second line creates a top-level window for the application. Finally, we get to the interesting part:

```
button = TkButton.new(root) {
  text "Hello, World!"
  command proc { puts "I said, Hello!" }
}
```

Here we're creating a button whose parent widget is the main window. Like all of the GUI toolkits we'll look at, Ruby/Tk uses a composition-based model where parent widgets can contain one or more child widgets, some of which may themselves be containers. This code fragment also demonstrates one way to specify various configuration options for a widget by following it with a code block. Inside the code block, you can call methods that change aspects of the widget's appearance or behavior; in this example, the *text* method is used to set the text displayed on the button, while the *command* method is used to associate a procedure with the button's callback (more on this in the next section). An alternate (but equivalent) form for specifying widget options is to pass them as hash-style (*key, value*) pairs, for the second and following arguments to the widget's *new* function, as follows:

```
button = TkButton.new(root, text => "Hello, World!",
   command => proc { puts "I said, Hello!" })
```

The second line is important because it instructs the button's parent container (the root window) to place it in the correct location. For this example that's not too difficult, since the root window only has one child widget to deal with. As we'll see later, real applications have much more complicated layouts with deeply nested structures of widgets contained within other container widgets. For those cases, we'll pass additional arguments to the widget's *pack* method to indicate where it should be placed in the parent container, how its size should change when its parent's size changes, and other aspects related to the layout.

This example program "ends", as most Ruby/Tk programs do, with a call to *Tk.mainloop*; but this is actually where the action begins. At this point, the program loops indefinitely, waiting for new user interface events and then dispatching them to the appropriate handlers. A lot of your work in developing GUI applications with Ruby/Tk is deciding which events are of interest and then writing code to handle those events; this is the topic of the following section.

Creating Responses to Tk's Callbacks and Events

Tk's event model is split along two closely-related lines. On one hand, the window system generates low-level events such as "the mouse cursor just moved into this window" or "the user just pressed the **S** key on the keyboard". At a higher level, Tk invokes *callbacks* in your program to indicate that something significant happened to a widget (a button was clicked, for example). For either case, you can provide a code block or a Ruby *Proc* object that specifies how the application responds to the event or callback.

First, let's take a look at how to use the *bind* method to associate basic window system events with the Ruby procedures that handle them. The simplest form of *bind* takes as its inputs a string indicating the event name and a code block that Tk uses to handle the event. For example, to catch the *ButtonRelease* event for the first mouse button on some widget, you'd write:

```
someWidget.bind('ButtonRelease-1') {
  … code block to handle this event …
}
```

For some event types, it's sufficient to use the basic event name, like "Configure" or "Destroy", but for others you'll want to be more specific. For this reason the event name can include additional *modifiers* and *details*. A modifier is a string like "Shift", "Control" or "Alt", indicating that one of the modifier keys was pressed. The detail is either a number from 1 to 5, indicating a mouse button number, or a character indicating a keyboard character. So, for example, to catch the event that's generated when the user holds down the **Ctrl** key and clicks the right mouse button (sometimes known as Button 3) over a window, you'd write:

```
aWindow.bind('Control-ButtonPress-3', proc { puts "Ouch!" })
```

The names of these events are derived from the names of the corresponding X11 event types, for mostly historical reasons; Tcl/Tk was originally developed for the Unix operating system and the X Window system. The Tk ports for Windows, Macintosh and other platforms use the same event names to represent their "native" windowing system events. The sample application we'll develop later uses a few other event types, but for a complete listing of the valid event names, modifiers and details you should consult the manual pages for Tk's **bind** command. A good online source for this kind of reference information is the Tcl/Tk documentation at the Tcl Developer Xchange Web site (http://tcl.activestate.com/doc).

It's useful to be able to intercept these kinds of low-level events, but more often you're interested in the higher-level actions. For example, you'd simply like to know when the user clicks on the **Help** button; you don't really need to know that the user pressed the left mouse button down on the **Help** button and then, a few milliseconds later, released the mouse button. Many Ruby/Tk widgets can trigger callbacks when the user activates them, and you can use the *command* call-back to specify that a certain code block or procedure is invoked when that happens. As with any other widget option, you can specify the *command* callback procedure when you create the widget:

```
helpButton = TkButton.new(buttonFrame) {
  text "Help"
  command proc { showHelp }
}
```

or you can assign it later, using the widget's *command* method:

```
helpButton.command proc { showHelp }
```

Note that since the *command* method accepts either procedures or code blocks, you could also write the previous code example as:

```
helpButton = TkButton.new(buttonFrame) {
  text "Help"
  command { showHelp }
}
```

Some widgets, like TkCanvas, TkListbox and TkText, may not be able to display all of their contents in the space allotted to them. For example, if you're using a TkText widget to display a very long document, at best you'll only be able to see a screen's worth of text at a time. For this reason you'll typically attach TkScrollbar widgets to one or more sides of the main widget to allow the user to scroll through the widget's contents. In order to properly interact with scrollbars, widgets like TkText or TkListbox can also generate callbacks when their contents are scrolled horizontally or vertically. To associate code blocks with these callbacks you can use the widget's *xscrollcommand* or *yscrollcommand* methods (for horizontal or vertical scrolling). We'll see an example of how this works in the sample application later in this chapter.

Working with Ruby/Tk's Layout Managers

When you're designing the behavior of your application, it's critical to understand how Ruby/Tk's events and callbacks work. An equally important aspect of the design is the layout of the user interface. Many widgets serve as interactive components upon which the user clicks on or types to get the program to perform an action. Other widgets, however, are more passive and should be used as containers (or parents) for yet other widgets. We've already seen that the top-level root window is one such container widget, and inside the main window you can use TkFrame widgets to group child widgets together in an organized way.

The layout manager for a container basically defines the strategy it's going to use when assigning positions and sizes to its child widgets. As you'll come to see, even after you understand how layout managers work, it takes some experimenting to translate your mental image of the user interface layout into code that correctly implements that layout. With Ruby/Tk, you can choose from three different layout managers, although you don't have to use the same layout manager for every container. In fact, for non-trivial user interfaces it's quite likely that you'll use more than one of them.

The simplest layout manager is the *placer*, which just places the child widgets using the positions and sizes that you specify. At first glance, this might sound reasonable; after all, a lot of the "GUI builder" tools that let you drag widgets off of a tool palette and drop them on to a work window use this approach in the source code that they generate. The drawbacks of this fixed layout become apparent as soon as you try to run the program on other computers, with different configurations and possibly running other operating systems. For example, if the system fonts are different, a button that requires only 40 pixels' width to display its text on your system might require 60 pixels on another system. If you had placed a text field at some fixed position immediately to the right of that button, those two widgets are now going to overlap each other. Because it's so inflexible, you probably won't use the placer much in practice.

The next layout manager is the *grid* layout manager, which places its child widgets in a table-like arrangement. When you add a child widget to a container using the grid layout manager, you specify the column and row in which it should be placed. The child widgets are arranged so that all of the widgets in the same column have the same width, and all of the widgets in the same row have the same height. For a quick example, here's a grid layout with 3 rows and 4 columns of label widgets:

```
require 'tk'
root = TkRoot.new
3.times { |r|
  4.times { |c|
    TkLabel.new(root) {
```

```
        text "row #{r}, column #{c}"
      }.grid('row' => r, 'column' => c, 'padx' => 10, 'pady' => 10)
   }
}
Tk.mainloop
```

Figure 2.1 shows the results when you run this program. The grid layout manager is more powerful than this simple example suggests, however. You can see that by default, the grid centers each child widget in its cell, but you can provide additional arguments to the grid method to specify that one or more sides of the child widget stretches to "stick" to the side(s) of its cell. Additionally, grid cells can span multiple rows or columns. For more information about advanced options for the grid layout manager, consult your favorite Tk reference.

Figure 2.1 Grid Layout Manager

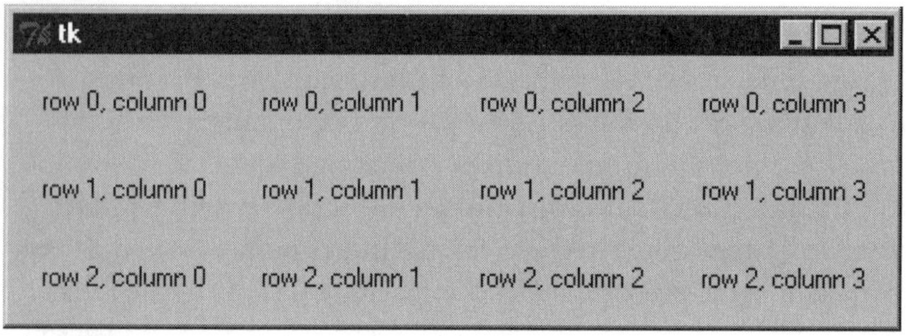

The last layout manager we'll discuss is the *packer*, which is the one you'll use most often because it is very flexible yet easy to use. The packer uses what is known as a "cavity" model for assigning the positions and sizes of its children. Imagine an empty frame widget, before any child widgets have been added to it. When you add the very first child widget to the frame, you specify which side (left, right, top or bottom) of the rectangular cavity against which the child widget should be packed (or aligned). The packer allocates that *entire* side of the cavity to this widget, and reduces the size of the cavity by the amount of space taken up by that first child. It's important to note that the packer allocates the entire side of the cavity to the newly added widget, even if that widget doesn't need the space. Successive child widgets are also packed against selected sides of the remaining cavity space until you're done.

It's also important to understand that the packer layout manager distinguishes between *packing space* and *display space*. The display space is the amount of space that a particular child widget would prefer to have to display itself properly. For example, a label or button widget's display space is a little wider than the space needed to display the text on that label or button. The packing space is the entire space that's available when positioning a widget in the cavity, which may be more or less than the display space for the widget.

When the amount of packing space exceeds the needed display space for a widget, the default behavior is to just center the child widget in that packing space, leaving gaps on the other sides. If you would instead like for the child widget to fill all the available packing space, you can set the *fill* parameter to one of three values (*x*, *y* or *both*), indicating the direction(s) in which the widget should fill. We'll see examples of this later, in the sample application.

A related parameter, *expand*, has to do with how the child widgets resize themselves when the parent container (the packer) itself is resized. By default, *expand* is false, meaning that even if the parent container grows (or shrinks) the child widgets will maintain their current positions and sizes. If you instead set *expand* to true, the child widgets will resize according to the new size of the parent. In general, if you've specified *fill* => *"both"* for a particular child widget, you'll also want to specify *expand* => *true* for that child widget.

It may help to work through a more concrete exercise to demonstrate how the packer's layout algorithm works. Remember that we start out with an empty, rectangular cavity. Let's start by adding a widget to the top side of the cavity (see Figure 2.2 [A]):

After this first step, the top section of the cavity is now claimed by the first child widget. Regardless of how we pack the remaining child widgets, this is the only one that can be adjacent to the top edge of the container; the bottom edge of this first widget has become the "top" of the remaining cavity space. Next, let's add a widget to the left side of the cavity (B).

Once again, the remaining space in the cavity shrinks, this time by the width of the second widget. The bottom edge of the first widget is still the top of the cavity, but the right edge of this second widget becomes the new left side of the cavity. Now let's add a third widget (C), this time to the bottom.

After adding this widget, the remaining space shrinks by the widget's height and its top edge becomes the new bottom side of the cavity. Finally, add the last widget (D), this time to the right side.

Figure 2.2 Tk Packer Layout Manager

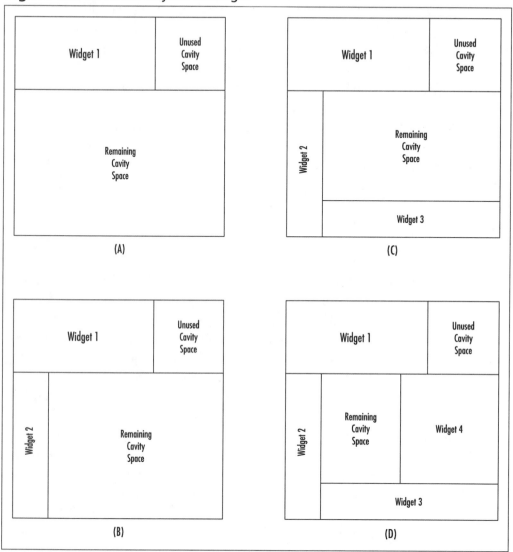

Ruby/Tk Sample Application

Figure 2.3 shows the source code for the Ruby/Tk version of our sample application. The source code for this application appears at www.syngress.com/solutions, under the file name *tk-xmlviewer.rb*.

Figure 2.3 Ruby/Tk Source Code for Sample Application (tk-xmlviewer.rb)

```ruby
#!/usr/bin/env ruby

require 'tk'
require 'nqxml/treeparser'

class XMLViewer < TkRoot
  def createMenubar
    menubar = TkFrame.new(self)
    fileMenuButton = TkMenubutton.new(menubar,
                                        'text' => 'File',
                                        'underline' => 0)
    fileMenu = TkMenu.new(fileMenuButton, 'tearoff' => false)

    fileMenu.add('command',
                 'label' => 'Open',
                 'command' => proc { openDocument },
                 'underline' => 0,
                 'accel' => 'Ctrl+O')
    self.bind('Control-o', proc { openDocument })

    fileMenu.add('command',
                 'label' => 'Quit',
                 'command' => proc { exit },
                 'underline' => 0,
                 'accel' => 'Ctrl+Q')
    self.bind('Control-q', proc { exit })

    fileMenuButton.menu(fileMenu)
    fileMenuButton.pack('side' => 'left')

    helpMenuButton = TkMenubutton.new(menubar,
                                        'text' => 'Help',
                                        'underline' => 0)
```

Continued

Figure 2.3 Continued

```ruby
  helpMenu = TkMenu.new(helpMenuButton, 'tearoff' => false)

  helpMenu.add('command',
                'label' => 'About...',
                'command' => proc { showAboutBox })

  helpMenuButton.menu(helpMenu)
  helpMenuButton.pack('side' => 'right')
  menubar.pack('side' => 'top', 'fill' => 'x')
end


def createContents
  # List
  listBox = TkListbox.new(self) {
    selectmode 'single'
    background 'white'
    font 'courier 10 normal'
  }
  scrollBar = TkScrollbar.new(self) {
    command proc { |*args|
      listBox.yview(*args)
    }
  }
  rightSide = TkFrame.new(self)
  attributesForm = TkFrame.new(rightSide)
  attributesForm.pack('side' => 'top', 'fill' => 'x')
  TkFrame.new(rightSide).pack('side' => 'top', 'fill' => 'both',
    'expand' => true)
  listBox.yscrollcommand(proc { |first, last|
    scrollBar.set(first, last)
  })
  listBox.bind('ButtonRelease-1') {
    itemIndex = listBox.curselection[0]
```

Continued

Figure 2.3 Continued

```ruby
  if itemIndex
    # Remove currently displayed attributes
    TkGrid.slaves(attributesForm, nil).each { |slave|
      TkGrid.forget(attributesForm, slave)
    }


    # Add labels and entry widgets for this entity's attributes
    entity = @entities[itemIndex]
    if entity.kind_of?(NQXML::NamedAttributes)
      keys = entity.attrs.keys.sort
      keys.each_index { |row|
        TkLabel.new(attributesForm) {
          text keys[row] + ":"
          justify 'left'
        }.grid('row' => row, 'column' => 0, 'sticky' => 'nw')
        entry = TkEntry.new(attributesForm)
        entry.grid('row' => row, 'column' => 1, 'sticky' => 'nsew')
        entry.value = entity.attrs[keys[row]]
        TkGrid.rowconfigure(attributesForm, row, 'weight' => 1)
      }
      TkGrid.columnconfigure(attributesForm, 0, 'weight' => 1)
      TkGrid.columnconfigure(attributesForm, 1, 'weight' => 1)
    else
    end
  end
}


listBox.pack('side' => 'left', 'fill' => 'both', 'expand' => true)
scrollBar.pack('side' => 'left', 'fill' => 'y')
rightSide.pack('side' => 'left', 'fill' => 'both', 'expand' => true)


@listBox = listBox
@attributesForm = attributesForm
```

Continued

Figure 2.3 Continued

```ruby
end

def initialize
  # Initialize base class
  super

  # Main Window Title
  title 'TkXMLViewer'
  geometry '600x400'

  # Menu bar
  createMenubar
  createContents
end

def populateList(docRootNode, indent)
  entity = docRootNode.entity
  if entity.instance_of?(NQXML::Tag)
    @listBox.insert('end', ' '*indent + entity.to_s)
    @entities.push(entity)
    docRootNode.children.each do |node|
      populateList(node, indent + 2)
    end
  elsif entity.instance_of?(NQXML::Text) &&
        entity.to_s.strip.length != 0
    @listBox.insert('end', ' '*indent + entity.to_s)
    @entities.push(entity)
  end
end

def loadDocument(filename)
  @document = nil
  begin
```

Continued

Figure 2.3 Continued

```ruby
      @document = NQXML::TreeParser.new(File.new(filename)).document
    rescue NQXML::ParserError => ex
      Tk.messageBox('icon' => 'error', 'type' => 'ok',
                    'title' => 'Error', 'parent' => self,
                    'message' => "Couldn't parse XML document")
    end
    if @document
      @listBox.delete(0, @listBox.size)
      @entities = []
      populateList(@document.rootNode, 0)
    end
  end


  def openDocument
    filetypes = [["All Files", "*"], ["XML Documents", "*.xml"]]
    filename = Tk.getOpenFile('filetypes' => filetypes,
                              'parent' => self)
    if filename != ""
      loadDocument(filename)
    end
  end


  def showAboutBox
      Tk.messageBox('icon' => 'info', 'type' => 'ok',
        'title' => 'About TkXMLViewer',
        'parent' => self,
        'message' => 'Ruby/Tk XML Viewer Application')
  end
end


# Run the application
root = XMLViewer.new
Tk.mainloop
```

The first few lines simply import the required Tk and NQXML modules, and the majority of the code consists of the *XMLViewer* class definition. The main application window class, *XMLViewer*, is derived from *TkRoot*. Its *initialize* method looks like this:

```
def initialize
  # Initialize base class
  super

  # Main Window Title
  title 'TkXMLViewer'
  geometry '600x400'

  # Menu bar
  createMenubar
  createContents
end
```

The first line of *initialize* calls *super* to initialize the base class; don't forget to do this! The next two lines call *TkRoot*'s *title* and *geometry* methods, respectively, to set the main window title string and its initial width and height in pixels. These two methods are actually provided by Ruby/Tk's *Wm* module, which defines a number of functions for interacting with the window manager.

The last two lines of the *initialize* method call out to other *XMLViewer* methods to create the window's menu bar and *contents* area. We could have included the code from these methods directly in the *initialize* method, but breaking up different parts of the GUI construction into different methods is a common way to organize larger, more complicated applications and so we'll use it here for consistency. Unlike some of the other tookits we'll look at, Ruby/Tk doesn't have a specific class for the "menu bar"; instead, we just use a *TkFrame* container widget stretched along the top of the main window.

A Ruby/Tk pulldown menu consists of a *TkMenubutton* object associated with a *TkMenu* object. The *TkMenubutton* is the widget that you see on the menu bar itself; its text is the name of the menu, such as File, Edit or Help. When the user clicks this button, the associated *TkMenu* will be displayed. You can add one or more menu options to a *TkMenu* using its *add* method. Let's look at the setup for our sample application's File menu:

```
fileMenuButton = TkMenubutton.new(menubar,

                                  'text' => 'File',

                                  'underline' => 0)
```

Menu buttons are created as child widgets of the menu bar itself. The *underline* attribute for *TkMenubutton* widgets is an integer indicating which letter in the menu button title should be underlined. Underlining a letter in the menu title is a commonly-used visual cue in GUI applications to identify the accelerator key that can be used to activate the menu; for example, in most Windows applications the **Alt+F** keyboard combination activates the File menu.

Next, we'll create the *TkMenu* associated with this *TkMenubutton* and add the first entry for that menu:

```
fileMenu = TkMenu.new(fileMenuButton, 'tearoff' => false)

fileMenu.add('command',
             'label' => 'Open',
             'command' => proc { openDocument },
             'underline' => 0,
             'accel' => 'Ctrl+O')
self.bind('Control-o', proc { openDocument })
```

Note that the *TkMenu* is created as a child of the menu button. Here we're specifying that it's not a tear-off style menu. The first entry we'll add to the menu is a command entry, for the **Open** command. The first argument to *add* is a string indicating the type of the menu entry; in addition to *command*, there are types for checkbutton entries (*check*), radiobutton entries (*radio*), separators (*separator*), and cascading sub-menus (*cascade*). The *command* attribute for this menu entry is a Ruby *Proc* object that calls a different *XMLViewer* instance method, *openDocument*, which we'll see shortly. Note that the *accel* attribute defines the keyboard accelerator string that is displayed alongside the *Open* menu entry but it doesn't automatically set up the keyboard binding for that accelerator; we need to call *bind* on the main window to do this ourselves.

Now let's take a look at the *createContents* method. This method sets up the main contents area of the application main window, which is divided into a listing of the XML document nodes on the left side and a listing of the node attributes on the right.

```ruby
listBox = TkListbox.new(self) {
  selectmode 'single'
  background 'white'
  font 'courier 10 normal'
}
scrollBar = TkScrollbar.new(self) {
  command proc { |*args|
    listBox.yview(*args)
  }
}
listBox.yscrollcommand(proc { |first, last|
  scrollBar.set(first, last)
})
```

Tk's list-box widget displays a list of strings that the user can select from. Our *TkListbox* instance sets the *selectmode* attribute to *single*, indicating that only one item can be selected at a time (other selection modes allow for multiple selections at the same time). We also set the *font* attribute to a fixed-pitch Courier font instead of the default GUI font, which is usually a system-dependent, proportionally-spaced font. Since the number of list items may become very large (too many to fit onscreen) we'll also attach a TkScrollbar widget to use with this listbox. The code block or procedure passed to the scrollbar's *command* method modifies the listbox's "view", the range of items displayed in its window. The number of parameters passed to the scrollbar's *command* method varies depending on what the user does to the scrollbar. For example, if the user adjusts the scrollbar position by clicking on one of the arrow buttons, the *command* method will receive three arguments (*scroll, 1, units*). For more details about the different arguments that can be passed, see the Tk reference documentation for Tk's *scrollbar* command. In general, you don't need to concern yourself with which set of arguments get passed to the command method, and you simply pass them along to the scrolled widget's *xview* or *yview* method. Similarly, the code block or procedure passed to the list's *yscrollcommand* method can adjust the position and range of the scrollbar when the list contents are modified. The next section of code sets up the right-hand side of the main window:

```ruby
rightSide = TkFrame.new(self)
attributesForm = TkFrame.new(rightSide)
attributesForm.pack('side' => 'top', 'fill' => 'x')
```

```
TkFrame.new(rightSide).pack('side' => 'top', 'fill' => 'both',
                                'expand' => true)
```

For now, this isn't very interesting, because the attributes form is still empty. But the next section of code, which handles list selections, makes its purpose a bit clearer:

```
listBox.bind('ButtonRelease-1') {
  itemIndex = listBox.curselection[0]
  if itemIndex
    # Remove currently displayed attributes
    TkGrid.slaves(attributesForm, nil).each { |slave|
      TkGrid.forget(attributesForm, slave)
    }
    # Add labels and entry widgets for this entity's attributes
    entity = @entities[itemIndex]
    if entity.kind_of?(NQXML::NamedAttributes)
      keys = entity.attrs.keys.sort
      keys.each_index { |row|
        TkLabel.new(attributesForm) {
          text keys[row] + ":"
          justify 'left'
        }.grid('row' => row, 'column' => 0, 'sticky' => 'nw')
        entry = TkEntry.new(attributesForm)
        entry.grid('row' => row, 'column' => 1, 'sticky' => 'nsew')
        entry.value = entity.attrs[keys[row]]
        TkGrid.rowconfigure(attributesForm, row, 'weight' => 1)
      }
      TkGrid.columnconfigure(attributesForm, 0, 'weight' => 1)
      TkGrid.columnconfigure(attributesForm, 1, 'weight' => 1)
    end
  end
}
```

This entire code block is bound to the *ButtonRelease* event for the left mouse button on the list box. This is the event that will be generated when the user selects a list item by first pressing, and then releasing, the left mouse button over the list. We start by calling the TkListbox's *curselection* method to get an array of the selected items' indices; since this is a single-selection list, we only expect one selected item (as the zeroth element of this array). Next, we clear the current *attributes* form's contents by calling *TkGrid.slaves* to get an array of the child widgets for the form, and then calling *TkGrid.forget* on each as we iterate through them. Whereas most GUI toolkits use the "parent-child" terminology to refer to the hierarchical composition of GUI containers, Tk often uses the terms "master" and "slave", especially when referring to layout managers like *TkGrid*.

The next section of this event handler loops over all of the attributes for the currently selected XML document node, and adds a *TkLabel* and *TkEntry* to the form for each. Note that we can override the default justification for the *TkLabel* through its *justify* attribute; valid values for this attribute are *left*, *center* and *right*, but the default label justification is centered text. Also, since we'd like grid columns and rows to be equally weighted, we're calling the *TkGrid.rowconfigure* and *TkGrid.columnconfigure* module methods to set the *weight* attribute for each row and column to *1*.

We need to look at some of the lower-level methods for the *XMLViewer* class. For starters, there's the *openDocument* method which is invoked when the user selects the **Open** entry from the **File** menu (or presses the **Ctrl+O** accelerator):

```
def openDocument
  filetypes = [["All Files", "*"], ["XML Documents", "*.xml"]]
  filename = Tk.getOpenFile('filetypes' => filetypes,
                            'parent' => self)
  if filename != ""
    loadDocument(filename)
  end
end
```

The important parts of this function are the call to *Tk.getOpenFile* and *loadDocument*. *Tk.getOpenFile* is a *Tk* module method that displays a system-specific file dialog box for selecting an existing file's name; a similar function, *Tk.getSaveFile*, can be used to get either an existing or new file name when saving documents. The *filetypes* attribute specifies a list of file type descriptions and patterns, while the *parent* attribute specifies the *owner* window for the *file* dialog. Assuming the user didn't cancel the dialog and provided a legitimate file name, we call the *XMLViewer* method *loadDocument* to actually read the XML document:

```
def loadDocument(filename)
  @document = nil
  begin
    @document = NQXML::TreeParser.new(File.new(filename)).document
  rescue NQXML::ParserError => ex
    Tk.messageBox('icon' => 'error', 'type' => 'ok',
                  'title' => 'Error', 'parent' => self,
                  'message' => "Couldn't parse XML document")
  end
  if @document
    @listBox.delete(0, @listBox.size)
    @entities = []
    populateList(@document.rootNode, 0)
  end
end
```

If the XML parser raises an exception while reading the XML file, we can display a simple dialog box stating this fact using the *Tk.messageBox* module method. The *icon* attribute can be one of the four strings *error*, *info*, *question* or *warning*, to provide a visual cue of the kind of message. The *type* attribute indicates which terminator buttons should be displayed on this message box. For our simple case, we'll just display the OK button to dismiss the dialog, but other options for *type* include *abortretrycancel*, *okcancel*, *retrycancel*, *yesno*, and *yesnocancel*.

Assuming there were no errors in reading the document, the instance variable *@document* should now hold a reference to an *NQXML::Document* object. We call the *delete* method to erase all of the current list entries and then call *populateList* to start filling the list with the new document's entities:

```
def populateList(docRootNode, indent)
  entity = docRootNode.entity
  if entity.instance_of?(NQXML::Tag)
    @listBox.insert('end', ' '*indent + entity.to_s)
    @entities.push(entity)
    docRootNode.children.each do |node|
      populateList(node, indent + 2)
    end
  elsif entity.instance_of?(NQXML::Text) &&
```

```
            entity.to_s.strip.length != 0
      @listBox.insert('end', ' '*indent + entity.to_s)
      @entities.push(entity)
   end
end
```

Other GUI toolkits we'll cover in this chapter have tree widgets that are well-suited for displaying hierarchical data like an XML document. Tk doesn't have such a widget, although Tix, a popular Tk extension does. For more information on Tix, see "Obtaining Tk Extensions: Tix and BLT" later in this section. Since Tix isn't always available, we'll approximate the tree widget using a regular *TkListbox* with the list items indented to indicate their depth in the tree. The *populateList* method is called recursively until the entire document is represented. In the earlier event handler code, we saw how the application handles selection of list items corresponding to different document entities.

Figure 2.4 shows the Ruby/Tk version of our sample application, running under Microsoft Windows 2000.

Figure 2.4 Ruby/Tk Version of Sample Application

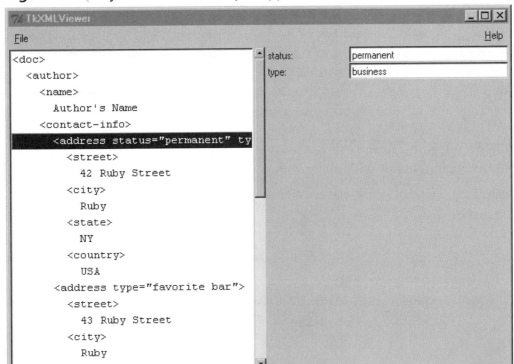

Using the SpecTcl GUI Builder

SpecTcl (http://spectcl.sourceforge.net) is a GUI building tool for Tk. It was originally developed by Sun Microsystems and has more recently been developed and maintained by a group of volunteers led by Morten Jensen. Although the original intent of SpecTcl was to generate Tcl source code based on the user interface design, people have since developed code generation backends for other scripting languages (such as Perl, Python, and Ruby) that use Tk as a GUI. An experimental version of the Ruby backend for SpecTcl, known as "specRuby," was developed by Conrad Schneiker and is currently maintained by Jonathan Conway. Figure 2.5 shows a sample specRuby session and the layout of a simple Tk user interface, while Figure 2.6 shows the result when you test this GUI.

Figure 2.5 A Sample SpecTcl Session

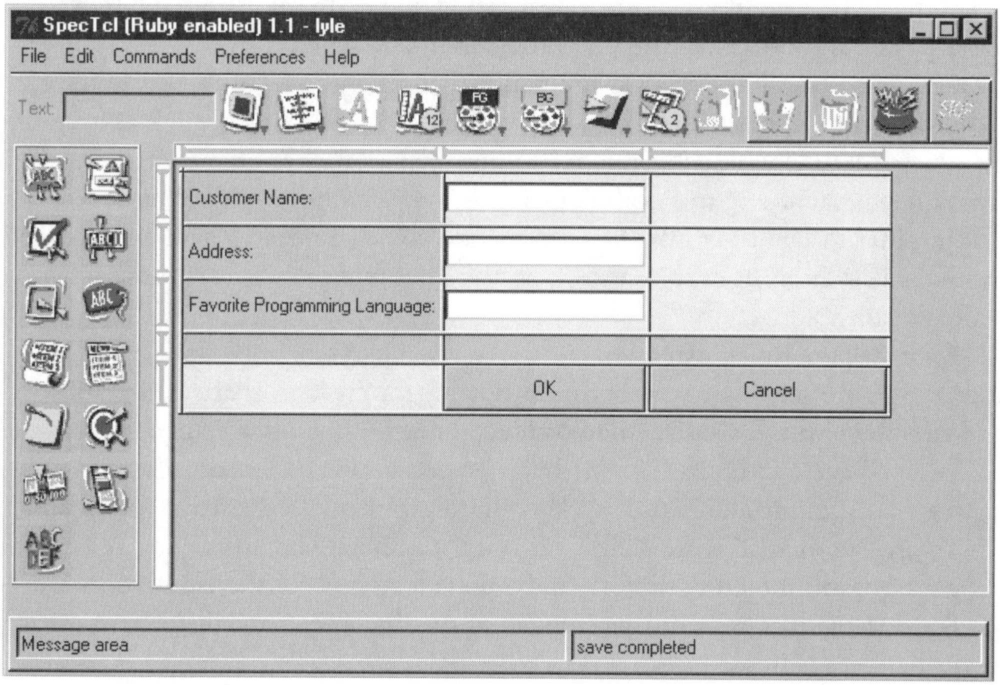

There is currently no home page for specRuby, but it is listed in the RAA and you should check there for the latest version and download site. Note that since SpecTcl is a Tcl/Tk application, you will need a working Tcl/Tk installation on your system.

Figure 2.6 Resulting Ruby/Tk GUI Generated by SpecTcl

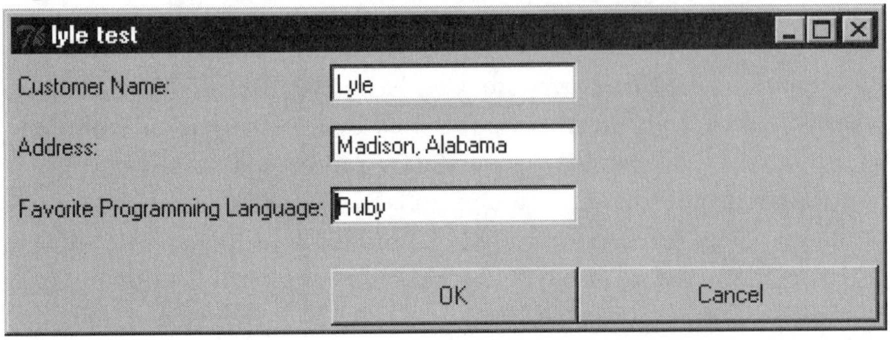

Obtaining Tk Extensions: Tix and BLT

In addition to Tk's core widgets, there are many third-party widgets (and widget collections) that are compatible with Tk. While the level of effort required to obtain these Tk extensions can be intimidating, the end result is often a much more powerful toolkit than the one provided by Tk alone.

One of the most popular Tk-compatible extensions is Tix, the Tk Interface Extension (http://tix.sourceforge.net). Tix offers a hierarchical list (a.k.a. "tree" list) widget, a notebook widget and a combo-box, as well as others. You can always download the source code for Tix from the Tix home page, but be aware that in order to build Tix from its source code you also need to have downloaded and built Tcl/Tk from its source code, as the Tix build process uses these source code directories directly.

Another popular Tk extension is BLT (www.tcltk.com/blt). Like Tix, BLT adds a variety of new functionality, most notably for creating charts and graphs. You can download the source code or precompiled binaries for Windows from the BLT home page, and unlike Tix, the build procedure for BLT is the standard **configure**, **make** and **make install** cycle common to many free software programs.

To use Tix or BLT with Ruby/Tk, you'll also need Hidetoshi Nagai's TclTk-ext package; you should be able to find a download link for the latest version in the RAA. Note that as of this writing, all of the documents for this extension are in Japanese.

Using the GTK+ Toolkit

GTK+ is a cross-platform GUI originally developed for use with the GNU Image Manipulation Program (GIMP) toolkit (available at www.gimp.org).

Although GTK+ is primarily designed for the X Window system, it has also been ported to Microsoft Windows. As a part of the GNU project, it is used for a lot of popular free software and is a core component of the GNU project's GNU Network Object Model Environment (GNOME) desktop environment.

Ruby/GTK is a Ruby extension module written in C that provides an interface from Ruby to GTK+. This extension was originally developed by Yukihiro Matsumoto (the author of Ruby) and is currently maintained by Hiroshi Igarashi.

Obtaining Ruby/GTK

The home page for Ruby/GTK is www.ruby-lang.org/gtk. If you're using the standard Ruby for Windows installation from the Pragmatic Programmers' site, there's a good chance that it includes precompiled binaries for Ruby/GTK. For other platforms (including Unix and Linux) you'll need to build Ruby/GTK from the source code.

In order to build Ruby/GTK from the source code, you will need a working installation of GTK+ itself. Most Linux distributions include a GTK+ development package as an installation option; in Red Hat Linux, for example, this is the *gtk+-devel* package. If your operating system doesn't already have a working GTK+ installation, the GTK+ home page (www.gtk.org) has plenty of information about how to download the source code and build it yourself. You can also download the sources for Ruby/GTK from its home page.

Once you've established a working GTK+ installation, you can download the Ruby/GTK sources from the Ruby/GTK home page. As of this writing, the latest version of Ruby/GTK is 0.25. The source code is distributed as a gzipped tar file named *ruby-gtk-0.25.tar.gz* and the build procedure is similar to that for other Ruby extensions. To extract this archive's contents on a Unix system, type:

```
gzip -dc ruby-gtk-0.25.tar.gz | tar xf -
```

These commands create a new directory named *gtk-0.25* (not *ruby-gtk-0.25*) containing the source code. To configure the build, change to the *gtk-0.25* directory and type:

```
ruby extconf.rb
```

This command automatically generates the Makefile for this extension. To start compiling Ruby/GTK, just type:

```
make
```

The Ruby/GTK source code distribution includes several example programs that you can use to verify that it's working properly. Once you're satisfied that it's working properly, you can install it by typing:

```
make install
```

Ruby/GTK Basics

Although the GTK+ library is written in C, its design is very object-oriented, and the Ruby/GTK extension reflects its class hierarchy. If you're already familiar with the GTK+ C API and its widget names (GtkLabel, GtkButton, etc.) then the transition to programming with Ruby/GTK should be very smooth. GTK+ widget names of the form *GtkWidgetName* become *Gtk::WidgetName* in Ruby/GTK; that is, the Ruby module name is *Gtk* and the widget's class name is *WidgetName*. Similarly, the Ruby/GTK instance methods are similar to the corresponding C function names; the C function *gtk_label_set_text()* becomes the *Gtk::Label* instance method *set_text*.

The minimal Ruby/GTK program will create a main window with one or more child windows, set up one more signal handlers and then start the main GTK+ event loop. Without further ado, we present the Ruby/GTK version of "Hello, World":

```
require 'gtk'

window = Gtk::Window::new
button = Gtk::Button::new("Hello, World!")
button.signal_connect(Gtk::Button::SIGNAL_CLICKED) {
  puts "Goodbye, World!"
  exit
}
window.add(button)
button.show
window.show
Gtk::main
```

The program begins by requiring the feature associated with Ruby/GTK; its name is "gtk". Next we create two new widgets: a GtkWindow widget, which by default is a top-level "main" window; and a GtkButton widget with the label

"Goodbye, World!". Note that so far, there's no connection between these two widgets; with Ruby/GTK, you compose complex user interfaces by explicitly adding child widgets to parent widgets.

The next line demonstrates one kind of event handler used by Ruby/GTK. The code inside the code block isn't executed immediately; instead, Ruby/GTK associates this code block with the button's *Gtk::Button::SIGNAL_CLICKED* signal which may be generated later, once the program's running. We'll get into this in more depth in the next section, but for the time being take it on faith that when this GtkButton widget is clicked, the program's response will be to print the string "Goodbye, World!" to the standard output and then exit.

The next two lines are critical, and they're somewhat unique to Ruby/GTK as far as the other toolkits are concerned. By default, newly-created Ruby/GTK widgets are not visible and you must explicitly make them visible by calling their *show* method. This step is easily forgotten by new Ruby/GTK programmers.

The last line of the program starts the GTK+ main event loop. At this point, GTK+ will wait for your inputs, paying special attention to those signals (like the button click) for which you've defined signal handler methods.

Now let's take a more detailed look at some of these basics and see how they work in real programs.

Programming Signals and Signal Handlers

Ruby/GTK's event model is based on the idea of user interface objects (widgets) emitting *signals* when something interesting happens. Some of these signals are low-level events generated by the window system, and indicate general information such as "the mouse moved" or "the left mouse button was clicked". Other signals are synthesized by GTK+ itself and provide more specific information, such as "a list item was selected". A widget can emit any number of signals, and every signal in Ruby/GTK has a name that indicates its significance. For example, a *GtkButton* widget emits a "clicked" signal when the button is clicked. Because GTK+ is an object-oriented toolkit, a given widget can emit not only its widget-specific signals, but also the signals emitted by all of its ancestor classes.

To associate a signal from a widget with some specific action, you can call the widget's *signal_connect* method. This method takes a string argument indicating the signal name (like "clicked") and a code block that will be evaluated in the caller's context. For example, if your Ruby/GTK-based spreadsheet program should save the spreadsheet's contents whenever the **Save** button is clicked, you might include the lines:

```
saveButton.signal_connect('clicked') {
  saveSpreadsheetContents if contentsModified?
}
```

Each class defines symbolic constants for the names of the signals it can emit, and these can be used instead of the literal strings. For example, we could have written the above code snippet as:

```
saveButton.signal_connect(Gtk::Button::SIGNAL_CLICKED) {
  saveSpreadsheetContents if contentsModified?
}
```

The advantage of using the symbolic constants like *Gtk::Button::SIGNAL_CLICKED* instead of literal strings like *clicked* is that if you make a typographical error, you're likely to discover the mistake much more quickly when you try to run your program. If you attempt to reference a constant and misspell its name, Ruby will raise a *NameError* exception; if you use a literal string, Ruby has no way to verify whether it is a valid signal name before passing it on to *signal_connect*.

As an application developer, it is up to you to decide which widgets' signals are of interest, and how your program should react when those signals are emitted. Also note that if it makes sense for your application, you can connect the same signal (from the same widget) to more than one signal handler code block. In this case, the signal handlers are executed in the order they were originally connected.

Once we start developing the sample application, you'll see a few more examples of how to connect signals to code blocks. For a complete listing of the signals emitted by different Ruby/GTK widgets, refer to the online API reference documentation at the Ruby/GTK home page (www.ruby-lang.org/gtk).

Working with Ruby/GTK's Layout Managers

Like Ruby/Tk, Ruby/GTK offers a variety of flexible layout managers. Each of the three layout managers we'll look at is a container widget to which you add one or more child widgets; the container itself is invisible for all practical purposes. The first two layout managers, the *horizontal packing box* (*Gtk::HBox*) and *vertical packing box* (*Gtk::VBox*) arrange their child widgets in a row or column, respectively. The third, *Gtk::Table*, arranges its child widgets in a *tabular* format like Ruby/Tk's grid layout.

The horizontal packing box (*Gtk::HBox*) arranges its children horizontally. All of the child widgets will have the same height, but their widths can vary according to the packing box parameters. Conversely, *Gtk::VBox* arranges its children vertically, and all of them will have the same width. Since the two packing boxes are so similar, we'll focus on *Gtk::HBox*.

The *new* method for *Gtk::HBox* takes two arguments:

```
hBox = Gtk::HBox.new(homogeneous=false, spacing=0)
```

The first argument is a Boolean value indicating whether the child widgets' sizes are "homogeneous" or not. If this argument is true (homogeneous), this simply means that the box will divide its width equally among its child widgets; if false (non-homogeneous), each child widget is allocated as much space as it needs, but no more. The second argument is the spacing (in pixels) placed between child widgets.

You add child widgets to a packing box using either its *pack_start* or *pack_end* instance methods. You may recall that in Ruby/Tk we always passed the parent widget in to as the first argument of the *new* function for its child widgets. Ruby/GTK takes a different approach: Child widgets are created and then added (or packed) into container widgets. To pack child widgets into a *Gtk::HBox* or *Gtk::VBox*, you can call its *pack_start* method:

```
hBox.pack_start(child, expand=true, fill=true, padding=0)
```

The first argument to *pack_start* is just a reference to the child widget you want to add to this packing box; the last three arguments require some additional discussion. The second argument (*expand*) is an instruction to the packing box that this widget is willing to take extra space if some becomes available (e.g. if the user resizes the window to make it wider). We've already commented on the difference between homogeneous and non-homogeneous packing boxes; homogeneous packing boxes divide their space evenly among the child widgets. Another way to think of this is that each child widget will be allocated as much space as the *widest* child widget. A side effect of this setting is that the child widgets that would have preferred a narrower space are now centered in their assigned spot in the packing box. By passing true for the *fill* argument of *pack_start*, you can instruct that child widget to grow and fill its assigned space. The last argument to *pack_start* simply indicates the padding (in pixels) you'd like to place around this child widget; this is in addition to the spacing already specified for the packing box in *Gtk::HBox.new*. If this child widget is either the first or last widget in the packing box, this is also the amount of space that will appear between the edge of the packing box and this child.

Ruby/GTK also provides the *Gtk::Table* layout manager for arranging widgets in rows and columns. The *new* method for *Gtk::Table* takes three arguments:

```
table = Gtk::Table.new(numRows, numColumns, homogeneous=false)
```

The first two arguments are the number of rows and columns for the table, and the *homogeneous* argument has the same meaning as it did for *Gtk::HBox* and *Gtk::VBox*. To specify the spacing between rows and columns, use one of the four instance methods:

```
table.set_row_spacing(row, spacing)
table.set_row_spacings(spacing)
table.set_column_spacing(column, spacing)
table.set_column_spacings(spacing)
```

The *set_row_spacings* and *set_column_spacings* methods assign a global spacing amount (in pixels) that applies to all table rows (or columns). If you need more fine-grained control, you can use *set_row_spacing* or *set_column_spacing* to assign the space that should appear below a particular row (or to the right of a particular column). The spacing amounts specified by calls to *set_row_spacing* and *set_column_spacing* override the global spacing amounts specified by *set_row_spacings* and *set_column_spacings*.

To add child widgets to a *Gtk::Table*, use its *attach* method:

```
table.attach(child, left, right, top, bottom,
             xopts=GTK_EXPAND|GTK_FILL, yopts=GTK_EXPAND|GTK_FILL,
             xpad=0, ypad=0)
```

This appears more complex than the argument lists for *pack_start* and *pack_end* (and it is) but observe that the last four arguments have default values. The first argument is again a reference to the child widget to be added. The next four arguments (*left*, *right*, *top* and *bottom*) are integers that indicate where in the table to place this child and how many rows and columns it spans. To understand how these arguments are used, it's better to think of the bounding lines of the table and its cells instead of the table cells themselves. For example, consider a table with 5 columns and 3 rows (see Figure 2.7). To draw this table, you'd need to draw 6 vertical lines (one on the left and right side of each of the 5 columns) and 4 horizontal lines (one on the top and bottom of the each of the 3 rows).

Figure 2.7 Edge Numbering for Sample GtkTable

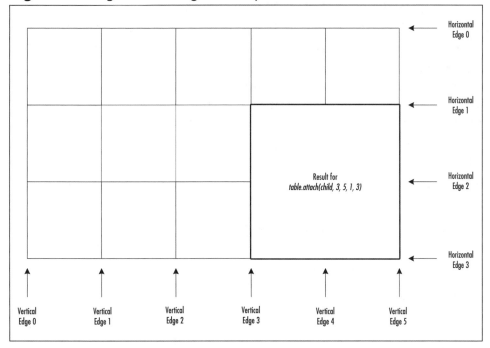

With this picture in mind, the meanings of the *left*, *right*, *top* and *bottom* arguments of *Gtk::Table.new* are as follows:

- *Left* indicates which vertical line of the table the left edge of this child widget is attached to.

- *Right* indicates which vertical line of the table the right edge of this child widget is attached to.

- *Top* indicates which horizontal line of the table the top edge of this child widget is attached to.

- *Bottom* indicates which horizontal line of the table the bottom edge of this child widget is attached to.

For widgets that occupy only one table cell, the value for *right* will always be one more than the value for *left* and the value for *bottom* will always be one more than the value for *top*. But for a widget that occupies the fourth and fifth columns of the second and third rows of a table, you'd use something like:

```
table.attach(child, 3, 5, 1, 3)
```

If your user interface layout looks incorrect, double-check the values you're passing to *attach*. Ruby/GTK *will* raise an exception if the arguments to attach would create a cell with zero width or height (i.e., if *left* is less than or equal to *right,* or *top* is less than or equal to *bottom*). But in many cases, Ruby/GTK will not raise an exception if the values for *left*, *right*, *top* or *bottom* are incorrect, even if they cause table cells to overlap one another.

The *xopts* and *yopts* arguments of *Gtk::Table#attach* specify how the table should allocate any additional space to this child widget. Valid values for *xopts* and *yopts* are *GTK_EXPAND*, *GTK_FILL* or *GTK_EXPAND|GTK_FILL* (both expand and fill). The meanings of these flags are the same as the corresponding parameters for the *pack_start* and *pack_end* methods for packing boxes. The final two arguments for *Gtk::Table#attach* specify the horizontal and vertical padding (in pixels) to apply around the outside of this widget, in addition to the spacing settings previously applied to the table in *Gtk::Table.new*.

Ruby/GTK Sample Application

Figure 2.8 shows the source code for the Ruby/GTK version of our sample application. The source code for this application appears at www.syngress.com/solutions, under the file name *gtk-xmlviewer.rb*.

Figure 2.8 Ruby/GTK Source Code for Sample Application (gtk-xmlviewer.rb)

```
require 'gtk'
require 'nqxml/treeparser'

class XMLViewer < Gtk::Window
  def initialize
    super(Gtk::WINDOW_TOPLEVEL)
    set_title('Ruby/Gtk XML Viewer')
    set_usize(600, 400)

    menubar = createMenubar

    @treeList = Gtk::Tree.new
    @treeList.show
```

Continued

Figure 2.8 Continued

```ruby
@columnList = Gtk::CList.new(['Attribute', 'Value'])
@columnList.show

bottom = Gtk::HBox.new(false, 0)
bottom.pack_start(@treeList, true, true, 0)
bottom.pack_start(@columnList, true, true, 0)
bottom.show

contents = Gtk::VBox.new(false, 0)
contents.pack_start(menubar, false, false, 0)
contents.pack_start(bottom, true, true, 0)
add(contents)
contents.show

signal_connect(Gtk::Widget::SIGNAL_DELETE_EVENT) { exit }
end

def createMenubar
  menubar = Gtk::MenuBar.new

  fileMenuItem = Gtk::MenuItem.new("File")
  fileMenu = Gtk::Menu.new

  openItem = Gtk::MenuItem.new("Open...")
  openItem.signal_connect(Gtk::MenuItem::SIGNAL_ACTIVATE) {
    openDocument
  }
  openItem.show
  fileMenu.add(openItem)

  quitItem = Gtk::MenuItem.new("Quit")
  quitItem.signal_connect(Gtk::MenuItem::SIGNAL_ACTIVATE) { exit }
```

Continued

Figure 2.8 Continued

```
    quitItem.show
    fileMenu.add(quitItem)

    fileMenuItem.set_submenu(fileMenu)
    fileMenuItem.show

    helpMenuItem = Gtk::MenuItem.new("Help")
    helpMenu = Gtk::Menu.new

    aboutItem = Gtk::MenuItem.new("About...")
    aboutItem.signal_connect(Gtk::MenuItem::SIGNAL_ACTIVATE) {
      showMessageBox('About XMLViewer', 'Ruby/GTK Sample Application')
    }
    aboutItem.show
    helpMenu.add(aboutItem)

    helpMenuItem.set_submenu(helpMenu)
    helpMenuItem.show

    menubar.append(fileMenuItem)
    menubar.append(helpMenuItem)
    menubar.show
    menubar
  end

  def selectItem(entity)
    @columnList.clear
    if entity.kind_of?(NQXML::NamedAttributes)
      keys = entity.attrs.keys.sort
      keys.each { |key|
        @columnList.append([key, entity.attrs[key]])
      }
```

Continued

Figure 2.8 Continued

```ruby
    end
  end

  def populateTreeList(docRootNode, treeRoot)
    entity = docRootNode.entity
    if entity.instance_of?(NQXML::Tag)
      treeItem = Gtk::TreeItem.new(entity.to_s)
      treeRoot.append(treeItem)
      if docRootNode.children.length > 0
        subTree = Gtk::Tree.new
        treeItem.set_subtree(subTree)
        docRootNode.children.each do |node|
          populateTreeList(node, subTree)
        end
      end
      treeItem.signal_connect(Gtk::Item::SIGNAL_SELECT) {
        selectItem(entity)
      }
      treeItem.show
    elsif entity.instance_of?(NQXML::Text) &&
          entity.to_s.strip.length != 0
      treeItem = Gtk::TreeItem.new(entity.to_s)
      treeRoot.append(treeItem)
      treeItem.signal_connect(Gtk::Item::SIGNAL_SELECT) {
        selectItem(entity)
      }
      treeItem.show
    end
  end

  def loadDocument(filename)
    @document = nil
```

Continued

Figure 2.8 Continued

```ruby
begin
  @document = NQXML::TreeParser.new(File.new(filename)).document
rescue NQXML::ParserError => ex
  showMessageBox("Error", "Couldn't parse XML document")
end
if @document
  @treeList.children.each { |child|
    @treeList.remove_child(child)
  }
  populateTreeList(@document.rootNode, @treeList)
end
end


def openDocument
  dlg = Gtk::FileSelection.new('Open File')
  dlg.ok_button.signal_connect(Gtk::Button::SIGNAL_CLICKED) {
    dlg.hide
    filename = dlg.get_filename
    loadDocument(filename) if filename
  }
  dlg.cancel_button.signal_connect(Gtk::Button::SIGNAL_CLICKED) {
    dlg.hide
  }
  dlg.show
end


def showMessageBox(title, msg)
  msgBox = Gtk::Dialog.new

  msgLabel = Gtk::Label.new(msg)
  msgLabel.show
```

Continued

Figure 2.8 Continued

```ruby
    okButton = Gtk::Button.new('OK')
    okButton.show
    okButton.signal_connect(Gtk::Button::SIGNAL_CLICKED) { msgBox.hide }

    msgBox.set_usize(250, 100)
    msgBox.vbox.pack_start(msgLabel)
    msgBox.action_area.pack_start(okButton)
    msgBox.set_title(title)
    msgBox.show
  end
end


if $0 == __FILE__
  mainWindow = XMLViewer.new
  mainWindow.show
  Gtk::main
end
```

Since most of the code is taken up by the *XMLViewer* class definitions, we'll start by examining the *initialize* method for that class.

XMLViewer is a subclass of *Gtk::Window* and so the first step is to initialize the base class by calling *super*. Note that the single argument to *Gtk::Window.new* is an optional integer indicating the window type; the default is *Gtk::WINDOW_TOPLEVEL*, but other valid values are *Gtk::WINDOW_POPUP* and *Gtk::WINDOW_DIALOG*. The next two lines set the window title and its initial width and height.

The next task is to create the application's menu bar and pulldown menus; we've purposely put this into a separate method *createMenubar* to keep things clear. Creating menus in Ruby/GTK requires creating a *Gtk::MenuBar* widget and then adding one or more *Gtk::MenuItem* objects to it. A menu item can represent an actual menu command or it can be used to display a sub-menu of *other* menu items contained in a *Gtk::Menu* widget. This excerpt from the *createMenubar* method illustrates the key points:

```
fileMenuItem = Gtk::MenuItem.new("File")
fileMenu = Gtk::Menu.new

openItem = Gtk::MenuItem.new("Open...")
openItem.signal_connect('activate') { openDocument }
openItem.show
fileMenu.add(openItem)

fileMenuItem.set_submenu(fileMenu)
fileMenuItem.show
menubar.append(fileMenuItem)
```

The *File* menu item (*fileMenuItem*) is a *Gtk::MenuItem* instance whose purpose is to display a sub-menu (*fileMenu*) containing other menu items. We call the *set_submenu* method to create this association between *fileMenuItem* and *fileMenu*. In contrast, the **Open...** menu item (*openItem*) represents a command for the application; we connect its *activate* signal to the *openDocument* method, which we'll see later.

Returning to the *initialize* method, we create and show the tree list widget:

```
@treeList = Gtk::Tree.new
@treeList.show
```

As well as the columned list widget:

```
@columnList = Gtk::CList.new(['Attribute', 'Value'])
@columnList.show
```

Here, we're using a constructor for *Gtk::CList* that specifies an array of column titles; an alternate constructor allows you to simply specify the number of columns and then set their titles later using the *set_column_title* method.

The entire layout of the main window widgets is handled using a horizontal packing box nested in a vertical packing box. The horizontal packing box (named *bottom*) holds the Gtk::Tree widget on the left and the *Gtk::CList* on the right. The vertical packing box (named *contents*) holds the menu bar along its top edge, and the rest of the space is taken up by the horizontal packing box. Note that the arguments to *pack_start* for the menu bar direct the vertical packing box to *not* stretch the menu bar vertically, even if there is extra space to do so:

```
contents.pack_start(menubar, false, false, 0)
```

The last line of initialize sets up a signal handler for the main window itself. When the main window is "deleted" (usually, by the user clicking the **X** button in the upper right-hand corner of the window), GTK+ will fire off the *Gtk::Widget::SIGNAL_DELETE_EVENT* (a symbolic constant for the *delete_event*). We'd like to catch this event and exit the program at that time.

Digging down to the next level of the application, we need to look at the signal handlers for the menu commands; these were assigned when we created the menu items in the *createMenubar* method. We can quickly see that the **Quit** menu command simply exits the application:

```
quitItem = Gtk::MenuItem.new("Quit")
quitItem.signal_connect(Gtk::MenuItem::SIGNAL_ACTIVATE) { exit }
```

The **About...** menu command displays a little dialog box containing a message about the application:

```
aboutItem = Gtk::MenuItem.new("About...")
aboutItem.signal_connect(Gtk::MenuItem::SIGNAL_ACTIVATE) {
  showMessageBox('About XMLViewer', 'Ruby/GTK Sample Application')
}
```

Here, *showMessageBox* is a helper method for the *XMLViewer* class that displays a dialog with a specified title and message string, plus an **OK** button to dismiss the dialog:

```
def showMessageBox(title, msg)
  msgBox = Gtk::Dialog.new

  msgLabel = Gtk::Label.new(msg)
  msgLabel.show

  okButton = Gtk::Button.new('OK')
  okButton.show
  okButton.signal_connect(Gtk::Button::SIGNAL_CLICKED) { msgBox.hide }

  msgBox.set_usize(250, 100)
  msgBox.vbox.pack_start(msgLabel)
  msgBox.action_area.pack_start(okButton)
  msgBox.set_title(title)
  msgBox.show
end
```

A more general-purpose method would give you more control over the message box's size, contents and layout, but this simple approach serves our purposes. As an aside, the GNOME library (built on top of GTK+) provides much more powerful and easy-to-use classes for putting message boxes and **About** boxes into your applications. You should be able to find information about Ruby bindings for GNOME at the Ruby/GTK home page.

The menu command that really gets things going, however, is the **Open...** command, which invokes *XMLViewer's openDocument* method:

```
def openDocument
  dlg = Gtk::FileSelection.new('Open File')
  dlg.ok_button.signal_connect(Gtk::Button::SIGNAL_CLICKED) {
    dlg.hide
    filename = dlg.get_filename
    loadDocument(filename) if filename
  }
  dlg.cancel_button.signal_connect(Gtk::Button::SIGNAL_CLICKED) {
    dlg.hide
  }
  dlg.show
end
```

The *new* method for *Gtk::FileSelection* takes a single string argument indicating the title for the file-selection dialog box. We're interested in catching the "clicked" signals for both the **OK** and **Cancel** buttons on this dialog, and we can use *Gtk::FileSelection's ok_button* and *cancel_button* accessor methods to set up those signal handlers. In particular, we'd like to retrieve the file name selected by the user (by calling *get_filename*) and then load that XML document by calling *XMLViewer's loadDocument* method:

```
def loadDocument(filename)
  @document = nil
  begin
    @document = NQXML::TreeParser.new(File.new(filename)).document
  rescue NQXML::ParserError => ex
    showMessageBox("Error", "Couldn't parse XML document")
  end
  if @document
```

```
    @treeList.children.each { |child|
      @treeList.remove_child(child)
    }
    populateTreeList(@document.rootNode, @treeList)
  end
end
```

If the XML parser raises an exception while creating the *NQXML::Document* object, we'll again use our *showMessageBox* helper method to alert the user to this error. Assuming the document loads successfully, we'll clear out the tree's previous contents and then refill it by calling *populateTreeList*. To clear the tree list's contents, we make a call to the *children* method (inherited from *Gtk::Container*) which returns an array containing the top-level tree items. Then we iterate over the child items and remove each of them in turn by calling the tree list's *remove_child* method.

The *populateTreeList* method calls itself recursively to build up the tree contents. The process of populating a *Gtk::Tree* widget is similar to the process for building pulldown menus that we saw in *createMenubar*. You can add *Gtk::TreeItem* objects to a *Gtk::Tree* and attach signal handlers to those items to receive notification when they are selected or deselected, expanded or collapsed, etc. But just as *Gtk::MenuItem* objects can have sub-menus associated with them (for cascading pulldown menus), *Gtk::TreeItem* objects can have sub-trees (that is, other *Gtk::Tree* objects) associated with them. In this excerpt from the *populateTreeList* method, we use this construct to model the XML document's nested nodes:

```
    treeItem = Gtk::TreeItem.new(entity.to_s)
    treeRoot.append(treeItem)
    if docRootNode.children.length > 0
      subTree = Gtk::Tree.new
      treeItem.set_subtree(subTree)
      docRootNode.children.each do |node|
        populateTreeList(node, subTree)
      end
    end
```

Here, *treeItem* is a child of the current *treeRoot* (which is itself a *Gtk::Tree* instance). If we see that this XML entity has one or more child entities, we spin off a new *Gtk::Tree* instance (named *subTree*) and make this the sub-tree of *treeItem* by calling its *set_subtree* method.

Whenever a tree item is selected, we want to update the attributes list (our *Gtk::CList* object) on the right-hand side of the main window. To do this, we attach a handler to each of the tree items that handles the *Gtk::Item::SIGNAL_SELECT* signal by invoking our *selectItem* method:

```
def selectItem(entity)

  @columnList.clear

  if entity.kind_of?(NQXML::NamedAttributes)

    keys = entity.attrs.keys.sort

    keys.each { |key|

      @columnList.append([key, entity.attrs[key]])

    }

  end

end
```

This handler begins by clearing out the old list contents and then, if there are some attributes associated with the currently-selected XML entity, it appends list items for each of them.

Figure 2.9 shows the Ruby/GTK version of our sample application, running under the X Window system on Linux.

Figure 2.9 Ruby/GTK Version of the Sample Application

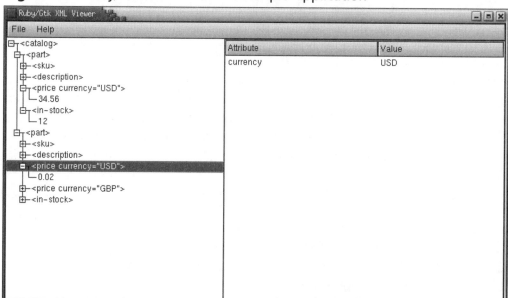

Using the Glade GUI Builder

Glade (http://glade.gnome.org) is a GUI building tool for GTK+ and GNOME. Its authors are Damon Chaplin and Martijn van Beers. You can obtain the source code for Glade from the Glade home page, and it comes as a standard installation option for many popular Linux distributions. This section does not cover the use of Glade in general, but good documentation is freely available. A plain text version of the Glade FAQ List is at http://glade.gnome.org/FAQ and the GNOME version of Glade includes on-line copies of the Glade FAQ List, Quick-Start Guide and Manual.

Glade's project file (the *.glade* file) is an XML file that includes all of the information about the user interface. James Henstridge developed a supporting library, *libglade*, that allows you to read Glade project files and dynamically create your user interface at run-time. This is significant because it allows you to use Glade to design user interfaces for a number of programming languages that Glade doesn't support directly. The home page for *libglade* is www.daa.com.au/~james/gnome, but like Glade itself, *libglade* comes as a standard installation option with most Linux distributions.

Ruby/LibGlade is an extension module, developed by Avi Bryant, that provides a wrapper for *libglade*. There is currently no home page for Ruby/LibGlade, but it is listed in the RAA and you should check there for the latest version and download site. The Ruby/LibGlade source code distribution includes installation and usage instructions, as well as a sample project file for testing purposes.

Ruby/LibGlade defines a single class, *GladeXML*. The *new* method for *GladeXML* takes the file name of the Glade project file and, optionally, the name of the root widget for the section of the user interface in which you're interested. If you want to load the entire user interface, you can omit the second argument. Finally, *GladeXML.new* also expects an iterator-style code block, which it uses to associate signal handler names with Ruby procedures or methods. While *libglade* starts loading information about your user interface from the Glade project file, it calls this iterator code block for each handler name that it encounters. Your code block should return either a Ruby *Proc* or *Method* object, which provides the code used to handle that GTK+ signal. For example, a version that returns *Proc* objects would look like this:

```
GladeXML.new('myproject.glade') { |handler_name|
  case handler_name
    when "on_button1_clicked"
```

```
      proc { puts "Goodbye, World!"; exit }
    when "on_button2_clicked"
      proc { puts "button2 was clicked" }
  end
}
```

If you've structured your code such that the Ruby methods that handle signals have the same names as the handler names you assigned in Glade, an even
cleaner approach would be to use Ruby's method *Kernel#method* to automatically
return references to those handler methods:

```
def on_button1_clicked
  puts "Goodbye, World!"
  exit
end


def on_button2_clicked
  puts "button2 was clicked"
end


GladeXML.new('myproject.glade') { |handler_name|
  method(handler_name)
}
```

The *GladeXML* class provides two other instance methods, *getWidget* and
getWidgetByLongName. Both methods return a reference to a specific widget in
the user interface, and both take a single string argument as input. The *getWidget*
method takes the short name for a widget (for example, "button1") while
getWidgetByLongName takes the full widget path name (for example,
"mainWindow.hbox.button1").

Figure 2.10 shows a sample Glade session, with our original Hello, World!
user interface consisting of a top-level window and a button as the child of that
window. Of particular importance is the **Properties** window for the button
widget. As shown in the Figure, we've added a signal handler for the button's
clicked signal, and have named that signal handler "on_button1_clicked". The
names of the signal handlers that you assign in Glade are significant for connecting the user interface to Ruby code using Ruby/LibGlade.

Figure 2.10 A Sample Glade Session

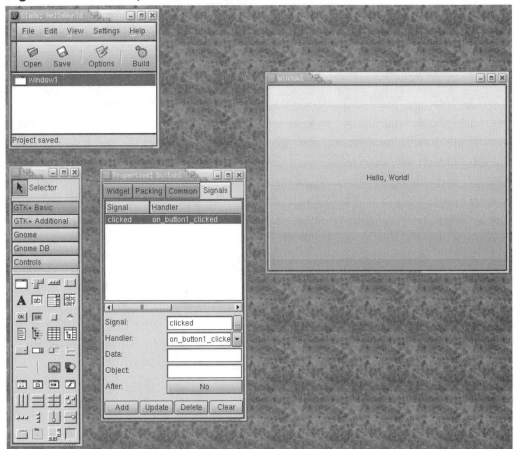

After saving this Glade project to a file (say, *helloworld.glade*) we can write a short Ruby program that uses Ruby/LibGlade to display this user interface:

```
require 'gtk'
require 'lglade'

def on_button1_clicked
  puts "Goodbye, World!"
  exit
end
```

```
GladeXML.new('helloworld.glade') { |handler_name|
  method(handler_name)
}
```

```
Gtk::main
```

The first two lines of this program import the Ruby/GTK and Ruby/LibGlade extensions, respectively (where "lglade" is the feature name for Ruby/LibGlade). The next section of the program defines the *on_button1_clicked* method which we'll use to handle the button's *clicked* signal. The new code for Ruby/LibGlade comes next, when we create a *GladeXML* object for the helloworld.glade project and associate the handler name, "on_button1_clicked", with the appropriate handler method, *on_button1_clicked*. Finally, as for all Ruby/GTK programs, the last line in the program kicks off the GTK+ main event loop. Figure 2.11 shows the results of running this program.

Figure 2.11 Resulting Ruby/GTK GUI Generated by Glade

Using the FOX Toolkit

Free Objects for X (FOX) is a cross-platform GUI toolkit developed by Jeroen van der Zijp. Compared to Tk and GTK+, FOX is the new kid on the block, but it is quickly gaining recognition among software developers looking for a cross-platform GUI toolkit.

FXRuby is the Ruby extension module that provides an interface to FOX from Ruby programs. It was developed by Lyle Johnson and its home page is at http://fxruby.sourceforge.net.

Obtaining FOX and FXRuby

A prerequisite for programming with FXRuby is to have a working FOX installation. If you're using the standard Ruby installation for Windows from the Pragmatic Programmers' site, you can download a compatible precompiled binary distribution of FXRuby from the FXRuby home page. Further, the most recent versions of the Windows installer for Ruby even include FXRuby as a standard installation option. Regardless of which source you use, the shared library in this distribution already incorporates the FOX library, so after downloading and installing the distribution you're ready to get started; There's no need to download and build FOX separately.

If you're running some other version of Ruby (including other non-Windows operating systems), you will most likely have some more work to do. Unlike Tk and GTK+, none of the Linux distributions include FOX as a standard installation package, and as of this writing, precompiled binaries for FOX aren't available at all; so you'll need to download, build and install FOX on your system. The FOX source code can be downloaded from the FOX home page (www.cfdrc.com/FOX/fox.html) and includes comprehensive build and installation instructions. For Linux and other Unix operating systems, the process is the standard **configure**, **make** and **make install**.

Once you have a working FOX installation, you can download the FXRuby source code from the FXRuby home page, and build and install that extension module. The build process for FXRuby begins by configuring the build by typing:

```
ruby setup.rb config
```

Then launch the build by typing:

```
ruby setup.rb setup
```

Once the build is completed, you can install FXRuby by typing:

```
ruby setup.rb install
```

For more detailed instructions about the build and installation options, check the FXRuby documentation.

FXRuby Basics

FXRuby's API follows FOX's C++ API very closely and, for the most part, you should be able to use the standard FOX class documentation to learn about the FXRuby class hierarchy and interfaces. All of the FXRuby classes, methods and constants live in a single Ruby module named *Fox*, and most of FXRuby is implemented in a C++ extension module whose feature name is "fox". The minimal FXRuby program would look something like this:

```
require 'fox'


include Fox
```

```
application = FXApp.new("Hello", "FoxTest")
application.init(ARGV)
main = FXMainWindow.new(application, "Hello", nil, nil, DECOR_ALL)
FXButton.new(main, "&Hello, World!", nil, application, FXApp::ID_QUIT)
application.create()
main.show(PLACEMENT_SCREEN)
application.run()
```

This program loads the *Fox* module by requiring the *fox* feature. Despite the fact that all FXRuby classes live in the *Fox* module's namespace, the class names begin with the *FX* prefix to avoid clashes with other class names. It's for this reason that most FXRuby applications can safely mix the *Fox* module's contents directly into the global namespace (using the *include Fox* statement).

The program begins by creating an *FXApp* object, with the application name "Hello" and the vendor name "FoxTest". Of the toolkits that we'll examine in this chapter, FOX is the only one that requires you to explicitly create and refer to an *application* object, which is used as a kind of central repository for global application resources (like default application fonts, colors and so on). It's also the entity responsible for managing the event loop, as we'll see toward the end.

The next step is to initialize the application. We call the application object's *init* method and pass in the command line arguments (Ruby's *ARGV* array), from which FOX can pick out selected meaningful options. For example, to enable FOX's tracing output from your FXRuby application, you can specify the −*tracelevel* option on the command line:

```
ruby hello.rb -tracelevel 301
```

For more information about which command line options FOX recognizes, consult the FOX documentation.

It's at this point that we finally get around to creating our first widget. The main window (named *main*) is an instance of the *Fox::FXMainWindow* class, and its *new* method expects a reference to the application object as well as a window title.

The next widget is a button (an instance of *Fox::FXButton*), and it's created as a child of the main window. This button will display the string "Hello, World!" and the first letter will be underlined because we placed an ampersand character ("&") before it. This is a special signal to the *FXButton* widget that this character should be underlined, and that the **Ctrl+H** accelerator key combination should have the same affect as directly clicking the button.

The fourth and fifth arguments to *FXButton*'s *new* method are significant in terms of how FOX processes user interface events. The fourth argument is a message target object (an instance of *FXObject* or one of its subclasses) and the fifth argument is a message identifier. In this case, the application is the message target for the button; any events generated on or by the button (button clicks, for example) will result in a message sent to the application. The message's identifier serves to distinguish between similar but different messages that the target object might receive; any given object can be the message target for *multiple* widgets.

The server-side resources (like windows, fonts and cursors) are created during the call to *FXApp*'s *create* method. FOX's distinction between the client side representation of objects (such as their instance variables) and server side resources associated with those objects is also unique to FOX. Once the windows and other resources have been created, the main window is shown centered onscreen and we enter the main event loop by calling the application's *run* method.

Targets and Messages

FOX's event model is based on the idea of application objects sending *messages* to other objects (their *targets*) when something interesting happens. It's your job as the application developer to decide how a target responds to a message. Because this target-message system is inherently bidirectional, part of that response often involves sending a message *back* to the original sender.

Every widget in your application has the ability to send messages, but some messages are more meaningful than others; for example, you'll probably want the application to respond in some way when the user types new text in a text field, or selects a new item from a tree list. You should specify a message target object for those widgets that you expect to send meaningful messages. Almost all FOX widgets allow you to specify their target as an argument to their constructors. For example, to construct a new *FXList* instance and specify that *anObject* is its target, you'd write:

```
myList = FXList.new(parent, numItems, anObject, …)
```

You can also change the target after the widget has been constructed by calling the widget's *setTarget* method:

```
myList.setTarget(anotherObject)
```

Every message has a *type* that indicates its significance. Some messages represent low-level events generated by the window system; for example, the

SEL_LEFTBUTTONPRESS message is sent when the left mouse button is pressed down while the *SEL_LEFTBUTTONRELEASE* message is sent when the same button is released. Other messages are generated by FOX and indicate more useful user interface events, like deleting text from a text widget or selecting a cell in a table. The message types are just integers (unlike the strings used for Ruby/Tk's events or Ruby/GTK's signals) but you'll always use the symbolic constants with names of the form *SEL_name*.

One message type that you'll encounter frequently in FOX applications is the *SEL_COMMAND* message; it generically means that the widget has just completed its primary action. For example, an FXButton widget will send a *SEL_COMMAND* message to its target after the user clicks on the button, while an FXTextField widget will send a *SEL_COMMAND* message after the user presses the **Enter** key in the text field or clicks outside of the text field.

It's a common practice in FOX applications to make one object the target of multiple widgets' messages. For example, your application might include multiple menu buttons for operations like **Open File**, **Save File**, and **Print File**, all sending their *SEL_COMMAND* messages to a single target. But you might wonder how that target object is able to distinguish between similar messages from different widgets. When the target receives a *SEL_COMMAND* message, how does it know *which* button sent the message? The answer is that each message includes an *identifier* (in addition to its type) to provide additional information about the source or significance of the message.

The message identifier is just an integer, usually represented by a symbolic constant that is defined by the *receiver* of the message. A class defines the different message identifiers it understands and, since FOX is an object-oriented toolkit, an object also understands all of the message identifiers defined by its ancestor classes. For example, since *FXButton* is a subclass of *FXLabel*, it inherits the message identifiers defined by *FXLabel* and *FXLabel*'s base class.

In order for an object to receive and respond to messages, it needs to register message handler functions for the different message types and identifiers. This registering is taken care of in the class *initialize* function, using the *FXMAP-FUNC* method to associate a message type and identifier with the name of an instance method for that class. For example, if we wanted to catch the *SEL_COMMAND* message with an *ID_OPEN_FILE* identifier, and use the *onOpenFile* method to handle that message, we'd write:

```
FXMAPFUNC(SEL_COMMAND, ID_OPEN_FILE, "onOpenFile")
```

Message handler functions (like our *onOpenFile* method) always take three arguments:

```
def onOpenFile(sender, sel, ptr)
  … handle this message …
end
```

The first argument (*sender*) is just a reference to the sender of the message, which is some other object in your application. It's often useful to know who sent the message, especially if part of the response involves sending a message *back* to the original sender.

The second argument (*sel*) is a number, sometimes referred to as the *selector*, which encodes both the message type and the message identifier. If necessary, you can extract the message type and identifier from the selector using the *SELTYPE* and *SELID* functions:

```
def onOpenFile(sender, sel, ptr)
  messageType = SELTYPE(sel)
  messageId   = SELID(sel)
  … handle this message …
end
```

The last argument passed to the message handler (*ptr*) contains message-specific data; the type of this data depends on both the sender and the message type. For example, when an FXTextField widget sends the *SEL_COMMAND* message to a target, the data sent along with the message is a string containing the text field's contents. When an *FXColorWell* widget sends a *SEL_COM-MAND* message to a target, however, the message data is an integer indicating the color well's current color. Our sample application will demonstrate some of the kinds of messages that get sent during a FOX application, but for a complete listing you should consult the FOX reference documentation (available at the FOX home page).

Working with FOX's Layout Managers

FOX's choices of layout managers are very similar to those for Tk and GTK+, with a few differences. We're going to focus on the four powerhouse layout managers: *FXPacker*, *FXHorizontalFrame*, *FXVerticalFrame* and *FXMatrix*. Like their counterparts in Tk and GTK+, these are the layout managers you'll use most often in real-world applications. For information about how to use some of the more special-purpose layout managers (like *FXSwitcher*, *FXSplitter* and *FX4Splitter*) check the FOX documentation.

As in GTK+, FOX layout managers are themselves just invisible container widgets that hold one or more child widgets. They're not strictly "invisible," since you have some control over how the outer border of the container is drawn (it's frame style), but we're mostly interested in how they arrange their child widgets.

As with Tk, FOX widgets are always constructed by passing in the parent widget as the first argument. You can later reparent a child window (that is, move it from one parent window to another) but unlike in Ruby/GTK, a child window cannot exist without a parent.

Unlike either of the other toolkits, FOX child widgets specify their layout preferences (or layout "hints") as part of their constructors. You can change a widget's layout settings after it exists by calling its *setLayout* instance method, but it's still a different model than those used in Tk and GTK+. As a FOX layout manager works its way through its unique layout strategy, it requests the layout hints from each of its children and uses those to assign the positions and sizes of those widgets.

We'll start by looking at *FXPacker* since it is both the most general of all the layout managers and it serves as the base class for the other three we'll cover (*FXHorizontalFrame*, *FXVerticalFrame* and *FXMatrix*). FXPacker uses roughly the same layout strategy as Tk's packer, and the names of the layout hints reflect its heritage. The *new* method for *FXPacker* goes like this:

```
aPacker = FXPacker.new(parent, opts=0,
                       x=0, y=0, w=0, h=0,
                       pl=DEFAULT_SPACING, pr=DEFAULT_SPACING,
                       pt=DEFAULT_SPACING, pb=DEFAULT_SPACING,
                       hs=DEFAULT_SPACING, vs=DEFAULT_SPACING)
```

You might take a few moments to recover from the shock at seeing such a long argument list. On closer examination, it should give you some relief to see that all but the first of its arguments are optional and have reasonable default values. As you start taking a look at the new methods for other FOX widgets, you'll see this pattern repeated: long argument lists with default values for most of the arguments. And in fact, most or all of these arguments can be changed after the widget has been constructed using its accessor methods, so that a call such as the following:

```
aPacker = FXPacker.new(parent, LAYOUT_EXPLICIT,
                        0, 0, 150, 80)
```

is equivalent to these four lines of code:

```
aPacker = FXPacker.new(parent)              # accept default values
aPacker.width = 150                         # fixed width (in pixels)
aPacker.height = 80                         # fixed height (in pixels)
aPacker.layoutHints = LAYOUT_EXPLICIT  # make sure width and height
                                            # values are actually enforced!
```

But we need to say more about the meanings of the arguments. Let's temporarily skip over the second argument (*opts*) and consider the remaining ones.

The *x*, *y*, *w* and *h* arguments are integers indicating the preferred position (in *its* parent's coordinate system) and size for a widget, with the caveat that any of these parameters is ignored if we don't also set the corresponding layout hint (*LAYOUT_FIX_X*, *LAYOUT_FIX_Y*, *LAYOUT_FIX_WIDTH* or *LAYOUT_FIX_HEIGHT*). These arguments show up in almost every widget's new method and they are not unique to *FXPacker.new*. In the above code example, we used a shortcut option, *LAYOUT_EXPLICIT*, that simply combines the four *LAYOUT_FIX* options; this makes sense, since a layout that uses fixed positions and sizes for its child widgets will need all of these options set.

The next four arguments to *FXPacker.new* are the left, right, top and bottom padding values, in pixels. Padding refers to the extra space placed around the inside edges of the container; if the layout of a particular packer in your program looks like it could use some extra breathing room around its edges, try increasing the padding values from their default value of *DEFAULT_SPACING* (a constant equal to 4 pixels).

The last two arguments for *FXPacker.new* indicate the horizontal and vertical spacing, in pixels, to be placed between the packer's children. As with the internal padding, this spacing defaults to four pixels.

Now let's come back to the second argument for *FXPacker.new*, its options flag (*opts*). Most FOX widgets' *new* methods use this value to turn on or off different bitwise flags describing their appearance or behavior. We've already seen that some of the flags include *layout hints*, hints from a child widget to its parent container about how it should be treated during the layout procedure. In addition to the *LAYOUT_FIX* hints, you can use:

- *LAYOUT_SIDE_LEFT* or *LAYOUT_SIDE_RIGHT*, and *LAYOUT_SIDE_TOP* or *LAYOUT_SIDE_BOTTOM* indicate which side(s) of the packing cavity this child widget should be packed against

- *LAYOUT_FILL_X* or *LAYOUT_CENTER_X*, and *LAYOUT_FILL_Y* or *LAYOUT_CENTER_Y* indicate how the child widget should make use of any leftover space assigned to it (should it grow to fill the space, or merely center itself in that space?)

There are two packer-specific options (or *packing styles*) that can be binary OR-ed into the optionsflag: *PACK_UNIFORM_WIDTH* and *PACK_UNI-FORM_HEIGHT*. Similar to the "homogeneous" property for Ruby/GTK's layout managers, these two options constrain the layout manager to assign equal widths (and/or heights) for its children. These packing styles apply to all of the packer's child widgets and override their preferences (including *LAYOUT_FIX_WIDTH* and *LAYOUT_FIX_HEIGHT*). These options are more appropriate for the other layout managers derived from *FXPacker*, but you can use them with the general packer if you know what you're doing.

We'll consider the next two layout managers, *FXHorizontalFrame* and *FXVerticalFrame*, together since they're so similar. As you might expect by now, these two arrange their child widgets horizontally and vertically, respectively. The *new* method for *FXHorizontalFrame* looks like this:

```
aHorizFrame = FXHorizontalFrame.new(parent, opts=0,
                                    x=0, y=0, w=0, h=0,
                                    pl=DEFAULT_SPACING,
                                    pr=DEFAULT_SPACING,
                                    pt=DEFAULT_SPACING,
                                    pb=DEFAULT_SPACING,
                                    hs=DEFAULT_SPACING,
                                    vs=DEFAULT_SPACING)
```

By default, the child widgets for a horizontal frame are arranged from left to right, in the order they're added. To request that a particular child should be packed against the right side of the horizontal frame's cavity, pass in the *LAYOUT_RIGHT* layout hint. Vertical frames arrange their children from top to bottom by default, and the *LAYOUT_BOTTOM* hint can be used to alter this pattern.

The last layout manager we'll review is *FXMatrix*, which arranges its children in rows and columns. The *new* method for *FXMatrix* is:

```
aMatrix = FXMatrix.new(parent, size=1, opts=0,
                        x=0, y=0, w=0, h=0,
                        pl=DEFAULT_SPACING, pr=DEFAULT_SPACING,
                        pt=DEFAULT_SPACING, pb=DEFAULT_SPACING,
                        hs=DEFAULT_SPACING, vs=DEFAULT_SPACING)
```

FXMatrix introduces two options, *MATRIX_BY_ROWS* and *MATRIX_BY_COLUMNS*, to indicate how the *size* argument for *FXMatrix.new* should be interpreted. For *MATRIX_BY_ROWS* (the default), *size* indicates the number of rows; the number of columns is ultimately determined by the total number of children for the matrix. In this configuration, the first *size* child widgets added to the matrix make up its first column: the first child becomes the first widget on the first row, the second child becomes the first widget on the second row, and so on. Alternately, the *MATRIX_BY_COLUMNS* option means that *size* is the number of columns and the number of rows varies.

Fox Sample Application

Figure 2.12 shows the complete source code for the FXRuby version of our sample application. The source code for this application appears on the CD accompanying this book, under the file name *fox-xmlviewer.rb*.

Figure 2.12 Source Code for Sample Application—FXRuby Version (fox-xmlviewer.rb)

```ruby
#!/bin/env ruby


require "fox"
require "fox/responder"


require "nqxml/treeparser"


include Fox


class XMLViewer < FXMainWindow


    include Responder
```

Continued

Figure 2.12 Continued

```ruby
# Define message identifiers for this class
ID_ABOUT, ID_OPEN, ID_TREELIST =
  enum(FXMainWindow::ID_LAST, 3)


def createMenubar
  menubar = FXMenubar.new(self, LAYOUT_SIDE_TOP|LAYOUT_FILL_X)


  filemenu = FXMenuPane.new(self)
  FXMenuTitle.new(menubar, "&File", nil, filemenu)
  FXMenuCommand.new(filemenu,
    "&Open...\tCtl-O\tOpen document file.", nil, self, ID_OPEN)
  FXMenuCommand.new(filemenu,
    "&Quit\tCtl-Q\tQuit the application.", nil,
    getApp(), FXApp::ID_QUIT, MENU_DEFAULT)


  helpmenu = FXMenuPane.new(self)
  FXMenuTitle.new(menubar, "&Help", nil, helpmenu, LAYOUT_RIGHT)
  FXMenuCommand.new(helpmenu,
    "&About FOX...\t\tDisplay FOX about panel.",
    nil, self, ID_ABOUT, 0)
end


def createTreeList
  listFrame = FXVerticalFrame.new(@splitter,
    LAYOUT_FILL_X|LAYOUT_FILL_Y|FRAME_SUNKEN|FRAME_THICK)
  @treeList = FXTreeList.new(listFrame, 0, self, ID_TREELIST,
    (LAYOUT_FILL_X|LAYOUT_FILL_Y|
      TREELIST_SHOWS_LINES|TREELIST_SHOWS_BOXES|TREELIST_ROOT_BOXES))
end


def createAttributesTable
  tableFrame = FXVerticalFrame.new(@splitter,
```

Continued

Figure 2.12 Continued

```ruby
            LAYOUT_FILL_X|LAYOUT_FILL_Y|FRAME_SUNKEN|FRAME_THICK)
    @attributesTable = FXTable.new(tableFrame, 5, 2, nil, 0,
        (TABLE_HOR_GRIDLINES|TABLE_VER_GRIDLINES|
          FRAME_SUNKEN|FRAME_THICK|LAYOUT_FILL_X|LAYOUT_FILL_Y))
  end

  def initialize(app)
    # Initialize base class first
    super(app, "XML Editor", nil, nil, DECOR_ALL, 0, 0, 800, 600)

    # Set up the message map
    FXMAPFUNC(SEL_COMMAND, ID_ABOUT,      "onCmdAbout")
    FXMAPFUNC(SEL_COMMAND, ID_OPEN,       "onCmdOpen")
    FXMAPFUNC(SEL_COMMAND, ID_TREELIST,   "onCmdTreeList")

    # Create the menu bar
    createMenubar

    @splitter = FXSplitter.new(self, LAYOUT_FILL_X|LAYOUT_FILL_Y)

    # Create the tree list on the left
    createTreeList

    # Attributes table on the right
    createAttributesTable

    # Make a tool tip
    FXTooltip.new(getApp(), 0)
  end

  # Create and show the main window
  def create
```

Continued

Figure 2.12 Continued

```ruby
    super
    show(PLACEMENT_SCREEN)
  end


  def loadDocument(filename)
    @document = nil
    begin
      @document = NQXML::TreeParser.new(File.new(filename)).document
    rescue NQXML::ParserError => ex
      FXMessageBox.error(self, MBOX_OK, "Error",
        "Couldn't parse XML document")
    end
    if @document
      @treeList.clearItems()
      populateTreeList(@document.rootNode, nil)
    end
  end


  def populateTreeList(docRootNode, treeRootNode)
    entity = docRootNode.entity
    if entity.instance_of?(NQXML::Tag)
      treeItem = @treeList.addItemLast(treeRootNode, entity.to_s, nil,
                                       nil, entity)

      docRootNode.children.each do |node|
        populateTreeList(node, treeItem)
      end
    elsif entity.instance_of?(NQXML::Text) &&
          entity.to_s.strip.length != 0
      treeItem = @treeList.addItemLast(treeRootNode, entity.to_s, nil,
                                       nil, entity)
    end
  end
```

Continued

Figure 2.12 Continued

```ruby
def onCmdOpen(sender, sel, ptr)
  dlg = FXFileDialog.new(self, "Open")
  dlg.setPatternList([
    "All Files (*)",
    "XML Documents (*.xml)"])
  if dlg.execute() != 0
    loadDocument(dlg.getFilename())
  end
  return 1
end


def onCmdTreeList(sender, sel, treeItem)
  if treeItem
    entity = treeItem.getData()
    if entity.kind_of?(NQXML::NamedAttributes)
      keys = entity.attrs.keys.sort
      @attributesTable.setTableSize(keys.length, 2)
      keys.each_index { |row|
        @attributesTable.setItemText(row, 0, keys[row])
        @attributesTable.setItemText(row, 1, entity.attrs[keys[row]])
      }
    end
  end
  return 1
end


# About box
def onCmdAbout(sender, sel, ptr)
  FXMessageBox.information(self, MBOX_OK, "About XMLViewer",
    "FXRuby Sample Application")
  return 1
end
end
```

Continued

Figure 2.12 Continued

```ruby
if $0 == __FILE__

  # Make application
  application = FXApp.new("XMLViewer", "FoxTest")


  # Open the display
  application.init(ARGV)


  # Make window
  mainWindow = XMLViewer.new(application)


  # Create the application windows
  application.create


  # Run the application
  application.run
end
```

The FXRuby version of our sample application begins by requiring the *fox* and *fox/responder* features, which correspond to the main FOX library as well as the code used by widgets to register their message handler methods:

```ruby
require "fox"
require "fox/responder"


require "nqxml/treeparser"


include Fox


class XMLViewer < FXMainWindow


  include Responder


  # Define message identifiers for this class
  ID_ABOUT, ID_OPEN, ID_TREELIST =
    enum(FXMainWindow::ID_LAST, 3)
```

As we'll see shortly, we want the main window class (*XMLViewer*) to respond to three message identifiers: *ID_ABOUT*, which is related to the **About...** menu command; *ID_OPEN*, which is related to the **Open...** menu command, and *ID_TREELIST*, which is related to selections in the tree list. In order to register message handler functions for a class, you need to first mix-in the *Responder* module. The *enum* function is a helper provided by this module, and it simply constructs an array of integers beginning with its first input and continuing for a number of elements equal to its second argument. In this case, we make sure that the enumerated values begin with *FXMainWindow::ID_LAST* so that we don't clash with any of *FXMainWindow*'s message identifiers. This is a standard programming idiom for FXRuby applications.

The first step in the initialize method is to initialize the base class (*FXMainWindow*):

```
super(app, "XML Editor", nil, nil, DECOR_ALL, 0, 0, 800, 600)
```

It's important not to omit this step! Here, the second argument to *FXMainWindow*'s initialize method is the window title ("XML Editor"). The fifth argument is a set of flags that provide hints to the window manager about which window decorations (for example, a title bar or resize handles) should be displayed for this window. In our case, we'll request all possible decorations, *DECOR_ALL*. The last two arguments specify the initial width and height for the main window.

The next step is to set up the message map for this object:

```
FXMAPFUNC(SEL_COMMAND, ID_ABOUT,    "onCmdAbout")
FXMAPFUNC(SEL_COMMAND, ID_OPEN,     "onCmdOpen")
FXMAPFUNC(SEL_COMMAND, ID_TREELIST, "onCmdTreeList")
```

The *FXMAPFUNC* method is mixed-in from the *Responder* module and its arguments are the message type, identifier, and message handler method name. The first call, for example, declares that if an *XMLViewer* object is asked to handle a *SEL_COMMAND* message with the message identifier *XMLViewer::ID_ABOUT*, it should do so by calling its *onCmdAbout* method.

The remainder of the *initialize* method sets up the contents and layout of the main window. The first point of interest is the application's menu bar, created in the *createMenubar* method:

```
def createMenubar
  menubar = FXMenubar.new(self, LAYOUT_SIDE_TOP|LAYOUT_FILL_X)
```

```
filemenu = FXMenuPane.new(self)

FXMenuTitle.new(menubar, "&File", nil, filemenu)

FXMenuCommand.new(filemenu,

  "&Open...\tCtl-O\tOpen document file.", nil, self, ID_OPEN)

FXMenuCommand.new(filemenu,

  "&Quit\tCtl-Q\tQuit the application.", nil,

  getApp(), FXApp::ID_QUIT, MENU_DEFAULT)


helpmenu = FXMenuPane.new(self)

FXMenuTitle.new(menubar, "&Help", nil, helpmenu, LAYOUT_RIGHT)

FXMenuCommand.new(helpmenu,

  "&About FOX...\t\tDisplay FOX about panel.",

  nil, self, ID_ABOUT, 0)
end
```

An *FXMenubar* acts as a horizontally-oriented container for one or more *FXMenuTitle* widgets. The *FXMenuTitle* has a text string associated with it for the menu title (like 'File') as well as an associated popup *FXMenuPane* that contains one or more *FXMenuCommand* widgets. The text for the menu title can include an ampersand character ("&") in front of one of the title's characters; when this is present, that letter will be underlined and FOX will install a keyboard accelerator to activate that menu. For example, the *FXMenuTitle* for the **File** menu:

```
FXMenuTitle.new(menubar, "&File", nil, filemenu)
```

will display the text "File" with the "F" underlined, and the **Alt+F** keyboard combination can be used to post that menu. Similarly, the text for menu commands can contain special control characters and delimiters:

```
FXMenuCommand.new(filemenu,

  "&Open...\tCtl-O\tOpen document file.", nil, self, ID_OPEN)
```

The ampersand in front of the "O" in "Open…" defines a hot key for that menu command; if the **File** menu is already posted, you can press the **O** key to activate the **Open…** command. The tab characters ("\t") are recognized by FOX as field separators. The first field is the primary text displayed on the *FXMenuCommand*. The second field is an optional string indicating an accelerator key combination that can be used to directly access that command, even if the menu isn't posted. The optional last field's string is the status line help text for this menu command.

Although we don't use any menu separators in this example, it is often helpful to add one or more horizontal separators to a pulldown menu to group together closely related menu commands. To add a menu separator to an *FXMenuPane*, simply create an instance of the *FXMenuSeparator* class in the desired position:

```
FXMenuSeparator.new(filemenu)
```

The left-hand side of the main window houses a tree listing of the XML document nodes; it's created in the *createTreeList* method:

```
def createTreeList
  listFrame = FXVerticalFrame.new(@splitter,
    LAYOUT_FILL_X|LAYOUT_FILL_Y|FRAME_SUNKEN|FRAME_THICK)
  @treeList = FXTreeList.new(listFrame, 0, self, ID_TREELIST,
    (LAYOUT_FILL_X|LAYOUT_FILL_Y|
     TREELIST_SHOWS_LINES|TREELIST_SHOWS_BOXES|TREELIST_ROOT_BOXES))
end
```

Because the *FXTreeList* class isn't derived from *FXFrame*, it doesn't directly support any of the frame style flags. In order to get a nice-looking sunken border around the tree list, we need to enclose it in some kind of *FXFrame*-derived container; here, we're using an *FXVerticalFrame*.

From the third and fourth arguments passed to *FXTreeList.new* we can see that the message target for this *FXTreeList* is the main window (*self*) and its message identifier is *XMLViewer::ID_TREELIST*. As we saw in the *initialize* function when we were setting up the message map, a *SEL_COMMAND* message sent with this identifier should lead to the *onCmdTreeList* method being invoked:

```
def onCmdTreeList(sender, sel, treeItem)
  if treeItem
    entity = treeItem.getData()
    if entity.kind_of?(NQXML::NamedAttributes)
      keys = entity.attrs.keys.sort
      @attributesTable.setTableSize(keys.length, 2)
      keys.each_index { |row|
```

```
        @attributesTable.setItemText(row, 0, keys[row])
        @attributesTable.setItemText(row, 1, entity.attrs[keys[row]])
      }
    end
  end
  return 1
end
```

When *FXTreeList* sends a *SEL_COMMAND* to its message target, the message data (the third argument passed to the message handler method) is a reference to the selected tree item, if any. Assuming that the selected item (named *treeItem*) is not *nil*, we get a reference to the user data associated with this tree item. As we'll see later, when we review the *populateTreeList* method that created these tree items, the user data associated with the tree items are references to the XML entities that the tree items represent. If the entity has attributes associated with it, we modify the table's row count by calling its *setTableSize* method and then iterate over the attributes to update the table cells' contents.

The attributes table on the right-hand side of the main window is created by the *createAttributesTable* method, and it consists of an *FXTable* widget, which is also enclosed in an *FXVerticalFrame*:

```
def createAttributesTable
  tableFrame = FXVerticalFrame.new(@splitter,
    LAYOUT_FILL_X|LAYOUT_FILL_Y|FRAME_SUNKEN|FRAME_THICK)
  @attributesTable = FXTable.new(tableFrame, 5, 2, nil, 0,
    (TABLE_HOR_GRIDLINES|TABLE_VER_GRIDLINES|
    FRAME_SUNKEN|FRAME_THICK|LAYOUT_FILL_X|LAYOUT_FILL_Y))
end
```

For some of the other GUI toolkits we've looked at, the name *table* refers to a layout manager that arranges its children in rows and columns (what FOX calls the *FXMatrix* layout manager). For FOX, the *FXTable* is more of a spreadsheet-like widget. We're creating an *FXTable* widget that initially has 5 visible rows and 2 visible columns, although, as we'll see later, the table dimensions are changed dynamically while the program's running.

The *onCmdOpen* method handles the *SEL_COMMAND* message generated when the user clicks the **Open...** menu command from the **File** menu:

```ruby
def onCmdOpen(sender, sel, ptr)
  dlg = FXFileDialog.new(self, "Open")
  dlg.setPatternList([
    "All Files (*)",
    "XML Documents (*.xml)"])
  if dlg.execute() != 0
    loadDocument(dlg.getFilename())
  end
  return 1
end
```

We construct a new *FXFileDialog* object, initialize its pattern list and then display the dialog by calling its *execute* method. The *execute* method returns non-zero if the user pressed the **OK** button, and when this is the case, we query the filename entered by the user and call *loadDocument* to load that XML document:

```ruby
def loadDocument(filename)
  @document = nil
  begin
    @document = NQXML::TreeParser.new(File.new(filename)).document
  rescue NQXML::ParserError => ex
    FXMessageBox.error(self, MBOX_OK, "Error",
      "Couldn't parse XML document")
  end
  if @document
    @treeList.clearItems()
    populateTreeList(@document.rootNode, nil)
  end
end
```

If the XML parser raises an exception while trying to create the *NQXML::Document* object, we call the *FXMessageBox.error* singleton method to display a simple dialog box explaining to the user what happened. The first argument to *FXMessageBox.error* identifies the owner window for this dialog box, i.e. the window above which this message box should float until it's dismissed. The second argument is a flag indicating which terminator buttons should be displayed on the message box; other options include *MBOX_OK_CANCEL, MBOX_YES_NO, MBOX_YES_NO_CANCEL, MBOX_QUIT_CANCEL* and *MBOX_QUIT_SAVE_CANCEL*. The *FXMessageBox* class supports a handful of other convenient singleton methods for displaying common messages (*information, question* and *warning*). If there were no errors, we clear the tree list's contents and then build up the tree list's contents with recursive calls to *populateTreeList*:

```
Parameter "self" in parens looks as if it is an argument to
FXMessageBox.errordef populateTreeList(docRootNode, treeRootNode)
  entity = docRootNode.entity
  if entity.instance_of?(NQXML::Tag)
    treeItem = @treeList.addItemLast(treeRootNode, entity.to_s, nil,
                                     nil, entity)
    docRootNode.children.each do |node|
      populateTreeList(node, treeItem)
    end
  elsif entity.instance_of?(NQXML::Text) &&
        entity.to_s.strip.length != 0
    treeItem = @treeList.addItemLast(treeRootNode, entity.to_s, nil,
                                     nil, entity)
  end
end
```

Here, we're using *FXTreeList*'s *addItemLast* method to add new tree items to the tree list. The first argument to *addItemLast* is a reference to a tree item, the parent for the item to be created; to create tree items at the top level, you can instead pass in *nil* for this argument. The second argument to *addItemLast* is the text to be displayed on the tree item and the third and fourth (optional) arguments are the "opened" and "closed" icons to be displayed alongside the tree item's text. If no icons are provided, *FXTreeList* will draw either a plus or minus sign in a square as the default icons. The last argument to *addItemLast* is optional user data; it's any Ruby object that you'd like to associate with the newly created tree item. In our case, we'll store a reference to the XML entity that this tree item represents.

Figure 2.13 shows the FXRuby version of our sample application, running under Microsoft Windows 2000.

Figure 2.13 The FXRuby Version of the XML Viewer Application

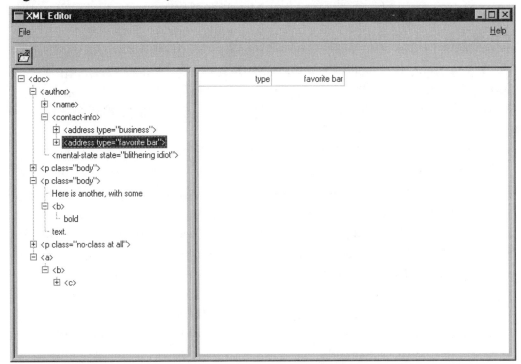

Using the SWin / VRuby Extensions

SWin and VRuby are the two primary components of the VisualuRuby project. SWin is a Ruby extension module, written in C, that exposes much of the Win32 API to the Ruby interpreter. VRuby is a library of pure Ruby modules built on top of SWin, that provides a higher-level interface to the Win32 programming environment.

As is the case with many Ruby extensions, most of the documentation for SWin and VRuby is only available in Japanese. And although the example programs from the VisualuRuby Web site will give you some idea about what's possible with SWin and VRuby, there's an implicit assumption that you're already familiar with basic Windows programming concepts. This section provides enough of an overview of the VRuby API to develop our sample application, but for a real appreciation of SWin/VRuby you need a stronger background in Windows programming. There are some excellent books on this subject, and although they may discuss the Win32 API from a C programming standpoint, they should help you to fill in a lot of the blanks about programming with

VRuby as well. Along those lines, another invaluable reference is the Win32 API reference from the Microsoft Developer Network (MSDN) CDs and DVDs.

Obtaining SWin and VRuby

SWin and VRuby are included in the Ruby installer for Windows from the Pragmatic Programmers' Web site. The source code for SWin can be downloaded from the VisualuRuby project home page, and you should be able to find pre-compiled binaries there as well.

VRuby Library Basics

Because there is so little English-language documentation available for SWin and VRuby, we're going to take an additional section here to provide a brief overview of the VRuby library and the classes and modules it provides. Most of this information has been extracted from the source file comments, which themselves are pretty sketchy, but this may give you a head start when you set out to begin working with VRuby.

The VRuby library is organized as a set of Ruby source files installed under the *vr* package directory. Table 2.1 lists some of the most important files that you'll be using in your applications (and the corresponding *require* statements). Note that most or all of the non-core files depend on the core classes and modules from vr/vruby.rb, so you probably won't need to import this file explicitly.

Table 2.1 VRuby Library Contents

Description	How to Import
Core Classes and Modules	require 'vr/vruby'
Layout Managers	require 'vr/vrlayout'
Standard Controls	require 'vr/vrcontrol'
Common Controls	require 'vr/vrcomctl'
Multipane Windows	require 'vr/vrtwopane'

The core classes and modules for VRuby (Table 2.2) consist of very high-level base classes and mix-in modules that you won't use directly in most programs. Two notable exceptions, however, are *VRForm* and *VRScreen*. *VRForm* is the base class used for top-level windows, such as your application's main window. As we'll see in the sample application, you typically want to derive your main window class from *VRForm*, possibly mixing in some other behaviors, and handling most customization in that class' *construct* method.

Table 2.2 Core Classes and Modules for VRuby

Class/Module Name	Description
VRMessageHandler	This module should be mixed in to any class that needs to receive Windows messages; it provides module methods *acceptEvents* and *addHandler*.
VRParent	This module provides module methods used by parent windows (windows that can function as containers of other child windows). It is mixed in to *VRForm* and *VRPanel* (among others) since they're the most popular container classes you'll use.
VRWinComponent	This is the base class of all windows.
VRControl	Base class for all controls (widgets); a subclass of *VRWinComponent*.
VRCommonDialog	This module offers several convenience functions for using common Windows dialogs; provides module methods *openFilenameDialog*, *saveFilenameDialog*, *chooseColorDialog* and *chooseFontDialog*.
VRForm	This is the base class for all top-level windows, like your application's main window, and it mixes in the *VRMessageHandler*, *VRParent* and *VRCommonDialog* modules.
VRPanel	This is the base class for all child windows (like controls); a subclass of *VRControl*.
VRDrawable	This module should be mixed in to any class that needs to handle the paint message (indicating that the window's contents need to be redrawn); that class should override the *self_paint* method.
VRResizeable	This module should be mixed in to any class that needs to intercept window resize events; that class should override *self_resize* method.
VRUserMessageUseable	This module should be mixed in to any class that needs to register user-defined messages with the operating system.
VRScreen	This class represents the Windows desktop, and provides methods to create and show new top-level windows and manage the event loop. VRuby defines exactly one global instance of this class, *VRLocalScreen*.

Some of the Windows controls have existed since the pre–Windows 95 days, and this set has come to be known as the *standard* controls. The standard controls (like buttons, labels and text fields), are accessible when you require 'vr/vrcontrol.rb'. Table 2.3 lists the classes exposed by this module.

Table 2.3 Standard Controls for VRuby

Class/Module Name	Description
VRStdControl	This class (a subclass of *VRControl*) is just the base class of all the standard controls.
VRButton	This is a standard push button; you can assign the button's text using the *caption=* instance method.
VRGroupbox	Group box
VRCheckbox	This is a check box control. You can set or remove the check mark using the *check* instance method, and test for its current setting using the *checked?* instance method.
VRRadioButton	This is a radio button, usually displayed as one of a group of radio buttons used to indicate mutually exclusive choices. Because it is a special case (a subclass) of *VRCheckbox*, it also supports the *check* and *checked?* instance methods.
VRStatic	This is a static text control, which simply displays a non-editable text label. The label text can be assigned using its *caption=* instance method.
VREdit	This is a single-line, editable text control. It provides a number of instance methods related to getting and setting the text, as well as working with the selected (highlighted) text and transferring text between the *VREdit* control and the Windows clipboard.
VRText	This is a multi-line editable text control. It's similar to the single-line version (*VREdit*) but provides a number of additional instance methods related to navigating through the text.
VRListbox	This is a vertically-oriented list of strings from which the user can select one or more items.
VRCombobox	This is a drop-down list of strings, similar to the *VRListbox* but with the difference that only one string can be selected.

Continued

Table 2.3 Continued

Class/Module Name	Description
VRMenu	This is a menu bar, populated with pulldown menus, that typically appears along the top edge of the application's main window.
VRMenuItem	This is a single menu item that appears in a *VRMenu* (for example, the **Save As...** command in an application's **File** menu). You'll usually create these implicitly when you call a menu's *set* method.
VRMenuUseable	This module should be mixed in to any window class that needs to use menus; it provides the *newMenu* and *setMenu* module methods.
VRBitmapPanel	This is a special kind of panel used to display a (static) bitmap image.
VRCanvasPanel	This is a special kind of panel used to display drawable bitmap images; you specify its width and height and can then use GDI functions to draw into it.

Windows 95 introduced a host of new user interface controls known as the *common* controls. These included controls such as the list views and tree views used extensively in the Windows Explorer. The VRuby classes representing common controls are listed in Table 2.4.

Table 2.4 Common Controls for VRuby

Class Name	Description
VRNotifyControl	This class (a subclass of *VRControl*) is just the base class of all the common controls.
VRListview	This is an enhanced list control that can be configured to display its data in a variety of formats (as icons with simple descriptions, or in a more detailed list form). The most familiar use of this control is in the Windows Explorer.
VRTreeview	This control, also commonly known as a tree list, is used to display hierarchically structured data. It's a popular choice for many Windows programs, used, for example, in the Registry Editor utility.

Continued

Table 2.3 Continued

Class Name	Description
VRProgressbar	This control is used during time-consuming operations to provide the user with some feedback on how far the operation has progressed and how much time is left before it's completed.
VRTrackbar	This control consists of a slider and optional tick marks. It is useful when you want the user to select a discrete value from a range of values.
VRUpdown	This control consists of a pair of arrow buttons (usually one pointing up and one pointing down) that the user can use to increment or decrement some value in the application. It is almost always paired with a buddy window, such as a *VREdit* control, to display its current setting.
VRStatusbar	This control is a horizontal strip that can appear at the bottom of the main window and is used to display status information.
VRStatusbarDockable	This module should be mixed in to a *VRForm* that will include a status bar control. It defines an *addStatusbar* method for adding a statusbar to the form.
VRTabControl	This control displays one or more tabs which can be used as the basis of a property sheet or tabbed panel.
VRTabbedPanel	This control combines the *VRTabControl* with a series of panels to create a tabbed *notebook* control.

Layout Managers

In contrast to all the other GUI toolkits we've seen so far, VRuby doesn't offer much in terms of layout managers. This is primarily due to the fact that the Win32 API on which SWin and VRuby are based doesn't include any layout management at all. Although the layout managers currently packaged with VRuby are somewhat limited, one would expect this situation to improve as VRuby matures.

The three layout managers for VRuby are *VRHorizLayoutManager*, *VRVertLayoutManager* and *VRGridLayoutManager*. Instead of serving as standalone container classes, these layout managers are modules that you mix in to a VRuby

container class like *VRPanel*. Like their counterparts in Ruby/GTK and
FXRuby, the first two arrange their children either horizontally or vertically. To
use them, first mix the desired layout manager module into your container class:

```
require 'vr/vrlayout'

class MyPanelClass < VRPanel
   include VRHorizLayoutManager
end
```

   Then add one or more child widgets (or, in Windows-speak, *controls*) to the
container using *addControl*:

```
aPanel = MyPanelClass.new ...

aPanel.addControl(VRButton, "button1", "Caption for First Button")
aPanel.addControl(VRButton, "button2", "Caption for Second Button")
```

   The full argument list for *VRHorizLayoutManager#addControl* (or
VRVertLayoutManager#addControl) is:

```
addControl(type, name, caption, style=0)
```

where *type* is the VRuby class for the control, *name* is its name, and *caption* is the
text to display on the control (for controls that support captions). The last argument, *style*, can be used to pass in additional Windows style flags for this control.
By default, VRuby will create a control with only the basic style flags; for
example, *VRButton* controls are created with the *WStyle::WS_VISIBLE* and
WStyle::BS_PUSHBUTTON flags. Unlike their counterparts in other GUI
toolkits, you'd don't really have any control over the child controls' resizing
parameters. For *VRHorizLayoutManager*, each child's height is the same as the
container's height and the width of the container is equally divided amongst the
child controls. Furthermore, each child is automatically stretched (horizontally
and vertically) to fill its assigned space.

   The *VRGridLayoutManager* roughly corresponds to Tk's *grid* layout, GTK's
Gtk::Table and FOX's *FXMatrix*, but with the same kinds of limitations of child
control sizing that we saw for *VRHorizLayoutManager* and *VRVertLayoutManager*.
Before adding any controls to a container using the *VRGridLayoutManager* layout
manager, you should first set the number of rows and columns using
VRGridLayoutManager#setDimension:

```
require 'vr/vrlayout'

class MyPanel < VRPanel
  include VRGridLayoutManager
end
aPanel = MyPanel.new ...
aPanel.setDimension(5, 3)
```

where the two arguments are the number of rows and number of columns, respectively. After that you can add child controls using *VRGridLayoutManager#addControl*:

```
addControl(type, name, caption, x, y, w, h, style=0)
```

Here, the first three arguments are the same as for the previous layout managers' *addControl* methods. The next two arguments (*x* and *y*) are used to indicate the upper-left cell of the range of cells occupied by this control, and the *w* and *h* arguments indicate the width and height (in numbers of table cells) of the range. For a control that only takes up one table cell's space, you'd use a width and height of one.

Event Handling

VRuby uses a callback-based approach for event handling that is quite unlike any of the others we've looked at. You may have wondered about why you specify a name for each control that you add to a form. For example, when adding a button control you might use:

```
aForm.addControl(VRButton, "button1", "Caption for Button", …)
```

The third argument is the caption string that is displayed on the button. The name string doesn't appear to be used anywhere, but in fact, whenever you add a new control to a *VRForm* or *VRPanel* (actually, any class that mixes in the *VRParent* module), that container object also adds new instance variable and accessor methods with the name you specified in the call to *addControl*. This new instance variable is just a reference to the child control. So, after executing the previous line of code, you could later change the button's caption with:

```
aForm.button1.caption = "New Caption for Button"
```

The controls' names are also used when they generate callbacks, and these callback methods must have names of the form:

```
def controlname_eventname
  … handle this event …
end
```

So, for example, if you wanted to catch the *clicked* event for the **button1** control, you'd need a method named *button1_clicked*:

```
def button1_clicked
  puts "Button 1 was clicked!"
end
```

These callback methods must be defined as instance methods for the container window, that is, if we had created *button1* as a child of *aForm*, *button1_clicked* would need to be an instance method of *aForm*. We'll see a few examples of how this works in the sample application, but Tables 2.5 and 2.6 provide listings of the event names for all the VRuby controls you might use.

Table 2.5 Event Names for Standard Controls

Control Class	Event Name(s)
VRButton	clicked, dblclicked
VREdit	changed
VRListbox	selchange
VRCombobox	selchange

Table 2.6 Event Names for Common Controls

Control Class	Event Name(s)
All Common Controls	clicked, dblclicked, gotfocus, hitreturn, lostfocus, rclicked, rdblclicked
VRListview	itemchanged, itemchanging, columnclick, begindrag, beginrdrag
VRTreeview	selchanged, itemexpanded, deleteitem, begindrag, beginrdrag
VRUpdown	changed
VRTabControl	selchanged

VRuby Sample Application

Figure 2.15 (found at the close of this section) shows the VRuby version of the sample application in its entirety. The source code for this application appears on the CD accompanying this book, under the file name *vruby-xmlviewer.rb*. It begins by importing the various VRuby library files that we'll need:

```
require 'vr/vruby'
require 'vr/vrcontrol'
require 'vr/vrcomctl'
require 'vr/vrtwopane'
```

Next, we define the global constants that we'll need to display message boxes later in the program:

```
# The values of these constants were lifted from <winuser.h>
MB_OK                 = 0x00000000
MB_ICONEXCLAMATION    = 0x00000030
MB_ICONINFORMATION    = 0x00000040
```

The Win32 API uses a large number of named constants (like *MB_OK*, *MB_ICONEXCLAMATION* and *MB_ICONINFORMATION*) to specify style flags for controls. In our case, the last argument of VRuby's *messageBox* function specifies message box options such as the displayed buttons and icon. Since these named constants are not yet exposed by SWin/VRuby, you need to dig around in the Windows header files to determine the actual numeric values of those constants. As you might have guessed, this is one of those times that a Windows programming background is a must!

The next major block of code defines the *XMLViewerForm* class and its instance methods; this is the focal point of the program. Before we jump into this, let's skip ahead for a moment and take a look at the last few lines of the program:

```
mainWindow = VRLocalScreen.newform(nil, nil, XMLViewerForm)
mainWindow.create
mainWindow.show


# Start the message loop
VRLocalScreen.messageloop
```

After defining the *XMLViewerForm* class (which is just a subclass of *VRForm*) we call *VRLocalScreen's newform* method to create an instance of *XMLViewerForm*.

Recall that *VRLocalScreen* is a special variable in VRuby; it's the single, global instance of *VRScreen* and it loosely corresponds to the Windows desktop. The first two arguments to *VRScreen#newform* are the parent window and the style flags for this window. In our case, this is the application's top-level main window and so we pass *nil* for the parent window. We also pass *nil* for the style flags, to indicate that we want the default style.

The call to *mainWindow.create* actually creates the real window backing this Ruby object. Since this is also a container window, the call to *create* triggers a call to *mainWindow's construct* method (which we'll see in a moment) to create its child controls and menus. The last step before entering the main event loop is to make the main window visible by calling *show*.

Now let's go back and look at the code for our form class, *XMLViewerForm*. We begin by mixing-in two modules that add useful functionality to the basic *VRForm*:

```
include VRMenuUseable

include VRHorizTwoPane
```

The *VRMenuUseable* module gives us the *newMenu* and *setMenu* methods for setting up the application's pulldown menus. The *VRHorizTwoPane* module adds the *addPanedControl* method and enables a horizontally-split paned layout for the main window contents. Next, we define the form's *construct* method, which actually creates the menus and adds child controls to the main window:

```
def construct
  # Set caption for application main window
  self.caption = "XML Viewer"

  # Create the menu bar
  @menu = newMenu()
  @menu.set([ ["&File", [ ["&Open...", "open"], ["Quit",  "quit"] ] ],
             ["&Help", [ ["About...", "about"] ] ]
           ])
  setMenu(@menu)

  # Tree view appears on the left
  addPanedControl(VRTreeview, "treeview", "")

  # List view appears on the right
```

```
    addPanedControl(VRListview, "listview", "")
    @listview.addColumn("Attribute Name", 150)
    @listview.addColumn("Attribute Value", 150)
end
```

The call to *newMenu* simply creates an empty menu and assigns it to our
@menu instance variable; the call to *set* actually defines the menu's contents. It's a
bit difficult to read, but *set* takes a single argument that is an array of arrays, one
per pulldown menu. The sub-array for each pulldown menu is itself a two-element array. Consider the first nested array, corresponding to the *File* menu:

```
["&File", [ ["&Open...", "open"], ["Quit",   "quit"] ] ]
```

The first array element is the name of the pulldown menu. By placing an
ampersand ("&") before the "F" in "File", we can make the **Alt-F** keyboard combination an accelerator for this menu choice. The second element in this array is
another array, this time of the different menu items. Each element in the menu
items array is either a two-element array providing the caption and name for the
menu item, or the caption and yet another array of menu items (for defining
nested or *cascading* menus). All of these nested arrays were making me a little dizzy
and so for this example I stayed with single-level (non-cascading) menus.

In the earlier section on event handling, we saw that the names of controls
are significant because they are used in the names of VRuby's callback methods.
In the same way, the names you assign to menu items are significant; when the
user clicks on one these menu items, VRuby will look for a callback method
named *name_clicked*. Soon we'll see that the *XMLViewerForm* class defines callback
methods *open_clicked*, *quit_clicked* and *about_clicked* to handle these three menu
commands.

After setting up the application's menus in *XMLViewerForm*'s *construct* method,
we add exactly two controls to our horizontal pane:

```
# Tree view appears on the left
addPanedControl(VRTreeview, "treeview", "")


# List view appears on the right
addPanedControl(VRListview, "listview", "")
```

Recall that the names of child controls added to a *VRParent* become the
names of instance variables. We'll take advantage of this to further configure the
list view widget (named *listview*):

```
@listview.addColumn("Attribute Name", 150)
@listview.addColumn("Attribute Value", 150)
```

Next, let's take a look at the three callback methods that handle the **Open…**, **Quit** and **About…** menu commands. Because the name associated with the **Open…** menu command was *open*, its callback method is named *open_clicked*:

```
def open_clicked
  filters = [["All Files (*.*)", "*.*"],
             ["XML Documents (*.xml)", "*.xml"]]
  filename = openFilenameDialog(filters)
  loadDocument(filename) if filename
end
```

The *openFilenameDialog* method is a convenience function for displaying a standard Windows file dialog. It is a module method for the *VRCommonDialog* module, which is mixed in to the *VRForm* class, so you can call this method for any form. Its input is an array of filename patterns (or *filters*) that will be displayed in the file dialog and returns the name of the selected file (or *nil* if the user cancelled the dialog). The callback for the **About…** menu command is handled by the *about_clicked* method:

```
def about_clicked
  messageBox("VRuby XML Viewer Example", "About XMLView",
    MB_OK|MB_ICONINFORMATION)
end
```

The *messageBox* method is another kind of convenience function, and is actually an instance method of the *SWin::Window* class (a distant ancestor class of our form). As you can probably surmise, the three arguments are the message box's message, its window title, and the style flags indicating which icon and terminating buttons to display. The callback for the **Quit** menu command is the easiest to understand, since it just calls Ruby's *exit* method:

```
def quit_clicked
  exit
end
```

Figure 2.14 shows the VRuby version of our sample application, running under Microsoft Windows 2000.

Figure 2.14 The VRuby Version of the XML Viewer Application

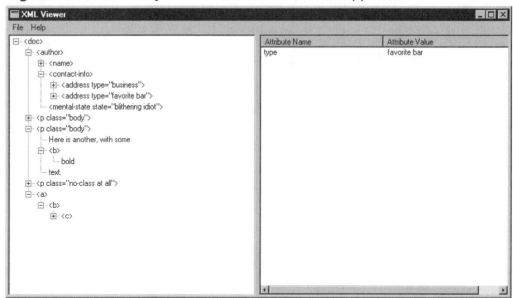

Figure 2.15 Source Code for Sample Application—VRuby Version (vruby-xmlviewer.rb)

```ruby
require 'vr/vruby'
require 'vr/vrcontrol'
require 'vr/vrcomctl'
require 'vr/vrtwopane'

require 'nqxml/treeparser'

# The values of these constants were lifted from <winuser.h>
MB_OK                = 0x00000000
MB_ICONEXCLAMATION   = 0x00000030
MB_ICONINFORMATION   = 0x00000040

class XMLViewerForm < VRForm

  include VRMenuUseable
  include VRHorizTwoPane
```

Continued

Figure 2.15 Continued

```ruby
def construct
  # Set caption for application main window
  self.caption = "XML Viewer"

  # Create the menu bar
  @menu = newMenu()
  @menu.set([ ["&File", [ ["&Open...", "open"], ["Quit", "quit"] ] ],
              ["&Help", [ ["About...", "about"] ] ]
          ])
  setMenu(@menu)

  # Tree view appears on the left
  addPanedControl(VRTreeview, "treeview", "")

  # List view appears on the right
  addPanedControl(VRListview, "listview", "")
  @listview.addColumn("Attribute Name", 150)
  @listview.addColumn("Attribute Value", 150)
end


def populateTreeList(docRootNode, treeRootItem)
  entity = docRootNode.entity
  if entity.instance_of?(NQXML::Tag)
    treeItem = @treeview.addItem(treeRootItem, entity.to_s)
    @entities[treeItem] = entity
    docRootNode.children.each do |node|
      populateTreeList(node, treeItem)
    end
  elsif entity.instance_of?(NQXML::Text) &&
        entity.to_s.strip.length != 0
    treeItem = @treeview.addItem(treeRootItem, entity.to_s)
    @entities[treeItem] = entity
  end
```

Continued

Figure 2.15 Continued

```ruby
end

def loadDocument(filename)
  @document = nil
  begin
    @document = NQXML::TreeParser.new(File.new(filename)).document
  rescue NQXML::ParserError => ex
    messageBox("Couldn't parse XML document", "Error",
      MB_OK|MB_ICONEXCLAMATION)
  end
  if @document
    @treeview.clearItems()
    @entities = {}
    populateTreeList(@document.rootNode, @treeview.root)
  end
end

def open_clicked
  filters = [["All Files (*.*)", "*.*"],
             ["XML Documents (*.xml)", "*.xml"]]
  filename = openFilenameDialog(filters)
  loadDocument(filename) if filename
end

def quit_clicked
  exit
end

def about_clicked
  messageBox("VRuby XML Viewer Example", "About XMLView",
    MB_OK|MB_ICONINFORMATION)
end
```

Continued

Figure 2.15 Continued

```ruby
  def treeview_selchanged(hItem, lParam)
    entity = @entities[hItem]
    if entity and entity.kind_of?(NQXML::NamedAttributes)
      keys = entity.attrs.keys.sort
      @listview.clearItems
      keys.each_index { |row|
        @listview.addItem([ keys[row], entity.attrs[keys[row]] ])
      }
    end
  end
end


mainWindow = VRLocalScreen.newform(nil, nil, XMLViewerForm)
mainWindow.create
mainWindow.show


# Start the message loop
VRLocalScreen.messageloop
```

Other GUI Toolkits

There are a number of other GUI toolkits under development for Ruby, and as always, you should check the RAA for the latest word.

The Fast Light Toolkit (FLTK) (www.fltk.org) is a nice cross-platform GUI developed in part by Bill Spitzak. FLTK is very efficient in terms of memory use and speed, and provides excellent support for OpenGL-based applications as well. It is currently available for both Windows and X (Unix) platforms. A Ruby interface to FLTK is being developed by Takaaki Tateishi and Kevin Smith, and the home page for this effort is at http://ruby-fltk.sourceforge.net.

Qt (www.trolltech.com) is an excellent cross-platform GUI toolkit that has been ported to Unix, Microsoft Windows and, most recently, Mac OS X. It is the basis of the popular KDE desktop for Linux. The Ruby language bindings for Qt (http://sfns.u-shizuoka-ken.ac.jp/geneng/horie_hp/ruby/index.html) are developed by Nobuyuki Horie.

Apollo (www.moriq.com/apollo/index-en.html), developed by Yoshida Kazuhiro, is a project whose goal, in the author's words, is to provide a "dream duet" of Delphi and Ruby. Delphi is a commercial application development environment from Borland/Inprise. The specific interest for Ruby GUI developers is in the Ruby extension that provides access to Delphi's Visual Component Library (VCL). As of this writing, Delphi is only available on Windows, but very soon, Kylix (the Unix port of Delphi) should be available for Linux and other platforms.

Choosing a GUI Toolkit

It can be both a blessing and a curse to have so many options when choosing a GUI for your Ruby application. Ultimately, there is no magic formula to make this decision for you, but here are a few considerations to keep in mind:

- Upon which platforms will your application need to run? If you need support for the Macintosh, Tk is really your only choice at this time. Similarly, if you need to support platforms other than Microsoft Windows, you probably don't want to develop the GUI using SWin/VRuby.

- If you do intend for your application to run on different platforms, do you prefer a uniform look-and-feel for the GUI, or would you rather have a native look-and-feel for each target platform? Tk provides a native look-and-feel on each platform, but "theme-able" toolkits like GTK can provide extremely customizable interfaces (possibly different from any platform's native GUI). FOX provides a consistent look-and-feel for both Unix and Windows (but that look-and-feel is decidedly Windows-like).

- Software licensing issues can be a significant concern, especially if you're developing commercial software applications. Most of the GUI toolkits for Ruby use some kind of open-source software license, but you should study their licenses carefully to understand the terms.

All other issues aside, the great intangible factor is how comfortable you are developing programs with a given toolkit. From a programmer's standpoint, every GUI toolkit has its own unique character and feel and you may not be able to put a finger on just what it is that you like about a particular toolkit. If you have some free time, take the opportunity to learn more about all the toolkits we've introduced in this chapter before settling on the one or couple that you like best.

Summary

This chapter has taken you on a tour of some of the most popular GUI toolkits for Ruby. It's good to have a number of options at your disposal, but to be an effective application developer it's in your best interests to experiment with several GUI toolkits and then pick the one that seems like the best fit for what you're trying to accomplish. Most GUI programming wisdom can't be taught in a book; it requires some trial and error.

We started out by looking at Ruby/Tk, the standard for Ruby and a sentimental favorite for many application developers. Tk was one of the first cross-platform GUIs, and the easy application development afforded by Tcl/Tk opened up the world of GUI programming to a lot of programmers who were struggling with earlier C-based GUI libraries like Motif and the Windows Win32 API. Of all the toolkits we've looked at, it's also usually true that Ruby/Tk will require the least amount of code to get the GUI up and running. This simplicity, however, is at the expense of more recent GUI innovations like drag and drop, or advanced widgets like spreadsheets and tree lists.

The next GUI toolkit we considered was Ruby/GTK. For developers who work primarily on the Linux operating system and are already familiar with GTK+ and GNOME-based applications in that environment, this is an obvious choice. The Ruby/GTK bindings are quite complete and there's extensive online documentation to get you started, including tutorial exercises. The only drawback seems to be for Windows developers, where it's sometimes difficult to get GTK+ and Ruby/GTK to work properly.

FXRuby is a strong cross-platform GUI toolkit for Ruby, and it works equally well under Unix and Windows. In addition to a full complement of modern widgets, FOX and FXRuby provide a lot of infrastructure for features like OpenGL-based 3-D graphics, drag and drop, and a persistent settings registry. In its relatively short time on the Ruby GUI scene, FXRuby has become one of the most popular GUI toolkits for Ruby. Its disadvantages can't be ignored, however: due to its close conformance to the C++ library, FXRuby's event handling scheme is awkward compared to that used by most other Ruby GUI toolkits. The lack of comprehensive user manuals and reference documentation for FOX and FXRuby is also a sore spot for many new developers.

Speaking of poor documentation, SWin/VRuby is a hard sell for anyone other than experienced Windows programmers. On the other hand, if your programming experience is such that you are already well-versed in the fine art of

Win32 programming, and you'd like to transfer that knowledge to Ruby applications development on Windows, SWin and VRuby may be the right choice for you.

Finally, while these are four of the more popular choices, this is only the tip of the iceberg. There are a number of other choices for GUI toolkits and new ones may have appeared by the time you read this. Take the time to check the RAA as well as newsgroup and mailing list posts to learn about the latest developments.

Solutions Fast Track

Using the Standard Ruby GUI: Tk

☑ Tk is still the standard GUI for Ruby, and this alone is a compelling reason to consider Tk for your application's user interface. It offers the path of least resistance in terms of distributing your Ruby applications, because you're almost guaranteed that your end users will already have a working Ruby/Tk installation in place.

☑ The most serious problem with Tk is its lack of more modern widgets like combo-boxes, tree lists, and the like. While it's true that Tk can be extended with third-party widget sets like BLT and Tix, and at least one Ruby extension module exists to take advantage of these Tk extensions, the build and installation efforts are non-trivial.

Using the GTK+ Toolkit

☑ Because it serves as one of the core components of the popular GNOME desktop for Linux, GTK+ development should be strong for the foreseeable future. The Ruby/GTK extension is likewise under ongoing development and already exposes most or all of the GTK+ functionality.

☑ One potential source of problems for GTK+ (and hence Ruby/GTK) is the weakness of the Windows port of GTK+, which typically lags behind the main X Window version. It is likely, however, that these problems will be sorted out at some point with the redesigned GTK+ 2.0.

Using the FOX Toolkit

☑ FOX provides an excellent cross-platform GUI solution, and unlike GTK+, it works very well out of the box on both Linux *and* Windows. In addition to its extensive collection of modern widgets, FOX offers built-in support for drag-and-drop, OpenGL, and a wide variety of image file formats.

☑ One drawback for choosing FOX is the lack of printed documentation. Most of the large chain bookstores (or online booksellers) will have a large selection of reference books for both Tk and GTK+, but you're not going to find any books on FOX programming.

Using the SWin/VRuby Extensions

☑ SWin and VRuby provide a fast, native solution for developing graphical user interfaces on Windows. If you don't need to run your Ruby application on non-Windows systems, or have some alternative user interface plan for those systems, this may be the right solution for you.

☑ Documentation is a bit of a problem when you're getting started with these extensions, especially if you're not already an experienced Windows programmer. It will probably help immensely to first educate yourself about the basics of Windows programming using one of the many fine reference books on Win32 programming.

Other GUI Toolkits

☑ We chose to cover a handful of popular GUI toolkits for Ruby in this chapter, but that shouldn't discourage you from investigating any of the others that look interesting to you. You should pay attention to posts on the Ruby newsgroup and mailing list, and check the Ruby Application Archive (RAA) regularly, because you never know when new choices will become available.

Choosing a GUI Toolkit

☑ Although Ruby is a powerful programming language for any single platform, many programmers are drawn to it because of its cross-platform nature. If you want your GUI applications written in Ruby to be similarly cross-platform, you need to be mindful of the target platforms when choosing a GUI toolkit.

☑ The bottom line is that there is no one-size-fits-all solution when choosing a GUI toolkit. Instead of being swayed by the hype about one toolkit versus another, invest some time to try out two or three that look promising and decide for yourself which is the best fit.

Frequently Asked Questions

The following Frequently Asked Questions, answered by the authors of this book, are designed to both measure your understanding of the concepts presented in this chapter and to assist you with real-life implementation of these concepts. To have your questions about this chapter answered by the author, browse to **www.syngress.com/solutions** and click on the **"Ask the Author"** form.

Q: Are any of the GUI toolkits for Ruby thread-safe?

A: The answer depends very much on your definition of "thread-safe." In the most general sense, none of the GUI toolkits we've looked at are thread-safe; that is to say, the GUI objects' instance methods don't provide proper support for reentrancy. A good practice for multithreaded GUI applications is to let the GUI operate in the main thread and reserve non-GUI "worker" threads for background tasks whenever possible.

Q: Ruby/GTK and FXRuby come with some good example programs but I didn't find much for Ruby/Tk. What's a good source for additional Ruby/Tk example programs?

A: Check the Ruby Application Archives for the latest version of a set of "Ruby/Tk Widget Demos" maintained by Jonathan Conway. These are a Ruby/Tk port of the original Tcl/Tk widget demos and should give you a good head start on writing your own Ruby/Tk applications. You should also scan the Ruby Application Archives for other Ruby/Tk applications from which you can learn.

Q: I built and installed FOX, and then built and installed FXRuby, and both appeared to build without errors. When I try to run any of the FXRuby example programs under Linux, Ruby responds with an error message that begins "LoadError: libFOX.so: cannot open shared object file". I checked the FOX installation directory and confirmed that libFOX.so is indeed present, so why does Ruby report this error?

A: The problem has to do with how the operating systems locate shared libraries that Ruby extensions like FXRuby depend on. Ruby is finding the FXRuby extension properly, but it cannot find the FOX shared library that FXRuby needs because it's not in the standard path searched for dynamically-loaded shared libraries. To correct the problem you simply need to add the FOX library's installation directory (usually, /usr/local/lib) to your LD_LIBRARY_PATH environment variable. See the FXRuby installation instructions for more information about this problem.

Accessing Databases with Ruby

Solutions in this chapter:

- **Accessing Databases with Ruby/DBI**
- **Accessing Databases with Ruby/ODBC**
- **Accessing LDAP Directories with Ruby/LDAP**
- **Utilizing Other Storage Solutions**

- ☑ **Summary**
- ☑ **Solutions Fast Track**
- ☑ **Frequently Asked Questions**

Introduction

The existence of a variety of data-storage solution interfaces is essential for broad acceptance of a language like Ruby. Certainly, interfaces to relational databases such as Oracle, MySql, PostgreSQL, or DB2 are the most important, with those to hierarchical databases like Lightweight Directory Access Protocol (LDAP) and Berkley DBM file databases; or flat-file databases like Comma Separated Values (CSV) coming in a close second. That being said, the ability to access databases of different vendors with the same interface is also a desirable trait.

In Ruby, all of the aforementioned is already reality. Ruby's equivalent to Perl's DataBase Interface (DBI) is Ruby/DBI which acts as a uniform way to access a lot of different databases (for example, Oracle, DB2, InterBase, PostgreSQL or MySql) with a simple yet powerful interface. And with Ruby/ODBC, the Open Database Connectivity (ODBC) binding for Ruby, you can access any database for which an ODBC driver exists. Besides Ruby/DBI and Ruby/ODBC, a lot of other database-dependent libraries for Ruby exist, including sybase-ctlib for Sybase databases, Ruby/LDAP for accessing LDAP directories, gdbm, ndbm, bdb, and cbd for Berkeley DBM files or library csv for comma separated flat-files, to mention only those not yet incorporated into Ruby/DBI.

This chapter gives an in-depth introduction into Ruby/DBI, briefly introduces Ruby/ODBC, and shows how to use Ruby/LDAP to access LDAP directories. Other solutions to store data are also exhibited, for example how to use the Berkley DB embedded database system or CSV files.

Accessing Databases with Ruby/DBI

Ruby/DBI is a unique database-independent interface for accessing numerous relational databases from within Ruby. It is designed after Perl's DBI, but pays special attention to Ruby's features that are *not* found in Perl (especially code blocks). For now, drivers for the following databases exist:

- Oracle, DB2 and InterBase
- PostgreSQL, MySql and mSQL
- ODBC and ActiveX Data Objects (ADO)
- SQLRelay, SQLite
- Proxy (remote database access over Transmission Control Protocol/ Internet Protocol [TCP/IP])

Developing & Deploying…

Ruby/DBI's Interactive SQL Shell

Ruby/DBI is distributed with the small interactive SQL shell, or command-line processor, *sqlsh.rb*. It uses Ruby's *readline* module, which features command line history and keyword completion, as well as the ability to run SQL scripts. This works with every database driver, be it Oracle, DB2 or even a remote connection to a MS Access database.

Let us start now and launch *sqlsh.rb* from the command line (it resides in the bin/commandline directory of Ruby/DBI's package and should have been installed into your system's binaries directory):

```
sqlsh.rb
```

This outputs which parameters it accepts and which Database Drivers (DBDs) and datasource names (DSNs) it is aware of, as follows:

```
USAGE: sqlsh.rb [—file file] driver_url [user [password] ]


Available driver and datasources:


dbi:Oracle:


dbi:DB2:
   dbi:DB2:SAMPLE
   dbi:DB2:CRTLN
```

Notice that the list of datasource names may be incomplete, as was the case for the *dbi:Oracle* driver in the output shown above, but this does not mean that you can't connect to an Oracle database. It is possible to connect in another way; here we connect to the Oracle database with the Transparent Network Substrate (TNS) name "oracle.neumann" using user "scott" and password "tiger":

```
sqlsh.rb dbi:Oracle:oracle.neumann scott tiger
```

Continued

If you have specified a valid TNS name, username, and password (and no error occurred during the connection phase), a prompt will appear, where you can input any SQL statement, be it Data Control Language (DCL), Data Definition Language (DDL) or Data Manipulation Language (DML):

```
CONNECT TO dbi:Oracle:oracle.neumann USER scott PASS tiger


dbi =>
```

As with some common UNIX shells (like bash or zsh), you can use the **Tab**-key to complete keywords, and pressing **Tab** twice shows all possible keywords for the current input. (This will only work if you have compiled Ruby with "readline" support, otherwise command line history and completion are disabled.)

Now let us execute a SQL statement. Note that you have to end it with a semicolon:

```
dbi => SELECT EMPNO, ENAME, JOB, COMM, DEPTNO
dbi =| FROM EMP WHERE COMM IS NOT NULL ORDER BY SAL;
```

And sqlsh.rb responds with the following output:

```
+---------+--------+------------+--------+---------+
| EMPNO   | ENAME  | JOB        | COMM   | DEPTNO  |
+---------+--------+------------+--------+---------+
| 7521.0  | WARD   | SALESMAN   | 500.0  | 30.0    |
| 7654.0  | MARTIN | SALESMAN   | 1400.0 | 30.0    |
| 7844.0  | TURNER | SALESMAN   | 0.0    | 30.0    |
| 7499.0  | ALLEN  | SALESMAN   | 300.0  | 30.0    |
+---------+--------+------------+--------+---------+
4 rows in set (0.001 sec)
```

To leave the SQL shell, type **\q** followed by a carriage return. To get a list of other internal sqlsh.rb commands, press **\h** (Table 3.1).

To use sqlsh.rb to execute files containing multiple SQL commands, use the command line option **--file**:

```
sqlsh.rb --file script.sql dbi:Pg:rdg matz 123
```

Continued

   This would execute the commands in file **script.sql**. After that the usual command prompt of sqlsh.rb would occur. If this is not desired, simply pipe a "\q" on *Stdin* as shown:

```
echo \\q| sqlsh.rb --file script.sql dbi:Pg:rdg matz 123
```

Table 3.1 Internal sqlsh.rb Commands

Command	Explanation
\h[elp]	Displays help screen listing all available commands.
\t[ables]	Lists all tables and views of the connected database.
\dt *table*	Describes columns of *table*.
\s *table*	Short-cut for "SELECT * FROM *table*".
\c[ommit]	Commits the current transaction.
\r[ollback]	Rolls the current transaction back.
\a[utocommit]	Shows current autocommit mode.
\a[utocommit] *on|off*	Switches autocommit mode on/off.
\i[nput] *filename*	Reads and executes lines read from file *filename*.
\o[utput]	Disables output to a file.
\o[utput] *filename*	Sets output to file *filename*. All SQL statements (and transaction control) the user enters are stored in this file.
\pl *n*	Sets the page length to *n*.
\rb ...	Executes the rest of the line as Ruby command.
\irb	Starts irb (interactive Ruby interpreter) in the current conext. Constant **Conn** refers to the current connection.
\q[uit]	Quits sqlsh.rb.

Obtaining and Installing Ruby/DBI

You can download a package containing the complete sources of Ruby/DBI and all of its database drivers (not including their dependent libraries) from www.ruby-projects.org/dbi. You'll also find a link to this page by following Ruby/DBI's Ruby Application Archive (RAA) entry in the Library section, under Database (www.ruby-lang.org/en/raa.html), but don't mix it up with John Small's Ruby/dbi package! Besides the official releases, there is also a Concurrent Versioning System (CVS) snapshot available, but be careful using this unless you know exactly what you are doing! Users of Debian Linux, FreeBSD, or NetBSD, may also check out the packages collections, where there are easy-to-install packages of Ruby/DBI as well.

Dependent on the database(s) you want to access, you will probably have to install other libraries before being able to use Ruby/DBI:

- **ADO (dbd_ado)**   RAA entry Library | *Win32* | *Win32OLE*

- **DB2 (dbd_db2)**   RAA entry Library | *Database* | *Ruby/DB2*

- **InterBase (dbd_interbase)**   RAA entry Library | *Database* | *interbase*

- **mSQL (dbd_msql)**   RAA entry Library | *Database* | *Ruby/mSQL*

- **MySql (dbd_mysql)**   RAA entry Library | *Database* | *MySQL/Ruby*

- **ODBC (dbd_odbc)**   RAA entry Library | *Database* | *Ruby/ODBC*

- **Oracle (dbd_oracle)**   RAA entry Library | *Database* | *oracle*

- **PostgreSQL (dbd_pg)**   RAA entry Library | *Database* | *postgres*

- **Proxy-Server (dbd_proxy)**   RAA entry Library | *comm* | *druby*

- **SQLite (dbd_sqlite)**   www.hwaci.com/sw/sqlite

- **SQLRelay (dbd_sqlrelay)**   www.firstworks.com/sqlrelay

After installing the dependent libraries, unpack the downloaded Ruby/DBI package (as of this writing, this is ruby-dbi-all-0.0.12.tar.gz) and change into the newly-created directory:

```
tar -xvzf ruby-dbi-all-0.0.12.tar.gz
cd ruby-dbi-all
```

As Ruby/DBI consists of multiple database drivers (and you usually don't want to install all of them), you can choose what to install by using the *--with* option:

```
ruby setup.rb config --with=dbi,dbd_oracle,dbd_pg
```

This would configure installation of the DBI module (which is necessary to run any database driver) and the two database drivers for Oracle (dbd_oracle) and PostgreSQL (dbd_pg). After that, execute the following command, which compiles and builds C extensions if necessary:

```
ruby setup.rb setup
```

Before installing Ruby/DBI into the appropriate directories, make sure you have the rights to do this (UNIX users might have to login as, or su to, the root user). Then execute:

```
ruby setup.rb install
```

Now, Ruby/DBI should be installed on your system and you can start using it.

Programming with Ruby/DBI

In this section we'll give you an in-depth introduction to programming with Ruby/DBI, showing many of its methods and features. You may also use this as a function reference. But first, let's have a look at an initial example that we'll implement using Ruby/DBI, Perl's DBI, and Python's DB API 2.0. All examples will complete the same tasks:

1. Connect to a database.
2. Query a table.
3. Output the result of the query.
4. Close the connection to the database.

Our first example uses Ruby/DBI. It connects to an Oracle database with the TNS name "oracle.neumann," and uses the user "scott," the password "tiger." and which queries the table "EMP":

```
require "dbi"

URL = "dbi:Oracle:oracle.neumann"

# establish connection to Oracle database
dbh = DBI.connect(URL, "scott", "tiger")

# query table EMP
```

```
rows = dbh.select_all("SELECT * FROM EMP")


# output the result
p rows


# disconnect from database
dbh.disconnect
```

The same example using Perl's DBI looks like this:

```
use DBI;


$URL = "dbi:Oracle:oracle.neumann";


# establish connection to Oracle database
$dbh = DBI->connect($URL, "scott", "tiger");


# query table EMP
$rows = $dbh->selectall_arrayref("SELECT * FROM EMP");


# output result
foreach $row (@$rows) {
  print join(',', $@row), "\n";
}


# disconnect from database
$dbh->disconnect();
```

Besides the language differences between Perl and Ruby (there's less punctuation in Ruby, for one), there are only minor differences between the two examples, the usage of the *selectall_arrayref* method in Perl and *select_all* in Ruby, for instance.

Now we'll modify our initial Ruby example to make use of Ruby's code blocks. This frees us from calling the *disconnect* method or other methods in order to free resources.

```
require "dbi"
URL = "dbi:Oracle:oracle.neumann"
```

```
DBI.connect(URL, "scott", "tiger") do | dbh |
  p dbh.select_all("SELECT * FROM EMP")
end
```

Finally, let's see how the same would look using Python's DB API 2.0. The example below uses the Python API, and connects to a DB2 database instead of an Oracle database.

```python
import DB2

# establish connection to DB2 database
conn = DB2.connect(dsn='SAMPLE', uid='', pwd='')

# create new cursor object
curs = conn.cursor()

# execute SQL statement ...
curs.execute('SELECT * FROM EMPLOYEE')

# ... and fetch all rows
rows = curs.fetchall()

# close/free the cursor
curs.close()

# output result
print rows

# disconnect from database
conn.close()
```

Understanding Ruby/DBI Architecture and Terminology

Ruby/DBI features a driver-based architecture similar to Perl's DBI. This architecture consists of two parts:

- The Database Interface (DBI), which is database-independent. This is the interface with which the programmer works.

- The Database Drivers (DBDs), which implement the database-dependent parts.

In the following text, we'll use the term *DBI module* or simply *DBI* when we refer to the Database Interface as a part of Ruby/DBI, and *Ruby/DBI* to refer to both DBI and DBD as a whole.

Figure 3.1 depicts Ruby/DBI's architecture. Each Ruby application exclusively calls DBI methods, which dispatch the method calls to the DBDs. The figure also indicates that it's possible to have multiple connections open to different databases at the same time, or to one and the same database.

Ruby/DBI mainly consists of three classes. These are the three *Handle* classes, *DriverHandle*, *DatabaseHandle* and *StatementHandle*, which all inherit from the same abstract superclass *Handle*. Each class wraps one of the database-depended classes defined by a DBD (classes *Driver*, *Database*, and *Statement* of module DBI::DBD::*DriverName*).

- A **DriverHandle** is created for each loaded DBD, and is stored internally by the DBI in a hashtable. It provides methods for connecting to a database (creates a *DatabaseHandle*) and to get more information about the underlying driver (for example, which datasources are available, the default username, and so on). You'll rarely call methods of this class directly, because most of its methods are wrapped by the module *DBI* as module functions (such as method *connect*).

- A **DatabaseHandle** is created for each connection to a database. It provides methods mainly for transaction control, gathering more information about the database, or for preparing (creates a *StatementHandle*) or immediately executing SQL statements. We'll name variables of this class *dbh*.

- A **StatementHandle** represents a prepared statement and provides methods mainly for binding values to parameter markers, executing the statement and fetching the resulting rows. We'll name variables of this class *sth*.

Connecting to Databases

Before we can use any of DBI's methods, we have to load the feature *dbi*. Once that is done, we can establish a database connection by calling the module function *DBI.connect*, either with or without code block, as the code snippet below shows:

```
require 'dbi'

# (1) without code block
dbh = DBI.connect(dsn, user=nil, auth=nil, params=nil)
   # ...use DatabaseHandle dbh...
dbh.disconnect

# (2) with code block
DBI.connect(dsn, user=nil, auth=nil, params=nil) do |dbh|
   # ...use DatabaseHandle dbh...
end
```

Figure 3.1 Ruby/DBI's Architecture

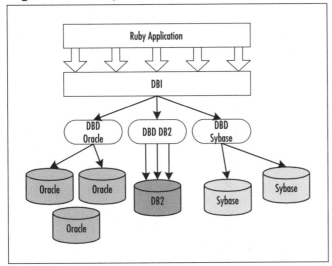

Invoking *DBI.connect* without code block returns a *DatabaseHandle* object that has to be closed explicitly by calling the *disconnect* method, whereas the code block variant implicitly closes the connection at the end of the block. So, the block form fits very well into the behavior of *File.open* or *File.new* of Ruby's standard library.

DBI.connect takes the following parameters:

- Parameter *dsn* must be a valid datasource name. The DBI uses this to load the DBD (if it's not yet loaded) and to connect with the specified database.

- Parameters *user* and *auth* specify the username and password to use for the connection and all following operations performed on it. If both parameters are omitted, default values provided by the underlying DBD are taken instead. For example, the default username and password for an Oracle database is "scott" and "tiger," and empty strings "" and "" for DB2; some others require you to specify both explicitly.

■ The last parameter *params* lets you specify several database-related options, for example, whether autocommit mode should be on or off by default for this connection (option *AutoCommit*). Because it is the last parameter of the method, Ruby allows us to leave off the curly braces ("{" and "}") around the key/value pairs.

The *connected?* method of the *DatabaseHandle* class lets us find out whether the connection was already closed by a call to the *disconnect* method. The *ping* method will check if the connection is still alive, usually by executing some SQL.

Rarely there will be a need for closing all connections established by one specific DBD or even of all loaded DBDs. Both is possible with the *DBI.disconnect_all* method, which you pass a datasource name of the DBD whose connections should be closed or call it without arguments to close really all connections of all loaded DBDs:

```
# close all connections established by DBD Pg (PostgreSQL)
DBI.disconnect_all('dbi:Pg')
```

```
# close all established connections
DBI.disconnect_all
```

Using Driver URLs and Datasource Names

Driver URLs and datasource names are almost the same thing. Both are used by the DBI with the difference that a driver URL is just used to represent a specific DBD (such as *dbi:Pg* for the PostgreSQL DBD) whereas a datasource name (for example "dbi:Pg:database") also includes the driver-specific parameters needed to establish a connection to a database. So each datasource name is a valid driver URL, whereas the reverse is not true.

The format of a driver URL is as follows:

```
dbi:driver_name
```

A datasource name includes additional driver-specific data:

```
dbi:driver_name:driver_specific_data
```

Table 3.2 lists all currently available DBDs with an explanation of their driver-specific parameters. A *db* in the table stands for the name of the database with which the DBD connects, whereas *host* and *port* are placeholders for the location of the database. Parameters with default values are optional and may be omitted.

Note that since Ruby/DBI version 0.0.6, database driver names are case-insensitive, so that both "dbi:Mysql:..." and "dbi:mysql:..." refer to the same DBD.

Table 3.2 Format of the Datasource Names

Database	Datasource Name	Explanation
ADO	dbi:ADO:*dns*	*dns*: ODBC Datasource name.
IBM DB2 UDB	dbi:DB2:*db*	
InterBase	dbi:InterBase:database=*db*;charset=*chrset* dbi:InterBase:*db*	*chrset*: Character set, defaults to NONE.
mSQL	dbi:Msql:database=*db*;host=*host* dbi:Msql:*db*:*host*	*host:* Defaults to the local host.
MySql	dbi:Mysql:database=*db*;host=*host*;port=*port*;socket=*socket*;flag=*flag* dbi:Mysql:*db*:*host*	*host:* defaults to "localhost". *port, socket, flag:* optional.
ODBC	dbi:ODBC:*dns*	*dns*: ODBC Datasource name.
Oracle 7/8(i)	dbi:Oracle:*tnsname*	*tnsname*: Oracle TNS name.

Continued

Table 3.2 Continued

Database	Datasource Name	Explanation
PostgreSQL	dbi:Pg:database=*db*; host=*host*;port=*port*; options=*options*;tty=*tty* dbi:Pg:*db:host*	*host, port, options, tty:* default to the default settings of PostgreSQL.
Proxy-Server	dbi:Proxy:hostname=*host*; port=*port*;dsn=*dsn*	*host, port*: location of the DBI-Proxyserver, defaults to localhost:9001. *dns*: DBI datasource name of the database to connect with.
SQLite	Dbi:SQLite:*db*	
SQLRelay	dbi:SQLRelay:*host:port* dbi:SQLRelay:host=*host*; port=*port*;socket=*socket*; retrytime=*retrytime*; tries=*tries*	*host*: defaults to "localhost". *port*: defaults to 9000. *retrytime*: defaults to 0 *tries*: defaults to 1 *socket*: optional

If you want to see which database drivers are installed on your system, you can execute the code in Figure 3.2. It calls method *DBI.available_drivers* to get an array containing the driver URL of each installed DBD. Then calls *DBI.data_sources* for each DBD, which returns all known datasources for the specified DBD.

Preparing and Executing SQL Statements

The Structured Query Language (SQL) consists of the three sub-languages, *DDL*, *DCL* and *DML*, each of which has a different purpose.

- Data Definition Language (DDL): Create databases, tables or views, for example: *CREATE TABLE, CREATE VIEW*.

- Data Control Language (DCL): Create users, grant and revoke privileges, for example: *GRANT, REVOKE, CREATE USER*.

- Data Manipulation Language (DML): Query, insert, delete and update tables or views, for example: *INSERT, SELECT, DELETE, UPDATE*.

Figure 3.2 List All DBDs with Their DSNs

```
require 'dbi'

DBI.available_drivers.each do |driver|
  puts "Driver: " + driver
  DBI.data_sources(driver).each do |dsn|
    puts "    Datasource: " + dsn
  end
end
```

Executing this might result in the following output:

```
Driver: dbi:DB2:
    Datasource: dbi:DB2:SAMPLE
    Datasource: dbi:DB2:CRTLN
Driver: dbi:Mysql:
    Datasource: dbi:Mysql:database=database
    Datasource: dbi:Mysql:database=michael
    Datasource: dbi:Mysql:database=mysql
    Datasource: dbi:Mysql:database=test
```

Executing SQL statements can be classified into three categories:

1. Executing *DDL*, *DCL* or *INSERT*, *UPDATE* and *DELETE* statements. All have the common characteristic that they return no result-set (no need to provide methods for fetching rows): Use the *DatabaseHandle#do* method.

2. Immediately executing SELECT statements without former preparation. Use the *DatabaseHandle#execute* method.

3. Executing prepared DML SQL statements. Useful if the same structural statement is executed repetitively. Use the *DatabaseHandle#prepare* and *StatementHandle#execute* methods.

Tables 3.3 and 3.4 list all methods related to preparing and executing SQL statements. The methods listed in Table 3.3 belong to the *DatabaseHandle* class, whereas Table 3.4 lists the methods of the *StatementHandle* class.

Table 3.3 Methods of the *DatabaseHandle* Class for Preparing and Executing SQL Statements

Method	Explanation
do(stmt, *bindvars) => rpc	Executes *stmt* immediately with binding *bindvars* to parameter markers beforehand. Returns the Row Processed Count (RPC).
execute(stmt, *bindvars) => sth execute(stmt, *bindvars) { |sth| aBlock }	Executes *stmt* immediately with binding *bindvars* to parameter markers beforehand. Returns a *StatementHandle* object (*sth*) which is ready for fetching rows. The block form ensures that the *StatementHandle* is freed, that is, its *finish* method is called.
prepare(stmt) => sth prepare(stmt) { |sth| aBlock }	Prepares *stmt* and returns a *StatementHandle* object (*sth*). The block form ensures that the *StatementHandle* is freed, that is, its *finish* method is called.

Table 3.4 Methods of the *StatementHandle* Class for Preparing or Executing SQL Statements

Method	Explanation
bind_param (param_marker, value, attribs=nil)	Binds *value* to the parameter marker represented by *param_marker*, which is either an integer (position) or a string (for example ":name"; which is only supported by Oracle). Parameter *attribs* is currently unused and should be omitted.
execute(*bindvars)	Executes an already prepared *StatementHandle* with binding *bindvars* to parameter markers beforehand. Afterwards the *StatementHandle* is ready for fetching rows.

Using Parameter Markers

Parameter markers are to SQL statements what a programming language's arguments or parameters are to methods, procedures or functions. That is, they are placeholders that must be bound to real values prior to execution. They are applicable for all but DDL and DCL-SQL statements.

Parameter markers are usually represented by question marks, whereas the Oracle DBD additionally supports arbitrary strings preceded by a colon (for example ":mymarker") or positional parameters such as ":1", ":2" etc. To bind them to real values, either use one of the methods listed in Table 3.3 or 3.4 that takes a *bindvars* parameter, or the *bind_param* method of the *StatementHandle* class. Oracle's textual parameter markers can only be bound to values using the latter method.

The values you bind to parameter markers are converted to SQL datatypes, as Table 3.5 shows.

Table 3.5 Ruby to SQL Type Conversion

Ruby Type	SQL Type
NilClass (**nil**)	NULL
TrueClass, FalseClass (**true, false**)	CHAR(1), BOOL
String	VARCHAR, CHAR, TEXT
Integer (Fixnum or Bignum)	INT, BIGINT
Float	FLOAT, DOUBLE, REAL
DBI::Binary	BLOB, CLOB, LONG, LONG RAW
DBI::Time (or String)	TIME
DBI::Date (or String)	DATE
DBI::Timestamp (or String)	TIMESTAMP

To create an instance of class *DBI::Binary*, simply pass its *new* method a *String* object that contains the following binary data:

```
aBinary = DBI::Binary.new( "Binary data\000\001..." )
```

Similarly, you can create instances of classes *DBI::Date*, *DBI::Time* and *DBI::Timestamp* as follows:

```
aTs = DBI::Timestamp.new(year=0, month=0, day=0, hour=0,
                         minute=0, second=0, fraction=0)
```

```
aTime = DBI::Time.new(hour=0, minute=0, second=0)


aDate = DBI::Date.new(year=0, month=0, day=0)
```

The three classes also have accessor methods for their attributes with the same names as the parameters in their *new* method. For example, you can set the hour of a *DBI::Time* object using its *time=* method or get it via the *time* method.

Immediately Executing Statements without Result-set

As we already know, immediate execution without result-set is provided by the *DatabaseHandle* class' *do* method. We will use it here to create a table called *Lang* (see Figure 3.3) that will store some of the most famous languages together with their creators.

Figure 3.3 Model of Table *Lang* using UML Data Profile

First we create the table:

```
require 'dbi'
DBI.connect('dbi:Pg:rdg', 'matz', '123',
            'AutoCommit' => true) {|dbh|


  # create table
  dbh.do "CREATE TABLE Lang (
     id      INTEGER NOT NULL PRIMARY KEY,
     name    VARCHAR(10) NOT NULL,
     creator VARCHAR(10) NOT NULL,
     age     INTEGER
     )"

}
```

Then we insert some rows into it. In all following examples we assume that *dbh* is an already established connection:

```
dbh.do "INSERT INTO Lang VALUES (1, 'C', 'Dennis', 28)"
```

This is not very elegant, so we'll insert the next two rows using parameter markers:

```
sql = "INSERT INTO Lang VALUES (?, ?, ?, ?)"

dbh.do( sql, 2, 'Python', 'Guido', 10 )
dbh.do( sql, 3, 'Tcl',    'John',  12 )
```

With an Oracle database, we could have instead written the following as the first line:

```
sql = "INSERT INTO Lang VALUES (:1, :2, :3, :4)"
```

Now if everything went well and no exception occurred, we should have three rows in our table. Unfortunately we cannot proof this yet, because the *do* method returns no result-set that we could output. Instead we update the three rows and increment each row's *age* field by one.

```
sql = "UPDATE Lang SET age=age+? WHERE age IS NOT NULL"

rpc = dbh.do( sql, 1 )

puts "#{ rpc } row(s) updated"
```

Here is the output:

```
3 row(s) updated.
```

What the *do* method returned in the last example is called the Row Processed Count (RPC), which is the number of rows processed by the execution of the statement (and *not* the number of returned rows!). The RPC is *nil* if no one exists for that statement, as is usually the case for *DDL*, *DCL* or *SELECT* statements.

Immediately Executing Statements with Result-set

Immediate statement execution with result-set is provided by the *DatabaseHandle* class' *execute* method. Don't mix this up with the method of the same name associated with the *StatementHandle* class, which executes an already prepared statement!

In the example below we use this method to output all languages of the table *Lang* that have existed for more than 12 years:

```
sql = "SELECT name FROM Lang WHERE age > ?"

sth = dbh.execute( sql, 12 )
p sth.fetch_all
sth.finish
```

Here is the output:

```
[ ["C"], ["Tcl"] ]
```

As a result of calling the *execute* method we get back a *StatementHandle* object, which we use in the next line to fetch the resulting rows via the *fetch_all* method. At the end we close the *StatementHandle* by calling the *finish* method, which frees all the resources it holds internally. This should not be forgotten, as it prevents too many open database cursors. Instead of explicitly calling *finish*, we could use the block form of the *execute* method, as the next example shows:

```
sql = "SELECT name FROM Lang WHERE age > ?"

dbh.execute( sql, 12 ) do |sth|
  p sth.fetch_all
end
```

The output is:

```
[ ["C"], ["Tcl"] ]
```

Executing Statements Preceded by Preparation

Execution preceded by preparation is a method best applied when executing a large number of structurally similar DML SQL statements (*structurally similar* meaning that they differ only in the values bound to parameter markers).

This kind of execution consists of two phases:

1. **Preparation**. Good databases create an execution plan for a given statement, which makes subsequent (repetitive) executions faster. This is supported by the *DatabaseHandle* class' *prepare* method, which returns a *StatementHandle* object.

2. **Execution**. Bind concrete values to the parameter markers of the prepared statement and execute it. This is supported by the *StatementHandle*
class' *execute* method.

Up to now, our table *Lang* just contains the three languages: C, Tcl, and
Python. Perl and Ruby are still missing, so we will add them:

```
sql = "INSERT INTO Lang VALUES (?, ?, ?, ?)"


dbh.prepare( sql ) do |sth|

  # add singleton method to sth
  def sth.insert(*values)
    execute(*values)
  end

  sth.insert(4, 'Perl', 'Larry', 14)
  sth.insert(5, 'Ruby', 'Matz' , 6)


end
```

Of course in Ruby, as in Perl, there are many ways of doing the same thing.
We could have inserted both languages also with the following piece of code:

```
sql = "INSERT INTO Lang VALUES (?, ?, ?, ?)"


sth = dbh.prepare( sql )
  sth.execute(4, 'Perl', 'Larry', 14)
  sth.execute(5, 'Ruby', 'Matz' , 6)
sth.finish
```

Or, if we used the *bind_param* method, we'd write:

```
sql = "INSERT INTO Lang VALUES (?, ?, ?, ?)"


dbh.prepare( sql ) do |sth|
  # first row
  sth.bind_param(1, 4)
```

```
    sth.bind_param(2, 'Perl')

    sth.bind_param(3, 'Larry')

    sth.bind_param(4, 14)

    sth.execute


    # proceed with the second row in the same way...

end
```

Fetching the Result

After you've successfully executed a SQL query, you will normally want to fetch some rows of its result-set. To do this, the DBI provides several different methods (Tables 3.6 and 3.7).

Table 3.6 Short-cut Methods of the DatabaseHandle Class to Fetch Rows

Method	Explanation
select_one(stmt, *bindvars) => aRow | nil	Executes the *stmt* statement with the *bindvars* binding beforehand to parameter markers. Returns the first row or *nil* if the result-set is empty.
select_all(stmt, *bindvars) => [aRow, ...] select_all(stmt, *bindvars) { |aRow| aBlock }	Executes the *stmt* statement with the *bindvars* binding beforehand to parameter markers. Calling this method without block returns an array containing all rows. If a block is given, this will be called for each row.

Table 3.7 Methods of the StatementHandle Class

Method	Explanation
fetch => aRow | nil	Returns the next row. Returns *nil* if no further rows are in the result-set.
fetch { |aRow| aBlock }	Invokes the given block for the remaining rows of the result-set.
fetch_all => [aRow, ...]	Returns all remaining rows of the result-set collected in an array.

Continued

Table 3.7 Continued

Method	Explanation
fetch_many(cnt) => [aRow, ...]	Returns the next *cnt* rows collected in an array.
fetch_scroll(direction, offset=1) => aRow | nil	Returns the row specified by the *direction* parameter (one of the constants listed in Table 3.8) and *offset*. Parameter *offset* is discarded for all but SQL_FETCH_ABSOLUTE and SQL_FETCH_RELATIVE.
fetch_array => anArray | nil fetch_array { |anArray| aBlock }	(Obsolete) Returns or passes an array instead of a *DBI::Row* object.
fetch_hash => aHash | nil fetch_hash { |aHash| aBlock }	(Obsolete!) Returns or passes a hash instead of a *DBI::Row* object.
each { |aRow| aBlock }	Behaves like the *fetch* method, called as iterator.
All other methods of module Enumerable	The *StatementHandle* class mixes in the *Enumerable* module so you can use all of its methods, such as *collect*, *select* etc.
column_names => anArray	Returns the names of the columns.
column_info => [aColumnInfo, ...]	Returns an array of *DBI::ColumnInfo* objects. Each object stores information about one column and contains its name, type, precision and more.
rows => rpc	Returns the Row Processed Count of the executed statement or *nil* if no such exist.
fetchable? => true | false	Returns *true* if it's possible to fetch rows, otherwise *false*.
cancel	Frees the resources held by the result-set. After calling this method, it is no longer possible to fetch rows until you again call *execute*.
finish	Frees the resources held by the prepared statement. After calling this method no further methods can be called onto this object.

Table 3.8 The *direction* Parameter of the fetch_scroll Method

Constant	Explanation
DBI::SQL_FETCH_FIRST	Fetch first row.
DBI::SQL_FETCH_LAST	Fetch last row.
DBI::SQL_FETCH_NEXT	Fetch next row.
DBI::SQL_FETCH_PRIOR	Fetch previous row.
DBI::SQL_FETCH_ABSOLUTE	Fetch row at position *offset*.
DBI::SQL_FETCH_RELATIVE	Fetch the row that is *offset* rows away from the current.

The DBI represents a row as an instance of the *DBI::Row* class. This makes it easy to access columns by name or index without the need for two separate methods, as is the case for Perl's DBI or Ruby/ODBC. A common error when fetching rows is:

```
sql, rows = 'SELECT creator FROM Lang ORDER BY age DESC'

dbh.execute( sql ) do |sth|
  rows = sth.collect { |row| row }      # WRONG !!!
end

p rows
```

This code outputs the following incorrect result:

```
[["Matz"], ["Matz"], ["Matz"], ["Matz"], ["Matz"]]
```

The reason for this is that due to performance reasons, the *DBI::Row* object passed to the block as parameter *row* (or returned when not called with the block) is always one and the same object, except that the values it holds are different each time. To fix this problem we could simply duplicate the object before storing it in the array, as shown here:

```
sql, rows = 'SELECT creator FROM Lang ORDER BY age DESC'

dbh.execute( sql ) do |sth|
  rows = sth.collect { |row| row.dup }
```

```
end
```

```
p rows
```

This time it would output the correct result:

```
[["Dennis"], ["Larry"], ["John"], ["Guido"], ["Matz"]]
```

But we could also use the *fetch_all* method:

```
sql = 'SELECT creator FROM Lang ORDER BY age DESC'

rows = dbh.execute( sql ) do |sth|
  sth.fetch_all
end
```

```
p rows
```

Or we could have written the following more Perl-ish code:

```
sql  = 'SELECT creator FROM Lang ORDER BY age DESC'
rows = []

sth = dbh.execute( sql )
while row=sth.fetch do
  rows << row.dup
end
sth.finish
```

```
p rows
```

Instead of storing whole *DBI::Row* objects in an array, we could instead store only the column values, as below. The advantage here is that we do not have to duplicate the *DBI::Row* object.

```
sql = 'SELECT creator FROM Lang ORDER BY age DESC'

creators = dbh.execute( sql ) do |sth|
  sth.collect { |row| row['creator'] }
end
```

```
p creators
```

This outputs our desired result:

```
["Dennis", "Larry", "John", "Guido", "Matz"]
```

Table 3.9 lists the methods of the *DBI::Row* class. As a side note, the *DBI::Row* class is currently implemented using the *delegator* pattern (*delegate.rb*) and delegates all but some specific method calls to an internally held *Array* object, which is used to store the column values.

Some different methods for accessing one or multiple columns of a *DBI::Row* object are demonstrated in the following example:

```
row = dbh.select_one('SELECT * FROM Lang WHERE age < 10')


p row                     # => [5, "Ruby", "Matz", 6]


p row[1]                  # => "Ruby"
p row['creator']          # => "Matz"
p row[:age]               # => 6


p row[1, 3]               # => ["Ruby", "Matz" 6]
p row[:name, 3]           # => ["Ruby", "Matz", 6]


p row[[:age, :name]]      # => [6, "Ruby"]
p row[:age, :name, :age]  # => [6, "Ruby", 6]
p row[/n/]                # => [5, "Ruby"]


p row['name'..'age']      # => ["Ruby", "Matz", 6]
p row[1..'age']           # => Error!!!


p row.field_names         # => ["lang_id", "name",
                          #      "creator", "age"]


p row.is_a? Array         # => false
p row.to_a.is_a? Array    # => true
```

Table 3.9 Methods of the DBI::Row Class

Method	Explanation
column_names => anArray field_names => anArray	Returns an array of all column names.
by_index(index) => anObj	Returns the column at position *index.*
by_field(field_name) => anObj	Returns the column named *field_name.*
each_with_name { |value, name| aBlock }	Calls for each column *aBlock* with two arguments, the column's *value* and its *name.* Note that the order of arguments differ from that of the *Hash#each* method.
to_h => aHash to_a => anArray	Converts the *DBI::Row* object into a hash or array. Both methods return newly created objects.
[aString | aSymbol | anInteger] => anObj	Equal to the *by_field* method for *aString* and *aSymbol* and to *by_index* for *anInteger.*
[anArray | aRegexp | aRange] => anArray	Returns the array of columns specified by *anArray*, *aRegexp* (all columns whose name match the regular expression) or *aRange.*
[aString | aSymbol | anInteger, length] => anArray	Returns *length* columns starting at the column specified by *aString*, *aSymbol* or *anInteger.*
[*more than two values*] => anArray	Calls the one-parameter form of method *[]* for each parameter. Collects the results and returns them as array.
[aString | aSymbol | anInteger] = anObj	Set the column specified by *aString*, *aSymbol* or *anInteger* to *anObj.*
[aRange] = anObj	Behaves like calling the same method of the *Array* class with the difference that strings in ranges are converted to integers before (position of column with that name).
[aString | aSymbol | anInteger, length] = anObj	Behaves like calling the same method of the *Array* class, only that the first parameter is converted to an integer if it's a string or symbol.

Finally, Table 3.10 lists the mappings between SQL and Ruby types. User-defined PostgreSQL datatypes, as well as values (except *NULL*) from MySql or mSQL databases, are returned as strings.

Table 3.10 SQL to Ruby Type Conversion

SQL Type	Ruby Type
BOOL	TrueClass, FalseClass (or String)
VARCHAR, CHAR	String
INT, BIGINT	Integer (Fixnum or Bignum)
FLOAT, DOUBLE, REAL	Float
BLOB, CLOB, LONG, LONG RAW	String
TIME	DBI::Time (or String)
DATE	DBI::Date (or String)
TIMESTAMP	DBI::Timestamp (or String)

Performing Transactions

Transactions are a mechanism that ensures data consistency. An often-recited example of where transactions are essential is that of transferring money between two accounts. If the system crashes just after debiting one account, or credits before it crashes, way it harms either the bank or the user. Therefore, both operations must be performed as one atomic operation in order for the transaction to be viable.

Transactions (should) have the following four properties (which form the acronym "ACID"):

- **Atomicity**: Either a transaction completes or nothing happens at all.

- **Consistency**: A transaction must start in a consistent state and leave the system is a consistent state.

- **Isolation**: Intermediate results of a transaction are not visible outside the current transaction.

- **Durability**: Once a transaction was committed, the effects are persistent; even after a system failure.

The DBI provides two methods to either commit or rollback a transaction. These are the *commit* and *rollback* methods of the *DatabaseHandle* class. If you call one of them for a database that does not support transactions (for example MySql or mSQL), the current default behavior is to do nothing, though this may change to raising an exception or something similar in future versions of Ruby/DBI.

Generally, there are two different ways that databases handle transactions. Some databases implicitly start new transactions and provide *COMMIT* and *ROLLBACK* commands, whereas others require an explicit start for transactions with commands, *BEGIN WORK* or *BEGIN TRANSACTION*, for instance. An example for the latter is PostgreSQL. Its DBD has to emulate the *commit* and *rollback* behavior.

The DBI provides a third transaction control method. This is the *transaction* method, which takes a block as argument and behaves as follows:

```
# assuming dbh is a DatabaseHandle


def dbh.transaction
  dbh.commit
  begin
    yield dbh
    dbh.commit
  rescue Exception
    dbh.rollback
    raise           # reraise exception
  end
end
```

It first commits the current transaction, then executes the code block. If the block raises an exception, the transaction is rolled back and the exception is raised again. Otherwise, the transaction is committed. Use this method to ensure that the database operations inside the block execute atomically – either all of them complete or nothing happens at all.

Enabling or Disabling Autocommit Mode

You can enable or disable autocommit mode either by setting the *AutoCommit* option in the last parameter of *DBI.connect,* or via the *DatabaseHandle* class' *[]=* method.

```
# disable AutoCommit from the beginning on
dbh = DBI.connect('dbi:Pg:rdg', 'matz', '123',
                  'AutoCommit' => false)


# enable AutoCommit
```

```
dbh['AutoCommit'] = true


# print current value of AutoCommit
p dbh['AutoCommit']          # => true


# disable AutoCommit
dbh['AutoCommit'] = false
```

If your application depends on whether *AutoCommit* mode is on or off, make sure to set it explicitly. Don't rely on a default setting!

Transaction Behavior on Disconnect

If the connection to a database is closed by the user with the *disconnect* method, any outstanding transactions are rolled back by the DBI. However, instead of depending on any of DBI's implementation details, your application would be better off calling *commit* or *rollback* explicitly.

Handling Errors

There are many sources of errors. A few examples are a syntax error in an executed SQL statement; a connection failure; or calling the *fetch* method for an already canceled or finished *StatementHandle* — just to mention a few. To see what happens when an error occurs, try executing the following at the command line:

```
ruby -r dbi -e "DBI.connect('dbi:Oracel:')"
```

This tries to connect to the non-existent DBD "Oracel" (note the typo). As a consequence we'll get the following message on the screen, which shows us that a *DBI::InterfaceError* exception was raised:

```
/usr/pkg/lib/ruby/site_ruby/1.6/dbi/dbi.rb:244:in `load_driver': Could
    not load driver (No such file to load - DBD/Oracel/Oracel)
    (DBI::InterfaceError)
```

The DBI defined exception class hierarchy is shown in Figure 3.4. Note that all exceptions but *RuntimeError* are defined under the *DBI* module.

- **DBI::Warning**: Its purpose is to signal a (usually unexpected) misbehavior such as data truncation. This exception is currently neither used by the DBI nor by any of the DBDs.

- **DBI::Error**: Base class of all other exception classes defined by the DBI. Use it in a rescue clause to catch all DBI-related errors.

- **DBI::InterfaceError**: Raised due to an error related to the DBI's interface; if, for example, the DBI is not able to load a DBD, or if you call the *fetch* method after you called *cancel* or *finish*.

- **DBI::NotImplementedError**: Raised due to a mandatory DBD method that was not implemented. If you are using stable DBDs, this exception should never be raised.

- **DBI::DatabaseError**: Base class for all exceptions related to database errors.

Figure 3.4 Hierarchy of DBI's Exception Classes

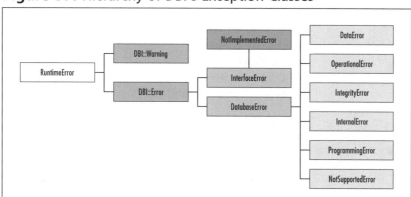

The two most important exception classes are *DBI::InterfaceError* and *DBI::DatabaseError*. The latter implements three methods of getting more information about the reason of the underlying database error, which are:

- *err*: Returns an integer representation of the occurred error or **nil** if this is not supported by the DBD. The Oracle DBD for example returns the numerical part of an "ORA-XXXX" error message.

- *errstr*: Returns a string representation of the occurred error.

- *state*: Returns the SQLSTATE code of the occurred error. The SQLSTATE is a five-character-long string. Most DBDs do not support this and return **nil** instead.

In the example below we implement the *try_connect* method, which tries to connect to a database; if necessary, repeat this up to a specified number of times (the *tries* parameter) with a delay between each attempt (the *sleep_sec* parameter).

```
require 'dbi'

def try_connect(dsn, user, pass, tries=3, sleep_sec=5)
  1.upto(tries) do |n|
    print "#{n}. Try ..."
    begin
      dbh = DBI.connect(dsn, user, pass)
      puts "connected"
      return dbh
    rescue DBI::DatabaseError => err
      puts "failed with error (#{err.errstr})"
      sleep sleep_sec
    end
  end
  raise 'could not connect to database #{ dsn }'
end

# try 10 times to connect, wait 20 secs between each try
dbh = try_connect('dbi:Pg:rdg', 'matz', '123', 10, 20)


# ...
```

Tracing the Execution of DBI Applications

Tracing DBI method calls can save you some time if your database application does some strange things that it shouldn't be doing. However, before you can use tracing in Ruby/DBI, you have to install the *AspectR* module by Robert Feldt and Avi Byrant.

The DBI provides two methods of controlling the tracing behavior of *DatabaseHandle* and *StatementHandle* objects or the default behavior for all new created handles:

- DBI.trace(level=nil, output=nil)
- DBI::Handle#trace(level=nil, output=nil)

The *level* parameter specifies the tracing level, which is a value from 0 to 3 (see Table 3.11). With the *output* parameter, you can define where the tracing messages should be written to. This is usually an object of the *IO* or *File* classes, but may also be any object implementing the << method. If one of the parameters is *nil*, its current value is not changed. This is useful for modifying only one value while keeping the others unchanged. An example would be to increase the tracing level without modifying the output location.

By default, the trace-level is set to *2*, and the output to *StdErr*, but unless you require *"dbi/trace"*, no tracing at all is performed. To modify the default settings, call the *DBI.trace* method. This will affect all newly created handles. Note that trace settings are inherited to subsequently created sub-handles.

Table 3.11 Tracing Levels and Their Meaning

Level	Meaning
0	No Tracing at all.
1	Show only return values and exceptions.
2	Show method calls (with parameters), return values and exceptions. (default)
3	Like *2*, but uses *inspect* instead of *to_s* to output objects. This often results in much more output.

To enable tracing without changing any line of code, just run your application like this:

```
ruby -r dbi/trace yourapp.rb
```

The example below demonstrates some aspects of tracing an application. Note that each handle could have a different output location, which is not possible in Perl's DBI.

```
require 'dbi'
require 'dbi/trace'


# disable tracing for all subsequent created Handles
DBI.trace(0)


dbh = DBI.connect('dbi:Pg:rdg', 'matz', '123')


dbh.do('CREATE TABLE trace_test (name VARCHAR(30))')
```

```
# enable tracing for this and all subsequent created
# StatementHandles
dbh.trace(1, File.new('trace.log', 'w+'))

sql = 'INSERT INTO trace_test VALUES (?)'
dbh.prepare(sql) do |sth|
  # sth inherits the trace settings from dbh
  sth.execute('Michael')

  # increase trace-level
  sth.trace(2)
  sth.execute('John')
end

dbh.do('DROP TABLE trace_test')

# generate an exception
dbh.select_one('SELECT * FROM trace_test')

dbh.disconnect
```

After execution, the *trace.log* file should contain something like the following (some lines were cut in this example):

```
<= cancel for #<DBI::StatementHandle:0x80ae2f8> = nil
<= column_names for #<DBI::StatementHandle:0x80ae2f8> =
<= execute for #<DBI::StatementHandle:0x80ae2f8> =
-> execute for #<DBI::StatementHandle:0x80ae2f8> ("John")
[... some lines cut ...]
!! ERROR:  Relation 'trace_test' does not exist
<= select_one for #<DBI::DatabaseHandle:0x80b9694>
<= connected? for #<DBI::DatabaseHandle:0x80b9694> = true
<= disconnect for #<DBI::DatabaseHandle:0x80b9694> = nil
```

Lines starting with "->" show method calls whereas "<-" shows method's returns. In trace mode *1* only one line for a method call and its return value is shown. These are the lines starting with "<=". Exceptions are denoted by "!!".

Values between parentheses at the end of a line denote arguments to methods, whereas a value after an equal sign denotes a return value.

Accessing Metadata

"Metadata" are data about data. In the case of database tables, this is mainly information stored about a table's columns, such as name, type, scale and precision; as well as whether or not it's nullable, unique, a primary key; or whether it's indexed or not. A list of tables and views (and other database objects) is also part of a database's stored metadata .

Because most databases store this metadata differently, the DBI provides a common interface for accessing the metadata.

First let us look at the *DatabaseDriver* class' *tables* method. It is supported by all but the ADO DBD, and returns a list of all the current connected database's tables. For example, we could use this to output all tables of a PostgreSQL database other than the system tables that start with "pg_":

```
require 'dbi'


DBI.connect(ARGV[0], ARGV[1], ARGV[2]) do |dbh|
  p dbh.tables.select {|t| t !~ /^pg_/ }
end
```

Which outputs (on my system):

```
["tab_referer", "tab_user_agent", "tab_log_data", "tab_url", "language",
    "person", "demo"]
```

Now let us try to gather more information about the table's columns. In Figure 3.5 (its output is shown in Figure 3.6) we use the *DatabaseHandle* class's *columns* method, which returns an array of *DBI::ColumnInfo* objects for a given table. Each *DBI::ColumnInfo* object represents one column of the table, and has the following attributes:

- *name*: The column's name.

- *type_name*: String representation of its type.

- *sql_type*: Portable integer representation of its type (DBI::SQL_XXX constants).

- *precision*: Number of bytes or digits.

- *scale*: Number of digits from right.
- *default*: Default value for this column.
- *nullable*: Is NULL allowed for this column?
- *indexed*: Is there an index on this column?
- *primary*: Is this column a primary key?
- *unique*: Is this column unique to the table?

Figure 3.5 Using the *columns* Method to Access Metadata

```
require 'dbi'

DBI.connect(ARGV[0], ARGV[1], ARGV[2]) do |dbh|

  dbh.do %[
    CREATE TABLE test (
      pk   INTEGER NOT NULL PRIMARY KEY,
      name VARCHAR(30) DEFAULT 'nobody',
      flt  DECIMAL(10,2) NOT NULL UNIQUE
    )
  ]

  head = %w(name type_name precision scale default
            nullable indexed primary unique)

  rows = dbh.columns('test').collect do |col|
    head.collect{|a| col[a]}
  end

  DBI::Utils::TableFormatter.ascii(head, rows)
  dbh.do 'DROP TABLE test'
end
```

If an attribute is *nil* then it was not possible to get information about it.

Figure 3.6 Output of Figure 3.5

```
+------+-----------+-----------+-------+---------+----------+---------+---------+--------+
| name | type_name | precision | scale | default | nullable | indexed | primary | unique |
+------+-----------+-----------+-------+---------+----------+---------+---------+--------+
| pk   | int       | 11        | NULL  | 0       | NULL     | true    | true    | true   |
| name | varchar   | 30        | NULL  | nobody  | true     | NULL    | NULL    | NULL   |
| flt  | decimal   | 10        | 2     | 0.00    | NULL     | true    | NULL    | true   |
+------+-----------+-----------+-------+---------+----------+---------+---------+--------+
```

Using Driver-specific Functions and Attributes

The DBI lets database drivers provide additional database-specific functions, which can be called by the user through the *func* method of any *Handle* object. Furthermore, driver-specific attributes are supported and can be set or gotten using the *[]=* or *[]* methods. Driver-specific attributes are lowercase and preceded by the DBD name, *pg_client_encoding* or *odbc_ignorecase*, for instance.

PostgreSQL

The DBD for PostgreSQL implements the driver-specific functions listed below for *DatabaseHandle* objects, all related to handling Binary Large OBjects (BLOBs).

```
blob_import(file)

blob_export(oid, file)

blob_create(mode=PGlarge::INV_READ)

blob_open(oid, mode=PGlarge::INV_READ)

blob_unlink(oid)

blob_read(oid, length=nil)
```

To import binary data or a file into a table, we could either use *blob_import,* which returns an object identifier (OID) for the inserted file; *blob_create,* which returns a *PGlarge* object; or we could simply insert a *DBI::Binary* object. Say we have an existing table *BlobTest* with two columns. *name* of type VARCHAR(30) and *data* of type OID and an already established database connection *dbh,* we could insert a file into this table in three different ways:

```
SQL = 'INSERT INTO BlobTest (name, data) VALUES (?,?)'


# (1) using blob_import
```

```
dbh.do(SQL, 'test.rb', dbh.func(:blob_import, 'test.rb'))


# (2) using DBI::Binary
data = DBI::Binary.new( File.readlines('test.rb').to_s )
dbh.do(SQL, 'test.rb (2)', data)


# (3) using blob_create
data = File.readlines('test.rb').to_s
blob = dbh.func(:blob_create, PGlarge::INV_WRITE)
blob.open
blob.write data
dbh.do(SQL, 'test.rb (3)', blob.oid)
blob.close
```

To read the BLOB back, we could use *blob_export* to store the BLOB into a file, *blob_read* to read the whole or a part of the BLOB into a *String* object, or *blob_open* to handle the BLOB similarly to a file. The latter is especially useful for streaming applications.

To get the BLOB with name "test.rb" out of the database and print it to *Stdout*, we could write:

```
SQL = "SELECT data FROM BlobTest WHERE name=?"
oid = dbh.select_one(SQL, 'test.rb')['data']


# (1) using blob_export
dbh.func(:blob_export, oid, '/tmp/test.rb')
puts File.readlines('/tmp/test.rb').to_s


# (2) using blob_read
puts dbh.func(:blob_read, oid)


# (3) using blob_open
blob = dbh.func(:blob_open, oid, PGlarge::INV_READ)
blob.open
puts blob.read
blob.close
```

You can also use *blob_open* to modify already existing BLOBs. To delete a BLOB, use *blob_unlink* and pass it the OID of the BLOB to remove it from the database.

MySql

MySql implements the following driver-specific functions for the *DriverHandle* class:

```
createdb(db, host, user, pass [, port, sock, flag])
dropdb(db, host, user, pass [, port, sock, flag])
shutdown(host, user, pass [, port, sock, flag])
reload(host, user, pass [, port, sock, flag])
```

And for the *DatabaseHandle* class, the following functions are defined:

```
createdb(db)
dropdb(db)
shutdown()
reload()
```

With the driver-specific functions of the *DriverHandle* class, it is possible to create or drop a database, or to shutdown or restart the database server without connecting to a database, using the *connect* method. Thus, to create a database we could write:

```
require "dbi"


# get DriverHandle object for DBD MySql
drh = DBI.get_driver('dbi:Mysql')


# create a datbase
drh.func(:createdb, 'demo', 'localhost', 'user', 'pw')
```

Whereas using a *DatabaseHandle* object we would write instead:
```
require "dbi"


DBI.connect('dbi:Mysql:test', 'user', 'pw') do |dbh|
  dbh.func(:createdb, 'demo')
end
```

ODBC

The ODBC database driver implements one driver-specific attribute: *odbc_ignore-case*. It has the same effect as the Ruby/ODBC method with the same name ("ignorecase"). If enabled, all column names are reported upper case.

Accessing Databases Remotely Using DBD::Proxy

With Ruby/DBI it is very easy to remotely connect to databases, even if the databases themselves do not support remote connections. This is achieved by a server component: the proxy server which runs on the machine where the database resides, and a database driver which communicates with that proxy server.

Note that there is currently no compression or encryption implemented. If security is important for your application, you might consider using a Virtual Private Network (VPN) that implements both encryption and compression transparently for all TCP/IP connections.

NOTE

Free VPN implementations are FreeS/WAN (www.freeswan.org) for Linux or KAME (www.kame.net) for BSDs.

Now to start the proxy server, change into the DBI distribution's *bin/ proxyserver* directory and enter the following at the command line:

```
ruby proxyserver.rb work 9001
```

This would start a proxy server listening on port *9001* and accepting connections for the *work* host. To test whether or not you can access the remote database, use *sqlsh.rb*:

```
REMOTE_DSN=dbi:Pg:dbname
URI=dbi:Proxy:hostname=work;port=9001;dsn=$REMOTE_DSN
sqlsh.rb $URI user passwd
```

On the remote host, this would establish a connection to the database specified by REMOTE_DSN. The proxy server would then forward this connection to you.

Copying Table Data between Different Databases

Have you ever tried to transfer whole tables from one database to another of a different type or vendor (for example, PostgreSQL and MS Access), and possibly even over TCP/IP? With Ruby/DBI this is a simple task that can be done in less than 40 lines of code, as we'll demonstrate below.

This example assumes that the table already exists in the destination database. Furthermore, we don't care about possible referential constraints, which would make our life unnecessarily hard.

We start with writing a helper function that lets us pass the username and password together with the DSN in one string of the form *user:pass@dsn*:

```ruby
def parse_uri( uri )
  auth, uri = uri.split('@')
  if uri.nil?
    return auth
  else
    user, pass = auth.split(':')
    return uri, user, pass
  end
end
```

The real work is done by the *replicate_table* method, which inserts all rows of table *src_tab* from database *src* into the table *dst_tab* of database *dst*. It loops over each row of the source table and prepares a statement for inserting a row into the destination table once it knows the number of fields. The prepared statement is then executed in each iteration.

```ruby
def replicate_table(src, dst, src_tab, dst_tab)
  stmt = nil
  src.select_all("SELECT * FROM #{src_tab}") do |row|
    if stmt.nil?
      fields = row.field_names.join(",")
      qs     = (['?'] * row.size).join(",")
      stmt   = dst.prepare %[
        INSERT INTO #{dst_tab} (#{fields}) VALUES (#{qs})
      ]
    end
```

```
        stmt.execute(*row.to_a)
    end
end
```

In the main program we just have to connect to both databases, turn *auto commit* mode off for the destination database to increase performance, and finally call the *replicate_table* method.

```
require 'dbi'

unless (3..4) === ARGV.size
  puts 'USAGE: #$0 src_dsn dst_dsn src_table [dst_table]'
  exit 1
end


SRC_DSN = ARGV[0]
DST_DSN = ARGV[1]
SRC_TAB = ARGV[2]
DST_TAB = ARGV[3] || SRC_TAB

DBI.connect(*parse_uri(SRC_DSN)) do |src|
  DBI.connect(*parse_uri(DST_DSN)) do |dst|
    dst['AutoCommit'] = false
    dst.transaction do
      replicate_table(src, dst, SRC_TAB, DST_TAB)
    end
  end
end
```

If the insertion of one row should fail or another error should occur, all changes already made to the destination database are rolled back and the program is aborted.

Getting Binary Objects Out of a Database

Suppose you develop a Web application. It is an online auction platform that allows users to upload pictures of objects they want to sell. You extend your already complex data model and add one more table (see Figure 3.7) that stores the pictures inside the database. In the same table, we also store the content type (for example, image/jpeg) as well as a primary key to uniquely access each image.

To insert a binary object into a database, simply use DBI's *DBI::Binary* class; pass the binary data as a string to its *new* method, and bind this object to a parameter marker as usual. This works for all databases including PostgreSQL (note that the column must be of the OID type) and MySql (TEXT column type).

To get the binary object out of the database, we write a little Common Gateway Interface (CGI) application, taking the primary key as of the image to show as CGI parameter *id*.

```ruby
#!/usr/bin/env ruby

require "cgi"
require "dbi"

DSN, USER, PWD = 'dbi:Pg:rdg', 'matz', '123'

SQL = 'SELECT data, content_type FROM picture WHERE ' +
      'picture_id = ?'

cgi = CGI.new
id = cgi['id'][0].to_i

DBI.connect(DSN, USER, PWD) do |dbh|
  row = dbh.select_one(SQL, id)

  puts "Content-Type: %s"    % row['content_type']
  puts "Content-Length: %s"  % row['data'].size
  puts "Date: %s"            % Time.now
  # cache image three minutes
  puts "Expires: %s"         % (Time.now + 3*60)
  puts

  # output image data
  print row['data'].to_s
end
```

This works for all databases. For PostgreSQL databases (currently the only DBD supporting streaming operations on BLOBs) we could modify this so that we don't need to load the whole image in memory. Instead, we read in the image in fixed-sized blocks (*BLK_SIZE*) and pass them, one after the other, to the Web server. Of course, this only makes sense if the images' binary data is large or is frequently requested.

```ruby
#!/usr/bin/env ruby

require "cgi"
require "dbi"

DSN, USER, PWD = 'dbi:Pg:rdg', 'matz', '123'

SQL = 'SELECT data, content_type FROM picture WHERE ' +
      'picture_id = ?'

BLK_SIZE = 8 * 1024

cgi = CGI.new
id = cgi['id'][0].to_i

DBI.connect(DSN, USER, PWD) do |dbh|
  row = dbh.select_one(SQL, id)

  stream = dbh.func(:blob_open, row['data'])

  puts "Content-Type: %s"    % row['content_type']
  puts "Content-Length: %s"  % stream.size
  puts "Date: %s"            % Time.now
  # cache image three minutes
  puts "Expires: %s"         % (Time.now + 3*60)
  puts

  # output image data
  loop {
    data = stream.read(BLK_SIZE)
```

```
      print data
      break if data.size != BLK_SIZE
   }
   stream.close
end
```

Figure 3.7 Data Model of Table to Store Images

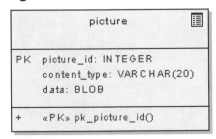

Transforming SQL-query Results to XML

XML is everywhere, so it's not very surprising that most of today's commercial database systems integrate it by default, or at least provide XML extensions. Microsoft's SQL Server, for example, makes the generation of XML very easy by extending the syntax of SQL's *SELECT* statement to *SELECT … FOR XML*, whereas Oracle takes a more solid approach and provides functions returning XML documents as Character Large OBjects (CLOBs) similar to the statement

```
SELECT xmlgen.getXML('select * from ....') FROM DUAL
```

Again, others use different approaches with different features and capabilities.

In this section we don't want to limit XML generation to the databases of only one or two vendors. Instead, we want to achieve this capability independently of specific databases, for which Ruby/DBI provides an excellent solution. Indeed, Ruby/DBI comes with some methods for generating XML by default, which are the following methods, defined in module *DBI::Utils::XMLFormatter*.

```
row(row, rowtag='row', output=STDOUT)


extended_row(row, rowtag='row', cols_in_row_tag=[],
             cols_as_tag=nil, add_row_tag_attrs={},
             output=STDOUT)


table(rows, roottag='rows', rowtag='row', output=STDOUT)
```

Use the *row* method if you don't need extra control over how the generated XML should look. Passing it a *DBI::Row* object as the *row* parameter and the name of the enclosing tag (the *rowtag* parameter), this method writes the generated XML to the *output* parameter (using the << method). The generated XML would look as shown below, where each column has its own tag:

```
<row>
   <name>Michael Neumann</name>
   <email>...</email>
   .
   .
</row>
```

The *extended_row* method has more options that let you specify the following:

- Which columns should go into the row-tag as attributes (*cols_in_row_tag*)
- Which column should have its own tag (*cols_as_tag*; **nil** means all but those specified in *cols_in_row_tag*)
- Additional attributes for the row-tag (*add_row_tag_attrs*)

Finally, the *table* method calls the *row* method for each row of its parameter *rows* and puts an XML tag named *roottag* around it.

To demonstrate the usage of the *extended_row* method, let's write a little CGI application that returns an XML document for a supplied SQL query (see Figure 3.8).

```
#!/usr/bin/env ruby
require "cgi"
require "dbi"


XML  = '<?xml version="1.0" encoding="utf-8"?>'
cgi  = CGI.new
sql  = cgi["sql"][0]              # sql query
root = cgi["root"][0] || "root"  # name of root element
row  = cgi["row"][0]  || "row"   # name of row tag
id   = cgi["id"][0]   || ""      # columns shown in the tag

exit if sql.nil? or sql.empty?


print cgi.header("text/xml")
```

```
puts XML, "<#{root}>"
DBI.connect("dbi:Pg:db", "user", "pass") do |dbh|
  dbh.select_all(sql) do |r|
    DBI::Utils::XMLFormatter.extended_row(r, row,
      id.split(/\s*,\s*/))
  end
end
puts "</#{root}>"
```

To get this example to work, you probably have to modify the DBI connection string appropriately.

Figure 3.8 Generated XML for SQL Query

All three above-mentioned methods work well for generating flat XML documents, but generating nested documents with them is not possible. Therefore, I decided to write an add-on (*xmlgen.rb*) using Sean Russell's XML parser, REXML. The add-on is included in the DBI package's *examples* directory—

additionally, you'll find it in this book's accompanying CD in the *xsql* directory. It extends the *DBI::Utils::XMLFormatter* module for two further methods:

```
row_to_xml(row, rowtag="row", include_nulls=true,
          colmap={})


table_to_xml(rows, roottag="rows", rowtag="row",
            include_nulls=true, colmap={})
```

Again, the *table_to_xml* method is just a wrapper around *row_to_xml* to conveniently process multiple rows. The difference between the methods mentioned earlier and *row_to_xml* or *table_to_xml* is that the latter ones make it possible to easily generate arbitrary nested XML documents. To demonstrate this, let's take a table that we'll call *Test,* with columns *entry_id, author_id, author_name, author_email, title* and *body.* Then we can specify within the *SELECT* statement which column creates which XML tag or attribute by misusing the column name for exactly this purpose:

```
SELECT title, body,
       entry_id     AS "@id",
       author_id    AS "author/@id",
       autor_name   AS "author/name",
       author_email AS "author/email"
FROM Test
```

When we now call the *row_to_xml* method for one row of the above statement's resultset and with the *rowtag* parameter set to *ROW*, we would get an XML document structured like the one below:

```
<ROW id="...">
  <title>...</title>
  <body>...</body>
  <author id="...">
    <name>...</name>
    <email>...</email>
  </author>
</ROW>
```

Instead of specifying the structure of the XML document within the SQL statement, we could also pass a mapping to the method as last parameter, in which case a simple *SELECT * FROM Test* would suffice:

```
row_to_xml(row, "ROW", true,
  "entry_id"     => "@id",
  "author_id"    => "author/@id",
  "author_name"  => "author/name",
  "author_email" => "author/email")
```

The return value of both *row_to_xml* and *table_to_xml* methods is an object of the *REXML::Element* class, which we can transform into a string as follows:

```
anElement = row_to_xml(...)
asString  = ""


anElement.write(asString)
# asString now contains the XML document as string
```

So far so good, except that we now want to write an application that comes close to Oracle's XSQL servelet. Never heard of XSQL? Doesn't matter! That won't affect our example at all. What our (very limited) version of XSQL should be able to do is the following:

- Execute the SQL queries surrounded by a **<xsql:query>** tag and substitute it with the result-set transformed to XML.

- Substitute parameters in the SQL statement before executing them (e.g. {@ID}).

- Forward the resulting XML document to an Extensible Stylesheet Language Transformations (XSLT) processor or return it as is if none was specified.

To implement this in Ruby we will make use of the following libraries:

- Ruby/DBI

- REXML

- XSLT4R (would also use any other external XSLT processor)

Figure 3.9 shows a sample XSQL document. Of course, an arbitrary number of <xsql:query> tags are allowed in one XSQL document, though it may be that only one <xsql:query> tag will occur as the root tag.

Figure 3.9 Sample XSQL Document

```
<?xml version="1.0"?>
<?xml-stylesheet type="text/xsl"
  href="http://www.syngress.com/rdg/page.xsl"?>
<page>
  <xsql:query xmlns:xsql="urn:ruby-xsql" connection="demo"
   rowset-element="nav-bar" row-element="link">

    SELECT href AS "@href", title, imgsrc
    FROM navigation WHERE nav_id = {@ID}

  </xsql:query>

  <p>Welcome to...</p>
  .
  .
  .
</page>
```

So let's start with the part of the application that does the really hard job, which is parsing and transforming the XSQL-XML document, executing the SQL statements, and finally triggering the XSLT processor. The source code for this is shown in Figure 3.10; it also appears at www.syngress.com/solutions under the *xsql* directory as the file named *xsql.rb*.

Figure 3.10 Sourcecode of XSQL Application (xsql.rb)

```
require "rexml/document"
require "xslt"
require "dbi"
require "xmlgen"
require "net/http"

class XSQL
  XSQL_URI = 'urn:ruby-xsql'
```

Continued

Figure 3.10 Continued

```ruby
def initialize(connections)
  @connections = connections
end

def process(stringOrReadable, params)
  doc = REXML::Document.new stringOrReadable
  stylesheet = getStylesheet(doc)['href']
  processQueries(doc, params)

  xml = ""; doc.write(xml)

  applyStylesheet(fetchURL(stylesheet), xml) rescue xml
end

private # ------------------------------------------------

def fetchURL(url)
  if url =~ /^http:\/\//
    addr, path = $'.split("/", 2)
    host, port = addr.split(":")
    Net::HTTP.start(host, (port||80).to_i) do |sess|
      res = ""
      sess.get("/" + (path || ""), nil, res)
      return res
    end
  else
    File.readlines(url).to_s
  end
end

def processQueries(doc, params)
  doc.elements.each("//query") do |q|
```

Continued

Figure 3.10 Continued

```ruby
        next unless q.namespace == XSQL_URI

      begin
        conn = @connections[q.attributes["connection"]]
        sql = q.text.gsub(/\{\s*@(\w+)\s*\}/) {params[$1]}
        raise "No connection specified" if conn.nil?

        DBI.connect(*conn) do |dbh|
          q.replace_with DBI::Utils::XMLFormatter.
          table_to_xml(
            dbh.select_all(sql),
            q.attributes["rowset-element"] || "ROWSET",
            q.attributes["row-element"]    || "ROW",
            !(q.attributes["include-nulls"] == "no")
          )
        end
      rescue Exception => err
        elt = REXML::Element.new("xsql:exception")
        elt.attributes["class"] = err.type.to_s
        elt.attributes["xmlns:xsql"] = XSQL_URI
        elt.add_text(err.message)
        q.replace_with(elt)
      end
    end
  end

  def applyStylesheet(stylesheet, xml)
    output = ""
    xslt = XSLT::Stylesheet.new(stylesheet, {})
    xslt.output = [output]
    xslt.apply(xml)
    output
  end
```

Continued

Figure 3.10 Continued

```ruby
def getStylesheet(doc)
  arr = doc.select { |i|
    i.is_a? REXML::Instruction and
    i.target == 'xml-stylesheet'
  }.collect { |i|
    i.remove
    keyValuePairsToHash(i.content)
  }
  arr.empty? ? {} : arr.first
end


def keyValuePairsToHash(str)
  hash = {}
  str.scan(/\s*([\w_]+)\s*=\s*(['"])(.*?)\2/).each{
    |k, d, v|
    hash[k] = v
  }
  hash
end

end
```

To explain what you've seen in Figure 3.10, note the following points regarding the methods of the *XSQL* class:

- The *fetchURL* method fetches the document with the specified URL from a Web server, or reads it from the local file system and returns its content.

- The *processQueries* method substitutes all <xsql:query> tags through the result-set (converted to XML) of executed SQL statements, or in the case of an error, through a <xsql:exception> tag.

- The *applyStylesheet* method, as the name suggests, applies the XSLT stylesheet supplied as a string by the first parameter onto the XML document (second parameter) and returns the transformed document.

- The *getStylesheet* method looks in the XSQL–XML document for <?xml-stylesheet ...?> processing instructions, parses the key/value pairs (using the *keyValuePairsToHash* method), and returns a hash. This hash then contains for example the key *href,* which points to the stylesheet to use.

An *XSQL* object is initialized with a hash containing all valid database connection names (key), and the DBI connection string, username, and password as values. After that, we can trigger the transformation by calling the *process* method and passing it the filename or IO object of the XSQL–XML document to transform, along with a list of parameters that get substituted inside the <xsql:query> tag, as hash (for example, Figure 3.9 contains one {@ID} parameter, which gets substituted by the value of the key *ID*). It returns the transformed document as a string.

Before we go on, we want to try this out using a little script that processes the following XSQL document (*test.xsql*):

```
<?xml version="1.0"?>
<xsql:query xmlns:xsql="urn:ruby-xsql" connection="test">
  SELECT 1+2 AS "{@COLUMN}"
</xsql:query>
```

Here is the script I used:

```
require "xsql"
conns  = { 'test'   => ["dbi:Pg:db", "pass", "auth"] }
params = { 'COLUMN' => '@expr' }
puts XSQL.new(conns).process("test.xsql", params)
```

Please modify the DBI connections string, username, and password. On execution, this script would respond with the following output, which reveals that it works as we expected it to:

```
<?xml version="1.0"?>
<ROWSET>
  <ROW expr="3"/>
</ROWSET>
```

However, which exact attributes can or must one <xsql:query> tag contain?

- *connection:* Name of the connection—mandatory
- *rowset-element:* Name of all rows surrounding element—defaults to *ROWSET*

- *row-element*: Name of the element which surrounds one single row—defaults to *ROW*

- *include-nulls*: Either *yes* or *no* for whether to include NULLs or not—defaults to include NULLs

Note that because we don't want to process our XSQL documents from the command line each time, but instead want them to be publicly available around the Internet, a CGI application is the way to go. Figure 3.11 shows this CGI application. Again, you should modify the DBI connection string appropriately.

Figure 3.11 XSQL CGI Application

```
#!/usr/bin/env ruby

require "xsql"
require "cgi"


CONNECTIONS = {
  'test' => ["dbi:Mysql:test", "user", "auth"],
  'demo' => ["dbi:DB2:SAMPLE", "", ""]
  # add more if you want
}


cgi  = CGI.new
xsql = XSQL.new(CONNECTIONS)


# collect CGI parameters in params
params = {}
cgi.params.each {|k, v| params[k] = v[0] }


# process XSQL file
data = xsql.process(File.new(cgi.path_translated), params)


# and finally output it
content_type = data =~ /^\s*<?\s*xml/ ? 'xml' : 'html'
cgi.out('text/' + content_type) { data }
```

Put this CGI script into the cgi-bin directory, make it executable (chmod +x xsql.cgi) and modify Apache's *httpd.conf* file, where we add the following into the main section (<Directory "/path/to/document-root">):

```
AddHandler xsql .xsql
Action     xsql /cgi-bin/xsql.cgi
```

Now save the *.xsql* file anywhere in the htdocs directory, do the same with the XSLT stylesheet (don't forget to refer to it from within the XSQL file using its complete URL) and direct your browser to its URL (for example, http://127.0.0.1/test.xsql?COLUMN=@expr) to display.

If you develop such an application yourself you should always have a shell open and showing Apache's error log file so you can see any errors that occur in your script. You can do this under Unix by executing the following code:

```
tail -f /var/log/httpd/error_log
```

Below is a list of some additional extensions that you could make to the XSQL application:

- Recognize the <?xml-stylesheet?> media attribute and apply only the matching stylesheet (different stylesheets for Netscape and Internet Explorer or for WAP cellular phones).

- Extend the <xsql:query> tag for attributes *max-rows* and *skip-rows*.

- Supply tags <xsl:if>, <xsql:param-for-stylesheet>, and <xsql:for-each-row>.

- Supply a tag to emit table schemas into the XML document.

- Improve speed by using FastCGI (or a similar approach) instead of CGI.

- Improve speed by using connection pooling, or at least reuse opened connections within one XSQL file.

Accessing Databases with Ruby/ODBC

An alternative to Ruby/DBI for accessing different types of databases is Christian Werner's Ruby/ODBC package, which enables us to access any ODBC data-source from within Ruby.

An installed ODBC driver manager is a requirement to use Ruby/ODBC, as well as an ODBC driver for the database you want to access. On Windows, there is an ODBC driver manager installed by default, whereas on Unix you have to either install UnixODBC (www.unixodbc.org) or iODBC (www.iodbc.com) before you can use Ruby/ODBC.

Shown below is a sample configuration file for use with iODBC and the ODBC driver for MySql. Just save this as file *.odbc.ini* in your home directory and modify the paths to the driver library and the host and database name, if needed.

```
[Myodbc]
Driver          = /usr/local/lib/libmyodbc-2.50.36.so
Host            = localhost
Database        = rdg
```

To install Ruby/ODBC, download it from its homepage at www.ch-werner .de/rubyodbc (As of this writing the newest version is 0.94). A precompiled binary for Windows is available there, though if you don't want to use the pre-compiled binary, you can compile and install the uncompiled Ruby/ODBC via the following commands:

```
ruby extconf.rb
make
make install
```

On Unix, you'll probably have to specify the directory for the ODBC libraries and header files. Do this with the command line option —*with-odbc-dir*.

```
ruby extconf.rb --with-odbc-dir=/usr/pkg
```

Now that you've successfully installed Ruby/ODBC, let's look at an example (Figure 3.12) where we connect to an ODBC datasource (in our case the data-source Myodbc), create a table, insert several rows into it and afterwards query the table. Finally we close the connection.

Figure 3.12 Sample Ruby/ODBC Application

```
require "odbc"


# modify settings below
DSN, USER, PWD = "Myodbc", "matz", "123"


ODBC.connect(DSN, USER, PWD) do |dbh|
```

Continued

Figure 3.12 Continued

```ruby
# enable autocommit (fails e.g. with Mysql)
dbh.autocommit = true

# drop table 'test' (if it already exists)
begin
  dbh.do("DROP TABLE test")
rescue ODBC::Error; end

# create table 'test'
dbh.do("CREATE TABLE test (id INT, name VARCHAR(30))")

# insert one row
dbh.do("INSERT INTO test VALUES (?,?)", 1, 'Michael')

# pull autocommit mode off (fails e.g. with Mysql)
dbh.autocommit = false

# insert some more rows
dbh.prepare("INSERT INTO test VALUES(?,?)") do |sth|
  name = "AAAAA"
  99.times {|n| sth.execute(n+2, name.succ!) }
end

# commit changes (fails e.g. with Mysql)
dbh.commit

# count rows in table 'test'
dbh.run("SELECT COUNT(*) FROM test") do |sth|
  p sth.fetch[0]   # => 100
end

# query table 'test' again
```

Continued

Figure 3.12 Continued

```
sql = "SELECT name FROM test WHERE id BETWEEN ? AND ?"
sth = dbh.run(sql, 49, 50)


# convert column names to uppercase
sth.ignorecase = true


# fetch the resulting rows
sth.fetch_hash do |row|
  p row['NAME']                 # => "AAABW", "AAABX"
end


# close and free the statement
sth.drop


end
```

Note that you can call most methods of Ruby/ODBC similarly to those in Ruby/DBI, with or without code block. The behavior is the same except that you don't have to duplicate row objects if you want to store them somewhere else using methods *fetch* or *fetch_hash* (or similar), which you must do in Ruby/DBI. To do this in Ruby/DBI, execute the following code:

```
arr = []
sth.fetch { |row| arr << row.dup }
```

This is equivalent to the following in Ruby/ODBC:

```
arr = []
sth.fetch { |row| arr << row }
```

Table 3.12 lists some Ruby/ODBC methods together with their Ruby/DBI counterparts. Not all methods are covered below; only the most important ones. Sometimes parameters or return values differ, so you should consult Ruby/ODBC's documentation for the exact behaviors.

Table 3.12 Comparing Ruby/DBI's and Ruby/ODBC's Methods

Ruby/ODBC	Ruby/DBI	Comments
module ODBC	*module DBI*	
connect	connect	
drivers	available_drivers	Different return value.
datasources	data_sources	Different return value.
class Database	*class DatabaseHandle*	
connected?	connected?	
disconnect	disconnect	
tables	tables	Ruby/ODBC returns a Statement.
columns	columns	Ruby/ODBC returns a Statement.
do	do	
run	execute	
prepare	prepare	
commit	commit	
rollback	rollback	
transaction	transaction	
autocommit	['AutoCommit']	
class Statement	*class StatementHandle*	
cancel	cancel	
close		Closes (but not frees) Statement.
drop	finish	
fetch	fetch	Ruby/ODBC returns an Array, Ruby/DBI a DBI::Row
fetch_hash		Not necessary in Ruby/DBI.
fetch_many	fetch_many	Same as for method *fetch*.
fetch_all	fetch_all	Same as for method *fetch*.
execute	execute	
columns	column_info	Different return value.
fetch_scroll	fetch_scroll	Same as for method *fetch*.

Ruby/ODBC provides several methods that are not found in Ruby/DBI, for example metadata access methods like *indexes*, *types*, *primary_keys*, *foreign_keys*, *table_privileges* or *procedures* of the *ODBC::Database* class. Furthermore Ruby/ODBC lets you query and set a variety of different attributes using the *ODBC::Driver* class.

The conversion from SQL to Ruby types (and vice versa) takes place as shown in Table 3.13.

Table 3.13 Datatype Conversion

SQL	Ruby
INTEGER, SMALLINT, TINYINT, BIT	Fixnum, Bignum
FLOAT, DOUBLE, REAL	Float
DATE	ODBC::Date
TIME	ODBC::Time
TIMESTAMP	ODBC::TimeStamp
All others	String

All in all, Ruby/ODBC is a good alternative to Ruby/DBI if an ODBC driver exists for the database you want to access and if you're able and willing to install and use an ODBC driver manager—especially as performance is currently better than that of Ruby/DBI.

Accessing LDAP Directories with Ruby/LDAP

As the Lightweight Directory Access Protocol (LDAP) gets more and more important, its good to know that we can access LDAP directories from within our Ruby applications using the Ruby/LDAP library (see the RAA's Database section). This library enables us to perform a search on the entries in an LDAP directory, add new entries, and modify or delete existing ones.

Using Ruby/LDAP

After requiring the feature *ldap*, we connect to a LDAP directory with:

```
conn = LDAP::Conn.new
```

which is equivalent to:

```
conn = LDAP::Conn.new('localhost', LDAP::LDAP_PORT)
```

Then we login. This is where we usually specify the username and password we will use for the rest of the session:

```
conn.bind('cn=Manager,dc=syngress,dc=com', 'pwd') do
  ...
end
```

Or without using code blocks, this is:

```
conn.bind('cn=Manager,dc=syngress,dc=com', 'pwd')
  ...
conn.unbind
```

We can now perform search, add, modify or delete operations inside the block of the *bind* method (between *bind* and *unbind*), provided we have the proper permissions.

Adding an LDAP Entry

We can add an entry to the directory using the *add* method:

```
conn.add 'cn=Michael Neumann,dc=syngress,dc=com',
        'objectclass'       => ['person'],
        'cn'                => ['Michael Neumann'],
        'sn'                => ['Neumann'],
        'telephoneNumber'   => ['private: 0333444',
                                'mobile: 333-444']
```

The *add* method's first parameter is the distinguished name for the new entry to be added. A distinguished name is comparable to a primary key in RDBMS - it is unique and identifies only one row. The second parameter is a hash that contains the attributes of the new entry.

Modifying an LDAP Entry

Modifying an entry is similar to adding one. Just call the *modify* method instead of *add* with the attributes to modify. For example, to modify the surname of the entry we added in the previous section, we'd write:

```
conn.modify 'cn=Michael Neumann,dc=syngress,dc=com',
        'sn' => ['New surname']
```

Deleting an LDAP Entry

To delete an entry, call the *delete* method with the distinguished name as parameter:

```
conn.delete('cn=Nobody,dc=syngress,dc=com')
```

Modifying the Distinguished Name

It's not possible to modify the distinguished name of an entry with the *modify* method. Instead, use the *modrdn* method.

Suppose we have the following entry (in LDIFF format):

```
dn: cn=Michal Neumann,dc=dyngress,dc=com

cn: Michal Neumann

sn: Neumann

objectclass: person
```

Then we modify its distinguished name with the following code:

```
conn.modrdn('cn=Michal Neumann,dc=syngress,dc=com',
            'cn=Michael Neumann', true)
```

If the last parameter of *modrdn* is *true*, the attribute that is part of the distinguished name ('cn=Michal Neumann') is deleted before the new (cn=Michael Neumann) is added. This would result in the following entry:

```
dn: cn=Michael Neumann,dc=dyngress,dc=com

cn: Michael Neumann

sn: Neumann

objectclass: person
```

If we specify *false* as last parameter, we get:

```
dn: cn=Michael Neumann,dc=dyngress,dc=com

cn: Michal Neumann

cn: Michael Neumann

sn: Neumann

objectclass: person
```

Performing a Search

Finally, to perform a search on a LDAP directory, use the *search* method with one of three different search modes:

- *LDAP_SCOPE_BASE*: Search only the base node.

- *LDAP_SCOPE_ONELEVEL*: Search all children of the base node.

- *LDAP_SCOPE_SUBTREE*: Search the whole subtree including the base node.

For example, to search the whole subtree of entry *dc=syngress,dc=com* for *person* objects, we'd write:

```
base    = 'dc=syngress,dc=com'
scope   = LDAP::LDAP_SCOPE_SUBTREE
filter  = '(objectclass=person)'
attrs   = ['sn', 'cn']


conn.search(base, scope, filter, attrs) do |entry|
  # print distinguished name
  p entry.dn

  # print all attribute names
  p entry.attrs

  # print values of attribute 'sn'
  p entry.vals('sn')

  # print entry as Hash
  p entry.to_hash
end
```

This invokes the given code block for each matching entry where the LDAP entry is represented by an instance of the *LDAP::Entry* class. With the last parameter of *search* you can specify the attributes in which you are interested, omitting all others. If you pass *nil* here, all attributes are returned (same as "SELECT *" in relational databases).

The *dn* method (alias for *get_dn*) of the *LDAP::Entry* class returns the distinguished name of the entry, and with the *to_hash* method you can get a hash representation of its attributes (including the distinguished name). To get a list of an entry's attributes use the *attrs* method (alias for *get_attributes*). Also, to get the list of one specific attribute's values, use the *vals* method (alias for *get_values*).

Handling Errors

Ruby/LDAP defines two different exception classes. In case of an error, the *new*, *bind* or *unbind* methods raise an *LDAP::Error* exception, whereas the methods related to modifying (add, modify, delete) or searching an LDAP directory instead raise a *LDAP::ResultError*— if, for example, you try to delete or modify a non-existing entry, or you try to add an entry with an existing distinguished name or without specifying a mandatory attribute.

Utilizing Other Storage Solutions

There are several other solutions for storing data persistently on disk with Ruby. In the following sections we'll introduce you into the following solutions:

- Reading and writing CSV files

- Berkeley DBM file databases like *gdbm*, *sdbm* or *dbm*

- The more advanced Berkeley DB database system

- Storing marshaled objects in a relational database

Storing Ruby objects as XML files is handled in Chapter 5, in the *XML-RPC* and *SOAP* sections.

Reading and Writing Comma-Separated Value Files

With Nakamura Hiroshi's CSV module (see the RAA's *csv* entry in the *Text* section) we can read and write Comma Separated Value files from within Ruby. To install this library, simply take the *csv.rb* file from the downloaded archive and put it into your *site_ruby* directory (for example, /usr/local/lib/ruby/site_ruby/1.6).

Suppose we have the following CSV file, which we have named *test.csv*:

```
id,name,creator,age
1,C,Dennis,
4,Perl,"Larry Wall",14
5,Ruby,Matz,6
```

To parse this we could write:

```
require "csv"
```

```
File.each("test.csv") do |line|
  p CSV.parse(line.chomp)
end
```

This outputs the following:

```
["id", "name", "creator", "age"]
["1", "C", "Dennis", nil]
["4", "Perl", "Larry Wall", "14"]
["5", "Ruby", "Matz", "6"]
```

Notice that we have to remove the line ending character (**\n**) before we pass the string to method *CSV.parse*.

To create a CSV file simply use the *CSV.create* method for each row:

```
require "csv"
rows = [
  ["id", "name", "creator", "age"],
  [1, "C", "Dennis", nil],
  [4, "Perl", "Larry Wall", 14],
  [5, "Ruby", "Matz", 6]
]

rows.each do |row|
  puts CSV.create(row)
end
```

This outputs:

```
id,name,creator,age
1,C,Dennis,
4,Perl,Larry Wall,14
5,Ruby,Matz,6
```

Using Berkley DBM-file Databases

Ruby's standard library has three classes for accessing Berkeley DBM databases. These are *DBM*, *GDBM* and *SDBM*. They behave similarly to the *Hash* class, with the difference that the values are stored in a file instead of in memory.

The following example demonstrates how to use the *DBM* class. To use one of the other two classes, simply modify the first line to require *gdbm* or *sdbm* and create an instance of class *GDBM* or *SDBM* in the second line.

```
require 'dbm'

db = DBM.open('test')

db['ruby'] = "matz"
db['perl'] = "larry"

db.keys      # => ['ruby', 'perl']
db.values    # => ['matz', 'larry']

db.each do |k, v|
  puts "#{k} => #{v}"´    # ruby => matz; perl => larry
end

db['obj'] = Marshal.dump [1,2,3]
p Marshal.load(db['obj'])    # => [1,2,3]

db.close
```

Using the Berkeley DB Interface BDB

With Guy Decoux's BDB module (see the RAA's *bdb* entry in the Database section), you can use the embedded Berkeley DB database system from within Ruby. This module is already included in the Pragmatic Programmers Windows Installer version of Ruby, but to use it on Unix systems you have to download and install.

BDB supports transactions, cursors, locking and three different access methods:

- B+tree: *BDB::Btree*
- Hashing: *BDB::Hash*
- Fixed and Variable Length Records: *BDB::Recno* or *BDB::Queue*

This module also lets you write your own sorting methods to be used by the database in Ruby.

Next we'll implement a little translator application that can translate words from German into English and vice versa. We'll take Frank Richter's German to English/English to German word list (www.tu-chemnitz.de/dict), parse it, and store the translations in two language-specific databases (using *BDB::Recno*). Also, because some translations include more than one word, we'll create two further databases (using *BDB::Btree*) to index the words of the translations.

First let us create the four databases. This is done in Figure 3.13. You'll also find its source code at www.syngress.com/solutions in the file create_dbs.rb under the *bdb* directory. Note that the execution of this application may take several minutes to complete.

Figure 3.13 Create Databases for Translator Application (create_dbs.rb)

```ruby
require "bdb"

FILE_NAME = "ger-eng.txt"

# here we store the translations
ger_db = BDB::Recnum.open "ger.db", nil, BDB::CREATE, 0644
eng_db = BDB::Recnum.open "eng.db", nil, BDB::CREATE, 0644

# here we store the indices
ger_inx = BDB::Btree.open "ger.inx", nil, BDB::CREATE,
          0644, "set_flags" => BDB::DUP | BDB::DUPSORT
eng_inx = BDB::Btree.open "eng.inx", nil, BDB::CREATE,
          0644, "set_flags" => BDB::DUP | BDB::DUPSORT

# extracts the words contained in one line
def words(line)
  line.scan(/\b[\w]+/).each{|w| w.downcase!}.uniq
end
```

Continued

Figure 3.13 Continued

```ruby
rec_no = 0        # current record number

File.foreach( FILE_NAME ) do | line |
  # skip line if comment or empty
  next if line[0] == ?# or line.strip.empty?

  g, e = line.split("::")
  e ||= ""
  g.strip! ; e.strip!

  # append translations to database
  ger_db << g
  eng_db << e

  # extract words to index
  inx = [rec_no].pack("L")    # store rec_no as LONG word
  words(g).each {|w| ger_inx[w] = inx}
  words(e).each {|w| eng_inx[w] = inx}

  rec_no += 1

  # display progress in percent
  puts "#{(rec_no*100 / 126_000)} %" if rec_no % 1000 == 0
end

# close all databases
[ger_db, eng_db, ger_inx, eng_inx].each {|d| d.close}
```

Now let us write the application that queries the databases to translate the words. Follow the example shown by Figure 3.14. Its sourcecode also appears on the accompanying CD. To translate the word "hello" from English to German, invoke the application as follows:

```
ruby query.rb hello en_de
```

which outputs:

```
DE: (jemandem) guten Tag sagen
EN: to say hello (to someone)


DE: Hallo allerseits!
EN: Hello everybody!


DE: Hallo!; Guten Tag!
EN: Hello!
```

Figure 3.14 English to German/German to English Translator (query.rb)

```ruby
require "bdb"

# open databases
ger_db  = BDB::Recnum.open "ger.db", nil, BDB::RDONLY
eng_db  = BDB::Recnum.open "eng.db", nil, BDB::RDONLY
ger_inx = BDB::Btree.open "ger.inx", nil, BDB::RDONLY,
          "set_flags" => BDB::DUP | BDB::DUPSORT
eng_inx = BDB::Btree.open "eng.inx", nil, BDB::RDONLY,
          "set_flags" => BDB::DUP | BDB::DUPSORT

word = (ARGV[0] || raise).downcase
inx  = if ARGV[1] == "en_de" then eng_inx else ger_inx end

# output translations
inx.each_dup_value(word) {|i|
  x = i.unpack("L").first
  print "DE: ", ger_db[x], "\n"
  print "EN: ", eng_db[x], "\n"
  puts
}

# close all databases
[ger_db, eng_db, ger_inx, eng_inx].each {|d| d.close}
```

Storing Ruby Objects in a Relational Database

To make Ruby objects persistent, you'll have to store them somewhere, either in a plain file, a Berkeley DBM-like database or a relational database. Storing a large number of objects in a plain file is very inflexible and slow, because you have to load and store the whole file even to read or write just one object. A better choice is a DBM database; these are fast but allow only one key to access an object. The best would be to map the instance variables of Ruby objects to fields of SQL tables, but that's not so easy to accomplish.

Another approach is to store Ruby objects of one class in a database table that contains N+2 fields:

- **Obj_id**: Unique ID for each stored object

- **Data**: Stores the marshaled Ruby object

- **N-keys**: N user-definable fields, which are mapped to attributes of the stored object

This approach allows you to access the stored Ruby objects with more than one key. You find the implementation in the DBI distribution's *examples/persistence.rb* file .

Suppose we have a *Language* class defined as follows:

```
class Language
  attr_accessor :name, :creator, :age, :info
  def initialize(name, creator, age)
    @name, @creator, @age = name, creator, age
  end
  def to_s
    "#@name, #@creator, #@age. " +
    (@info ? @info[:home] : '')
  end
end
```

And we want to store our *Language* objects in the *Language* table. To achieve this, we have to enable the class for persistency.

```
require 'persistence'
Persistence.new('Language', Persistence::Pg) {
  index_on :name,     'VARCHAR(10) NOT NULL'
```

```
    index_on :creator, 'VARCHAR(10) NOT NULL'
    index_on :age,        'INT'
}.add(Language)
```

Note that instead of *Persistence::Pg* for PostgreSQL databases we could also have used *Persistence::Oracle* for Oracle databases. Others are not currently supported.

With *index_on* we declared three additional fields for the *Language* table. Now we can establish a database connection and create the table if it does not yet exist:

```
dbh = DBI.connect('dbi:Pg:rdg', 'matz', '123',
                      'AutoCommit' => true)


# set the connection used for Language objects
Language.connection = dbh


# if the table not yet exists, create it!
Language.install unless Language.installed?
```

Then we create some Ruby objects of the *Language* class with:

```
l1 = Language.new('C',    'Dennis', 28)
l2 = Language.new('Ruby', 'Larry',  13)
l3 = Language.new('Perl', 'Matz',    5)


l3.info = {:home => 'http://www.ruby-lang.org'}
```

Note that the objects are not stored in the database unless you call the *store* method:

```
l1.store
l2.store
l3.store
```

To read the objects back from the database, we can either use *get_where*, *get_all* or *each*. Thus to increase the age of each language we simply write:

```
Language.each {|lang| lang.age += 1; lang.store }
```

Have you recognized that we mixed up Perl with Ruby above? Well, we can easily correct this and delete language C:

```
perl = Language.get_where('name = ?', 'Ruby')[0]
ruby = Language.get_where('name = ?', 'Perl')[0]

perl.name, ruby.name = ruby.name, perl.name
perl.store; ruby.store

Language.get_where("name = 'C'")[0].delete
```

Finally, we check to see if everything went well and print out all objects:

```
Language.each {|lang| puts lang.to_s}
```

This outputs the following:

```
Perl, Larry, 14.
Ruby, Matz, 6. http://www.ruby-lang.org
```

Summary

In this chapter we mainly looked at Ruby/DBI and developed several applications with it. Ruby/DBI is a database-independent interface for a large number of different databases, similar to Perl's DBI. However, we also showed how to access ODBC datasources using Ruby/ODBC, and we confronted methods of both interfaces in the *Accessing Databases with Ruby/ODBC* section. Furthermore we gave an introduction into Ruby/LDAP and other alternative data storage solutions, such as Berkeley DBM.

Solutions Fast Track

Accessing Databases with Ruby/DBI

☑ Ruby/DBI provides an easy-to-use, database-independent interface for a large number of relational databases. Currently most database drivers still depend on other database libraries. This results in harder installations and decreases performance.

☑ Due to its short existence, Ruby/DBI has not yet reached the same level of maturity as other comparable database interfaces, for example Perl's DBI or Python DB API 2.0.

Accessing Databases with Ruby/ODBC

☑ Ruby/ODBC is the ODBC binding for Ruby. Its API is very similar to Ruby/DBI's, which makes it very easy to switch between the two. Ruby/ODBC's performance is better than that of Ruby/DBI.

☑ Ruby/ODBC works not only on Windows, but also on UNIX systems using the unixODBC or iODBC driver manager.

Accessing LDAP Directories with Ruby/LDAP

☑ With Ruby/LDAP we can access LDAP directories from within our Ruby applications.

Utilizing Other Storage Solutions

☑ There are numerous other data storage solutions for Ruby. Berkeley DBM files provide a hash-like interface for storing data, whereas the

Berkeley DB system has more advanced features (like transactions and cursors), and provides three different access methods (B+tree, Hashing and Fixed or Variable Length Records). A very simple solution is to store data in plain text files using the Comma Separated Values (CSV) format.

Frequently Asked Questions

The following Frequently Asked Questions, answered by the authors of this book, are designed to both measure your understanding of the concepts presented in this chapter and to assist you with real-life implementation of these concepts. To have your questions about this chapter answered by the author, browse to **www.syngress.com/solutions** and click on the **"Ask the Author"** form.

Q: Using Ruby/DBI, I have set the tracing level to *2* and output to standard error, but nothing happened. What's wrong?

A: You may have forgotten to require the *dbi/trace* file at the top of your program.

Q: Using Ruby/DBI, I installed the DBI and some DBDs, but when I start my application, I get a "No such file to load" error.

A: You have probably forgotten to install one of the libraries upon which a DBD depends.

Q: Using Ruby/DBI, I use the *StatementHandle#collect* method to get all rows of a SQL query, but all the rows have the same content. What's wrong?

A: All *DBI::Row* objects passed to the *StatementHandle#collect* method refer to one and the same object. Use *dup* to copy the object.

Q: I'm experiencing problems compiling a database library required by Ruby/DBI. Where can I get help?

A: Either write the author of the library an email, or post a message on Ruby's mailing list (ruby-talk).

XML and Ruby

Solutions in this chapter:

- **Why XML?**
- **XML Parser Architectures and APIs**
- **Parsing and Creating XML in Ruby**
- **Using XSLT in Ruby**

☑ **Summary**

☑ **Solutions Fast Track**

☑ **Frequently Asked Questions**

Introduction

Since its inception, Extensible Markup Language (XML) has been turning heads in the programming and development world. It used to be that creating a database required pre-made and sometimes costly tools, such as MySQL or Microsoft Access; but the advent of XML, with its open architecture and extremely supple simplicity, has completely changed that.

If you know what you are doing, you can have Ruby take advantage of its own architecture and apply it to XML fairly simply. If you are new to Ruby, you can always spend time by yourself, learn Ruby, and create a parser by yourself. However, XML has simple needs; all it requires from a parser is that it reads and formats the file –nothing more.

Instead of working with our own parser, let's take a look at some of the more popular parsing options available for Ruby and XML. Remember, all we are doing here is looking at and understanding XML parsers—which you can always use to develop a more robust engine, if that's what you need.

NOTE

This chapter examines XML *with* Ruby, not how XML works. If you need a good reference for XML, pick up Syngress Publishing's *XML.NET Developer's Guide* (ISBN 1-928994-47-4).

Why XML?

XML is the frequent subject of both marketing hyperbole and heated predictions of its imminent decline, but at heart it's a very straightforward and useful technology: Plain text files are combined with a simple but powerful markup scheme. Much of XML's appeal to programmers lies in its embrace of the so-called "80/20 Rule." The 80/20 Rule simply states that:

- 80% of a problem can be solved with 20% of the code.

- The remaining 80% of the code solves only 20% of the problem.

Which, in essence, means that a little work goes a long way. XML exemplifies this with its simplicity in design, allowing us to easily create solutions for various problems.

For a quick XML example, look at Figure 4.1. There, we define a *root* element, which is used by XML parsers to determine the top-level node. A root-level element can be named anything, just like the rest of XML elements and attributes, but it is very good practice (and good for your sanity!) to keep all elements and attributes relevant, easy to read, and easy to parse. In this example, we have named our root element *PhoneBook* (line 01; and its closing tag on line 11), which also defines for us that this XML file will probably be used as a personal phone book of some kind.

Line 02 begins our first actual phone book entry. *Entry*, as we have so aptly named the element, is the *parent node*; for those with database experience it can be viewed as the beginning of a new row. Each node within the parent node is referred to as a *child node*. Child nodes can be thought of as the columns within a row of data in a database. Lines 03 through 09 are our child nodes; each one written in plain English, readable, and easy to analyze if any other programmer views our XML code.

Figure 4.1 Small XML Example

```
01: <PhoneBook>
02:     <Entry>
03:       <Title>Cacawatha Construction Company</Title>
04:       <Name>Fred Williams, Jr.</Name>
05:       <Position>CEO</Position>
06:       <Phone1>555-555-1234</Phone1>
07:       <Phone2>555-554-4567</Phone2>
08:       <Fax>555-555-8910</Fax>
09:       <Comments>Nice Guy!</Comments>
10:     </Entry>
11: </PhoneBook>
```

There's another reason why we want to use names that are easy to read – they are also easy to remember. With XML files like the one in Figure 4.1, a simple set of entries allows us to remember the name of each entry while we are coding and makes our parser code easier to read as well. For example, if we were to see this file in a browser, we would see the output shown in Figure 4.2.

Figure 4.2 Phonebook XML File In A Browser

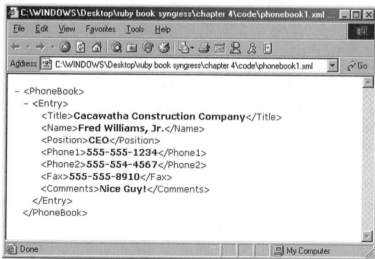

While this is nicely organized and displayed, why can't we view XML in a more orderly fashion, such as in a table view, like in traditional databases? Also, even though the XML file is small and tidy, where are the database capabilities? Several side projects from the W3 have answered these questions; they have created a couple of extra languages that make XML a more manageable—and prettier to look at.

Making XML Manageable

So just how do you deal with XML then? Well, we have already introduced parsers, but does XML need to depend on hand-coded parsers alone? The answer is no; there are several languages available that we can use in order to augment XML. We can use either a Document Type Definition (DTD) or a Schema to provide an XML file with proper validation; Extensible Stylesheet Language Transformations (XSLT) to provide the XML file with a graphical look and/or transform from XML to text files or Hypertext Markup Language (HTML); XPath allows us to travel through an XML file, and XPointer extends XPath's capabilities. Let's take a look at how XML is validated first through the DTD and the Schema.

Validation though DTD

A *Document Type Definition* is a file that XML can use to validate itself. You may be familiar with this term from working with HTML files. The DTD defined an

HTML document that would be matched against the HTML you wrote to make sure your code was up to a specific standard, such as "strict" HTML or "transitional" HTML. The DTD format did not change its syntax for XML, and kept its own method of doing things, so if you're familiar with DTDs for HTML, you're well on your way to using them for XML.

Figure 4.3 has our XML phonebook example with an inline DTD added. The only modification done to the XML file itself is that we have changed <ENTRY> from being a parent node with child nodes to just another child node. An inline DTD is a DTD that is defined within the XML file, sort of like declaring a class within the same file as the main code. Line 01 starts off our DTD by wrapping it around a DOCTYPE definition. The *DOCTYPE* definition tells the client that a new type, *Phonebook* is being created and its description is within the open and close brackets ("[" and "]"). Elements within the *DOCTYPE* are defined using the <!ELEMENT> tag; even the document's *Type* (root element) has to be declared as an *ELEMENT*.

The value within captions (in this case *#PCDATA* for all of the elements) is used to describe the element content, (referred to as the element-content space) or the type of value stored within the element – pretty much like declaring a variable, storing the value 19 to it and declaring the variable an integer. The element-content space can also store the number of times it appears. A DTD can also be included externally by using the *DOCTYPE* element; if we were to reference the DTD in Figure 4.3 externally it would look like <!DOCTYPE Phonebook SYSTEM "phonebook.dtd"> where SYSTEM defines the location of the DTD file.

Figure 4.3 Phonebook XML with an Inline DTD

```
00: <?xml version = "1.0">
01: <!DOCTYPE Phonebook [
02:<!- -The following line wraps- ->
03:    <!ELEMENT Phonebook (Entry, Title, Name, Position, Phone1,
    Phone2, Fax, Comments)>
04:    <!ELEMENT Entry      (#PCDATA)>
04:    <!ELEMENT Title      (#PCDATA)>
05:    <!ELEMENT Name       (#PCDATA)>
06:    <!ELEMENT Position   (#PCDATA)>
07:    <!ELEMENT Phone1     (#PCDATA)>
```

Continued

Figure 4.3 Continued

```
08:      <!ELEMENT Phone2      (#PCDATA)>

09:      <!ELEMENT Fax         (#PCDATA)>

10:      <!ELEMENT Comments    (#PCDATA)>

11: ] >

12:

13: <PhoneBook>

14:      <Entry>Work</Entry>

15:      <Title>Cacawatha Construction Company</Title>

16:      <Name>Fred Williams, Jr.</Name>

17:      <Position>CEO</Position>

18:      <Phone1>555-555-1234</Phone1>

19:      <Phone2>555-554-4567</Phone2>

20:      <Fax>555-555-8910</Fax>

21:      <Comments>Nice Guy!</Comments>

22: </PhoneBook>
```

NOTE

Even though DTD can check the value, it actually only makes sure the XML file conforms to the syntax within the DTD file.

Validating With XML–Schemas

It's obvious from the start that DTD has some drawbacks. First, its language is not XML, which is rather an academic point, but it still forces a requirement on XML in terms of requiring a different, external tool and language for validation. DTD also falls short that validating complex hierarchies using DTD can be quite daunting. Finally, DTD has poor support for data types; *#PCDATA* is really the one that gets the most use. In light of these drawbacks, the alternative Schema was propositioned to the W3C and accepted as a recommendation in Autumn 2001. Schema has been widely accepted and has already begun to replace DTDs as the validation technique of choice for XML.

Technically, Schema is superior to DTD in the following areas:

It validates data as well as form – Remember, DTD only validates the formation (or the document's conformance to XML syntax rules), and not the data types per se.

Both sender and receiver know what to expect – While DTD can say PCDATA, Schema can break it down as *String, Character, Integer, Date,* and other various formats, giving both parties a good expectation of what they are about to get.

It allows data facets, data patterns, data type creation, and data conversion – DTD can't even begin to figure out how to do this.

It is written with XML syntax – Possibly the biggest reason that many programmers have taken to Schema; Schema is able to benefit from XML syntax perks, such as manipulation via DOM and use of XSLT.

Since we know that a Schema is XML we can start right off the bat without having to go into too much detail. Figure 4.4 is an example of how an inline Schema may appear in the same Phonebook file.

Figure 4.4 Phonebook XML With Inline Schema

```
00: <?xml version = "1.0"?>
01: <xs:schema xmlns:xs="http://www.w3.org/2001/XMLSchema">
02:
03: <xs:element name="Phonebook">
04:    <xs:complexType>
05:       <xs:sequence>
06:          <element name="Entry" type="xs:string"/>
07:          <element name="Title"  type="xs:string"/>
08:          <element name="Name"  type="xs:string"/>
09:          <element name="Position"  type="xs:string"/>
10:          <element name="Phone1"  type="xs:string"/>
11:          <element name="Phone2"  type="xs:string"/>
12:          <element name="Fax"  type="xs:string"/>
```

Continued

Figure 4.4 Continued

```
13:            <element name="Comments"  type="xs:string"/>
14:        </xs:sequence>
15:    </xs:complexType>
16: </xs:element>
17:
18:</xs:schema>
```

XPath

XPath is an official W3 recommendation that uses XPath expressions. For example, say you want to find the *Name* element in our previous phonebook example. To find the *Name* variable, our XPath syntax would be:

```
/Phonebook/Name
```

Pretty simple, right? However, this simplicity hides a very robust system. XPath can use the same type of syntax throughout an XML document, and literally filter for what you are looking for if you perform a search. XPath can even accept the wild card indicator "★". Attributes can also be located by including an "@" symbol before the attribute name. For example, */Root/★[@test]* would look for any element one level under the root element that has an attribute named "test". There are also features available, such as *Count()* and *Postition()*, which would select elements based on the count of their children or on their position. XPath can also use Boolean expressions.

> **NOTE**
>
> The XPath expressions work just like the URI (Uniform Resource Indicator, similar to URL) style mapping in order to navigate through an XML document. You can find out more information about XPath at www.w3.org/xpath.

XML Parser Architectures and APIs

XML parsers and the Application Programming Interfaces (APIs) they offer generally come in two fundamentally different flavors: event streams and object trees.

Event streams are typified by the *Simple API for XML* interface (SAX) that grew out of the xml-dev mailing list discussions. To use the SAX interface, you register callbacks for events of interest and then let the parser proceed through the document. In contrast, the Document Object Model (or DOM, currently a World Wide Web Consortium recommendation [www.w3.org]) builds an in-memory tree of objects to represent all the features of an XML document. Both can be used for most tasks, but there are certain niche applications for which one or the other is better suited.

Stream interfaces have certain inherent performance advantages: memory consumption for the parser itself is roughly constant since only the current event, the callback routines and whatever data structures they construct need be kept in memory, and document processing doesn't have to wait for the entire document to be parsed. With very large documents or very tight memory and response time constraints, stream interfaces often enjoy a critical advantage, whereas for more linear documents or those in which only small subset of the elements are of interest, it is often simplest to use a callback interface to specify the handling of relevant entities and completely ignore the rest.

Object tree interfaces tend to have memory demands that grow with the size of the document and must wait for parsing to complete before any processing can begin, but they really shine for more complex manipulations and highly dynamic requirements. Their DOM-style interfaces allow one to walk the object tree in any manner desired, completely free of the event stream's linear constraints. They generally allow you to manipulate the contents and arrangements of the nodes as needed, and tend to provide a wider variety of methods for each object. When you have a complex document (one with extensive use of ID/IDREF pairs), a requirement to revisit nodes, or perhaps a need to manipulate the structure of the document prior to further processing the object tree is a natural fit.

Several of the Ruby parsers offer a third alternative: *iterators*. Like SAX-style callback interfaces, these parsers function on a stream of events (with the performance advantages that implies), but they take a more natural approach for Ruby by using iterators to walk the event stream. This approach (as implemented by both XMLParser and NQXML) is often the simplest solution for a Ruby program that needs to extract data from XML. An experienced Ruby programmer is likely to be very comfortable working with enumerable collections, and that experience can translate directly to working with the entities present in XML.

A rather unscientific benchmark, executed by running each of the sample scripts several times with the Unix time command on a 500MHz Pentium III, gave the results shown in Table 4.1:

Table 4.1 CPU Times for Sample Scripts

Program / Parser	User CPU
libgdome.rb / libgdome-ruby	65 ms
nqxml_stream.rb / nqxml	220 ms
nqxml_tree.rb / nqxml	240 ms
xmlparser_iterator.rb / XMLParser	85 ms

Developing & Deploying…

When to Use SAX and DOM Together?

SAX obviously can't process information as fast as DOM can when working with large files. On the other hand, using DOM exclusively can really kill your resources, especially if used on a lot of small files. SAX is read-only, while DOM allows changes to the XML file. Since these two different APIs literally complement each other there is no reason why you can't use them both for large projects.

Here are some situations that would require a combination of SAX and DOM:

- The application will experience large changes between small XML files and large XML files.

- The application has a system in which small, inconsequential or referential data is stored in small XML files.

- The application will require extensive traversing of a centralized XML file.

A good example would be a huge XML file that needed to be updated and have a report generated for each section that changed. You could use DOM to build the tree and move freely as you find the areas that need change, then generate smaller XML files containing the items that were changed. SAX could then come in, look through the smaller files, and generate a customized report for each change.

Parsing and Creating XML in Ruby

Ruby's extensibility has always been one of its strong points; its ease of use can easily rival C/C++'s header file system, and with the added Ruby perks it is definitely a simple process to enhance Ruby itself for whatever is needed. Several users have already created parsers for Ruby that work either directly with XML or with one of XML's APIs. In this section we'll take a look at some of the more popular parsers available and how they work.

The best way possible to show the differences between the parsers is to provide a single set of XML that each parser needs to work with and display the output for which we are looking. The application with which each parser will be working will provide the following tasks in XML:

1. Parse an XML file.

2. Properly identify the needed tags.

3. Return information as required.

The application itself is a semi-functional port-scanning tool that will operate based on a central list of servers. When fed an XML file with a list of settings and ports for which to scan on each server, it will check these ports and return their status.

Figure 4.5 (servers.xml) is a very lengthy XML file that is our standard server input file (this can be found at www.syngress.com/solutions in the *shared* directory). The server's file has the following information stored within it:

- <servers> root tag;

- <hosts> complex type, with the host's *name* and *primary ip* address as attributes;

- <owner> for owner information;

- <department> for department information;

- <service> complex type with the attributes *type* for usage (domain, dsn, email, etc.), *role*, *name*, *version*, and *source*;

- <port> with *number* and *protocol* attributes.

Figure 4.5 Sample Server's Input File: servers.xml

```xml
<?xml version="1.0" encoding="UTF-8" standalone="yes"?>
<servers>
  <host name="alecto" primary_ip="10.0.11.2">
    <owner>John Q. Admin</owner><department>MIS</department>
    <alias>ns-1</alias><alias>www-2</alias><alias>sql-3</alias>
    <service type="Domain" role="primary" name="Bind"
             version="9.1.2" source="www.isc.org">
      <port number="53" protocol="tcp"/>
      <port number="53" protocol="udp"/>
      <port number="1486" protocol="udp"/>
    </service>
    <service type="Web Server" role="cluster-member" name="Apache"
             version="1.3.19" source="httpd.apache.org">
      <port number="80" protocol="tcp"/>
      <port number="443" protocol="tcp"/>
    </service>
    <service type="PostgreSQL" role="backup" name="PostgreSQL"
             version="7.1.3" source="www.postgresql.org">
      <port number="5432" protocol="tcp"/>
    </service>
    <service type="ident" role="support">
      <port number="113" protocol="tcp"/>
      <port number="113" protocol="udp"/>
    </service>
    <service type="ssh" role="support" name="OpenSSH"
             version="2.9p1" source="www.openssh.com">
      <port number="22" protocol="tcp"/>
    </service>
  </host>
  <host name="megaera" primary_ip="10.0.11.3">
    <owner>John Q. Admin</owner><department>MIS</department>
```

Continued

Figure 4.5 Continued

```
    <alias>sql-1</alias><alias>ns-2</alias><alias>www-3</alias>
    <service type="Domain" role="secondary" name="Bind"
            version="9.1.2" source="www.isc.org">
      <port number="53" protocol="tcp"/>
      <port number="53" protocol="udp"/>
      <port number="1486" protocol="udp"/>
    </service>
    <service type="Web Server" role="cluster-member" name="Apache"
            version="1.3.19" source="httpd.apache.org">
      <port number="80" protocol="tcp"/>
      <port number="443" protocol="tcp"/>
    </service>
    <service type="PostgreSQL" role="primary" name="PostgreSQL"
            version="7.1.3" source="www.postgresql.org">
      <port number="5432" protocol="tcp"/>
    </service>
    <service type="ident" role="support">
      <port number="113" protocol="tcp"/>
      <port number="113" protocol="udp"/>
    </service>
    <service type="ssh" role="support" name="OpenSSH"
            version="2.9p1" source="www.openssh.com">
      <port number="22" protocol="tcp"/>
    </service>
  </host>
  <host name="tisiphone" primary_ip="10.0.11.4">
    <owner>John Q. Admin</owner><department>MIS</department>
    <alias>www-1</alias><alias>sql-2</alias><alias>ns-3</alias>
    <service type="Domain" role="secondary" name="Bind"
            version="9.1.1" source="www.isc.org">
      <port number="53" protocol="tcp"/>
```

Continued

Figure 4.5 Continued

```
      <port number="53" protocol="udp"/>
      <port number="1486" protocol="udp"/>
    </service>
    <service type="Web Server" role="cluster-member" name="Apache"
             version="1.3.19" source="httpd.apache.org">
      <port number="80" protocol="tcp"/>
      <port number="443" protocol="tcp"/>
    </service>
    <service type="PostgreSQL" role="backup" name="PostgreSQL"
             version="7.1.3" source="www.postgresql.org">
      <port number="5432" protocol="tcp"/>
    </service>
    <service type="ident" role="support">
      <port number="113" protocol="tcp"/>
      <port number="113" protocol="udp"/>
    </service>
    <service type="ssh" role="support" name="OpenSSH"
             version="2.9p1" source="www.openssh.com">
      <port number="22" protocol="tcp"/>
    </service>
  </host>
</servers>
```

Figure 4.6 (scans.xml) is our sample XML file that tells the application where and which ports to check, based on the general information provided in the servers.xml file (it can be found at www.syngress.com/solutions). It has the following structure:

1. <scans> root tag

    a. <host> complex type with *ip, scan_time, scanner_name, scanner_version, scanner_arch* attributes

        i. <port> element with *number, protocol,* and *service* attributes

Figure 4.6 Sample Scans Input File: scans.xml

```xml
<?xml version="1.0" encoding="utf-8" standalone="yes" ?>
<scans>
  <host ip="10.0.11.2" scan_time="2001-10-31 20:14:33"
        scanner_name="nmap" scanner_version="2.53"
        scanner_arch="i686-linux">
    <port number="22"   protocol="tcp" service="ssh"/>
    <port number="53"   protocol="tcp" service="domain"/>
    <port number="53"   protocol="udp" service="domain"/>
    <port number="80"   protocol="tcp" service="http"/>
    <port number="443"  protocol="tcp" service="https"/>
    <port number="1486" protocol="udp" service="nms_topo_serv"/>
    <port number="5432" protocol="tcp" service="postgres"/>
    <port number="6000" protocol="tcp" service="X11"/>
  </host>
  <host ip="10.0.11.3" scan_time="2001-10-31 20:15:13"
        scanner_name="nmap" scanner_version="2.53"
        scanner_arch="i686-linux">
    <port number="22"   protocol="tcp" service="ssh"/>
    <port number="53"   protocol="udp" service="domain"/>
    <port number="80"   protocol="tcp" service="http"/>
    <port number="113"  protocol="tcp" service="auth"/>
    <port number="113"  protocol="udp" service="auth"/>
    <port number="443"  protocol="tcp" service="https"/>
    <port number="1486" protocol="udp" service="nms_topo_serv"/>
    <port number="5432" protocol="tcp" service="postgres"/>
  </host>
</scans>
```

Figure 4.7 displays a sample output file based on the information provided in the previous samples (this can be found at www.syngress.com/solutions).

Figure 4.7 Sample Output File: output.xml

```xml
<?xml version="1.0"?>
<scan_report report_time="Tue Oct 09 00:35:54 MDT 2001">
  <host ip="10.0.11.2" name="alecto" owner="John Q. Admin"
    department="MIS">
    <port port_number="22" protocol="tcp" status="Normal">
      <comment>Service status normal for ssh on 22/tcp.</comment>
    </port>
    <port port_number="53" protocol="tcp" status="Normal">
      <comment>Service status normal for Domain on 53/tcp.</comment>
    </port>
    <port port_number="53" protocol="udp" status="Normal">
      <comment>Service status normal for Domain on 53/udp.</comment>
    </port>
    <port port_number="80" protocol="tcp" status="Normal">
      <comment>Service status normal for Web Server on 80/tcp.</comment>
    </port>
    <port port_number="443" protocol="tcp" status="Normal">
      <comment>Service status normal for Web Server on
443/tcp.</comment>
    </port>
    <port port_number="1486" protocol="udp" status="Normal">
      <comment>Service status normal for Domain on 1486/udp.</comment>
    </port>
    <port port_number="5432" protocol="tcp" status="Normal">
      <comment>Service status normal for PostgreSQL on
5432/tcp.</comment>
    </port>
    <port port_number="6000" protocol="tcp" status="Unexpected Open
Port">
      <comment>An undocumented open port was found at 6000/tcp which may
be the X11 service.</comment>
    </port>
```

Continued

Figure 4.7 Continued

```
   <port port_number="113" protocol="tcp" status="Not Found">
     <comment>The ident service at 113/tcp was not detected. Please
   check service status.</comment>
   </port>
   <port port_number="113" protocol="udp" status="Not Found">
     <comment>The ident service at 113/udp was not detected. Please
   check service status.</comment>
   </port>
</host>
<host ip="10.0.11.3" name="megaera" owner="John Q. Admin"
   department="MIS">
   <port port_number="22" protocol="tcp" status="Normal">
     <comment>Service status normal for ssh on 22/tcp.</comment>
   </port>
   <port port_number="53" protocol="udp" status="Normal">
     <comment>Service status normal for Domain on 53/udp.</comment>
   </port>
   <port port_number="80" protocol="tcp" status="Normal">
     <comment>Service status normal for Web Server on 80/tcp.</comment>
   </port>
   <port port_number="113" protocol="tcp" status="Normal">
     <comment>Service status normal for ident on 113/tcp.</comment>
   </port>
   <port port_number="113" protocol="udp" status="Normal">
     <comment>Service status normal for ident on 113/udp.</comment>
   </port>
   <port port_number="443" protocol="tcp" status="Normal">
     <comment>Service status normal for Web Server on
   443/tcp.</comment>
   </port>
   <port port_number="1486" protocol="udp" status="Normal">
     <comment>Service status normal for Domain on 1486/udp.</comment>
   </port>
```

Continued

Figure 4.7 Continued

```
    <port port_number="5432" protocol="tcp" status="Normal">
      <comment>Service status normal for PostgreSQL on
    5432/tcp.</comment>
    </port>
    <port port_number="53" protocol="tcp" status="Not Found">
      <comment>The Domain service at 53/tcp was not detected. Please
    check service status.</comment>
    </port>
  </host>
  <unscanned_host>tisiphone</unscanned_host>
  <missing_ports>3</missing_ports>
  <extra_ports>1</extra_ports>
  <good_ports>15</good_ports>
</scan_report>
```

Shared Code for Examples

To facilitate things a bit, we are going to create two Ruby files; one for defining the *Host* and *Port* classes, named "hosts.rb" and another file for defining the *Report* class, which generates our output. We'll name this one "report.rb". We are going to be using the XML parser *Not Quite XML* (NQXML) for our two shared files; however, since we have not looked at NQXML yet, we'll concentrate on the design portion of hosts.rb and reports.rb. This rule applies to XMLParser, NQXML, and libgdome-ruby. Ruby Electric XML (REXML) will have its own file set.

> **NOTE**
>
> In order to save time, we are using NQXML to handle the light reading and writing stuff. While this does not mean that NQXML is the best parser out there, it is one of the faster ones to work with and its Ruby architecture allows us to override whatever methods we need to provide the required functionality. It also makes the functionality required for the hosts.rb and report.rb files easier to use than if we'd used XMLParser and libgdome-ruby.

Defining and Implementing Classes Host and Port

In Figure 4.8 we find the *Host* class as defined in hosts.rb. *Host* takes the following attributes: *ports*, *ip*, *name*, *owner*, *department*, *aliases*, and *scanned*. For all intents and purposes it follows the general layout of servers.xml. The *ports* attribute is a hash that stores port numbers and port protocols (80/HTTP, for example); *aliases* contains an array of possible aliases used by the server.

Figure 4.8 Host Class Definition

```
class Host
   attr_accessor :ports, :ip, :name, :owner, :department, :aliases,
                    :scanned
   def initialize(ip, name="unknown")
     @ports = Hash.new
     @ip = ip
     @name = name
     @owner = ""
     @department = ""
     @aliases = Array.new
     @scanned = false
   end
end
```

In Figure 4.9 we find the *Port* class as defined in hosts.rb.

Figure 4.9 Port Class Definition

```
class Port
   attr_accessor :port_number, :protocol, :service_data, :status
   def initialize(port_number, protocol, service_data=Hash.new)
     @port_number = port_number
     @protocol = protocol
     @service_data = service_data
     @status = "Not Found"
   end
end
```

Defining and Implementing the Report Class

Figure 4.10 contains our *initialize* method for the *Report* class. We are going to be using *Report* not only to write our output, but also to keep track internally of the number of extra ports (that is, ports not listed in the server.xml file), the number of missing ports, and the number of good ports in order to provide a summary at the end of the output.xml file from Figure 4.9. The writer is defined and started, and a root tag of <scan_report> is listed in the new output.xml file as well as the date and time, The *Report* class will also check to see which scans did not go through and which scans failed, and include them in the report it generates.

Figure 4.10 Report Class, Initialize Method

```
def initialize
  @extra_ports = 0
  @missing_ports = 0
  @good_ports = 0

  @writer = NQXML::Writer.new($stdout, true)
  @writer.processingInstruction('xml', 'version="1.0"')

  @writer.startElement('scan_report')

  @writer.attribute('report_time', Time.new)
end
```

Figure 4.11 shows an override of a pre-existing method inside the NQXML writer that is modified to add a new line character after the *prettify* method. The *nopretty* method is used to tell *Report* not to use the *pretty* override. Figure 4.12 displays the *start_host* and *end_host* methods, which generates the <host> tag. Figure 4.13 displays the *add_port*, *unscanned_host*, and *finish* methods.

Figure 4.11 Report Class, def pretty and def nopretty

```ruby
# the default printing behavior doesn't interact well with our
# report structure, so we'll handle it manually
def pretty
    @writer.prettify = true
    @writer.write("\n")
end


def nopretty
  @writer.prettify = false
end
```

Figure 4.12 Report class, def start_host and def end_host

```ruby
def start_host(ip, name, owner, department)
  # a host element has ip, name, owner and department attributes
  @writer.startElement('host')
  @writer.attribute('ip', ip)
  @writer.attribute('name', name)
  # for the owner attribute we'll use startAttribute, write and
  # endAttribute since write will handle escaping for us
  @writer.startAttribute('owner')
  @writer.write(owner)
  @writer.endAttribute
  # and we'll do the same for department
  @writer.startAttribute('department')
  @writer.write(department)
  @writer.endAttribute
end

def end_host
      @writer.endElement('host')
end
```

Figure 4.13 Report class, def add_port, def unscanned_port, and def_finish

```ruby
def add_port(port_number, protocol, status,
               reported_service, expected_service)
  @writer.startElement('port')
  @writer.attribute('port_number', port_number)
  @writer.attribute('protocol', protocol)
  @writer.attribute('status', status)
  # we need to set the appropriate comment and update our statistics
  comment = ""
  case status
  when /Not Found/i
    @missing_ports += 1
    comment = "The #{expected_service} service at #{port_number}/" +
      "#{protocol} was not detected. Please check service status."
  when /Unexpected Open Port/i
    @extra_ports += 1
    if (reported_service == "unknown") then
      comment = "An undocumented open port was found at " +
        "#{port_number}/#{protocol}."
    else
      comment = "An undocumented open port was found at " +
        "#{port_number}/#{protocol} which may be the " +
        "#{reported_service} service."
    end
  when /Normal/i
    @good_ports += 1
    comment = "Service status normal for #{expected_service} on " +
      "#{port_number}/#{protocol}."
  end
  @writer.startElement('comment')
  nopretty
  @writer.write(comment)
  @writer.endElement('comment')
  pretty
```

Continued

Figure 4.13 Continued

```ruby
      @writer.endElement('port')
  end

  def unscanned_host(host)
    # an unscanned host is simple element with only text content
    @writer.startElement('unscanned_host')
    nopretty
    @writer.write(host.name)
    @writer.endElement('unscanned_host')
    pretty
  end

  def finish
    # as are the port counts
    @writer.startElement('missing_ports')
    nopretty
    @writer.write(@missing_ports.to_s)
    @writer.endElement('missing_ports')
    pretty
    @writer.startElement('extra_ports')
    nopretty
    @writer.write(@extra_ports.to_s)
    @writer.endElement('extra_ports')
    pretty
    @writer.startElement('good_ports')
    nopretty
    @writer.write(@good_ports.to_s)
    @writer.endElement('good_ports')
    pretty
    # ending the root element completes the output
    @writer.endElement('scan_report')
  end
end
```

Using XMLParser

XMLParser, developed by Yoshida Masato, is a Ruby wrapper around everyone's favorite XML Parser, *expat*. Expat, developed by James Clark, uses a SAX-like API to traverse through XML and is relied upon by users worldwide. XMLParser has some major drawbacks however, though many of them are inherited from expat and are no fault of Yoshida Masato's:

- Can generate segfault errors easily, depending on installation (see the Note sidebar in this section);

- No support for Namespaces.

However, XMLParser has the following excellent advantages:

- Full XML conformance;

- Very stable due to its existence;

- Very fast.

NOTE

Frequently generating segfault errors seems like a serious claim to make about a program that's been around (and worked for as long as) expat. However, it's a serious issue that has been documented and is, ironically, due to the open source nature of the application. Several developers have integrated expat as a statically-compiled application. When called by anything that dynamically loads expat, the result will be a segfault because expat is already there. For example, Apache and PHP have their own static expat, so if you add a module (like XMLParser) that loads expat dynamically, it will result in a segfault.

The true beauty of expat lies in its speed when dealing with XML files. Its flexible C code makes it a powerful tool for working with XML, and the "pure" version of expat works great without requiring extensive mods or files.

To successfully install and run XMLParser, you first need the expat parser. You may already have expat from an earlier Apache or PHP installation, so take a look around before downloading and installing it. Once you have installed expat, you install XMLParser by compiling it and using the following lines to point to the expat header file or library file:

```
—with-xmlparse-lib=/path/to/expat/xmlparse

—with-xmlparse-include=/path/to/expat/xmlparse
```

Developing & Deploying…

libgdome-ruby

Libgdome-ruby is a wrapper for an existing Unix XML parser called libgdom, which relies on yet another existing XML parser called libxml. Libgdome-ruby is maintained by Tobias Peters and is currently in Beta. This beta release is unstable and suffers from a memory leak as a result of a libgdom fault. Unlike XMLParser, libgdome-ruby uses DOM to traverse through an XML file.

Since libgdome-ruby has not been in active development for the last seven months, we won't be covering it in detail in this book. However, if you want to see the libgdome-ruby code for this particular application, feel free to view the source code on the CD that accompanies this book, in Chapter 4's *libgdome-ruby* directory. You'll have to procure your own copy of libgdome-ruby but it can work with Windows (albeit with difficulty) provided you can install libgdom. The file, and instructions on installing it, are available at http://libgdome-ruby.berlios.de/.

XMLParser is currently only available to work with Unix but can be compiled for Windows through Cygwin as well.

Figure 4.14 has our XMLParser example.

Figure 4.14 Sample Application Using XMLParser's Iterator Interface

```
#! /usr/bin/ruby -w


require 'hosts'
require 'ports'
require 'report'
require 'xmlparser'
```

Continued

Figure 4.14 Continued

```ruby
def server_host_start(ip, name, hosts)
  host = Host.new(ip, name)
  hosts[ip] = host
  return host
end

begin
  parser = XMLParser.new

  current_host = nil
  current_service = nil
  hosts = Hash.new

  # since there is no "parent" object to provide context in a stream
  # we'll have to track it with flags to handle text elements
  in_owner = false
  in_dept  = false
  in_alias = false

  # the each method iterates over all entities in the file
  servers = File.open('servers.xml').readlines.join
  parser.parse(servers) { |event, name, data|
    # events are returned as the values of constants in the XMLParser
    # class so our case statement switches on constants
    case event
    when XMLParser::START_ELEM
      case name
      when "host"
        # we need to create and record in the hosts Hash an object for
        # the host entity we've entered
        current_host = Host.new(data["primary_ip"],
                                data["name"])
```

Continued

Figure 4.14 Continued

```ruby
      hosts[ data["primary_ip"] ] = current_host
   when "owner" then in_owner = true
   when "department" then in_dept = true
   when "alias" then in_alias = true
   when "service"
      current_service = data.dup
   when "port"
      port_number = data["number"]
      protocol = data["protocol"]
      port_pair = port_number + "/" + protocol
      current_host.ports[ port_pair] =
         (Port.new( port_number, protocol, current_service))
   end
when XMLParser::END_ELEM
   case name
   when "host"
      current_host = nil
   when "owner" then in_owner = false
   when "department" then in_dept = false
   when "alias" then in_alias = false
   when "service"
      current_service = nil
   when "port" # no action necessary
   end
when XMLParser::CDATA
   if (data !~ /\S/m or data =~ /^[\s\n]+$/)
      next
   else
      # set parts of the host record based on our context flags
      if in_owner then current_host.owner = data end
      if in_dept then current_host.department = data end
      if in_alias then current_host.aliases.push(data) end
```

Continued

Figure 4.14 Continued

```
      end
   else
     next
   end
}
# parsers can't be reused, so we create a new one
parser = nil
parser = XMLParser.new

report = Report.new
scans = File.open('scans.xml').readlines.join
parser.parse(scans) { |event, name, data|
   case event
   when XMLParser::START_ELEM
     case name
     when "host"
       # get the correct host record and start a report section for
       # it in the hosts hash
       current_host = hosts[ data["ip"] ]
       current_host.scanned = true
       report.start_host(current_host.ip, current_host.name,
                           current_host.owner,
                           current_host.department)
     when "port"
       # update port status in the host record
       port_number = data["number"]
       protocol = data["protocol"]
       port_pair = port_number + "/" + protocol
       status = ""

       # open ports need to be added to to the report with a status
       # based on the presence or lack of a port record
```

Continued

Figure 4.14 Continued

```
      if current_host.ports.has_key?( port_pair )
        current_host.ports[port_pair].status = "Normal"
        service =
          current_host.ports[port_pair].service_data["type"]
        report.add_port(port_number, protocol, "Normal",
                        nil, service)
      else
        report.add_port(port_number, protocol,
                        "Unexpected Open Port",
                        data["service"], nil)
      end
    end
  when XMLParser::END_ELEM
    case name
    when "host"
      # add reports for ports not found in the scan
      current_host.ports.each { |key, port|
        if (port.status == "Not Found") then
          report.add_port(port.port_number, port.protocol,
                          "Not Found", nil,
                          port.service_data["type"])
        end
      }
      report.end_host
      current_host = nil
    when "port" # no action necessary
    end
  when XMLParser::CDATA
    if (data !~ /\S/m or data =~ /^[\s\n]+$/)
      next
    else
      if in_owner then current_host.owner = data end
```

Continued

Figure 4.14 Continued

```
        if in_dept then current_host.department = data end
        if in_alias then current_host.aliases.push(data) end
      end
    else
      next
    end
  }


  # print a sorted report of hosts not scanned
  hosts.values.sort { |hosta, hostb|
    hosta.name <=> hostb.name
  }.
    each { |host|
    if (! host.scanned ) then report.unscanned_host(host) end
  }


  report.finish

rescue XMLParserError => exception
  print "Parser exception at line #{parser.line()}: #{$!}\n"
end
```

Using NQXML

NQXML is the brainchild of Jim Menard. It's exactly what its name means ("Not Quite XML"); not all of XML's functions are available for use. Here's a list of what is missing (this is also available from the LIMITATIONS text in the package):

- The only encoding supported in NQXML is ASCII-8; there is no support for UTF-8 or UTF-16. This essentially means that you can forget about using NQXML for any projects or applications that require international characters.

- It checks for well-formed documents only.

- There is no DTD support.

- There are no external references (which basically shoots down Schema as well).

- ELEMENT, ATTLIST, and NOTATION tags return their attributes as string only.

However, even with the somewhat basic items it is missing, NQXML has some advantages:

- It is built with Ruby.

- It does not require external applications.

- It is not a wrapper for any existing parser.

- Its functionality is easy to remember and easy to find.

So, in essence, items that are part of standard XML, such as Unicode Transformation Format (UTF) and DTD/external link support, are missing; but we are able to use NQXML for basic XML parsing and maybe a few more advanced strategies with some tinkering. Also, since NQXML is written in Ruby, any Ruby programmer can open up any of the files and edit them as they see fit. Figure 4.15 and Figure 4.16 in the next section show two different ways of approaching our application.

Installing NQXML

Installing NQXML on Unix is quite simple since it comes with a handy install.rb file. Just untar/ungzip the NQXML archive to the directory of your choice and run *install.rb*.

On Windows, open the DOS shell and use *ruby install.rb* from within the NQXML application folder. This a little bit trickier if the installer doesn't work, but it can still be done: download the NQXML.tar file and use either WinRAR or WinZIP (or the free PowerArchiver) to extract the files. Once the files are extracted, copy the folder NQXML to the *C:\ruby\lib\ruby\1.6* directory (assuming you first installed it in the default directory). This will work for both Windows 9x and Windows 2000. Let's take a look at Figure 4.15 and Figure 4.16.

Figure 4.15 Sample Application Using NQXML's Iterator Interface

```
#! /usr/bin/ruby -w

require 'hosts'
require 'ports'
require 'report'
require 'nqxml/streamingparser'

begin
  servers_parser =
NQXML::StreamingParser.new(File.open('servers.xml'))

  current_host = nil
  current_service = nil
  hosts = Hash.new

  # since there is no "parent" object to provide context in a stream
  # we'll have to track it with flags to handle text elements
  in_owner = false
  in_dept  = false
  in_alias = false

  # the each method iterates over all entities in the file
  servers_parser.each { |entity|
    # skip the XML Declaration
    if (entity.is_a?(NQXML::XMLDecl) or
        # and all whitespace or newline only text entities
        (entity.is_a?(NQXML::Text) and
          ((entity.text !~ /\S/m) or (entity.text == "\n"))) or
        # and the servers tags
        (entity.is_a?(NQXML::Tag) and entity.name == "servers")
        ) then
      next
    end
```

Continued

Figure 4.15 Continued

```
if entity.is_a?(NQXML::Tag) then
  case entity.name
  when "host"
    # for host entries we have to set up the current_host variable
    # we're using for context
    if entity.isTagStart then
      current_host = Host.new(entity.attrs["primary_ip"],
                              entity.attrs["name"])
      hosts[ entity.attrs["primary_ip"] ] = current_host


    # or tear it down on exit from the element
    elsif entity.isTagEnd
      current_host = nil
    end
  when "owner" then in_owner = entity.isTagStart
  when "department" then in_dept = entity.isTagStart
  when "alias" then in_alias = entity.isTagStart
  when "service"
    if entity.isTagStart then
      current_service = entity.attrs.dup
    else
      current_service = nil
    end
  when "port"
    if entity.isTagStart then
      port_number = entity.attrs["number"]
      protocol = entity.attrs["protocol"]
      port_pair = port_number + "/" + protocol
      current_host.ports[ port_pair] =
        (Port.new( port_number, protocol, current_service))
    end
  else
    raise "Unhandled tag: #{entity.name}\n"
  end
```

Continued

Figure 4.15 Continued

```ruby
    elsif entity.is_a?(NQXML::Text) then
      # text values are set based on which kind of element we're in
      if in_owner then current_host.owner = entity.text end
      if in_dept then current_host.department = entity.text end
      if in_alias then current_host.aliases.push(entity.text) end
    else
      raise "Unhandled entity type: #{entity.type}\n"
    end
}
servers_parser = nil


scans_parser = NQXML::StreamingParser.new(File.open('scans.xml'))
report = Report.new


scans_parser.each { |entity|
  # skip the XML Declaration
  if (entity.is_a?(NQXML::XMLDecl) or
      # and all whitespace or newline only text entities
      (entity.is_a?(NQXML::Text) and
        ((entity.text !~ /\S/m) or (entity.text == "\n"))) or
      # and the scans tags
      (entity.is_a?(NQXML::Tag) and entity.name == "scans")
    ) then
    next
  end


  if entity.is_a?(NQXML::Tag) then
    case entity.name
    when "host"
      if entity.isTagStart then
        # get the correct host record and start a report section for
        # it
        current_host = hosts[ entity.attrs["ip"] ]
        current_host.scanned = true
```

Continued

Figure 4.15 Continued

```
                report.start_host(current_host.ip, current_host.name,
                              current_host.owner,
                              current_host.department)
        elsif entity.isTagEnd then
          # add reports for ports not found in the scan
          current_host.ports.each { |key, port|
            if (port.status == "Not Found") then
              report.add_port(port.port_number, port.protocol,
                            "Not Found", nil,
                            port.service_data["type"])

            end

          }
          report.end_host
          current_host = nil
        end
      when "port"
        if entity.isTagStart then
          # update port status in the host record
          port_number = entity.attrs["number"]
          protocol = entity.attrs["protocol"]
          port_pair = port_number + "/" + protocol
          status = ""

          # open ports need to be added to to the report with a status
          # based on the presence or lack of a port record
          if current_host.ports.has_key?( port_pair )
            current_host.ports[port_pair].status = "Normal"
            service =
              current_host.ports[port_pair].service_data["type"]
            report.add_port(port_number, protocol, "Normal",
                          nil, service)
          else
            report.add_port(port_number, protocol,
                          "Unexpected Open Port",
```

Continued

Figure 4.15 Continued

```
                                    entity.attrs["service"], nil)
          end
        end
      end
    end


  }
  scans_parser = nil


  # print a sorted report of hosts not scanned
  hosts.values.sort { |hosta, hostb|
    hosta.name <=> hostb.name
  }.
    each { |host|
    if (! host.scanned ) then report.unscanned_host(host) end
  }


  report.finish


rescue NQXML::ParserError => exception
  print "Parser exception at line #{exception.line()}: #{$!}\n"
end
```

Figure 4.16 Sample Application Using NQXML's Tree Interface

```
#! /usr/bin/ruby -w


require 'hosts'
require 'report'
require 'nqxml/treeparser'


def host_child(child, host)
  if (child.entity.is_a?(NQXML::Tag)) then
```

Continued

Figure 4.16 Continued

```ruby
    # only the text content is relevant for the first three types
    case child.entity.name
    when "owner" then
      # take the text value of the first (only) child's entity
      host.owner = child.firstChild.entity.text
    when "department" then
      host.department = child.firstChild.entity.text
    when "alias" then
      host.aliases.push( child.firstChild.entity.text )
    when "service" then
      # services are more complex since the service data needs to be
      # applied to each port in turn
      service_data = Hash.new
      # the service data fields are accessible from the attributes
      # hash of the child's entity object
      service_data["type"] = child.entity.attrs["type"]
      service_data["role"] = child.entity.attrs["role"]
      # we iterate over the ports for each service and create a Port
      # object to place in the host's ports list
      child.children.each { |service_node|
        if (service_node.entity.is_a?(NQXML::Tag)) then
          port_number = service_node.entity.attrs["number"]
          protocol = service_node.entity.attrs["protocol"]
          # create a key in /etc/services style port/protocol format
          port_pair = port_number + "/" + protocol
          host.ports[ port_pair] =
            (Port.new( port_number, protocol, service_data))
        end
      }
    end
  end
end

def scan_child(port_node, host, report)
```

Continued

Figure 4.16 Continued

```
    port_number = port_node.entity.attrs["number"]
    protocol = port_node.entity.attrs["protocol"]
    port_pair = port_number + "/" + protocol

    status = ""
    if host.ports.has_key?( port_pair )
      host.ports[port_pair].status = "Normal"
      report.add_port(port_number, protocol, "Normal", nil,
                       host.ports[port_pair].service_data["type"])
    else
      report.add_port(port_number, protocol, "Unexpected Open Port",
                       port_node.entity.attrs["service"], nil)
    end
  end
end

begin
  # first we build an array of Host objects and their expected
  # services from the servers.xml file

  # skip directly to the root node
  server_root = NQXML::TreeParser.new(File.open("servers.xml")).
    document.rootNode
  hosts = Hash.new()
  server_root.children.each { |host_node|
    # we ignore all none tag nodes at this level
    if (host_node.entity.is_a?(NQXML::Tag)) then
      # index the hosts by ip (retrieved from the attrs hash)
      ip = host_node.entity.attrs["primary_ip"]
      name = host_node.entity.attrs["name"]
      host = Host.new(ip, name)
      hosts[ip] = host

      host_node.children.each { |child_node|
        if (child_node.entity.is_a?(NQXML::Tag)) then
          host_child(child_node, host)
```

Continued

Figure 4.16 Continued

```
        end
    }


  end
}
server_root = nil


# now we compare the results from our scanner (scans.xml) to our
# expected hosts and services
scan_root = NQXML::TreeParser.new(File.open("scans.xml")).
  document.rootNode
report = Report.new
scan_root.children.each { |host_node|
  # we ignore all none tag nodes at this level
  if (host_node.entity.is_a?(NQXML::Tag)) then
    # index the hosts by ip (retrieved from the attrs hash)
    host = hosts[ host_node.entity.attrs["ip"] ]
    host.scanned = true
    report.start_host(host.ip, host.name,
                        host.owner, host.department)
    # now we build the report from the ports found open by the scan
    host_node.children.each { |port_node|
      if (port_node.entity.is_a?(NQXML::Tag)) then
        scan_child(port_node, host, report)
      end
    }
  host.ports.each { |key, port|
      if (port.status == "Not Found") then
        report.add_port(port.port_number, port.protocol,
                        "Not Found", nil,
                        port.service_data["type"])
      end
    }
    report.end_host
```

Continued

Figure 4.16 Continued

```
    end
  }


  # print a sorted report of hosts not scanned
  hosts.values.sort { |hosta, hostb|
    hosta.name <=> hostb.name
  }.
    each { |host|
    if (! host.scanned ) then report.unscanned_host(host) end
  }


  report.finish
rescue NQXML::ParserError => exception
  print "Parser exception at line #{exception.line()}: #{$!}\n"
end
```

Developing & Deploying…

Xmlscan

The xmlscan library by Ueno Katsuhiro is another pure-Ruby XML parser that offers limited DTD support and one of the few XPath implementations available for Ruby, among other features. It's been used as the basis for MoonWolf's MWDOM (a DOM implementation) and Michael Neumann's XSLT module for Ruby. As of this writing, xmlscan is undergoing a complete rewrite and its API is in a state of flux. In the previous releases, the author paid special attention to standards conformance and performance issues, making xmlscan a strong contender in the native parser niche. The older version is available from the author's home page at www.blue.sky.or.jp/atelier/ruby/xmlscan-0.0.10.tar.gz, and the next release will almost certainly be announced on the ruby-talk mailing list and the Ruby Application Archive. Ruby-talk has also carried occasional mentions of the development version (available as of October 2001 from www.blue.sky.or.jp/.tmp/xmlscan-snapshot.tar.gz) so a search of the archives is probably your best bet for current information.

Using REXML

REXML can be chalked up as a frustrated developer's dream; Sean Russell created REXML after fidgeting with two Ruby XML parsers and finding both to be insufficient. Instead of sitting back and waiting for someone to make a good one, Sean took it upon himself to make a XML Parser using the foundations of Ruby. REXML has the following advantages:

1. It is written 100 percent in Ruby.

2. It can be used for both SAX and DOM parsing.

3. It is small—approximately 1845 lines of code.

4. Methods and classes are in easy-to-understand and remember English.

All of the hard-core parsing in REXML is done using Ruby's powerful built-in regular expression support and are likewise coded in native code. If you have used Electric XML you may find some similarities in the simplicity of this parser; in fact Sean Russell was inspired by the Electric XML code, and was even given permission by TheMind to hack it. You can find Electric XML at www.themindelectric.com/products/xml/xml.html. Let's examine our sample XML in Figure 4.17, and then we will look at our small REXML application, written specifically in Windows (these can be found at www.syngress.com/ solutions in the *rexml* directory). Our output will just display the names of the movies we have in our list.

Figure 4.17 movies.xml

```
<collection>
<movie title="Left Behind">
  <type>Reality, Religious</type>
  <format>DVD</format>
  <year>2000</year>
  <rating>PG</rating>
  <stars>10</stars>
  <description>Talk about a straight shot</description>
  </movie>
<movie title="Transformers">
  <type>Anime, Science Fiction</type>
  <format>DVD</format>
```

Continued

Figure 4.17 Continued

```
  <year>1999</year>
  <rating>R</rating>
  <stars>8</stars>
  <description>Until all are one!</description>
  </movie>
<movie title="Trigun">
  <type>Anime, Action</type>
  <format>DVD</format>
  <episodes>4</episodes>
  <rating>PG</rating>
  <stars>10</stars>
  <description>Vash the Stampede!</description>
  </movie>
<movie title="Ishtar">
  <type>Comedy</type>
  <format>VHS</format>
  <rating>PG</rating>
  <stars>2</stars>
  <description>Viewable boredom</description>
  </movie>
</collection>
```

Now let's take a look at our quick little app. All we need to do is generate a list of our movie titles so we can keep track of what we have:

```
require "rexml/document"
include REXML

xmfile = File.new( "movies.xml" )

xmdoc = Document.new xmfile

xmdoc.elements.each("collection/movie") {|element|
puts element.attributes["title"] }
```

Simple, no? REXML has been gifted with perhaps the simplest API available. As you may remember from the NQXML and XMLParser examples, doing something as simple as cycling though a list of elements and plucking out the content of just one element was tricky and tedious. REXML made it as easy as writing one line. We can enhance the output on this one a little bit by generating the movie list with ratings and comments associated with it:

```
require "rexml/document"
include REXML


xmfile = File.new( "movies.xml" )


xmdoc = Document.new xmfile


puts "Current movie list:"
xmdoc.elements.each("collection/movie") {|element|
    puts element.attributes["title"] }


puts "\n"


puts "with ratings of:"
xmdoc.elements.each("collection/movie/rating") { |element|
    puts element.text }


puts "\n"


puts "and the following descriptions:"
xmdoc.elements.each("collection/movie/description") { |element|
    puts element.txt }
```

Using XSLT in Ruby

XSLT is not completely out of the Ruby picture; there are two XSLT parsers available that Ruby can use, namely Ruby-Sablotron and XSLT4R.

Ruby-Sablotron

Technically, this module is named "Sablotron module for Ruby" and is written primarily for Linux. It is written and maintained by Masayoshi Takahashi and requires the following libraries in order to properly work with Sablotron:

- Sablot
- Iconv (when used)
- Expat

The author does not provide any English documentation (at the time of this writing, accessing the "pseudo-english" section of the website results in a 404 error) and has a lot of heavy dependencies on the libraries it uses. You can find this module at www.rubycolor.org/sablot.

XSLT4R

XSLT4R is the brainchild of Michael Neumann (whose name may ring a bell to those readers who checked the name of this book's editor), and can be found at the RAA in the Library section under *XML*. XSLT4R uses a simple command-line interface, though it can alternatively be used within a third-party application to transform an XML document.

XSLT4R needs XMLScan to operate, which is included within the XSLT4R archive and which is also a 100 percent Ruby module. Installation is easy too; just run *ruby install.rb*. If you have any problems with it, just copy the XSLT4R and XMLScan files to the ruby directory (*C:\ruby\lib\ruby\1.x*). As I mentioned, XSLT can run either from the command line or from within an application. From the command line, XSLT4R has the following syntax:

```
ruby xslt.rb stylesheet.xsl document.xml [arguments]
```

If you want to useXSLT4R from within an application, you can include XSLT and input the parameters you need. For example:

```
require "xslt"

stylesheet = File.readlines("stylesheet.xsl").to_s
xml_doc     = File.readlines("document.xml").to_s
arguments  = { 'image_dir' => '/....' }

sheet = XSLT::Stylesheet.new( stylesheet, arguments )

# output to StdOut
sheet.apply( xml_doc )

# output to `str'
str = ""
sheet.output = [ str ]
sheet.apply( xml_doc )
```

Summary

XML can be as extensible as it needs to be; it does not need any particular platform to operate on or any particular application from which to be read and/or processed. This can allow a developer to create files from one application that will be read with another application on a different platform. Also, XML itself is easy to read and follow, provided the author wrote it correctly, so there is usually no need to hunt down arcane names. The fact that XML is basically a text database organized in a hierarchal system allows languages with speedy string methods, such as Ruby, to fully exploit XML.

There are currently two widely-used, Ruby-compatible APIs for the parsing of XML: SAX and DOM. SAX beats DOM in terms of memory requirements and forward-read speed, while DOM allows a developer to jump back and forth in an XML file, at a memory cost. DOM's storing of the XML tree allows for faster traversing when dealing with larger XML files. Since both APIs have fairly open architectures, they can both be used simultaneously without damaging one another.

Ruby can use a number of widely available Open Source parsers; in this chapter we looked at XMLParser, NQXML, and REXML for standard XML. XMLParser and Libgdome-ruby (which has example code in the CD that accompanies this book) have dependencies on the expat XML parser; NQXML and REXML are true Ruby parsers that have been written completely in Ruby. While XMLParser and Libgdome-ruby have the ability to use a tried-and-true parser, NQXML and REXML load up faster since they don't have to rely on loading expat. Because they don't depend on expat, NQXML and REXML are also less segault-prone than the other parsers.

Ruby for Sablotron and XSLT4R are two libraries that are available for XSLT, and which currently work with both Unix/Linux and Windows. Ruby for Sablotron requires the Sablotron parser, but XSLT4R is entirely Ruby-based, giving it a speed edge. Neither one of the parsers are 100 percent complete, and both are missing implementations.

Solutions Fast Track

Why XML?

☑ XML is a portable, open source language that allows programmers to develop applications that can be read by other applications, regardless of operating system and/or developmental language.

☑ XML is extremely useful for keeping track of small to medium amounts of data without requiring a SQL-based backbone.

XML Parser Architectures and APIs

☑ SAX (Simple API for XML), is based on the xml-dev list. It offers low memory consumption and high speed but tedious coding and jumping when dealing with complex XML files.

☑ DOM (Document Object Model), is based on a recommendation from the W3C. Its memory consumption is higher but it can fly through an XML file, regardless of its location within the tree.

Parsing and Creating XML in Ruby

☑ NQXML and REXML are the only two totally Ruby-only parsers that we looked at extensively in this chapter (though we briefly mentioned xmlscan, a third 100-percent pure Ruby parser).

☑ XMLParser provides a reasonably reliable system since it is based on expat. Because of this, many of the possible errors in XMLParser arise out of problems with expat, and not with XMLParser itself.

☑ NQXML does not fully support XML, but rather provides quick functionality due to its English-readable methods.

☑ REXML is a fairly complete XML parser and uses XPath and regular expression for many of its actions. It is very fast and its functionality also uses English-readable methods.

Using XSLT in Ruby

- ☑ The two XSLT parsers in Ruby are Ruby-Sablotron and XSLT4R

- ☑ Ruby-Sablotron depends on the Sablotron XSLT parser.

- ☑ XSLT4R depends on the XMLScan library but both XSLT4R and XMLScan are written in pure Ruby.

Frequently Asked Questions

The following Frequently Asked Questions, answered by the authors of this book, are designed to both measure your understanding of the concepts presented in this chapter and to assist you with real-life implementation of these concepts. To have your questions about this chapter answered by the author, browse to **www.syngress.com/solutions** and click on the **"Ask the Author"** form.

Q: Isn't part of the Ruby philosophy that whatever runs in one operating system should run in another?

A: Yes, it is, but many of the current Ruby developers are running Unix/Linux on their machines, since Ruby was originally a language made to be a substitute for Perl. Many developers are bringing their modules up to Windows, though this will take time.

Q: I am currently using Windows; do I need to run the install file that the module comes with?

A: On a majority of modules, the answer is "no"; even some apparently Unix/Linux-only modules will run fine if placed within the correct folder in your Ruby directory. Usually, you will want to place the folder in the TAR/GZIP file that has all of the Ruby files (usually the folder that contains the files for the module will be within a folder with the name and revision of the module) into the C:\ruby\lib\ruby\1.x folder (*x* being the current Ruby build you are using).

Q: I am using REXML and am receiving the following (or similar) error:

```
/cygdrive/c/RUBY/lib/ruby/1.6/rexml/parent.rb:59:in `[]': no
implicit conversion from string(TypeError)
```

A: More than likely you tried to use the following line in your code:

```
Document.elements.each("root/element") { |element| puts element
    ["rating"]
```

which is wrong, as *element* does not respond to method []. However, you can use *element.text* to return what you need as long as you define the element you need in the *XPath* string being passed to *Document.elements.each*.

Q: I run a Cobalt server; can I run Ruby and the parser described in this book?

A: Yes, you will be able to without any problems, but keep an eye out for the segfault problems when you work with any of the parsers that require expat.

Web Services and Distributed Ruby

Solutions in this chapter:

- **Using XML-RPC for Ruby**
- **Using SOAP for Ruby**
- **Using Distributed Ruby**

☑ **Summary**

☑ **Solutions Fast Track**

☑ **Frequently Asked Questions**

Introduction

In this chapter we'll introduce you into three libraries, XML-RPC for Ruby (xmlrpc4r), Simple Object Access Protocol for Ruby (SOAP4R) and Distributed Ruby (DRb). The first two are interfaces to XML-RPC and SOAP, which are XML-based and language-independent protocols; both are used for writing or accessing Web services. The third library is a pure Ruby solution for remote method calls, and is limited to Ruby That is, it's not possible to write a client or a server in a language other than Ruby using Distributed Ruby.

Developing & Deploying…

Monitoring TCP/IP Based Services

We can monitor Web services, or any TCP/IP-based client and server, by using a very simple monitor application that comes with XML-RPC for Ruby (see file *samples/monitor/monitor.rb*) or TCPSocketPipe (available from the Ruby Application Archive [RAA]).

Suppose you are running a SOAP service on port 8070. To display the traffic between that service and a SOAP client, start the monitor with the following:

```
ruby monitor.rb 8060 localhost 8070
```

The SOAP client should now access the service through port 8060 instead of port 8070.

In addition to the graphical user interface (GUI) displaying the traffic, a hex dump of the TCP/IP traffic and some logging messages are stored in the directory's TCPSocketPipe.log file.

Using XML-RPC for Ruby

XML-RPC takes a pragmatic approach to distributed computing between different systems and languages, based on two major Internet standards: HTTP for transmission, and XML to encode information in a human-readable and portable way.

XML-RPC's specification (see www.xmlrpc.com/spec) defines a set of datatypes: *Integer*, *Float*, *Boolean*, *String*, *Hash*, *Array*, *DateTime*, *Base64*, and *Nil—nil* values are a non-standard extension to the XML-RPC specification; it also defines Remote Procedure Call (RPC) elements (for example, method name, parameters, return value, or fault information), for simple, hard-wired, relatively easy-to-parse encoding in XML. Unlike SOAP, XML-RPC does not directly support user-defined datatypes, but with little effort we can emulate them using hashes, as we'll see later.

The Ruby XML-RPC implementation, called xmlrpc4r, is a pure Ruby solution. Some of its features include the following:

- Support for Introspection and multiCall extensions;
- HTTP Basic Authentication and Secure Sockets Layer (SSL) (client-only);
- Asynchronous RPCs and connection-alive;
- Common Gateway Interface (CGI), FastCGI, standalone and mod_ruby servers.

Obtaining and Installing xmlrpc4r

Xmlrpc4r was developed by Michael Neumann. Its homepage is at www.fantasy-coders.de/ruby/xmlrpc4r, though you'll also find it at Ruby's Application Archive (RAA) in the Library section under *XML*.

It requires either Jim Menard's NQXML or Yoshida Masato's XMLParser package, both of which can be obtained from the RAA.

After you've downloaded the *xmlrpc4r* package (which, as of this writing, is xmlrpc4r-1_7_4.tar.gz), extract and install it as follows:

```
tar -xvzf xmlrpc4r-1_7_4.tar.gz
cd xmlrpc4r-1_7_4
ruby install.rb
```

To run some test-cases for xmlrpc4r, change into the extracted archive's *test* directory and execute:

```
ruby test.rb
```

Note that the test-cases require both NQXML and XMLParser to be installed, otherwise running the tests will result in a lot of failure messages being thrown.

Configuring xmlrpc4r

You may configure xmlrpc4r globally by setting several options in the xmlrpc/config.rb file, located at Ruby's *site_ruby* directory (e.g. /usr/local/lib/ruby/site_ruby/1.6). Table 5.1 lists the possible settings.

Table 5.1 Configuration Options of xmlrpc4r (file xmlrpc/config.rb)

Option	Default value	Meaning (when option = true)
DEFAULT_WRITER	XMLWriter::Simple	The default XML writer. Other possible value is XMLWriter::XMLParser.
DEFAULT_PARSER	XMLParser::NQXMLStreamParser	The default XML parser. Other possible values are XMLParser::NQXMLTreeParser, XMLParser::XMLStreamParser and XMLParser::XMLTreeParser.
ENABLE_BIGINT	false	Allow **Bignum**s with more than 32 bits. **Non-standard!**
ENABLE_NIL_CREATE	false	Allow passing/returning nil to/from a RPC. **Non-standard!**
ENABLE_NIL_PARSER	false	Accept a <nil> tag. **Non-standard!**
ENABLE_MARSHALLING	true	Convert objects which classes include module **XMLRPC::Marshallable** into hashes and reconstruct them later from that hash.
ENABLE_MULTICALL	false	Enable the *multiCall* extension by default.
ENABLE_INTROSPECTION	false	Enable the *Introspection* extension by default.

Writing XML-RPC Clients

Our first XML-RPC client, presented below, will output all entries of the RAA as well as detailed information about the entry *XML-RPC*. This is possible because the RAA is accessible (read-only) through a SOAP and XML-RPC interface. For more information about the XML-RPC interface, see the directory *samples/raa* of xmlrpc4r's distribution.

```
require "xmlrpc/client"

client = XMLRPC::Client.new2(
   'http://www.ruby-lang.org/~nahi/xmlrpc/raa/')

p client.call('raa.getAllListings')
p client.call('raa.getInfoFromName', 'XML-RPC')
```

The XML-RPC request that the client application sends to the server, caused by the second RPC *raa.getInfoFromName*, looks like this:

```
<?xml version="1.0" ?>

<methodCall>

  <methodName>raa.getInfoFromName</methodName>

  <params>

    <param>

      <value><string>XML-RPC</string></value>

    </param>

  </params>

</methodCall>
```

To play with some other public XML-RPC services, take a look at the Services section of XML-RPC's homepage (www.xmlrpc.com), where you can find examples such as a real-time news client interface, a search engine, or a spell checker.

In the above example, we used the *new2* method to create an instance of the *XMLRPC::Client* class. However, there are three constructor methods that can do the job:

```
client = XMLRPC::Client.new(

  host='localhost', path='/RPC2', port=80,

  proxy_host=nil, proxy_port=8080, user=nil,

  password=nil, use_ssl=false, timeout=30)


client = XMLRPC::Client.new2(

  uri='http://localhost:80/RPC2' , proxy=nil, timeout=30)


# 'hash' takes same keys as the names of method new's parameters
client = XMLRPC::Client.new3(hash)
```

If you pass one of the three methods *nil* as parameter, the default value (for example, *port=80* or *path="/RPC2"*) is taken instead.

Again, in our first example, we used the *call* method to invoke a remote procedure, but there are other methods designed for the same purpose. We divide them into two major categories, *return value convention*, and *concurrent behavior*:

- Return value convention

  - Raise a *XMLRPC::FaultException* if a fault-structure was returned from a RPC. This applies to methods *call*, *proxy*, *multicall*, *call_async*, *proxy_async*, and *multicall_async*.

  - Raise no exception. Instead, return two values: The first indicates whether or not the second is an instance of *XMLRPC::FaultException* (false) or if it is a regular return value (true). This applies to the following methods: *call2*, *proxy2*, *multicall2*, *call2_async*, *proxy2_async*, and *multicall2_async*.

- Concurrent behavior

  - *Synchronous*. All remote procedure calls use the same *Net::HTTP* object. If the server supports HTTP connection-alive, only one connection is used for all remote procedure calls. This saves network bandwidth and increases overall performance. The disadvantage is that you cannot concurrently call two (or more) remote procedures using the same *XMLRPC::Client* object. This applies to all methods without "async" in their name.

  - *Asynchronous*. A new connection to the server is established for each remote procedure call. Therefore it's no problem to call two (or more) remote procecure using the same *XMLRPC::Client* object concurrently. This applies to all methods with "async" in their name.

Regarding the *return value* convention, both forms are equivalent:

```
# (1)
begin
  param = client.call('raa.getInfoFromName', 'XML-RPC')
  p param
rescue XMLRPC::FaultStructure => err
  p err.faultCode; p err.faultString
end


# (2)
ok, param = client.call2('raa.getInfoFromName', 'XML-RPC')
if ok
  p param
else            # param is a fault-structure
```

```
    p param.faultCode; p param.faultString
end
```

Of course the above example applies to methods *proxy* and *multicall* as well as their asynchronous counterparts (*proxy_async*, etc.).

The concurrent behavior category establishes whether or not we can call remote procedures concurrently. Using threads, we now rewrite our initial example and call both remote procedures *getAllListings* and *getInfoFromName* concurrently:

```
require "xmlrpc/client"

client = XMLRPC::Client.new2(
  'http://www.ruby-lang.org/~nahi/xmlrpc/raa/')


list = info = nil

t1 = Thread.new {
  list = client.call_async("raa.getAllListings")
}

t2 = Thread.new {
  ok, param = client.call2_asnyc("raa.getInfoFromName", "XML-RPC")
  info = param if ok
}

# wait for the threads to complete
t1.join; t2.join

p list, info
```

We have to use threads because the asynchronous methods block the execution of the program in the same way any synchronous method would.

Instead of using the *call* method and specifying the remote procedure's name as the first parameter, we could use method *proxy*, which creates a *XMLRPC::Proxy* object:

```
# creates a XMLRPC::Proxy object
raa = client.proxy("raa")
```

```
p raa.getAllListings
```

```
p raa.getInfoFromName("XML-RPC")
```

Similar to the *call* method, also exist the *proxy2*, *proxy_async*, and *proxy2_async* methods. Note that using a service method named *to_s* or *inspect* (all methods defined in class *Object* and module *Kernel*) will not work using an *XMLRPC::Proxy* object (due to using *method_missing*).

Using the MultiCall Extension

MultiCall is an extension by Eric Kidd, the author of XML-RPC for C/C++ (MultiCall's RFC: www.xmlrpc.com/discuss/messageReader$1208). Its intent is to enhance performance for applications that need to invoke many short (in terms of time) remote procedures. In this situation, the overhead of each XML-RPC message can be very high; sometimes too high, in fact.

MultiCall allows us to call an arbitrary number of remote procedures with one RPC to the remote procedure *system.multicall*. This procedure then calls all specified procedures on the server side and returns a return value for each called procedure.

Note that MultiCall is not supported by every XML-RPC server. To enable a server written with XML-RPC for Ruby, read the section *Configuring xmlrpc4r*.

Let's look at an example:

```
res = client.multicall(
  ["num.div", 10, 5],      # divide 10 by 5 => 2
  ["num.add", 4, 12],      # add 4 and 12 => 16
  ["num.div", 51, 0]       # 51/0 => division by zero
)


p res    # => [2, 16, <XMLRPC::FaultException#...>]
```

Each array in the parameter list of the *multicall* method specifies one RPC; the first element is the remote procedure's name, and the rest is its arguments. Note that there are also other methods, such as *multicall2*, *multicall_async*, etc.

Introspecting XML-RPC Servers

The *Introspection* extension, as proposed by Edd Dumbill (http://xmlrpc.use-fulinc.com/doc/reserved.html), specifies three service methods for introspecting XML-RPC servers:

- **array system.listMethods()** Returns a list of all available methods.
- **array system.methodSignature(string methodName)** Returns the method signature(s) of the *methodName* method
- **string system.methodHelp(string methodName)** Returns the help text of the *methodName* method

The application presented below introspects an introspection-enabled XML-RPC server and outputs the method signatures together with their help texts. The source code also appears as file *introspect.rb* on the CD accompanying this book.

```ruby
# file: introspect.rb
require "xmlrpc/client"


uri = ARGV[0] || "http://localhost:8080"
system = XMLRPC::Client.new2(uri).proxy("system")


puts "Introspecting #{ uri }"
for meth in system.listMethods.sort
  puts '=' * 70
  for sig in system.methodSignature(meth)
    puts "- %s %s( %s )" % [
      sig[0], meth, (sig[1..-1] || []).join(', ')
    ]
  end
  puts "", system.methodHelp(meth)
end
```

We can test our application by introspecting O'Reilly's Meerkat server. At the command line we type:

```
ruby introspect.rb http://www.oreillynet.com/meerkat/xml-rpc/server.php
```

This outputs:

```
Introspecting http://www.oreillynet.com/meerkat/xml-rpc/server.php

======================================================================

- array meerkat.getCategories(  )
```

```
Returns an array of structs of available Meerkat categories each with
its associated category Id.
=======================================================================
- array meerkat.getCategoriesBySubstring( string )


Returns an array of structs of available Meerkat categories each with
its associated category Id
given a substring to match (case-insensitively).
=======================================================================
- array meerkat.getChannels(  )


Returns an array of structs of available RSS channels each with its
associated channel Id.
=======================================================================
- array meerkat.getChannelsByCategory( int )


Returns an array of structs of RSS channels in a particular category
(specified by integer
category id) each with its associated channel Id.
=======================================================================


[.. More snipped ..]
```

With such a nice output, it should be an easy to start writing a client for that service. As an exercise you might write a WWW or GUI adapted version of the introspector.

Writing XML-RPC Servers

XML-RPC for Ruby supports three different types of servers:

- Standalone server (*XMLRPC::Server*)

- CGI/FastCGI-based server (*XMLRPC::CGIServer*)

- mod_ruby-based server (*XMLRPC::ModRubyServer*) *Mod_ruby* embeds a Ruby interpreter into the Apache Web server. This speeds up the execution of Ruby applications because it removes the process creation for each request.

All three server classes inherit from the same abstract *XMLRPC::BasicServer* superclass. This common superclass implements methods that are used by all sub-classes for adding service handlers or internally-used methods for dispatching RPCs etc.

Look at the following XML-RPC server, which introduces all important aspects:

```
require "xmlrpc/server"

class Num
  INTERFACE = XMLRPC::interface("num") {
    meth 'int add(int, int)', 'Add two numbers', 'add'
    meth 'int div(int, int)', 'Divide two numbers'
  }

  def add(a, b) a + b end
  def div(a, b) a / b end
end

server = XMLRPC::Server.new(8080, "0.0.0.0")
server.add_handler(Num::INTERFACE, Num.new)
server.serve
```

The example implements a standalone server that exposes two services (*num.add* and *num.div*) and specifies a signature and a help text for them. The constructor method *new* of the *XMLRPC::Server* class takes the following parameters:

```
server = XMLRPC::Server.new(port=8080, host="127.0.0.1",
                            maxConnections=4, stdlog=$stdout,
                            audit=true, debug=true)
```

The first two parameters, *port* and *host*, specify the port the server listens on and for which host it should accept requests. All further parameters are bypassed to the HTTP server framework (John Small's generic server framework *GServer*, available at RAA) and specify the maximum number of concurrent connections as well as the server's logging and debugging behavior.

Once you've started a standalone server (initiated by method *serve*) it will start up a *TCPServer* and wait for connections. To quit the server, either call the *shut-*

down method or send the process a SIGHUP signal (by typing *kill –HUP pid* at the command line, where *pid* is the process' ID).

To use a CGI- or mod_ruby-based server in the example above, simply change this line:

```
server = XMLRPC::Server.new(8080, "0.0.0.0")
```

into this:

```
server = XMLRPC::CGIServer.new
# or
server = XMLRPC::ModRubyServer.new
```

For a FastCGI-based server you have to change a bit more. The example would then look like:

```
require "xmlrpc/server"
require "fcgi"    # or "fastcgi"

class Num
  # ..same as above..
end


server = XMLRPC::CGIServer.new
server.add_handler(Num::INTERFACE, Num.new)

FCGI.each_request do |f|
  $stdin = f.in
  server.serve
end
```

There are currently two FastCGI implementations for Ruby — the *fastcgi* module (written in pure Ruby) and *fcgi*, a C-extension module. Both are available from Eli Green's homepage at http://fenris.codedogs.ca/~eli/fastcgi.html. Alternatively, follow the link from the FastCGI entry in the RAA's Library section, under *WWW*.

To add a service handler to the server, there are several other possible ways we have not yet handled. For example:

```
# using a code-block
server.add_handler("num.add", ["int", "int", "int"],
  "Add two numbers") { |a, b| a + b }
```

```
# the same without method signature and help text
server.add_handler("num.add") { |a, b| a + b }


# add all public methods of class Num under namespace "num"
server.add_handler(XMLRPC::iPIMethods("num"), Num.new)
```

The datatypes in the method signature should be one of the following strings: *int*, *boolean*, *double*, *string*, *dateTime.iso8601*, *base64*, *array*, or *struct*.

Some other methods of class *BasicServer* are listed in Table 5.2.

Table 5.2 Further Methods of Class BasicServer

Method	Explanation
add_multicall	Enables the multiCall extension (unless enabled by default).
add_introspection	Enables the introspection extension (unless enabled by default).
set_parser(parser)	Uses *parser* instead of the default one.
set_writer(writer)	Uses *writer* instead of the default one.
set_default_handler { |meth, *params| }	Calls the block if no service handler for a request was found; *meth* is the name of the not-found service method, *params* its arguments.
set_service_hook { |obj, *params| }	The block is called instead of each service handler; *obj* is the **Proc** object of the original service handler, *params* its arguments. The return value of the block is the result of the RPC.

For instance, we could use the *set_service_hook* method to convert return values passed to, or returned from, service handlers to types recognized by XML-RPC in order to catch exceptions etc. So, with the little code snippet below, we convert all arguments that are *Integer* types to *String*s before we pass them to the service handler:

```
server.set_service_hook { |obj, *args|
  args.collect! { |e|
    e.kind_of?(Integer) ? e.to_s : e
  }


  obj.call(*args)
}
```

Project: A File Upload Service

In this section we'll implement a XML-RPC file upload service that will enable us to upload a compressed file to the server, where it will be uncompressed and stored in a predefined directory (in our case /tmp/). For compressing and uncompressing we use the *Ruby/zlib* module, available from RAA. Furthermore, we pass a MD5 checksum of the file to the service, so that it can check whether data–loss has happened or not.

Figure 5.1 shows the source code of this application (it can also found at www.syngress.com/solutions under the file named *fileupload.rb*).

Figure 5.1 Source Code of file-upload service (fileupload.rb)

```ruby
require "xmlrpc/server"
require "xmlrpc/client"
require "md5"
require "zlib"


class FileUpload
  NS = "file"
  INTERFACE = XMLRPC::interface(NS) {
    meth 'boolean upload(string, string, base64)',
         'Upload a file to the servers file system.'
  }


  FAULT_BASE    = 9000
  MAX_FILE_SIZE = 1024*1024

  def initialize(upload_dir, max_file_size=MAX_FILE_SIZE)
    @upload_dir    = upload_dir
    @max_file_size = max_file_size
  end

  def upload(name, md5, data)
```

Continued

Figure 5.1 Continued

```
  if data.size > @max_file_size
    fault(0, 'File too large.')
  elsif name.include? '/' or name.include? '\\'
    fault(1, 'Invalid name.')
  elsif File.exists?( @upload_dir + name )
    fault(2, 'File already exists.')
  elsif MD5.new(data).hexdigest != md5
    fault(3, 'MD5 checksum mismatch.')
  else
    data = Zlib::Inflate.inflate(data)
    if data.size > @max_file_size
      fault(0, 'File too large.')
    else
      File.open(@upload_dir + name, "w+") { |f| f << data }
      return true
    end
  end
end


private # ------------------------------------------------

def fault(code, message)
  raise XMLRPC::FaultException.new(FAULT_BASE + code, message)
end


# --------------------------------------------------------

class Client
  def initialize(uri, compression=Zlib::Deflate::BEST_COMPRESSION)
    @file = XMLRPC::Client.new2(uri).proxy(NS)
    @compression = compression
  end
```

Continued

Figure 5.1 Continued

```
    def upload(localfile, remotefile)
      content = File.readlines(localfile).to_s
      content = Zlib::Deflate.deflate(content, @compression)
      content = XMLRPC::Base64.new(content)
      md5     = MD5.new(content).hexdigest

      @file.upload(remotefile, md5, content)
    end
  end
end



if __FILE__ == $0
  PORT = (ARGV.shift || 8080).to_i

  # starts a FileUpload server
  XMLRPC::Server.new(PORT, "0.0.0.0").
  add_handler(FileUpload::INTERFACE, FileUpload.new('/tmp/')).
  serve
end
```

We test our service by uploading a file (/etc/hosts) to the server and storing it there as *hosts*. We do this with the following script (make sure the server is running before you execute the script):

```
require "fileupload"

file = FileUpload::Client.new("http://localhost:8080/")
file.upload('/etc/hosts, 'hosts')
```

XML-RPC Datatypes

Table 5.3 lists the mappings between Ruby and XML-RPC types (column 1 and 2) and vice versa (column 2 and 3). You can pass all types listed in column 1 as parameters to a RPC or return them from a service-handler. The types you get back from an RPC (for example, return value of *Client#call*) or that a service handler receives as arguments are listed in column 3.

Table 5.3 Mapping of Ruby to XML-RPC Types and Vice Versa

Ruby type =>	XML-RPC type =>	Ruby type
Fixnum, Bignum	\<i4> \<int>	Fixnum, Bignum
TrueClass, FalseClass (true, false)	\<boolean>	TrueClass, FalseClass (true, false)
Float	\<double>	Float
String, Symbol	\<string>	String
Hash, Struct	\<struct>	Hash
Array	\<array>	Array
Date, Time, XMLRPC::DateTime	\<dateTime.iso8601>	XMLRPC::DateTime
XMLRPC::Base64	\<base64>	String
NilClass (nil) **Non-Standard!**	\<nil>	NilClass (nil)

To transfer binary data (as we did in out file upload service) use a *XMLRPC::Base64* object:

```
aBase64 = XMLRPC::Base64.new( aString )
```

To pass dates before 1970 that include the time, you have to use instances of class *XMLRPC::DateTime*:

```
aDateTime = XMLRPC::DateTime.new(year, month, day, hour, min, sec)
```

Otherwise, you may use class *Time* for dates after 1970 that include the time, or class *Date* for dates without the time.

An instance of *XMLRPC::DateTime* has attribute accessor methods with the same names as the parameter names of the *new* method shown above. Additionally, it has the *to_date*, *to_time* and *to_a* methods that return a *Date*, *Time* or *Array* object respectively.

Instances of *XMLRPC::FaultException* represent XML-RPC fault structures. They provide two attribute readers, *faultCode* and *faultString*. To return a fault-structure, simply raise them in the service-handler:

```
aFaultException = XMLRPC::FaultException.new(faultCode, faultString)
```

User-defined Datatypes

There is a convenient way of passing Ruby objects other than the default types listed in Table 5.3. All you need to do is to include the *XMLRPC::Marshallable* module into their classes. An example follows:

```
class Person
  include XMLRPC::Marshallable
  attr_reader :name, :father, :mother
  def initialize(name, father=nil, mother=nil)
    @name, @father, @mother = name, father, mother
  end
end
```

This only works if the *Config::ENABLE_MARSHALLING* option is true. If this applies, XML-RPC for Ruby converts instances of *Person* into a *hash*. This hash contains all instance variables and one additional key "___class___" storing the class name. If the *Config::ENABLE_NIL_CREATE* option is true (it is false by default), then all instance variables with a value of *nil* are left out.

Note that both the client and server application must be aware of the class definition, otherwise a *hash* is returned instead of a *Person* object.

Dumping and Loading XML-RPC Messages

If we leave off the distributed component of XML-RPC, we end up in its XML encoding specification. We could use this to store Ruby objects in XML-RPC's encoding, or to communicate between two programs without the need of establishing a TCP/IP connection, simply by exchanging XML-RPC messages using files or pipes.

For this purpose there is a *XMLRPC::Marshal* class defined in *xmlrpc/marshal.rb* (the output is shown in bold):

```
require "xmlrpc/marshal"


str = XMLRPC::Marshal.dump( { 'Ruby' => 'is cool' } )
puts str


<?xml version="1.0" ?><methodResponse><params><param><value>
<struct><member>  <name>Ruby</name><value><string>is cool</string>
</value></member></struct></value>  </param></params></methodResponse>
```

```
p XMLRPC::Marshal.load( str )
```

{"Ruby"=>"is cool"}

The methods *Marshal.load* and *Marshal.dump* are aliases for *Marshal.load_response* and *Marshal.dump_response*. To create or load XML-RPC method calls instead, use the *Marshal.dump_call(methodName, *args)* or *Marshal.load_call(stringOrReadable)* methods respectively.

Communicating with Python's xmlrpclib

Exchanging XML-RPC messages between Ruby's *xmlrpc4r* and Python's *xmlrpc-lib* is problematic, because messages created with xmlrpclib have *<params>* as the root tag whereas xmlrpc4r requires this to be either *<methodCall>* or *<methodResponse>*. We can fix this by surrounding Python's output with a *<methodResponse>* tag and by adding a XML declaration at the top:

```
require "xmlrpc/marshal"


def load_from_python( stringOrReadable )

  XMLRPC::Marshal.load_response( %{

    <?xml version="1.0"?>

    <methodResponse>

    #{ stringOrReadable }

    </methodResponse>

  } )

end
```

Below you see a little Python script that marshals an array (a tuple in Python) of two values:

```
# file: xmlrpc.py
import xmlrpclib
data = ( ("From Python", 2), )
print xmlrpclib.dumps( data )
```

We now try to unmarshal the output generated by the Python script *xmlrpc.py* shown above, using our new *load_from_python* method:

```
# back in Ruby
p load_from_python( `python xmlrpc.py` )
```

This outputs:

```
["From Python", 2]
```

To unmarshal a XML-RPC message in Python we write a second script *xmlrpc2.py*:

```
# file: xmlrpc2.py
import xmlrpclib, sys
print xmlrpclib.loads( sys.stdin.read() )[0][0]
```

This script reads the XML-RPC documents from standard input, parses it and outputs the native Python value to standard output. We call it at the command-line together with a Ruby *one-liner*, creating a XML-RPC message (this line just wraps in our book layout):

```
ruby -r xmlrpc/marshal -e "puts XMLRPC::Marshal.dump(
    ['From Ruby, 1.7])" | python xmlrpc2.py
```

This outputs:

```
['From Ruby', 1.7]
```

Securing XML-RPC Services

Due to the usage of HTTP as transport protocol, it is very easy to transparently add security mechanisms without changing the XML-RPC specification by making use of standards like SSL or HTTP authentication (*403 Authentication Required* status code). You can use SSL to encrypt the communication between the client and server and HTTP authentication (it is currently impossible to use the Digest method, as only the Basic method is implemented) to restrict access to a specified group of persons.

Currently, both are supported by only the client-side of xmlrpc4r.

Client-side Support

To enable SSL, either call *Client.new* or *Client.new3* with the *use_ssl* parameter set to *true,* or use *https* as the protocol (instead of *http*) in the Uniform Resource Identifier (URI) passed to *Client.new2.*

If you want to access XML-RPC services restricted by HTTP authentification, pass the parameters *user* and *password* to *Client.new* or *Client.new3* or specify them in the URI (http://user:pass@host) passed to *Client.new2.* You can also set the user or password later through the setter methods *user=* and *password=*.

> **NOTE**
>
> Before you can use client-side SSL, you have to install the *SSL_Socket* extension, which is available at the RAA. Note that the client side will not (yet) validate a certificate sent by an SSL-enabled server.

Server-side Support

As mentioned above, there is no direct support in xmlrpc4r for server-side HTTP authentification or SSL, but by using a SSL and/or HTTP authentification-capable Web server together with a CGI (or FastCGI) based XML-RPC server, it is possible to support these authentication protocols.

An Apache Web server, for example, supports SSL through *mod_ssl* and HTTP authentication by putting a *.htaccess* file inside the directory to be protected. Figure 5.2 shows a sample *.htaccess* file. Note that you have to use the program *htpasswd* to create a password file, first. For example, to create a new password file (*password.file*) with one user called *michael*, type the following at the command-line:

```
htpasswd -c password.file michael
```

When prompted, enter the password twice for the new user. For more information on *htpasswd* see its man page (in Unix type *man htpasswd* at the command line).

Figure 5.2 A Sample .htaccess File

```
AuthType Basic
AuthName "XML-RPC Restricted Area"
AuthUserFile "/path/to/password.file"
Require valid-user
```

Performance Comparisons

XML-RPC for Ruby comes with four different XML-RPC parsers; a tree and stream parser each for NQXML and XMLParser. For small XML documents, tree parsers perform almost equally to stream parsers, but they are totally unusable for really large XML documents with many tags, due to the huge performance decrease and memory usage.

The major difference between xmlrpc4r's tree and stream parsers is that the tree parsers validate their XML-RPC documents whereas the stream parsers don't, or at least not at the same degree. That is, if you want to make sure that only valid XML-RPC documents are processed and they are not very large, go for a tree parser. Otherwise, if speed is most important, consider using a stream parser.

Table 5.4 compares the four parsers and shows their performance levels relative to *NQXMLTreeParser*. You can see from the numbers that *XMLStreamParser* is the fastest parser overall; for example, it parses a really huge document (many tags, 561796 bytes) about 316 times faster than *NQXMLTreeParser* and still 17 times as fast as *XMLTreeParser*. But we also see that *XMLTreeParser* is incredibly slow at parsing one (or more) large Base64 elements; this makes it relatively unusable for many tasks; uploading files, for example.

There are two reasons why *XMLStreamParser* is so incredibly fast:

1. It uses the XMLParser module (the wrapper for James Clark's XML Parser toolkit, *expat*), an XML parser written in C.

2. Unlike *NQXMLTreeParser* or *XMLTreeParser*, it does not build a DOM-like tree in memory. It's a stream parser, which means that it streams on-the-fly through the XML document.

Table 5.4 Performance Comparison of the XML Parsers Supported by xmlrpc4r

XML Document	NQXMLTree Parser	NQXMLStream Parser	XMLTree Parser	XMLStream Parser
Small (343 bytes)	1	1,14	1,6	22,66
Middle (6687 bytes)	1	1,2	2,54	25,85
Large (14390 bytes)	1	1,2	2,43	22,38
Huge (561796 bytes)	1	1,67	18,5	316,39
Base64 (1421526 bytes) (One Base64 element, 1 MB in size)	1	0,97	1/3877	1,92

Developing & Deploying…

XML-RPC - SandStorm Component Architecture

SandStorm (developed by Idan Sofer and found at http://sstorm.source-forge.net) is a "loose framework for creating cross-platform, multi-language, modular and distributed middle-ware Web applications" that uses XML-RPC as its communication protocol. It is mostly written in Python and PHP, but that should not deter us from using it.

One of SandStorm's main components is a *central service registry* (which is itself a XML-RPC service), where components (XML-RPC services) located anywhere on a network can be registered with a name. Thereafter, clients can easily access the components by name without knowledge of its current location.

Each registered SandStorm component must have a unique namespace (for example *my.component*), under which all its methods are defined. This is also the name stored in the central registry for this component.

The SandStorm architecture implements a simple load balancing mechanism that allows multiple components to be registered with the same name. SandStorm supposes that all these components have the same implementation, but are located on different servers. Each time a client requests a component with that name, SandStorm returns different one in a round-robin fashion.

To access the central service registry: Use the *Active::Registry* class defined in xmlrpc4r's samples/sandstorm/active.rb file or the file *lib/ruby/active.rb* from the SandStorm distribution.

The location of the service registry server must be supplied either in the environment variables ACTIVE_REGISTRY_HOST, ..._PORT and ..._URI, or by passing it to *Active::Registry#new*:

```
registry = Active::Registry.new(uri=nil, host=nil,
                                 port=nil)
```

Default values are taken in the case that both parameters and environment variables are not given.

The *getComponents* method returns a list of all registered components, whereas *getComponent(comp)* returns a *XMLRPC::Proxy* object for the component specified by parameter *comp*:

Continued

```
registry = Active::Registry.new


# assuming that the XML-RPC interface of RAA

# was registered before as component 'Ruby.RAA'

raa = registry.getComponent('Ruby.RAA')


p raa.getAllListings
```

To get more information about a component, such as its location, call the *getComponentInfo(comp)* method. It returns a Hash containing the keys "host", "port" and "uri".

To add components to the registry: Two methods exist to add components to the registry:

```
Active::Registry#setComponent(name, uri, host, port)


Active::Registry#addComponent(name, uri, host, port)
```

They add or set the component located at *host*, *port* and *uri*, under the name *name*, to the registry and return *true* on success or *false* if not. The *addComponent* method is different in that it allows multiple components with the same name (for load balancing, as noted above).

To remove a component from the registry: call the following to remove a component:

```
Active::Registry#removeComponent(name)
```

It returns *true* on success. Note that this removes all components registered as *name*.

Using SOAP for Ruby

Similar to XML-RPC, the *Simple Object Access Protocol* (SOAP) is a cross-platform and language-independent RPC protocol based on XML and, usually (but not necessarily) HTTP. It uses XML to encode the information that makes the remote procedure call, and HTTP to transport that information across a network from clients to servers and vice versa.

SOAP was not designed to compete in performance with binary communication protocols like Sun's RPC or Common Object Request Broker Architecture

(CORBA), nor for massive parallel computing like the Message Passing Interface (MPI) or Parallel Virtual Machine (PVM). Instead, SOAP has several other advantages: for example, its relatively cheap deployment and debugging costs (because XML is human readable, SOAP is as well), its extensibility and ease-of-use, and the existence of several implementations for different languages and platforms (see Table 5.5 for a list of some SOAP implementations).

Table 5.5 References to Some SOAP Implementations, Ordered by Language

Language	Name of Implementation	Info on the Web
C++	WASP Server for C++ (IdooXoap for C++)	www.zvon.org www.idoox.com
COM/Windows	MS SOAP Toolkit 2.0	http://msdn.microsoft.com/ library/default.asp?url=/ library/en-us/soap/htm/ kit_intro_19bj.asp
Java	Apache SOAP	http://xml.apache.org/soap
	WASP Server for Java (IdooXoap for Java)	www.zvon.org www.idoox.com
Perl	SOAP::Lite	www.soaplite.com
Python	SOAPPy	http://soapy.sourceforge .net
	soaplib.py	www.pythonware.com/ products/soap
Ruby	SOAP4R	www.jin.gr.jp/~nahi/ Ruby/SOAP4R

Initially developed by companies like Microsoft (.NET platform), IBM (Websphere Application Server), DevelopMentor, Lotus and UserLand, the SOAP 1.1 specification was submitted to the World Wide Web Consortium (W3C) as W3C Note and is now likely to become SOAP 1.2 (details of the specification can be found at www.w3.org/TR/SOAP). Many companies have shown interest in SOAP, and by now many tools and implementations are available, with many more on the way — it's good to know that Ruby is not an exception in this.

In the following sections we'll introduce you to the SOAP implementation for Ruby (SOAP4R). We'll explain how to write clients and servers, mention logging and exception handling, and marshaling and datatype conversion between SOAP and Ruby. At the end, we present one large example of an authentication server for SOAP services.

Obtaining and Installing SOAP4R

SOAP4R is the SOAP implementation for Ruby developed by Hiroshi Nakamura. Its homepage is at www.jin.gr.jp/~nahi/Ruby/SOAP4R; alternatively, you'll find it by looking for the SOAP4R entry in the Library section under *XML* at the RAA.

SOAP4R depends on the use of one of the following packages:

- NQXML, the pure-Ruby XML parser by Jim Menard
- XMLParser, the expat wrapper by Yoshida Masato

Both are available from RAA. All other libraries upon which SOAP4R depends are redistributed in its *redist* directory.

Extract and install the SOAP4R package (as of this writing this is *soap4r-1_4_1.tar.gz*) as follows:

```
tar -xvzf soap4r-1_4_1.tar.gz
cd soap4r-1_4_1
ruby install.rb
```

Writing SOAP4R Client and Server Applications

In this section, we will learn how to write client and server applications using SOAP4R. Before we dive too deep into SOAP4R's details, let's implement a very simple client/server SOAP application, the client/server version of "Hello World."

Figure 5.3 shows the server (file *hw_s.rb*), and Figure 5.4 shows the client application (file *hw_c.rb*). Note that both applications can also be found at www.syngress.com/solutions as files *hw_s.rb* and *hw_c.rb*.

When executed, the server application starts a standalone SOAP server on localhost and listens for requests on port 8080. It exposes one service method, *helloWorld,* which takes one parameter *from* and returns the string *Hello World, from #{from}* to the client.

Figure 5.3 Sourcecode of the Hello World SOAP Server (hw_s.rb)

```
require "soap/standaloneServer"

class HelloWorldServer < SOAP::StandaloneServer
  def methodDef
    addMethod(self, 'helloWorld', 'from')
  end

  def helloWorld(from)
    return "Hello World, from #{ from }!"
  end
end

server = HelloWorldServer.new('HelloWorld-Server',
  'urn:ruby:hello-world', 'localhost', 8080)
server.start
```

Figure 5.4 Sourcecode of Hello World SOAP Client (hw_c.rb)

```
require "soap/driver"

driver = SOAP::Driver.new(nil, nil,
  'urn:ruby:hello-world', 'http://localhost:8080/')

driver.addMethod('helloWorld', 'from')

puts driver.helloWorld("Ruby")
```

We test our client/server application by first starting the server in a separate shell:

```
ruby hw_s.rb
```

Then we start the client:

```
ruby hw_c.rb
```

If everything went well, this results in the following output:

```
Hello World, from Ruby!
```

The SOAP request sent by our client application to the server is shown in Figure 5.5.

Figure 5.5 SOAP Request Sent by Client Application

```
<?xml version="1.0" encoding="utf-8" ?>
- <env:Envelope xmlns:xsi="http://www.w3.org/2001/XMLSchema-instance"
    xmlns:env="http://schemas.xmlsoap.org/soap/envelope/"
    xmlns:xsd="http://www.w3.org/2001/XMLSchema">
  - <env:Body>
    - <n2:helloWorld xmlns:n2="urn:ruby:hello-world"
        env:encodingStyle="http://schemas.xmlsoap.org/soap/encoding/"
        xmlns:n1="http://schemas.xmlsoap.org/soap/encoding/">
        <from xsi:type="xsd:string">Ruby</from>
    </n2:helloWorld>
  </env:Body>
</env:Envelope>
```

Choosing an XML Parser

SOAP4R operates with three different XML parsers:

- NQXML (default)
- XMLParser
- SAX driver for XMLParser

To use XMLParser or the SAX driver of XMLParser instead of the default parser (which is NQXML), simply put the line *require "soap/xmlparser"* or *require "soap/saxdriver"* after other SOAP4R related *requires*.

Note that XMLParser is the fastest parser; NQXML is a bit slower — but even slower than NQXML is the SAX driver for XMLParser. However, an advantage of using NQXML is that it is written in pure Ruby and is therefore easy to install on every platform.

Writing SOAP4R Clients

The *SOAP::Driver* class provides support for writing SOAP client applications. In this section we will describe this class and demonstrate its usage on the basis of an application.

The following list includes some of the information needed to invoke a SOAP service:

- The URL of the SOAP service (SOAP Endpoint URL)

- The namespace of the service methods (Method Namespace URI)

- The *SOAPAction* field used inside the HTTP header (not required by all services)

- The names of the service methods and their parameters

Increasingly, all this information is optionally provided within a Web Service Description Language (WSDL) file. WSDL is a standardized XML document-type for encoding Web-Service-related information, not only SOAP services. For instance, some SOAP implementations make use of WSDL to automate the generation of wrapper classes for accessing SOAP services. Unfortunately, SOAP4R is not (yet) able to parse WSDL files, but I am sure that this is in the works and will arrive on the scene at some point in the future.

The aforementioned *SOAPAction* field gives a Web server or firewall the chance to make a decision (the Web server to invoke different CGI scripts, and the firewall to reject a request) for a HTTP request without parsing the XML SOAP message—which would be too time-consuming.

With this initial information in mind, let's start writing a SOAP client in Ruby; this one will invoke a service, named *BabelFish,* to translate text up to 5 KB in size from one language to another. You can find out more about that service at Xmethods' Web Service List (www.xmethods.com), a page especially suited to finding interesting SOAP services with which to experiment.

Our application (shown in Figure 5.6, and found in the file *babelfish.rb* at www.syngress.com/solutions) wraps the BabelFish service and provides an easy-to-use command-line interface; it can even act as a filter by translating the text read from *Stdin* and having it output to *Stdout*. Note that for the command-line parsing we used the *getoptlong*, library, which is part of Ruby's standard library.

Figure 5.6 Client Application Using the SOAP Service "BabelFish" (babelfish.rb)

```ruby
#!/usr/bin/env ruby

require 'soap/driver'
require 'getoptlong'

NAMESPACE    = 'urn:xmethodsBabelFish'
URL          = 'http://services.xmethods.net:80/perl/soaplite.cgi'
SOAP_ACTION  = 'urn:xmethodsBabelFish#BabelFish'
HTTP_PROXY   = nil

# default values for the arguments
input, output, lang = STDIN, STDOUT, "en_de"

# process the command-line arguments
opts = GetoptLong.new(
  [ "--file",    "-f", GetoptLong::REQUIRED_ARGUMENT ],
  [ "--output", "-o", GetoptLong::REQUIRED_ARGUMENT ],
  [ "--lang",    "-l", GetoptLong::REQUIRED_ARGUMENT ]
)
opts.each do |opt, arg|
  case opt
  when "--file"
    input = File.open(arg, "r")
  when "--output"
    output = File.open(arg, "w+")
  when "--lang"
    lang = arg
  end
end

# create a SOAP::Driver object
```

Continued

Figure 5.6 Continued

```
driver = SOAP::Driver.new(nil, nil, NAMESPACE, URL, HTTP_PROXY,
                          SOAP_ACTION)


# add the SOAP method "BabelFish" that takes two arguments
# "translationmode" and "sourcedata" to driver
driver.addMethod('BabelFish', 'translationmode', 'sourcedata')


# finally call the SOAP service
result = driver.BabelFish(lang, input.read)


output.puts result
```

To test our application and translate a short message from French to English, we specify on the command line that our application should read a text message from *Stdin*, translate it from French to English (option *--lang*) and finally write the result into the file *english.txt* (option *--output*). After that, we output the file english.txt (*cat english.txt*) to display the translated output.

```
ruby babelfish.rb --lang fr_en --output english.txt
Allo mon ami,
Je suis Michael et j'habite dans une petit village en Allemagne.
Au revoir.
^D
cat english.txt
```

This outputs the following:

```
Hello my friend,
I am Michael and I live in a small village in Germany.
Goodbye.
```

The essence of our application, that is, the part that performs the SOAP RPC can be cut down to a few lines of code:

```
require 'soap/driver'
```

```
NAMESPACE    = 'urn:xmethodsBabelFish'

URL          = 'http://services.xmethods.net:80/perl/soaplite.cgi'

SOAP_ACTION = 'urn:xmethodsBabelFish#BabelFish'

HTTP_PROXY  = nil


driver = SOAP::Driver.new(nil, nil, NAMESPACE, URL, HTTP_PROXY,
                          SOAP_ACTION)


driver.addMethod('BabelFish', 'translationmode', 'sourcedata')


result = driver.BabelFish(lang, input.read)
```

In the first line, we load the feature *'soap/driver,'* which implements the *SOAP::Driver* class. Then we define four constants and use them in the next line, where we create an instance of *SOAP::Driver* by calling its *new* method (Table 5.6 lists the parameters of *SOAP::Driver.new*):

```
aDriver = SOAP::Driver.new(log, logId, namespace, endPoint,
                           httpProxy=nil, soapAction=nil)
```

Table 5.6 Parameters of SOAP::Driver.new

Parameter	Explanation
log	An object of class *Log*, or *nil* to disable logging (see the section "Client-side Logging" for more information).
logId	A string that is used in each log-line to distinguish multiple clients using the same logfile. Only useful if parameter *log* is not *nil*.
namespace	The namespace to use for all RPCs done with this *SOAP::Driver* object (Method Namespace URI).
endPoint	URL of the SOAP server to connect with (SOAP Endpoint URL).
httpProxy	Unless *nil*, this parameter specifies the HTTP-Proxy through which to communicate instead of a direct connection to the SOAP server. It takes the form "http://host:port".
soapAction	A value for the SOAPAction field of the HTTP header. If *nil* this defaults to the empty string "".

After that, we call the *addMethod* method, passing it the name of the SOAP service method we want to invoke later on as well as its parameter names. As you might know, SOAP's method parameter names are often not taken into account on the server side. In this case, what really counts is the order in which the parameters were passed to the service. For services, this assumption applies you may forego calling *addMethod* and invoke BabelFish directly. However, I wouldn't recommend this for anything other than small scripting tasks.

To add a SOAP service method to a *SOAP::Driver* we can use one of the two following methods (Table 5.7 lists the parameters of *addMethod* and *addMethodWithSOAPAction*):

```
SOAP::Driver#addMethod(name, *paramArg)
```

or

```
SOAP::Driver#addMethodWithSOAPAction(name, soapAction, *paramArg)
```

Table 5.7 Parameters of addMethod and addMethodWithSOAPAction

Parameter	Explanation
name	The name of the remote procedure.
soapAction	SoapAction header to use instead of the default one specified in *SOAP::Driver.new*
paramArg	Specifies the names and modes (in/out/inout/retval) of the remote procedures' parameters. It has two different forms:
	(1) If it is an array of strings, each string represents an parameter name of mode "in". A parameter "return" with mode "retval" is automatically added.
	(2) If it is an array of size one and the single element is itself an array, then the inner array contains itself arrays each containing two strings, the first representing the mode and the second the name of the parameter.

To understand the usage of the *paramArg* parameter, regard the two different, but equivalent, calls to the *addMethod* method, where the second one explicitly uses parameter mode specifiers:

```
driver.addMethod('BabelFish', 'translationmode', 'sourcedata')
```

```
driver.addMethod('BabelFish', [
```

```
    ['in',      'translationmode'],
    ['in',      'sourcedata'],
    ['retval', 'return']
])
```

Possible parameter mode specifiers are *in*, *out*, *inout* and *retval*. You can combine them with an arbitrary number of other specifiers simply by separating them either through whitespace or commas; SOAP4R will just ignore the unknown ones.

Finally, in the last line of our example, we invoke the SOAP service:

```
result = driver.BabelFish(lang, input.read)
```

Note that *addMethod* creates a singleton method in the *SOAP::Driver* object. This method then invokes the SOAP service. If you don't call *addMethod*, *method_missing* will do the same, but it will use random parameter names.

As mentioned earlier, SOAP lets you declare a parameter as *in*, *out*, *inout* or *retval* — but how can we call a method that takes *inout* or *out* parameters? Consider the following:

```
# define service method
driver.addMethod('aMeth', [
    ['in',      'inParam'],
    ['inout',   'inoutParam'],
    ['out',     'outParam'],
    ['retval', 'return']
])


# invoke it
ret, inoutParam, outParam = driver.aMeth(inParam, inoutParam)
```

That is, you have to pass all *in* and *inout* parameters in the order in which they were defined in the call to *addMethod*. Similar, the *inout* and *out* parameters are returned in the same order they occur, but after the return value (mode *retval*).

Up to this point, we haven't yet discussed the datatypes you can pass as parameters to SOAP RPCs or which are returned from the same. Basically, you can pass any standard Ruby type, but for complex datatypes or types that cannot be represented directly in Ruby, you have to use special classes or special creator methods. All this will be explained in detail in section "SOAP Datatypes and Type Conversion."

Exceptions

What happens if the execution of a SOAP service method fails? Unless the whole service fails (which would result in a *500 Internal Server Error*), a *SOAP Fault* is returned, indicating that an error occurred on the server-side. In this case, SOAP4R raises in the client application either a *RuntimeError* or the same exception as occurred on the server side, if you accessed a server running SOAP4R (SOAP4R marshals the exception and passes it in the *detail* tag of the SOAP Fault structure).

To distinguish remote from local exceptions, all remote exceptions include module *SOAP::RPCServerException*. The following example demonstrates this:

```
begin
  driver.rpcThatRaisesAnException(someParams)
  raise                      # local exception
rescue SOAP::RPCServerException => err
  # remote exception
  ...
rescue
  # local exception
  ...
end
```

Client-side Logging

Logging is useful for detecting possible errors, especially for autonomously running applications like HTTP servers and daemons. Not only can logging save a lot of time, but it can also make an application more readable if logging is implemented as a basic service, as is the case for SOAP4R.

We already came across the *log* parameter of *SOAP::Driver.new* which takes *nil* to disable logging or an object of class *Log*:

```
aLog = Log.new(log, shiftAge=3, shiftSize=102400)
```

Table 5.8 lists the parameters of *Log.new*.

Table 5.8 Parameters of Log.new

Parameter	Explanation
log	Specifies the file to use for logging; it is either the name of a file (*String*) or an instance of class *IO* or *File*. The file gets opened or created in append mode.
shiftAge	Specifies when to switch to another log file. It is either one of the strings *'daily'*, *'weekly'* or *'monthly'*, or an integer specifying the number of log files to keep.
shiftSize	If the *shiftAge* parameter is an integer, *shiftSize* specifies the size a log file must exceed to trigger the switch to another one. Otherwise it is not used.

A sample log line generated by a *SOAP::Driver* object with a *logId* of CLIENT1 looks like this:

```
D, [Thu Jul 05 22:09:29 CEST 2001 161940 #8584] DEBUG — SOAP::Driver:
   <CLIENT1> call: parameters '["DE", "AU"]'.
```

The *SOAP::Driver* class provides two further methods for logging:

```
SOAP::Driver#setWireDumpDev(dumpDev)
```

and

```
SOAP::Driver#setWireDumpFileBase(fileBase)
```

The *setWireDumpDev* method writes all HTTP requests and responses, together with the complete SOAP XML message, to the *File* or *IO* object specified by the *dumpDev* parameter. The *setWireDumpFileBase* method instead logs the SOAP XML messages without the HTTP headers and stores them in two files, of which the *fileBase* parameter is part of the name:

- **fileBase**_*SOAPmethodName*_request.xml (The SOAP message for the RPC to *SOAPmethodName*)

- **fileBase**_*SOAPmethodName*_response.xml (The server's response for the above RPC)

WARNING

Each SOAP RPC overwrites its two corresponding files. It does not append its log messages!

The example in Figure 5.7 is an advanced version of our "Hello World" client application from Figure 5.4. It also appears as file *hw_c2.rb* at www.syngress.com/ solutions. What's new here is that it makes use of the *Application* class.

Figure 5.7 Advanced Hello World SOAP Client (hw_c2.rb)

```
require "soap/driver"

class HelloWorldClient < Application
  NS      = 'urn:ruby:hello-world'
  AppName = 'HelloWorldClient'

  def initialize(server, proxy=nil)
    super(AppName)
    @server = server
    @proxy  = proxy
    @logId  = AppName
    @driver = nil

    # Log to HelloWorldClient.log instead of STDERR
    setLog(AppName + '.log')
  end

  def run
    # Driver initialization and method definition
    @driver = SOAP::Driver.new(@log, @logId, NS, @server, @proxy)
    @driver.addMethod('helloWorld', 'from')

    # Method invokation
    puts @driver.helloWorld("Ruby")
  end
end

if __FILE__ == $0
  HelloWorldClient.new('http://localhost:8080/').start
end
```

Writing SOAP4R Services

SOAP4R currently supports two different types of servers:

- CGI/FastCGI based (*SOAP::CGIStub*)
- Standalone (*SOAP::StandaloneServer*)

Both the *SOAP::CGIStub* (defined in "soap/cgistub") and *SOAP::StandaloneServer* (defined in "soap/standaloneServer") classes inherit from *SOAP::Server*, which itself inherits from the *Application* class.

The implementation of a SOAP server hardly differs between a CGI, FastCGI or a standalone one; a general template is given below (replace the occurrences of "XXX" with the appropriate values):

```
require "soap/XXX"
class MyServer < SOAP::XXX
  def methodDef
    addMethod(self, 'add', 'a', 'b')
    # add further service methods here
  end

  def add(a, b)
    a + b
  end
  # add further implementations of service methods here
end


# ..put here the code to start the server..
```

The *methodDef* method is implicitly called from *SOAP::Server's initialize* method and has the purpose of exposing service methods with one of the two following methods (Table 5.9 lists the parameters of *addMethod* and *addMethodWithNS*):

```
SOAP::Server#addMethod(receiver, methodName, *paramArg)
```

or

```
SOAP::Server#addMethodWithNS(namespace, receiver, methodName,
                             *paramArg)
```

Table 5.9 Parameters of addMethod and addMethodWithNS

Parameter	Explanation
receiver	The object that contains the *methodName* method. If you define the service methods in the same class as the *methodDef* method, this parameter is *self*.
methodName	The name of the method that is called due to a RPC request. It is a *String*.
paramArg	Specifies, when given, the parameter names and parameter modes. It takes the same values as the parameter with the same name of the *SOAP::Driver#addMethod* method (see Table 5.6).
namespace	Overwrites the default namespace you specified with the second argument to *SOAP::Server#initialize* for the current method.

To demonstrate the usage of *inout* or *out* parameters, imagine the following service method that takes two parameters (*inParam* and *inoutParam*), returns one *normal* return value (*retVal*) and two further parameters: *inoutParam* and *outParam*:

```
def aMeth(inParam, inoutParam)
  retVal     = inParam + inoutParam
  outParam   = inParam - inoutParam
  inoutParam = inParam * inoutParam
  return retVal, inoutParam, outParam
end
```

To expose it from within *methodDef*, call:

```
addMethod(self, 'aMeth', [
  %w(in     inParam),
  %w(inout  inoutParam),
  %w(out    outParam),
  %w(retval return)
])
```

At this point, we complete the template from the beginning of the section and implement three working SOAP servers. We start with a CGI-based server:

```ruby
#! /usr/bin/env ruby
require "soap/cgiStub"

class MyCGIServer < SOAP::CGIStub
  def methodDef
    addMethod(self, 'add', 'a', 'b')
    addMethod(self, 'div', 'a', 'b')
  end

  # handler methods -----------------
  def add(a, b) a + b end
  def div(a, b) a / b end
end

if __FILE__ == $0
  server = MyCGIServer.new("CGIServer", "urn:ruby:test1")
  server.start
end
```

The arguments to *MyCGIServer.new* are the application's name (this is similar to *SOAP::Driver.new*'s *logId* parameter) and the default namespace for all via *addMethod*-exposed service methods. The application's name distinguishes multiple servers using the same log file.

We should mention here that a CGI-based server has one major disadvantage: performance. It gets even worse if it needs to query a database, because each request has to establish a new connection unless a persistent connection mechanism is used (such as using DRb).

Below the same example using FastCGI is shown. For more information about the FastCGI module, see Eli Green's homepage at http://fenris.codedogs.ca/~eli/fastcgi.html, or alternatively, the RAA entry *FastCGI* in the Library section, under *WWW*.

```ruby
#! /usr/bin/env ruby
require "soap/cgiStub"

class MyFastCGIServer < SOAP::CGIStub
  # ..same as for the CGI-based server..
```

```
end

if __FILE__ == $0
  require "fcgi"          # or "fastcgi"

  server = MyFastCGIServer.new("FastCGIServer", "urn:ruby:test2")

  FCGI.each_request do |f|
    $stdin = f.in
    server.start
  end
end
```

The implementation of a standalone server is very similar, except that the constructor takes two further parameters, *host* and *port*. The standalone server shown in Figure 5.8 exposes one service method, *getInfoFromName*, which returns the result-set of a SQL query (using Ruby/DBI. See Chapter 3). Note that we established only one database connection for all requests; so to prevent concurrent access, we have to use a *Mutex*. The source code of this application can also be found at www.syngress.com/solutions, under the file named *dbserver.rb*.

Figure 5.8 Standalone SOAP Server (dbserver.rb)

```
require "soap/standaloneServer"
require "dbi"            # for database access
require "thread"         # for Mutex

# change to appropriate values!
DB_URL  = 'dbi:Mysql:database=testdb'
DB_USER = 'UserName'
DB_PASS = 'MySecret'

class DBServer < SOAP::StandaloneServer

  def initialize(appname, namespace, host, port)
    super
```

Continued

Figure 5.8 Continued

```
    @mutex = Mutex.new

    # establish database connection
    @dbh = DBI.connect(DB_URL, DB_USER, DB_PASS)

    # use build-in logging features
    log( SEV_INFO,
        "Established database connection <#{DB_URL}>" )

    # prepare SQL query (change this appropriately)
    sql = "SELECT * FROM test WHERE name = ?"
    @query = @dbh.prepare(sql)
  end


  def methodDef
    addMethod(self, 'getInfoFromName', 'name')
  end


  def shutdown
    @dbh.disconnect
    log( SEV_INFO,
        "Closed database connection <#{DB_URL}>" )
  end


  # handler methods --------------------------------

  def getInfoFromName(name)
    result = @mutex.synchronize { @query.execute(name) }
    result.to_a unless result.nil?
  end


end # class DBServer
```

Continued

Figure 5.8 Continued

```
if __FILE__ == $0
  server = DBServer.new('SOAP-Server', 'urn:ruby:dbserv',
                        'localhost', 8080)
  server.start
  server.shutdown    # closes database connection
end
```

Once the server was started with the *start* method, it will serve until the process receives a SIGHUP signal (for example, by typing *kill -HUP pid* at the command-line).

Exceptions

To return a *SOAP Fault* from a service method instead of a regular return value, simply raise an exception. SOAP4R will use the exceptions' *message* attribute as the value for the *faultString* tag and will pass the marshaled exception in the *detail* tag. This way, a SOAP4R client is able to reconstruct the original exception by unmarshaling the *detail* tag.

Server-side Logging

By default, logging is enabled because the *SOAP::Server* class inherits from *Application*. The default logging device is *StdErr*. Thus, using a CGI or FastCGI-based server, the log messages are written to the Web server's error log file (for example, */var/log/httpd/error_log* in Apache). To change the logging device and other logging-related parameters, the *Application* class provides the public *setLog* method which takes the same parameters as *Log.new* (see Table 5.7). For example, to disable the nerving log messages of our "Hello World" SOAP service (see Figure 5.3) we could set the log device to */dev/null* respectively to a Windows equivalent, by simply adding the line:

```
server.setLog('/dev/null')
```

SOAP Datatypes and Type-Conversion

SOAP and Ruby use different representations for datatypes as well as different names, value ranges and semantics. For this reason, SOAP4R must perform a translation from Ruby to SOAP types and vice versa. This takes place in the following manner:

1. SOAP4R converts a *build-in* Ruby object into a special type defined in module *SOAP* (For example: *SOAPInt, SOAPString, SOAPArray*), also called *SOAP4R type* (see Table 5.9).

2. It converts the SOAP4R types into SOAP's XML encoding (see Table 5.10).

The XML namespaces we use in the two tables are as follows:

```
xsi     = http://www.w3.org/2001/XMLSchema-instance

xsd     = http://www.w3.org/2001/XMLSchema

xsd1999 = http://www.w3.org/1999/XMLSchema

n1      = http://schemas.xmlsoap.org/soap/encoding/

n2      = http://xml.apache.org/xml-soap

rb      = http://www.ruby-lang.org/xmlns/ruby/type/1.6
```

Of course, step one only takes place if the object is not yet a SOAP4R type. The translation from SOAP's XML representation into Ruby objects is similar — simply reverse the two steps.

By default, SOAP4R uses the 2001 XML Schema Definitions. To use the 1999 XML Schema Definitions, require the file *soap/XMLSchema1999* just after *soap/driver*, *soap/cgistub*, *soap/server* or *soap/standaloneServer*.

Table 5.9 Conversion from "Build-in" Ruby Types to SOAP4R Types

"Build-in" Ruby Type	SOAP4R type
NilClass (nil)	SOAPNil
TrueClass, FalseClass (true, false)	SOAPBoolean
Integer (Fixnum, Bignum)	SOAPInt, SOAPLong, SOAPInteger
Float	SOAPFloat
String	SOAPString
Date, Time	SOAPDateTime
Array	SOAPArray
Hash, Struct	SOAPStruct

Table 5.10 Conversion from SOAP4R Types to SOAP's XML Encoding

SOAP4R type (range)	SOAP's encoding (XMLSchema 1999)
SOAPNil	xsi:nil="true" (xsi:null="1")
SOAPBoolean	xsi:type="xsd:boolean"
SOAPInt (-2^31 to 2^31-1)	xsi:type="xsd:int"
SOAPInteger	xsi:type="xsd:integer"
SOAPLong (-2^63 to 2^63-1)	xsi:type="xsd:long"
SOAPFloat (32 bit)	xsi:type="xsd:float"
SOAPDouble (64 bit)	xsi:type="xsd:double"
SOAPDecimal	xsi:type="xsd:decimal"
SOAPString	xsi:type="xsd:string"
SOAPBase64	xsi:type="n1:base64"
SOAPHexBinary	xsi:type="xsd:hexBinary"
SOAPDate	xsi:type="xsd:date"
SOAPTime	xsi:type="xsd:time"
SOAPDateTime	xsi:type="xsd:dateTime" (xsi:type="xsd1999:timeInstant")
SOAPArray	xsi:type="n1:Array"
SOAPStruct (from Struct)	xsi:type="rb:Struct..*Classname*"
SOAPStruct (from Hash)	xsi:type="n2:Map"

Instead of passing a built-in Ruby type to a remote procedure, you could also directly pass a SOAP4R type. Below we create some SOAP4R types directly:

```
aLong     = SOAP::SOAPLong.new( 123_456_789_012_345 )

anInt     = SOAP::SOAPInteger.new( 123456789 )

aDecimal = SOAP::SOAPDecimal.new( "-123456789.012345678" )

aFloat    = SOAP::SOAPFloat.new( 123.456 )


aHex      = SOAP::SOAPHexBinary.new( "binary string" )

aBase64   = SOAP::SOAPBase64.new( "binary string" )


aDate     = SOAP::SOAPDate.new( Date.today )

aTime     = SOAP::SOAPTime.new( Time.now )
```

Creating Multi-dimensional or Typed SOAP Arrays

Ruby has no built-in multi-dimensional arrays. Despite this fact, we can encode a Ruby *Array* as a multi-dimensional SOAP array:

```
three_dim_ary = [ [ [1,2], [3,4] ], [ [5,6], [7,8] ] ]
obj = SOAP::RPCUtils.ary2md(three_dim_ary, 3)
# now pass "obj" as argument to a SOAP-RPC
```

SOAP::RPCUtils.ary2md takes two further parameters that let you specify the element's datatype and one to specify the mapping registry to use:

```
SOAP::RPCUtils.ary2md( ary, rank, typeNamespace = SOAP::XSD::Namespace,
   type = SOAP::XSD::AnyTypeLiteral,
   mappingRegistry = SOAP::RPCUtils::MappingRegistry.new )
```

By default, the elements are of the type *anyType*, but you may specify another type and namespace. See the *soap/XMLSchema* file for existing namespaces and type literals.

The *ary2soap* method behaves similarly to *ary2md*, with the difference that it creates one-dimensional arrays.

```
SOAP::RPCUtils.ary2soap( ary, typeNamespace = SOAP::XSD::Namespace,
   type = SOAP::XSD::AnyTypeLiteral,
   mappingRegistry = SOAP::RPCUtils::MappingRegistry.new )
```

To create a typed SOAP array whose elements are *String* objects, we'd write:

```
ary = ["this", "is", "an", "array"]
obj = SOAP::RPCUtils.ary2soap( ary, SOAP::XSD::Namespace,
   SOAP::XSD::StringLiteral )
```

Creating User-defined Datatypes

Creating user-defined datatypes with SOAP4R is very easy: all you have to do is specify a *type name* (class variable *@@typeName*) and a *type namespace* (class variable *@@typeNamespace*) for your own class that distinguishes it from others. For various reasons, you should include the *SOAP::Marshallable* module into the class. Below we implement the user-defined *Human* datatype with the type name *human* and the namespace *urn:ruby-dev-guide*:

```
class Human
  include SOAP::Marshallable

  @@typeName      = 'human'
  @@typeNamespace = 'urn:ruby-dev-guide'

  attr_reader :name, :sex, :birth

  def initialize( name, sex, birth = Date.now )
    @name, @sex, @birth = name, sex, birth
  end

  def say( text = "hello" )
    print @name, " says '#{text}'.\n"
  end
end
```

An instance of this class in SOAP's XML encoding would look like Figure 5.9 (without the SOAP envelope).

Figure 5.9 Sample Human Class in SOAP's XML Encoding

```
<Human xmlns:n2="urn:ruby-dev-guide" xsi:type="n2:human">
  <birth xsi:type="xsd:dateTime">1815-01-01T00:00:00Z</birth>
  <sex xsi:type="xsd:string">f</sex>
  <name xsi:type="xsd:string">Ada Lovelace</name>
</Human>
```

More formally, SOAP4R proceeds as follows to convert the instance to XML:

- **Type name** of object *obj* is examined as:

  `@typeName || @@typeName || obj.class.to_s`

- **Type namespace** is examined as:

  `@typeNamespace || @@typeNamespace ||`
  `'http://www.ruby-lang.org/xmlns/ruby/type/custom'`

Then it generates a *SOAPStruct* containing the instance variables of the object as key/value pairs and with the *type name* and *type namespace* as examined above. Finally, SOAP4R converts the *SOAPStruct* into XML, as usual.

The conversion back from such a user-defined datatype encoded in XML to a Ruby object is a bit more complicated. Therefore, SOAP4R performs the following steps:

1. It first tries to find a class with the capitalized *type name* (xsi:type argument; *human* in the example above) as name. If this fails it returns a *Struct*.

2. If the class was found and includes the *SOAP::Marshallable* module, it returns an object of this class.

3. If the class was found but do not include the *SOAP::Marshallable* module, the class must have, for each instance variable, an attribute writer method and an *initialize* method callable without parameters. If both are present, a new object of that class is created and returned, otherwise a *Struct* is returned.

Now back to our example. In step one, the *xsi:type* value is *human*. Capitalized, this is "Human." Therefore, SOAP4R searches for and finds a class named *Human*. In step 2, it checks whether this class includes the module *SOAP::Marshallable*, which is true; thus it returns an object of class *Human*.

What would happen if the *type name* differs from the class name in Ruby? Imagine that in our above example the *xsi:type* argument would have been "n5:human_type" instead of "n5:human". SOAP4R would capitalize "human_type" to "Human_type", but it wouldn't find a class *Human_type*; it would fail in Step one and return a *Struct::Human_type* object.

A solution for this problem is presented in the next section.

Changing the Default Type-Mapping

SOAP4R gives you the ability to customize the mapping between Ruby and SOAP types. There are two possible ways:

■ Extend the *SOAP::RPCUtils::MappingRegistry::UserMapping* array. This has a global effect.

■ Set the *mappingRegistry* attribute of *SOAP::Driver* or *SOAP::Server* instances to an object of the *SOAP::RPCUtils::MappingRegistry* class. This only affects the particular object.

For instance, to map an *Integer* to a *SOAPLong* (64 bit integer), we could write:

```
MR    = SOAP::RPCUtils::MappingRegistry    # abbreviation
entry = [Integer, SOAP::SOAPLong, MR::BasetypeFactory]


## 1. solution (global effect)
MR::UserMapping << entry


## 2. solution (local effect)
# obj is either a SOAP::Driver or a SOAP::Server object
obj.mappingRegistry = MR.new
obj.mappingRegistry.set( *entry )
```

In the same way, you can change the mappings of all other base datatypes. Compound or array types are a bit more difficult to change.

The following example adds a mapping between the *IntArray* class and a typed *SOAP::SOAPArray* (type and namespace specified by the last element of *entry*) using the *MR::TypedArrayFactory* factory. Note that we use class *SOAP::Marshal* to marshal and unmarshal Ruby objects; you'll read more about this in the section "Using SOAP as Marshaling Format."

```
require "soap/marshal"


MR = SOAP::RPCUtils::MappingRegistry    # abbreviation


class IntArray < Array; end            # Integer-only Array


entry = [
  IntArray, SOAP::SOAPArray, MR::TypedArrayFactory,
  [XSD::Namespace, XSD::IntLiteral]
]


MR::UserMapping << entry


# ------ test the mapping ------


obj  = IntArray[1, 2, 3]
```

```
str  = SOAP::Marshal.marshal(obj)
obj2 = SOAP::Marshal.unmarshal(str)


puts "before: #{obj.inspect} : #{obj.type}"
puts "after:  #{obj2.inspect} : #{obj2.type}"
```

This outputs:

```
before: [1, 2, 3] : IntArray
after:  [1, 2, 3] : IntArray
```

Do you remember the problem we discussed at the end of the section "Creating User defined Datatypes?" We got a *Struct::Human_type* instead of an instance of the *Human* class due to the type name "human_type". The following mapping fixes this:

```
Human, SOAP::SOAPStruct, MR::TypedStructFactory, ['urn:ruby-dev-guide',
   'human_type']
```

Note that if you add such an entry to the mapping registry, the class variables *@@typeNamespace* and *@@typeName* of the *Human* class become superfluous.

There is even more possible with the mapping registry; to gather more information about it, take a look at the file *soap/mappingRegistry.rb*.

Using SOAP as Marshalling Format

SOAP's specification consists of three (independent) parts:

- The SOAP envelope.
- The encoding rules.
- The RPC representation.

In this section, we'll use only the first two parts of SOAP without the RPC representation, to store Ruby objects as a human readable XML document. For this purpose, SOAP4R provides two class methods of *SOAP::Marshal*, defined in the file *soap/marshal*:

```
str = SOAP::Marshal.marshal( obj,
   mappingRegistry = SOAP::RPCUtils::MappingRegistry.new )
```

to marshal *obj* into a string representation, and

```
obj = SOAP::Marshal.unmarshal( str,
  mappingRegistry = SOAP::RPCUtils::MappingRegistry.new,
  parser          = SOAP::Processor.loadParser )
```

to unmarshal *str* back to a Ruby object. The *mappingRegistry* parameter provides a way to change the default mapping between Ruby and SOAP types (see the earlier section "Changing the Default Type-Mapping").

In the following example, we marshal some instances of the *Human* class and store the resulting XML document in the humans.xml file (see Figure 5.10):

```ruby
require "soap/marshal"

class Human
  include SOAP::Marshallable

  @@typeName      = 'human'
  @@typeNamespace = 'urn:ruby-dev-guide'

  attr_reader :name, :sex, :birth

  def initialize( name, sex, birth = Date.now )
    @name, @sex, @birth = name, sex, birth
  end

  def say( text = "hello" )
    print @name, " says '#{text}'.\n"
  end
end


people = [
  Human.new( 'Ada Lovelace',    'f', Date.new(1815) ),
  Human.new( 'Albert Einstein' 'm', Date.new(1879,3, 14) )
]

File.open( 'humans.xml', 'w+' ) do |f|
  f << SOAP::Marshal.marshal( people )
```

```
end
```

Then we unmarshall the XML representation back to Ruby objects:

```
require "soap/marshal"

class Human
  # ..same as above..
end

str     = File.readlines( 'humans.xml' ).to_s
people = SOAP::Marshal.unmarshal( str )

p people[0]
p people[1]
```

This outputs:

```
#<Human:0x80c9548 @birth=#<Date: 4767949/2,0,2299161>, @sex=
    "f", @name="Ada Lovelace">
 #<Human:0x80c7ae0 @birth=#<Date: 4814845/2,0,2299161>, @sex=
    "m", @name="Albert Einstein">
```

Figure 5.10 SOAP XML Representation of Marshaled Ruby Objects

```
<?xml version="1.0" ?>
- <env:Envelope xmlns:xsi="http://www.w3.org/2001/XMLSchema-instance"
   xmlns:env="http://schemas.xmlsoap.org/soap/envelope/"
   xmlns:xsd="http://www.w3.org/2001/XMLSchema">
 - <env:Body>
   - <Array n1:arrayType="xsd:anyType[2]"
      env:encodingStyle="http://schemas.xmlsoap.org/soap/encoding/"
      xsi:type="n1:Array" xmlns:n1="http://schemas.xmlsoap.org/soap/encoding/">
     - <item xmlns:n2="urn:ruby-dev-guide" xsi:type="n2:human">
        <birth xsi:type="xsd:dateTime">1815-01-01T00:00:00Z</birth>
        <sex xsi:type="xsd:string">f</sex>
        <name xsi:type="xsd:string">Ada Lovelace</name>
       </item>
     - <item xmlns:n3="urn:ruby-dev-guide" xsi:type="n3:human">
        <birth xsi:type="xsd:dateTime">1879-03-14T00:00:00Z</birth>
        <sex xsi:type="xsd:string">m</sex>
        <name xsi:type="xsd:string">Albert Einstein</name>
       </item>
     </Array>
   </env:Body>
  </env:Envelope>
```

Project: A SOAP Authentification Server

How we can make sure that only authorized users are allowed to access our SOAP services? As we have seen in the section "Securing XML-RPC Services," we could use HTTP authentication. Implementing this for SOAP4R wouldn't be that hard, but we want to take another approach: Authentication at the application level instead of at the HTTP protocol layer.

The method we will use for Authentication works with symmetrical keys, and can be described as follows:

1. The user sends his username to the Authentication server.

2. The Authentication server creates a "nonce" (a random number), and sends this back to the user.

3. The user encrypts the nonce with his password and sends this back to the Authentication server.

4. The Authentication server compares the initial created nonce encrypted with the users password and the nonce sent by the user. If both are equal, the user has been successfully authenticated.

To implement this in Ruby we need:

1. A random number generator: We will use a simple linear congruence generator for this.

2. An encryption algorithm: We will use RC4 for this.

Ideally both the random number generator and the encryption algorithm should be cryptographically secure, whereas the algorithms we use are not!

First let us implement a linear congruence generator (LCG). LCGs generate sequences of pseudo random numbers and are described with the following equation:

$X(n) = (a * X(n-1) + b) \bmod m$

X(n) is the nth created random number, and *X(n-1)* is its forerunner. Variable *a* is the multiplier, *b* the increment and *m* the modulo; all three are constant values. There are several good values for *a*, *b* and *m* and they differ in the period of the generated sequence. We choose for *a*, *b* and *m* the values *2416, 374441* and *1771875* respectively, which result in a generator with a maximal period of *m*, that is, all numbers from 0 to 1771874 are generated in a pseudo random order.

```
# file: lcg.rb
# Linear Congruence Generator
class LCG
  def initialize(seed=Time.now.to_i, a=2416, b=374441, m=1771875)
    @x, @a, @b, @m = seed % m, a, b, m
  end
  def next() @x = (@a * @x + @b) % @m end
end
```

It follows the implementation of the encryption algorithm RC4:

```
# file: rc4.rb
# RC4, algorithm by Ron Rivest (RSA)
# symetrical algorithm (stream cipher)
class RC4

  def RC4.crypt(key, str)
    RC4.new(key).crypt(str)
  end

  def initialize(key)
    raise "Empty key" if key.empty?

    s, j = (0..255).to_a, 0
    k = (key * ((256 / key.size)+1))[0,256].unpack('C*')

    for x in 0..255 do
      j = (j + s[x] + k[x]) & 0xFF
      s[x], s[j] = s[j], s[x]
    end
    @i, @j, @s = 0, 0, s
  end

  def crypt(str)
    str = str.dup
    (0...(str.size)).each {|i| str[i] ^= next_rand }
```

```
      str
   end


   private # -----------------------------


   def next_rand
     i, j, s = @i, @j, @s
     i = (i + 1) & 0xFF
     j = (j + s[i]) & 0xFF
     s[i], s[j] = s[j], s[i]
     t = (s[i] + s[j]) & 0xFF
     @i, @j = i, j
     s[t]
   end

end
```

Figure 5.11 shows the implementation of our SOAP Authentication server. It can be divided into two parts: The Authentication model implemented by the *Auth* class (it does the hard work), and the standalone SOAP server, which exposes the two methods *initAuth* and *validateAuth* as SOAP services.

Figure 5.11 The SOAP Authentication Server (auth.rb)

```
# The SOAP Authentication Server
require "md5"
require "lcg"        # linear congruence generator
require "rc4"        # RC4 encryption algorithm
require "thread"     # for Mutex


class Auth
  def initialize(user_info, ticket_life=30, gc_interval=120)
    @user_info   = user_info
    @ticket_life = ticket_life
```

Continued

Figure 5.11 Continued

```ruby
    @rng           = LCG.new
    @rng_mutex     = Mutex.new

    @nonce_list  = {}
    @nonce_mutex = Mutex.new

    # garbage collects @nonce_list
    install_gc(gc_interval)
  end

  def initAuth(user)
    pass = @user_info[user]
    return nil if pass.nil?

    nonce, nonce_enc = nonce_pair(pass)
    @nonce_mutex.synchronize {
      @nonce_list[nonce_enc] = [user, Time.now + @ticket_life]
    }
    nonce
  end

  def validateAuth(enc_nonce)
    user, time = @nonce_mutex.synchronize {
      @nonce_list.delete(enc_nonce)
    }
    (time.nil? or Time.now > time) ? nil : user
  end

  private # --------------------------------------

  def install_gc(interval)
    Thread.new {
```

Continued

Figure 5.11 Continued

```
      loop do
        sleep interval
        @nonce_mutex.synchronize {
          @nonce_list.delete_if {|k, v| Time.now > v[1] }
        }
      end
    }
  end

  def nonce_pair(pass)
    rng       = @rng_mutex.synchronize { @rng.next }
    nonce     = MD5.new(rng.to_s).hexdigest
    nonce_enc = Auth.enc_nonce(pass, nonce)
    [nonce, nonce_enc]
  end

  # class methods ------------------

  def self.enc_nonce(pass, nonce)
    MD5.new(RC4.crypt(pass, nonce)).hexdigest
  end

end


if __FILE__ == $0
  require "soap/standaloneServer"

  class AuthServer < SOAP::StandaloneServer

    USERS = {
      'john'  => 'ahgr',
```

Continued

Figure 5.11 Continued

```
      'wayne' => 'h98xh'
    }

    def methodDef
      auth = Auth.new(USERS)
      addMethod(auth, 'initAuth',      'user')
      addMethod(auth, 'validateAuth', 'enc_nonce')
    end
  end

  # start SOAP AuthServer
  server = AuthServer.new('Auth-Server', 'urn:ruby:authsvr',
    ARGV[0] || 'localhost', (ARGV[1] || 9876).to_i)
  server.start
end
```

Note that we prevent concurrent access to the variables *@rng* and *@nonce_list* by making use of two instance of the *Mutex* class stored in *@rng_mutex* and *@nonce_mutex*. Furthermore, we run a concurrent thread (started by the *install_gc* method) that every *n* seconds activates and removes timed-out nonces.

To authenticate, we use the model illustrated in Figure 5.12. The SOAP client requests a nonce (*initAuth*) from the SOAP authserver (1). It encrypts this nonce with its password and sends it to the SOAP service (2). To validate the encrypted nonce sent by the client, the SOAP service calls *validateAuth* of the SOAP authserver (3). If the Authentication succeeded, the SOAP service can proceed with its original task and sends the result to the client (4).

To test the SOAP Authentication Server, we'll adapt our "Hello World" client/server application and add Authentication to it.

Here is the source code for the server:

```
# file: ahw_s.rb
require "soap/standaloneServer"
require "soap/driver"
```

```ruby
module AuthMixin

  AUTH_NS  = 'urn:ruby:authsvr'
  AUTH_URL = 'http://localhost:9876/'

  class UnauthorizedError < Exception; end

  def setupAuth
    @auth = SOAP::Driver.new(nil, nil, AUTH_NS, AUTH_URL)
    @auth.addMethod('initAuth', 'user')
    @auth.addMethod('validateAuth', 'enc_nonce')

    addMethod(self, 'initAuth', 'user')
  end

  def initAuth(user)
    @auth.initAuth(user)
  end

  private

  def validate(enc_nonce)
    raise UnauthorizedError unless @auth.validateAuth(enc_nonce)
  end

end

class HelloWorldServer < SOAP::StandaloneServer
  include AuthMixin

  def methodDef
    addMethod(self, 'helloWorld', 'enc_nonce', 'from')
  end
```

```ruby
  def helloWorld(enc_nonce, from)
    validate(enc_nonce)
    return "Hello World, from #{ from }!"
  end
end



if __FILE__ == $0
  server = HelloWorldServer.new('HelloWorld-Server',
    'urn:ruby:hello-world', 'localhost', 8080)


  server.setupAuth
  server.start
end
```

And here the client's source code:

```ruby
# file: ahw_c.rb
require "soap/driver"
require "auth"          # for Auth.enc_nonce

USER, PASS = 'john', 'ahgr'

driver = SOAP::Driver.new(nil, nil, 'urn:ruby:hello-world',
  'http://localhost:8080/')

driver.addMethod('helloWorld', 'enc_nonce', 'from')
driver.addMethod('initAuth', 'user')

nonce = driver.initAuth(USER)                # get nonce from service
enc_nonce = Auth.enc_nonce(PASS, nonce)    # encrypt nonce with password

puts driver.helloWorld(enc_nonce, "Ruby") # call the service
```

The source code for all applications presented in this section appear at www.syngress.com/solutions.

Figure 5.12 Authentication Model

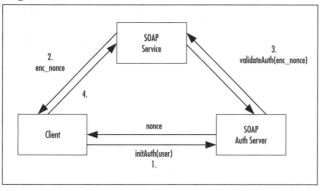

Using Distributed Ruby

What Remote Method Invocation (RMI) is to Java programmers, Distributed Ruby (DRb) is to Ruby programmers. With DRb, a Ruby application can transparently call the methods of remote objects simply by doing a method call. DRb was written by Masatoshi Seki in pure Ruby and is only around 500 lines long. To install it on your computer, download it from RAA (it's the *druby* entry in the Library section, under *comm*), extract it and invoke *install.rb*.

DRb uses a *front server architecture*. That means that every DRb application, be it a client or server, runs a front server (a *TCPServer*) that acts as interface to exposed Ruby objects. A DRb server initially exposes exactly one object, the *front* object, whereas a DRb client does not expose any object explicitly—this is the only difference between a client and a server.

A client that makes contact for the first time with a DRb server can only access its front object. This object's methods may return other remote objects, which the client can then access directly. The client's front-server comes into play when you (as client) pass an object as argument to a remote method, which is either an instance of a non-marshalable class like *IO, File, Process, Proc, Thread,* or an object that includes the *DRbUndumped* module and thus should be passed as reference and not as value (to pass an object as reference simply include the *DRbUndumped* module into its class). In this case, DRb wraps the object's ID together with the front-server's URI in a *DRbObject*, marshals this, and passes it to the server. If the server (or better yet, one of its methods) calls a method of this object, it turns into a client, and the client into a server.

Let's have a look at an example, for which we'll use the obligatory "Hello World" application. The source code of the server is given below:

```
require "drb/drb"

uri = ARGV.shift || 'druby://0.0.0.0:0'

class HelloWorld
  def helloWorld() "Hello World from DRb!" end
end

DRb.start_service(uri, HelloWorld.new)
puts DRb.uri
puts '[return] to exit'
gets
```

The call to *DRb.start_service* is important. Its first parameter specifies the URI of the front server to start, and the second parameter specifies the front object to expose. If the URI is *nil* then DRb generates its own URI (which we output using *DRb.uri*). Similarly, when the URI specifies a port number of 0 (as in *druby://0.0.0.0:0*), DRb searches for a port number which is not in use and uses it. We use an IP number of 0.0.0.0 if no other URI is given on the command line. It gets replaced by the IP address of the machine where you start the application.

Now for the "Hello World" client application:

```
require "drb/drb"

uri = ARGV.shift

DRb.start_service(nil, nil)
ro = DRbObject.new(nil, uri)
puts ro.helloWorld
```

Again, we call *DRb.start_service*, but this time without specifying a URI and without exposing a front object. Note also that we could omit the two *nil* arguments. Then we create a proxy for the remote object exposed by the server with the URI specified by the *uri* variable. Using this object (*ro*) we can call methods of the remote object as we do in the last line.

To run our Hello World application, let us first start the server (file named *hw_s.rb*) with this:

```
ruby hw_s.rb
```

This outputs something similar to the following (port number may vary):

```
druby://0.0.0.0:61782
[return] to exit
```

Now we start the client in another shell:

```
ruby hw_c.rb druby://localhost:61782
```

This outputs:

```
Hello World from DRb!
```

Below, we demonstrate a more advanced example which remotely iterates over the elements of an array:

```
# file_s.rb
require "drb/drb"


front = [1, 2, 3, 4, "aString"]
primary = DRb::DRbServer.new(ARGV.shift, front)
puts primary.uri
primary.thread.join
```

This example also shows the usage of the *DRb::DRbServer* class, which can be used in place of calling *DRb.start_service*; the effect is the same, except that it's now possible to instantiate more than one *DRb::DRbServer*.

The client that iterates over the lines of the exposed *Array* object looks like this:

```
# file_c.rb
require "drb/drb"


primary = DRb::DRbServer.new
ro = DRb::DRbObject.new(nil, ARGV.shift)
ro.each do | elt |
  p elt
end
```

When a remote method is called with a code block, the *Proc* object of the block is passed by reference to the remote method. When the remote method yields control to that code block, it gets executed on the client machine and the result is transferred back to the remote method.

If executing the example above results in a *Connection refused* error, you probably have to change the third line of the client as follows:

```
primary = DRb::DRbServer.new
# to
primary = DRb::DRbServer.new("druby://0.0.0.0:0")
```

Or when calling *DRb.start_service*, this is:

```
DRb.start_service
# to
DRb.start_service("druby://0.0.0.0:0")
```

A Name Server for DRb

A central name server can be very useful if you want to expose more than one object to the client applications. We implement one below:

```
# file: ns.rb
require "drb/drb"

class NS
  def initialize
    @services = {}
  end

  def [](name)
    @services[name]
  end

  def []=(name, obj)
    @services[name] = obj
  end
end

DRb.start_service(ARGV[0], NS.new)
puts DRb.uri
```

```
puts '[enter]'
gets
```

To register or lookup an object from the name server, you have to create a proxy for the remote name server object first, with:

```
require "drb/drb"
DRb.start_service

ns = DRbObject.new(nil, 'druby://here:65333') # modify URI
```

Then you can register or lookup a service. Note that this is usually done in separate processes/applications:

```
# register a service
ns['anArray'] = (1..10).to_a

# lookup a service
ro = ns['anArray']
ro.each { |i| p i }
```

Using DRb to Speed Up CGI Scripts

CGI applications have one major disadvantage: a new process is created for each request, and it's not possible to hold values in memory across multiple requests. To hold information across multiple requests, you have to store them persistently on disk or in a database; or simply use DRb to access a long-running process, which returns the requested data and itself stores them in memory.

In the following examples we'll use DRb to write a page access counter. First, the CGI script shown below demonstrates one possible solution (without using DRb):

```
#!/usr/bin/env ruby

f = File.new('counter', File::CREAT | File::RDWR)
counter = f.gets.to_i
f.rewind
f << (counter + 1).to_s
f.close

puts "Content-type: text/html"
```

```
puts

puts "<html>"

puts "<body>Accessed #{counter} times.</body>"

puts "</html>"
```

Of course, for a simple page access counter, this is probably the best solution, but when storing/retrieving more information (for example, the entries of RAA), reading each instance into memory, modifying them all and then writing them back would be slow. Another example where DRb would be useful is for CGI scripts that have to access an Oracle database; for example, where the time to establish a connection is relatively high (several seconds).

Below, we implement the DRb page access counter service:

```
# file: counter.rb
require "drb/drb"


class Counter
  def self.load(name)
    if test(?e, name)
      new( Marshal.load(File.readlines(name).to_s) )
    else
      new
    end
  end


  def initialize(count = nil)
    @count = count || {}
    @changed, @mutex = false, Mutex.new
  end


  def value(s)
    @count[s] || 0
  end


  def next(s)
    @mutex.synchronize {
```

```
        @changed = true
        @count[s] = value(s) + 1
      }
    end


    def store(name)
      @mutex.synchronize {
        break unless @changed
        File.open(name,'w+') {|f| f << Marshal.dump(@count)}
        @changed = false
      }
    end
  end
end


if __FILE__ == $0
  URI = 'druby://0.0.0.0:12000'


  counter = Counter.load("counter")


  # store all 5 minutes counters to disk
  Thread.new do
    loop {
      sleep 300
      counter.store("counter")
    }
  end


  DRb.start_service(URI, counter)


  puts "[return]"; gets


  # store on exit
  counter.store("counter")
end
```

When running this application, we can access the counter from our CGI script as shown below:

```ruby
#!/usr/bin/env ruby
require "drb/drb"


URI = 'druby://localhost:12000'


DRb.start_service
cnt = DRbObject.new(nil, URI)


puts "Content-type: text/html"
puts
puts "<html>"
puts "<body>Accessed #{ cnt.next('cnt') } times.</body>"
puts "</html>"
```

Using Rinda and Distributed TupleSpaces

Rinda, Ruby's equivalent of Linda (for information on Linda, see www.cs.yale .edu/Linda/linda.html), uses DRb to distribute a *TupleSpace* across a TCP/IP network. A TupleSpace is a space in which you can store arbitrary tuples of any length and type. Three operations are defined on it:

- **in**: Removes a matching tuple from the TupleSpace and returns it.

- **rd**: Same as *in* but does not remove the tuple from the TupleSpace.

- **out**: Stores a tuple in the TupleSpace.

All three operations are performed atomically, that is, they are thread-safe. The pattern-matching on tuples is performed using Ruby's ===; *nil* in a pattern matches everything.

An example of how to use a TupleSpace is shown below, where we implement the consumer-producer scenario that the Petri-Net in Figure 5.13 depicts. (For more about Petri Networks see www.daimi.au.dk/PetriNets or www.cis.um.edu.mt/~jskl/petri.html.) Both the consumer and the producer thread synchronize to each other using the TupleSpace. The tokens in the "Cars" place of Figure 5.13 are represented in the TupleSpace by *car* tuples, and the "Credit" tokens by *credit* tuples, whereas all others are not required.

The transitions of the Petri-Net are marked in the source code below with comments.

```ruby
# file: prod_cons.rb
require "tuplespace"

ts = TupleSpace.new

# init with 2 credits
2.times do
  ts.out ['credit']
end

producer = Thread.new {
  loop do
    # produce
    ts.get ['credit']
    puts "P: produce car"
    sleep 1

    # deliver
    ts.out ['car']
    puts "P: car delivered"
  end
}

consumer = Thread.new {
  loop {
    # consume
    ts.out ['credit']
    puts "C: car ordered"

    # receive
    ts.get ['car']
```

```
      puts "C: car received"

      sleep 4
   }
}


gets
```

Figure 5.13 Petri-Net Consumer-Producer Example

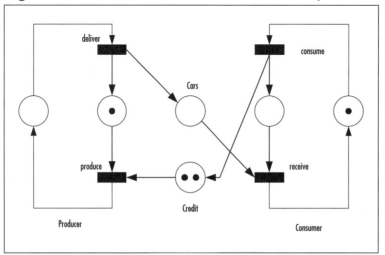

To distribute a TupleSpace, simply expose it via DRb as shown in the example below or invoke the *drb/rinda.rb* file from the command line.

```
# A distributed TupleSpace
require "drb/rinda"

uri = ARGV.shift || 'druby://0.0.0.0:0'

DRb.start_service(uri, TupleSpace.new)
puts DRb.uri
puts '[return] to exit'
gets
```

After starting this, you can access the distributed TupleSpace from everywhere if you know its URI (ARGV[0] below):

```
require "drb"

DRb.start_service

ts = DRbObject.new( nil, ARGV[0] )

# ...
```

Load-Balancing

Suppose we own a computation server, and the number of clients using it reaches a critical limit and slows it down too much. What we could do is either buy a new, faster server to replace the old one, or distribute the load to one or multiple additional servers. The second solution is more flexible and scalable; at any time we can add or remove a server to suit our changing needs.

To balance the requests of multiple clients to multiple servers we make use of a distributed TupleSpace. The server-side code that multiplies two numbers and puts the result back to the TupleSpace is listed below:

```
# file: comp_s.rb
require "drb"

DRb.start_service

ts = DRbObject.new( nil, ARGV[0] )


loop {
  # get a request from the TupleSpace
  req, a, b = ts.in( ['req', nil, nil] )

  # compute the result
  res = a * b

  # to identify the server on the client side
  host = DRb.uri.split('//')[1].split(':')[0]

  # put the result back into the TupleSpace
  ts.out( ['res', a, b, res, host] )
}
```

Start as many servers as you want (even on different machines or located anywhere on the Internet), and pass all the URI of the distributed TupleSpace as the parameter. Now let's write a client that uses any number of servers to perform some multiplications:

```
# file: comp_c.rb
require "drb"
DRb.start_service
ts = DRbObject.new( nil, ARGV[0] )

for a in 6..9 do
  for b in 3..5 do
    ts.out( ['req', a, b] )
  end
end

for a in 6..9 do
  for b in 3..5 do
    _, a, b, res, host = ts.in( ['res', a, b, nil, nil] )
    puts "#{a} * #{b} = #{res}    (#{host})"
  end
end
```

Looking at the output confirms that the load is distributed across multiple computational servers. With five different machines, each running one server application, I got the following output:

```
6 * 3 = 18    (server3)
6 * 4 = 24    (server1)
6 * 5 = 30    (server2)
7 * 3 = 21    (server4)
7 * 4 = 28    (server1)
7 * 5 = 35    (server2)
8 * 3 = 24    (server4)
8 * 4 = 32    (server3)
8 * 5 = 40    (server5)
9 * 3 = 27    (server4)
9 * 4 = 36    (server5)
9 * 5 = 45    (server1)
```

Security Considerations

DRb implements neither encryption nor authentication, but it still has some mechanisms to protect a server against malicious clients. The considerations we must bear in mind when using DRb are:

1. Marshaled objects should not exceed a maximal size. Larger objects should be rejected;

2. We don't want to allow more than a maximum number of arguments to remote methods;

3. We don't want certain methods to be called (e.g. *instance_eval*);

4. We want to allow or deny specific hosts;

5. We want the user to self-authenticate.

6. *DRbObject*s are passed with the object's *id*. If a malicious user changes this id, he or she can get access to objects that should normally not be accessible. We don't want this!

And so what can we do to protect against each of these points?

1. Limit the maximum size a marshaled object may reach, with either the *DRb::DRbServer#load_limit=* or *DRb::DRbServer.default_load_limit* methods;

2. Limit the maximum number of allowed arguments, with the *DRb::DRbServer#argc_limit=* or *DRb::DRbServer.default_argc_limit* methods;

3. Override the *DRb::DRbServer#insecure_methods?* method. This method gets passed a *Symbol* of the called method. Return *true* to disallow calling this method. (Another solution is provided below);

4. Set an Access Control List (ACL) to allow/deny specific hosts. Use *DRb::DRbServer#install_acl* or *DRb::DRbServer.default_acl*;

5. Use Kerberos authentication. Masatoshi Seki's *DRbAuth* implements this on DRb(for information on *DRbAuth*, see www2a.biglobe.ne.jp/~seki/ruby/drbauth-0.9.tar.gz);

6. Write an ID-to-object converter. For Ids, use a cryptographically secure random number generator and store a mapping between the random and the real ID.

In the third point, we mentioned that there is another solution to disallow the calling of specific methods. We can achieve this by using a restricted or a specific delegator:

```ruby
# file: deleg.rb
require "delegate"

class RestrictedDelegator < SimpleDelegator
  def initialize(obj, *without_methods)
    super(obj)
    eval %[
      class << self
        #{ without_methods.collect { |m| "undef :#{m}" }.
                          join("\n") }
      end
    ]
  end
end


class SpecificDelegator
  def initialize(obj, *exposed_methods)
    @obj = obj
    eval %[
      class << self
        #{ exposed_methods.collect { |m|
             "def #{m}(*a, &b)
                @obj.send(:#{m}, *a, &b)
              end"
           }.join("\n")
        }
      end
    ]
  end
end
```

If, for example, we now want to expose an *Array* object but allow the client to only call its *each* and *collect* methods, we could write:

```
obj = [1, 2, 3, 4]


new = SpecificDelegator.new(obj, :each, :collect)


# now pass 'new' to the clients
```

Or if we want to disable only specific methods, e.g. method *freeze*, we could write:

```
obj = [1, 2, 3, 4]


new = RestrictedDelegator.new(obj, :freeze)


# now pass 'new' to the clients
```

Summary

The first section of this chapter covered writing XML-RPC clients and servers, including service-introspection. Furthermore we learned how to use the *MultiCall* extension to increase performance and marshal Ruby objects to a XML-RPC document, as well as how to secure Web services using HTTP Authentication and SSL.

In the following section, we handled many aspects regarding SOAP services, such as writing SOAP client and server applications, client and server-side logging, datatype-conversion, user-defined datatypes, marshaling and more.

The last section covered DRb, Ruby's equivalent to Java's Remote Method Invocation (RMI). We used it to write a little name server for DRb services and a CGI-interface to a DRb page access counter. Furthermore we introduced Rinda – Ruby's version of Linda, which uses DRb to distribute a TupleSpace across a TCP/IP network. We used a Distributed TupleSpace to balance load to multiple servers.

At the end we listed some points and solutions to make DRb more secure.

Solutions Fast Track

Using XML-RPC for Ruby

☑ XML-RPC is a simple, hard-wired XML document type that makes distributed computing as easy as possible. If you want to represent user-defined datatypes with it, you have to misuse a struct (a Hash in Ruby) for this purpose.

Using SOAP for Ruby

☑ The Simple Object Access Protocol (SOAP) is an XML document type for Remote Procedure Calls (RPCs). It uses XML-Namespaces and XML Schemas extensively and allows user-defined datatypes.

Using Distributed Ruby

☑ DRb is Ruby's equivalent to Java's Remote Method Invocation (RMI). It allows for calling the methods of remote objects, even remote iterators.

☑ A Distributed TupleSpace allow for easy communication and synchronization between different threads and processes. Load-Balancing can also be implemented easily.

Frequently Asked Questions

The following Frequently Asked Questions, answered by the authors of this book, are designed to both measure your understanding of the concepts presented in this chapter and to assist you with real-life implementation of these concepts. To have your questions about this chapter answered by the author, browse to **www.syngress.com/solutions** and click on the **"Ask the Author"** form.

Q: I started a server using localhost as host. When I try to connect to it using the IP address 127.0.0.1, I get a *Connection refused* error. What's happening?

A: Try the IP-address 0.0.0.0 as host, which allows each host to connect to the server.

Q: When starting a SOAP server on my Linux machine's port 80, I get a *Permission denied* error.

A: On Unix-like systems, the ports below 1024 are usually reserved for the administrator and cannot be used by a normal user. But it should work if you login as root-user before you start the server.

Q: When calling the *type* method of a remote object using DRb, I get *DRb::DRbObject* as a result instead of the remote objects' type. How can I determine the remote objects' type?

A: Assuming *ro* is the remote object, simply call *ro.method_missing(:type)*. The same works for other methods, too.

Q: I can call methods of a DRb server, but when I call a method with iterator, I get a *Connection refused* error. What's wrong?

A: Pass method *DRb.start_service* a URI containing the special IP 0.0.0.0 as the first parameter and retry.

Q: Using DRb, how can I pass an object by reference instead of by value?

A: Include the module *DRb::DRbUndump* into the objects' class.

Q: I am running Linux and I get a SocketError telling me *getnameinfo: ai_family not supported*. What can I do?

A: You have to recompile your Ruby interpreter (*make* and *make install*), first configuring it with *./configure --enable-ipv6 --with-lookup-order-hack=INET*.

WWW and Networking with Ruby

Solutions in this chapter:

- **Connecting to the Web with Ruby**

- **Looking at WWW and Networking Classes**

- **Using Ruby on the Web**

- **Implementing an Online Shop**

- **Using mod_ruby and eruby**

- **Installing and Configuring IOWA**

☑ **Summary**

☑ **Solutions Fast Track**

☑ **Frequently Asked Questions**

Introduction

Just like Perl, Ruby's reach extends into the field of networking and the Web. When Perl/CGI applications popped up all over the Web, people who were not exactly expectant of the phenomenon failed to react properly. Part of the train of thought driving Ruby, on the other hand, is that it needs to be extensible in order to cover the unexpected—hence we find that Ruby can swim quite well in the world of the Web.

Ruby's socket library is very robust; everything from Network Interface Card (NIC) connections to FTP connections can be configured through this library.

Ruby can also be set up to run within a server like running a standard Perl file through a couple of modules which are readily available, such as eruby and pRuby. There are even a couple of small servers out there that run on pure Ruby.

In this chapter, we'll develop a Web-based, database-driven online-shop application, at first taking a CGI/FastCGI approach, then rewrite the same utilizing mod_ruby and eruby; finally we'll implement it using Interpreted Objects for Web Applications (IOWA), Ruby's powerful application server. Furthermore, we'll show how to apply mod_ruby and eruby for rendering RDF Site Summary (RSS) news channels to an HTML representation or to dynamically generate XML. In the last section, we'll implement a reusable and attractive tree-view component for IOWA.

Go to www.syngress.com/solutions for supplemental material: "Writing a TCP/IP-based server in Ruby" and "Parsing and Creating HTML with Ruby."

Connecting to the Web with Ruby

Like any other network, the Web is one big connection of client-servers; each home computer is a client connecting to a machine acting as a server. All of the "server" machines together, simply put, create what we know today as the Internet. The system used by computers to connect is called the socket system; one can think of them as the endpoints of a bi-directional connection.

Ruby's socket library is very robust; it is split between low-level functions (within the *Socket* class) and high level functions (within the *Net* class).

Low-Level Functions: The Socket Class

The *Socket* class contains all of the information you need to create raw connections. For example, you can use the *IPSocket* class to create a base class that relies on IP to provide transport while *TCPSocket* creates a base class that relies on TCP/IP connections; there's even the *TCPServer* class which awaits all incoming connections, essentially giving you a base class with which to build a Web server.

High-Level Functions: The Net Class

The *Net* class brings with it a lot of ready functionality, such as FTP, HTTP, POP/SMTP, and even Telnet, allowing for quick and easy creation and programming of these services. Its internal ease of use makes writing these applications feel like simple scripting.

POP/SMTP

The Internet mail protocols POP and SMTP are commonly used by developers who want to integrate their applications with an existing and reliable e-mail system. Let's take a look at the simple SMTP application shown in Figure 6.1 (this is also provided at www.syngress.com/solutions in the *smtp.rb* file).

Figure 6.1 SMTP Application (smtp.rb)

```
Require 'net/smtp'

mail = SMTP.new

# -- set smtp server

mail.start ('syngress.com')

# -- create mail; start with "from" field

# -- we're also using "do" to set the rest

# -- of the SMTP process.

mail.read ('you@syngress.com', 'you') do |msg|

# -- write out the subject

msg.write "Subject: hi!\r\n"

# -- jump to body

msg.write "\r\n"

# -- write the body

msg.write "This is the body"

# -- end & send

end
```

With the same simplicity we can write a POP3 interface.

```
Require 'net/pop'

# -- create the pop3 object & connect to the pop3 server
Getmail = Net::POP3.new('pop3.server')

# -- login and start a do loop for emails
Getmail.start('user', 'login') do |Getmail|
   Mailmsg = Getmail.mails[0]

# -- show a list of emails on the server
   Print "From :" + Mailmsg.header.split("\r\n").grep(/^From: /)
   Print "\n"
   Print "Subject: " + Mailmsg.header.split("\r\n").grep(/^Subject: /)
   Print "\n\n""

# -- close connection
end
```

An alternative to using *POP* is using *Net::POPMail*, which is a bit higher-level. *POP* will create the "raw" POP connection but *POPMail* has a more basic set of methods and classes so it is a bit easier to work with when time is of the essence.

HTTP

The *Net* class offers two ways to work with HTTP data: *Net::HTTP* and *Net::HTTPResponse*. *Net::HTTP* handles many of the basic HTTP functions such as retrieving the header using GET and POST in order to send data. You can combine *Net:HTTP* with *Net::HTTPResponse* in order to create some custom code that reacts differently based on responses from the server.

FTP

The *Net* class has a single class for working with FTP, aptly named *Net::FTP*. *Net::FTP* has the basic functionality of an FTP server, such as OPEN, CLOSE, and GET. However, *Net::FTP* has also methods that can output the traffic to and from the server (*debug_mode*), get a file in binary (*getbinaryfile*) or in ASCII (*gettextfile*) mode, login (*login*), and even set the connection as passive (*passive*). Let's take a look at a quick example in Figure 6.2 (the ftp.rb file at www.syngress.com/solutions) that connects us to ftp.simtel.net.

Figure 6.2 Connecting to FTP (ftp.rb)

```
require 'net/ftp'

ftploc=Net::FTP.new('ftp.simtel.net')
ftploc.login

# -- display welcome msg
puts ftploc.welcome
puts "\r\n"

# -- display directory list
puts "Getting list... \n"
puts ftploc.list('*')
puts "\r\n"

# -- chdir to pub
puts "Going to pub... \n"
ftploc.chdir('pub')
puts "\r\n"

# -- list directory in pub
puts "Getting pub list... \n"
puts ftploc.list('*')
puts "\r\n"

# Uncomment the line below & pick a file to
# download. Make sure it's in the right dir!
# IMPORTANT! rename file to a SAFE DIRECTORY
# and a SAFE FILE NAME (i.e. don't accidently
# overwrite something important!)
# ftploc.getbinaryfile('filename', 'saveas')

ftploc.close
```

> **N**OTE
>
> Even though we used ftp.simtel.net in the example in Figure 6.2, any anonymous FTP server will work. Keep in mind that if you want to use ftp.simtel.net you will be redirected to one of many FTP servers in the ftp.simtel.net network; while most mirror networks are 100 percent accurate, you may find some that are missing a minor file (such as a README or a welcome.msg file).

If you are using Windows you can get a more "complete" look at what's going by just redirecting the output to a text file. For example, assuming ftp.rb is on the C:\code directory, the command to run ftp.rb from DOS would appear like this:

```
C:\code> ruby ftp.rb >> debug.txt
```

This would create a file named "debug.txt" in your C:\code directory that you can open and read to view what ftp.rb did when it connected to ftp.simtel.net.

Telnet

The Telnet functionality within Ruby is substantial as well. Basic functions, such as login (*login*), running commands (*cmd*), and a raw write to the server (*write*) are all available. Let's take a look at some dead code to get an idea of how a basic Telnet application would function. In the CD that comes with this book under the Chapter 6 folder (chap06/code) you can find a small but great Telnet client written in Ruby by Mike Wilson (http://members.home.net/wmwilson01/myindex.html) that you can glance over.

> **N**OTE
>
> In order to test the Telnet applications you will need shell access to a server or be running your server and configure it to allow telnet access (port 23). If you do not have a server and are having a hard time finding a shell provider, just use a search engine like Google and do a search for "shell accounts."

Writing a Server in Ruby

If you would like to start writing your own server, the first thing that you need to keep in mind is what type of server architecture you want to follow. We'll take a look at the main three first and then take a look at a small, yet efficient Web server.

Models of Server Architectures

There are three popular and common server models; a server without forking, a server with forking, and a server with pre-forking. Forking is the creation of a child process in response to a request, or because it is needed. Each one of these models has their advantages and disadvantages, as shown in Table 6.1.

Table 6.1 Server Models

Server Model	Advantage	Disadvantage
Server without Forking	Highly portable, no context switching	Does not scale well for multi-processor systems
Server with Forking	Great for machines that can not thread	Constant fork creation increases overhead and resource consumption
Server with Pre-forking	Since forks are just "waiting", it bypasses the fork creation overhead and resource consumption	Mutual exclusion needed in some systems to make it work properly

Server without Forking

Server without forking is a model in which no child processes are created and there is nothing to clean up. It sounds simple but it's actually quite difficult to properly write a stable server without forking that can scale well. Figure 6.3 displays the server without forking model.

The common technique for writing a server that will not fork involves either an array or object array of concurrent connections that the server keeps track of. You can see that you would have to code responses for each object in an array, and at the same time produce diligent and constant clean up to prevent any type of overruns or other ailments associated with an array being bombarded by a thousand connections at a time.

Figure 6.3 Server Without Forking Model

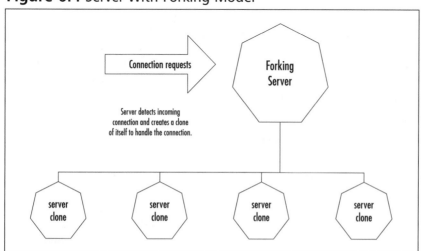

Server with Forking

Server with forking is a model in which the server *forks* a process which is a clone of itself, to handle new connections to the server. Once the connection disconnects, the fork will either be immediately cleaned up or cleaned up following a specific interval. Figure 6.4 displays the server with forking model.

Server with forking commonly requires the knowledge of how to work with child processes. In Ruby you should be able to create clones of the server object itself and keep track of them within a master array.

Figure 6.4 Server With Forking Model

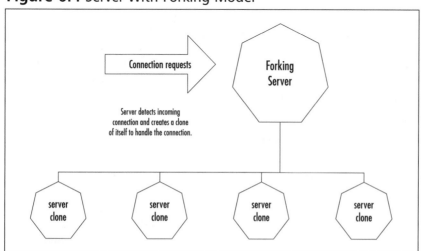

Server with Pre-Forking

Server with pre-forking has become very popular. It is the server model architecture for the Apache Web server, one of the Web's most widely used servers, since version 1.3. Using pre-forking, a "pool" of forks is available at any time without requiring a connection to be initiated. This way, when a connection starts, all the server needs to do is "dip" the connection into the pool and get a fresh fork for the connection. This is essentially a server with forking without the requirement of the creation process. Figure 6.5 displays the server with pre-forking model.

Figure 6.5 Server With Pre-Forking Model

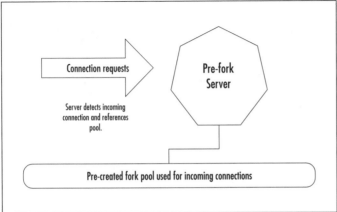

Basic Web Servers Using Ruby

There are several Web servers that rely completely on Ruby. Many of these servers supply what appear to be bare-bones support but that is because many are still under development; however, most have support for CGI. The current Ruby Web servers that are stable are the following:

- httpd by Michel van de Ven
- httpserv by Michael Neumann

There are also a couple of other servers that are in alpha or beta stages of development:

- wwwsrv.rb by Yoshinori Toki
- wwwd by ringo

And, believe it or not, there's even an upcoming game server developed for MUD/RPG games called MUES (pronounced "muse")–check it out at http://mues.faeriemud.org.

Building your own Web server can be extremely simple and fulfilling as well. A good place to start would be by looking at the httpd code as well as the httpserv code. Let's take a quick look at the httpserv code as an example.

```ruby
#! /usr/bin/env ruby
# A simple HTTP-server
# $Id: httpserv.rb,v 1.5 2001/06/02 11:46:58 michael Exp $
# Michael Neumann (neumann@s-direktnet.de)


# -- required classes
require 'cgi'
require 'socket'
# -- for some weird reason, I needed to copy mime to the
# -- Ruby library directory for it to work.
require 'mime'


# -- load config file
unless ARGV.size == 1
  puts "USAGE: #$0 config-file"
  exit 1
else
  begin
    load ARGV[0]
  rescue LoadError => err
    puts "Couln't load config-file #{err.to_s}"
    exit 2
  end
end


Thread.abort_on_exception = true


# -- declare our header versions
```

```ruby
SERVER_SOFTWARE = "httpserv (1.0)"

CGI_VERSION = "CGI/1.1"

HTTP_PROTOCOL = "HTTP/1.0"

ENDL = "\r\n"


# -- notice how the environment variable is
# -- read from the Config file
ENV["DOCUMENT_ROOT"] = Config::DOCUMENT_ROOT

ENV["GATEWAY_INTERFACE"] = CGI_VERSION

ENV["SERVER_NAME"] = "localhost"
# -- again, the SERVER_PORT variable is
# -- read from the Config file
ENV["SERVER_PORT"] = Config::HTTP_PORT.to_s

ENV["SERVER_PROTOCOL"] = HTTP_PROTOCOL

ENV["SERVER_SOFTWARE"] = SERVER_SOFTWARE


ENV["REMOTE_HOST"] = ""

ENV["REMOTE_ADDR"] = ""

ENV["REMOTE_IDENT"] = ""

ENV["AUTH_TYPE"] = ""

ENV["PATH_INFO"] = ""               # Not Used



# -- Get the MIME types supported on the server
$mime = MIME::open(Config::MIMETYPES_FILE)



# returns true if line is empty
def empty_line? (line)
   line == nil or line =~ /^(\n|\r)/
end


def _header(status_nr, status_code, header_hash)
  buf = format("%s %d %s", HTTP_PROTOCOL, status_nr, status_code) + ENDL
```

```ruby
    header_hash.each do |key,val|
      buf += format("%s: %s", key, val) + ENDL if val != nil
    end
    return buf
  end


  def header( mime_type, length = nil )
    _header(200, "OK", {
      "Content-Type"   => mime_type,
      "Content-Length" => length,
      "Server"         => SERVER_SOFTWARE,
      "Connection"     => "close",
      "Date"           => CGI::rfc1123_date(Time.now)
    })
  end


  # f, sock
  def copy_data_from_to(from, to)
    while (buf=from.read 1)
    to.write buf
    print buf if $DEBUG
    #while ! from.eof?
    #   buf = from.read 1 #1024
    #   to.write buf
    #   print buf if $DEBUG
    end
  end


  def process_request( command, path, protocol, hash, sock )

    ENV["CONTENT_TYPE"] = hash["CONTENT-TYPE"] || ""
    ENV["CONTENT_LENGTH"] = hash["CONTENT-LENGTH"] || ""
```

```
ENV["HTTP_ACCEPT"] = hash["ACCEPT"] || ""
ENV["HTTP_REFERER"] = hash["REFERER"] || ""
ENV["HTTP_USER_AGENT"] = hash["USER-AGENT"] || ""
ENV["REQUEST_METHOD"] = command

Config::URL_MAPPING.each do |map_re, map_url|
  # mostly a string is used => convert it into Regexp
  if map_re.is_a? String
    map_re = /^#{Regexp.escape(map_re)}/
  end

  if path =~ map_re then
    ENV["REQUEST_URI"] = path
    path = map_url
    break    # only one mapping
  end
end


path =~ /^(.*?)(\?(.*))?$/
whole_path = $1
query = $3 || ""
whole_path =~ /^(.*?)\/([^\/]*)$/
only_path = $1
script_name = $2


ENV["QUERY_STRING"] = query
ENV["SCRIPT_NAME"] = script_name
path_translated = Config::DOCUMENT_ROOT + only_path.gsub("/"
    , Config::PATH_SEP)
ENV["PATH_TRANSLATED"] = path_translated
file = path_translated + Config::PATH_SEP + script_name
```

```ruby
    script_name =~ /\.([^\.]*)$/
    file_ext = $1 || ""
    mime_type = $mime.mimetype_for_extension(file_ext) || "unknown"

    if $DEBUG then
      puts "path: #{path}"
      puts "whole_path: #{whole_path}"
      puts "query: #{query}"
      puts "only_path: #{only_path}"
      puts "script_name: #{script_name}"
      puts "path_translated: #{path_translated}"
      puts "file: #{file}"
      puts "file_ext: #{file_ext}"
      puts "mime_type: #{mime_type}"
    end

    # file is a script (recognize later by mime-type)
    if ["rb", "cgi"].include? file_ext then
        # examine first line of the script #!...
        prog = ""
        File.open(file,"r") do |f|
          if f.readline =~ /^#!(.*)$/ then
          prog = $1
        else
            # Error!
        end
        end
        puts "prog: #{prog}" if $DEBUG

        # executes the script and prints its output into the socket
        pipe = IO::popen("#{prog} #{file}", "r+")
        if command == "POST" then
            pipe.print sock.read(ENV["CONTENT_LENGTH"].to_i)
        end
```

```ruby
          if script_name =~ /^nph/ then
              copy_data_from_to(pipe, sock)
          else
              data_from_pipe = pipe.read
              puts data_from_pipe if $DEBUG
              sock.print data_from_pipe
          end
      else
          size = File::size(file)
          puts "size: #{size}" if $DEBUG
          head = header( mime_type, size )
          puts head if $DEBUG

          p sock if $DEBUG

          sock.print head
          sock.print ENDL

          # returns the whole file
          File::open(file,"r") {|f|
              f.binmode
              copy_data_from_to(f, sock)
          }
      end
end


def handle_request(new_sock)
    begin
        sock = new_sock
        hostname, ip_addr = sock.addr[2..3]

        # read first line and parse it
```

```ruby
      line = sock.readline
      if line =~ /^(\S+)\s+(\S+)\s+(\S+)/
          puts "command: #{$1}, path: #{$2}, protocol: #{$3}" if $DEBUG

          command = $1
          path = $2
          protocol = $3
      end

      hash = {}
      # params which goes over more than one line not yet implemented!
      # read all parameter
      while not empty_line?(line=sock.readline)
          if line =~ /^([\w-]+):\s*(.*)$/
              hash[$1.upcase] = $2.strip
          #elsif line =~ /^\s+(.*)$/
          end
      end

      process_request( command, path, protocol, hash, sock )
      sock.close
      print sock, " closed\n" if $DEBUG
   rescue
      print "Internal Server Error\n"
      p sock
      p path
      puts $!
      puts $@
      #exit
   end
 end

puts "host: #{Config::HTTP_HOST}, port: #{Config::HTTP_PORT}"
server = TCPserver.open(Config::HTTP_HOST, Config::HTTP_PORT)
```

```
print "wait for connections...\n\n"
while true do
   new_sock = server.accept
   print new_sock, " accepted\n" if $DEBUG

   if Config::THREADED
     Thread.start { handle_request(new_sock) }
   else
     handle_request(new_sock)
   end
end
```

Using Ruby on the Web

Now that we have taken a look at how Ruby can work with the functionality that the Web offers, such as network connections, FTP clients, and Web servers, we can start looking at how Ruby can be used to provide Web content and dynamic interaction to Web clients. This perhaps illustrates Ruby's versatility better than the networking protocols Ruby supports.

Perl and CGI, by nature, are stand-alone applications that are scripted, exactly like Ruby. However, since Ruby is a full OOP language, it can take advantage of its flexible structure and apply itself to any existing system of Web application development, such as scripting or templating.

As a scripting language, Ruby provides several approaches for generating HTML for Web sites that PHP can not perform. In this section we'll take a look at these solutions briefly. Specifically, we are going to take a look at solutions that Ruby can use to generate, to provide a scripting language, and to provide a template solution for HTML.

NOTE

The programmatic or code-embedding solutions are not usable for larger projects or Web sites for which the programmer and designer are two different individuals. Also of note is that many of the items we are going to look at as far as scripting and templates are still in some sort of developmental phase. If you want to use them, make sure it is on a non-essential server and running Linux for best results.

Generating HTML with Ruby

Ruby can generate HTML in any number of ways, the most basic of which is just like a standard CGI script; just run a Ruby file that has the information in it to generate the HTML page. If you are accustomed to CGI, however, Ruby has a built-in class library containing CGI methods that can be used to maximize your capabilities on a Linux/Unix machine. Let's use both standard Ruby and the Ruby CGI class to generate a simple HTML page that reads "Hello World" with the following structure:

```
<HTML>
<HEAD>
<TITLE>Generated World HTML</Title>
</HEAD>
<BODY>
HELLO WORLD!
</BODY>
</HTML>
```

Ruby HTML Code Generation

Ruby can generate HTML easily by using the standard IO, **print**. Figure 6.6 displays our simple code (found at www.syngress.com/solutions in the hello1.rb file in the html directory):

Figure 6.6 Ruby HTML Code Generation (hello1.rb)

```
print "HTTP/1.0 200 OK\r\n"
print "Content-type: text/html\r\n\r\n"
print "<html>"
print "<head>"
print "<title>Hello World - Pure Ruby!</title>"
print "</head>"
print "<body>"
print "Hello World!"
print "</body>"
print "</html>"
```

Ruby CGI HTML Generation

You can also use Ruby's *CGI* class to generate and interact with users of your Web page. The *CGI* class functions with a very "natural" flow: Each section of a standard HTML page when passed with the *CGI* class is a method that returns the output of the method, and they follow a specific order. For example:

```
cgi.out    #--all the stuff under here is printed
{
    cgi.html #-- the <HTML> tag start point
    {
        cgi.head #-- the <head> tag
        {
            #head-relevant code here
        } #-- close <head> tag

        cgi.body #-- the <body> tag
        {
            #body-relevant code here
        } #-- close <body> tag
    } #-- close <html> tag
} #-- close cgi output
```

Instead of kicking out a simple "Hello World" page, let's present the user with a form page that can display a certain form or message depending on whether or not the **Submit** button is pressed; if the button is pressed that means that a message has been input and a new page will be displayed with the new message and no visible form. Notice the use of string concatenation with the different CGI methods after the use of cgi.html.

```
require "cgi"
cgi = CGI.new("html3")

#-- let's see if the "text" variable has been filled
    # if it's been filled then we can assume the form
    # has been filled out. This can be implemented better
    # but works as a visible action example.
cgi.out
```

```
{
    cgi.html
    {
        cgi.head{ "\n"+cgi.title{"CGI Form Page"} +
        cgi.body
        {
            if cgi['text'] == ""
              cgi.form
                {
                   cgi.h2 {"form area"} +
                   cgi.textarea("text") +
                   cgi.br +
                   cgi.submit
                }
            else
              cgi.h2 {"The text is: "} +
              cgi.br +
              cgi.h1 { cgi['text'] }
            end
        }
    }
}
```

Scripting With Ruby Using eruby and ERb

As we mentioned earlier, Ruby can be used as a scripting language in a variety of ways. Eruby and ERb allow you to embed your Ruby code within an HTML file, like PHP or ASP; it essentially allows Ruby to be treated as a script file. Eruby files end with the .rhtml extension. A simple eruby file may look like this:

```
<HTML>
<HEAD>
<TITLE>ERuby Sample</TITLE>
</HEAD>
<BODY>
Hello <% print "coder!" %>
```

```
</BODY>
</HTML>
```

Eruby does not only need "<%" in order to work; you can start a line with the prefix "%" and Ruby will automatically compile the line information and display the output. In our previous code we used **<% print "coder!" %>** after **Hello** to display an HTML page that read "Hello coder!" Let's try to do it again, but let's see how it would look like with the simple "%":

```
<HTML>
<HEAD>
<TITLE>ERuby Sample</TITLE>
</HEAD>
<BODY>
% print "Hello Coder!"
</BODY>
</HTML>
```

Obviously you need to be careful with how you use the percentage symbol when working with eruby!

Templating With Ruby

Templating is a method that allows you to separate your Ruby code from your HTML code yet be able to access it through tags on your HTML page; this creates an abstraction layer between presentation (HTML files, or templates) and the actual content (Ruby code). Some templating solutions have the Ruby code inline while other templating solutions have a Ruby file which in turns calls the HTML file.

Using the HTML/Template Extension

HTML/Template has been coded by Tomohiro Ikebe and it is currently in version 0.15 beta (it will work fine if you are testing it out, but don't test it on important items). It can be found at the RAA in the Library section under *HTML*.

HTML/Template works by referencing the Ruby file with the HTML/Template code, which in turn references the HTML file where the "template" of the output is stored. Let's take a look at "Hello, World" with HTML/Template, shown in Figures 6.7 and 6.8.

Figure 6.7 Hellot.rb

```
require "html/template"

# -- it's good coding practice with HTML/Template
     # to name the HTML file the same as the
     # Ruby source.
hellot = HTML::Template.new("hellot.html")

# -- this is where you declare any variables that
     # are viewed
hellot.param
(
  {
    "msg" => "Hello World!"
  }
)

# -- let's output the file
     # HTML/Template will read the HTML file
     # and output the Ruby code according to
     # the way it's presented in the HTML file.
print "Content-Type: text/html\n\n"
print hellot.output
```

Figure 6.8 Hellot.html

```
<HTML>
<HEAD><TITLE>Hello World, HTML/Template Style!</TITLE></HEAD>
<BODY>
<FONT FACE="Arial, Helvetica" Size="2"><!var:msg></FONT>
</BODY>
</HTML>
```

Using Ruby-tmpl

Ruby-tmpl can work alone or can be combined with mod_ruby to provide slightly faster results. Just like HTML/Template, it provides an abstraction layer between content and templates. Ruby-tmpl includes the following features:

- Recursive file includes
- Custom error messages
- Removal of whitespace from output (munging)
- Default values for variable substitution
- XML-compliant template tag syntax

It was written by Sean Chittenden and can be found at the RAA in the Library section under *WWW/textproc*.

Putting It All Together

Web templating and scripting solutions for Ruby allow us to create robust and exciting applications online that previously may have been limited. It's also very nice to have an alternative to PERL/CGI come out in the last couple of years that has already shown that it can handle the rigors we usually place on those languages. Let's take a look at an online shopping application using various Ruby applications we have worked with.

Implementing an Online Shopping Application

In this section we'll implement a CGI and FastCGI-based online shop. We'll use a PostgreSQL database to store the articles, orders, and customers, and use sessions and cookies to hold information about the articles in the shopping cart across multiple requests. Figure 6.9 illustrates our sample application. All examples and files shown in this section can also be found on the accompanying CD in the *online-shop* directory; the Ruby source files and CGI scripts reside in the *src* sub-directory, the SQL scripts in the *sql* subdirectory, and the images in the *images* subdirectory.

Figure 6.9 The Online Shop Example

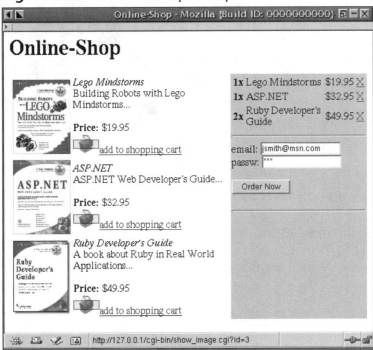

Designing the Data Model

The organization of the tables (the data model) used by the online shop application is shown in Figure 6.10. A *customer* can place an arbitrary number of orders. Each *order* consists of at least one order item. An *order item* stores the ID of the ordered article and the quantity ordered. The *inventory* stores the current stock of an article, whereas the *article* stores the name, description, and price, and a link to the *picture* of the article.

Figure 6.11 lists the SQL script for PostgreSQL (file sql/create.sql) that creates the necessary tables and sequences. Note that all table and column names should be lowercase when using a PostgreSQL database; if this is not the case, you have to surround them with double quotes whenever you use them in an SQL statement. We attended to this implementation detail of PostgreSQL and converted the table and column names as used in Figure 6.10 to lowercase, and inserted underscores whenever the case changes.

Figure 6.10 Data Model of the Online Shop

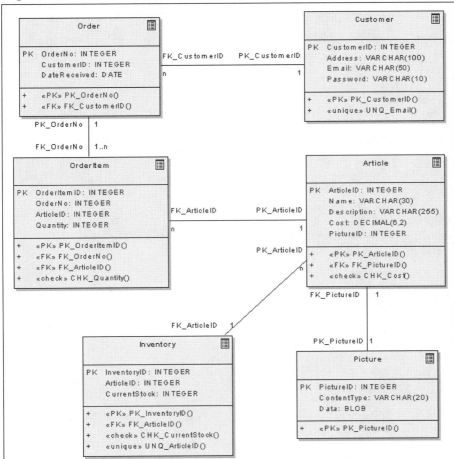

Figure 6.11 SQL Script to Create Tables and Sequences (sql/create.sql)

```
CREATE SEQUENCE seq_customer_id;

CREATE SEQUENCE seq_picture_id;

CREATE SEQUENCE seq_article_id;

CREATE SEQUENCE seq_inventory_id;

CREATE SEQUENCE seq_order_no;

CREATE SEQUENCE seq_order_item;


CREATE TABLE customer (
  -- Columns
```

Continued

Figure 6.11 Continued

```
  customer_id    INTEGER NOT NULL DEFAULT NEXTVAL('seq_customer_id'),
  address        VARCHAR(100) NOT NULL,
  email          VARCHAR(50) NOT NULL,
  password       VARCHAR(10) NOT NULL,
  -- Constraints
  CONSTRAINT pk_customer_id PRIMARY KEY (customer_id),
  CONSTRAINT unq_email UNIQUE (email)
);


CREATE TABLE picture (
  -- Columns
  picture_id    INTEGER NOT NULL DEFAULT NEXTVAL('seq_picture_id'),
  content_type VARCHAR(20) NOT NULL,
  data          OID,
  -- Constraints
  CONSTRAINT pk_picture_id PRIMARY KEY (picture_id)
);


CREATE TABLE article (
  -- Columns
  article_id    INTEGER NOT NULL DEFAULT NEXTVAL('seq_article_id'),
  name          VARCHAR(30) NOT NULL,
  description   VARCHAR(255),
  cost          DECIMAL(6,2) NOT NULL,
  picture_id    INTEGER,
  -- Constraints
  CONSTRAINT pk_article_id PRIMARY KEY (article_id),
  CONSTRAINT fk_picture_id FOREIGN KEY (picture_id)
                            REFERENCES picture,
  CONSTRAINT chk_cost CHECK (cost::FLOAT >= 0.0)
);


CREATE TABLE inventory (
  -- Columns
  inventory_id   INTEGER NOT NULL DEFAULT NEXTVAL('seq_inventory_id'),
```

Continued

Figure 6.11 Continued

```
   article_id     INTEGER NOT NULL,
   current_stock INTEGER NOT NULL,
   -- Constraints
   CONSTRAINT pk_inventory_id PRIMARY KEY (inventory_id),
   CONSTRAINT fk_article_id FOREIGN KEY (article_id)
                                 REFERENCES article,
   CONSTRAINT unq_article_id UNIQUE (article_id),
   CONSTRAINT chk_current_stock CHECK (current_stock >= 0)
);


CREATE TABLE "order" (
   -- Columns
   order_no       INTEGER NOT NULL DEFAULT NEXTVAL('seq_order_no'),
   customer_id    INTEGER NOT NULL,
   date_received DATE NOT NULL DEFAULT 'now',
   -- Constraints
   CONSTRAINT pk_order_no PRIMARY KEY (order_no),
   CONSTRAINT fk_customer_id FOREIGN KEY (customer_id)
                              REFERENCES customer
);


CREATE TABLE order_item (
   -- Columns
   order_item_id INTEGER NOT NULL DEFAULT NEXTVAL('seq_order_item'),
   order_no       INTEGER NOT NULL,
   article_id     INTEGER NOT NULL,
   quantity       INTEGER NOT NULL,
   -- Constraints
   CONSTRAINT pk_order_item_id PRIMARY KEY (order_item_id),
   CONSTRAINT fk_order_no FOREIGN KEY (order_no)
                        REFERENCES "order",
   CONSTRAINT fk_article_id FOREIGN KEY (article_id)
                                 REFERENCES article,
   CONSTRAINT chk_quantity CHECK (quantity > 0)
);
```

The Database Access Layer

We use a single class that handles all interaction with the database tables. This is the *DB* class defined in file *src/db.rb* (see Figure 6.12). It provides several methods that we'll use later to insert new customers, orders, or articles into the database or for querying the same:

- **new_article**: This method first inserts the supplied image into the *picture* table, then inserts a new row into the *article* table, and finally one row into the *inventory* table. If any action should fail, all operations are rolled back.

- **new_customer**: Creates a new customer.

- **new_order**: Places a new order. Touches the *order* and *order_item* tables.

- **get_customer_id**: Returns the customer's ID that matches the supplied e-mail and password.

- **get_articles_in_inventory**: Returns all articles of the inventory.

To make the same work with a MySQL database or any other database, you probably have only to change the private method *next_val*. This method returns the next value of the sequence specified by the parameter. Using a MySQL database, you have to use here in the SQL statement *last_insert_id* and a column type of *auto_increment* or something similar.

Figure 6.12 The Database Access Layer, Class DB (src/db.rb)

```
require "dbi"
require "config"
require "forwardable"


class DB

  attr_reader :connection


  def DB.connect(url = DB_URL, user = DB_USER, pass = DB_PASS)
    DBI.connect(url, user, pass, 'AutoCommit' => false) do |dbh|
      # create new instance of class DB and yield it to outer program
      yield DB.new(dbh)
```

Continued

Figure 6.12 Continued

```ruby
    end
  end

  def initialize(connection)
    @connection = connection
  end

  def new_article(name, description, cost, current_stock,
                  picture_content_type, picture_data)

    transaction do
      # 1. insert picture
      execute(
        sql_insert_into('picture', :picture_id, :content_type, :data),
        picture_id = next_val('seq_picture_id'),
        picture_content_type, DBI::Binary.new(picture_data) )

      # 2. insert article
      execute(
        sql_insert_into('article', :article_id, :name, :description,
          :cost, :picture_id),
        article_id = next_val('seq_article_id'),
        name, description, cost, picture_id )

      # 3. insert inventory
      execute(
        sql_insert_into('inventory', :inventory_id, :article_id,
          :current_stock),
        inventory_id = next_val('seq_inventory_id'),
        article_id, current_stock )
    end
  end
```

Continued

Figure 6.12 Continued

```
def new_customer(address, email, password)
  transaction do
    execute(
      sql_insert_into('customer', :customer_id, :address,
        :email, :password),
      customer_id = next_val('seq_customer_id'),
      address, email, password )
  end
end


def new_order(customer_id, article_id_quant)
  transaction do
    execute(
      sql_insert_into('"order"', :order_no, :customer_id),
      order_no = next_val('seq_order_no'),
      customer_id )

    article_id_quant.each do |id, quant|
      execute(
        sql_insert_into("order_item", :order_no, :article_id,
          :quantity),
        order_no, id, quant )
    end
  end
end


def get_customer_id(email, password)
  connection.select_one("SELECT customer_id FROM customer
    WHERE email=? AND password=?", email, password)[0]
end


def get_articles_in_inventory
```

Continued

Figure 6.12 Continued

```ruby
    sql = "SELECT a.* FROM article a, inventory i
            WHERE a.article_id = i.article_id"
    connection.select_all(sql)
  end


  private


  def next_val(sequence)
    connection.select_one("SELECT NEXTVAL('#{sequence}')")[0]
  end


  def sql_insert_into( table, *fields )
    "INSERT INTO #{ table } (" +
      fields.map{|f| f.to_s}.join(",") +
    ") VALUES ("   +
      fields.map{'?'}.join(",") +
    ")"
  end


  extend Forwardable
  def_delegators(:@connection, :execute, :execute)
  def_delegators(:@connection, :transaction, :transaction)
end
```

Initializing the Database

Now it's time to insert some customers and articles into the empty database. But before we can do this, we have to execute the SQL script shown in Figure 6.11. To do this, invoke Ruby/DBI's interactive SQL shell *sqlsh.rb* as shown below (modify database name, user, and password):

```
echo "\q" | ruby sqlsh.rb dbi:Pg:db —file sql/create.sql user pass
```

The **echo "\q"** is necessary in order to leave sqlsh.rb after the SQL script is executed. For convenience, we wrote a Makefile (see Figure 6.13) that does this job—and much more—with a simple **make create**. The src/config.rb file which is included by the Makefile (and by the online shop application) is listed below; you have to modify it appropriately to match your database settings. Also modify the second and third line of the Makefile.

```
# file: src/config.rb

# modify these values to your database settings
DB_URL  = 'dbi:Pg:michael'
DB_USER = 'michael'
DB_PASS = 'michael'
```

After having initialized the database (with **make create**), we insert some customers and articles into it; For this purpose we write a Ruby script (src/db-init.rb at www.syngress.com/solutions), shown in Figure 6.14. Execute it by invoking the Makefile with **make db-init** or change into the *src* directory and execute **ruby db-init.rb**.

Figure 6.13 Makefile

```
include src/config.rb

SQLSH=/usr/local/bin/sqlsh.rb        # modify
TARGET=/home/michael/htdocs          # modify


CGI_FILES  = src/shop.cgi src/shop2.cgi src/show_image.cgi
FCGI_FILES = src/shop.fcgi src/show_image.fcgi
RB_FILES   = src/components.rb src/config.rb src/db.rb src/session.rb


all: db-init install


install:
    cp ${CGI_FILES}  ${TARGET}/cgi-bin
    cp ${FCGI_FILES} ${TARGET}/cgi-bin
    cp ${RB_FILES}   ${TARGET}/cgi-bin


    cp images/trolley.gif ${TARGET}
```

Continued

Figure 6.13 Continued

```
db-init: drop create
    (cd src; ruby db-init.rb)

drop:
    echo "\q" | ${SQLSH} ${DB_URL} --file sql/$@.sql \
        ${DB_USER} ${DB_PASS}
create:
    echo "\q" | ${SQLSH} ${DB_URL} --file sql/$@.sql \
        ${DB_USER} ${DB_PASS}
```

SYNGRESS syngress.com

Figure 6.14 The Database Initialization Script (db-init.rb)

```
require "db"

DB.connect do |db|
  # add two customers
  db.new_customer(
    'John Smith, Downing Street 1, Little Rock, Arkansas',
    'jsmith@msn.com',
    '123'
  )
  db.new_customer('James Last', 'last@yahoo.com', 'secret')

  # add three articles
  db.new_article(
    'Lego Mindstorms', 'Building Robots with Lego Mindstorms...',
    19.95, 1000,
    'image/gif', File.readlines('../images/mindstorm.gif').to_s
  )
  db.new_article(
    'ASP.NET', "ASP.NET Web Developer's Guide...",
    32.95, 500,
```

Continued

Figure 6.14 Continued

```
   'image/jpg', File.readlines('../images/aspnet.jpg').to_s
 )
 db.new_article(
   "Ruby Developer's Guide", 'A book about Ruby in Real World
       Applications...',
   49.95, 1200,
   'image/jpg', File.readlines('../images/rdg.jpg').to_s
 )
end
```

Developing the Web Interface

This section develops the *view* and *controller* of our online shop application. It mainly consists of the two files *shop.cgi* (Figure 6.15) and *components.rb* (Figure 6.16). The first is the CGI script that is directly invoked by the Web server when the user opens up his or her browser at http://yourhost/cgi-bin/shop.cgi. The second implements classes that generate the HTML code and react on user actions:

- *Component*: Is the base class of all other classes.

- *Article*: Generates the output of one article.

- *ArticleList*: Uses the *Article* class to output multiple articles.

- *Cart*: Displays the HTML code for the shopping cart on the right.

- *MainPage*: Outputs the whole page using the *ArticleList* and *Cart* classes.

- *Controller*: This class is special because it does not generate HTML code. Instead it performs actions like adding an article to the shopping cart, or performing an order when the user clicks one of the **Add to shopping cart** links, clicks on the **X** to remove an article from the cart, or on the **Order** button on the right side. As we don't want to see something like "shop.cgi?add=1" in the URL of our browser, we redirect after performing an action to shop.cgi.

We use a session object to hold the articles in the cart, and pass the session ID around using cookies. In file *session.rb* (Figure 6.17) we extend the standard session class *CGI::Session* and enable it to store marshaled Ruby objects instead of just strings.

There's one further CGI script, *show_image.cgi* (Figure 6.18), which you'll recognize if you've read Chapter 3. Its purpose is to view an article's picture, which is stored in the database in the *picture* table. It will respond with the image data when it is passed the picture's ID.

Before you can open up your browser to see the online shop in action, you'll have to install the CGI scripts and the Ruby files into your Web server's *cgi-bin* directory. Do this by invoking the already introduced Makefile (Figure 6.13) with **make install**. Also make sure that the CGI scripts are world readable and executable (**chmod 755 *.cgi**), otherwise it will not work. Now open up your browser, point it to http://yourhost/cgi-bin/shop.cgi, and enjoy!

Figure 6.15 The Online Shop CGI Script (file src/shop.cgi)

```ruby
#!/usr/bin/env ruby
require "session"
require "components"


session = Session.new(cgi = CGI.new("html4"), SESSION_PARAMS)


puts Controller.new(cgi, session).output
```

Figure 6.16 Implement the View and Controller (src/components.rb)

```ruby
require "db"


class Component
  attr_reader :cgi, :session
  def initialize(cgi, session)
    @cgi, @session = cgi, session
  end


  def url(path, params={})
    str = params.collect {|k, v| "#{k}=#{v}"}.join('&')
    if str.empty?
```

Continued

Figure 6.16 Continued

```
      path
    else
      path + "?" + str
    end
  end

  def script_name(params={})
    url(cgi.script_name, params)
  end
end

class Article < Component
  attr_accessor :row

  def output
    img_url  = url('show_image.cgi', 'id' => row[:picture_id])
    cart_url = script_name('add' => row[:article_id])
    trolley_url = '/trolley.gif'

    cgi.table { cgi.tr {

      cgi.td {
        cgi.a('target' => '_new', 'href' => img_url) {
          cgi.img('src' => img_url, 'width' => '90',
                  'height' => '113', 'border' => '0') }
      } +

      cgi.td {
        cgi.i {row[:name] } + cgi.br + row[:description] + cgi.br +
        cgi.br + cgi.b { 'Price: ' } + "$#{ row[:cost] }" +
        cgi.br + cgi.a('href' => cart_url) {
          cgi.img('src' => trolley_url, 'border' => '0') +
                  'add to shopping cart' } }
      }
```

Continued

Figure 6.16 Continued

```ruby
      }
    end
  end

class Cart < Component
  attr_accessor :articles

  def output
    article_ids = {}
    articles.each { |i| article_ids[ i[:article_id] ] = i }

    cart = session['cart'] || {}

    cgi.table {
      cart.map do |id, count|
        cgi.tr {
          a = article_ids[id]
          cgi.td { cgi.b {"#{ count }x"} } +
          cgi.td { a[:name] } +
          cgi.td { '$' + a[:cost] } +
          cgi.td {
            cgi.a('href' => script_name('drop' => id)) {'X'}
          }
        }
      end.to_s
    } +
    cgi.hr +
    cgi.form('action' => script_name()) {
      'email: ' + cgi.text_field('name' => 'email') + cgi.br +
      'passw: ' + cgi.password_field('name' => 'password') + cgi.br +
      cgi.br + cgi.submit('value' => 'Order Now', 'name' => 'order')
    } + cgi.hr
  end
end
```

Continued

Figure 6.16 Continued

```ruby
class ArticleList < Component
  attr_accessor :articles

  def output
    article = Article.new(@cgi, @session)
    articles.collect do | row |
      article.row = row
      article.output
    end.join("")
  end
end

class MainPage < Component
  attr_accessor :articles
  def output
    cgi.html {
      cgi.head { cgi.title {'Online-Shop'} } +
      cgi.body {
        cgi.h1 {'Online-Shop' } +
        cgi.table {
          cgi.tr {
            cgi.td('valign' => 'top', 'width' => '50%') {
              al = ArticleList.new(cgi, session)
              al.articles = articles
              al.output
            } +
            cgi.td('bgcolor' => '#CCCCCC', 'valign' => 'top',
                   'width' => '25%') {
              c = Cart.new(cgi, session)
              c.articles = articles
              c.output
            } } } } }
  end
end
```

Continued

Figure 6.16 Continued

```ruby
class Controller < Component
  def output
    cart = session['cart'] || Hash.new(0)

    if id = cgi['add'][0]
      # add article to cart
      cart[id.to_i] += 1

    elsif id = cgi['drop'][0]
      # drop article from cart
      cart.delete(id.to_i)

    elsif cgi['order'][0]
      # place order
      DB.connect do |db|
        cust_id =
db.get_customer_id(cgi['email'][0],cgi['password'][0])
        db.new_order(cust_id, cart)
      end
      cart = nil     # empty the cart

    else
      # show the online-shop
      mp = MainPage.new(cgi, session)
      mp.articles = DB.connect { |db| db.get_articles_in_inventory }
      return cgi.header('pragma' => 'no-cache') + mp.output

    end

    # store the cart back to the session and redirect
    session['cart'] = cart
    cgi.header('status' => 'REDIRECT', 'Location' => script_name())
  end
end
```

Figure 6.17 Extended Session Class (src/session.rb)

```ruby
require "cgi/session"

SESSION_PARAMS = {
  'session_key' => 'sid',
  'prefix'      => 'online-shop'
}

class Session < CGI::Session
  def [](key)
    if val = super then Marshal.load(val) else val end
  end
  def []=(key, val)
    super(key, Marshal.dump(val))
  end
end
```

Figure 6.18 Display an Article's Image Stored in the Database
(src/show_image.cgi)

```ruby
#!/usr/bin/env ruby

require "cgi"
require "db"

BLK_SIZE = 8 * 1024

cgi = CGI.new
id = cgi["id"][0].to_i

DB.connect do |db|
  dbh = db.connection
  row = dbh.select_one("SELECT data, content_type FROM picture WHERE " +
                       "picture_id = ?", id)
```

Continued

Figure 6.18 Continued

```
stream = dbh.func(:blob_open, row['data'])

puts "Content-Type: %s"    % row['content_type']
puts "Content-Length: %s" % stream.size
puts "Date: %s"            % Time.now
puts "Expires: %s"         % (Time.now + 3*60) # cache images three
                                               # minutes
puts
loop {
  data = stream.read(BLK_SIZE)
  print data; $stdout.flush
  break if data.size != BLK_SIZE
}
  stream.close
end
```

Improving the Online Shop

There are lots of things we can do to improve the online shop. Here is a short "wish list:"

- Use URL-rewriting (make the session ID a part of the URL) instead of cookies to pass the session ID between multiple requests, like many online shops.

- Use FastCGI instead of CGI to increase performance.

- Use a templating toolkit instead of class CGI to generate the HTML code.

- Extend the data model. Add a *category* table and extend the *article* table to store more information about an article. Also decrement the *current_stock* field of the *inventory* table when fulfilling an order.

In the following we'll implement the first two points. Because we designed our application so carefully, the first point is very easy to implement. All we have to do is to modify method *script_name* of the *Component* class and add the session ID to the URL:

```
class Component
  alias old_script_name script_name
  def script_name(params={})
    params[ SESSION_PARAMS['session_key'] ] = session.session_id
    old_script_name(params)
  end
end
```

This results in the file *shop2.cgi* shown in Figure 6.19. Now our online shop works with every browser, whether cookies are enabled or not, even in a text-mode browser like w3m or Links.

Figure 6.19 Online Shop with URL Rewriting (src/shop2.cgi)

```
#!/usr/bin/env ruby
require "session"
require "components"

class Component
  alias old_script_name script_name
  def script_name(params={})
    params[ SESSION_PARAMS['session_key'] ] = session.session_id
    old_script_name(params)
  end
end


session = Session.new(cgi = CGI.new("html4"), SESSION_PARAMS)


puts Controller.new(cgi, session).output
```

The second item in our "wish list" was to make our online shop work with FastCGI as a protocol instead of CGI. FastCGI is much faster, due to the lack of process creation and because we can hold the session data in memory instead of storing it to disk.

File *shop.fcgi* (see Figure 6.20) implements the FastCGI version of our online shop. Some important tasks we must address include the following:

1. Use *CGI::Session::MemoryStore* instead of the default database manager for storing sessions.

2. Assign *f.in* to *$stdin*.

3. Add a singleton method *binmode* to *$stdin*. This is only required when you use the *CGI* class and the script is invoked with the HTTP POST method (as is the case in our example when the user presses the **Order** button).

4. Remove the *CGI_PARAMS* and *CGI_COOKIES* constants from the *CGI* class.

Finally, Figure 6.21 implements *show_image.fcgi*, the FastCGI version of *show_image.cgi* (Figure 6.18). It uses one connection to the database for all requests, instead of one for each picture as with the CGI version. Also, don't forget to modify file components.rb where you'll change the URL to the FastCGI version.

Figure 6.20 FastCGI Version of the Online Shop (src/shop.fcgi)

```ruby
#!/usr/bin/env ruby
require "session"
require "components"
require "fcgi"      # or "fastcgi"

SESSION_PARAMS['database_manager'] = CGI::Session::MemoryStore

FCGI.each_request {|f|
  $stdin = f.in
  def $stdin.binmode() end     # required for HTTP POST method

  session = Session.new(cgi = CGI.new("html4"), SESSION_PARAMS)

  f.out << Controller.new(cgi, session).output

  # remove constants of class CGI
  class CGI
    remove_const :CGI_PARAMS
    remove_const :CGI_COOKIES
  end
}
```

Figure 6.21 FastCGI Version of show_image.cgi (src/show_image.fcgi)

```ruby
#!/usr/bin/env ruby

require "db"
require "fcgi"      # or "fastcgi"


BLK_SIZE = 8 * 1024

DB.connect do |db|
  dbh = db.connection

  FCGI.each_request do |f|
    id = ENV['QUERY_STRING'].split("=")[1].to_i
    row = dbh.select_one("SELECT data, content_type FROM picture
                          WHERE picture_id = ?", id)

    stream = dbh.func(:blob_open, row['data'])

    f.out << "Content-Type: %s\r\n"   % row['content_type']
    f.out << "Content-Length: %s\r\n" % stream.size
    f.out << "Date: %s\r\n"           % Time.now
    f.out << "Expires: %s\r\n"        % (Time.now + 3*60)
    f.out << "\r\n"
    loop {
      data = stream.read(BLK_SIZE)
      f.out << data; f.out.flush
      break if data.size != BLK_SIZE
    }
    stream.close
  end
end
```

Developing & Deploying…

Installing FastCGI For Ruby

There are two different FastCGI implementations for Ruby, an implementation in C and one written in pure Ruby.

Both are available from Eli Green's home page at http://fenris .codedogs.ca/~eli/fastcgi.html (or in the RAA in the Library section under *WWW*). The pure Ruby implementation even supports multiplexing, which means that the FastCGI adaptor communicates with multiple FastCGI applications through *one* socket.

The pure Ruby version requires the *stringio* module, which you can download from the same page. To compile the C version, you'll also need the devkit from FastCGI's homepage at www.fastcgi.com.

In any case, you need *mod_fastcgi* when using an Apache Web server. After installing it, modify Apache's *httpd.conf* configuration file and add these two lines at the very beginning:

```
LoadModule fastcgi_module lib/httpd/mod_fastcgi.so

AddModule mod_fastcgi.c
```

To let Apache handle all files ending with .fcgi, add one more line:

```
AddHandler fastcgi_script .fcgi
```

Alternatively, use *SetHandler* inside a location:

```
SetHandler fastcgi_script
```

See mod_fastcgi's documentation (on UNIX, usually: /usr/local/share/ httpd/htdocs/manual/mod/mod_fastcgi.html) for more information.

Using mod_ruby and eruby

The mod_ruby package embeds the Ruby interpreter into the Apache Web server similar to mod_perl or mod_php for Perl and Php respectively. It allows Ruby scripts to be executed natively without creating a new process as is the case for CGI scripts. This increases performance significantly.

Installing and Configuring mod_ruby

Download the mod_ruby package from www.modruby.net. Unpack the archive, then issue the following command:

```
./configure.rb
```

If Apache's *apxs* tool cannot be found, specify it explicitly:

```
./configure.rb —with-apxs=/path/to/apxs
```

You can also build mod_ruby with support for *eruby* (Ruby code embedded in HTML). To do this, first download the eruby archive from www.modruby.net, and compile and install it with the three commands **./configure.rb**, **make**, and **make install**. Then configure mod_ruby as shown below (modify the path to eruby's libraries/header files if necessary):

```
./configure.rb —enable-eruby                          \
             —with-eruby-includes=/usr/local/include \
             —with-eruby-libraries=/usr/local/lib
```

Then compile and install mod_ruby:

```
make
make install
```

Now edit Apache's *httpd.conf* configuration file and add the following lines to it (modify the path to mod_ruby.so if necessary):

```
LoadModule ruby_module /usr/local/apache/libexec/mod_ruby.so
AddModule  mod_ruby.c
```

This will tell Apache to load mod_ruby, after restarting.

To execute all files under the /ruby directory (for example, http://yourhost/ruby/myscript) as Ruby scripts, as well as all files ending in *.rbx*, add the following to *httpd.conf*:

```
<IfModule mod_ruby.c>
  RubyRequire apache/ruby-run

  <Location /ruby>
    SetHandler ruby-object
    RubyHandler Apache::RubyRun.instance
```

```
    Options ExecCGI

  </Location>


  <Files *.rbx>

    SetHandler ruby-object

    RubyHandler Apache::RubyRun.instance

  </Files>

</IfModule>
```

If you want to execute Ruby code embedded in HTML, in addition, add one of the following sections. For eruby, this is:

```
<IfModule mod_ruby.c>

  RubyRequire apache/eruby-run


  # handle files under /eruby as eRuby files by eruby

  <Location /eruby>

    SetHandler ruby-object

    RubyHandler Apache::ERubyRun.instance

    Options ExecCGI

  </Location>


  # handle *.rhtml as eruby files.

  <Files *.rhtml>

    SetHandler ruby-object

    RubyHandler Apache::ERubyRun.instance

  </Files>

</IfModule>
```

And for ERb, eruby's equivalent written in pure Ruby, this is:

```
<IfModule mod_ruby.c>

  RubyRequire apache/erb-run


  # handle files under /erb as eRuby files by ERb.

  <Location /erb>

    SetHandler ruby-object
```

```
    RubyHandler Apache::ERbRun.instance
    Options ExecCGI
  </Location>

  # handle *.rhtml as eRuby files by ERb.
  <Files *.rhtml>
    SetHandler ruby-object
    RubyHandler Apache::ERbRun.instance
  </Files>

</IfModule>
```

When developing mod_ruby scripts, a last directive is very useful, too:

```
RubyRequire auto-reload
```

Put this anywhere in one of the above sections. This will reload modified scripts that you load into your script using Ruby's *require* directive. Alternatively, use *load* instead of *require*.

Before you can use mod_ruby, make sure to restart the Apache Web server:

```
apachectl restart
```

If you are still running mod_ruby, a restart will not free the resources held by the embedded Ruby interpreter. Therefore, you'd better stop and then start Apache again, with the following:

```
apachectl stop
apachectl start
```

Using mod_ruby and eruby in the Online Shop Example

In this section we'll rewrite the Web interface of our online shop application from the previous sections, this time using mod_ruby instead of CGI or FastCGI. Also, instead of generating HTML with the *CGI* class, we'll embed our Ruby code into HTML using eruby. Note that the database model stays the same, as well as the database access layer (file *src/db.rb* shown in Figure 6.12).

You'll find the source codes shown in this section in directory *mod_ruby-shop* at www.syngress.com/solutions. The Ruby sourcefiles reside there in subdirectory *src*. Again, for convenient installation, there is a Makefile available (Figure 6.22).

Figure 6.22 Makefile

```
TARGET=/home/michael/htdocs            # modify


RB_FILES     = src/config.rb src/db.rb src/session.rb
RBX_FILES    = src/show_image.rbx src/action.rbx
RHTML_FILES = src/articles.rhtml src/cart.rhtml src/shop.rhtml


FILES        = ${RB_FILES} ${RBX_FILES} ${RHTML_FILES}


install:
        cp ${FILES} ${TARGET}
```

Let's first rewrite the show_image.cgi application, resulting in *show_image.rbx* (Figure 6.23). For this one we don't need to use eruby, because we will output image data, not HTML.

Figure 6.23 Show_image.rbx

```
#!/usr/bin/env ruby
require "db"
require "cgi"


BLK_SIZE = 8 * 1024


req = Apache::request
id  = CGI.parse(req.args)["id"][0].to_i


DB.connect do |db|
  dbh = db.connection
  row = dbh.select_one("SELECT data, content_type FROM picture
                        WHERE picture_id = ?", id)

  stream = dbh.func(:blob_open, row['data'])
```

Continued

Figure 6.23 Continued

```
req.status                         = 200
req.content_type                   = row['content_type']
req.headers_out["Content-length"]  = stream.size.to_s
req.headers_out["Date"]            = Time.now.to_s
req.headers_out["Expires"]         = (Time.now + 3*60).to_s
req.send_http_header
loop {
  data = stream.read(BLK_SIZE)
  req << data
  break if data.size != BLK_SIZE
}
stream.close
end
```

At the beginning, we invoke *Apache::request* to get an object representing the current request. This object provides the method for querying the request information and for generating a response. Then we call the *args* method of the request object to get the arguments passed in the URL (everything after the "?", which in our case is "id=*ImageID*"). We pass its return value to *CGI.parse*, which in turn returns a hash, similar to the return value of *CGI* class's instance method *params*.

After opening the database connection and executing the SQL statement to get the OID, (we need to open the image data stream), we create the response header. With the *status* method, we set the HTTP status code to 200 (OK) and set the content type with the *content_type* method. The other HTTP headers we set using *headers_out*. Note that to access the HTTP headers of the request, we use *headers_in*. Finally we send the headers to the Web server by calling the *send_http_header* method; do this before you send any response data. The response data is sent using the << method; alternatively, you can use the *write* or *print* methods of the *Apache::Request* object.

Note that mod_ruby will *not* recognize the first line of Figure 6.23 as is the case for CGI scripts:

```
#!/usr/bin/env ruby
```

Developing & Deploying…

Using DRbSession as Database Manager for Storing Sessions

DRbSession is a database manager you may use with the *CGI::Session* class instead of the two managers *FileStore* and *MemoryStore* that come with Ruby by default. DRbSession consists of two parts, a client component (*CGI::Session::DRbSession* class) and a server component (*session-server*) that stores the session data in memory and exposes it via DRb (see the DRb section in Chapter 5 for more information).

To install it, download the package (from the RAA in the Library section under *WWW*), unpack the archive, and copy the *drbsession.rb* file into the same directory where the *cgi/session* feature resides (for example, /usr/local/lib/ruby/1.6/cgi). Then add two key/value pairs to the hash you pass to *Session.new* for the second *option* parameter:

```
'drbsession_uri'   => 'druby://localhost:4999',
'database_manager' => CGI::Session::DRbSession
```

Also, do not forget to require *cgi/drbsession*, and make sure that DRb is installed. Then run the session server:

```
./sessionserver
```

To modify the URI under which the session server is available (this is druby://localhost:4999 by default), edit the *sessionserver* file and modify the *SERVER_URI* constant appropriately.

Nevertheless it is useful, because some editors (such as VIM) will use it to determine the type of language used in the file—Ruby in our case—so that it can correctly syntax-highlight it without your having to modify any of its configuration files.

After testing that *show_image.rbx* works correctly, let's proceed with the *view* of our Online shop. This consists of three eruby files, *shop.rhtml* (Figure 6.24), *articles.rhtml* (Figure 6.25), and *cart.rhtml* (Figure 6.26). The first is the main script, directly invoked by the user by specifying the URL http://yourhost/shop.rhtml. It inclues the two other eruby files (by calling *ERuby.import*); this makes the whole application easier to read and easier to maintain.

Obviously then, *articles.rhtml* displays the articles (*Article* and *ArticleList* classes in the CGI version of the online shop) while *cart.rhtml* generates the HTML for the cart on the right (the *Cart* class in the CGI version of the online shop).

We use a slightly modified session class compared to the one we used in the CGI version of the online shop. We added one *url* method to it that returns the "*session_key=session_id*" string. We use this to pass the session ID inside the URL instead of passing it as a cookie. The class is implemented in the *session.rb* file shown in Figure 6.27.

Notice that we call *session.close* at the end of *shop.rhtml* (and *action.rbx*). This is absolutely neccessary because the *FileStore* manager that stores the content of a session on disk will not unlock the session file until the session object is garbage collected, or the *close* method is called. This is no problem using CGI scripts, because the Ruby interpreter terminates after each request and therefore will garbage collect all objects, but using mod_ruby the Ruby interpreter will (almost) never terminate!

An additional piece of advice is not to use class *MemoryStore* for storing sessions in memory, as mod_ruby does not make the assumption that each request is handled by the same instance of the Ruby interpreter. But you can safely use *DRbSession* (available at the RAA in the Library section under *WWW*), which also works for CGI scripts.

Figure 6.24 Shop.rhtml

```
<%
require "db"
require "session"

session  = Session.new(CGI.new, SESSION_PARAMS)
articles = DB.connect {|db| db.get_articles_in_inventory }
%>


<html>
<head><title>Online-Shop</title></head>
<body>
   <h1>Online-Shop</h1>
```

Continued

Figure 6.24 Continued

```
<table><tr><td valign="top" width="50%">

  <% ERuby.import "articles.rhtml" %>

</td><td bgcolor="#CCCCCC" valign="top" width="25%">

  <% ERuby.import "cart.rhtml" %>

</td></tr></table>


</body>

</html>


<% session.close %>
```

Figure 6.25 Articles.rhtml

```
<table>
<% articles.each do |row| %><tr>
<td>
  <% img_url = "show_image.rbx?id=" + row[:picture_id].to_s %>
  <a target="_new" href="<%= img_url %>"><img src="<%= img_url %>"
    width="90" height="113" border="0"></a></td>
<td>
  <i><%= row[:name] %></i><br><%= row[:description] %><br><br>
  <b>Price: </b>$<%= row[:cost] %><br>
  <a href="action.rbx?add=<%= row[:article_id] %>&<%= session.url %>">
    <img src="/trolley.gif" border="0">add to shopping cart</a>
  </td></tr>
<% end %>
</table>
```

Figure 6.26 Cart.rhtml

```
<%
cart = session['cart'] || {}
article_ids = {}
articles.each { |i| article_ids[ i[:article_id] ] = i }
%>


<% unless cart.empty? %>


<table>
<% cart.each do |id, count| %>
  <% a = article_ids[id] %>
  <tr>
    <td><b><%= count %>x</td>
    <td><%= a[:name] %></td>
    <td>$<%= a[:cost] %></td>
    <td><a href="action.rbx?drop=<%= id %>&<%= session.url
      %>">X</a></td>
  </tr>
<% end %>
</table>


<hr>
<form action="action.rbx" method="POST">
  email: <input type="text" name="email"><br>
  passw: <input type="password" name="password"><br>
  <br><input type="submit" name="order" value="Order Now">
</form>
<hr>


<% end %>
```

Figure 6.27 Session Class (session.rb)

```ruby
require "cgi/session"

SESSION_PARAMS = {
  'session_key' => 'sid',
  'prefix'      => 'online-shop'
}

class Session < CGI::Session
  def initialize(req, option={})
    @opt = option; super
  end

  def url
    [@opt['session_key'] || '_session_id', session_id].join("=")
  end

  def [](key)
    if val = super then Marshal.load(val) else val end
  end

  def []=(key, val)
    super(key, Marshal.dump(val))
  end
end
```

If you click any of the **Add to shopping cart links**, click the **X** to remove an item from the cart, or if you press the **Order** button to order the items in the cart, the *action.rbx* script (Figure 6.28) will be invoked. Its purpose is very similar to that class *Controller* of file components.rb in the CGI version of the online shop. It either adds or removes an article from the cart or inserts an order into the database. Then it redirects the browser back to shop.rhtml. Redirecting is done in mod_ruby using the following two lines:

```
Apache::request.headers_out["Location"] = "/url/to/redirect"
exit Apache::REDIRECT
```

or with:

```
Apache::request.status = 302
Apache::request.headers_out["Location"] = "/url/to/redirect"
Apache::request.send_http_header
```

Figure 6.28 Action.rbx

```
#!/usr/bin/env ruby
require "db"
require "session"

session   = Session.new(cgi = CGI.new, SESSION_PARAMS)
cart      = session['cart'] || Hash.new(0)

if id = cgi['add'][0]
  # add article to cart
  cart[id.to_i] += 1

elsif id = cgi['drop'][0]
  # drop article from cart
  cart.delete(id.to_i)

elsif cgi['order'][0]
  # place order
  DB.connect do |db|
    cust_id = db.get_customer_id(cgi['email'][0], cgi['password'][0])
    db.new_order(cust_id, cart)
  end
  cart = nil     # empty the cart
end

# store the cart back to the session and redirect
```

Continued

Figure 6.28 Continued

```
session['cart'] = cart
session.close


# redirect
Apache::request.headers_out["Location"] = "shop.rhtml?" + session.url
exit Apache::REDIRECT
```

Dynamically Generating XML with eruby

You can also generate XML with eruby and mod_ruby. This is useful, for example, if you want to deliver XML to the browser, which then (on the client-side) invokes an XSLT script to transform it to HTML. Not many browsers support this; in fact only Microsoft's Internet Explorer can do this for certain. Make sure you have MSXML 3.0 (Microsoft's XML parser package) installed, so that you can use a full-fledged XSLT processor for your XSLT scripts, otherwise you can't do anything particularly useful with it.

Below is an eruby script that creates XML, for use with mod_ruby:

```
<%
ERuby.noheader = true
req = Apache.request
req.content_type = "text/xml"
req.send_http_header
%><?xml version="1.0"?>


<root>
  <% [1,2,3].each do |r| %>
  <row id="<%= r %>">
    <% [1, 2].each { |c| %> <col id="<%= c %>"/> <% } %>
  </row>
  <% end %>
</root>
```

This would output the following XML document:

```
<?xml version="1.0"?>


<root>


  <row id="1">
     <col id="1"/>  <col id="2"/>
  </row>


  <row id="2">
     <col id="1"/>  <col id="2"/>
  </row>


  <row id="3">
     <col id="1"/>  <col id="2"/>
  </row>


</root>
```

Note that for some XML parsers, it is necessary that the *<?xml?>* processing instruction comes first; they do not accept a new line before it. This is why we put it after the closing "%>":

```
%><?xml version="1.0"?>
```

Displaying RSS News Channels

In this section, we'll implement an eruby component that renders an RDF Site Summary (RSS) news channel to HTML. Note that Ruby/RSS only supports RSS version 0.91 (or older). The location of the RSS channel can be given by an URI; our component will support the HTTP and FTP protocols. The source code for these files are available on the accompanying CD in the *rss-view* directory.

For parsing the RSS in XML format, we use Chad Fowler's Ruby/RSS library. This is dependent on Yoshida Masato's XMLParser and Uconv module, which implement UTF-16 and UTF-8 conversion. (All are available from the RAA's Library section: Ruby/RSS and XMLParser under *XML* and Uconv under *I18N*.) To install Ruby/RSS, simply copy the *rss.rb* file into your *site_ruby* directory (for example, /usr/local/lib/ruby/site_ruby/1.6).

To parse the URIs, we make use of Akira Yamada's URI package called URb (found in the RAA's Library section under *Net*, or available directly from http://arika.org/ruby/uri.html.en).

First, we develop a *RSSModel* class (see Figure 6.29), which fetches an RSS file from a given HTTP or FTP URI, and parses it. Note that we add an *element_accessor* to the *RSS::Item* class. This tells the RSS library to recognize an item's *<description>* tag and makes its content accessible through the *description* method. After calling *fetchFile* to fetch the RSS file from the given URI, we pass the RSS data to the *from_xml* method (included in the RSS module) to parse it.

Next we develop a HTML view for the *RSSModel* class, resulting in the *RSSView* class, as shown in Figure 6.30. Last, we write an eruby application (see Figure 6.31) that outputs two channels. The result is shown in Figure 6.32.

Figure 6.29 The RSSModel Class (rssmodel.rb)

```
require "uri"
require "net/http"
require "net/ftp"
require "rss"

module RSS
  class Item
    element_accessor :description
  end
end


class RSSModel
  include RSS

  attr_reader :rss
  def initialize(uri)
    @uri = uri
    @rss = from_xml(fetchFile(@uri))
  end

  private
```

Figure 6.29 Continued

```ruby
def fetchFile(uri)
  case uri = URI.parse(uri)
  when URI::HTTP
    http = Net::HTTP.new(uri.host, uri.port)
    resp = http.get2(uri.request_uri)
    if resp.code =~ /^2\d\d$/        # 2xx
      resp.body
    elsif resp.code == "301"         # REDIRECT
      fetchFile(resp['location'])
    else
      raise "Could not fetch file! #{ resp.code }"
    end
  when URI::FTP
    ftp = Net::FTP.new(uri.host)
    ftp.login(uri.user || 'anonymous', uri.password)
    data = ""
    ftp.gettextfile(uri.path, '/dev/null') {|line| data << line}
    data
  else
    raise "URI class not supported"
  end
end
```

Figure 6.30 The RSSView Class (rssview.rhtml)

```ruby
<%
require "rssmodel"

class RSSView
  def initialize(modelOrURI)
    modelOrURI = RSSModel.new(modelOrURI) if modelOrURI.kind_of? String
```

Continued

Figure 6.30 Continued

```
      @rss = modelOrURI.rss
   end


   def toHTML
%>
<table>


<tr><td>
<!-- display image -->
<% unless @rss.image == [] %>
<a href="<%= @rss.image.link %>"><img src="<%= @rss.image.url %>"
   title="<% @rss.image.title %>" width="<%= @rss.image.width %>"
   height="<%= @rss.image.height %>" border="0"></a>
<% end %>


<!-- display title -->
<font size="+2"><b><a href="<%= @rss.link %>"><%= @rss.title %></a>
   </b></font>
</td></tr>


<!-- display items -->
<% @rss.each_item do | item | %>
<tr><td bgcolor="#DDCCD0">
   <a href="<%= item.link %>"><%= item.title %></a>
</td></tr>
<tr><td>
   <%= item.description || "" %>
<td></tr>
<% end %>


</table>
<% end end %>
```

Figure 6.31 The RSS Demo-Viewer (test.rhtml)

```
<% ERuby.import "rssview.rhtml" %>
<% URI1 = 'http://linuxcentral.com/backend/lcnew.rdf' %>
<% URI2 = 'http://www.multiagent.com/mynetscape.rdf'  %>


<html>
<body>
<table><tr>
<td valign="top">
  <% RSSView.new(URI1).toHTML %></td>
<td valign="top">
  <% RSSView.new(URI2).toHTML %></td>
</tr></table>
</body>
```

Figure 6.32 Output of test.rhtml

Installing and Configuring IOWA

Interpreted Objects for Web Applications (IOWA) is a powerful, *truly* object-oriented application server written in pure Ruby by Avi Bryant. Its architecture is similar to that of Apple's WebObjects, but uses an interpreted language (Ruby) instead of a compiled one (Objective-C or Java, in the case of WebObjects).

Some features of IOWA include the following:

- IOWA separates logic (model and controller) from presentation (view), so that the HTML designer and programmer can do their work independently. Both parts, code and HTML, are joined together using an optional bindings-section, freeing both from using specified names. Also, this makes changes in both HTML and code easier to maintain.

- It offers intuitive program flow.

- IOWA pages are stateful objects.

- It provides reusable components.

> **NOTE**
>
> For an introduction to the basics of IOWA, have a look through IOWA's tutorial (www.beta4.com/iowa), or, for more in-depth information about the concepts behind it, see the documentation and tutorials for Apple's WebObjects available at http://developer.apple.com.

Let's have a look at two more advanced IOWA applications, the Online Shop introduced earlier in this chapter, and a reusable tree-view component with which we will build a file-viewer application.

As IOWA is a pure Ruby solution, it is very simple to install. Download it from www.beta4.com/iowa (use the 0.14a version) and extract the archive (use **tar –xvzf iowa-0-14.tar.gz** on UNIX or use a program like PowerArchiver or WinZip on Windows). Then install the IOWA sources with a simple **ruby install.rb**. Easy? Well, that was the *first* step!

Next, you have to install the IOWA adaptor for your Web server. This passes requests through a Unix socket to the long-running IOWA-applications and delivers the response back to the Web server. By taking this approach, IOWA is capable to work with (almost) every Web server. The adaptor need not to be written in Ruby itself—C, Perl, or any other language that can handle Unix sockets would also work.

For the adaptor, we can currently choose between three different implementations/approaches:

- **The CGI adaptor iowa.cgi** This should work with every Web server that can handle CGIs and which is able to forward requests of a specific

URL to the handler (for example, a CGI script). I tried it with Apache and with the pure Ruby Web server httpserv (found at the RAA in the Application section under *WWW*). Both worked, even on Windows!

- **The Apache module mod_iowa**   This only works for Apache Web servers.

- **The IOWAServlet**   This is for use with the pure Ruby Web server framework WEBrick. With this, the only requirement is an installed Ruby interpreter plus the WEBrick and IOWA libraries.

We'll not discuss how to install the Apache module *mod_iowa*, because it may not work for some systems; see the README document of the IOWA package for installation instructions.

To access IOWA applications using the CGI adaptor, simply put the *iowa.cgi* script which is delivered with IOWA into your Web server's *cgi-bin* directory. Then, for an Apache Web server, edit its configuration file *httpd.conf* and add the following four lines:

```
Action iowa /cgi-bin/iowa.cgi
<Location /iowa>
  SetHandler iowa
</Location>
```

After making the changes to Apache, restart the server.

```
apachectl restart
```

To use the *IOWAServlet* adaptor, first download the WEBrick package (found in the RAA's Library section under *Net*) and install it via **ruby install.rb**. Then invoke the Ruby file *webrick-adaptor.rb* (shown in Figure 6.33 and available at www.syngress.com/solutions in the *iowa-utils* directory). Modify the *:DocumentRoot* and *:Port* settings appropriately to match your needs.

NOTE

WEBrick supports SSL and authentification, and there are WEBrick "servlets" or "plug-ins" available for XML-RPC and SOAP services.
    Another full-featured Web server for Ruby is Yoshinori Toki's *wwwsrv*, which can be found at the RAA in the Application section under *WWW*. Plug-ins for XML-RPC are available for this as well.

Figure 6.33 IOWA Adaptor for WEBrick (webrick-adaptor.rb)

```ruby
require 'webrick'
require 'socket'
require 'iowa/config'

class IOWAServlet < WEBrick::HTTPServlet::AbstractServlet
  def service(req, res)
    url, = req.request_uri.to_s.split("?")
    params = if req.request_method == "GET"
      req.query_string || ""
    else
      req.body
    end

    url =~ ".*?/iowa/([^/]*)"
    socket_name = "#{$tempDir}iowa_#{$1}"
    socket = UNIXSocket.new(socket_name)
    socket.putc(url.length)
    socket.write(url)
    socket.putc(params.length)
    socket.write(params)
    socket.shutdown(1)

    body = ""
    while (recv = socket.recv(1000)) != "" do
      body << recv
    end

    res['Content-type'] = "text/html"
    res.body = body
  end
end

if __FILE__ == $0
```

Continued

Figure 6.33 Continued

```
s = WEBrick::HTTPServer.new(
  :Port              => 2000,
  :DocumentRoot      => '/home/michael/htdocs',
  :Logger            => WEBrick::Log::new($stderr, WEBrick::Log::DEBUG)
)


s.mount("/iowa", IOWAServlet)
trap("INT"){ s.shutdown }
s.start
end
```

Using IOWA for the Online Shop Example

In this section we'll rewrite the Web interface of the online shop application we introduced earlier, but this time using IOWA instead of CGI, FastCGI, or mod_ruby. Again, the database model, as well as the database access layer (file db.rb, shown in Figure 6.12), are the same as for the CGI-based one. We'll use the *show_image.cgi* script (shown in Figure 6.18) to display an article's image, because with IOWA it is currently impossible to output anything other than HTML data, due to a hard-coded HTTP content-type header (text/html) in the IOWA adaptor.

You'll find the source code of the files shown in this section in the *iowa-shop* directory of the accompanying CD.

Let's start by explaining the purpose of the *shop.rb* file, shown in Figure 6.34. All definitions of this file are available in the IOWA components we'll write (files ending with .html). First we define our own *MySession* session class; this will be used instead of the default *Iowa::Session* for all sessions of this application. It has one attribute, *cart*, which will store the articles in the cart. Note that there is no need to tell IOWA to use this class instead of the default one, because IOWA will take notice of this when you subclass *Iowa::Session*, by overwriting the *inherited* class method. The same applies to IOWA's *Iowa::Application* class.

Next, we define our own application class, *MyApplication*. There will be exactly one instance of this class; all components have access to it through their *application* method. In its *initialize* method, we connect to the database, get all information about the articles, and store them in *@articles* and *@article_ids*. The reason for storing them in the application class is to improve performance; however, any changes to the articles in the database will not affect this application unless you restart. To avoid a restart, we could also set up a thread that gets the newest information about the articles out of the database every five minutes and stores them in the application object—something similar to the following:

```
Thread.new {
  loop {
    @articles = DB.connect {|db| db.get_articles_in_inventory }
    @article_ids = {}
    @articles.each { |i| @article_ids[ i[:article_id] ] = i }
    sleep 5*60
  }
}
```

Still in *shop.rb*, we add two methods *takeValueForKey* and *valueForKey* to class *DBI::Row*. This is necessary so that we can access the row's columns using the dot notation (for example, @row.name) in IOWA bindings.

Last, we invoke *Iowa.run*. This will start the application; you can access it in your browser at the URL http://yourhost/iowa/shop.

Figure 6.34 Global Definitions, Startup File (shop.rb)

```
require "iowa"
require "db"


class MySession < Iowa::Session
  attr_accessor :cart

  def initialize(*args)
    @cart = Hash.new(0)
    super
  end

  # just to show you that it exists...
  def handleRequest(context) super end
end
```

Continued

Figure 6.34 Continued

```
class MyApplication < Iowa::Application
  attr_reader :articles, :article_ids

  def initialize(*args)
    @articles = DB.connect {|db| db.get_articles_in_inventory }
    @article_ids = {}
    @articles.each { |i| @article_ids[ i[:article_id] ] = i }
    super
  end


  # just to show you that it exists...
  def handleRequest(context) super end
end


module DBI
  class Row
    def takeValueForKey(value, key)
      self[key] = value
    end
    def valueForKey(key)
      self[key]
    end
  end
end


Iowa.run('shop')
```

The view of our online shop consists of three components:

- **Main**   This is the start page; it uses the two other components to display the whole online shop (see Figure 6.35).

- **Article**   This displays one article; it implements the *addToShoppingCart* action (see Figure 6.36).

- **Cart**   This displays the cart on the right; it implements the *removeFromCart* and *order* actions (see Figure 6.37).

You can see that the components are clearly structured, with well-defined, intuitive responsibilities. This is one of the main advantages of using IOWA—this is object-oriented Web development!

Figure 6.35 Main Component (Main.html)

```
<%
  import "Article"
  import "Cart"

  class Main < Iowa::Component
    attr_accessor :item
  end
%>
<?
  articleList : Repeat {
    list = application.articles
    item = item
  }

  article : Article {
    row = item
  }
?>
<html>
<head><title>Online-Shop</title></head>
<body>
  <h1>Online-Shop</h1>
  <table><tr><td valign="top" width="50%">
    <repeat oid="articleList">
      <Article oid="article"/>
    </repeat>
  </td><td bgcolor="#CCCCCC" valign="top" width="25%">
    <Cart oid="cart"/>
  </td></tr></table>
</body>
</html>
```

Figure 6.36 Article Component (Article.html)

```
<%
  class Article < Iowa::Component
    attr_binding :row

    def img_url
      "/cgi-bin/show_image.cgi?id=" + row[:picture_id].to_s
    end

    def addToShoppingCart
      session.cart[row[:article_id]] += 1
    end
  end
%>
<table>
<tr>
<td><a target="_new" href="@img_url"><img src="@img_url" width="90"
    height="113" border="0"></a></td>
<td>
  <i>@row.name</i><br>@row.description<br><br>
  <b>Price: </b>$@row.cost<br>
  <a oid="addToShoppingCart"><img src="/trolley.gif" border="0">add to
  shopping cart</a>
</td></tr>
</table>
```

Figure 6.37 Cart Component (Cart.html)

```
<%
  class Cart < Iowa::Component
    attr_accessor :cartItem, :email, :password

    def article
```

Continued

Figure 6.37 Continued

```
        application.article_ids[cartItem[0]]
    end

    def removeFromCart
      session.cart.delete(cartItem[0])
    end

    def cartNotEmpty
      not session.cart.empty?
    end

    def order
      DB.connect do |db|
        cust_id = db.get_customer_id(email, password)
        db.new_order(cust_id, session.cart)
      end
      session.cart = Hash.new(0)  # empty cart
    end
  end
%>
<?
  cartList {
    list = session.cart
    item = cartItem
  }
?>
<table oid="cartList">
  <tr>
    <td><b>@cartItem.1</b></td>
    <td>@article.name</td>
    <td>$@article.cost</td>
    <td><a oid="removeFromCart">X</a></td>
```

Continued

Figure 6.37 Continued

```
    </tr>
</table>


<if oid="cartNotEmpty">
<hr>
<form oid="order">
    email: <input type="text" oid="email"><br>
    passw: <input type="password" oid="password"><br>
    <br><input type="submit" value="Order Now">
</form>
<hr>
</if>
```

Implementing a TreeView Component

Implementing a tree-view in HTML—impossible, you say? No, it is entirely possible, as we'll demonstrate by implementing one here in this section. To get an idea of what it will look like, see Figure 6.42 at the end of this section.

The tree-view we'll develop is partitioned into three classes, *TreeModel*, *TreeController*, and *TreeView* (Model View Controller [MVC] pattern). Only the last class, the view, depends on IOWA, whereas the others are pure Ruby classes (the *TreeView* class is also pure Ruby, but it's an IOWA component) and could be used elsewhere as well, such as for a GUI-TreeView component.

The *TreeModel* class (see Figure 6.38) is a simple, recursive data structure that stores the nodes of the tree, together with additional information such as the name of a node (this will be displayed later) and user-definable attributes. A *TreeModel* either stores its children (subnodes) directly in an array, which is optimal for trees with a less number of elements, or generates them on demand, that is, lazily. The latter is especially useful if you want to display deeply nested trees with lots of nodes (for example, the Unix filesystem—try iterating recursively over each file starting at '/'!). Of course, it's possible to mix both arbitrarily. We implement the laziness using *Proc* objects that, when called, return an array containing its children. Once you have requested the children of a *TreeModel* object, they are stored internally and the next call will return them directly without invoking the *Proc* object for a second time. Of course, we could free the children of a subtree when it gets collapsed (and call the Proc object again when requested the next time), but we won't do that here, because we would lose the information about which of the children (not being leaves) were expanded and which were not.

Each instance of the *TreeModel* class can have its own controller object (it should be of the *TreeController* class). Simply assign one using the *controller=* attribute accessor. If no controller was assigned and you call the *controller* method, it returns the controller of its parent, possibly recursive. This way, all subnodes inherit the controller from the root node, if none was explicitly specified. Of course you should make sure that at least the root node was assigned a controller, otherwise an exception will result.

Figure 6.38 The Tree's Model: Class TreeModel (TreeModel.rb)

```ruby
class TreeModel
  attr_accessor :name, :parent, :expanded, :attrs
  attr_accessor :controller

  def initialize(name, parent=nil, expanded=false, *childs,
                 &childs_proc)
    @name, @parent, @expanded,  = name, parent, expanded
    @attrs = {}
    if block_given?
      @childs = nil
      @childs_proc = childs_proc
    else
      @childs = childs
      @childs.each {|c| c.parent = self}
      @childs_proc = nil
    end
  end

  def childs
    if @childs.nil?
```

Continued

Figure 6.3.8 Continued

```
        @childs = @childs_proc.call
        @childs.each {|c| c.parent = self}
      else
        @childs
      end
  end

  def level
    isRoot ? 0 : @parent.level + 1
  end

  def isLeaf
    childs.empty?
  end

  def isRoot
    @parent.nil?
  end

  def isLastChild
    isRoot or (parent.childs[-1] == self)
  end

  def controller
    if @controller.nil? and not isRoot
      @parent.controller
    else
      @controller
    end
  end
end
```

The *TreeController* class (see Figure 6.39) implements the action that will be performed when you click onto a node of the *TreeView*. If it's not a leaf you click on, then it will either expand and show its children, or will fold or collapse. You can customize the action performed when clicking on it, either by inheriting from the *controller* class, or, if this is not possible due to single-inheritance, by including the *TreeControllerMixin* module into your class. In either case, you have to overwrite the *action* method to implement your customized action. From here you should call the original *action* method, either with *super*, or when mixing the *TreeControllerMixin* in; then call __*action* (as we'll do later in our sample application).

Figure 6.39 The Tree's Controller: The TreeController Class (TreeController.rb)

```
module TreeControllerMixin
  def action(model, view)
    model.expanded = ! model.expanded
  end


  alias __action action
end


class TreeController
  include TreeControllerMixin
end
```

The *TreeView* IOWA component renders a *TreeModel* into HTML. If the TreeView's model is not a leaf, then it applies itself recursively to display all of its children. The source code is shown in Figure 6.40 and is contained on the accompanying CD in the TreeView.html file. To use the TreeView component from within another IOWA component, put the following into the HTML section:

```
<TreeView oid="treeview"/>
```

Then, in the bindings section (between <? and ?>), specify its model with the following:

```
treeview : TreeView {
  model = treeModel
}
```

This binding additionally requires a method defined in the "calling" component, named *treeModel*, which returns an instance of the *TreeModel* class.

Figure 6.40 The TreeView Component (TreeView.html)

```
<%
  class TreeView < Iowa::Component
    attr_binding  :model
    attr_accessor :child

    def action
      model.controller.action(model, self)
    end

    # indentation of this components' parent
    def parentIndent
      model.isRoot ? "" : @parent.indent
    end

    # indentation for this components' childs
    def indent
      parentIndent +
      if model.isLeaf
        ' '
      elsif model.isLastChild
        '<img src="/images/blank.gif" width="16" height="22">'
      else
        '<img src="/images/vertline.gif" width="16" height="22">'
      end
    end

    def getBranchIcon
      name = 'node'
      name = 'last' + name if model.isLastChild
```

Continued

Figure 6.40 Continued

```
        name = (model.expanded ? 'm' : 'p') + name if not model.isLeaf
        '/images/' + name + '.gif'
      end

      def getNodeIcon
        name = if model.isLeaf
          'doc'
        elsif model.expanded
          'folderopen'
        else
          'folderclosed'
        end
        '/images/' + name + '.gif'
      end

  end
%>
<?
  nodeList : Repeat {
    list = model.childs
    item = child
  }

  subtree : TreeView {
    model = child
  }
?>
<table cellspacing="0" cellpadding="0" border="0"><tr>
<td nowrap>@parentIndent<a oid="action"><img border="0" width="16"
  height="22" src="@getBranchIcon"><img border="0" width="24"
  height="22" src="@getNodeIcon"></a></td>
```

Continued

Figure 6.40 Continued

```
<td valign="middle" nowrap>@model.name</td>
</tr></table>
<if oid="model.expanded">
<repeat oid="nodeList"><TreeView oid="subtree"/></repeat>
</if>
```

Now with the help of the TreeView component (and the *TreeModel* and *TreeController* classes), we can simply implement the file viewer application as shown in Figure 6.42. You can find the source code of this application (the file Main.html, shown in Figure 6.41) and all files making up the TreeView component (TreeView.html, TreeModel.rb, and TreeController.rb) at www.syngress .com/solutions under the *iowa-treeview* directory. The images necessary to display the tree can be found in the subdirectory *images*; put them into a directory known by your Web server, so that they become available through the URL */images/XXX* where *XXX* is the name of the image.

To start the file viewer application, invoke Ruby from the *iowa-treeview* directory, as shown:

```
ruby -r iowa -e 'Iowa.run("fileviewer")'
```

Then point your browser to the URL http://yourhost/iowa/fileviewer, and enjoy!

Figure 6.41 File Viewer Application (Main.html)

```
<%
  require "TreeModel"
  require "TreeController"
  import  "TreeView"

  class Main < Iowa::Component
    attr_reader :rootNode, :selected


    include TreeControllerMixin


    DIR = "/home/michael/devel"
```

Continued

Figure 6.41 Continued

```ruby
def action(model, view)
  __action(model, view)
  @selected = model
  yield self     # display page
end

def awake
  @rootNode = TreeModel.new(DIR) { genNodes(DIR) }
  @rootNode.attrs['filename'] = DIR
  @rootNode.controller = self
  @selected = @rootNode
end

def fileName
  @selected.attrs['filename']
end

def fileContent
  require "cgi"
  if File.directory? fileName
    CGI.escapeHTML `ls -la #{ fileName }`
  else
    CGI.escapeHTML File.readlines(fileName).to_s
  end
end

private

def genNodes(path)
  Dir[path+"/*"].collect do |name|
    bn = File.basename(name)
    n = if FileTest.directory? name
      TreeModel.new(bn) { genNodes(name) }
```

Continued

Figure 6.41 Continued

```
          else
             TreeModel.new(bn)
          end
          n.attrs['filename'] = name
          n
       end
     end


  end
%>
<?
  nd : TreeView {
    model = rootNode
  }
?>
<html>
<head><title>File Viewer</title></head>
<body>
  <table cellspacing="5">
    <tr>
      <td valign="top">
        <TreeView oid="nd"/>
      </td>
      <td valign="top" bgcolor=#BBBBBB>
        <b>@fileName</b>
        <pre>@fileContent</pre>
      </td>
    </tr>
  </table>
</body>
</html>
```

Figure 6.42 File Viewer Application Using the TreeView Component for IOWA

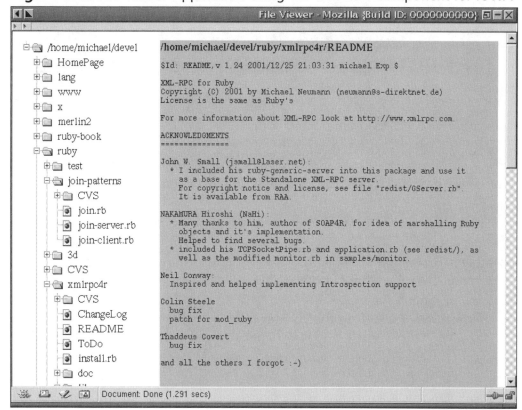

Summary

Ruby's full Web ability is still in development in many areas, so just how much of an impact it will develop on the Internet side of the open source programming field is still to be determined; however, it is already a strong Web language alternative.

The *Socket* class contains everything the Ruby programmer will need to work with the low-level networking/Web services, such as TCP/IP and raw socket creation. If all you need to do, however, is work with a server or create a thin HTTP client, you can always use the *Net* class, which contains pre-built high-level Internet objects that handle many of the popular protocols, such as HTTP and FTP.

Ruby does not always need to stand alone as a CGI/Perl language; with some modifications, Ruby has been able to work together with PHP as an embedded scripting language and can be optimized through mod_ruby. IOWA provides Ruby programmers with yet another alternative by creating a framework that has Ruby as its central language.

Through our example in this chapter using the online shop component, we have been able to see that Ruby is not only a language for desktop applications. It is also a full-bodied Web language that can stand alone or work with any existing scripting language. Ruby can interact easily with database components as well, showing that Ruby is just as flexible as the other languages available.

Solutions Fast Track

Connecting to the Web with Ruby

☑ The NET package stores the functionality that you will need to create high-level applications, such as HTTP clients and FTP clients.

☑ The SOCKET package stores the functionality that you will need to create low-level connections, such as raw TCP/IP sockets or UDP sockets.

Using Ruby on the Web

☑ You can use Ruby's *CGI* class to generate and interact with users of your Web page.

☑ Templating is a method that allows you to separate your Ruby code from your HTML code yet be able to access it through tags on your HTML page. Some templating solutions have the Ruby code inline while other templating solutions have a Ruby file which in turns calls the HTML file.

☑ HTML/Template and Ruby-tmpl are templating extensions for Ruby.

Implementing an Online Shop

☑ CGI and FastCGI, while standards of programming, required more coding than the Ruby and eruby counterparts.

☑ Mod_Ruby is an excellent utility for speeding up the programming process of Ruby.

☑ Eruby, a scripting language for Ruby, can also take advantage of the resources provided by mod_Ruby.

Using mod_ruby and eruby

☑ Ruby is not limited to being just like a CGI/Perl file.

☑ Using the eruby module, Ruby can be interwoven with HTML and PHP to create a style that incorporates not only one scripting language, but three different languages.

☑ Mod_ruby can speed up the speed of your Ruby (*.rb) files by optimizing the compiler.

Installing and Configuring IOWA

☑ IOWA installation is as easy as running the setup.rb file from the command line.

☑ IOWA works best with an Apache Web server, but does not depend on an Unix server. It can even run on a Windows 2000 machine.

Frequently Asked Questions

The following Frequently Asked Questions, answered by the authors of this book, are designed to both measure your understanding of the concepts presented in this chapter and to assist you with real-life implementation of these concepts. To have your questions about this chapter answered by the author, browse to **www.syngress.com/solutions** and click on the **"Ask the Author"** form.

Q: Are the *Socket* and *Net* class extra modules?

A: No, the *Socket* and *Net* class are part of the standard Ruby installation.

Q: It seems as though it is difficult to install some of these applications on Windows. Is there a way to facilitate this?

A: Many of the module programmers have released versions for Windows DOS and they have been able to install without any problems. To get the best out of these modules under Windows it is best to stay with either Windows 98 SE or Windows 2000; Windows ME and Windows XP remove the user interface with DOS.

Q: I am having trouble running IOWA on a Windows 2000 machine running Apache; Windows says I am not authorized to work with these files. Where could the trouble be?

A: Check the ownership of the IOWA and Apache files and see if you have permission to access them.

Q: Are there any other types of server architectures?

A: Recently there has been talk of G-Server Architecture but it has been implemented on only one Ruby application so far. The majority of the servers widely used today use one of the three implementations mentioned in this chapter.

Miscellaneous Libraries and Tools

Solutions in this chapter:

- **Graphics Programming in Ruby**
- **Mathematical Programming in Ruby**
- **Using C/S Data-Structure Tools**
- **Using Random Numbers, Genetic Algorithms, and Neural Nets**
- **Working with Ruby and Windows**
- **Using OOP-Related Tools**
- **Using Text-Processing, Date, and Calendar Tools**
- **Using Language Bindings**

- ☑ **Summary**
- ☑ **Solutions Fast Track**
- ☑ **Frequently Asked Questions**

Introduction

Ruby is a new, exciting, object-oriented scripting language—but due to its status as a relative newcomer to the world of programming, one might expect that there is little support in the way of libraries and packages. On the contrary, because of Ruby's ease of extendibility, there exists a rapidly growing list of libraries and extensions. In this chapter we explore a small subset of that list, with the hope of both being immediately applied to current projects and also encouraging the reader to explore the marvelous contributions out there.

In this chapter we discuss five broad categories of topics. The first topic we describe will be *graphics*. Since the topic is rather broad and involved, we will expend our energy exposing some methodology. The second topic is *algorithms and data structures*; this will be broken up into two groups, those that deal with primarily mathematical notions and those that are of a more computer-science nature. The third topic to be discussed involves *Ruby and Windows*. Since we discussed GUI development in Chapter 2, we can focus here on other topics, such as COM and Active Script. The fourth topic is an examination of some convenient *libraries* which aid in object-oriented development. The final topic discusses cutting edge technologies that allow Ruby to interface with code written in *other languages*. This gives us as developers the ability to take advantage of the ease of Ruby development inside other environments such as Java and Python.

> **NOTE**
>
> There are basically two types of libraries, those written in pure Ruby, and those that are C extensions to Ruby. Generally, pure Ruby extensions only require being on the search path. The C extensions to Ruby are usually installed by unzipping or untarring, and then at the command line typing **ruby extconf.rb**, which builds a Makefile. A *make* is then performed, followed often by a *make site-install* or *make install*.

Graphics Programming in Ruby

There are many different graphics-related packages that are supported in Ruby. For example, inside the Library section under *Graphics* in the Ruby Application

Archives (RAA), you can find support for OpenGL, GD, GD::Graph, PGPlot and Imlib2 (http://ruby-lang.org/en/raa.html). In this section we will discuss Ruby support for both OpenGL and GD Graph.

Using OpenGL in Ruby

OpenGL is probably one of the most well-known and powerful graphics library in the programming community. To this end, an OpenGL interface module has been developed by Yoshiyuki Kusano. In the sections that follow, we will create a simple application that will illustrate how to use OpenGL in a Ruby environment.

Defining the Goal and the Strategy

First let's define the goal of our sample application. The return on treasuries (bonds) maturing at different times generates a curve called a *yield curve*, which will be the focus of our application. The rate of return for long-term bonds is usually better than the rate of return for short-term bonds. However, the shape of this curve varies over time, and a bond trader may be interested in seeing how the shape has evolved over the last 12 months. Our example involves plotting and comparing 12 different curves (one for each month). What we want to do is to line these curves up next to each other, forming a three-dimensional picture. (We might want to do the same thing to analyze a spectrogram, the evolution of the frequency distribution over time of a voice sample) The general problem is to create a sequence of 2D graphs lined up against each other; since several sample programs are included with the OpenGL package, it seems reasonable to start with one of the samples and evolve it in such a way that it eventually satisfies our desired requirements.

Starting with a Sample Program

The first thing we do is to peruse the collection of samples that have been included with the OpenGL interface. Some, such as teapot.rb, are quite striking. But remember, what we want to do is represent a sequence of curves. If we can represent a single curve, then we should be able to replicate it. A curve is easier to see if we fill the area below the curve, and since this curve is to reside in three dimensions, it should probably have a thickness. Looking at the sample programs, the closest and simplest thing that is similar is cube.rb. When we run **ruby cube.rb** from the command line we will see a window similar to that shown in Figure 7.1.

Figure 7.1 Ruby cube.rb Image

Although this is not the most exciting figure, it is a start. What we will do is create our curve by piecing blocks together to form a row. The blocks will vary in height, and thus trace out the value of the curve. So let's first examine the code of *cube.rb* (shown in Figure 7.2 and found at www.syngress.com/solutions).

Figure 7.2 cube.rb

```
require "opengl"
require "glut"


$light_diffuse = [1.0, 0.7, 0.7, 1.0]
$light_position = [1.0, 1.0, 1.0, 0.0]
$n = [
  [-1.0, 0.0, 0.0], [0.0, 1.0, 0.0], [1.0, 0.0, 0.0],
  [0.0, -1.0, 0.0], [0.0, 0.0, 1.0], [0.0, 0.0, -1.0] ]
```

Continued

Figure 7.2 Continued

```
$faces = [
  [0, 1, 2, 3], [3, 2, 6, 7], [7, 6, 5, 4],
  [4, 5, 1, 0], [5, 6, 2, 1], [7, 4, 0, 3] ]

def drawBox
  for i in (0..5)
    GL.Begin(GL::QUADS)
    GL.Normal(*($n[i]))
#     GL.Vertex3f(*$v[$faces[i][0]])
#     GL.Vertex3f(*$v[$faces[i][1]])
#     GL.Vertex3f(*$v[$faces[i][2]])
#     GL.Vertex3f(*$v[$faces[i][3]])
    GL.Vertex($v[$faces[i][0]])
    GL.Vertex($v[$faces[i][1]])
    GL.Vertex($v[$faces[i][2]])
    GL.Vertex($v[$faces[i][3]])
    GL.End()
  end
end

display = Proc.new {
  GL.Clear(GL::COLOR_BUFFER_BIT | GL::DEPTH_BUFFER_BIT)
  drawBox
  GLUT.SwapBuffers
}

def myinit
#   $v[0,0] = $v[1,0] = $v[2,0] = $v[3,0] = -1;
#   $v[4,0] = $v[5,0] = $v[6,0] = $v[7,0] = 1;
#   $v[0,1] = $v[1,1] = $v[4,1] = $v[5,1] = -1;
```

Continued

Figure 7.2 Continued

```
#   $v[2,1] = $v[3,1] = $v[6,1] = $v[7,1] = 1;
#   $v[0,2] = $v[3,2] = $v[4,2] = $v[7,2] = 1;
#   $v[1,2] = $v[2,2] = $v[5,2] = $v[6,2] = -1;

    $v = [[-1, -1,1],[-1, -1,-1], [-1,1,-1], [-1,1,1], [1, -1,1],
        [1, -1,-1], [1, 1,-1], [1,1,1]]

    GL.Light(GL::LIGHT0, GL::DIFFUSE, $light_diffuse)
    GL.Light(GL::LIGHT0, GL::POSITION, $light_position)
    GL.Enable(GL::LIGHT0)
    GL.Enable(GL::LIGHTING)

    GL.Enable(GL::DEPTH_TEST)

    GL.MatrixMode(GL::PROJECTION)
    GLU.Perspective(40.0, 1.0, 1.0,  10.0)
    GL.MatrixMode(GL::MODELVIEW)
    GLU.LookAt(0.0, 0.0, 5.0, 0.0, 0.0, 0.0, 0.0, 1.0, 0.0)

    GL.Translate(0.0, 0.0, -1.0)
    GL.Rotate(60, 1.0, 0.0, 0.0)
    GL.Rotate(-20, 0.0, 0.0, 1.0)
end
GLUT.Init
GLUT.InitDisplayMode(GLUT::DOUBLE | GLUT::RGB | GLUT::DEPTH)
GLUT.CreateWindow("red 3D lighted cube")
GLUT.DisplayFunc(display)
myinit
GLUT.MainLoop()
```

This code can be described in roughly five pieces. The first piece defines some constants to be used later. The second piece, *drawBox*, is a drawing routine that draws a box. The third piece defines a process, *display*, which calls the *drawBox* method. The fourth piece, *myinit*, is an initialization method which sets up some lighting and perspectives. The final piece does some more initialization, calls the *myinit*, creates the window via *CreateWindow*, and runs the *MainLoop*.

We will keep the general form, but replace *drawBox* with *draw*, which will call *makeRow* and *drawRow*. The row can be thought of as being composed of 20 rectangular-based columns, with a rectangular front and back, and with trapezoids on the sides. We fill a row with data inside *makeRow* and we render that data inside *drawRow*. Actually, *drawRow* will have to draw its top and four sides: top, front, back, left and right. This is accomplished by calling *drawFront*, *drawBack*, *drawSide*, and *drawTop*. Now the front and back faces are just rectangular sides like the cube. We note that in addition to the corners, we must provide an outward-pointing normal vector (that is, a vector perpendicular to the surface). For the front, back, and sides, it's pretty easy to figure out what the normal vector is, but for the top we must compute it. This is done by taking the cross product of the vector, determined by two adjacent edges. The sides are composed of trapezoids. Now, it would be tempting to use GL::POLYGON for the sides and do it in one step, but GL::POLYGON requires that the shape of the polygon is convex, which will generally not be the case. Thus, the sides need to be pieced together as 20 individual trapezoidal strips. Fortunately, there is a relatively easy way to do this, namely to use QUAD::STRIP. Thinking of z as a function of x and y, it seems appropriate to have the z-axis pointing upward. However, by default OpenGL has the z-axis point out of the screen. Therefore, at the end of our *myinit* we perform a couple of rotations. We also edit the constants to create a change in the lighting. Putting it all together, we have the code shown in Figure 7.3 (this is the *ParabolaGraph.rb* file at www.syngress.com/solutions).

Figure 7.3 ParabolaGraph.rb

```ruby
require "opengl"
require "glut"


$light_diffuse   = [0.0, 1.0, 1.0, 1.0]
$light_position  = [1.0, 1.0, 1.0, 0.0]


$light_ambient   = [0.3, 0.0, 0.2, 1.0]
$material_specular = [0.7, 0.9, 0.9, 1.0]
$material_emitted  = [0.7, 0.7, 0.7, 1.0]
$material_specular = [0.7, 0.7, 0.7, 1.0]
```

Continued

Figure 7.3 Continued

```
shininess = 0.7
nTheta = 70
nPhi    = 30


def drawTop( row, width)
    x1,y1,z1=row[0]
    x2=x1+width
    (1...row.length).each do |i|
        y2, z2 = row[i][1], row[i][2]
        normal = [0.0, z1-z2, y2-y1]
        l = Math.sqrt( normal[1]*normal[1]+normal[2]*normal[2])
        normal.collect!{ |x| x=x/l }
        GL.Begin(GL::POLYGON)
        GL.Normal(*normal)
        GL.Vertex(x1,y1,z1)
        GL.Vertex(x1,y2,z2)
        GL.Vertex(x2,y2,z2)
        GL.Vertex(x2,y1,z1)
        GL.End
        y1, z1 = y2, z2
    end
end

def drawSide( row, width=0.0, side = 1.0)
    x=row[0][0]+width
    GL.Begin(GL::QUAD_STRIP)
    normal = [side, 0.0, 0.0]
    GL.Normal(*normal)
    (0...row.length).each do |i|
        y, z = row[i][1], row[i][2]
        GL.Vertex(x,y,0.0)
        GL.Vertex(x,y,z)
```

Continued

Figure 7.3 Continued

```
    end
    GL.End
end

def drawFront(row, width)
    normal = [0.0, 1.0, 0.0]
    x, y, z = row.last
    GL.Begin(GL::QUADS)
    GL.Normal(*normal)
    GL.Vertex(x,y,0.0)
    GL.Vertex(x,y,z)
    GL.Vertex(x+width,y,z)
    GL.Vertex(x+width,y,0.0)
    GL.End
end

def drawBack(row, width)
    normal = [0.0, -1.0, 0.0]
    x, y, z = row.first
    GL.Begin(GL::QUADS)
    GL.Normal(*normal)
    GL.Vertex(x,y,0.0)
    GL.Vertex(x,y,z)
    GL.Vertex(x+width,y,z)
    GL.Vertex(x+width,y,0.0)
    GL.End
end

def drawRow row
    dx=.3
    drawTop( row, dx )
    drawSide(row, dx , 1.0) #left
    drawSide(row, 0.0, 1.0) #right
```

Continued

Figure 7.3 Continued

```
    drawFront(row, dx)
    drawBack(row, dx)
end

def makeRow
    dy=.1
    row= []
    x, y =  0.0, -1.0
    (-10..10).each do |i|
        z = y*y
        row << [x, y, z]
        y = y+dy
    end
    return row
end

def draw
    row = makeRow
    drawRow row
end

display = Proc.new {
  GL.Clear(GL::COLOR_BUFFER_BIT | GL::DEPTH_BUFFER_BIT)
  draw # this is where we do the drawing
  GLUT.SwapBuffers
}

def myinit

  GL.Light(GL::LIGHT0, GL::DIFFUSE, $light_diffuse)
  GL.Light(GL::LIGHT0, GL::POSITION, $light_position)
  GL.Light(GL::LIGHT0, GL::SPECULAR, $material_specular)
  GL.Material(GL::FRONT, GL::SPECULAR, $material_specular)
```

Continued

Figure 7.3 Continued

```
GL.Material(GL::FRONT, GL::SPECULAR, $material_specular)
GL.Material(GL::BACK,  GL::SPECULAR, $material_specular)
GL.Material(GL::BACK,  GL::SPECULAR, $material_specular)


GL.Enable(GL::LIGHT0)
GL.Enable(GL::LIGHTING)


GL.Enable(GL::DEPTH_TEST)


GL.MatrixMode(GL::PROJECTION)
GLU.Perspective(40.0, 1.0, 1.0,  10.0)
GL.MatrixMode(GL::MODELVIEW)
GLU.LookAt(0.0, 0.0, 5.0, 0.0, 0.0, 0.0, 0.0, 1.0, 0.0)


# standardize the coordinates so that z iR pointing up
# and use spherical coord phi and theta, where phi == 0
# means the z axis is pointing up: and if in adition theta ==0
# then the y axis is pointing directly at the viewer


phi = 20 # phi is the angle between the z-axis and the eyeball
theta = -30 # theta is the rotation of the about the z axis
GL.Rotate(phi-90.0, 1.0, 0.0, 0.0)
GL.Rotate(theta-90.0, 0.0, 0.0, 1.0)


end


GLUT.Init
GLUT.InitDisplayMode(GLUT::DOUBLE | GLUT::RGB | GLUT::DEPTH)
GLUT.CreateWindow("graph test")
GLUT.DisplayFunc(display) # this sets the display rendering function
myinit
GLUT.MainLoop()
```

This produces an image similar to the one seen in Figure 7.4.

Figure 7.4 Ruby 3-D Parabola Image

Creating Multiple Curves

Now we adjust the code to create several curves at once by replacing *makeRow* with *makeRows*:

```
def makeRows
    dy=.1
    row1, row2, row3 = [], [], []
    x1, x2, x3,  y = 0.0, 0.4, 0.8,  -1.0
    (-10..10).each do |i|
        z = 0.5-y/2.0
        row1 << [x1, y, z]
        z=  y* y
        row2 << [x2, y, z]
        z= 3.0/8.0 + y*(y-1.0)*(y+1.0)
        row3 << [x3, y, z]
        y = y+dy
```

```
      end
      return row1, row2, row3
end


def draw
      rows = makeRows
      rows.each{ |row| drawRow row }
end
```

This produces our graph test, similar to the image seen in Figure 7.5.

Figure 7.5 Ruby 3-D Multi BarGraph

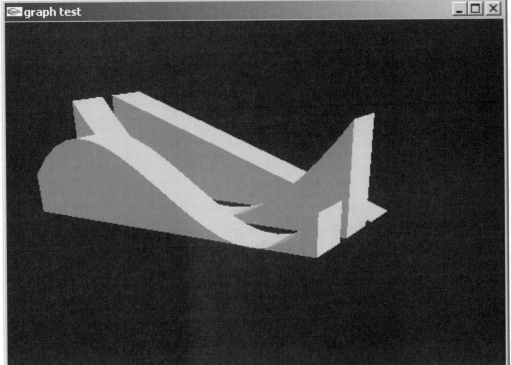

For a final touch, we will set the amplitude of the curves to be radially sinu-soidal and modulate by an exponential of the radius. Additionally, we touch up some of the surface lighting. The complete listing is shown in Figure 7.6. and can be found in the *ExpModCos.rb* file at www.syngress.com/solutions.

Figure 7.6 ExpModCos.rb

```ruby
require "opengl"
require "glut"


$light_diffuse  = [0.0, 0.5, 0.5, 1.0]
$light_position = [1.0, 1.0, 1.0, 0.0]


$light_ambient  = [0.3, 0.1, 0.2, 1.0]
$light_specular = [0.6, 0.7, 0.9, 1.0]
$material_specular = [0.5, 0.5, 0.7, 1.0]
$shininess = 0.7
Pi = 3.14
def drawTop( row, width)
    x1,y1,z1=row[0]
    x2=x1+width
    (1...row.length).each do |i|
        y2, z2 = row[i][1], row[i][2]
        normal = [0.0, z1-z2, y2-y1]
        l = Math.sqrt( normal[1]*normal[1]+normal[2]*normal[2])
        normal.collect!{ |x| x=x/l }
        GL.Begin(GL::POLYGON)
        GL.Normal(*normal)
        GL.Vertex(x1,y1,z1)
        GL.Vertex(x1,y2,z2)
        GL.Vertex(x2,y2,z2)
        GL.Vertex(x2,y1,z1)
        GL.End
        y1, z1 = y2, z2
    end
end


def drawSide( row, width=0.0, side = 1.0)
    x=row[0][0]+width
    GL.Begin(GL::QUAD_STRIP)
```

Continued

Figure 7.6 Continued

```
    normal = [side, 0.0, 0.0]
    GL.Normal(*normal)
    (0...row.length).each do |i|
        y, z = row[i][1], row[i][2]
        GL.Vertex(x,y,0.0)
        GL.Vertex(x,y,z)
    end
    GL.End
end


def drawFront(row, width)
    normal = [0.0, 1.0, 0.0]
    x, y, z = row.last
    GL.Begin(GL::QUADS)
    GL.Normal(*normal)
    GL.Vertex(x,y,0.0)
    GL.Vertex(x,y,z)
    GL.Vertex(x+width,y,z)
    GL.Vertex(x+width,y,0.0)
    GL.End
end


def drawBack(row, width)
    normal = [0.0, -1.0, 0.0]
    x, y, z = row.first
    GL.Begin(GL::QUADS)
    GL.Normal(*normal)
    GL.Vertex(x,y,0.0)
    GL.Vertex(x,y,z)
    GL.Vertex(x+width,y,z)
    GL.Vertex(x+width,y,0.0)
    GL.End
end
```

Continued

Figure 7.6 Continued

```
def drawRow row
    dx=.1
    drawTop( row, dx )
    drawSide(row, dx , 1.0) #left
    drawSide(row, 0.0, 1.0) #right
    drawFront(row, dx)
    drawBack(row, dx)
end

def makeRow( x )
    dy=.05
    row = []
    y = -1.0
    (-20..20).each do |i|
        z = yield(y)
        row << [x, y, z]
        y = y+dy
    end
    return row
end

def makeRows
    rows=[]
    (-20..20).each{ |i|
      x=.1*i
    rows<<makeRow(x){ |y|
            .5*(1+Math.cos(Math.sqrt(x*x+y*y)*2*3.14 ))*
            Math.exp(-(x*x+y*y))
    }
    return rows
end

def draw
```

Continued

Figure 7.6 Continued

```
      rows = makeRows
      rows.each{ |row| drawRow row }
end

display = Proc.new {
  GL.Clear(GL::COLOR_BUFFER_BIT | GL::DEPTH_BUFFER_BIT)
  draw # this is where we do the drawing
  GLUT.SwapBuffers
}

def myinit

  GL.Light(GL::LIGHT0, GL::DIFFUSE, $light_diffuse)
  GL.Light(GL::LIGHT0, GL::POSITION, $light_position)
  GL.Light(GL::LIGHT0, GL::SPECULAR, $material_specular)
  GL.Material(GL::FRONT, GL::SPECULAR, $material_specular)
  GL.Material(GL::FRONT, GL::SHININESS, $shininess)


  GL.Enable(GL::LIGHT0)
  GL.Enable(GL::LIGHTING)


  GL.Enable(GL::DEPTH_TEST)


  GL.MatrixMode(GL::PROJECTION)
  GLU.Perspective(40.0, 1.0, 1.0,  10.0)
  GL.MatrixMode(GL::MODELVIEW)
  GLU.LookAt(0.0, 0.0, 5.0, 0.0, 0.0, 0.0, 0.0, 1.0, 0.0)


  # standardize the coordinates so that z iR pointing up
  # and use spherical coord phi and theta, where phi == 0
  # means the z axis is pointing up: and if in adition theta ==0
  # then the y axis is pointing directly at the viewer


  phi = 20 # phi is the angle between the z-axis and the eyeball
```

Continued

Figure 7.6 Continued

```
theta = -30 # theta is the rotation of the about the z axis
GL.Rotate(phi-90.0, 1.0, 0.0, 0.0)
GL.Rotate(theta-90.0, 0.0, 0.0, 1.0)
GL.Translate(0.0, 0.0, -0.5)
end

GLUT.Init
GLUT.InitDisplayMode(GLUT::DOUBLE | GLUT::RGB | GLUT::DEPTH)
GLUT.CreateWindow("graph test")
GLUT.DisplayFunc(display) # this sets the display rendering function
myinit
GLUT.MainLoop()
```

The final result looks like the image seen in Figure 7.7.

Figure 7.7 Ruby 3D-Exponentially Modulated Cosine

Generating Diagrams with GD::Graph

GD::Graph is a wrapper around Perl's GD::Graph and GD::Graph3D libraries written in Ruby. Because the two Perl libraries depend only on the widely used library GD.pm, they are easy to install and very portable.

Effectively, GD::Graph does nothing more than to convert the method calls it receives to appropriate Perl code, fork a Perl interpreter, and feed that with the generated Perl code. The Perl code gets executed and sends the picture data back through a pipe, and finally the picture arrives by the Ruby application calling the GD::Graph library.

You can download GD::Graph from the RAA in the Library section under *Graphics*. Additionally, you will need a Perl interpreter, GD.pm, and at least one of the Perl libraries (GD::Graph or GD::Graph3D).

The code shown in Figure 7.8 generates a very simple three-dimensional bar-diagram with two data sets (seee the *gdBarGraph.rb* file at www.syngress.com/ solutions).

Figure 7.8 gdBarGraph.rb

```
require 'gd/graph'


# create new diagram object
graph = GD::Graph::Bars3d(400,200) # widht, height


# set some options
graph.set(
  :x_label => 'Day of week',       # x-axis label
  :y_label => 'Number of hits',    # y-axis label
  :title   => 'Diagram Title'      # diagram title


  # you may set here any other options available
  # in Perl's GD::Graph or GD::Graph3d
)


# plot the diagram...
graph.plot([
  # x-axis values
```

Continued

Figure 7.6 Continued

```
['Sun', 'Mon', 'Tue', 'Wed', 'Thu', 'Fri', 'Sat'],
# data-sets
[123, 555, 1200, 7, 4000, 401, 1913],
[339, 8393, 421, 876, 5143, 56, 737]
])


# ... and save it as image
f = File.new("my_diag.jpg", "w+")
graph.jpeg(f)
f.close
```

Use the methods *png* and *gif* to create .png or .gif images instead of .jpegs.

Ruby's GD::Graph library currently supports the *Bars, Lines, Points, LinesPoints, Area, Mixed, Pie, Bars3d, Lines3d,* and *Pie3d* diagram types, all classes under module *GD::Graph.* They work in the same way as shown in Figure 7.8.

For more information consult the man pages of Perl's GD::Graph or GD::Graph3D.

Mathematical Programming in Ruby

In this section we will discuss NArray, an array handling package, and BigFloat, a package for dealing with floats of almost unlimited size, as well as Polynomial, a package which deals with prime factorizations, polynomials, and infinitesimals. Last, we'll take a look at a package called Algebra, which deals with algebraic mathematical concepts such as rings, matrices, polynomial factorization and Gaussian elimination.

Using the NArray Library

Suppose that you are working on a project that requires the addition of two vectors. If it's sufficiently late at night and you are sufficiently sleepy, you might be tempted to try something like this:

```
[1,2]+[3,4]
```

But you shouldn't be too surprised if instead of [4,6], Ruby returns:

```
>> [1,2,3,4]
```

Obviously, you wanted component-wise addition instead of concatenation. Now, clearly you can overload **+** for the Array class, but this is rather hazardous, since it might break a lot of other code that relies on the *Array* class. You could define a new member method for the *Array* class, called, for example, *plus*. However, this is not elegant and one might wonder what should happen when the components are not numeric. The most satisfactory choice is to construct a numerical array class. This new array class could contain all sorts of methods besides just **+**; in addition, since you would like this class to perform its operations quickly, this numerical array library should interface with native C code. Fortunately, there is already such a numerical array library, namely *NArray*. To demonstrate, we will use it to write a small piece of code to add two vectors:

```
require 'narray'
a= NArray.int(2)
b= NArray.int(2)
a[0]=1
a[1]=2
p a
b[0]=3
b[1]=4
p b
p a+b
```

This results with an output of:

```
NArray.int(2):
[ 1, 2 ]
NArray.int(2):
[ 3, 4 ]
NArray.int(2):
[ 4, 6 ]
```

So NArray certainly satisfies the minimal functionality demanded—and in fact, it does much more: It is a general matrix-processing library. The following code sample exhibits some of the basic matrix operations:

```
require 'narray'
require 'irb/xmp'
```

```
# xmp :: http://www.ruby-lang.org/en/raa-list.rhtml?name=xmp


m1 = NMatrix.float(2,2).indgen!
m2 = NMatrix[[0,1.2],[1.5,0]]


v1 = NVector[0.5,1.5]
v2 = NVector.float(2,2).indgen!


a   = NArray.float(2,2).indgen!


xmp 'm1'
xmp 'm1.inverse'
xmp 'm2'
xmp 'm1*m2'
xmp 'm2*m1'
xmp 'm1+m2'
xmp '3.14*m1'
xmp 'm2*1.25'
xmp 'v1'
xmp 'v2'
xmp '1.25*v1'
xmp 'NMath.sqrt(v2**2)'
xmp 'v1*v2'
xmp 'm1*v1'
xmp 'v2*m2'
xmp 'm1.diagonal([98,99])'
xmp 'NMatrix.float(4,3).unit'
```

The resulting output is as follows:

```
m1
    ==>NMatrix.float(2,2):
[ [ 0.0, 1.0 ],
  [ 2.0, 3.0 ] ]
m1.inverse
    ==>NMatrix.float(2,2):
```

```
[ [ -1.5, 0.5 ],
  [ 1.0, 0.0 ] ]
m2
    ==>NMatrix.float(2,2):
[ [ 0.0, 1.2 ],
  [ 1.5, 0.0 ] ]
m1*m2
    ==>NMatrix.float(2,2):
[ [ 1.5, 0.0 ],
  [ 4.5, 2.4 ] ]
m2*m1
    ==>NMatrix.float(2,2):
[ [ 2.4, 3.6 ],
  [ 0.0, 1.5 ] ]
m1+m2
    ==>NMatrix.float(2,2):
[ [ 0.0, 2.2 ],
  [ 3.5, 3.0 ] ]
3.14*m1
    ==>NMatrix.float(2,2):
[ [ 0.0, 3.14 ],
  [ 6.28, 9.42 ] ]
m2*1.25
    ==>NMatrix.float(2,2):
[ [ 0.0, 1.5 ],
  [ 1.875, 0.0 ] ]
v1
    ==>NVector.float(2):
[ 0.5, 1.5 ]
v2
    ==>NVector.float(2,2):
[ [ 0.0, 1.0 ],
  [ 2.0, 3.0 ] ]
1.25*v1
```

```
      ==>NVector.float(2):
[ 0.625, 1.875 ]
NMath.sqrt(v2**2)
      ==>NArray.float(2):
[ 1.0, 3.60555 ]
v1*v2
      ==>NArray.float(2):
[ 1.5, 5.5 ]
m1*v1
      ==>NVector.float(2):
[ 1.5, 5.5 ]
v2*m2
      ==>NVector.float(2,2):
[ [ 1.5, 0.0 ],
  [ 4.5, 2.4 ] ]
m1.diagonal([98,99])
      ==>NMatrix.float(2,2):
[ [ 98.0, 1.0 ],
  [ 2.0, 99.0 ] ]
NMatrix.float(4,3).unit
      ==>NMatrix.float(4,3):
[ [ 1.0, 0.0, 0.0, 0.0 ],
  [ 0.0, 1.0, 0.0, 0.0 ],
  [ 0.0, 0.0, 1.0, 0.0 ] ]
```

You can see that matrix addition, multiplication, and inverse are supported (and also transpose—not shown). Of course, in matrix algebra, the dimensions of the matrices involved must be taken into account. For example, to perform addition of matrices, the dimensions should match. This means if we try to add two matrices whose dimensions do not match, an exception should be thrown. For example, if we append the following lines to the above code:

```
puts "\n=== following will fail ...\n"
xmp 'm1+v1'
xmp 'm1+1'
```

then an "Illegal operation: NMatrix + NVector" exception will be thrown. Using *xmp*, the error will be recorded by an output similar to this:

```
=== following will fail ...
m1+v1
TypeError: Illegal operation: NMatrix + NVector/...
/1m1+1
TypeError: Illegal operation: NMatrix + Fixnum/...
```

Here we used "…" to indicate that we have truncated the message.

NArray is a C extension of Ruby, which gives it a significant performance advantage over pure Ruby libraries such as Vector and Matrix. Additionally, NArray includes support of basic statistical operations such as mean, median, standard deviation (hence variance), covariance, etc. NArray also includes support for LU factorization and Fast Fourier Transforms. NArray is authored by Masahiro Tanaka and available through the RAA in the Library section under *Numerical*. It is a requirement for several other packages, such as Pgplot.

Using the BigFloat Library

As the name suggests, BigFloat is a library for handling big floating-point numbers. It is a C extension to Ruby developed by Shigeo Kobayashi. It is available in the RAA in the Library section under *Numerical*. This short example illustrates its usage:

```ruby
require 'BigFloat'


bf1 = BigFloat.new("01111111111.11111")
puts 'bf1=BigFloat.new("01111111111.11111")',bf1


bf2 = BigFloat.new("09999999999.99999")
puts 'bf2=BigFloat.new("09999999999.99999")',bf2


bf3 = bf2 * bf1
puts 'bf3 = bf2 * bf1',bf3


bf4 = bf2 + bf1
puts 'bf4 = bf2 + bf1',bf4


bf5 = bf2.power(5)
puts 'bf5 = bf2.power(5)',bf5
```

```
bf6 = BigFloat.new("")
puts 'bf6 = BigFloat.new("")',bf6


bf7 = BigFloat.new("xyzabc")
puts 'bf7 = BigFloat.new("xyzabc")',bf7
```

The resulting output is:

```
bf1=BigFloat.new("01111111111.11111")
0.111111111111111000E10
bf2=BigFloat.new("09999999999.99999")
0.999999999999999000E10
bf3 = bf2 * bf1
0.1111111111111110888888888888900E20
bf4 = bf2 + bf1
0.111111111111111E11
bf5 = bf2.power(5)
0.999999999999995000000000000009899999999999401000E50
bf6 = BigFloat.new("")
0.0
bf7 = BigFloat.new("xyzabc")
0.0
```

The constructor for BigFloat requires a string representation of a float. If the string does not represent a legitimate float, then 0.0 is assumed.

Using the Polynomial Library

Polynomial, developed by K. Kodama (also found in the RAA in the Library section under *Numerical*), is written in pure Ruby. It consists of several pieces, and is designed to give a synthetic approach to differentiation by use of non-standard analysis or hyperreals. The idea is simple: The real numbers (reals) are extended to include infinitesimals, so that differentiation may be performed by algebraic manipulations and then taking the standard part.

To explain further, in non-standard analysis, *hyperreals* are created when we extend the real numbers to include infinitesimals. Just as each complex number can be decomposed into an imaginary and real part, each finite hyperreal can be decomposed uniquely into the sum of a standard part (an ordinary real) and a non-standard part (an infinitesimal). A hyperreal, ε, is infinitesimal provided that $\varepsilon > 0$ and $\varepsilon < 1/n$ for every standard positive natural number n. Thus, if ε is an infinitesimal, then $0 < \varepsilon < 1$, $0 < \varepsilon < 1/2$, $0 < \varepsilon < 1/3$, etc. With infinitesimals available, limits are no longer necessary in expressing differentiation. For a standard real x and a function F, the derivative of F evaluated at x, denoted by $F'(x)$, is given by the standard part of:

[F(x+ε)-F(x)] / ε

Here ε is an infinitesimal. For example, if F(x) is squaring function x*x, then we see by doing the algebra that *F'(2)* is just the standard part of:

[F(2+ε)-F(2)] / ε= [4+4*ε+ ε*ε– 4]/ ε= 4+ε

But the standard part of 4+ε is just 4, so F'(2)=4. This is a special case of a more general problem; compute the limit as *h* approaches *0* of a function *G(x+h)*. The non-standard solution is to plug in $x+\varepsilon$ where ε is an infinitesimal. This process has been codified inside Polynomial. To demonstrate the non-standard approach more explicitly, consider the problem of computing the limit of rational polynomial:

(x-1)(3x+2)/(x-1)(2x+1)

as x approaches *1*. The astute reader will note that plugging in *1* for x gives *0/0*. In the non-standard approach, we plug in *1+ε* for x where ε is an infinitesimal and take the standard part. This is precisely what is done in the following code fragment:

```
require "hyperreal" # Non-standard real class
require "mathext" # extension for math.


def f1(x)
    return (3*x**2-x-2)/(2*x**2-x-1)
    #  (x-1)(3x+2)/(x-1)(2x+1)
end


print "-- Let f1=(3*x**2-x-2)/(2*x**2-x-1).\n"


x=1+HyperReal::Epsilon
printf "f1(%s)=%s\n",x, f1(x)
```

Here the function f1 is given by the following equation:

$$f1(x) = \frac{3x^2 - x - 2}{2x^2 - x - 1}$$

And in order to compute $\lim_{x \to 1} f(x)$, we simply evaluate $f(1+\varepsilon)$ where ε is an infinitesimal, and take the standard part. In the code, *HyperReal::Epsilon* is ε. Also note that *print* automatically extracts the standard part of an expression. The output is:

```
-- Let f1=(3*x**2-x-2)/(2*x**2-x-1).
f1(1)=5/3
```

If ε is an infinitesimal, *1divided by* ε is infinitely large, thus plugging in *infinity=1/ε* gives us the limit as h approaches infinity. We demonstrate this in the following code fragment:

```
x=HyperReal::Infinity # infinity
printf "f1(%s)=%s\n",x, f1(x)
```

This results with the output of:

```
f1(Infinity)=3/2
```

The following code exhibits both the polynomial algebraic manipulations and utilizes the non-standard approach to differentiation. Here, two rational polynomials are constructed, symbolically manipulated, and then differentiated:

```
require "rationalpoly"
# require "complex" # Complex coefficients


def sampleRationalPoly
        r1=RationalPoly("x^2+1","x+2")
        r2=RationalPoly("x+2","x+1")

        printf "%s+%s = %s\n",r1,r2,r1+r2
        printf "%s-%s = %s\n",r1,r2,r1-r2
        printf "%s*%s = %s\n",r1,r2,r1*r2
        print "-- We need to write reduction explicitly.\n"
        printf "%s*%s = %s\n",r1,r2,(r1*r2).reduce
        printf "%s/%s = %s\n",r1,r2,r1/r2
        printf "(%s)**2=%s\n",r2,r2**(2)
```

```
        q,r=r1.divmod(r2)
        printf "(%s).divmod(%s)=%s...%s\n",r1,r2,q,r
        printf "(%s)'= %s\n",r1,r1.derivative
        printf "(%s)''= %s\n",r1,r1.derivative(2)
        printf "(%s)'''= %s\n",r1,r1.derivative(3)
end
```

```
sampleRationalPoly
```

The resulting output is:

```
(x^(2)+1)/(x+2)+(x+2)/(x+1) = (x^(3)+2x^(2)+5x+5)/(x^(2)+3x+2)
(x^(2)+1)/(x+2)-(x+2)/(x+1) = (x^(3)-3x-3)/(x^(2)+3x+2)
(x^(2)+1)/(x+2)*(x+2)/(x+1) = (x^(3)+2x^(2)+x+2)/(x^(2)+3x+2)
-- We need to write reduction explicitly.
(x^(2)+1)/(x+2)*(x+2)/(x+1) = (x^(2)+1)/(x+1)
(x^(2)+1)/(x+2)/(x+2)/(x+1) = (x^(3)+x^(2)+x+1)/(x^(2)+4x+4)
((x+2)/(x+1))**2=(x^(2)+4x+4)/(x^(2)+2x+1)
((x^(2)+1)/(x+2)).divmod((x+2)/(x+1))=x-3...(9x+13)/(x^(2)+3x+2)
((x^(2)+1)/(x+2))'= (x^(2)+4x-1)/(x^(2)+4x+4)
((x^(2)+1)/(x+2))''= (10)/(x^(3)+6x^(2)+12x+8)
((x^(2)+1)/(x+2))'''= (-30)/(x^(4)+8x^(3)+24x^(2)+32x+16)
```

Note the first, second, and third derivatives of the rational polynomial *r1* are transparently computed. For more information on non-standard analysis and hyperreals, see Robert Goldblatt's *Lectures on the Hyperreals*, volume 188 of the *Graduate Texts in Mathematics Series* published by Springer Verlag, or see Nigel Cutland's *Nonstandard Analysis and its Applications,* volume 10 of the *London Mathematical Society Student Texts* published by Cambridge University Press. Also worth mentioning is J.E. Rubio's *Optimization and Nonstandard Analysis* published by Marcel Dekker.

Let's discuss briefly the *Number* module, which is also included in the Polynomial package. An example of the usage of *Number* is as follows:

```
require "number"
include Number
```

```ruby
pr=7;n=5;
# inverse of n mod pr is given by inv(n, pr)
puts "#{n}*#{inv(n,pr)}= 1 (mod #{pr})"
# factorial is given by factorial
puts "#{n}!=#{factorial(n)}"

# lcm give the least common multiple
a = [24,81,56]
s=a.join(',')
theLCM=lcm(a)
puts "lcm(#{s})=#{theLCM}"

# gcd2 gives the greatest common divisor and some other info
theGCD,*aj=gcd2(a)
arr=[]
a.each_index{ |i| arr<<"(#{a[i]})*(#{aj[i]})" }
srr= arr.join('+')
puts "gcd(#{s}) = #{theGCD} = #{srr}"

# prime number test is given by
n=10000000019
puts "prime?(#{n})=#{prime?(n)}"
n=10000000017
puts "prime?(#{n})=#{prime?(n)}"
puts "Factorization of #{n} is given by"+
  #{n}=#{factor2s(factorize(n),'*')}"

puts "---converting notational base---\n"
n=14;
b=2;
c=Number.i_to_notation_array(n,b)
puts "#{n} (base 10) = #{c.reverse} (base #{b})"
b=3;
c=Number.i_to_notation_array(n,b)
puts "#{n} (base 10) = #{c.reverse} (base #{b})"
```

```
c=Number.i_to_notation_factorial(n); c.shift
printf "%d=%s(factorial)\n",n, c.reverse.join(",")


str="1010"
b=2; a=Number.notation_str_to_i(str,b)
puts "#{str} (base #{b}) = #{a} (base 10)"
b=3; a=Number.notation_str_to_i(str,b)
puts "#{str} (base #{b}) = #{a} (base 10)"


print "----first 10 primes above 10**10 ----\n"
pr=10**10
10.times{ pr = nextPrime(pr); puts pr }
```

The output is as follows:

```
5*3= 1 (mod 7)
5!=120
lcm(24,81,56)=4536
gcd(24,81,56) = 1 = (24)*(-190)+(81)*(57)+(56)*(-1)
prime?(10000000019)=true
prime?(10000000017)=false
Factorization of 10000000017 is given by
10000000017=3*3*3*7*7*7*1079797
----converting notational base----
14 (base 10) = 1110 (base 2)
14 (base 10) = 112 (base 3)
14=2,1,0(factorial)
1010 (base 2) = 10 (base 10)
1010 (base 3) = 30 (base 10)
----first 10 primes above 10**10 ----
10000000019
10000000033
10000000061
10000000069
10000000097
10000000103
```

```
10000000121
10000000141
10000000147
10000000207
```

Using the Algebra Extension

Algebra is a pure Ruby package devoted to algebraic tools. Authored by Shin-ichiro Hara, it includes such diverse topics as multi-variate polynomials, quotient fields, and matrix manipulations. This package is well documented with a series of Web pages. Being pure Ruby, it is easy to install and extend. *Algebra* is available in the RAA in the Library section under *Math*. The following sections show a few examples of its usage.

Working with Polynomials

Both monomials and multi-variate polynomials are supported. As a simple example, consider the following:

```
# testPoly1
require "algebra"
P = Polynomial(Integer, "y", "x")
y, x = P.vars
a=x+y
b=x-y
c=a*b


puts "(#{a})*(#{b})=#{c}"
```

Here *Integer* is the base *ring* whose role is to provide the coefficients of the polynomial, and x and y are the variables. (A *ring* is a structure with + and ★ appropriately defined.) We reversed the order of x and y (that is, "y", "x") since the last element appears as the first in the output and we wanted x to be first. The output is:

```
(x + y)*(x - y)=x^2 - y^2
```

Exponentiation is easily handled as shown by the following:

```
# testPoly2
require "algebra"
```

```
P = Polynomial(Integer, "x")
x = P.var
a = x + 1
puts "(#{a})^3=#{a**3}"
```

Which gives an output of:

```
(x + 1)^3=x^3 + 3x^2 + 3x + 1
```

What makes this interesting is that we can replace *Integer* with any ring. For example, consider Z_3. This ring embodies integer arithmetic mod 3. (Actually, since 3 is prime, all non-zero elements have inverses and hence this is called a *field*.) We modify the above code to use Z_3 for coefficients, as follows:

```
# testPoly3
require "algebra"
Z3 = ResidueClassRing(Integer, 3)

P = Polynomial(Z3, "x")
x = P.var
a, b = x + 1, x+2
puts "(#{a})^3=#{a**3}"
puts "(#{a})^5=#{a**5}"
puts "(#{b})/2 =#{b/2}"
```

Since $3 \equiv 0 \pmod 3$, $2 \equiv -1 \pmod 3$ and $2 * 2 \equiv 1 \pmod 3$, the result becomes:

```
(x + 1)^3=x^3 + 1
(x + 1)^5=x^5 - x^4 + x^3 + x^2 - x + 1
(x + 2)/2 =-x + 1
```

Working with Matrices

Algebra similarly supports *matrices*. We form a class of matrices by supplying both the dimension (number of rows and number of columns) and the ring from which the matrix elements are to be drawn. A simple example demonstrating matrix multiplication is shown as follows:

```
# testMatrix1
require "algebra"
```

```
M54 = MatrixAlgebra(Rational, 5, 4)
M43 = MatrixAlgebra(Rational, 4, 3)
a = M54.matrix{|i, j| i + j}
b= M43.matrix{|i, j| i + j}
puts " a is"
a.display
puts " b is"
b.display
c=a*b
puts "a*b is"
c.display
```

The resulting output is:

```
a is
   0,    1,    2,    3
   1,    2,    3,    4
   2,    3,    4,    5
   3,    4,    5,    6
   4,    5,    6,    7
  b is
   0,    1,    2
   1,    2,    3
   2,    3,    4
   3,    4,    5
a*b is
  14,   20,   26
  20,   30,   40
  26,   40,   54
  32,   50,   68
  38,   60,   82
```

Again we can choose the ring elements to be something more interesting, such as Z_2, and the integers mod 2:

```
# testMatrix2
require "algebra"
```

```
Z2 = ResidueClassRing(Integer, 2)
M = SquareMatrix(Z2, 2)
a = M[[1,1], [1,1]]
puts " a is"
a.display
c=a*a
puts "a*a is"
c.display
```

Which, since $1+1 \equiv 0 \pmod 2$, gives an output of:

```
a is
  1,   1
  1,   1
a*a is
  0,   0
  0,   0
```

Now, matrices form a ring, so we may use them as coefficients of a polynomial. Here we multiply two polynomials whose coefficients are drawn from the ring of 2 by 2 matrices with entries in Z_3 (integers mod 3):

```
# testMatrix3
require "algebra"
Z3 = ResidueClassRing(Integer, 3)
M = SquareMatrix(Z3, 2)
c1 = M[[1,0], [1,1]]
c2 = M[[0,1], [1,1]]
puts " c1 is #{c1}"
puts " c2 is #{c2}"

P = Polynomial(M, "x")
x = P.var
a, b = c1*x + 1, x+c2
puts "a=#{a}"
puts "b=#{b}"
puts "a*b=#{a*b}"
```

The result is:

```
c1 is [[1, 0], [1, 1]]
c2 is [[0, 1], [1, 1]]
a=([[1, 0], [1, 1]])x + [[1, 0], [0, 1]]
b=([[1, 0], [0, 1]])x + [[0, 1], [1, 1]]
a*b=([[1, 0], [1, 1]])x^2 + ([[1, 1], [1, 0]])x + [[0, 1], [1, 1]]
```

At this point, everyone should agree that the algebra package is extremely flexible!

However, any discussion of matrices would be remiss if we did not address the eigenvector problem and diagonalization. To give a concrete example, consider the engineering problem consisting of two first order linear differential equations given by:

$$d(Y_1)/dt = -7\,Y_1 + -6\,Y_2$$
$$d(Y_2)/dt = 18\,Y_1 + 14\,Y_2$$

This can be put into a matrix form as $Y' = A\,Y$, where $Y = [Y1, Y2]$ and $A=[[-7, -6], [18, 14]]$. We solve this by finding a matrix P such that $D=P-1\,A\,P$ is diagonal. Then the problem becomes $Z'= DZ$, which we can solve readily. Now the solution for Y can be gotten as $Y=PZ$, since $Y'=(PZ)'=P(Z)'=P(DZ)=PP-1APZ=APZ=AY$. Or if you prefer, you can think of this as a coordinate transformation by P into a system where the original differential equations become transformed into a system with no interdependence. In any case, the vector Z is given by $Z=[\,C_1\exp(\lambda_1 t), C_2\exp(\lambda_2)\,]$ where λ_1, λ_2 are the eigenvalues of A, and columns of P are the corresponding eigenvectors e_1, e_2 of A. (As usual, C_1, C_2 are arbitrary constants to be determined by appropriate initial conditions.) In order to solve the original problem, we compute the eigenvalues and corresponding eigenvectors of A. Using the eigenvalues, we form the vector Z. Using the eigenvectors, we form the matrix P. The solution Y is the product $Y=PZ$. Now, enough talk, let's do it!

```
require "algebra"


eq1 = "d(y1)/dt = -7 y1  + -6  y2"
eq2 = "d(y2)/dt = 18 y1  + 14 y2"



def makerow eq
```

```
    r = eq.split
    return [r[2].to_i, r[5].to_i]
end



M = SquareMatrix(Rational, 2)
r1 = makerow(eq1)
r2 = makerow(eq2)


a = M[r1, r2]


puts "A = "; a.display; puts


extfield, roots, tmatrix, eigenvalues, addelms, eigenvectors, espaces,
    charactoristic_polynomial, facts = a.diagonalize


puts "eigenvalues are"
p eigenvalues
puts "eigenvectors are"
p eigenvectors


l = eigenvalues.collect{|x| x.to_f}
e = eigenvectors.collect{ |e| e.collect{|x| x.to_f}}
puts "\n\nsolutions are"
puts "y1= #{e[0][0]} C1 exp(#{l[0]} t)+ #{e[1][0]} C2 exp(#{l[1]} t)"
puts "y2= #{e[0][1]} C1 exp(#{l[0]} t)+ #{e[1][1]} C2 exp(#{l[1]} t)"
```

Let's walk our way through the code. First, using *makerow* we parse the text eq1, eq2 to create the matrix A. Next, we display the matrix, then diagonalize it, and display the eigenvalues and eigenvectors. Then we convert the Rational entries in eigenvalues and eigenvectors into floats. Finally we write down the solutions. The output is as follows:

```
A =
 -7,  -6
 18,  14
```

```
eigenvalues are
[Rational(5, 1), Rational(2, 1)]
eigenvectors are
[[Rational(-1, 2), Rational(1, 1)], [Rational(-2, 3), Rational(1, 1)]]
```

The solutions are:

```
y1= -0.5 C1 exp(5.0 t)+ -0.6666666667 C2 exp(2.0 t)
y2= 1.0 C1 exp(5.0 t)+ 1.0 C2 exp(2.0 t)
```

There is great deal more to this package and the reader is encourage to explore the possibilities. For references on algebra, consider Trefethen and Bau's *Numerical Linear Algebra* published by the Society for Industrial and Applied Mathematics (SIAM), or Gilbert Strang's *Linear Algebra and its Applications* published by Harcourt Brace Jovanovich.

Exploring C/S Data-Structure Tools

The Computer Science-related data structure packages we introduce here are *BinaryTree* and *BitVector*. You may recall from your first computer science course on data structures that a binary tree is a finite set of nodes which either is empty, or consists of a root and two disjoint binary trees called the left and right subtrees of the root node. A bit vector, also called a *dyadic sequence*, is a finite sequence of 0s and 1s. We begin our discussion with BinaryTree.

Using the BinaryTree Extension

BinaryTree is authored by Toki Yoshinori and is available at www.freedom.ne.jp/toki/ruby.html. This pure Ruby package consists of several pieces. The core functionality of the tree class is given in the file base.rb, and additional functionality is added requiring binary.rb. Binary.rb requires base.rb. Both avl.rb and splay require both base.rb and binary.rb. This layout demonstrates that we can add additional functionality to a class in Ruby by just requiring more files which contain that functionality—this is in distinction to Java or C++, where if we had a base class and wanted to add additional functionality by including (importing) more files, then we must resort to adding the desired functionality to a derived class of the base class and not to the base class itself. The package is very well written and comes complete with a test program that provides a series of tests. The five parts of the program and what they contain are:

- Tree/Base: Tree interface and parts classes

- Tree/Binary: Simple and basic binary search tree algorithm

- Tree/AVL: Balanced AVL tree algorithm

- Tree/splay: Self-adjustment splay tree algorithm

- Tree/Lock: Tree lock of multithreaded access

We demonstrate a simple application of the BinaryTree package by a simple (albeit contrived) example. Suppose we have a collection of farm animals. We want to maintain a record of the each animal's weight by modeling this with a binary tree, using the animal names as the keys and their weights as the values. We begin by entering the names and weights of our farm animals into a binary tree and then we display the list sorted by name.

```
require "tree/binary"


tree = Tree.new_binary


farm_animals=[ ['dog', 13.5], ['old cat', 10.2], ['bird', 3.4],
          [ 'young kitten', 3.5], ['bull', 978.3],
          ['pig', 304.4], ['cow', 800.3], ['chicken', 3.2],
          ['horse', 663.9], ['donkey', 356.6] ]


# now add all the animals
farm_animals.each do |key, value|
tree.put(key,value)
end


# now lets see the tree (without  traversing)
tree.each_with_index do |(key, value), i|
      puts "index=#{i} key=#{key} value=#{value} "
end
```

This results in the following output:

```
index=0 key=bird value=3.4
index=1 key=bull value=978.3
index=2 key=chicken value=3.2
```

```
index=3 key=cow value=800.3
index=4 key=dog value=13.5
index=5 key=donkey value=356.6
index=6 key=horse value=663.9
index=7 key=old cat value=10.2
index=8 key=pig value=304.4
index=9 key=young kitten value=3.5
```

We note that internally the tree looks like an array, and that it's not sorted. We want to see the resulting tree sorted by name, so we add the following code:

```
# now we traverse the tree
tree.each_pair{ |key, value|
       puts "key=#{key} value=#{value} "
}
```

This will produce the output:

```
key=bird value=3.4
key=bull value=978.3
key=chicken value=3.2
key=cow value=800.3
key=dog value=13.5
key=donkey value=356.6
key=horse value=663.9
key=old cat value=10.2
key=pig value=304.4
key=young kitten value=3.5
```

Now, alas, the old cat passes away, and after the funeral, we need to remove him from our list. This is accomplished by adding the following code snippet:

```
# old cat has died, we delete him from the tree
tree.delete('old cat')
```

We decide to convert the weight from pounds to kilos. Since 2.2 pounds equals 1 kilo, we divide each weight by 2.2. We also decide to change the format of the names to uppercase.

```
# now convert the weight from pounds to kilos
```

```
# and change the names to upper case
tree.collect!{ |key, value| key.upcase!; value/=2.2 ;}
# traversing tree to see our animals in order
tree.each_pair{ |key, value|
        puts "key=#{key} value=#{value} "
}
```

This results in:

```
key=BIRD value=1.545454545
key=BULL value=444.6818182
key=CHICKEN value=1.454545455
key=COW value=363.7727273
key=DOG value=6.136363636
key=DONKEY value=162.0909091
key=HORSE value=301.7727273
key=PIG value=138.3636364
key=YOUNG KITTEN value=1.590909091
```

We leave town for the weekend, and the automatic feeder breaks. The animals get hungry and break into our computer and post a protest message.

```
# Animal protest hunger
tree.fill('I am hungry')
# traversing tree to see our animals in order
tree.each_pair{ |key, value|
        puts "traversing key=#{key} value=#{value} "
}
```

This results in the following:

```
traversing key=BIRD value=I am hungry
traversing key=BULL value=I am hungry
traversing key=CHICKEN value=I am hungry
traversing key=COW value=I am hungry
traversing key=DOG value=I am hungry
traversing key=DONKEY value=I am hungry
traversing key=HORSE value=I am hungry
traversing key=PIG value=I am hungry
```

```
traversing key=YOUNG KITTEN value=I am hungry
```

Although somewhat silly, this example should be sufficient to get started. If you prefer a more serious example, think of the animals as bank customers and the weights as account balances.

Also included in this library is support for dynamically balanced AVL trees. Additionally, we have support for the splay tree algorithm, which shifts an accessed node and its neighborhood nodes to the root direction to transform the tree structor in order to more quickly access recently used nodes. Finally, when you separate threads, there is a tree lock mechanism that should be used.

For more information on trees, see Aho, HopCroft, and Ullman's *The Design and Analysis of Computer Algorithms*, or Knuth's classic *Fundamental Algorithms*, both published by Addison Wesley.

Using the BitVector Extension

BitVector is a C extension to Ruby. It was developed by Robert Feldt and is available at the RAA in the Library section under *Datastructure*. It is fairly extensive and fast, handling sequences of up to $2**31-1$ bits. It is implemented as a wrapper around Bit::Vector version 6.0 by Steffen Beyer. It is very similar to the Perl class *Bit::Vector*. BitVector comes with a convenient test suite. We begin our exploration of this library by examining the constructor *BitVector.new(n, s="")*. The first argument *n* represents the total number of digits that is to be allocated to the bit vector. The second argument, *s*, is an optional string which represents the data that is to be right-aligned within the BitVector. If the length of the string *s* is less than number *n*, padding of 0s occurs on the left. If the string *s* is of length greater than *n*, the most significant bits of the string are lost. Hence it is prudent to have n>=s.length. This is demonstrated by the following code fragment:

```
require 'bitvector'

b = BitVector.new(30)
puts "b=#{b.inspect}"


b = BitVector.new(2, "1011")
puts "b=#{b.inspect}"


b = BitVector.new(30, "1011")
puts "b=#{b.inspect}"
```

Which produces the following:

```
b=00000000000000000000000000000000
b=11
b=00000000000000000000000000001011
```

Of course, any package that deals with bits must supply some basic methods for manipulating these bits. The following code snippet demonstrates unary bitwise operations:

```
require 'bitvector'
b1 = BitVector.new(16, "10011011")
puts " b1              =#{b1.inspect}"
puts " b1.flip         =#{(b1.flip).inspect} (reverses bits)"
puts " b1              =#{b1.inspect}"
puts " b1.rotate_left  =#{(b1.rotate_left).inspect}"
puts " b1              =#{b1.inspect}"
puts " b1.rotate_right =#{(b1.rotate_right).inspect}"
puts " b1              =#{b1.inspect}"
puts " b1.randomize    =#{(b1.randomize).inspect}"
puts " b1              =#{b1.inspect}"
puts " b1.to_i         =#{b1.to_i} (as an integer)"
puts " b1              =#{b1.inspect}"
```

This produces the following:

```
b1              =0000000010011011
b1.flip         =1111111101100100 (reverses bits)
b1              =1111111101100100
b1.rotate_left  =1
b1              =1111111011001001
b1.rotate_right =1
b1              =1111111101100100
b1.randomize    =1100110101011001
b1              =1100110101011001
b1.to_i         =-12967 (as an integer)
b1              =1100110101011001
```

Note that all of the above operations change the value of *b1*, and all except *rotate_left*, and *rotate_right* return the current value of *b1*. The bit which was rotated is returned by *rotate_left*, and *rotate_right*.

However binary bit-wise operations do not change the value of the participants, and are demonstrated in the following code:

```
require 'bitvector'
b1 = BitVector.new(16, "10011011")
b2 = BitVector.new(16, "10111001")
puts " b1              =#{b1.inspect}"
puts " b2              =#{b2.inspect}"
puts " b1^b2           =#{(b1^b2).inspect} (Xor)"
puts " b1*b2           =#{(b1*b2).inspect} (multiplication)"
puts " b1/b2           =#{(b1/b2).inspect} (division)"
puts " b1.difference b2 =#{(b1.difference b2).inspect} (set difference)"
puts " b1+b2           =#{(b1+b2).inspect} (add)"
puts " b1-b2           =#{(b1-b2).inspect} (subtract)"
```

This produces the following output:

```
b1                   =0000000010011011
b2                   =0000000010111001
b1^b2                =0000000000100010 (Xor)
b1*b2                =00000000000000000111000000000011 (multiplication)
b1/b2                =0000000000000000 (division)
b1.difference b2 =0000000000000010 (set difference)
b1+b2                =0000000101010100 (add)
b1-b2                =1111111111100010 (subtract)
```

The position of the digits 1 or 0 in a BitVector can be gotten rather easily, namely:

```
require 'bitvector'


b1 = BitVector.new(16, "10011011")
puts "     b1              =#{b1.inspect}"
puts "     b1.ones         =#{(b1.ones).inspect}"
puts "     b1.zeroes       =#{(b1.zeroes).inspect}"
```

which produces:

```
b1               =0000000010011011
    b1.ones      =[0, 1, 3, 4, 7]
    b1.zeroes    =[2, 5, 6, 8, 9, 10, 11, 12, 13, 14, 15]
```

It should be noted that the position is given from left to right. That is, in the above, *0* in *b1.ones* indicates that the least significant bit is a 1.

This is just a sampling of the methods available to BitVector; for further information, see www.ce.chalmers.se/~feldt/ruby/extensions/bitvector.

Using Random Numbers, Genetic Algorithms, and Neural Nets

In this section we discuss some packages that implement some sophisticated algorithms. In particular, we explore a random-number generator package called *RandomR*, a genetic programming package called *Ruby/GP*, and a neural net package called *LibNeural*.

Working with a Random-Number Generator

In this section we introduce Robert Feldt's RandomR, which is a wrapper around *Mersenne Twister*, a fast random number generator written in C. Developed in 1997 by Makoto Matsumoto and Takuji Nishimura, this algorithm was originally called *Primitive Twisted Generalized Feedback Shift Register Sequence*. Subsequently it has been renamed to the less verbose *Mersenne Twist*er. Since it is written in C and is divide- and mod-free, it is four times faster than the standard rand. It has a period of $2^{199937}-1$ and gives a sequence that is 623-dimensionally equi-distributed. The installation is quite easy and usage is equally easy, as shown in the following example:

```
require 'random/mersenne_twister'
mt = Random::MersenneTwister.new 4357


puts "Random reals"
(0..10).each{ |x|  puts mt.rand(0) }
puts "Rand integers"
(0..10).each{ |x|  puts mt.rand(100) }
```

The output is as follows:

```
Random reals
0.6675764778
0.3690838726
0.7248306949
0.6877586338
0.5736469451
0.8107781868
0.27108403
0.8377701905
0.1373637365
0.9574540583
0.1786079517
Rand integers
57
12
84
25
88
24
31
0
12
46
```

RandomR is available at http://rubyvm.sourceforge.net/subprojects/randomr or in the RAA in the Library section under *Math*.

Genetic Programming in Ruby

Genetic Programming (GP) is a very nice package in Ruby dedicated to genetic programming, written by Akimichi Tatsukawa. Genetic programming is the art of applying *genetic algorithms* to solve programming problems that involve some optimization (by this we mean finding the x such that $f(x)$ is a minimum, or maximum). This is similar to evolution as it occurs in nature, whereby a population evolves over time to produce individuals that are best fit to a given environment.

More specifically, the first step is to randomly generate a fixed number N of an initial population consisting of a collection of individuals or chromosomes. Historically, the chromosomes are often characterized as binary sequences. The next generation of the population is generated by gene splicing (called *crossover*) and mutation. Each member of the new population is evaluated (or ranked) according to some fitness criteria. The population is then reduced until the population is again of size N. The reduction in population is done more or less by lottery, where those who are most fit have a better chance of survival. Generation after generation evolves until there is no significant improvement in the best individuals in subsequent generations. At this time the process stops and the most fit individual is returned as the optimal solution.

Given a maximization (or minimization) problem, we can turn it into a genetic algorithm, as follows. Suppose the problem is to find x such that f(x) is a maximum. Then x plays the role of the chromosome, and f is the fitness function. The problem becomes to find a chromosome that is most fit.

The GP package (available in the RAA in the Library section under *AI*) has several sample programs included with its distribution. Let's consider the following program, called Logic.rb. The stated purpose of Logic.rb is to perform a symbolic regression of a Boolean function. The quest is to create a Boolean expression, whose valuation A is identical that given by the truth table seen in Table 7.1.

Table 7.1 Truth Table

Truth Table								
P	True	True	True	True	False	False	False	False
Q	True	True	False	False	True	True	False	False
R	True	False	True	False	True	False	True	False
A	False	True	False	True	False	True	False	False

By this we mean we want to find some Boolean expression like **(not P or Q) and R** which is equivalent to A, where the behavior of A relative to P, Q, and R is given above. To be more machine-friendly, we use Polish notation—that is, we will write **and(or(not(P), Q), R)** instead of **(not P or Q) and R**.

Our chromosomes, in this case, should be well formed expressions such as **and(or(not(P), Q), R)** which will be evaluated across each case (vertical column in the Truth Table) to give a measure of fitness. Actually, all we need to do is to count the number of disagreements of a given expression (chromosome) with the desired value of A. In this case, the lower the number, the more fit the individual. Expressions that are not well-formed are rejected as unfit.

We are now ready to examine the code for *Logic.rb* (shown in Figure 7.9 and at www.syngress.com/solutions). The first class in the file is *GPIndividual*.

Figure 7.9 Logic.rb

```
class GPIndividual
  def evaluate_standardized_fitness() # should be the smaller the better
    fitness = 0.0
    GPSystem.fitness_cases.case_size.times do |the_case|

      GPSystem.fitness_cases.inputs.each{|variable,value|
        GPSystem.table.set_variable_value(variable,value[the_case])
      }
      output = GPSystem.fitness_cases.output(the_case)

      @genome.each do |gene|
        fitness += 1 if (output != gene.evaluate())
        gene_length = gene.length()
        if (gene_length > 30) # to supress huge genes
          fitness += gene_length * gene_length * 0.1
        end
      end
    end
    return @standardized_fitness = fitness
  end
end
```

GPIndividual is just a wrapper around the individual's chromosomes, which is called *genome* and defined originally in gpsystem.rb. What we see in Logic.rb in Figure 7.9 is a fitness function, *evaluate_standardized_fitness*, which must be supplied for every application using genetic algorithms. Each case that we loop around corresponds to a column in the table; all we are doing is counting the number of disagreements between *A* and the evaluation using the individuals genome.

Next we add the code that tells GPSystem how to evaluate the genome:

```
# table setting
GPSystem.table.add_function("and",2,Proc.new{|arg1,arg2| arg1 && arg2})
GPSystem.table.add_function("or",2,Proc.new{|arg1,arg2| arg1 || arg2})
GPSystem.table.add_function("not",1,Proc.new{|arg| !arg})
GPSystem.table.add_function("->",2,Proc.new{|arg1,arg2|
                    if (arg1 == true and arg2 == false)
                      false
                    else
                      true
                    end})
GPSystem.table.add_variable("P")
GPSystem.table.add_variable("Q")
GPSystem.table.add_variable("R")
```

Now we set some parameters used in the evolutionary process:

```
# GP parameters setting
GPSystem.population_size = 120
GPSystem.max_generations = 30
GPSystem.probability_of_crossover = 0.9
GPSystem.probability_of_mutation = 0.1
GPSystem.grow_method = GPGlobal::GROW
GPSystem.max_depth_of_tree = 5
GPSystem.genome_size = 1
GPSystem.allow_const = false
# now set selection pressure in the argument of new method.
GPSystem.selection_strategy = GPTruncationRandomly.new(3)
```

Most of the parameters should be self-explanatory. For example, *GPSystem.probability_of_mutation = 0.1* means that we expect some mutation of the genome to occur one-tenth of the time. What this means is that an "or" may be replaced by an "and," or maybe a "P" is replaced by a "Q." We also set a condition for early termination—that is, if we find an expression which is equivalent under all cases, then quit the evolution, and return that expression. This is what is done in the next code snippet:

```
# the condition of early termination
def GPSystem.terminate_early(best_individual)
  return (best_individual.adjusted_fitness == 5.0)
end
```

Finally, we input the truth table:

```
# the configuration for the fitness cases
fitness_cases = GPCases.new()
rowP = [true,true,true,true,false,false,false,false]
rowQ = [true,true,false,false,true,true,false,false]
rowR = [true,false,true,false,true,false,true,false]
rowA = [false,true,false,true,false,true,false,false]
fitness_cases.set_inputs("P", rowP)
fitness_cases.set_inputs("Q", rowQ)
fitness_cases.set_inputs("R", rowR)
fitness_cases.set_outputs(rowA)
# now register the fitness_cases to the GPSystem
GPSystem.fitness_cases = fitness_cases
```

The easiest way to run this is from another script, *testLogic.rb*, which contains the code shown in Figure 7.10 (also included at www.syngress.com/solutions).

Figure 7.10 testLogic.rb

```
require "gp/gpsystem"


gpMAIN = GPSystem.new
gpMAIN.startup("Logic.rb")
gpMAIN.run
```

Alternatively, add the following to the beginning of Logic.rb:

```
require "gp/gpsystem"


gpMAIN = GPSystem.new
```

and this to the end of Logic.rb:

```
gpMAIN.report_config()
gpMAIN.create_population()
gpMAIN.run()
```

Then save it as Logic2.rb and just run via *ruby Logic2.rb*. Both alternatives are included on the CD.

Running this, we get an output similar to the following (I say *similar to*, because Genetic Algorithms have a random ingredient):

```
<<The configulation of the genetic programming library >>


population_size = 120
max_generations = 30
probability_of_crossover = 0.9
probability_of_mutation = 0.1
max_depth_of_tree = 5
selection_strategy = truncation according to the selection
                    pressure 3 after overproduced randomly
grow_method = 0
genome_size = 1
allow_const = false


   <<The report of the current run >>


The best of the generation 1 is:
standardized_fitness: 1.0
adjusted_fitness    : 0.5
normalized_fitness  :
genome:
  (not  R)


The best of the run so far is:
standardized_fitness: 1.0
adjusted_fitness    : 0.5
```

```
normalized_fitness   :

genome:

   (not   R)



        <<The  report  of  the  current  run  >>


The best of the generation 2 is:
standardized_fitness: 1.0
adjusted_fitness      : 0.5
normalized_fitness   :
genome:
   (not   (and   (->   R R)  (and   R R)))


The best of the run so far is:
standardized_fitness: 1.0
adjusted_fitness      : 0.5
normalized_fitness   :
genome:
   (not   R)



        <<The  total  report  of  the  run>>


The best of the run is acquired at 3th generation:
standardized_fitness: 0.0
adjusted_fitness      : 1.0
normalized_fitness   :
genome:
   (not   (->   (and   (->   R Q)  (->   (or   R (->   P Q))  Q))  (not   (not
      R))))
```

As you can see, the best was found at the third generation. To interpret this, we see that we have *(not R)* and *(Q or P)*. A quick check of the table shows we have a match.

Genetic Algorithms is an interesting technology that has been used for the study of non-linear dynamical systems, neural nets, robotics, and more. For further information, start with Lawrence Davis's *Handbook of Genetic Algorithms* published by Van Nostrand Reinhold.

Neural Nets

Written by Akimichi Tatsu, *Ruby-LibNeural* is a wrapper around the C-based neural net library, *LibNeural*, originally written by Daniel Franklin.

Neural nets are used for both prediction and pattern classification. Common uses are speech recognition, fingerprint identification, character recognition, financial market prediction, credit risk, detection of money laundering, and diagnostics for X-rays, ultrasounds, electrocardiograms (ECGs), and electroencephalograms (EEGs).

LibNeural is a three-layered back-prop model. That means there is an input layer, a hidden layer, and an output layer. Each layer consists of nodes. Each node of the input layer feeds into each node of the hidden layer, and each node of the hidden layer feeds into each node of the output layer. Weights are attached to the connects between the node. It is often visualized as shown in Figure 7.11.

Figure 7.11 Three Layer Neural Net

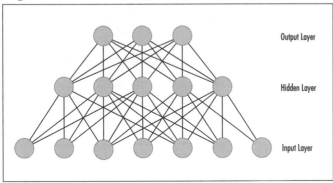

The network can be thought of as a function: Patterns of values are input into the nodes of the input layer and values are extracted from the nodes of output layer. Each node of the hidden layer and of the output layer performs a computation by taking the weighted sum of its inputs (coming from the nodes feeding into it), and applying a squashing function (sigmoid) to obtain an output. It is well-known that the standard feed-forward network architectures using arbitrary squashing functions can approximate virtually any continuous function of interest to any degree of accuracy, provided a sufficient number of hidden units are available. Thus, the only question is to find the appropriate weights. That is what training (in our case, this is called *backpropagation*) is about. Weights are initially selected at random. Sample patterns are given as inputs to the network, and the outputs are observed and graded. The weights are adjusted to improve the network's performance. When the performance is sufficient, training halts and the network is ready to use. Rather than going into further detail, let's consider a sample problem.

We will choose a rather simplistic problem to illustrate our neural net. Our goal will be to classify a curve as being either a straight line (linear), a parabola (quadratic), or cubic. The first question that comes to mind is: What do we want as an input? One obvious choice is to take the values of the curve at fixed set points. We will do this using the values at the seven points, from x = -3 to x = 3.

The next question is: How do we want our neural net to indicate which type of curve a given curve belongs to? Since we have three possibilities, one way is to use three output nodes. If node one is active, it is to be linear; if node 2 is active, it is to be quadratic; and if node three is active, then it will be cubic. The output of a given neuron is limited to be strictly between 0 and 1, so we will settle for a value of 0.8 to be considered *active* (on), and a value of 0.2 to be considered *inactive* (off). In this case, linear corresponds to an output of [0.8, 0.2, 0.2]. Putting the last two pieces together we see that we will want a neural net with seven input nodes and three output nodes.

We now appeal to a little intuition, and will try five nodes for the hidden layer. Before doing any coding, however, let's review our strategy. First we will train the neural net on a set of data, which we will call the *training data*. In order to decide when the training is sufficient enough that we may stop, we need to test the net against some data. However, it is inappropriate to test the net against the same data as was used for training (all that proves is that it can recognize the specific examples shown to it during the training). What we require of the neural net is the ability to generalize from the training samples presented to it and see the patterns we are looking for. In fact, we want to avoid over-training (also called *over-fitting*), otherwise we risk the net losing its ability to generalize. For this reason, we use a set of data called the *testing set*, which is not used in the training process to determine the stopping criteria. Finally, when we are finished with training and testing, we wish to validate the nets with a measure of performance on how well it can deal with completely new data. For this, a third set of data, called the *final validation data*, is to be used.

Now we begin by creating the data we want to use (code for this example is included at www.syngress.com/solutions in the *curveClassifer.rb* file):

```ruby
# We create a class to Build Data Sets
class DataSet < Array
  def initialize aCoffArry, bCoffArry
    for a in aCoffArry
      for b in bCoffArry
          self << (-3..3).collect{ |i| yield( i.to_f, a, b) }
      end
    end
  end
end


# Now build the data sets
linearTrainingSet    = DataSet.new( [1.0, 2.0, 3.0], [0.0] ) {
     |x, a, b| a * x + b }
quadradicTrainingSet = DataSet.new( [1.0, 2.0, 3.0], [0.0] ){
     |x, a, b| a * x * x + b }
qubicTrainingSet     = DataSet.new( [1.0, 2.0, 3.0], [0.0] ){
     |x, a, b| a * x * x * x+ b }


linearTestingSet     = DataSet.new( [1.2, 3.2, ], [0.0] ){
     |x, a, b| a * x + b }
quadradicTestingSet = DataSet.new( [1.2, 3.2, ], [0.0] ){
     |x, a, b| a * x * x + b }
qubicTestingSet      = DataSet.new( [1.2, 3.2, ], [0.0] ){
     |x, a, b| a * x * x * x+ b }


linearValidationSet    = DataSet.new( [1.1, 3.1], [0.0] ){
     |x, a, b| a * x + b }
quadradicValidationSet = DataSet.new( [1.1, 3.1], [0.0] ){
     |x, a, b| a * x * x + b }
qubicValidationSet     = DataSet.new( [1.1, 3.1], [0.0] ){
     |x, a, b| a * x * x * x+ b }
```

```
trainingSets  =[ linearTrainingSet,    quadradicTrainingSet,
    qubicTrainingSet]
testingSets   =[ linearTestingSet,     quadradicTestingSet,
    qubicTestingSet]
validationSets=[ linearValidationSet, quadradricValidationSet,
    qubicValidationSet]
```

Here we have limited ourselves to polynomials whose leading coefficient is positive and has a 0 y-intercept. Typically, in real world applications, the data is preprocessed. So in our case, we would preprocess the real world data by subtracting off the y-intercept whenever necessary, and maybe reflecting if the global behavior is decreasing, etc. In any case, we are now ready to set up our desired or targeted outputs. That is, the system should respond with approximately [.8, .2, .2] if the curve is linear, [2., .8, .2] if the curve is quadratic, etc. Also we need to include some helper functions to measure how close we are to the targeted output.

```
# set up the desired target outputs
linTarget   = [.8, .2, .2]
quadTarget  = [.2, .8, .2]
qubicTarget = [.2, .2, .8]
Targets = [linTarget, quadTarget, qubicTarget]


# Mean Square Error of a result with a given target
def Targets.MSError(whichOne, result)
  t = self[whichOne]
  s=0.0
  for i in (0...t.length)
    d=result[i]-t[i]
    s=s+d*d
  end
  return s
end
def testMSError( nnBrain , tsSets)
  # test if good enough
  totError=0.0
```

```
for indx in (0...tsSets.length)
  ts=tsSets[indx]
  targ= Targets[indx]
  for i in (0..1)
    result = nnBrain.work(ts[i])
    err = Targets.MSError(indx, result)
    totError=totError+err
    return true if totError > .01
  end
end
false
end
```

Next we create the net and do the actual training. The net is constructed in a single statement specifying the number of input nodes, hidden nodes, and output nodes. The training is accomplished by a call to *Neural#learn(input training vector, output target vector, tolerance, eta)*. *Input training vector* is the sequence of values to be applied to the input nodes, *output target vector* is the sequence which is the desired output for that sequence, and *tolerance* is the root mean square error allow for that output. Finally, *eta* is the learning rate parameter η, which arises in the optimization of the least mean square error.

```
# create a new neural net with 7 inputs, 5 hidden nodes and 3 outputs
brain = Neural.new(7,5,3)

more = true
while more do
  for i in (0..2)
    for indx in (0...trainingSets.length)
      ts=trainingSets[indx]
      targ= Targets[indx]
      brain.learn(ts[i],  targ,   0.0005, 0.2)
    end
  end
  more = testMSError(brain, testingSets)
end
```

Note that when a neural net is first constructed, weights are selected at random. Sometimes the initial weights are not very good, and take a long time to converge at an acceptable solution, so we restart with a different set if it fails to converge quickly enough. (In fact, genetic algorithms are applied to facilitate a faster convergence.) Finally we give our results:

```
# Just for curiosities sake, let's see how it does on the training data
puts "on trainingData"
for vs in trainingSets
  puts "*"*8
  for data in vs
    result=brain.work(data)
    p result
  end
  puts

end


# Now check the validation
indx=0
puts "validationSets"
for vs in validationSets
  puts "*"*8
  for data in vs
    result=brain.work(data)
    p result
  end
  puts

end
```

We see this output:

```
on trainingData
********
[0.7467244864, 0.2234046161, 0.2251292616]
[0.7764865756, 0.2254813612, 0.194798857]
```

```
[0.7790427804, 0.2257776409, 0.1922256351]
********
[0.2256926745, 0.7805635929, 0.1958302706]
[0.2251456231, 0.7814783454, 0.1951233]
[0.2251440585, 0.7814799547, 0.1951220185]
********
[0.2234400213, 0.1783940196, 0.7954290509]
[0.2225975692, 0.178310141, 0.7963095903]
[0.2225959301, 0.178309992, 0.7963113189]
validationSets
********
[0.7535769343, 0.2236442566, 0.2180884331]
[0.7790927887, 0.2257836014, 0.1921753436]
********
[0.2254521549, 0.7810022831, 0.1954940706]
[0.2251440585, 0.7814799547, 0.1951220185]
********
[0.2230481505, 0.1783550382, 0.795838654]
[0.2225959301, 0.178309992, 0.7963113189]
```

As stopping is a criterion for the training, we checked against our testing set (which was not seen during training) to determine if the mean square error was sufficiently small. This suffices for our purposes, but it is a bit simple; we should note that another approach is to continue training until performance on the testing set becomes worse—at which point we stop, back up, and use the weights of the previous iteration. Remember, the goal is to preserve the ability of the net to generalize, that is, to avoid over-training. Additionally, the number of nodes in the hidden layer can be adjusted by successively building and training nets with a decreasing number of hidden nodes until performance deteriorates. That procedure is justified by the belief that fewer hidden nodes allow better generalization, but that is usually computationally expensive. Be aware that some practitioners may only use two data sets, and call the set used for the stopping criteria the validation set.

For further information about neural nets, consult Simon Haykin's *Neural Networks*, published by Macmillan, or Robert Hect-Nielsen's *Neurocomputing*, published by Addison Wesley.

Working with Ruby and Windows

There are several alternatives to writing Windows programs with Ruby. In Chapter 2 we saw several interesting toolkits for building GUIs with Ruby that will run on a Windows-based platform. In this section we will discuss ActiveScript and Win OLE, two more alternatives for exploiting the Windows environment using Ruby.

Using ActiveScript in Ruby

ActiveScriptRuby can live inside your Internet Explorer. Just download it from the RAA from the Application section under *devel*, and do a one-click install. Of course, you need a *Windows Scripting Host* (WSH) installed—if you have Internet Explorer 4.0 or later on your system, then you already have one installed. ActiveScriptRuby is a Win32 ActiveScripting bridge component, and is supported by Anton. The example in Figure 7.12 is a variant of a script attributable to Yo-Ko-So.

Figure 7.12 The ActiveScriptRuby inside Internet Explorer

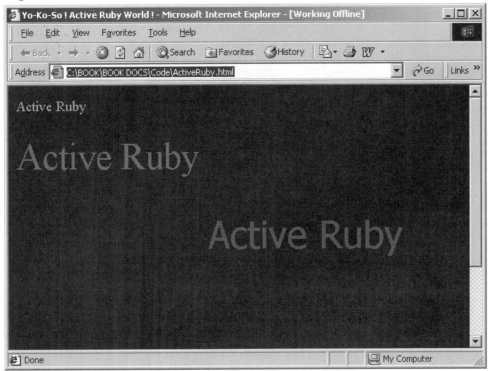

The script has such a nice appearance that we are compelled to examine the source—see Figure 7.13 (it can also be found at www.syngress.com/solutions).

Figure 7.13 ActiveRuby.html

```
<html>
<head>
 <title>Yo-Ko-So ! Active Ruby World !</title>
 <script language="RubyScript">
  ActiveScriptRuby.settrace false


  @ctbl = %w(red firebrick deeppink hotpink lightpink darksalmon
             darkorange coral crimson)


  @stbl = %w(x-small small medium large x-large xx-large)


  @ftbl = %w(Times\ New\ Roman Modern Tahoma Arial Century
             Courier\ New)


  def timeout(meth, arg)
    @window.setTimeout("#{meth}(#{arg})", rand(1000) + 1, "RubyScript")
  end


  def changeColor(s)
    @window.document.all(s).style.color = @ctbl[rand(@ctbl.length)]
    timeout('changeColor', s)
  end


  def changeFont(s)
    @window.document.all(s).style.fontFamily = @ftbl[rand(@ftbl.length)]
    timeout('changeFont', s)
  end


  def changeSize(s)
    @window.document.all(s).style.fontSize = @stbl[rand(@stbl.length)]
```

Continued

Figure 7.13 Continued

```
    timeout('changeSize', s)
  end

  def changePos(s)
    style = @window.document.all(s).style
    style.posTop  = rand(@window.screen.availHeight)
    style.posLeft = rand(@window.screen.availWidth)
    timeout('changePos', s)
  end

  def run
    @window.document.body.innerHTML = (1..7).collect do |s|
      %w(Color Font Size Pos).each {|m| timeout("change#{m}", s) }

      "<SPAN ID=#{s} style='position:absolute'>Active Ruby</SPAN>"
    end.to_s
  end

 </script>
</head>
<body language="RubyScript" onload="run" bgcolor="black">
</body>
</html>
```

It's actually pretty self-explanatory, it uses *setTimeout* to randomly pop up the word "Active Ruby" in different fonts, colors, and locations on the screen.

Using WinOLE in Ruby

OLE automation is supported in Ruby. Unless you built Ruby from the source, you probably obtained OLE support when you downloaded the Pragmatic Programmer's Windows installer. If for some reason, you do not have OLE automation support, you can get the necessary download at the RAA. Win32OLE (found at the RAA in the Library section under *Win32*) is maintained by Masaki Suketa.

OLE automation is easy to use. Consider the example shown in Figure 7.14 (and available at www.syngress.com/solutions).

Figure 7.14 Excel.rb

```ruby
require 'win32ole'
# Creates OLE object to Excel
excel = WIN32OLE.new("excel.application")
excel['Visible'] = true
workbook = excel.Workbooks.Add(1)
worksheet= workbook.Worksheets("Sheet1")
worksheet.name="Ruby Greetings"
worksheet.Cells(1, 1)['Value']='Hello Ruby Fans'
worksheet.Cells(1, 1).Font['Bold']=true
worksheet.Cells(1, 1).font['size']=18


# Now add some more sheets
for name in ['dog', 'cat', 'rabbit', 'bird']
   worksheet = workbook.Worksheets.Add
   worksheet.name=name
   for row in 2..6
      for col in 2..10
         worksheet.Cells(row, col)['Value']="(#{row}, #{col})"
      end
   end
   for col in 2..10
      worksheet.Columns(col).AutoFit
   end
end
```

This produces an output similar to the image seen in Figure 7.15. Examining the code we first wake up Excel by calling:

```ruby
excel = WIN32OLE.new("excel.application")
excel['Visible'] = true
```

Figure 7.15 Ruby meets Excel

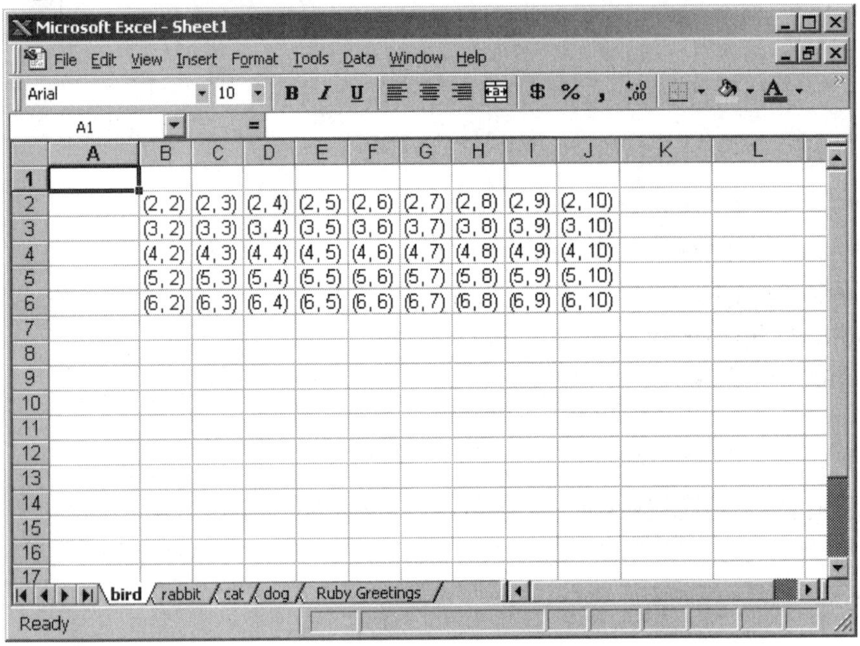

We then add a workbook and grab the first worksheet from that workbook called "Sheet1" and rename it "Ruby Greetings" by calling:

```
worksheet= workbook.Worksheets("Sheet1")
worksheet.name="Ruby Greetings"
```

We next set the text of the first cell of that first sheet:

```
worksheet.Cells(1, 1)['Value']='Hello Ruby Fans'
```

We set the font and size:

```
worksheet.Cells(1, 1).Font['Bold']=true
worksheet.Cells(1, 1).font['size']=18
```

We then loop around adding more sheets:

```
worksheet = workbook.Worksheets.Add
```

We name each sheet:

```
worksheet.name=name
```

We fill the cells of that sheet:

```
worksheet.Cells(row, col)['Value']="(#{row}, #{col})"
```

Finally we adjust the width of each column to fit the data in that column:

```
worksheet.Columns(col).AutoFit
```

The same techniques can be applied to a Microsoft Word document. For example, consider the following code snippet:

```
require 'win32ole'
# Creates OLE object to word
word = WIN32OLE.new("word.application")
word['Visible'] = TRUE;
word.documents.Add
0.upto(10){
        word.selection.TypeText(Text="Hello Ruby Relatives!")
        word.selection.TypeParagraph
}
#word.close()
```

A quick inspection of the code reveals that it opens a new Word document and places ten lines of the text "Hello Ruby Relatives!" Note the code to close the document has been commented out, so the document will remain open after the program exits. Running this will result in the document shown in Figure 7.16.

Figure 7.16 Ruby Running Word

NOTE

Call *#ole_methods* to obtain a list of OLE methods.

Using OOP-Related Tools

It should not be surprising that Object-Oriented Programming (OOP) is a central theme in the Ruby community. The nature of the language makes it easy to extend Ruby with additional OO features as needed. In this section we explore some of those extensions, which are written in pure Ruby. These extensions can be both useful in themselves and can serve as a model for the developer when the need arises for some possibly exotic future OO programming requirement.

Using the EachDelegator Library

EachDelegator is a pure Ruby library that adds enumerable capabilities to iterators. (EachDelegator is written by Okada Jun and can be found in the Ruby Archives in the Library section under *Syntax*.)

For example, consider the following:

```
require 'eachdelegator'
p "hoge".each_byte.each_with_index.collect{|a, i| [ i, a ]}
```

The output will be:

```
[[0, 104], [1, 111], [2, 103], [3, 101]]
```

Here's another example:

```
require 'eachdelegator'
class Array
   def all_pair
     for i in 0..(size/2-1)
       yield at(i), at(size - i-1)
     end
     self
   end
   each_delegator :all_pair
```

```
end

p [1, 2, 3, 4, 5, 6].all_pair.collect{|a, b| b + a}
```

Here the addition is applied pair-wise, so the result is:

```
[7, 7, 7]
```

Using the Preserved, Forwardable, and Finalize Modules

In C++ and Java, a class definition occurs in exactly one place, and that class definition cannot directly be augmented or enhanced by additional methods in any other place. And certainly any method's implementation cannot be redefined at a later time. Ruby, as we all know, breaks this rule. We may define a class method such as this:

```
class Furry
  def list_it(a)
    a.each{ |x| puts x }
  end
end
```

However, you could later decide to alter the method's implementation by using the following:

```
class Furry
    def list_it(a) return [a] end
end
```

In fact, the code defining these methods may reside in different files. While this gives the developer great freedom, this is not always desirable. Sometimes we would like to define a method and disallow any subsequent modifications of its behavior. In particular, two developers might accidentally use the same name to extend a class but with completely different desired behaviors, causing the code to break or produce bad results. We prevent this by guaranteeing our method's behavior is preserved when we use the *preserved* module. Using it is just a matter of declaring the *preserved* method, as shown in the following code:

```
require "preserved"


class MyPets
```

```
    def dog_sound
      puts "bow wow"
    end
    def cat_sound
      puts "meow"
    end
    def bird_sound
      puts "chirp chirp"
    end
    preserved :dog_sound, :cat_sound
end
```

Here both *dog_sound* and *cat_sound* are preserved, but *bird_sound* is not. What this means is that we can alter the behavior of *bird_sound* by including this code:

```
class MyPets
  def bird_sound
    puts "tweet tweet"
  end
end
```

But any similar attempt to alter *dog_sound* or *cat _sound* will generate an error that is something like:

```
./preserved.rb:67:in `method_added':
    preserved method `dog_sound' redefined
    for class MyPets (NameError)
```

A list of the preserved methods of an object is easily obtained by using the *preserved_methods* method, as shown in the following:

```
p MyPets.preserved_methods
```

Which returns this:

```
["dog_sound", "cat_sound"]
```

One final note: *preserved* applies only to class methods; singleton methods can override the behavior of a preserved class method.

Forwardable.rb allows an object to forward or delegate tasks to another object. As an example, consider the following:

```
require "forwardable"
class Programmer
  def work(n)
    puts "work "*n
  end
end

class Manager
  extend Forwardable
  def initialize
    @employee = Programmer.new
  end

  def_delegator("@employee", "work", "project")
end

manager = Manager.new
manager.project 3
```

Here the manager is assigned the project and his programmer does the actual work, as evidenced in the output:

```
work work work
```

Ruby's *define_finalizer* is augmented by the finalize.rb library. Generally, in finalize.rb we send notification of an object's eminent demise to another object so that it may handle any necessary cleanup (such as closing sockets, database connections, and so on). One way to do this is to use the *FinalObservable* module as shown below:

```
require "finalize"
class Foo
  include FinalObservable
end

class Bar
  def initialize
```

```
      foo = Foo.new
      @foo_id = foo.id
      foo.add_final_observer(self)
   end
   def terminate(theId)
      puts "inside bar terminating id=#{theId}"
      puts "bye bye foo" if theId == @foo_id
   end
end


bar = Bar.new
GC.start
puts "bar type=#{bar.type}"
```

What is interesting here is that when a new *bar* object is created, its initializer creates a new *foo*, which then adds *bar* as a final observer of *foo*. When leaving the initializer of *bar*, *foo* is released. *Bar* is notified of *foo*'s eminent disappearance by a call to *bar*'s terminate. The output thus becomes:

```
inside bar terminating id=83984164
bye bye foo
bar type=Bar
```

An alternative approach is to use the *Finalizer* module directly. Consider this example:

```
require "finalize"
dog="bow wow"
cat="meow"
Dog_id = dog.id

def cat.terminate id
   puts self
   puts "dog gone" if id == Dog_id
end
Finalizer.add(dog, cat)
dog = nil
```

Here *Finalizer#add* adds *dog* to the list of objects to be notified upon *cat's* eminent departure. Thus the output becomes:

```
meow
```

```
dog gone
```

Using Text-Processing, Date, and Calendar Tools

In this section we'll examine several new tools for handling different sorts of Date Logic: Soundex (a text processing tool), Date, and Calendar.

Using the Soundex Extension

Soundex is a pure Ruby extension of the Soundex algorithm. Soundex can be obtained in the RAA in the Library section under *Text*, and is written by Michael Neumann.

The Soundex algorithm was first applied in the 1880 census. Its purpose is to consolidate disparate spellings of surnames in census reports. Soundex is a phonetic index; its key feature is that it codes surnames (last names) based on the way a name sounds rather than how it is spelled. The intent is to allow one to quickly find the surname even if the spelling has changed (not an unusual occurrence). Names like Smith and Smyth are indexed together, that is, they have the same Soundex code. A Soundex code consists of one letter followed by three numbers. The algorithm is as follows:

1. Drop spaces, punctuations, accents, and other marks.

2. Drop the vowels A, E, I, O, and U, and the letters H, W, and Y.

3. Drop the second letter of any duplicate characters.

4. Drop the second letter of adjacent characters with the same Soundex numbering.

5. Convert remaining characters in positions 2 to 4 to numbers via Soundex numbering.

6. Truncate or pad with 0 to make the result of length 4.

Soundex numbers are coded as follows: The letters B, P, F, and V are numbered 1; the letters C, S, K, G, J, Q, X, and Z are numbered 2; the letters D and T are numbered 3; the letters M and N are numbered 5; the letter R is numbered 6.

Consider the following example:

```
require "soundex"
include Text::Soundex
x = "Smith"
puts "Soundex code for #{x} #{soundex(x)}"
x = "Smyth"
puts "Soundex code for #{x} #{soundex(x)}"
```

This results in the following:

```
Soundex code for Smith S530
Soundex code for Smyth S530
```

A possible application of Soundex might be to assist a telephone operator to look up telephone numbers quickly.

Using the Date2 and Date3 Extensions

Date2 and Date3 are pure Ruby extensions, which add more sophisticated date operations to include holidays of various sorts. These extension are written by Tadayoshi Funaba and are included together under *date2* in the RAA, in the Library section under *Date*. Included in this release are several sample programs, the simplest of which is *daylight*, which calculates when daylight savings time occurs in the US.

```
#! /usr/bin/env ruby

# daylight.rb: Written by Tadayoshi Funaba 1998, 2000
# $Id: daylight.rb,v 1.3 2000-07-16 10:28:50+09 tadf Exp $

require 'date2'
require 'holiday'

year = Date.today.year
[[ 4,  1, 0, 'US Daylight Saving Time begins'], # first Sunday in April
 [10, -1, 0, 'US Daylight Saving Time ends']].  # last Sunday in October
each do |mon, n, k, event|
  puts (Date.nth_kday(n, k, year, mon).to_s + '   ' + event)
end
```

The current year is obtained by a call to *Date.today.year*; the date is gotten by specifying the week, day of the week, year, and month. Another interesting example illustrates the call to *Date.easter* that is included in goodfriday.rb:

```
#! /usr/bin/env ruby

# goodfriday.rb: Written by Tadayoshi Funaba 1998, 2000
# $Id: goodfriday.rb,v 1.4 2000-07-16 10:28:50+09 tadf Exp $

require 'date2'
require 'holiday'

es = Date.easter(Date.today.year)
[[-9*7, 'Septuagesima Sunday'],
 [-8*7, 'Sexagesima Sunday'],
 [-7*7, 'Quinquagesima Sunday (Shrove Sunday)'],
 [-48,  'Shrove Monday'],
 [-47,  'Shrove Tuesday'],
 [-46,  'Ash Wednesday'],
 [-6*7, 'Quadragesima Sunday'],
 [-3*7, 'Mothering Sunday'],
 [-2*7, 'Passion Sunday'],
 [-7,   'Palm Sunday'],
 [-3,   'Maunday Thursday'],
 [-2,   'Good Friday'],
 [-1,   'Easter Eve'],
 [0,    'Easter Day'],
 [1,    'Easter Monday'],
 [7,    'Low Sunday'],
 [5*7,  'Rogation Sunday'],
 [39,   'Ascension Day (Holy Thursday)'],
 [42,   'Sunday after Ascension Day'],
 [7*7,  'Pentecost (Whitsunday)'],
 [50,   'Whitmonday'],
 [8*7,  'Trinity Sunday'],
 [60,   'Corpus Christi (Thursday after Trinity)']].
```

```
each do |xs|
  puts ((es + xs.shift).to_s + '  ' + xs.shift)
end
```

This gives the following output:

```
2001-02-11   Septuagesima Sunday
2001-02-18   Sexagesima Sunday
2001-02-25   Quinquagesima Sunday (Shrove Sunday)
2001-02-26   Shrove Monday
2001-02-27   Shrove Tuesday
2001-02-28   Ash Wednesday
2001-03-04   Quadragesima Sunday
2001-03-25   Mothering Sunday
2001-04-01   Passion Sunday
2001-04-08   Palm Sunday
2001-04-12   Maunday Thursday
2001-04-13   Good Friday
2001-04-14   Easter Eve
2001-04-15   Easter Day
2001-04-16   Easter Monday
2001-04-22   Low Sunday
2001-05-20   Rogation Sunday
2001-05-24   Ascension Day (Holy Thursday)
2001-05-27   Sunday after Ascension Day
2001-06-03   Pentecost (Whitsunday)
2001-06-04   Whitmonday
2001-06-10   Trinity Sunday
2001-06-14   Corpus Christi (Thursday after Trinity)
```

Finally, we should note that Date3 has an advantage over Date and Date2 by allowing us to include a time portion with our date.

Using the Calendar Extension

Calendar is a C extension of Ruby, which features various international calendars and operations. It features the Julian, Gregorian, Islamic, Hebrew, and Kyureki calendars. Calendar is authored by Tadayoshi Funaba and can be found in the RAA in the Library section under *Calendar*.

A simple example is "cal.rb":

```ruby
require 'calendar'
include Calendar

def cal(m, y)
  printf("    %s %d\n", MONTH_NAMES[m], y)
  printf(" S  M Tu  W Th  F  S\n")
  fst = absolute_from_gregorian(m, 1, y)
  print('   ' * day_of_week_from_absolute(fst))
  days = gregorian_last_day_of_month(m, y)
  for i in 1..days
    printf('%2d', i)
    if day_of_week_from_absolute(fst + i) != 0
      print(' ')
    else
      print("\n")
    end
  end
  if ((day_of_week_from_absolute(fst) + days) / 7) < 5
    print("\n")
  end
  print("\n")
end

def main()
  if $*.length > 2
    printf($stderr, "usage: cal [ month [year] ]\n")
    exit(1)
  end
  now = Time.now
  m = now.mon
  y = now.year
```

```
  m = $*[0].to_i if $*.length >= 1
  y = $*[1].to_i if $*.length >= 2
  cal(m, y)
end


main()
```

The year and month are taken from the current time: *Time.now*. When run, the output appears as the following:

```
November 2001
  S  M Tu  W Th  F  S
              1  2  3
  4  5  6  7  8  9 10
11 12 13 14 15 16 17
18 19 20 21 22 23 24
25 26 27 28 29 30
```

Using Language Bindings

Language bindings is a general term for how we call code written in one language from another. The most familiar example to any Ruby master is Ruby and C. The fact that Ruby can interface with C should not be too surprising, since Ruby was in C. All of the C library extensions presented in this chapter are examples of calling C from Ruby. In Chapter 10, we will see how Ruby can call C programs and how C programs can call Ruby. What this means is that any language that can interface with C can interface with Ruby by going through C. Using this technique, bindings have been written for Java, Perl, and Python, among others. But there is another technique—namely, Ruby has been recently rewritten in Java. This makes it very easy for Ruby to call Java and for Java to call Ruby.

Using JRuby

Probably one of the most exciting recent developments in the growth of Ruby is the introduction of JRuby, which is a pure Java implementation of Ruby. This provides a seamless way of accessing Ruby from Java and Java from Ruby. JRuby can be obtained at http://JRuby.sourceforge.net.

Ruby Calling Java

Ruby can call Java effortlessly. Moreover, we can write a swing application completely inside of Ruby. Consider the following example:

```
JavaObject.load_class "javax.swing.JFrame"

JavaObject.load_class "javax.swing.JLabel"

JavaObject.load_class "javax.swing.JButton"

JavaObject.load_class "javax.swing.JList"

JavaObject.load_class "java.awt.BorderLayout"



frame = JFrame.new("Java loves Ruby")

label = JLabel.new("Cats have nine lives")



button = JButton.new("press me")

listContents=[]

(1..9).each{ |x| listContents<<("cat number "+x.to_s)}

alist = JList.new(listContents)



frame.getContentPane().add(button,BorderLayout::SOUTH)

frame.getContentPane().add(alist,BorderLayout::CENTER)

frame.getContentPane().add(label,BorderLayout::NORTH)

frame.setDefaultCloseOperation(JFrame::EXIT_ON_CLOSE)

frame.pack()

frame.setVisible(true)
```

We can make several observations from this example. *Importing* a Java class XXX in a Java program corresponds to loading the corresponding Java object in JRuby, which is done by *JavaObject.load_class(XXX)*. More generally, *JavaObject.load_class* may take two arguments: The first is still the name of the Java class, while the second may specify the Ruby name of the class when it is to differ from the Java name (by default, the Ruby name is the Java name without the package). Each Java object is loaded individually—that is, we don't load all of *javax.swing*. Ruby strings correspond to Java strings, and a Ruby list is passed directly into the constructor of the JList. *JavaObjects* have the same methods as in Java, so we can use JDK documentation to look up the methods.

For example, *setDefaultCloseOperation* is a method of *JFrame* in the JDK. Also *JFrame.EXIT_ON_CLOSE* becomes *JFrame::EXIT_ON_CLOSE* in Ruby.

Putting it all together, we run the program from the command line by invoking the following:

```
java -jar jruby.jar RubyToJava.rb
```

This produces the resulting swing application window seen in Figure 7.17.

Figure 7.17 A Ruby Swing Application

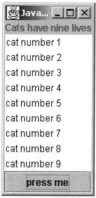

Note that arguments are converted from Ruby to Java types, as shown in Table 7.2.

Table 7.2 Ruby and Java Type Conversion

Ruby Type	Java Type
nil (NilClass)	null (Object)
true (TrueClass)	true (boolean/Boolean)
false (FalseClass)	false (boolean/Boolean)
Fixnum	Int/long/Integer/Long
Float	Float/Double/float/double
String	String
JavaObject	Object
Fixnum	Char
Array	Java array object (for example Object[] or String[])

Now since we have a button labeled **press me**, it would be nice if when we pressed it, something happened. So our next goal is to add an ActionListener. We will do this by adding the call:

```
button.addActionListener(JavaInterface.listener "ActionListener",
    "actionPerformed", action)
```

Here *action* is a Proc object which will handle the response to an action performed on our button. The action we choose to perform will be to pop up a dialog box with a message from Ruby telling us what action was performed. To this end, we will add the following:

```
action = Proc.new() do |evt|
  JOptionPane.showMessageDialog NIL,
    "Hello from Jruby. The button was:"+evt.getActionCommand
end
```

And while we're at it, we can drop the *javax.swing* from the *JavaObject.load_class* statements, provided we import *swing* via a *JavaObject.import* statement. We likewise can drop *java.awt* from the *JavaObject.load_class*. Putting this together, we get a complete listing, as shown in Figure 7.18.

Figure 7.18 Ruby2Java.rb

```
JavaObject.import "java.awt"
JavaObject.import "javax.swing"
JavaObject.import "java.awt.event"


JavaObject.load_class "JFrame"
JavaObject.load_class "JLabel"
JavaObject.load_class "JButton"
JavaObject.load_class "JList"
JavaObject.load_class "BorderLayout"
JavaObject.load_class "JOptionPane"


# create frame
frame = JFrame.new("Java loves Ruby")
```

Continued

Figure 7.18 Continued

```
# create label
label = JLabel.new("Cats have nine lives")


# create button
button = JButton.new("press me")


# create proc object to show MessageDialog box
action = Proc.new() do |evt|
    JOptionPane.showMessageDialog NIL,
    "Hello from JRuby\n Responding button: "+evt.getActionCommand
end


# add an action to the button
button.addActionListener(JavaInterface.listener "ActionListener",
    "actionPerformed", action)


# create contents
listContents=[]
(1..9).each{ |x| listContents<<("cat number "+x.to_s)}
alist = JList .new(listContents)

frame.getContentPane().add(button,BorderLayout::SOUTH)
frame.getContentPane().add(alist,BorderLayout::CENTER)
frame.getContentPane().add(label,BorderLayout::NORTH)
frame.setDefaultCloseOperation(JFrame::EXIT_ON_CLOSE)

frame.pack()
frame.setVisible(true)
```

We run as before; however, this time when we push the button, we get what's shown in Figure 7.19.

Figure 7.19 Resulting Action from Pressing Button

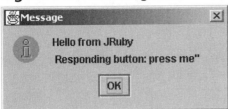

Be aware that subclassing a *JavaObject* or extending that object via an instance method may not always work.

Java Calling Ruby

In the previous example, Ruby called Java to implement a swing application. The JList in that application had its contents generated by ordinary Ruby code. Turning the problem around, we want to call Ruby from a Java program. More specifically, we will transform the Ruby swing application, Ruby2Java.rb, into a Java swing application, Java2Ruby.java, with Java calling Ruby to again generate the contents of the JList. This provides a nice insight on how to invoke Ruby from Java. We will proceed in two steps: First we begin by creating the Java-only portion of the program, then we will add the call to Ruby. The Java-only portion follows:

```
import javax.swing.JFrame;

import javax.swing.JLabel;

import javax.swing.JButton;

import javax.swing.JList;

import java.awt.BorderLayout;


public class Java2Ruby{

  public static void main(String[] args){

    JFrame frame = new JFrame("Java loves Ruby");
```

```
    JLabel label = new JLabel("Cats have nine lives");
    JButton button = new JButton("press me");


    //add an action to the button
    button.addActionListener( new ActionListener(){
      public void actionPerformed(ActionEvent evt){
        JOptionPane.showMessageDialog( null,
          "Hello from Java\n Responding button:" +
            evt.getActionCommand());
      };
      }
    );


    // The next 2 lines will be replaced by ruby code
    String[] listContents = new String[1];
    listContents[0]="temporary filler";


    JList alist = new JList(listContents);
            frame.getContentPane().add(button,BorderLayout.SOUTH);
            frame.getContentPane().add(alist,BorderLayout.CENTER);
            frame.getContentPane().add(label,BorderLayout.NORTH);
            frame.setDefaultCloseOperation(JFrame.EXIT_ON_CLOSE);
            frame.pack();
            frame.setVisible(true);

      }
}
```

Here we have temporarily placed a single string into the *listContents* so that we can test it and make sure that the Java only portion works properly. Running this we see the result shown in Figure 7.20.

Figure 7.20 The Swing Application with No Ruby

We now want to remove the two lines:

```
// The next 2 lines will be replaced by ruby code
String[] listContents = new String[1];
listContents[0]="temporary filler";
```

and replace them by Ruby code. Now the first thing is to create a JRuby runtime object. This is accomplished as follows:

```
// Create and initialize Ruby intpreter
Ruby ruby = Ruby.getDefaultInstance(GNURegexpAdapter.class);
```

Or alternatively by this:

```
// Create a new JRuby runtime object
Ruby ruby = new Ruby();
// set the Rexexp class
ruby.setRegexpAdapterClass(GNURegexpAdapter.class);
// initialize the JRuby runtime
ruby.init();
```

We next form a string which embodies what we want to do inside of Ruby:

```
String rubySource = "listContents=[]\n"+
"(1..9).each{ |x| listContents << (\"cat number \"+x.to_s)}\n";
```

Evaluating the string is simply a call to method *evalScript*:

```
String[] listContents = (String[])ruby.evalScript(rubySource,
    String[].class);
```

Adding the appropriate headers, the complete listing looks like this:

```
import javax.swing.JFrame;
import javax.swing.JLabel;
import javax.swing.JButton;
import javax.swing.JList;
import java.awt.BorderLayout;
import org.jruby.*;
import org.jruby.regexp.*;
import org.jruby.javasupport.*;


public class Java2Ruby{
```

```
public static void main(String[] args){
  JFrame frame = new JFrame("Java loves Ruby");
  JLabel label = new JLabel("Cats have nine lives");
  JButton button = new JButton("press me");
  // Create and initialize Ruby intpreter
  Ruby ruby = Ruby.getDefaultInstance(GNURegexpAdapter.class);


  //add an action to the button
  button.addActionListener( new ActionListener(){
    public void actionPerformed(ActionEvent evt){
      JOptionPane.showMessageDialog( null,
        "Hello from Java\n Responding button:" +
          evt.getActionCommand() );
    };
  });
  String rubySource = "listContents=[]\n"+
  "(1..9).each{|x| listContents << (\"cat number \"+x.to_s)}\n";


  String[] listContents = (String[])ruby.evalScript(rubySource,
    String[].class);


  JList alist = new JList(listContents);
  frame.getContentPane().add(button,BorderLayout.SOUTH);
  frame.getContentPane().add(alist,BorderLayout.CENTER);
  frame.getContentPane().add(label,BorderLayout.NORTH);
  frame.setDefaultCloseOperation(JFrame.EXIT_ON_CLOSE);


  frame.pack();
  frame.setVisible(true);
}
}
```

Running this, we see the screen shown in Figure 7.21.

Figure 7.21 Swing Application calling Ruby

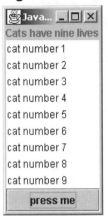

There are two other approaches to call Ruby from Java: The first allows for greater power, but is more involved: Instead of using *eval*, it calls all the Ruby methods directly. The second approach, which is to use Bean Scripting Framework (BSF), is much easier, but does not allow as much control (information on the Bean Scripting Framework can be found at www-124.ibm.com/developerworks/project/bsf and http://jruby.sourceforge.net/docs_bsf.html).

The JRuby development team includes Jan Arne Petersen, Alan Moore, Chad Fowler, Benoit Cerrina, and Stefan Matthias Aust.

Using the Ruby/Python Extension

Ruby/Python is a C extension of Ruby, which allows Ruby to easily access Python. Consider the following simple example:

```
require 'python'
require 'python/sys'

Py::Sys.stdout.write("Hello python world!\n")

Py.eval 'sys.stdout.write("Hello ruby world!\n")'

x = 1+2
line = "Ruby computes 1+2=#{x}"
```

```
puts line
```

```
x= Py.eval("1+2")
line = "Python computes 1+2=#{x}"
puts line
```

This produces the following output:

```
Hello python world!
Hello ruby world!
Ruby computes 1+2=3
Python computes 1+2=3
```

Note that we invoke the Python interpreter to add 1+2 using the **Py.eval** command. In general, a Python *import xxx* statement translates to a Ruby *require 'python/xxx'* statement, and a Python *XXX.xxx()* method becomes a Ruby *Py::XXX::xxx()*. To demonstrate the translation, consider the following sample Python program, *Html.py*, which is bundled with the Ruby/Python distribution. This program displays a formatted Web page.

```
import httplib
import htmllib
import formatter

import re, sys

match = None
if len(sys.argv) > 1:
    url = sys.argv[1]
    match = re.match('^http:\/\/([^\/]+)(\/.*)$', url)
if match:
    host, path = match.groups()
else:
    print "Usage: python ", sys.argv[0], " http://host/[path]"
    sys.exit(1)
h = httplib.HTTP(host)
h.putrequest('GET', path)
h.putheader('Accept', 'text/html')
```

```
h.putheader('Accept', 'text/plain')

h.endheaders()

errcode, errmsg, headers = h.getreply()


if errcode == 200:

    data = h.getfile().read()


    f = formatter.AbstractFormatter(formatter.DumbWriter())

    parser = htmllib.HTMLParser(f)

    parser.feed(data)

    parser.close()

else:

    print errcode, ": Failed to fetch", url

    sys.exit(1)
```

Html.py is a pure Python program, and is to be invoked from the command line with a Web page as an argument. For example, if we are running Linux with an Apache Web server, we might type the following at the command line to see a formatted text version of that Web page:

```
python Html.py  http://localhost/
```

The Ruby/Python version that is bundled with the distribution, Html.rb, is almost a direct translation:

```
require 'python'

require 'python/httplib'

require 'python/htmllib'

require 'python/formatter'


url = ARGV.shift

if url != nil && url =~ /^http:\/\/([^\/]+)(\/.*)$/

  host, path = $1, $2

else

  print "Usage: ruby ", $0, " http://host/[path]\n"

  exit(1)

end
```

```
h = Py::Httplib::HTTP.new(host)

h.putrequest('GET', path)

h.putheader('Accept', 'text/html')

h.putheader('Accept', 'text/plain')

h.endheaders()

errcode, errmsg, headers = h.getreply().to_a


if errcode == 200

  data = h.getfile().read()


  f =
Py::Formatter::AbstractFormatter.new(Py::Formatter::DumbWriter.new())

  parser = Py::Htmllib::HTMLParser.new(f)

  parser.feed(data)

  parser.close()

else

  print errcode, ": Failed to fetch ", url, "\n"

  exit(1)

end
```

Similarly, *Html.rb* is invoked from the command line:

```
ruby Html.rb  http://localhost/
```

The Ruby/Python extension allows us to leverage existing Python libraries and code with incredible ease. The Ruby/Python extension is due to Masaki Fukushima and can be found in the RAA in the Library section under *Language*.

Summary

In general, Ruby extensions are either written in pure Ruby or are Ruby wrappers around C code. Pure Ruby extensions are easy to install, easy to read, and easy to customize. Wrapping Ruby around C code allows us to have the ease of development that is inherent in Ruby while efficiently utilizing existing C libraries.

In this chapter we discussed using Ruby to create graphics. In particular, we discussed the *OpenGL Interface* package and also the *GD Graph* package. We surveyed some mathematical packages, for array manipulation, some of which were C-extensions (such as *NArray*) and some of which were pure Ruby extensions (such as *Algebra*). We discovered that *Polynomial* had an implementation of infinitesimals, an alternative to the theory of limits. We explored *BigFloat*, which allowed us to efficiently manipulate very large floating point numbers to a high degree of accuracy. More related to computer science, we found *BitVector* would allow to do bit-wise operations on large sequences of bit (or 0's and 1's). We built a binary tree using the *BinaryTree* package, and discovered how to use *RandomR* for random number generation. We explored genetic algorithms and artificial neural nets using the packages *GP* and *LibNeural*. We interfaced with Windows applications using *OLEWin32* and *ActiveScriptRuby*. We explored *Date* and *Calendar* libraries for date manipulation and discovered how *SoundEx* maps the sounds of surnames into Soundex codes. We explored tools to aid Object-Oriented Programming, namely *EachDelegator*, *Perserved*, *Forwardable*, and *Finalize*. Finally we saw that we can integrate Ruby with Python and Java by exploring the *JRuby* package, which is Ruby written in Java.

The Ruby community is one of the most exciting and fastest growing communities of software developers and the tools to develop new and innovative technologies is mushrooming. In this chapter we covered just a small portion of the publicly available solutions. What we discovered is that Ruby makes development for such diverse areas as OpenGL and Java transparently easy.

Solutions Fast Track

Graphics Programming in Ruby

☑ There are several outstanding alternatives for manipulating graphics in Ruby. OpenGL is high on that list since it is relatively well known and highly portable.

☑ The Ruby-OpenGL package allows full support of OpenGL. Usage is quite straightforward, and somewhat easier than in C.

☑ The Ruby-GD Graph package allows full support of Perl-based GD Graph.

Mathematical Programming in Ruby

☑ NArray is standard array package that allows for rapid array manipulations and is used by several other packages, such as PGPlot.

☑ BigFloat is a package dedicated to the manipulation of very large floating point numbers.

☑ Polynomial is a pure Ruby package that performs polynomial operations and differentiation using infinitesimals.

☑ Algebra is a package that performs all of the usual linear algebra operations, but has the additional capability of handling exotic fields and rings.

Using C/S Data-Structure Tools

☑ Binary Tree contains support for binary trees, avl trees, splay, and lock.

☑ Bit Vector supports 0-1 sequences of almost unlimited length.

Using Random Numbers, Genetic Algorithms, and Neural Nets

☑ RandomR is a sophisticated, but easy-to-use random number generator. It is well-suited when a large degree of randomness is necessary.

☑ GP is an extensive genetic algorithms programming toolkit.

☑ LibNeural is a very easy-to-use three-layered back propagation neural net engine.

Working with Ruby and Windows

☑ ActiveScriptRuby adds Active Script support to Ruby.

☑ Win32OLE makes working with OLE automation easy.

Using OOP-Related Tools

☑ EachDelegator is a delegator that adds Enumerable capabilities to iterators.

☑ Preserved.rb allows for preserving the definition of method—that is, protecting it from accidental change.

☑ Forwardable.rb allows an object to forward or delegate tasks to another object.

☑ Finalize.rb is an object-oriented enhancement of Ruby's *define_finalizer* method.

Using Text-Processing, Date, and Calendar Tools

☑ Soundex.rb is a program that codes names by one character and 3 digits, which are to represent the sound of the name as opposed to its spelling.

☑ Date2 and Date3 provide date manipulation programming with holiday support.

☑ Calendar features different international calendars.

Using Language Bindings

☑ JRuby is Ruby written in Java. It allows for easy access of Ruby from Java or Java from Ruby. It is easy to install, and one can rapidly develop code using Ruby within a Java environment.

☑ Ruby/Python allows for the Ruby programmer to call Python routines and libraries easily.

Frequently Asked Questions

The following Frequently Asked Questions, answered by the authors of this book, are designed to both measure your understanding of the concepts presented in this chapter and to assist you with real-life implementation of these concepts. To have your questions about this chapter answered by the author, browse to **www.syngress.com/solutions** and click on the **"Ask the Author"** form.

Q: I just found the latest and greatest tool, but the documentation is in Japanese. Where will I find a translation?

A: If the documentation is on a Web page, go to http://world.altavista.com and paste the message into Babel Fish, an online language translation program. If it's in code, or in a text file, then there are three possible formats (that are not Unicode). Copy the text from the source and place it into a Web page (set up for Japanese encoding) and display in your Web browser. Then copy from the Web browser and paste into Babel Fish and translate.

Q: I'm running Windows, and I want to use a Ruby extension, but it requires a C compiler—what do I do?

A: Try downloading and installing Cygwin from http://cygwin.com. The complete Cygwin package comes with gcc and f77. If you are using a pre-built version of Ruby for Windows that is Cygwin-based, take care that you do not have conflicting versions of the cygwin.dll on your path. I found that removing the cygwin.dll that came with Ruby (for Windows) seems to work.

Q: I want to use OLE automation to create some Excel spreadsheets, but I don't know the Ruby-OLE automation command for one of the operations I want to perform. Where can I find it?

A: Go to Excel, and record a macro for that operation. Then open the macro editor and read what was recorded. That will be sufficient to tell you what the appropriate Ruby script should be.

Profiling and Performance Tuning

Solutions in this chapter:

- **Analyzing the Complexity of Algorithms**
- **Improving Performance by Profiling**
- **Comparing the Speed of Ruby Constructs**
- **Further Performance Enhancements**

- ☑ **Summary**
- ☑ **Solutions Fast Track**
- ☑ **Frequently Asked Questions**

Introduction

Believe it or not, performance should not be the first thing on your mind when designing and writing programs. If you prematurely optimize your programs or designs, they will tend to be more complex and error-prone, harder to understand, and more difficult to maintain. Concentrate first on getting a given program to work and adding in the needed features before shifting your focus to how fast it will execute. Otherwise, you can prematurely alter your program by changing the algorithm, adding code to cache results or using different data structures. Another reason not to start optimizing early is that you simply will not know what parts of your program take the most time. Chances are, you'll have to focus on performance at some point because your program is too slow, but that should come later.

If you discover that the application you've developed is slow, the first thing to ask yourself is: Does it really matter? It does if endless tweaking causes your program to ship too late to be useful or if it does not arrive at all. But often, poor performance is more of a nuisance than a disaster. To settle this, you have to time your program using realistic input data, and you have to keep in mind that next year's computers will be twice as fast. If you put your efforts into performance instead of adding needed features and weeding out bugs, you may end up with a fast but useless program.

When you are sure your program has a performance problem, you need to understand why this is so. A good first step is to use a profiler to analyze where time is being spent. The standard Ruby distribution comes with a profiler that gives you information on the amount of time spent in each method. Armed with this knowledge, you can find the hot spots in your program, which are the lines of code where the majority of time is wasted. By using this information and thinking about the algorithms in your program, you can understand why the program executes slower than you'd expected.

There is a general strategy for improving performance: *reduce the total number of steps the computer needs to go through.* Often you will get the largest performance increase by considering your program's algorithms. This is because they are the factor that most affects the steps through which the computer must go. They affect a larger part of your program than detailed decisions, such as whether you should add elements to an array using *push* or *concat*. By considering the algorithm, you think about what your program actually does. Maybe you will find redundant computations that can be eliminated; or you will find that you're using data structures that allocate too much memory.

When you have worked on the "what" of your design and feel you cannot eliminate more of your program's steps, you may have to focus on smaller-scale issues. There are some Ruby constructs that you might prefer if you need that extra performance; we'll take a look at some of them and compare them in this chapter. First, let's start at the highest level: the algorithm.

Analyzing the Complexity of Algorithms

Your program describes a sequence of instructions for the computer to execute. It has lots of details to describe exactly how and where the computer should read data, calculate new values, call methods and store the results. In order to understand the time it takes for your program to perform its tasks, you would have to take all this information into account. You would *also* need to understand how these instructions interact during the run, the speed of the computer, and so on. To simplify things, study the general properties of programs and the complexity of their algorithms.

The algorithm is the essence of your program—what it does and in what order. It is basically a sequence of steps. The number of steps needed often grows as the size of the input grows. For example, look at the following Ruby code for sorting an array using the Bubblesort algorithm:

```ruby
def bubble_sort(ary)
  0.upto(ary.length-2) do |i|            # Outer loop
    (ary.length-2).downto(i) do |j|      # Inner loop
      if ary[j+1] < ary[j]
        ary[j], ary[j+1] = ary[j+1], ary[j]
      end
    end                                  # end of inner
  end                                    # end of outer
  ary
end
```

Let's call the length of *ary* "N" and see how the number of steps (and thus the execution time) of the algorithm increases as N does. The inner loop will be executed N-1 times. The statement in the inner loop will be executed N-1 times the first time, N-2 times the second time and so on down to 1 time for the last instance.

In total it will be executed N-1 + N-2 + ... + 1 = N*(N-1)/2 = (N^2 − N)/2 times.

When the inner loop statement is executed there is always a comparison and then sometimes, based on the outcome, two assignments. So if we want to predict the time, *T(N)*, that it will take to do a Bubblesort, we could use an expression of the following form:

T(N) = (N^2-N)/2*(Tcomp + Pswap * Tswap)

where *Pswap* is the probability that a swap is needed, *Tswap* is the time to perform the swap and *Tcomp* is the time to perform the comparison. But note that even at this detailed level there are lots of things we haven't considered; we have not included any time to set up the loops, nor any time to check the loop conditions and decide if we need to continue looping.

In general, you don't need this level of detail. You want an approximate measure to characterize and compare different algorithms, and that is independent of the actual computer and input data. If we skip the Ts and P from the equation above, we can say that "Bubblesort typically uses (N^2-N)/2 steps." When N grows larger, the N^2 term totally dominates the expression so we could simplify even more and say "Bubblesort needs on the order of N^2 steps". Formally, this is called the time complexity of the Bubblesort algorithm, which is denoted O(N^2) in the ordo notation and spelled "ordo-N-two".

The Ruby extension *benchmark.rb* by Goto Kentaro can be found in the Ruby Application Archive (RAA) at www.ruby-lang.org/en/raa.html, in the Library section under *devel*; it provides a simple way to time Ruby code.

It times how much user, system, total and wall clock (real) time is spent while executing a block of Ruby code. The method *bm* can be used to compare several blocks of code. Let's use it to call Bubblesort on some random arrays of different sizes:

```
require 'benchmark'
include Benchmark

array_generator = proc{|n| Array.new(n).map!{rand(n)}}

bm(12) do |t|
    t.report("N = 50")   { bubblesort(array_generator.call(50))   }
    t.report("N = 500")  { bubblesort(array_generator.call(500))  }
    t.report("N = 5000") { bubblesort(array_generator.call(5000)) }
end
```

which, when run, will report the following:

	user	system	total	real
N = 50	0.030000	0.000000	0.030000 (	0.030000)
N = 500	2.493000	0.000000	2.493000 (	2.574000)
N = 5000	257.591000	0.010000	257.601000	(271.560000)

The argument given to *bm* is simply the width (in number of characters), of the leftmost column of labels.

When increasing N from 50 to 500, one would expect a 100-fold increase in the running time of the algorithm, since it is O(N^2) and 500*500/50*50 = 100. This is indeed what we observe with *benchmark.rb*. There is a 83-fold increase (2.49/0.03). And when increasing N from 500 to 5000 there is a 103-fold increase (257.591/2.493) so the ordo notation seems to capture the essence of the algorithm's behavior.

What are your options if you need to speed up the sorting? You could go into the details of how Ruby will interpret the Bubblesort code and find ways to speed its execution up, but typically you can only gain a a factor of 1–2 with such low-level tuning.

Of course, this can be substantial in many applications, you should definitely try it if you need to squeeze that extra performance out of your program. You could also gain some speed by terminating the sorting when no swaps have occurred in the inner loop. However, a better alternative is often to try to find a faster algorithm.

Divide-and-conquer algorithms, which divide the input into smaller pieces, work on the pieces, and then assemble the solution from the pieces, often have good performance. The Quicksort algorithm is the canonical example of a divide-and-conquer algorithm, and is shown below in Ruby code:

```
def qsort(a)
  return a if a.length <= 1
  m, *r = a
  qsort(r.select{|x| x<=m}).push(m).concat(qsort(r.select{|x| x>m}))
end
```

The idea is to guess the median value *m* and then recursively sort the elements that are smaller and larger than the median. The version above simply takes the first element to be the median. Quicksort's complexity depends on how well you can guess the median. If you come close to the actual median, the array is effectively partitioned into two parts of equal size and you will need fewer recursive calls. Even if you make some bad guesses during the run, Quicksort is known to show good performance. Since it ideally halves the size of the array left to be sorted in each step, there will be on the order of log(N) steps. On average the complexity of Quicksort is O(NlogN).

Comparing Algorithms

In comparing Quicksort and Bubblesort, we will also include Array#sort, which would be the natural way to sort an array in Ruby. Array#sort is actually a heavily optimized Quicksort coded in C.

We want to compare the average behavior of the algorithms on arrays of different sizes. To get the average behavior we repeat the timing measurements several times for each size. We extend the Benchmark extension with *ordo_compare* to get a general way to compare algorithms:

```
def ordo_compare(inputSizes, generator, procHash, iterations = 10)
  width = procHash.keys.map{|k| k.length}.max
  inputSizes.each do |n|
    puts "\nN = #{n}"
    bm(width + 8) do |t|
      inputs = Array.new(iterations).map {generator.call(n)}
      procHash.keys.sort.each do |desc|
        p = proc do
          iterations.times {|i| procHash[desc].call(inputs[i].clone)}
        end
        t.report(desc, &p)
      end
    end
  end
end
```

There are four parameters to *ordo_compare*. The first is an array with the input sizes (the Ns) that should be used to compare the algorithms. The second parameter is a proc that will generate an input of a given size. Code to invoke each algorithm is supplied in the third parameter, which is a hash that maps descriptive strings to procs. Finally, the fourth parameter specifies the number of times to repeat the timings for each input size.

For example, when called as

```
ordo_compare([100, 1000, 10_000], array_generator,
                { "bubblesort" => proc{|i| bubblesort(i)},
                  "quicksort"  => proc{|i| qsort(i)},
                  "Array#sort" => proc{|i| i.sort} }
)
```

it will report (depending on the speed of your machine) as follows:

```
N = 100
                        user        system        total            real
Array#sort           0.000000     0.000000     0.000000  (  0.000000)
bubblesort           0.981000     0.000000     0.981000  (  1.082000)
quicksort            0.090000     0.000000     0.090000  (  0.100000)


N = 1000
                      user        system         total            real
Array#sort         0.010000     0.000000       0.010000    (  0.010000)
bubblesort       103.870000     0.020000     103.890000    (110.088000)
quicksort          1.372000     0.000000       1.372000    (  1.382000)


N = 10000
                      user        system         total            real
Array#sort         0.160000     0.000000       0.160000    (  0.161000)
bubblesort     12004.502000     1.221000    12005.723000   (30247.427000)
quicksort         19.668000     0.000000      19.668000    ( 20.320000)
```

From this you can see that, even for arrays with as few as 100 elements, the difference between Bubblesort and Quicksort is noticeable: Bubblesort is slower by a factor of 10. For 1000 and 10,000 elements, the difference is enormous. The difference between $O(N^2)$ and $O(NlogN)$ is a very important one.

It is also worth noting that Array#sort is more than 100 times faster than Quicksort. Even if this kind of increase in speed is not what you can normally expect when rewriting your Ruby methods in C, it can give a hint as to the difference between unoptimized Ruby code and highly optimized C code.

However, you should know that Array#sort is made out of more than 150 lines of C code, compared to the five lines of Ruby above. This highlights the fact that when optimizing for speed you often sacrifice the clarity and maintainability of your program. I can assure you that the more than 150 lines of C code took a considerably longer time to develop and debug than our 5 lines above!

The Different "Ordos"

There is a hierarchy of different algorithm complexities (ordos) you will frequently encounter when analyzing your algorithms:

- O(1) when something takes a constant time regardless of the size of the input. O(1) algorithms are very fast but very rare except for atomic operations such as accessing an array or hash element.

- O(N) or *linear complexity*. Linear algorithms are fast, but you will rarely find one for difficult problems.

- O(NlogN) or *logarithmic complexity* algorithms typically apply some kind of divide-and-conquer strategy, that is, they recursively divide the input into smaller pieces, work on them separately and assemble the solution from the pieces. The running time is often good even for large inputs.

- O(N^2) or *quadratic complexity* algorithms are acceptable for difficult problems or when the input is relatively small.

- O(N^3) or *cubic complexity* algorithms is rarely acceptable in practice for medium to large input sizes.

- O(b^N) for some *b* (typically 2 but sometimes N!) or *exponential complexity* algorithms are intractable and you will typically not have the time to wait for their result even for relatively small input.

In Figure 8.1 you can see the number of steps needed by algorithms of different complexities as N grows. To understand what this means in terms of seconds, let's assume that each step takes 10e-6 seconds (say 1000 CPU cycles per step on a 1 GHz machine). With an input size of 1000, it would take 0.001 seconds with an O(N), 0.007 seconds with an O(NlogN), 1 second with an O(N^2) and about 16 minutes with an O(N^3) complexity algorithm. For an O(2^N) algorithm you'd have to wait until the end of the universe, or 3.4E+284 millennia!

Figure 8.1 Comparison of Algorithm Complexities for Increasing the Size of the Input Data

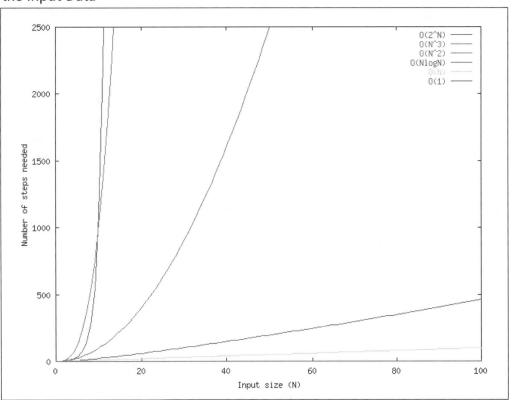

Average and Worst-case Complexity

Note the difference between average and worst-case complexity. If we give our implementation of Quicksort an already sorted array it will partition it into one part of size 1 and another one of size N-1. There will be no halving, so we will need on the order of O(N^2) steps. Since this is the worst-case behavior of Quicksort it is said to have a quadratic worst-case complexity (even if we choose the median in a different way, there will always be some input vectors giving quadratic behavior). This situation is rare and on average there will be some bad and some good guesses at the median. However, if you're doing a time-critical application where you cannot tolerate bad behavior, no matter how rare, you will have to pay attention to these kinds of details. Luckily, there are sorting algorithms with a worst-case complexity of O(NlogN), of which Mergesort is one example. Instead of partitioning the array by making a guess at the median, we simply halve it and sort the halves. Then we merge them together to get the sorted array.

Developing & Deploying…

Choosing an Algorithm

Keep in mind that the ordo notation gives an *approximation* of your algorithm's *order of growth* . You should never trust it blindly. There will typically be *hidden constants* that it does not reflect. For example, algorithms with exact time expressions $80*N^2+10*N$ and N^2+5 would both be characterized as $O(N^2)$, although the latter would be superior for all N. If you only compared them using the ordo notation, you might come to the erroneous conclusion that you can choose either of them.

You cannot even be sure that an algorithm with lower algorithmic complexity is always the best choice. An $O(N^3)$ algorithm might sometimes be a better alternative than an $O(N)$ algorithm if the latter has higher hidden constants and your input is typically small. However, note that these situations are unusual. In general you should go for the algorithm with the lowest complexity, especially as your input is probably not very small or you wouldn't be worrying about performance in the first place.

When comparing algorithmic complexities, you must also pay attention to the issue of worst-case versus average complexity. For example, from the discussion on sort algorithms, you might conclude that Mergesort would be a better alternative than Quicksort since the latter will take a very long time for some inputs. Since they both have the same average complexity, Mergesort looks like a more attractive choice. However, there are hidden costs in Mergesort so that it will typically take a longer time than Quicksort.

NOTE

There is often a trade-off between the memory used by your programs (*space*) and the time they take to complete. By using more memory you can save previously calculated results, and need not recalculate them. Thus the total time taken by your program decreases while the memory used during the run increases. Conversely, you can often re-calculate results instead of saving them in memory. Thus, you can decrease the amount of memory used at the expense of more time.

The general property of your program's memory use is called its *space complexity*. Space complexity is analyzed in much the same way as time complexity. Later in this chapter we will discuss the performance enhancement technique called *result caching* which gives you the power to trade space for time in a simple way.

Improving Performance by Profiling

If algorithm complexity is a theoretic approach to assessing and improving program performance, then profiling is its pragmatic sibling. Profiling harnesses unused CPU cycles to see where the program spends its time.

There are at least two solutions available for profiling in Ruby: *profile.rb*, found in the standard Ruby distribution, and *RbProf*, which is part of the *AspectR* extension. The former is easier to use, while the latter is faster and can give you more detailed information.

In the profiling examples that follow, we will use the following scenario as an example: You are developing a Ruby program where you have lots of large strings that need to be written to disc. You would like to compress them to save on disc space. Since you want your program to run on many different platforms, you do not want to assume there are any compression programs available. You will therefore need to compress the strings internally within your program. After doing some Internet searches on compression, you decide on the simplest possible solution: *Huffman compression*. You create a Ruby class and write the main compression loop:

```
class Huffman
  def compress(aString)
    count_symbols(@data = aString)
    build_tree
    @code = Hash.new
    assign_char_codes(0, @tree, 0)
    encode
    Marshal.dump([@tree, @bits, @data.length])
  end
end
```

The overall function of Huffman compression is to count the symbols in the data, build a binary tree with the symbols at the leaves, walk the tree to get the bit string to code for each symbol and finally encode the data by replacing each symbol by its code. Since we want to compress strings, it's natural to let each character be a symbol (depending on what you'd like to compress, you might get better compression ratios by trying other string-to-symbol mappings).

We thus count the symbols:

```
def count_symbols(data)
  @counts = Hash.new(0)
  data.each_byte {|c| @counts[c] += 1}
end
```

The substance of the Huffman encoding is in the construction of the binary tree. Huffman compression exploits the fact that some symbols appear more frequently than others. By coding those symbols with fewer bits, we can reduce the total number of bits needed to encode the data. So in Huffman codes there is one unique code for each symbol. The binary tree represents all of these codes. We get the code of a symbol by going from the root node to the leaf with the symbol and recording a zero (0) when going left, and a one (1) when going right. In the example in Figure 8.2 there are three symbols: *a* (char value 97), *b* (98) and *c* (99). From the tree we can see that they have the codes 1, 00 and 01 respectively. So the original string *aaabbc* would be coded as the bit string 111000001; a compression from 6*8=48 bits down to 9 bits (but we would also need to include the tree so that the string can be unpacked).

Figure 8.2 Huffman Tree for Coding the Symbols *a* (97), *b* (98) and *c* (99)

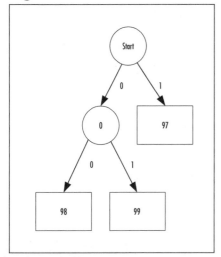

The tree is constructed iteratively by merging the two subtrees that have the smallest frequency counts. The count for the new tree is the sum of counts for its subtrees. If we represent the tree as an array of subtrees (array if a tree, or a symbol if a leaf) we can build the tree like this:

```
def build_tree
  pq = @counts.to_a.sort{|a,b| b[1] <=> a[1]}.map {|e| e.push 0}
  while pq.length > 1
    (e1, cnt1, depth1), (e2, cnt2, depth2) = pq.pop, pq.pop
    insert_sorted([e1, e2], cnt1+cnt2, [depth1, depth2].max+1, pq)
  end
  @tree, @max_length = pq.first.first, pq.first.last
end


def insert_sorted(elements, count, depth, priorityQueue)
  (priorityQueue.length+1).times do |i|
    if i == priorityQueue.length or count >= priorityQueue[i][1]
      return (priorityQueue[i,0] = [[elements, count, depth]])
    end
  end
end
```

We save the codes as an integer value and its number of bits and hold them in a hash. To get the code for each symbol, we simply traverse the tree in a recursive fashion. To encode the original data we simply loop over it and shift in the corresponding bits. Finally, we use a *Bignum* to represent the bitstring since it is simple.

```
def assign_char_codes(val, element, len)
  if element.kind_of?(Array)
    assign_char_codes(val, element[0], len+1)
    assign_char_codes(val + (1 << len), element[1], len+1)
  else
    @code[element] = [val, len]
  end
end


def encode
  @bits = 0                              # Use Bignum for bitstring
```

```
@data.reverse.each_byte do |symbol|
    @bits = (@bits << @code[symbol][1]) + @code[symbol][0]
  end
end
```

There it is—Huffman compression in 43 lines of Ruby code (the code can also be found on the CD accompanying the book, in the file *huffman.rb*). To decompress, we'll need some more lines:

```
def decompress(string)
  (array_tree, bits, length), decompressed = Marshal.load(string), ""
  length.times do
    element = array_tree
    while element.kind_of?(Array)
      element = element[bits & 1]
      bits >>= 1
    end
    decompressed << element
  end
  decompressed
end
```

We simply use the bits in the string to choose between left and right in the tree. When we get to a leaf, we have found the symbol.

After testing the Huffman class on some short strings, you can plug it into your program and try it in its real setting. You will quickly realize that your program takes forever to return a value. A bug! After some poking around, you'll notice that there are no bugs. Compression simply takes too long. Testing the codec on some strings of different sizes will return the following:

	user	system	total	real
N = 10000	11.557000	0.511000	12.068000	(12.138000)
N = 30000	94.045000	1.923000	95.968000	(97.400000)
N = 100000	1116.536000	10.044000	1126.580000	(1135.393000)

The time complexity seems to be quadratic in the length of the string. This was unexpected since the number of steps of the algorithms should be logarithmic according to the number of different symbols. We need some profiling to understand this!

Profiling Using profile.rb

Ruby's standard profiling solution is *profile.rb* which is included in the standard distribution. The simplest way to invoke the standard profiler is to simply require it on the command line when invoking Ruby:

```
ruby -r profile huffman.rb 1000
```

You can also require it from within your program:

```
require 'profile'
#... rest of the 'huffman.rb' file
```

In any case, the profiler will install itself and collect profiling information. When your program has finished, the profiler will print a report to *StdErr*.

Here is the report when compressing and then decompressing a string of length 1000 (only the top 25 entries are shown):

% time	cumulative seconds	self seconds	calls	self ms/call	total ms/call	name
51.06	15.29	15.29	254	60.21	90.64	Fixnum#times
10.40	18.41	3.11	23414	0.13	0.13	Array#[]
7.39	20.62	2.21	2	1107.00	1617.00	String#each_byte
3.51	21.67	1.05	9340	0.11	0.11	Kernel.kind_of?
3.31	22.66	0.99	7803	0.13	0.13	Bignum#>>
3.28	23.65	0.98	505	1.94	19.10	Huffman#assign_char_codes
2.84	24.50	0.85	7803	0.11	0.11	Bignum#&
2.48	25.24	0.74	1	742.00	1052.00	Array#sort
2.44	25.97	0.73	6133	0.12	0.12	Array#length
2.37	26.68	0.71	5626	0.13	0.13	Fixnum#>=
2.04	27.29	0.61	5627	0.11	0.11	Fixnum#==
1.61	27.77	0.48	1	482.00	12598.00	Huffman#build_tree
1.57	28.24	0.47	3000	0.16	0.16	Hash#[]
1.50	28.69	0.45	252	1.79	42.36	Huffman#insert_sorted
0.53	28.85	0.16	253	0.63	0.75	Array#each
0.50	29.00	0.15	2516	0.06	0.06	Fixnum#+

0.50	29.15	0.15	2000	0.08	0.08	String#<<
0.47	29.29	0.14	1253	0.11	0.11	Hash#[]=
0.40	29.41	0.12	996	0.12	0.12	Bignum#+
0.37	29.52	0.11	1163	0.09	0.09	Fixnum#<=>
0.30	29.61	0.09	1000	0.09	0.09	Kernel.rand
0.30	29.70	0.09	995	0.09	0.09	Bignum#<<
0.20	29.76	0.06	252	0.24	0.56	Enumerable.max
0.17	29.81	0.05	504	0.10	0.10	Array#pop
0.13	29.85	0.04	252	0.16	0.16	Array#[]=

. . .

The profile report is a table of data with a row for each method that was invoked during the run of your program. It is sorted on the total time spent inside each method (not counting the time spent in yet other methods called from the one in question). All times measured are the amounts of user CPU time.

The first column shows the percentage of the total time that was spent in the method. The third column shows the total time (absolute). The second column is the cumulative for the methods up to and including the current one. The fourth column gives the number of calls to the method. The fifth column is the time spent in the method on each call (the ratio between columns 4 and 3) and the sixth column is the total time for each call (including the time spent in called methods). Note that the last two columns report time in microseconds while columns 2 and 3 report seconds.

So what can we learn from this profile? The majority of the time is spent in *Fixnum#times*. This is a bit surprising since *Fixnum#times* really only calls a block a certain number of times. However, the time spent in the block is not measured since it is invoked with a yield and not via a method call. An additional problem is that *Fixnum#times* is called from two places in the program: *insert_sorted* and *Huffman#decompress*. It is not obvious which one of these takes the most time, but we need to know that in order to focus our efforts and enhance performance. We have the same problem with the next two entries in the profile: *Array#[]* is used all over our program and *String#each_byte* is used both when counting the symbols and when encoding.

This problem of not knowing the caller of a method occurs frequently when using the standard profiler. It will often be the case that the common Ruby methods you use take up the majority of the time. This may be normal, but it will not help you decide what part of your program to try speeding up. One solution may be to look at the total times spent in the methods you have defined yourself. By multiplying column 4 and 6 we can see that 12.6 seconds are spent while executing in *Huffman#build_tree*, 12.1 in *Huffman#decompress* and 9.6 seconds in *Huffman#assign_char_codes*. In this case we don't gain much from this information, since the times are pretty similar, but in general it can be a good way forward.

One thing to notice is that the times reported do not seem to add up. The profiler reports that we spent 17.7 seconds executing within *Huffman#compress* of which we used 1 second in *count_symbols*, 12.6 in *build_tree*, 9.6 in *assign_char_codes* and 2.1 in *encode* for a total of 25.3 seconds! This is probably because of inaccuracies in how time is measured, or because the normal flow of control is altered in order to profile the code.

WARNING

There is a law in physics called the *Heisenberg Uncertainty Principle*, which unfortunately has a counterpart that applies to profiling: You cannot profile a program without affecting it in a way that makes you unsure if you can trust your measurements!

Whatever causes this phenomenon, it should make you aware of the fact that profiling is not an exact science. Take all output from profilers with a grain of salt and interpret it in the context of your program. A general rule is to trust only large differences while disregarding smaller ones. In the profile above we can safely assume that there is potential to speed up the two uses of *Fixnum#times* and that we might have to check on our use of arrays. We shouldn't conclude from the profile that *Kernel#kind_of?* takes a longer time than *Bignum#>>*; the times reported for them are very similar.

Profiling with the standard profiler takes a long time. Without profiling, executing the Huffman program above with an input size of 1000 takes less than half a second, whereas it takes around half a minute when profiling. This is not because of some special property of the Huffman program; you will typically see slow-downs of a factor of 50-100 when using the standard profiler.

To understand why this is so we need to see how the standard profiler works.

How the Standard Profiler Works

The standard profiler installs a trace function (using *set_trace_func*) that traps calls to, and returns from, methods. The trace function is a Ruby *Proc* object. The interpreter invokes the trace function every time an evaluation event occurs. There are eight different events identified by strings:

- **class**   Start a class or module definition

- **end**   Finish a class or module definition

- **call**   Call a method (written in Ruby)

- **return**   Return from a method (written in Ruby)

- **c–call**   Call a method (written in C)

- **c–return**   Call a method (written in C)

- **line**   Execute code on a new line

- **raise**   Raise an exception

Most of them are self-explanatory, but *line* might be a bit hard to understand. A trace function will be invoked with the *line* event each time the Ruby interpreter is about to execute a separate piece of code on a new line in a program. So the code

```
1.times { ablock }
```

would invoke a trace function two times: one for the line's *1.times* portion and one for the *block* portion.

When a method is called, the profiler's trace function saves the start time (using *Time.times.utime* or *Process.times.utime* in Ruby version 1.7 and later) on an invocation stack. Later, when the program returns from the method in question, the trace function notes the end time, pops the start time from the invocation stack and calculates the time spent in the method. Information on the number of invocations and times spent in each method is saved in a hash. When the program is about to end and return back to the command line, the profiler summarizes the information in the hash and prints the profile to *StdErr*.

As you know from the profiles printed by *profile.rb*, both the *self ms/calls* and *total ms/calls* times are reported. The profiler handles this by saving extra information on the invocation stack: each time you return from a method, it adds the time spent in there to the entry for the caller. By subtracting the time spent in calls from the total time, you know how much time was spent in the method itself.

Drawbacks with the Standard Profiler

There are a number of drawbacks with the standard profiler:

- It adds a lot of time to the execution of the program.

- You cannot control which methods are profiled .

- You do not get any information on the callers of a method.

Using a trace function is very costly in terms of time, since it is called on each line executed in your program. The trace function used for profiling slows down your program by a factor of between 10 and 200, depending on your program. When you need to profile your code it typically takes a considerable amount of time in itself so a factor of 10 or more can be tedious to say the least. A faster profiling solution would be preferable.

When you use the standard profiler, the top entries in the profile will frequently be Ruby core methods such as *Array#each*, *Array#[]* and *Object#==*. However you're primarily interested in the methods you have written yourself since they are in your "circle of influence". It would be useful if you could specify which methods should be profiled.

If you got information on the callers of a frequently executed method you could focus your profiling and performance enhancement efforts. The standard profiler does not give you such information.

Profiling Using RbProf in AspectR

RbProf is a part of AspectR—the Ruby extension for aspect-oriented programming. It is faster than the standard profiler and can be told to profile the parts of a program you're interested in. RbProf also gathers more information than the standard profiler, and will tell you which methods called each other and, optionally, the distribution of arguments supplied when calling a method.

You use RbProf in much the same way as the standard profiler. Once you have installed AspectR and RbProf you can simply write:

```
ruby -r rbprof your_program.rb
```

and the profile will be printed on *StdErr*. In its default mode, RbProf gathers information only on the methods you have defined in your program. It will not profile Ruby's base methods (unless you have redefined them in your program). However you can add base methods in which you are interested. To accomplish this you have to invoke the profiler from within your program:

```
require 'rbprof'
$profiler.profile_method(:times, Fixnum)
# rest of your_program.rb follows here...
```

The *profile_method* method takes three arguments. The first one is the symbol ID of the method to be profiled, whereas the second one is the class in which the method is found. The third parameter is optional and specifies what kind of information should be gathered during the profiling of the method. It can be any combinations of the constants:

- *TIME* Time in each method

- *CALL_SITES* Count the number of times and from where this method is called

- *UNIQUE_ARGUMENTS* Count the number of unique arguments used when calling the method

- *UNIQUE_ARG_INSPECTS* Count the number of unique arguments used when calling this method and base uniqueness on the inspect of the arguments

- *LINE_PROFILE* Profile the time spent on each line of the method

The default value for the third parameter is TIME + CALL_SITES, that is, RbProf will time each method invocation and save information on from where the method is called. The three other alternatives are experimental, and you should consult the RbProf documentation to see to what degree they are currently supported. Basically, the UNIQUE_ARGUMENTS and UNIQUE_ARG_INSPECTS can be used to assess if result caching would speed up a method. They report how large a percentage of the calls to any given method have parameters that have been previously used in calls to that method. The LINE_PROFILE constant specifies that a detailed line-by-line profile of the method should be conducted.

RbProf is faster than the standard profiler, and this allows you to use more realistic input sets. Profiling the Huffman compression of a 30000 byte string with the standard profiler takes a little more than 16 minutes on my machine. With RbProf it takes 93 seconds, and without any profiling, it runs in 87 seconds. So the overhead with RbProf is less than 10 percent. Let's look at the profile from RbProf:

```
Profiling summary
*****************
for profile taken: Sat Aug 25 10:57:01 GMT+1:00 2001
for program huffman.rb with args '30000'
Total elapsed time: 92.823 seconds
Time in profiled methods:
```

%% time	cumulative seconds	self seconds	# calls	self ms/call	total ms/call	name
87.74	81.45	81.45	1	81447.00	81447.00	

Huffman#decompress

    Call sites:

             1 100.0% Object#compress_and_compare

| 11.62 | 92.23 | 10.79 | 1 | 10786.00 | 10786.00 | Huffman#encode |

    Call sites:

             1 100.0% Huffman#compress

| 0.22 | 92.43 | 0.20 | 1 | 200.00 | 92823.00 | TOPLEVEL |
| 0.18 | 92.60 | 0.17 | 1 | 170.00 | 170.00 | |

Huffman#count_symbols

    Call sites:

             1 100.0% Huffman#compress

| 0.09 | 92.68 | 0.08 | 511 | 0.16 | 1.15 | |

Huffman#assign_char_codes

    Call sites:

         510 100.0% Huffman#assign_char_codes

             1   0.0% Huffman#compress

| 0.06 | 92.74 | 0.06 | 255 | 0.24 | 0.24 | |

Huffman#insert_sorted

    Call sites:

        255 100.0% Huffman#build_tree

| 0.04 | 92.78 | 0.04 | 1 | 40.00 | 11156.00 | |

Huffman#compress

    Call sites:

```
              1 100.0% Object#compress_and_compare
  0.02     92.80       0.02        1    20.00    80.00
Huffman#build_tree
    Call sites:
              1 100.0% Huffman#compress
  0.02     92.82       0.02        1    20.00 92623.00
    Object#compress_and_compare
    Call sites:
              1 100.0% TOPLEVEL
```

As you can see, the information is much the same as from the standard profiler, but with some notable exceptions: since only the methods we defined have
been profiled, there are fewer entries. For example, *Array#[]* is not in this profile
even though it was the top method in the previous profile.

Another difference is that we can see a method's callers and how many times
they called the method. If there are more than one caller (as for
Huffman#assign_char_codes), the percentage of the total time spent in the method
caused by calls from each site is shown. This information is not very useful for
the profile above, but if we specify that RbProf should profile *Fixnum#times*, as
shown earlier, the top of that profile reads:

```
  %%    cumulative    self        #      self     total
 time    seconds    seconds     calls  ms/call  ms/call   name
 ------------------------------------------------------------
 87.92     82.04      82.04      257    319.21   319.21  Fixnum#times
    Call sites:
            1   99.8% Huffman#decompress
            1    0.2% TOPLEVEL
          255    0.0% Huffman#insert_sorted
```

We can immediately see that it is the call from *decompress* that takes up the
majority (99.8%) of the time spent in *Fixnum#times*. For larger programs with
lots of methods, this kind of information can be crucial.

So, we learn from the profile that we should focus on speeding up decompression, since over 80% of our time is spent there. Note that this fact was not
clear from the profiles we did with the standard profiler. One reason for this is
probably that we have now profiled while compressing a larger string. For shorter
strings, the methods calculating the Huffman codes dominate the profiles. When

profiling you should always try to use the most realistic input data possible; otherwise you might arrive at wrong conclusions. Since the standard profiler is slow you might be tempted to use smaller inputs, but you should avoid doing so.

While searching the Internet for Huffman compression algorithms you might come across the paper "Sub-linear Decoding of Huffman Codes Almost In-Place" by Andrej Brodnik and Svante Carlsson (www.iskrasistemi.se/~brodnik/Andrej/research.htm). It presents an efficient way to mutate the Huffman tree in order to give code words that can be decoded faster. We can code it up and profile it for a string of 30000 bytes (You can find the source code on the CD that accompanies this book, in the file called *huffman_fasterdecode.rb*).

Here's the top three entries without any caller information:

```
  %%   cumulative   self              self     total
 time    seconds   seconds   calls  ms/call  ms/call  name
 ------------------------------------------------------------
 49.09    11.57     11.57       1  11567.00 11567.00  Huffman#encode
 48.28    22.94     11.38       1  11376.00 11376.00  Huffman#decompress
  0.98    23.17      0.23       1    230.00 23563.00  TOPLEVEL
```

At the end of the profile, RbProf reports the timing differences from the previous profile (RbProf saves its profiles in binary form in the current directory and compares a new profile to the latest one if there are similar profiles in the current directory):

```
Compared to profile taken Sat Sep 01 11:21:40 GMT+1:00 2001
*************************************************************
                              New      Old       Diff
Total elapsed time          22.772   92.973    -75.51%

Huffman#decompress          11.066   81.547    -86.43%
Huffman#compress             0.01     0.04     -75.00%
Object#compress_and_compare  0.0      0.01    -100.00%
Huffman#insert_sorted        0.01     0.02     -50.00%
Huffman#count_symbols        0.17     0.17     -0.00%
Huffman#build_tree           0.05     0.05      0.00%
TOPLEVEL                     0.22     0.2      10.00%
Huffman#encode              11.116   10.846     2.49%
```

Such a report can be very handy when you iteratively update your program.

So the change in algorithm brought about a healthy 75 percent increase in speed, but 23 seconds is still way too long. In the profile we see that encoding and decompression are now the dominant methods. This is not surprising since they both loop over all of the strings. To gain more detailed knowledge we could use RbProf's line profiler to see which lines are the real hot spots. However, the line profiler has drawbacks similar to the standard profiler: since it installs a trace function it will be quite slow. A better approach might be to manually specify that the methods called from *encode* and *decompress* should be profiled. After inspecting the code, we'll add the following, since we suspect that the bit-shifting and pushing of characters might be problematic:

```
$profiler.profile_method(:<<, Bignum)
$profiler.profile_method(:<<, String)
```

The top of the new profile validates our suspicion:

```
%%      cumulative    self       #        self      total
time     seconds     seconds    calls   ms/call   ms/call  name
------------------------------------------------------------
37.10     13.47       13.47       1    13471.00  15543.00
   HuffmanDecodeSpec#decompress
   Call sites:
          1 100.0% TOPLEVEL
34.65     26.05       12.58     89996     0.14      0.14   Bignum#<<
   Call sites:
       29996  67.8% HuffmanDecodeSpec#encode
       30000  16.5% HuffmanDecodeSpec#decompress
       30000  15.8% TOPLEVEL
19.62     33.18        7.12       1     7123.00  15652.00
   HuffmanDecodeSpec#encode
   Call sites:
          1 100.0% HuffmanDecodeSpec#compress
 7.72     35.98        2.80       1     2805.00  36312.00   TOPLEVEL
```

Representing the bits in a *Bignum* does not seem to be a good idea, at least not if we are going to shift all the bits whenever we need to add a few. An alternative might be to use Robert Feldt's *BitVector* extension from RAA (found in the Library section under *Datastructure*). It is a Ruby wrapper class around a library of fast C functions for arbitrary length bit vectors. The BitVector class has got methods for writing to a block of consecutive bits in any position in the vector. This would solve our problems. Download it from the RAA and install it, then update our Huffman codec. The updated code can be found as *huffman_bitvector.rb* on the CD.

The time for compressing and decompressing a 30000 byte string is now down to 1.2 seconds. Note that the change in data structure had a larger effect than we would have expected from the profile above. The reason is that it not only affected the bitshifting, but also all operations that are working with the bit string.

We have seen that the iterative and focused profiling supported by RbProf can be a powerful tool. To understand how RbProf works, we need to understand a little about aspect-oriented programming and AspectR.

Understanding AOP and AspectR

In essence, aspect-oriented programming (AOP) allows you to add code to methods without having to copy-and-paste it there by hand. By giving a controlled way to alter the behavior of your methods you can separate concerns even more between your classes and flexibly add or delete functionality as needed. The idea has been around for some time and has been given many different names; but recently AOP has been popularized by a research group at Xerox Parc under the leadership of Gregor Kinscalez. They have released a tool called AspectJ, which supports AOP in Java.

The motivation for AOP is that when you design a program you often have to extend your classes with code that is unrelated to their purpose. An example would be a thread-safe (synchronized) queue. A *queue* is a data structure that allows you to add and take away elements. Thread safety has nothing to do with the queue in itself; sometimes you will need a thread-safe queue and sometimes you will not. The code for a queue will be easier to understand, debug, and maintain if it is separated from the synchronization code that is needed for a thread-safe queue. AOP lets you separate the code and gives you a way to express the bindings necessary to glue synchronization code onto a non-thread-safe queue to make a thread-safe queue.

In AOP lingo the synchronization code would be written in an *aspect* and this synchronization aspect would be woven into your queue.

The concept of AOP can be applied not only to synchronization but to most situations where there is a clear separation between orthogonal functionalities your classes need to support. Examples include:

- Tracing and logging
- Transactions in database accesses
- Security
- Fault-tolerance
- Caching strategies
- Profiling

Using AspectR

Let's see how we can add tracing to a class. Let's say you have a class *YourClass* and you want to log method entry and exit to trace the flow of events.

```
class YourClass
  def method1
    sleep 1
    puts "Hello!"
    [:t, "sd"]
  end
  def method2(*args)
    raise NotImplementedError
  end
end
```

In AspectR an aspect is simply a subclass of Aspect:

```
require 'aspectr'
include AspectR
class Tracer < Aspect
  def tick
    "#{Time.now.strftime('%Y-%m-%d %X')}"
  end

  def tracer_enter(method, object, exitstatus, *args)
    puts "#{tick} #{self.class}##{method}: #{args.inspect}"
  end
```

```
def tracer_exit(method, object, exitstatus, *args)
  print "#{tick} #{self.class}##{method}: exited "
  if exitstatus.kind_of?(Array)
    puts "normally returning #{exitstatus[0].inspect}"
  elsif exitstatus == true
    puts "with exception '#{$!}'"
  else
    puts "normally"
  end
end
end
```

The *Tracer* aspect contains two methods that can be added to other methods. In AspectJ they would be called *advices. tracer_enter* should be added so that it executes before (and *tracer_exit* after) the existing code. They will print the time, method and arguments for the call. We see that the arguments to advice methods are always the same: the ID for the method called, the object receiving the call, the *exitstatus* of the method if it has finished, and the arguments in the call. In advices that execute before the code in the base method (called *pre-advices*), the *exitstatus* is always nil. In advices that execute *after* the code in the base method (called *post-advices*), *exitstatus* is normally an array with the return values from the method. If *exitstatus* has the value *true*, that means that an exception was raised.

The basic way to add advice methods to methods in a class is to use *Aspect#add_advice*. For the example above this would be:

```
tracer = Tracer.new
tracer.add_advice(YourClass, PRE, :tracer_enter, :method1)
tracer.add_advice(YourClass, POST, :tracer_exit, :method1)
```

You simply specify the class, where to add the advice, ID for advice method, and the method to add to. Since it is very common to add both a pre- and a post-advice, the shorthand method *Aspect#wrap* can be used instead:

```
tracer.wrap(YourClass, :tracer_enter, :tracer_exit, :method1)
```

It is also common to want to wrap many methods with the same pre- and post-advices. *Aspect#wrap* supports this by allowing a *regexp* as a method specifier. The shortest way to add logging to both methods in *YourClass* would thus be:

```
tracer.wrap(YourClass, :tracer_enter, :tracer_exit, /method\d/)
```

since /method\d/ matches both method1 and method2. If we now run the following code:

```
YourClass.new.method1
begin
  YourClass.new.method2(1, true)
rescue Exception; end
```

we would get the output:

```
2001-06-15 14:36:17 Tracer#method1: args = []
Hello!
2001-06-15 14:36:18 Tracer#method1: exited normally returning [:t, "sd"]
2001-06-15 14:36:18 Tracer#method2: args = [1, true]
2001-06-15 14:36:18 Tracer#method2: exited with exception 'NotImplemen
tedError'
```

We can now see how AspectR can be used for profiling. We simply add a pre-advice that saves the entry time to a stack, and a post-advice that calculates the time elapsed and saves it in a database. When the program has finished, we go through the database and summarize the information in a profile. Indeed, this is how it is done even though some special tricks are used to decrease the overhead introduced by AOP.

How AspectR Works

AspectR simply aliases the existing method and defines a new version of it that calls advice methods before and after calling the original method. Here's a template for how it works:

```
class YourClass
  alias old_method1 method1
  def method1
    begin
      exitstatus = nil
      # code to call pre advices
      return exitstatus.push(old_method1).last
    rescue Exception
      exitstatus = true
    ensure
      # code to call post advices
```

```
          end
    end
end
```

Since AspectR calls methods on actual instances of aspects, it cannot simply call them with static code inserted above. Instead, it saves aspect instances and information on when and how they should be called in class variables in *YourClass*. So when you wrap other advices around an already wrapped method they are simply added to the class' variables; there is no need to redefine the methods again.

The way AspectR is implemented means that it adds considerable overhead to normal method dispatch. The authors of AspectR have traded speed for flexibility and power. But the extension is still in development and there is the possibility of doing the implementation in C to speed it up while retaining the power. There has even been a discussion in the ruby-talk postings on how to add support to the Ruby interpreter for AOP-style wrapping. In future Ruby versions, this might become part of Ruby itself since it supports so many powerful programming concepts in one framework.

Comparing AspectR and AspectJ

AspectR is 300 lines of Ruby code and AspectJ is a multi KLOC Java program—so how do they compare? AspectJ is actually a pre-processor for Java. You write your aspects and bind them to your Java classes in a superset of Java. The program is then parsed by AspectJ and turned into valid Java code that can be passed on to a compiler or interpreter. With this in mind, you can understand why the wrapping of advices is called *weaving* in AspectJ. Put another way, the tool helps you do sophisticated cut-and-paste. The advice code is statically added to the source code of the wrapped classes.

This is in stark contrast to AspectR, which makes heavy use of Ruby's dynamic features to redefine and extend methods. There is no cut-and-pasting of Ruby code in AspectR, since Ruby gives you the tools to do more powerful stuff. So there are a number of differences between the two. Here is a list of AspectJ features that AspectR is currently missing:

- Join points additional to method entry and exit: when a method is called and when an exception handler executes

- Composition of pointcut designators (you can specify several method calls in different classes and objects)

- Precedence and specificity among advices and aspects

AspectR only lets you add advices before and after the existing code. In AspectJ you have more power and can, for example, specify that an advice should be invoked each time a method calls other methods.

AspectJ has pointcut designator primitives to let you specify join points very finely. The primitives can be combined with boolean operators to say things like "Call this advice for all method calls in all methods that call both *a* and *b*". AspectR can only add advices to methods.

On the other hand, AspectJ does not support dynamically changing your advices the way AspectR does. Much of this may change over the next little while, as AspectR is still in development.

Comparing the Speed of Ruby Constructs

Ruby is a flexible language that gives you many ways to accomplish the same thing. Ruby's creator, Yukihiro Matsumoto, has sometimes quoted the motto of Larry Wall, the developer of Perl: "There is more than one way to do it!" Ruby certainly lives up to this motto. You can add elements to an array using push or *concat* or +, you can create arrays with *Array.new* or *[]*, there is a multitude of different ways to loop, and so on. In this section we will compare the speeds of some of these alternatives. We will also introduce some tricks that can be used to slightly increase the performance of your Ruby programs.

But first we need a method to time different Ruby constructs. There are a number of things that can complicate things if we want to make accurate comparisons:

- **Garbage collection** The GC might kick in and affect the timings.

- **Timing inaccuracies** Small constructs may execute so fast that the resolution of the clock used to time them is not high enough.

- **Memory allocation** The first things you time can be adversely affected because the GC needs to allocate memory for holding objects.

- **Dependence on the input** We should have general rules of thumb pertaining to what constructs to choose, independent of the input they work on.

To combat these effects you should repeat your measurements a large number of times and randomize as many things as possible. You should use randomly generated inputs. You should randomize the order in which you time the constructs in order to decrease the probability of systematic errors introduced by garbage collection. If you force garbage collection before the timings, you can further decrease the probability of it affecting your timings. You should repeat each construct many times so that there is no problem with the timing accuracy. You should also repeat the timings many times. And finally you should skip the first repetitions to lessen the effects of initial memory allocation.

On the accompanying CD you can find the file *stat_bench.rb,* which applies all of these tricks. It contains the method *stat_bench* (which will report the average time needed to execute each construct), the standard deviation for these averages, a comparison of the averages, the number of *outliers* (outliers are explained below) that have been deleted from the results, and the minimum and maximum time observed. It takes three arguments: a label describing what is being compared, a hash that maps descriptive strings to blocks with the constructs to be compared, and an input generator that will generate random input. Optionally you can also specify how many times to repeat the timings (M), the different sizes to use for the input, if outliers among the timings should be removed before calculating the average time, and finally, the number of repeated calls (N) to the construct within one timing.

For each iteration of the timing loop, *stat_bench* will create N inputs by repeatedly calling the input generator. It will then randomly choose a block and measure how long it takes to call it with the N inputs. For each iteration, it will also time N repeated calls to a *baseline block.* The baseline block is specified with the descriptive string *_base* in the hash given as parameter number two to *stat_bench.* This baseline time indicates how much time arises from support code (repeated calls to a block, accessing the input and so on). By subtracting the baseline block from the block timings, we get an estimate of the time to execute the code in each block. This whole procedure is repeated M times to get an average for different inputs.

Even though *stat_bench* applies many tricks to try to ensure that the timings reported are as accurate as possible, you will have to be careful when using large input since they will stress the Garbage Collector harder. If the GC kicks in, the time taken will be considerably longer than normal (called an outlier). A statistical procedure is used to eliminate these outliers. The number of such outliers that were removed before calculating the average time, and the standard deviation, is reported from *stat_bench.*

The key to accurate and reliable timings is to have a good, high-resolution timer. The standard method for timing things in Ruby is to use the *Time.times* method and compare the amount of user time used by the Ruby interpreter process. This method is used both in the standard profiler and in RbProf. On many platforms, this timing method will only give a resolution of 0.01 seconds, or about 10 milliseconds. The *stat_bench* method will use an alternative timer available in the *PerfCtr* extension, which is available from the RAA. This extension is currently in a beta state and will only work on some platforms. The resolution of which PerfCtr is capable depends on your computer hardware, but typically it can be a number of microseconds or even better. If PerfCtr is not available, stat_bench will use the standard method to try and overcome its limitations. If PerfCtr is available, one can use a small N and disable the Garbage Collector while timing. Note that there might be outliers in any case since PerfCtr is a wall-clock timer; on multitasking operating systems, other processes might kick in and affect the timings.

Below you can find comparisons between different Ruby constructs for common tasks. All of the timings were conducted with Ruby 1.6.4 (2001-06-04) on an IBM ThinkPad 600E with 266MHz Pentium II and 128 MB of memory, running Cygwin and Windows 2000 Workstation Professional . However, the underlying machine and operating system should not affect the general conclusions drawn in the sections below. The *PerfCtr* extension was installed and is used in the timings below. In all timings, the Garbage Collector was enabled and outliers were deleted.

Adding Elements to Arrays

There are many ways to add elements to an array. You can push them, use *concat*, <<, +=, element assignment, or you can even create a new array containing both the old and the new elements. Since array manipulation is such a common task there is potential for performance gains, so let's try them out. We start with the case in which we only add one element to an array:

```
one_element = {
   "<<"      => proc{|a, e| a << e},
   "concat"  => proc{|a, e| a.concat [e]},
   "push"    => proc{|a, e| a.push e},
   "+="      => proc{|a, e| a += [e]},
   "[,0]="   => proc{|a, e| a[a.length, 0] = [e]},
   "_base"   => proc{|a, e| a},
}

stat_bench("Adding one element to an array", one_element,
        IntArrayGen.new + FixnumGen.new, [10, 500], 100, 10)
```

which specifies that the blocks in *one_element* should be timed 100 times each with 10 invocations per timing. The procedure should be repeated two times for input sizes of 10 and 500. Also, we should use a combined input generator that generates an array of integers and a *Fixnum* object. When run it reports:

```
Input size: 10
Adding one element to an array
```
----

	usec	diff	std.dev	# outl.	min	max
push	21.30	2.997	4	17.04	32.13	
<<	23.25	+9.2%	2.912	3	19.56	31.57
concat	42.38	+99.0%	2.915	1	36.32	51.68
[,0]=	60.47	+184.0%	4.437	5	53.92	75.15
+=	61.33	+188.0%	4.116	5	53.64	73.75

```
Input size: 500
Adding one element to an array
```
----

	usec	diff	std.dev	# outl.	min	max
push	26.43	6.625	2	15.37	48.33	
<<	28.06	+6.2%	7.108	1	17.04	49.73
concat	51.34	+94.2%	6.443	4	39.39	68.17
[,0]=	70.39	+166.3%	9.402	3	53.64	99.45
+=	187.08	+607.9%	17.003	7	155.89	240.53

The difference between << and *push* is not large enough to be taken seriously (look at the standard deviations). However, we can conclude that, from a performance point of view, we should use them instead of *concat*, element assignment, or +=. Note also that += is noticeably slower for larger input since it creates a new array with all elements.

If we have more than one element to add:

```
array_concat = {
  "push"          => proc{|a, es| a.push(*es)},
  "concat"        => proc{|a, es| a.concat es},
  "loopeach <<" => proc{|a, es| es.each{|e| a << e}},
  "+="            => proc{|a, es| a += es},
```

```
    "[,0]="            => proc{|a, es| a[a.length, 0] = es}
}


stat_bench("Array concatenation", array_concat,
        IntArrayGen.new + IntArrayGen.new,
      [[10, 5], [10, 50]], 100, 10)
```

Note that we did not specify a base-line construct. If we don't, *stat_bench* will insert one with the same number of arguments as those specified. It will simply return the first argument. When run, *stat_bench* reports:

```
Input size: [10, 5]
Array concatenation

-------------------
```

	usec	diff	std.dev	# outl.	min	max
concat	28.03		3.165	5	22.63	36.88
push	28.82	+2.8%	3.132	4	23.75	40.23
[,0]=	44.99	+60.5%	3.739	3	39.39	55.59
+=	49.26	+75.7%	3.464	8	43.58	62.30
loopeach <<	194.58	+594.2%	3.894	4	186.62	205.33

```
Input size: [10, 50]
Array concatenation

-------------------
```

	usec	diff	std.dev	# outl.	min	max
+=	60.13		4.712	12	52.24	75.71
concat	65.99	+9.8%	4.673	8	58.67	81.85
push	76.34	+27.0%	4.841	8	69.28	89.96
[,0]=	83.91	+39.6%	5.371	9	75.43	99.17
loopeach <<	1630.96	+2612.6%	12.006	14	1613.33	1670.60

The picture is not as clear; the time needed depends on the size of the input, even though the awkward way of looping and adding the elements by hand is inferior. When the second array is larger += fares relatively better. Since the difference between += and *concat* is not significant, *concat* is probably the wisest general choice, as it does not stress the GC to the same degree.

Concatenating Strings

Concatenating strings is another common task that can be implemented in different ways. Let's compare a few of those ways:

```
string_concat = {
  "<<"    => proc{|s, ns| s << ns},
  "+="    => proc{|s, ns| s += ns},
  "join"  => proc{|s, ns| [s, ns].join},
  "_base" => proc{|s, ns| s},
}


stat_bench("String concatenation", string_concat,
          StringGen.new + StringGen.new, [10], 100, 10)
```

which reports:

```
String concatenation
--------------------
```

	usec	diff	std.dev	# outl.	min	max
+=	46.59		3.131	11	40.23	55.31
<<	56.48	+21.2%	3.809	8	51.40	68.72
join	132.28	+183.9%	7.206	7	113.98	155.33

It is a bit surprising that += is faster than << since the former always creates a new string while the latter appends to an existing one. However, there are probably more checks to be made for the append method, while the adding one simply creates a new instance and copies the existing characters. You shouldn't conclude from this that you should always use the former since its memory use will typically be worse, so there will be costs later when the Garbage Collector starts working. Our benchmarking method does not measure such memory effects. In fact, it actively tries to *avoid* measuring them.

The method using *join* fares badly, but this may be attributed to the fact that it has to create an array before calling the join method. This cost should go away when you have lots of strings to concatenate. Let's compare when the number of strings grow:

```
string_concat_many = {
  "<<"    => proc do |str_ary|
```

```
      str = ""
      for s in str_ary
        str << s
      end
      str
    end,
    "+="    => proc do |str_ary|
      str = ""
      for s in str_ary
        str += s
      end
      str
    end,
    "join"  => proc{|str_ary| str_ary.join},
    "_base" => proc{|str_ary| str_ary},
  }


stat_bench("Concatenating many strings", string_concat,
          ArrayOfGen.new(StringGen.new), [5, 25], 100, 10)
```

which gives the tables:

```
Input size: 5
Concatenating many strings

---------------------------
```

	usec	diff	std.dev	# outl.	min	max
join	158.45		7.526	7	146.67	183.54
+=	296.95	+87.4%	5.424	5	284.67	310.37
<<	312.26	+97.1%	7.806	8	289.70	328.25

```
Input size: 25
Concatenating many strings

---------------------------
```

	usec	diff	std.dev	# outl.	min	max
join	957.28		131.481	4	674.39	1164.11
<<	1667.14	+74.2%	147.983	2	1355.76	2122.34
+=	1817.37	+89.8%	33.172	10	1748.83	1911.42

Using join beats the other methods even when we have only 5 strings to concatenate. We also see that when we have many strings to concatenate, the method using += is slower than the one using <<. The larger number of strings created when adding strings now overtakes the extra code needed to append.

Predeclaring Variables

In Ruby, you do not have to declare variables. They are implicitly declared the first time you assign to them. However, you can often speed up your program by predeclaring variables. The gain is largest for iterator variables and variables used inside loops:

```
predeclaring_vars = {
  "no predecl"        => proc do |n|
    n.times do |i|
      intermediate_res = i+1
    end
  end,
  "predeclaring" => proc do |n|
    i = intermediate_res = nil
    n.times do |i|
      intermediate_res = i+1
    end
  end,
  "_base"             => proc{|n| n.times{}},
}


stat_bench("Predeclaring iterator variables", predeclaring_vars,
          SizeGen.new, [100], 100, 1)
```

which reports:

```
Predeclaring iterator variables
---------------------------------
```

	usec	diff	std.dev	# outl.	min	max
predeclaring	211.27		1.287	6	209.24	215.11
normal	252.44	+19.5%	1.228	15	250.59	255.90

Iterating Over Array Elements

There are many ways to loop in Ruby. Some of the most common methods for looping over an array are to use *each*, loop over the range from 0 to the length, use *length.times*, use *for-loops* or *while-loops*:

```
iterating_over_array = {
    "each"                  => proc{|a|  a.each{|e|  t=e}},
    "each_with_index"       => proc{|a|  a.each_with_index{|e,i|  t=e}},
    "length.times"          => proc{|a|  a.length.times{|i|  t=a[i]}},
    "(0...length).each"  => proc{|a|  (0...a.length).each{|i|  t=a[i]}},
    "0.upto(length-1)"   => proc{|a|  0.upto(a.length-1) {|i|  t=a[i]}},
    "for in"                => proc{|a|  for e in a do t=e end},
    "while < length"        => proc{|a|  i = -1; while i < a.length
                                                    t=a[i+=1]
                                                end},
    "_base"                 => proc{|a|  t = 1}
}


stat_bench("Iterating over array elements", iterating_over_array,
       IntArrayGen.new, [10], 100, 10)
```

which reports:

```
Iterating over array elements

-----------------------------
```

	usec	diff	std.dev	# outl.	min	max
for in	186.23		2.991	5	177.96	193.88
each	253.81	+36.3%	2.351	7	248.63	260.37
length.times	422.03	+126.6%	3.928	6	414.02	433.57
0.upto(length-1)	438.68	+135.6%	4.497	5	430.78	451.17
(0...length).each	506.26	+171.8%	7.097	12	494.20	530.51
each_with_index	636.22	+241.6%	12.001	16	605.94	668.52
while < length	668.01	+258.7%	3.837	4	659.58	679.70

Surprisingly, there is a benefit in using a *for-loop* instead of an *each*.

Iterating Over Array Elements with an Index

There is a special method for looping over all elements while simultaneously getting an index to each one. Since the *for*-loop was the fastest above, we'll compare it to the dedicated method. The *Array* class also has a method for iterating over the indices to its elements. For good measure , we include it as well. Note that we predeclare variables so that this effect does not affect the measurements:

```
iterating_with_index = {
  "each"                => proc do |a|
    e = i = -1
    a.each{|e| t=e; j=(i+=1)}
  end,
  "each_index"          => proc do |a|
    e = i = -1
    a.each_index {|i| t=a[i]; j=i}
  end,
  "each_with_index"     => proc do |a|
    e = i = -1
    a.each_with_index {|e,i| t=e; j=i}
  end,
  "for in"              => proc do |a|
    e = i = -1
    for e in a
      t=e; j=(i+=1)
    end
  end,
}


stat_bench("Iterating with index over array elements",
          iterating_with_index, IntArrayGen.new,
          [10], 100, 10)
```

which reports:

```
Iterating with index over array elements
----------------------------------------
```

	usec	diff	std.dev	# outl.	min	max
for in	461.68		3.674	10	452.85	472.41
each_index	517.48	+12.1%	5.341	4	506.49	532.47
each	536.00	+16.1%	4.680	13	525.49	552.58
each_with_index	724.22	+56.9%	15.571	15	686.68	774.96

Surprisingly, *each_with_index* is significantly slower. To understand this behavior we must look into the internals of Ruby. It turns out that *Enumerable#each_with _index* will create a new array of length 2 for each iteration. There is also a small overhead since *each_with_index* is not a method of *Array*, like *each* and *each_index*.

Destructive versus Non-destructive Methods

Destructive methods, such as *sort!, flatten!* and *collect!* can be faster than their non-destructive variants. The reason is that, unlike the destructive methods, the non-destructive variants simply clone and then use the destructive method on the clone.

```
destructive_vs_nondestructive = {
    "sort"              => proc{|a| b = a.sort},
    "sort!"             => proc{|a| a.sort!; b=a},
    "clone and sort!"   => proc{|a| b = a.clone; b.sort!},
}


stat_bench("Destructive vs non-destructive sort",
        destructive_vs_nondestructive,
        IntArrayGen.new, [10, 10000], 100, 1)
```

which reports:

```
Input size: 10

Destructive vs non-destructive sort

-----------------------------------
```

	usec	diff	std.dev	# outl.	min	max
sort	10.82		1.031	14	8.94	13.41
clone and sort!	14.71	+35.9%	1.274	2	12.57	18.44
sort	15.45	+42.7%	0.977	16	13.69	18.16

```
Input size: 10000

Destructive vs non-destructive sort
```

	msec	diff	std.dev	# outl.	min	max
sort	15.39		0.266	4	15.02	16.09
sort	15.63	+1.6%	0.227	5	15.28	16.28
clone and sort!	15.67	+1.8%	0.274	4	15.28	16.49

There is a difference between the two, though it decreases as the array gets larger. This is because the time to clone the array does not grow as fast as the time to sort it. However, from a performance point of view, you should use destructive methods whenever possible. You will actually gain more than indicated by the measurements above since you will decrease the amount of work for the memory system and Garbage Collector.

Accessing the First Array Element

There are two obvious ways to access the first element of an array: use *first* or *[0]*. However, there is also the less obvious trick of using a multiple assignment:

```
accessing_first_element = {
  "first"        => proc{|a| b = a.first},
  "[0]"          => proc{|a| b = a[0]},
  "massignment"  => proc{|a| b, = a}
}


stat_bench("Accessing first array element", acessing_first_element,
        IntArrayGen.new, [10], 100, 10)
```

which reports:

```
Accessing first array element
```

	usec	diff	std.dev	# outl.	min	max
massignment	6.46		1.784	7	3.35	11.17
first	12.62	+95.5%	1.690	7	9.22	17.32
[0]	18.35	+184.3%	1.327	11	15.92	22.63

It is not surprising that *[0]* is not very fast. Element reference is very general and can take many different types of parameters; it also takes time to distinguish between them. It is a bit of surprise that multiple assignment has such a *large* edge, though.

Creating Arrays and Hashes

There are syntactical shortcuts to creating arrays and hashes. Should we use them instead of calling *Array.new* or *Hash.new*? Well, it turns out the shorthand are significantly faster. For arrays:

```
creating_array = {
   "Array.new"   => proc{a = Array.new},
   "[]"          => proc{a = []},
   "_base"       => proc{a = 1}
}


stat_bench("Creating empty array", creating_array, ConstantGen.new([]),
           [1], 100, 1)
```

which reports:

```
Creating empty array

--------------------

                      usec      diff      std.dev   # outl.   min       max

[]                    2.85                0.784     12        1.68      5.59

Array.new             9.46      +232.0%   0.799     8         8.10      12.29
```

The situation is not as acute for hashes but the difference is still significant:

```
creating_hash = {
   "Hash.new"   => proc{h = Hash.new},
   "{}"         => proc{h = {}},
   "_base"      => proc{h = 1}
}


stat_bench("Creating hash", creating_hash, ConstantGen.new([]),
           [1], 100, 1)
```

which reports:

```
Creating hash

--------------

                      usec      diff      std.dev   # outl.   min       max

{}                    5.04                0.865     5         3.35      7.82

Hash.new              11.06     +119.5%   0.846     4         9.50      13.69
```

Calling Methods and Proc Objects

In Ruby, you can call methods dynamically by using *Method#call* or *Object#send*. Let's compare how efficient this is compared to an ordinary static call. We also include a call to a *proc* object implementing the same functionality as the method:

```ruby
class T
  def m(a)
    a
  end
end

t = T.new
m_method = t.method(:m)
m_proc = proc{|a| a}

calling_method = {
  "std call"    => proc{|a| t.m(a)},
  "Method#call" => proc{|a| m_method.call(a)},
  "Object#send" => proc{|a| t.send(:m, a)},
  "proc"        => proc{|a| m_proc.call(a)},
  "_base"       => proc{|a| a},
}

stat_bench("Calling a method", calling_method,
        FixnumGen.new, [1], 100, 10)
```

which reports:

```
Calling a method
----------------
```

	usec	diff	std.dev	# outl.	min	max
std call	33.56		1.471	4	30.73	37.71
Object#send	47.73	+42.3%	1.296	11	45.26	51.96
Method#call	49.24	+46.8%	1.714	6	46.10	54.20
proc	65.05	+93.9%	2.263	11	60.06	71.24

As expected, the ordinary call is the fastest. Somewhat surprisingly, however, the dynamic method calls are not much more expensive. Note that the significance of these differences will decrease when the code inside the method (or proc) is more complex.

Further Performance Enhancements

The techniques we used in comparing Ruby constructs above should help you decide which Ruby constructs you'd prefer from a performance standpoint. Such a choice affects your Ruby program on a low-level, line-by-line basis. In this section we look at techniques that have a wider scope. We take a look at how we can trade memory for speed by caching results, we discuss how the Garbage Collector affects performance and, finally, what effects to expect if you rewrite parts of your program in C.

Caching Results

A simple technique that can speed up some types of programs is *result caching* or *memoizing*. The idea is to save previously calculated results so that they can later be looked up instead of recalculated. The cache is typically a hash that maps the arguments to the return value(s).

One situation in which this is effective is with recursive and compute-intensive functions. Let's see how we can speed-up the *fibonacci* function with this technique:

```
$cache = Hash.new

def fibonacci_rc(n)
  if (t = $cache[n])
    return t
  end
  if n <= 1
  res = 1
  else
    res = fibonacci_rc(n-2) + fibonacci_rc(n-1)
  end
  $cache[n] = res
end
```

If we compare the speed of this version of fibonacci to the standard recursive one without result caching, the speed-up is substantial. fibonacci(30) takes over 15 seconds while fibonacci_rc(10000) takes about a second. But note that this is a special case that is very well suited to result caching. In general, you will not see these kinds of speed-ups. In fact, for methods that are seldom called with the same arguments, you will actually see a slowdown. To help you decide when to apply result caching, you might use RbProf's aforementioned argument summary feature.

Hand-coding result caching is a bit tedious and can clutter up your code. However, there is an extension in RAA to help you out. *Memoize* (found at the RAA in the Library section under *devel*) gives you an easy-to-use directive that modifies your methods to add result caching. Here's how we can use it on the fibonacci function:

```
require 'memoize'


def fibonacci(n)
  if n == 0 or n == 1
    1
  else
    fibonacci(n-2) + fibonacci(n-1)
  end
end
memoize :fibonacci
```

You can also use *memoize* inside a class definition:

```
class Fibonacci
  def calc(n)
    # calculation here...
  end
  memoize :calc
end
```

The *unmemoize* directive will take away result caching and restore a method to its normal state:

```
unmemoize :fibonacci
```

As a *memoize* option, you can specify the cache to be used. Use this feature to implement different expiration policies (when values in the cache should expire and require recalculation). Thus you can fine-tune the result caching behavior. Valid cache objects are objects that respond to the basic hash methods assignment ([]) and reference ([]=). One example is the *BoundeLruCache* that is included with *memoize*. It gives you a hash with a fixed maximum size that will delete the least recently used key-value pair when the hash is full. This way you can limit the memory used for caching results. To use a hash that can hold a maximum of 50 pairs for fibonacci you would execute:

```
memoize :fibonacci, BoundedLruCache.new(50)
```

The *BoundedLruCache* is a very simple example of a customized cache; you can implement more sophisticated schemes if you need them. For example, one possibility would be to write a persistent cache that will save results on disc between successive uses of the program.

When Not To Use Result Caching

You should not use result caching for methods that:

- Have side effects, such as printing output or writing to file, since the side effect will not be seen on successive calls.

- Depend on state other than its arguments.

- Return a data structure that is modified by its caller.

If you were to use *memoize* on methods with side effects, the side effect will not be seen on calls with previously used parameters. Since the result can be found in the cache, there is no need to execute the body of the method.

If a method depends on states other than the parameters, they cannot safely be used as keys in the cache. Subsequent calls with the same parameters will return the previously calculated result even though the state might have changed.

Note that the last two limitations above are due to the current implementation of *memoize*. If we write the code by hand we can overcome them. A fix for the last limitation would be to clone the cached value before returning it. To handle the situation with dependence on state, not in the parameters, we could include the actual state in the key in the cache. There are proposals to add these features to future versions of *memoize*. You should check the README file in the latest version for the most up-to-date information.

How Memoize Works

By now we are quite familiar with Ruby code that aliases and redefines methods to alter their behavior. As you have probably guessed, *memoize* is yet another example of this. It simply wraps code around your method to implement the caching behavior we wrote by hand in the example above and the caches are kept in a class variable. In fact, *memoize* can be seen as yet another aspect; it will actually be part of AspectR in a future release.

However, there is one interesting feature of *memoize* that we should probe some more. The *memoize* directive modifies methods, and it works both inside classes and in the top-level. How can we accomplish this?

When we are in a class definition, *self* is the class we are defining. So a directive should be an instance method of the *Class* class. Since we would also like our directives to be available when writing modules we add it to the *Module* class, which *Class* inherits from.

```
module MyDirective
  def my_directive(*args)
    args.each {|m| puts m}
  end
end


class Module
  include MyDirective
end


class T
  my_directive :m        # => "m"
end
```

To make your directive available at the top level simply *include MyDirective*:

```
include MyDirective


my_directive :t          # => "t"
```

Disabling the Garbage Collector

Disabling the Garbage Collector is a thing you should probably never do. By disabling the GC you leave the cozy and safe virtual room that is Ruby and enter a world full of evil goblins! If your program needs lots of memory while the GC is disabled, it will continue allocating it until the OS says no or starts swapping to disc. If this occurs on some operating systems, your whole system might come to a halt.

Ruby 1.6.4 has a conservative mark and sweep garbage collection algorithm. This algorithm will traverse all objects that are alive and mark them. It will then sweep all objects without a mark, (that are not alive). So the cost for garbage collection will be high if there are many objects alive and only a few of them die between each garbage collection. The following dummy code illustrates the problem:

```
h = {}
GC.disable if ARGV[0]
5e5.to_i.times {|i| h[i] = "dummy"}
h = nil
GC.enable
GC.start
```

It will create 500,000 strings and keep them in a hash until all of them have been created. It will then garbage collect all of the strings and the hash. This takes more than 16 seconds when run on my machine in Ruby 1.6.4 without disabling the GC. However, with the GC disabled it takes less than 5 seconds.

One situation where this technique might be called for is if you need to quickly get back with an answer, and you will then have lots of idle time where the Garbage Collector can get to work. One example of this sort of situation would be an interactive application where the user is waiting for your answer but there is plenty of time between user requests (while he or she is typing, for example). The technique might also be valid if you are sure that your program's total memory requirement is lower than the available memory on the computers where it will be run. However, it is very difficult to ensure this for all computers and in all situations where your program might run.

A major disadvantage with disabling the GC is that your program will not benefit from GC advances in the interpreter. A new Garbage Collector has been introduced in the Ruby 1.7 development series that will lead up to Ruby 1.8. It is a compacting, generational collector that shows better performance in general. Running the above program, without disabling the Garbage Collector, in Ruby version 1.7.1 2001-09-10 took 5 seconds which is about the same as with the GC disabled in 1.6.4. Disabling the GC only speeds execution up by 0.5 seconds

(10%). If you disable garbage collection you take a risk of running out of memory even though advances in the interpreter may speed up your program anyway.

Developing & Deploying...

A Process for Program Optimization

1. Question the need!

   - Is performance your highest priority at this stage?
   - Premature optimization is the root of much evil. Focus on correctness and maintainability first.

2. Look at the big picture!

   - Are you doing stuff that is not needed? Are you using the best available algorithms?
   - Changes at the highest level give the largest effect.

3. Find the hot-spots!

   - Where does the program spend its time?
   - Profile to find the 10% of the code using 90% of the time.

4. Check structure and data!

   - How is your data stored and accessed?
   - Implicit choices related to data, its generation and management is often the key.

5. Dig deep!

   - Can you use combinations of built-in methods instead of writing your own? Can you rewrite a method or a statement to execute faster?
   - Know your Ruby environment and use it wisely.

Writing a C Extension

And now for the method of last resort: abandoning Ruby and rewriting parts of your program in C. If you are sure that performance of your program is a problem, that you are using the best algorithm, and that you have tuned the implementation by using the speediest Ruby constructs, and your program is still not fast enough, there is no other way out. Luckily, Ruby has great support for integrating with C code. How you write and use a C extension from Ruby is covered in Chapter 10. However, some special issues arise in this context.

One problem is that your design often restricts your options since the interface to your methods is defined and may be difficult to change, and your data is in Ruby data structures (arrays and hashes, for example). Since your C-implemented method needs to take the same type of input as the Ruby-implemented one, you might end up writing Ruby in C — that is, you call the C variants of the Ruby methods you use in the Ruby-implemented code. This limits the performance gain compared to a pure C implementation that works with C data and then converts the result to a Ruby object. Beware of this situation and try to rethink your class. Often you can find an atomic method working on some basic Ruby data structure that will be the key to better performance. Or you can implement a custom data structure in C and use it throughout your program.

Summary

If your program runs too slowly you should first think about it at the highest level. What does it do and in what order? By looking at the overall algorithm you may find redundant computations or steps whose results are never used. Or maybe there is a totally different approach that will be faster. Try to think *out of the box* to find new ways of accomplishing the program's goals.

To compare algorithms you should know how to analyze their complexity. The ordo notation helps you to quickly characterize the growth rate of the execution time as the input data grows larger. It is a powerful tool that will help you choose between alternative algorithms.

Another powerful tool is a profiler that shows you your program's hot spots — that is, the handful of methods where the majority of time is spent. Use a profiler to focus your efforts and measure your progress. It is important that you use input data that is as realistic as possible. If not, the reported timings might lead you to the wrong conclusions so that you try to speed up the wrong methods, those that have little effect. For profiling, you can either use the standard profiler or RbProf in AspectR. The latter is faster and gives you additional information on the call graph and on the opportunity for result caching. However, both profilers rely on *Time.times.utime*. For small methods, its resolution might not be good enough to enable meaningful timings.

It is not easy to compare different Ruby constructs in a fair way. You have to make sure the Garbage Collector does not invalidate your timings; you should beware of timing inaccuracies; and you should repeat the timings many times on different inputs. It can often be very misleading to take out small portions of large programs and compare them. Always try to compare constructs in their real-world context and with realistic input. Also, ask yourself if the time you spend on getting that extra percentage of performance is worth it in the long run. Maybe it's better if you spend the time on extending the program or ensuring that it is bug-free.

Result caching trades space for time: by caching previously calculated results, you do not have to recalculate them later. The *memoize* extension provides an easy interface to result caching.

As a last resort you may have to consider writing a crucial part of you program in C to reach the desired performance levels. Try to avoid doing this before you really know which part of your program is the bottleneck. With a thorough understanding of the algorithm, and after doing a few profiles, you're in good shape to decide if and where you need to use lower-level languages.

Solutions Fast Track

Analyzing the Complexity of Algorithms

- ☑ The algorithm complexity gives an approximate measure of how the number of steps needed to execute an algorithm grows with increasing size of the input data. It is a basis for comparing and choosing between algorithms.

- ☑ The ordo notation gives a short-hand for describing algorithm complexity. $O(1)$ is very fast, $O(N)$ good, $O(N*logN)$ acceptable, $O(N^2)$ tedious, $O(N^3)$ slow and $O(N^N)$ infeasible.

- ☑ Remember that the big-O notation is a simplification and that you might sometimes have to take the "hidden constants" into account. One algorithm may be faster for your use than another one with better complexity.

Improving Performance by Profiling

- ☑ Profile your program to understand why its performance is not good enough. Then use the profiling information to focus your performance enhancement efforts.

- ☑ The standard profiler *profile.rb* is simple and easy to use. However, it is slow and does not give you information on the callers of often-used methods.

- ☑ The *AspectR* extension contains the profiler *RbProf,* which is faster than the standard profiler. It can show you how methods call each other and if methods are repeatedly called with the same arguments.

Comparing the Speed of Ruby Constructs

- ☑ Benchmarking different Ruby constructs in a fair way is difficult. Be sure to try them all before starting to time them. If possible, turn off garbage collection while timing, repeat the timings many times, repeat the constructs many times within the timing to avoid timing inaccuracies, randomize the order of invoking the constructs, and try on many different inputs of different sizes.

☑ Use *push* or << for adding an element to an *Array*.

☑ Use *for-in* loops instead of *each* to loop over the elements in an *Array*.

☑ Use *join* when concatenating many strings.

☑ Pre-declare loop variables.

☑ Use destructive methods. They are faster and put less stress on memory system and Garbage Collector.

Further Performance Enhancements

☑ Understand your algorithm and its complexity, and try to devise or find a better one with lower complexity.

☑ Do not change many different things at a time. You need to know how each one affects performance.

☑ By caching the results from your methods (memoizing a method) you can speed up algorithms that repeatedly call a method with the same arguments. You trade some memory for more speed.

☑ Reduce the number of temporary objects created in your program since a lot of time might go into allocating and garbage collecting them. If you cannot avoid creating them you should try to reuse them.

☑ If you really need speed consider implementing the central part of your program in a C extension. It can buy you the extra speed you need at the expense of a less maintainable, less portable and more error-prone program that is harder to install.

Frequently Asked Questions

The following Frequently Asked Questions, answered by the authors of this book, are designed to both measure your understanding of the concepts presented in this chapter and to assist you with real-life implementation of these concepts. To have your questions about this chapter answered by the author, browse to **www.syngress.com/solutions** and click on the **"Ask the Author"** form.

Q: The hot spots in my program reported by the standard profiler are all Ruby base methods. I use them all over so the profile doesn't tell me very much. What can I do?

A: Look at the column marked "total ms/calls" to see which of your own methods take majority of the time. The calls to the top base methods probably arise from within your hot spots, so focus your efforts there. As an alternative try RbProf and tell it to only benchmark your own methods.

Q: Which is the fastest way to loop over the elements of an array?

A: A *for-in*-loop is faster than using iterators or manually updating an index.

Q: Should I create an empty *Array* using *Array.new* or *[]*?

A: The shorthand, *[]*, is faster. The same goes for hashes.

Parser Generators

Solutions in this chapter:

- Creating the Parsing Library of your Dreams

- Parsing in Ruby with Rockit

- Parsing in Ruby with Racc

☑ Summary

☑ Solutions Fast Track

☑ Frequently Asked Questions

Introduction

When you program computers, you will sooner or later need to parse a text into something that your program can directly manipulate. Even though you will probably not write a compiler for a full programming language, there are countless other situations in which a parser would help you: extracting options specified in command-line arguments, reading configuration files, building a contact database from mails, or extracting information from XML documents. For common tasks there are often specialized solutions (there are ways to parse XML documents, for example, which are covered in Chapter 4, and there is the *optparse* extension for handling command-line arguments, which can be downloaded from RAA). However, when specialized tools do not address your problem, you will need to produce a parser for your needs. In this chapter we'll take a look at your options.

In general, to *parse* is to reconstruct the structure of some data in a linear form according to a grammar. The linear form is often ASCII text but can be any linear data such as binary data or Unicode text. The grammar is a description of all the valid forms the linear data can take and, at the same time, a description of the structure of the data.

You have two main options in producing a parser. You can write manually or you can use a parser generator that will generate a parser from the grammar. The benefits from writing your parser manually are that it can be very fast, you understand all aspects of it, and, most important, you can get a parser no matter how your grammar looks. The drawbacks to writing your parser manually are that it is more error-prone, you have to write code that can be automatically generated, and it is more time-consuming when there are changes in the grammar. Parser generators address these issues, but they force you to write your grammar in a form they understand and the resulting parser can be slower.

In Ruby there are many different packages for creating parsers. Racc and RBison are two solutions that mimic the GNU Bison program commonly used to generate table-driven parsers. Rockit is the more recent arrival with some new approaches to the parsing problem. In this chapter, we will focus on Racc and Rockit—the former because it is a very mature, tried-and-tested solution that can handle Yacc grammars, which are in common supply, and Rockit because it differs the most from the other two.

Let us start with the most important question: What kind of support have you been dreaming of getting from a parser extension?

Creating the Parsing Library of your Dreams

A parser is an object that analyses the structure of a given string and returns objects that reflects this structure. Instead of taking such an abstract sentence and idea any further, let's try a more hands-on description. The most hands-on thing I can think of is Ruby, of course, so let's describe our parsers and how they should work in pseudo-Ruby code. Even if we can't actually execute the code, it will act as a kind of requirements specification on how we want parsers in Ruby to work.

For the purpose of having a goal in mind for our illustration, I've chosen Basic—it was my first programming language with which I got programs to run and print output on the Commodore 128's Basic Interpreter (let's call it CBI). The full description of CBI can now be found on the Web at http://members.tripod.com/~rvbelzen/c128sg/index.html. Since we will not be implementing the full language supported by CBI we make our own. Let's write a parser for RdgBasic (Ruby Developer's Guide Basic)! We can decide how much to include as we go along.

To begin: what's the simplest parser we can start with? If we are going to analyze strings, we would need to be able to create parsers for substrings. How can we analyze a string without taking it to pieces? Since perhaps the most elementary Basic command is **PRINT**, let's try something like the following:

```
print_command = string_parser "PRINT"
```

In the parser library of our dreams, this would mean that we get a parser for strings looking like PRINT in the variable *print_command*. So *string_parser* is a function that generates a parser that matches the string we supply to it. It would be kind of awkward if we had to append *_parser* to every parser generation function, so let's assume there is a *Parse* module where the parser generators reside. We also include our dream parser library so that the earlier code would look like this:

```
require 'ploods'
include Parse


print_command = string "PRINT"
```

Nice! How should we use our parser? The simplest thing I can think of is that we call a *parse* method and supply a string, and the parser returns the string if there was a match, or returns an error otherwise. So we would have the following:

```
print_command.parse "PRINT"              #=> "PRINT"
print_command.parse "Print"              # Oh yes, all caps. What now?
```

But what kind of error message should we get on the second line? Remember, this is the parser library of our dreams, so nothing should hold us back! It would sure be handy to get the position of the offending character, a description of what went wrong, and a suggestion of what would have been a valid input. So when executing the second line above, we would instead get a ParseError which would read as follows when printed:

```
parse error at (line 1, column 2):
unexpected "r" when expecting "R" (trying to parse "PRINT")
```

That's what I would call a useful error message. But we're on a mission to an RdgBasic "Hello World," so let's press on! We need a way to specify a parser for string literals because we could combine it with our previously mentioned *print_command* and parse our first program.

A *string literal* in Basic is a sequence of characters enclosed in double quotes. Something like the following:

```
dquote = string '"'
string_literal = seq(dquote, mult(string_character), dquote)
```

would be natural if *mult(x)* meant "a parser repeatedly applying the parser *x* zero or more times" and if *seq(*parsers)* meant "apply the parsers given as arguments in turn and return their results in an array." It's good if *mult* returns the empty string if *x* didn't match at all, since our parser would then parse empty Basic strings (""). Note that *mult* has the same meaning as '*' in Regexps. For example, /\d*a/ would match zero or more digits followed by an '*a*'.

However, we need to specify a parser for string characters in Basic before this will really fly. We couldn't find a full specification of what characters are valid, but as a first approximation we'll start with ASCII values from 0x20 (space) up to 0x7E (~). To keep things simple we exclude the quote itself (or our strings will never end) and the backslash (or we will forget that RdgBasic is not Ruby and think the backslash could give us a string with a double quote in it). To specify a parser for this we could of course create a *seq* and write the 93 (0x7E-0x20-2+1) string parsers for all the different ASCII values. Or we could do the following:

```
valid_ascii = (0x20..0x7e).to_a.select {|c| c != ?" and c != ?\}
string_character = choice(valid_ascii.map{|c| string(c.chr)})
```

where *choice(*parsers)* would try each of the parsers in turn and return the result from the first one matching the input—definitely nicer. This would be a major strength of the parser library of our dreams—it is "embedded" in Ruby so we have the full Ruby language to lean on.

Let's add some more parsers so that we have a "full" grammar (for our very limited language) and can try it out. We need to sequence this:

```
white_space = skip(mult(choice(string(" "), string("\t"))))
command = seq(print_command, white_space, string_literal)
RdgBasicParser = command
p RdgBasicParser.parse 'PRINT "Hello, World!"'
```

where we use the new parser generator *skip(p)*, which matches if *p* matches but discards the parse result returned from *p*. We should probably skip the double-quotes around string literals also. After these updates the script evaluates to:

```
["PRINT", "Hello, World!"]
```

We can now add an evaluator and a *print-eval* loop to get an interactive interpreter. Let's call it *iba* (Interactive rdg BAsic):

```
class RdgBasicEvaluator
  def eval(res)
    if Array === res && res[0] == "PRINT"
      puts res[1]
    end
  end
end


def print_eval_loop(parser, evaluator, prompt = "rdg_basic")
  while true
    print "<#{prompt}> "
    prg = STDIN.gets.chomp
    exit if prg == ":quit"
    begin
      puts "#{evaluator.eval(parser.parse(prg))}"
    rescue Exception => e
      puts e.message
    end
```

```
      end
   end


   if $0 == __FILE__
      puts "Welcome to Rdg Basic version 0.1.0\n\n"
      parser = RdgBasicParser
      print_eval_loop(RdgBasicParser, RdgBasicEvaluator.new)
   end
```

Here's what a sample session could look like:

```
$ ruby iba.rb
Welcome to Rdg Basic version 0.1.0


<rdg basic> PRINT "Hello, World!"
Hello, World!
<rdg basic> :quit
$
```

It's really very simple (basic!) but it's what we needed—we can now start
adding to it. Natural additions are more literals, variables, assignment, and some
control structure. If we add the **INPUT** command, we should be able to do
quite complex programs with I/O and calculations.

However, before we start extending, we had better think of the structure of
our parser and the evaluator. Sure, it gets the work done, but in many ways it is
awkward and not easily extendable. One problem is that we have to make calls
to string all over the place. If you are a slow typist, this is not optimal. Also, each
character that isn't essential shouldn't be there, as it might cloud the important
things and make them harder to grasp. Fortunately this is easy to fix: All parser
generator functions should create string parsers from all arguments that are
strings. It should also create parsers from ranges of strings so that we can easily
give a range of allowed characters. An example would be "0"..."9" for a parser
for digits.

A similar problem is that it is rather awkward to have to use *seq* and *choice* all
the time since they are used a lot. What if parsers could be chained with "&" and
"|"? The former would correspond to *seq* and the latter to *choice*. Then we could
write our parsers in a clearer way. We could even define *String#|* and *String#&* to
generate string parsers from themselves. Look at this in code:

```
class String
  def to_parser
    Parse::string(self)
  end

  def |(o)
    self.to_parser | o
  end

  def &(o)
    self.to_parser & o
  end
end
```

A more serious problem with our current dream library is regarding the data structure returned from the parser. Currently it is an array with the parsed strings. We cannot simply push to this array when introducing more commands. If we do, we might loose the structure we are trying to restore from the linear representation in the string.

One solution would be to return an array of arrays indicating the structure in the input. So if:

```
integer = plus( "0".."9" )                        # One or more digit chars
expression = integer & "+" & integer
identifier = plus( "a".."z" | "A".."Z" )
assignment = identifier & "=" & expression
```

and we parse the string "temp=1+2" with the assignment parser, it would return:

```
["temp", "=", ["1", "+", "2"]]
```

which is adequate since the structure is still there. And it is basically a tree with the expression part in a subtree. But consider what would happen if we add alternative ways of constructing expressions. A single integer should also be an expression, but if we parse a string like "temp=1" we would get ["temp","=",["1"]] and we would have to check position 1 in the inner array to understand what kind of expression it was. This constitutes a kind of parsing yet again and we shouldn't have to do it. The solution is to build syntax trees as we go along. But before going in that direction, let's address a concern you might have with all this parsing.

Why Not Use Regexps?

You may have noticed that some of our parsers look very much like Regexps. A valid question at this stage might be to ask why we can't simply use Regexps. They are well-known, mature, reliable, and available in Ruby proper.

The answer is that they will not be strong enough for the things we want to do. The canonical example would be nested parentheses. There is no way to match nested parentheses (or any nested constructs) with a single Regexp. It can be done with two Regexps and some supporting code, but it will take multiple passes over the string to be matched and it will be hard to understand.

With the parser library of our dreams we would do this:

```
parens = recursive("(" & maybe(recurse) & ")")
```

and have *recurse* mean the parser we are currently defining. If we'd try it as follows:

```
parens.parse "((()))"    #=> "((()))"
parens.parse "((()"
```

then the second line should raise a ParseError with this message:

```
parse error at (line 1, column 5):
unexpected end of input
expected "))"
```

Getting this behavior when using Regexps would be considerably harder.

The question has real merit, though. Before starting to write a parser you should consider whether or not your task would lend itself to a concise solution using solely Regexps. Extracting information out of a larger body of text is the classic situation where Regexps will do. Examples could be to extract the comments out of Ruby programs, finding a certain entry in an XML document or finding the function signatures in a C program.

If a Regexp solution will suffice, it will generally be both faster and simpler than writing the full parser. However, you have to be on your guard so that the Regexp solutions do not grow with the requirements and match larger parts of the data until it gets unwieldy. If this happens you might be better off writing the full parser, which will typically give you a simple and more easily maintainable program. It is always up to you and your assessment of the problem. Now let's grow some trees!

Representing Recovered Structures with Abstract Syntax Trees

A natural way to represent the structure we recover when parsing is with a *syntax tree*. Each parsed item is a node; links between the nodes show how the parsed items relate to each other. Figure 9.1 shows an example of a parse tree used to represent the structure recovered from the string "temp=a+b".

Figure 9.1 Example Abstract Syntax Tree for the String "temp=a+b"

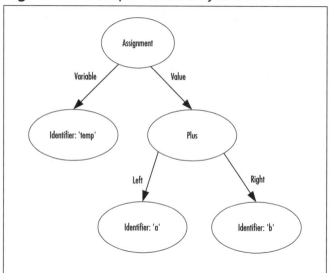

The top node is an *assignment* since that is the main characteristic of the string. The assignment node has two children: one is the variable assigned to and the other one is the value being assigned. The value is another tree because it is an expression saying that 'a' should be added to 'b'. The tree in Figure 9.1 is not the only one that we could use to represent the structure of the string. One alternative would be a general expression node with the Plus operator indicated in a child to the expression node, maybe on a link labeled "operator".

In this simple example it may not be obvious what we have gained by using a tree representation instead of simply arrays of arrays. However, the extra information added by having nodes of different types is crucial when we later work with the result from our parser. We can choose what actions to take based on the type instead of having to check the internals of the arrays. Another benefit is that we can give names to the children and access them by name instead of with an index. These advantages will become increasingly important as the strings we parse (and our trees!) grow larger.

Before we go on to decide how to describe and use these trees in our ideal parsing library, I had better explain why these trees are called *abstract*. The reason is simply that we throw away information that is superfluous and that can be easily inferred from the node types. For example, it could be a parser for a class declaration in Ruby. A *class declaration* is the string *class*, followed by the name of the class, an optional part specifying the super class, a set of statements inside the class, and the string *end*. In an abstract syntax tree we throw away the strings *class*, *end* and < (if there is a superclass specification);since we know that they should be there, having them in the tree would not add any information.

Okay, so we want to build trees that are typed and have named children. How should we use this from inside the Ruby code? Well, the natural way to represent the type of the nodes is to have each node type be a unique class. Then we can access its children by using attribute readers. For example, something like the following:

```
class Assignment < Tree
  attr_reader :variable, :value
  def initialize(var, val)
    @variable, @value = var, val
  end
end
```

would be a straightforward way to encode assignment nodes like the one used above. However, since there may be a large number of node types, and the code would be kind of boring to write each time, it would be better if we could simply write:

```
Assignment = Tree.new_subclass(:Assignment, :variable, :value)
```

And now for the really fun part: How should our parsers build these parse trees? We want them to return trees instead of strings, so we should modify them in some way. One simple way would be to call a method and supply the class of the tree to be built. For the assignment operator:

```
assignment = (variable & skip("=") & expression).build(Assignment)
```

With this new power let's modify our previous parsers and add some new parsers so that we can get some input from the user.

```
Int = Tree.new_sub_class(:Int, :lexeme)

Identifier = Tree.new_sub_class(:Identifier, :lexeme)

StringLit = Tree.new_sub_class(:StringLit, :lexeme)

Print = Tree.new_sub_class(:Print, :expr)

PrintLn = Tree.new_sub_class(:PrintLn)

Read = Tree.new_sub_class(:Read, :identifier)


newline = skip("\r\n" | "\n")
identifier = plus(choice("a".."z", "A".."Z")).build(Identifier)
expr = integer.build(Int)            \
     | identifier             \
     | string_literal.build(StringLit)
statement = (skip('PRINT') & ws & expr         & newline).build(Print) \
          | (skip('READ')  & ws & identifier & newline).build(Read)   \
          | skip('PRINTLN').build(PrintLn)
RdgBasicParser = plus(statement)
```

We also modify *iba* into an RdgBasic interpreter called *bint*:

```
class RdgBasicEvaluator
  def initialize
    @variables = Hash.new
  end

  def evaluate(res)
    case res
    when Array
      res.each {|s| evaluate(s)}
    when PrintLn
      puts ""; STDOUT.flush
```

```
      when Read
        print "? "; STDOUT.flush
        @variables[res.identifier.lexeme] = STDIN.gets.strip
      when Print
        print evaluate(res.expr)
      when Int
        res.lexeme.to_i
      when Identifier
        @variables[res.lexeme]
      when StringLit
        res.lexeme
      end
    end
end


if $0 == __FILE__
  File.open(ARGV[0], "r") do |f|
    ast = RdgBasicParser.parse(f.read)
    RdgBasicEvaluator.new.evaluate(ast)
  end
end
```

We can now write small basic programs and run them. Here's a simple one:

```
PRINT "What is your name"
READ name
PRINT "Hello "
PRINT name
PRINT "!"
PRINTLN
```

And here's what a sample session should look like:

```
$ ruby bint.rb name.bas
What is your name? Robert
Hello Robert!
$
```

We now have the rudimentary machinery to continue building our RdgBasic parser. With a pretty good feeling of how this library of our dreams should work, it's time to look at our options for building a parser in Ruby with the available tools. Let's start with Rockit and then tackle Racc.

Parsing in Ruby with Rockit

Perhaps this was obvious, but Rockit *is* the parser library of this author's dreams. When I designed it I thought much like we did in the previous section about what would be the simplest way to write parsers in Ruby. The result was the parser generators and combinators we used earlier—with only a few modifications, the basic parsers and interpreters program we built in that section will actually work. Let's start with the basics: What exactly is Rockit?

Ruby Object-oriented Compiler construction toolKIT (Rockit) is a Ruby extension available from RAA, or at http://rockit.sourceforge.net/. It was started as part of the vision to build a set of Ruby components to execute Ruby programs. Rockit will support this aim by supplying the basic building blocks needed to assemble parsers, interpreters, and compilers.

As it happens, parsing Ruby is not the easiest thing you can do—the grammar is context-sensitive and quite large. The parse.y file used to generate the parser for Ruby 1.6.5 is over 8000 lines long, and although all of it isn't doing parsing, a majority of it is. Matz's vision of human-oriented programming has led him to a parser that can almost guess what you mean. In the development effort to parse Ruby in Ruby code, Rockit has developed into a pretty competent tool in its own right. It might well be the parsing tool you need.

Rockit's main features include the following:

- Parsers are written in Ruby code and are first-class objects.

- It has basic parser building blocks and combinators that build larger parsers from basic ones.

- Both lexical analyzers and syntactical analyzers are built with the same building blocks. In fact, there is no need to separate lexical and syntactical analysis, unless you want to.

- All input to the parsers are via symbol streams so that Rockit can handle strings, Unicode, and binary input.

- Parsers produce either *abstract syntax trees* (ASTs) or call actions as parts are parsed (event-based).

- The abstract syntax trees can be dumped to many graphics formats such as .png, .tif, Postscript, and .jpg (if you have installed 'dot' from AT&T's GraphViz package).

- It supports non-context free languages; for example, it can parse nested comments.

- It has an extensive error detection and reporting system with reasonable automatic error messages and support for customized error messages as needed.

At the time of this writing the current version of Rockit is 0.4. It is still in alpha and some things might change as new ideas and implementation solutions are encountered. So far the development has focused on finding the Ruby way to specify and use parsers—that is, to get the syntax and semantics laid out. Almost no time has gone into getting good performance.

Older Rockit versions used a totally different parsing model which was even stronger in theory and had many nice properties, but it was slow and had poor error reporting. For compatibility reasons it is still supported but it is unclear if future Rockit versions will still support it. Maybe there is a good way to merge the two approaches and they will both be supported. However, the official way to use Rockit for constructing parsers is now with the combinator approach as shown earlier. You should avoid using the older style for new projects unless you have really good reasons for doing so.

Deviations from the Parsing Library of Our Dreams

Well, now you know that I was "cheating" and that the "parsing library of our dreams" is how it will look and feel when you build parsers in Ruby. But there are some differences between our RdgBasic and Rockit:

- You should require 'rockit/parse/combinator_parsers' and not 'ploods'.

- The combinators are in Rockit::Parse so if you want to access them directly you should include that module.

- The class for syntax trees (called *Tree* above) is called *Term* in Rockit. It supports pattern matching and simple pretty-printing.

- There is a standard library of parsers derived from the basic ones in std_library.

To show you a larger example, look at this larger grammar for RdgBasic as it would look in Rockit version 0.4:

```
require 'rockit/parse/combinator_parsers'
require 'rockit/parse/std_library'
include Rockit::Parse


class RdgBasicGrammar < Grammar
  language "RDG Basic"
  version  "1.0"


  WhiteSpace = mult(" " | "\t" | "\f" | "\v")
  Comments   = nest( "/*", "*/", mult(AnyChar) )


  Ident   = Upper & mult(Upper | Digit)                           ^
    (Identifier = term(:Identifier, :lexeme))
  Num       = plus(Digit)                                          ^
    (Number = term(:Number, :lexeme))
  valid_ascii = (0x20..0x7e).to_a.select {|c| c != %q{"} and c != ?\}
  string_char = one_of(valid_ascii.pack("c*"))
  StringP = skip('"') & mult(string_character) & skip('"')  ^
    (StringLit = term(:StringLit, :lexeme))


  BinExpr = term(:BinExpr, :left, :op, :right)
  Expr = expression_parser([
          [['*', :Left, BinExpr], ['/', :Left, BinExpr],
           ['MOD', :Left, BinExpr]],
          [['+', :Left, BinExpr], ['-', :Left, BinExpr]]],
          Num > Ident > "(" & recurse & ")" ^ lift(1))


  Cond = Expr & ('<' | '>' | '=') & Expr ^
          (Condition = term(:Condition, :left, :op, :right)


  Statement =
      'IF' & Condition & 'THEN' & Newline &
```

```
            Statements &
        maybe('ELSE' & Newline & Statements > term)
        'ENDIF' & Newline ^
          (If = term(:If, :_, :condition,:_,:_, :statements, :optelse))    \
    >   'FOR' & Identifier & ':=' & Expr & 'TO' & Expr & Newline &
            Statements &
        'NEXT' & Newline ^
          (For = term(:For, :_, :ident,:_, :from,:_, :to,:_,:statements) \
    >   'READ' & Identifier & Newline ^
          (Read = term(:Read, :_, :ident))                                 \
    >   'PRINT' & (Expr | String) & Newline ^
          (Print = term(:Print,:_,:message,:_))                            \
    >   'PRINTLN' & Newline ^
          (PrintLn = term(:PrintLn, :_))                                   \
    >    Identifier & ':=' & Expr & Newline ^
          (Assignment = term(:Assignment, :ident,:_,:expression))


  Statement.set_separator(skip(maybe(WhiteSpace | Comment)),
                          [Ident, Num, StringP])


  BasicProgram = plus(Statement) ^
    (Program = term(:Program, :statements))


  start BasicProgram
end
```

There are a number of new techniques used here:

- It is customary, but not required, to define your Rockit grammar in a
  separate class derived from *Grammar*. It is a nice way to collect things
  together. The *grammar* class also gives you a number of methods for
  specifying the language and setting the start symbol (the parser to start
  parsing with when you call *Grammar#parse*). Note that even though only
  one parser can be the start parser, intermediate parsers can still be
  accessed from the outside if they are defined as constants (for example,
  RdgBasicGrammar::Identifier for parsing the identifier in RdgBasic).

Parsers that you don't want to export in this way can be specified as local variables (*string_character* above).

- Parsers are specified on the form "parser ^ (Term = term(:Term, ...))" instead of the previously used "(parser).build(:Term, ...)" which allows us to drop the parentheses around the parser and save the *term* class for later use in evaluators. Since "^" has lower priority than "&", it can be used without parentheses. We also define ">" as an alias for "|". Since ">" has lower precedence than both "&" and "^" we can stack alternatives after each other without parentheses.

- Instead of explicitly marking all sub-parsers that should be skipped, one can specify this in the *term* function. The trick is to give the corresponding children the name ":_". When building the *term*, all results for children having that name will be skipped.

- A special parser generator can handle binary expressions (*Expr Op Expr*) with operators of different precedence and associativity. You can find more details in the reference material below.

- You can specify a separator parser that is allowed between "tokens" in parsers producing terms. In this way you do not have to add whitespace and comments parsers between every token parser in your grammar. The specified separator will be recursively applied to sub-parsers but will not affect parsers that you explicitly say are token parsers. Note that parsers specified as strings are always token parsers (that is, indivisible).

- The standard library contains predefined parsers for many situations. Examples in the grammar above include *Digit*, *AnyChar*, and *nest*.

With the parser above we can now execute relatively complex RdgBasic programs. We only have to extend the evaluator in *bint* to evaluate the new terms:

```
class RdgBasicEvaluator
  alias old_eval evaluator
  def evaluator(ast)
    case ast
    when Statements
      ast.statements.each {|stmt| mb_eval(stmt)}
    when If
      if evaluator(ast.condition)
```

```
          evaluator(ast.statements)
       elsif ast.optelse
          evaluator(ast.optelse[2])
       end
    when For
       for i in (evaluator(ast.from)..evaluator(ast.to))
          @variables[ast.ident.lexeme] = i
          evaluator(ast.statements)
       end
    when "Read"
       print "? "; STDOUT.flush
       input = STDIN.gets
       input = input.to_i if (?0..?9).include?(input[0])
       @variables[ast.ident.lexeme] = input
    when Assignment
       @variables[ast.ident.lexeme] = evaluate(ast.expression)
    when Condition, BinExpr
       map = {">" => :>, "<" => :<, "=" => :==, "+" => :+, "-" => :-,
              "*" => :*, "/" => "/".intern, "MOD" => "%".intern}
       evaluate(ast.left).send(map[ast.op.lexeme], evaluate(ast.right))
    else
       old_eval(res)
    end
  end
end
```

Let's try the program.

```
/* Sum even numbers between two user-supplied limits */
PRINT "I can sum even numbers."
PRINTLN
PRINT "At what number should I start summing"
READ START
PRINT "At what number should I stop"
READ STOP
SUM := 0
```

```
FOR I := START TO STOP
  IF (I MOD 2) = 0 THEN
    SUM := (SUM + I)
  ENDIF
NEXT
PRINT "The sum of all even numbers between (inclusive) "
PRINT START
PRINT " and "
PRINT STOP
PRINT " is = "
PRINT SUM
```

Here's a sample session:

```
$ ruby bint2.rb sumeven.rdb
I can sum even numbers.
At what number should I start summing? 10
At what number should I stop? 18
The sum of all even numbers between (inclusive) 10 and 18 is 80
$
```

If you want to play around with this parser and evaluator yourself you can find the latest versions of these files at www.syngress.com/solutions.

Using Rockit as a Parser Generator

If you think the combinator approach to parsing is cool but would like to write your grammars in even cleaner form, Rockit can also be used as a traditional parser generator. Note, however, that this feature was how Rockit was used prior to version 0.4. This old model and the new model are both supported in Rockit 0.4 but there may be changes in future Rockit versions. Here's what our RdgBasic grammar would look like:

```
Grammar RdgBasic
  Version = "1.0"
  Date    = "2001-10-06"
Tokens
  Blank      = /(( )|(\t)|(\v))+/                        [:Skip]
  Identifier = /[A-Z]([A-Z]|\d)*/
```

```
Number      = /\d+/
String      = /"[^\r\n]*"/
Newline     = /(\r\n)|(\r)|(\n)/
```

Productions
```
  Statements -> Statement+           [Statements: statements]
  Statement  -> 'IF' Condition 'THEN' Newline
                   Statements
                   ('ELSE' Newline Statements)?
                 'ENDIF' Newline    [If: _,condition,_,_,
                     statements,optelse,
                                        _,_]
              | 'FOR' Identifier ':=' Expr 'TO' Expr Newline
                  Statements
                 'NEXT' Newline      [For: _,ident,_,from,_,
                     to,_,statements,_,_]
              | 'READ' Identifier Newline
                                     [Read: _,ident,_]
              | 'PRINT' (Expr | String) Newline
                                     [Print: _,message,_]
              | 'PRINTLN' Newline    [PrintLn]
              | Identifier ':=' Expr Newline
                                     [Assignment: ident,_,expression,_]
  Condition -> Expr ('<' | '>' | '=') Expr
                                     [Condition: left, op, right]
  Expr      -> Number               [^]
            | Identifier            [^]
            | '(' Expr ')'          [^: _,expr,_]
            | Expr '+' Expr         [Plus: left, _, right]
            | Expr '-' Expr         [Minus: left, _, right]
            | Expr '*' Expr         [Mult: left, _, right]
            | Expr '/' Expr         [Div: left, _, right]
            | Expr 'MOD' Expr       [Mod: left, _, right]
```
Priorities
```
  Mult = Div = Mod > Plus = Minus
```

The following lists the most prominent features of this grammar format:

- Tokens are specified with Regexps.

- You specify the trees to be built with *arrays* to the right or below the corresponding rule.

- The first component of a tree specification is the name of the term (AST node to be created). The rest of the components are the children's names. Children to be skipped are given the name ":_".

- Precedence is specified by giving the relative priority of productions. In the earlier example we stated that multiplication, division, and module should have the same precedence and a higher precedence than plus and minus.

Case-Insensitive Parsing

In some grammars you don't care about the case-sensitivity of matched tokens. It would be cumbersome if you had to manually insert alternatives for each character. Fortunately, all Rockit parsers have an accessor named *case_sensitive*. By default its value is *true* but if you set it to *false* it will allow both uppercase and lowercase characters. For example:

```
p = string "query"
p.case_sensitive = false
p.parse "query"              #=> "query" as usual
p.parse "QUERY"              #=> "QUERY"
```

Note that this is applied at the *character level*. So although *p* is a string parser, if it is case insensitive, it will also parse "QuEry", "quERY" and any other combination of uppercase and lowercase characters.

Customizing Your Parser

There are four main groups of parser building blocks: *generators*, *combinators*, *transformers*, and *error-related*. In many of the groups there are both basic and derived building blocks. When you build a parser you can use and combine these basic and derived building blocks in any way you want, without thinking about their status. Below we separate them and show how the derived ones can be implemented with the basic ones. Note that you cannot assume that this is the way it is done in Rockit; for performance reasons they may be implemented in other ways. However, by showing the actual definitions of the derived building blocks, you can see some examples of how to write your own, tailored to your grammar and problem.

Parser Generators

In this section we'll take a look at the following building blocks: *symbol*, for matching one or more symbols in the input; *none_of*, for matching any character but the specified ones; and *succeed*, for always returning a result without consuming any input.

The most basic parser building block is one that matches a symbol in the output:

```
symbol("a")       # Matches a single "a"
```

but since it is so common to allow more than one symbol in a position, *symbol* is actually a derived building block implemented with the *symbols* parser generator:

```
def symbol(aSymbol)
  symbols(aSymbol)
end
```

Symbols can take a symbol, a range of symbols, or any combination of them as exemplified by the following:

```
symbols("a")                   # Matches a single "a"
symbols("0".."9")              # Matches a single digit
symbols("0".."9", "a".."f")    # Matches a single hexadecimal digit
symbols("a", "c".."d", "k")    # Matches one of "a", "c", "d" or "k"
```

The *none_of* generator is specific to strings of characters. The characters that will not be matched are specified in a string. There is a corresponding version for positive parsing called *one_of* but there is no need to use it since *symbols* will use it if needed. Here's an example of using *none_of* (the parser will match any character but "a" or "b"):

```
p = none_of "ab"
```

You can use the *succeed* parser generator when building larger parsers, even though it's not very useful on its own. It will simply return the result specified by you when calling the generator and will not consume any input. So the parser p defined as follows:

```
p = succeed("Yes")

p.parse "No"                          # Matches and returns "Yes"
```

will return "Yes" regardless of the input.

Parser Combinators

The basic way to combine parsers is to have two or more of them in sequence, or to allow a choice between two or more of them. In Rockit, the former is expressed with the *seq* function. The latter is expressed either with *choice* or with *alt* (short for *alternatives*). They have slight differences in semantics. For performance reasons you should use *choice* whenever possible.

With *seq* you can combine parsers in a sequence, stacking parsers after each other. The combined parser only matches if all of its component parsers match:

```
seq(symbols("a"), symbols("b"))   # Matches the string "ab"
```

To simplify the encoding of parsers, all of the parser combinators allow symbols as parameters. So the parser above could equally well be written as:

```
seq("a", "b")                     # Matches the string "ab"
```

This is implemented by simply calling *symbols* on every parameter that is not a parser so you can use ranges and combinations of ranges and symbols as shown above. This means that the following:

```
seq("a".."d", "k")                # Matches string /[a-d]k/
```

matches any string that matches the Regexp /[a-d]k/ and *not* the string "abcdk". In the rest of this chapter we use symbols or ranges of symbols without further mentioning the intermediate calls to the symbols generator.

With *seq* and symbols we can now build a derived parser building block which is very handy: a parser generator for strings:

```
string("def")                          # Matches the string "def"

string("'\"'")                         # Matches the string "'\"'"
```

The implementation is straightforward but shows the strength of Rockit's model of specifying parsers in Ruby itself:

```
def string(aString)

  seq(*aString.split(""))

end
```

As a matter of fact, the parser combinators accepts strings as well as symbols and symbol ranges. For strings they call the string parser generator, and for symbols and ranges they call symbols. A contrived example showing these possibilities would be:

```
seq("code", " ", "a".."z")    # Matches strings /code [a-z]/
```

The *choice* combinator is a deterministic way to specify a choice between parsers. The parsers given as parameters are tried in order. When the first one matches, its result is returned and none of the latter parsers are tried. If there is no match when all the alternatives have been tried, the choice parser fails. Here are some examples:

```
digit = symbols("0".."9")
choice(digit, seq("a", digit))          # Matches strings /a?\d/


choice(seq(digit, ".", digit), digit) # Matches strings /\d(\.\d)?/
```

When the latter parser is applied to a string "3.4", it will return "3.4" even though the *digit* parser, being the second parameter, would also match and return "3"—the *choice* parser will never apply the second parameter when the first one matches.

Next we'll consider the *repeat* parser, which specifies a range for the number of times a parser should apply. It is very common that a pattern matched by a parser repeats many times. The simplest example is probably a word which is constructed from one or more letters. The *repeat* parser combinator gives a general way to express such repetition. It takes a parser and two optional range limits: *min* (the minimum number of times the parser should match) and *max* (the maximum number of times it should match). Their default values are 0 and positive infinity. Some examples follow:

```
repeat(digit)                      # Matches zero or more digits
repeat(digit, 1)                   # Matches one or more digits
repeat(digit, 0, 1)                # Matches zero or one digit
repeat(digit, 2, 4)                # Matches two, three or four digits
```

With this parser combinator we can easily define the repeat constructs used in extended Backus–Naur Form (BNF) grammars and Regexps:

```
def maybe(parser)
  repeat(parser, 0, 1)
end
```

```
def mult(parser)
  repeat(parser, 0)
end
alias many mult


def plus(parser)
  repeat(parser, 1)
end
alias many1 plus
```

We introduced the aliases since they are commonly used. The *plus* and *mult* is closer to Regexp usage, where they are specified with '+' and '*' respectively. For example, *many1* is taken to mean "many but at least one repetitions of a parser."

Parser Transformers

In addition to building basic parsers and combining them, we can also transform parsers to change what they return or how they work. This is most commonly used to construct the parse tree but also to skip whitespace, keep track of the position, and so forth. We'll describe the parser transformers *build* and *term* for building a term for the abstract syntax tree; *apply* for applying a function to the result and parse state; *look_ahead* and *look_back* for context-sensitive parsing; and *capture* and *ref* for saving a parse result and referring to it later.

First we'll look at *build* and *term*. You can transform the result of a parser into a term for the AST. Terms are specified by giving their *term* class name as a symbol, followed by the children's names as symbols. Children's name in position 1 corresponds to the first parser in a sequence, children's name in position 2 to the second parser etc. If a children's name is ":_ ", the result from the corresponding parser is skipped when building the term. For example, the parser:

```
p = seq(plus(digit), "+", plus(digit)).build(:Plus, :left, :_, :right)
```

would return the term *Plus[1,2]* when applied to the string "1+2". Often you want to keep a reference to the *Term* class used to create terms. If so, you can tell a parser to send its results to a *term* class, thus producing a term. The following code has the same effect as the one above:

```
p = seq(plus(digit), "+", plus(digit)) ^ term(:Plus, :left, :_, :right)
```

but it allows you to save a reference to the term so that you can use it later:

```
p = seq(plus(digit), "+", plus(digit)) ^
    (Plus = term(:Plus, :left, :_, :right))
```

Apply is a powerful transformer that allows you to apply a function to the results of a parser. It is not common to use *apply* directly; its main use is in implementing other transformers. As an example, here is the implementation of the *build* transformer from earlier:

```
class BuildTerm < ResultMappingFunction
  def initialize(aTermClass)
   @term_class = aTermClass
  end


  def call(aParseResult, aParseState, aPosition)
   if Array === aParseResult
     @term_class[*aParseResult]
   else
     @term_class[aParseResult]
   end
  end
end

class Parser
  def build(aTermClass)
    self.apply(BuildTerm.new(aTermClass))
  end
end
```

We see that *apply* takes an object that is a kind of *ResultMappingFunction*. This is a long name for a simple concept: RMFs take a parse result, the parse state, and a position, and return a new parse result. Because it has access to the state of the parse, it can perform powerful operations such as rolling back the position or skipping ahead.

A common example of using *apply* would be to map an integer string to its integer value.

The parser transformers *look_ahead* and *look_back* are used to test the context of a parser but without matching any of its input. Essentially they peek into the future or history of the input sequence to check that some conditions apply, but they won't consume any input or alter the position in the sequence. Both transformers take a parser as an argument but the parsers supplied to *look_back* must have a constant length. The typical example would be a string. We need this restriction since we would otherwise not know where to start trying to match the parser. There is no such restriction on the parsers that can be transformed by *look_ahead*.

The parser building blocks *capture* and *ref* are also related to context-sensitivity. They can be used to capture the result from a parser and use it later. The *capture* transformer corresponds to using parentheses in a Regexp and *ref* corresponds to using a back-reference (\1 for the first parenthesized match, etc). The difference here is that the captured substring can be named by giving an object as the second parameter to capture. Here's an example for parsing a (simplified) XML block:

```
xml_block =
  capture("<" & Identifier & ">", :block_name) &
    plus(none_of("<")) &
  ref(:block_name)
```

Error-related Building Blocks

There are a number of transformers that relate to error handling, including *.expecting()* and *.or_raises* (also *.raises*).

Remember that everything in Ruby is an object, right? So are our parsers; what the building blocks are actually doing is constructing parser objects. All parsers are subclasses of the *Parser* class with an instance method named *expecting*. You use *expecting* to describe what you expect to parse with a parser. This information will be used to give meaningful error messages in case of a syntax error during parsing. in the following example we redefine *digit*:

```
digit = symbols("0".."9").expecting("a digit")
```

Here we are saying that when digit is used to parse you are expecting to see a digit on the input. The parser will still parse the same strings so you will only notice the difference when there is an error. If you try to parse the string "a" with the digit parser, Rockit will give you this error:

```
Parse error at (line = 1, column = 1):
  unexpected 'a' when expecting a digit
```

Even if you hadn't specified what you were expecting, Rockit will give some indication. If you tried to parse the "a" string with the parser:

```
digit_plain = symbols("0".."9")
```

Rockit would report this:

```
ParseError at (line = 1, column = 1):
  unexpected 'a'
  when expecting '0', '1', '2', '3', '4', '5', '6', '7', '8' or '9'
```

When you nest parsers the error messages at the higher levels override error messages at lower levels. Thus if we try to parse the string "★" with the parser:

```
hexdigit = choice(digit, "a".."z", "A".."Z").expecting("a
    hexdigit")
```

Rockit would report that it was expecting "a hexdigit" and not "a digit, 'a', 'b', ..., 'z', 'A', ..., 'Z'" as when we hadn't specified the top-level error message. For alternatives the error messages are merged so that the alphanum parser defined as the following:

```
alpha = symbols("a".."z", "A".."Z").expecting("an alpha
    character")
alphanum = choice(digit, alpha)
```

would report "expecting a digit or an alpha character."

The .or_raises parser transformer raises Parse errors unless (and .raises if) a parser matches. They take a string as parameter and use it as the error message. A typical use of or_raises is when we have parsed a prefix and now the rest of the string must match a certain parser—if it doesn't, we should raise an error. As an example let's look at a parser for lexing hexadecimal literals in Ruby (there is no difference between lexing and parsing for Rockit):

```
errorMessage = "numeric literal without digits"
hexlit = maybe("+"|"-") & ("0"&("x"|"X")) &
  plus(mult("_"), plus(hexdigit)).or_raises(errorMessage)
```

When we have seen *0x* we know that it must be a hex literal so if there is an error when trying to parse the digits we should raise an error. In this case we can see that an error can only arise if there are no digits, so we tailor the error message to this situation.

Parsing in Ruby with Racc

Racc is a pure-Ruby implementation of the famous GNU Bison parser generator. Bison is based on Yacc (Yet Another Compiler Compiler) which is the most used parser generator in the Unix world. It is a proven technology and has been used in countless projects over many years.

You describe your grammar in a file. Racc reads the file, calculates parser tables that will be used during the parsing, and outputs a file with your parser. By default the file is a pure-Ruby parser, but a nice feature is that you can choose to output C code and get a Ruby C extension with the parser. This will give you a faster parser with exactly the same interface as a pure-Ruby parser.

Racc's grammar files are basically Ruby variants of Yacc grammar files. They have up to four main sections: the grammar, a header section, an inner section, and a footer section. The header (or footer) goes to the head (or foot) of the generated file and the inner section is inserted into the parser class generated from the grammar. A typical use of the inner section is to add methods to connect the parser class to a lexical analyzer (or *lexer* for short). If the lexical analyzer is small, you can even write it directly in the inner section.

Here's an example Racc grammar file for simple numerical expressions:

```
class CalcParser
  prechigh
    nonassoc UMINUS
    left '*' '/'
    left '+' '-'
  preclow

  token NUMBER


rule
  target: exp
        | /* none */            { result = 0 }
        ;
  exp: exp '+' exp              { result += val[2] }
     | exp '-' exp              { result -= val[2] }
     | exp '*' exp              { result *= val[2] }
     | exp '/' exp              { result /= val[2] }
     | '(' exp ')'              { result = val[1] }
     | '-' NUMBER  = UMINUS { result = -val[1] }
     | NUMBER
     ;
end
```

The grammar section looks like a class declaration with the class name specifying the name of the parser class to be generated. If you use "::" notation in the class name, Racc will output modules around your parser class. For example, if you give the name *Java::Parser*, Racc will generate code like this:

```
module Java

  class Parser

    # parser code here...

  end

end
```

There are two main sections inside the "class": a meta section (with the *prechigh..preclow* declaration) and a rule section. The latter contains the grammar rules in Yacc-style BNF format with action code in blocks. Note that the code in the blocks should be valid Ruby code because it will be copied directly into the generated parser.

The meta section can be further divided into a precedence table (as shown earlier), token declarations, the expected number of shift/reduce conflicts, options, semantic value conversion, and a start rule specification. All of them are optional and need only be present when you do not want the default behavior. We'll briefly describe the most often used meta sections here; in the next chapter we'll dive into the details of writing the grammar rules.

The precedence section lists the precedence of your operators from high to low (or vice versa, which is less intuitive). You can also state their associativity by specifying *left*, *right*, or *nonassoc*. The associativity decides how repeated uses of an operator nests. The sequence **x op y op z** would be parsed as **(x op y) op z** for a left-associative operator and as **x op (y op z)** for a right associative. The precedence of an operator defines how tightly the operator binds. Operators with higher precedence bind tighter than operators with lower precedence. The grammar earlier in this section also shows an example of specifying the precedence of a particular rule. *UMINUS* is not a token in the grammar, it's a name given to the precedence level of the rule for *unary minus*.

The token declaration section lists all tokens in the grammar. It is customary to write the tokens in all uppercase letters, but you can also use lowercase letters, underscores, and strings. When you use strings, the lexer must return the string itself, whereas for the non-string tokens the lexer should return the corresponding symbol (that is, :NUMBER for the NUMBER token shown above). It is considered good style to declare your tokens in the token declaration section, although not mandatory.

Your action code can often be simplified if you specify the *no_result_var* option in the options section. This way you do not have to explicitly assign to the result variable upon exit from the action block. Examples of this are given in the next section.

Writing the Grammar Rules

In the rules section of a Racc grammar you specify the rules for how non-terminals are constructed from tokens and other non-terminals. You can also specify actions to be taken when a rule is matched against the input. The rules are written in BNF and are terminated by a semi-colon (;). They consist of a left-hand side with one non-terminal, a colon (:), and a right-hand side of symbols. Alternative rules for a non-terminal can be separated by a pipes (|) or given in multiple rules.

You can write *actions* after or in between the right-hand side symbols of a rule. An action looks like a Ruby block without input parameters. There are a few differences from ordinary Ruby blocks though: You cannot use %-delimited strings or %r-delimited Regexps or here documents, so stay with ordinary single- or double-quoted strings and /-delimited Regexps.

You can access the values that have been matched by the right-hand side symbols. They are available in the *val* array; the first element (*val[0]*) is the value matched by the first symbol on the right-hand side, and so forth. Note that if you have written actions in between right-hand symbols, their result will be inserted into the *val* array.

In your action code you can explicitly set the result to return as the value of the left-hand side non-terminal: Simply assign to the variable result. However, if you have specified the *no_result_var* option in the options section, the return value from the block will automatically be used as the result value. This is often quite handy because it enables you to write one-line actions.

When writing a grammar for Racc you cannot use the EBNF constructs that you can use in Regexps and Rockit (such as *one-or-more*, *many*, or *maybe*); instead, you will have to convert your grammar to a form suitable for Racc. Below we show some common patterns in doing these translations.

Repetition is very common in grammars. If you want one or more repetitions of a token (*plus(token)* in Rockit), this must be written as two rules:

```
nonterminal : TOKEN

            | nonterminal TOKEN

            ;
```

If you want zero or more repetitions (*mult(TOKEN)* in Rockit) you also need two rules. But this time you leave one of the right-hand sides empty. It is customary, but not necessary, to insert a comment saying that the right-hand side is empty, as in the following:

```
nonterminal : /* none */
            | nonterminal TOKEN
            ;
```

We see that Racc understands C-style comments with text surrounded by **/*** and ***/**. You can also use Ruby **#**-style comments.

The above pattern also gives us the pattern to write optional tokens (*maybe(token)* in Rockit) by simply omitting the recursive reference:

```
nonterminal : /* none */
            | TOKEN
            ;
```

These translations seem simple enough; the problems arise when there are multiple symbols in a rule that has repetition constructs. Expanding to new rules results in a state explosion and you need to write a large number of rules—unfortunately, there is no way to get away from this.

Writing a Lexical Analyzer for Use with Racc

You have to write a lexer by hand when using Racc. You will get adequate performance by creating a state machine and then stepping over the characters until a unique token has been matched. However, you might get a faster lexer if you use Regexps. Even though you might need multiple traversals over the input string, Regexps are significantly faster than Ruby code since they are implemented in C (actually, they are implemented in a kind of "virtual machine," but it is code in C and is pretty fast).

The interface between a Racc-generated parser and your hand-coded lexer is via the *next_token* method. You need to define it on the parser class generated by Racc. The simplest way is to do it is in the inner section. If the lexer is small you can even write your lexer directly in the inner section. However, it is probably easier to maintain your code if you separate the lexer from the parser and write it in a class on its own. Then you can instantiate the parser class with the lexer class, as in the following:

```
---- inner ----
def initialize(lexerClass)
  @lexer_class = lexerClass
end

def parse(aString)
  @lexer = @lexer_class.new(aString)
  do_parse  # Let's parse!
end

def next_token
  @lexer.next_token
end
```

To begin with, let's write a simple lexer using Regexps:

```
class LexerError < Exception; end

class Lexer
  def initialize(aString)
    @str = aString
  end

  def next_token
    token = nil
    until token
      if @str =~ /\A(\d+)/
        token = [:NUMBER, $1.to_i]
      elsif @str =~ /\A\s+/
        # do nothing => iterates once more since token still nil
      elsif @str =~ /\A(\+|-|\*|\/|\(|\))/ #\+|-|\*|\/|\(|\))/
        token = [$1, $1]
      elsif @str.length > 0
        raise LexerError, "Invalid token at: '#{@str[0,10]}'"
      else
        token = [false, :end]
        end
```

```
        @str = $'
      end

      token

    end
  end
end
```

We simply try a number of Regexps in order until one matches. We then update the *@str* instance variable to hold the unmatched rest of the string. Note the special treatment of whitespace; since the token variable is not updated we will loop another time and try to match the Regexps once more. Since we update *@str* also after matching whitespace, the next unmatched character will not be a whitespace character.

The above solution works pretty well for small grammars; however, it might not provide strong enough performance for larger grammars with a large number of token types. The performance problem has two main sources: $' will make a new string on each invocation and you might have to apply a large number of Regexps to the same position in the string until one matches. Let's address each part of the problem in turn.

The assignment "*@str* = $'" creates a new string from the unmatched part of *@str* and assigns it to the instance variable. This puts a heavy burden on the memory allocator and Garbage Collector. Let's say the string to be lexed is 10 KB large and that the average length of a token is 4 characters (since many will simply be short sequences of whitespace, this is probably close to reality). This means we will create 10000/4 strings of an average length of 5 KB, thus using over 10 MB of memory (5000*10000/4) that will have to be allocated and garbage-collected! We need some way to keep a pointer to the character we are currently at and then start matching at that position without having to allocate any new strings. Fortunately there is an excellent extension in RAA that can help us, called *strscan*, which was written by Minero Aoki (who also created Racc).

Strscan gives you the *StringScanner* class, which is simply a string with a pointer. When you match a Regexp to it you'll get the matching substring, and *StringScanner* will update its internal pointer to the start of the unmatched portion of the string. There is no allocation going on behind the scenes so there is no additional load on the memory system. Here's an implementation of the lexer shown earlier, using strscan to speed things up:

```
require 'strscan'


class StrScanLexer < Lexer
```

```ruby
  def initialize(aString)
    @str = StringScanner.new(aString)
  end

  def next_token
    @str.skip(/\s+/) # Skip white space
    if @str.scan /\d+/
      [:NUMBER, @str.matched.to_i]
    elsif @str.scan /\+|-|\*|\/|\(|\)/ # /\+|-|\*|\/|\(|\)/
      [@str.matched, @str.matched]
    elsif @str.rest_size > 0
      raise LexerError, "Invalid token at: '#{@str.rest[0,10]}...'"
    else
      [false, :end]
    end
  end
end
```

The three methods you will probably use the most are *scan*, *skip*, and *matched*. *Scan* tries to match a Regexp at the current position in the string. If a match is possible, the matched substring is returned; if no match is possible, *nil* is returned. *Skip* works the same way but returns the length of the matched substring instead of the matched string. This is more efficient if you don't care about the matched substring (as when skipping whitespace). If there is a match when calling *scan*, the matched string can be accessed with the *matched* method.

Let's generate some strings of different length and compare the speed of the lexers above to get a feel of the kind of speed ups involved. We need a way to generate random valid expressions on the form accepted by the grammar:

```ruby
def random_string(chars, maxLength)
  Array.new(1+rand(maxLength)).map do
    chars[rand(chars.length)]
  end.pack("c*")
end


Digits = (0..9).map {|d| ?0 + d}


def random_expression_string(maxStringLength)
```

```
  str = ""
  while str.length < maxStringLength - 10
    str << "-" if rand < 0.05
    str << random_string(Digits, 6)
    str << random_string([? , ?\t, ?\n], 2)
    str << random_string([?+, ?-, ?*, ?/], 1)
    str << random_string([? , ?\t], 3)
  end
  str << random_string(Digits, 6)
  str
end
```

Then we can use the Benchmark extension to compare the times to lex:

```
require 'benchmark'
include Benchmark

bm(15) do |x|
  s = random_expression_string(10000)
  l = Lexer.new s
  sl = StrScanLexer.new(s)
  x.report("StrScanLexer") {sl.lex}
  x.report("Lexer")       {l.lex }
end
```

I tried this for some different string lengths on my machine. The results can be seen in Table 9.1. The conclusion is clear: the lexer based on strscan is significantly faster, and the speed increases with the growth of the strings. The growth seems to be linear in the length of the string while the non-strscan-based lexer shows non-linear behavior.

When the number of token types to match grows larger, the performance might suffer even if you use strscan. This is because we repeatedly apply Regexps until one matches. You are left with the option of writing your own lexer as a state machine using the current unmatched character to guide the state transitions. Even if you take this approach, you should try to use strscan and Regexps as much as possible because your code will then execute in C. You can also contemplate using the current character as a look-ahead to divide the set of possible Regexps to match and then write the "smaller" lexers in the style above.

Table 9.1 Speed to Perform Lexical Analysis with and without the *strscan* Extension

String Size	StrScanLexer Time	Lexer Time	Times Slower
1000	0.01	0.04	4.00
10000	0.11	0.52	4.73
25000	0.23	2.92	12.69
50000	0.511	12.56	24.63
100000	1.10	61.00	55.45

Another option would be to write your lexer in Rockit. In its current state, the lexers produced by Rockit will likely not be fast enough to beat a hand-coded lexer but there are a number of optimizations techniques that will be applied in the next major version of Rockit. As always, you will have to follow the developments in the Ruby community to stay on top of the situation!

Invoking the Racc Command Line Tool

When you download and install Racc it will install a command line tool called *racc*, which is the command to use when you want to turn your grammar file into a parser. In the simplest case you supply the grammar file name as the sole argument to *racc*, as follows:

```
$ racc calc.y
```

This will produce the parser in the file calc.tab.rb. The *tab* stands for *table* and indicates that Racc produces a table-driven parser. The name of the output file can be changed by giving the 'o' or '--output-file' flag and supplying an alternative name.

The first line in the produced file loads the Racc runtime support code needed when using the parser. If you want to create a stand-alone parser that anyone can use without having Racc installed, you need to give the 'E' or '--embedded' flag. Here's a comparison:

```
$ racc calc.y
$ wc -l calc.tab.rb
    226 calc.tab.rb
$ racc --embedded --output-file calc.rb calc.y
$ wc -l calc.rb
    705 calc.rb
```

We see that the file is considerably larger because the Racc runtime is now included.

There are many more options for Racc but the above-mentioned ones will cover most of your usage. Check out Racc's documentation for complete reference.

Building Abstract Syntax Trees with Racc-generated Parsers

If you want to get an abstract syntax tree from a Racc-generated parser you will have to write the action code that builds the AST. To represent the AST you may use Structs (since they are built in Ruby), roll your own AST class, or use the *Term* class in Rockit. The advantage of using the *Term* class in Rockit is that you can create the *Term* classes in a hierarchy (which is not directly supported by Structs) and that you have support for pattern matching terms, traversing with visitors, and pretty-printing them. The advantage of using Structs is that they are available in all Ruby environments and well known by all Ruby programmers.

Once you have decided on a strategy for the *term* classes you need to write the action code in the grammar for building the ASTs. If you want a really flexible parser that you will not need to change for different outputs, you can introduce another level of indirection: The parser is initialized with an actions object and calls methods on it in response to matching a rule. The default actions object builds an AST, but if you want other behavior you simply instantiate the parser with your custom actions object. This technique is used in Rulator, a hybrid parser written in Ruby using both Racc and Rockit; it buys you flexibility while sacrificing some performance. Let's modify the *calcparser* to use an action object:

```
class CalcParser
  prechigh
    nonassoc UMINUS
    left '*' '/'
    left '+' '-'
  preclow

  no_result_var  # So we don't need to assign to result in actions

rule
    exp: exp '+' exp          { @actions.on_plus(val)   }
       | exp '-' exp          { @actions.on_minus(val)  }
```

```
     | exp '*' exp            { @actions.on_mult(val)    }
     | exp '/' exp            { @actions.on_div(val)     }
     | '(' exp ')'            { val[1]                   }
     | '-' NUMBER  = UMINUS   { @actions.on_uminus(val)  }
     | NUMBER                 { @actions.on_number(val)  }
     ;
end


---- inner ----
  def initialize(actionsObject = CalcAstBuilder.new,
                 lexerClass = CalcLexer)
    @actions, @lexer_class = actionsObject, lexerClass
  end

  def parse(aString)
    @actions.reset(aString)
    @lexer = @lexer_class.new(aString)
    do_parse
  end

  def next_token
    @lexer.next_token
  end
```

We are now free to change how the parser is used without having to change the parser itself. This may not seem like a big win in this small example, but it can be very powerful when the grammar is large. You simply subclass the actions class and define the methods for the events you want to detect and get an event parser for your grammar. To accomplish this we need to define a base class for actions objects that simply do nothing:

```
class CalcActions
  def reset(aString); end
  def on_plus; end
  def on_minus; end
  def on_mult; end
```

```
  def on_div; end
  def on_uminus; end
  def on_number; end
end
```

Now we can easily get a parser building abstract syntax trees:

```
require 'rockit/term/term'
include Rockit


Plus = Term.new_subclass(:Plus, :left, :right)
Minus = Term.new_subclass(:Minus, :left, :right)
Mult = Term.new_subclass(:Mult, :left, :right)
Div = Term.new_subclass(:Div, :left, :right)
UnaryMinus = Term.new_subclass(:UnaryMinus, :number)


class CalcAstBuilder < CalcActions
  def on_plus(results); Plus[*results.indices(0,2)]; end
  def on_minus(results); Minus[*results.indices(0,2)]; end
  def on_mult(results); Mult[*results.indices(0,2)]; end
  def on_div(results); Div[*results.indices(0,2)]; end
  def on_uminus(results); UnaryMinus[results[1]]; end
  def on_number(results); results[0]; end
end
```

We can also use the calc parser as an event parser by simply overriding the method handling of the event we are interested in. Here's an example for counting the numbers in the input.

```
class CountingNumbers < CalcActions
  attr_reader :count


  def reset(aString)
    @count, @str = 0, aString
  end


  def on_number(results); @count += 1; end
```

```
  def inspect
    "The string '#{@str}' contains #{count} numbers"
  end
end
```

Comparing Racc and Rockit

We've covered a lot of ground in this section. The following list summarizes some of the differences between Racc and Rockit.

- Racc is more stable than Rockit. Racc has existed for several years and many bug fixes have been made. Rockit is recent and has changed since its inception.

- The Bison algorithms used in Racc have been well studied since the 1970's. Rockit's parser combinator approach is relatively recent and from the functional programming area.

- Rockit's parsers are first-class objects in Ruby and ordinary Ruby code can be used when defining them, so you have the power of Ruby at your fingertips while writing your grammars.

- Racc's grammar cannot use repetition operators (+, * and ?) so you will have to rewrite your grammar in a form that Racc can understand. It is awkward, error-prone, and time consuming, but not particularly difficult. Rockit *can* use repetitions operators. It can also be used to parse context-sensitive constructs.

- Racc is used off-line and generates a Ruby file with a parser corresponding to a grammar given in a file. Rockit can be used both as an off-line parser generator and on-line from inside Ruby programs.

- The parsers generated by Racc are fast and show linear behavior as the input grows larger. Rockit's parsers have not yet been optimized for speed and are slower.

Summary

Parsing is about finding the structure in some text. It is a common task that you frequently encounter no matter what problem you're attacking. Parsing is frequently divided into lexical analysis and syntactical analysis. During lexical analysis the stream of characters is chopped up into consecutive lexical tokens. Syntactical analysis collects valid sequences of tokens together until no more input can be matched. Lexical analysis is frequently called *scanning* or *tokenizing* and the object doing the analysis is called a *lexer, scanner,* or *tokenizer.* The object doing the syntactical analysis is simply called the *parser.*

The standard solution to get a parser is to write the grammar in a file and give it to a parser generator which will create a parser for the grammar. There are two tried-and-tested Ruby solutions in taking this approach: Racc and RBison. They are very similar in features but totally different in implementation. Racc is the most updated and mature one, so we recommend you use it to get fast parsers. You should be aware that you will have to hand-code your lexer though, since Racc will only give you a parser.

In contrast to the parser generating programs, Rockit will allow you to define parsers as objects directly from within Ruby. It supplies a set of "building blocks" so you can build parsers from simple strings that can be combined in sequences, alternations, etc. The approach is very flexible and gives you a lot of control. It can also parse a larger class of languages than can Racc. However, Rockit is not as mature as Racc and the parsers it produces are not as fast.

Which solution you use is up to your application and needs—in fact, they can work very well together. For example, you could use Rockit to generate a lexer for a Racc-generated parser.

Solutions Fast Track

Creating the Parsing Library of your Dreams

☑ If you simply need to extract some information out of a larger text body, consider using some specialized Regexps and code to process what they match.

☑ If you have an existing Yacc grammar and want to get a parser for it, use Racc or RBison from the RAA. They are compatible with Yacc and

Bison and will work as you would expect. Write your actions as Ruby code and hand-code your lexer.

☑ If you need to write a new parser, or need to parse non-regular features such as nested comments or parentheses, consider using the simple parsing combinators of Rockit.

Parsing Ruby with Rockit

☑ In Rockit you write your parsers directly in Ruby code by combining simple building blocks into larger parsers.

☑ You can use the same parser generators and combinators for specifying lexer and parsers. In fact, you don't even have to separate lexing from parsing.

☑ You can use extended BNF constructs such as *one-or-more*, *many*, and *maybe*, so your parser is closer to the grammar you have in mind.

Parsing Ruby with Racc

☑ Racc is a mature application for generating fast Ruby parsers. It is based on Yacc and on Bison, which has been used successfully in a large number of parsers since the 1970's.

☑ Racc generates a pure-Ruby parser or a C parser that interfaces to Ruby.

☑ You can not use extended BNF operators but will have to rewrite your grammar to get repetition and other common constructs.

Frequently Asked Questions

The following Frequently Asked Questions, answered by the authors of this book, are designed to both measure your understanding of the concepts presented in this chapter and to assist you with real-life implementation of these concepts. To have your questions about this chapter answered by the author, browse to **www.syngress.com/solutions** and click on the **"Ask the Author"** form.

Q: I have to match nested parentheses but I don't need a full parser. What can I do?

A: Using Rockit you can specify this with a one-liner in pure-Ruby code. It is simple and fast.

Q: I need to extract some information out of a larger portion of text. How should I proceed?

A: Try specifying a Regexp for the text you need to extract, read the text in, and match to the Regexp. This is much simpler and faster than writing a full parser.

Q: I have a Yacc grammar that I need to port to Ruby. What tool should I use?

A: If you use Racc, you can use the file as is. You only have to rewrite the C code in the actions in Ruby.

Q: I find the Yacc style of writing grammars inflexible, and I cannot parse non-regular features such as XML tags without preprocessing the result. Is there a better way?

A: Rockit allows you to handle such non-regular features directly.

Extending and Embedding Ruby

Solutions in this chapter:

- **Writing C/C++ Extensions**
- **Using SWIG**
- **Embedding Ruby**
- **Configuring Extensions with Mkmf**

☑ **Summary**
☑ **Solutions Fast Track**
☑ **Frequently Asked Questions**

Introduction

You already know how to extend Ruby's built-in functionality by importing modules with the *require* statement. Although these extension modules are often written in Ruby, they can also be written in C (or C++) and then compiled into dynamically-loadable shared libraries that look like regular Ruby modules to the Ruby interpreter. Like regular Ruby modules, C extension modules can expose constants, methods, and classes to the Ruby interpreter. Several modules in the standard Ruby library (including *socket*, *tk*, and *Win32API*) are implemented as C extensions, and a survey through the Ruby Application Archive reveals a number of other popular Ruby extensions implemented using C/C++ code.

You might well ask why you would want to write a Ruby extension module in C/C++ instead of Ruby; after all, you've probably turned to Ruby as a more flexible and powerful alternative to traditional programming languages like C/C++. Nevertheless, there are two primary reasons for implementing an extension in C/C++:

- **Performance** For some applications, the performance requirements for your extension module may necessitate a C/C++ implementation. For example, the standard Ruby library's *Matrix* and *Vector* classes (defined by the *matrix.rb* module) don't perform well for large-scale numerical computing applications. Third-party extensions such as NArray have been developed to fill this gap.

- **Interfaces to already-available C/C++ libraries** If a library of useful C/C++ code already exists, it is generally quicker to develop an interface from Ruby to that library instead of reimplementing that library in Ruby. This is especially true when using a code generation tool like SWIG (discussed later in this chapter) that automates a lot of the tedious parts of the process.

A subject closely related to writing Ruby extensions in C is the practice of embedding the Ruby interpreter into your C/C++ applications. This is an increasingly popular choice for application developers who want to provide a scripting language for their application end-users, to allow them to easily write "plug-in" code modules that can run alongside the main application and extend its functionality. Ruby is a natural fit for this kind of application, because the Ruby interpreter is already packaged as a C library with APIs to facilitate embedding.

Writing C/C++ Extensions

A Ruby extension module, in its final form, is just a shared library that Ruby can load dynamically at runtime. Whereas Ruby modules written in Ruby will have file names that end with the ".rb" extension, C extension modules are compiled into shared library files that usually end with a ".so" extension (for *shared object*). When the Ruby interpreter encounters a statement like *require 'featurename'* in a Ruby program, it first searches its load path (the global array "*$:*" or "*$LOAD_PATH*") for a file named "featurename.rb" to load. If it can't find "featurename.rb," it will instead try to find a shared library by that name (for example, "featurename.so," or "featurename.dll"). As we'll see later in an example, it's a good practice to omit the ".rb" or ".so" extension from a feature name, even if you know how the extension module is packaged. By leaving the file extension unspecified, you give yourself the flexibility to quickly develop a Ruby implementation of the module and later replace it with a C implementation, without changing any of the other code that uses that module.

At a high level, the C source code making up a Ruby extension module consists of two major pieces: a feature initialization function and a number of C functions that implement the module's functionality. The initialization function name must be of the form *Init_featurename*; for example, a feature named *shapes* should have an initialization function declared like so:

```
#ifdef __cplusplus
extern "C"
#endif
void Init_shapes() {
    /* module initialization code goes here */
}
```

One of the first steps in the initialization function is to define a module using either the *rb_define_module()* or *rb_define_module_under()* function. Remember, in Ruby a module is itself an object: it is an instance of the Ruby class named *Module*. Both *rb_define_module()* and *rb_define_module_under()* return a Ruby *VALUE*, which is a reference to the new module; you'll use this variable in subsequent function calls. It's also important to point out at this point that strictly speaking, it's not necessary to define a module for your code to live in at all. Most Ruby APIs have variations that allow you to define classes, constants, and methods at the global level, and if you study a lot of Ruby extension modules you'll see that many of them follow this practice. For a lot of reasons (most notably, avoiding name clashes with other modules) it's a good practice to put related code into a self-contained module, and so for this example (and the following one) I'll take that approach.

So, continuing to build up our imaginary module, we'd add the code:

```
#ifdef __cplusplus
extern "C"
#endif
void Init_shapes() {
    VALUE mShapes;
    mShapes = rb_define_module("Shapes");
    /* more to follow */
}
```

The next step is to start creating classes and constants that live in this module. Let's suppose that the *Shapes* module defines a base class, *Shape*, and three subclasses, *Circle*, *Rectangle*, and *Triangle*. We can add to the initialization function (the new lines are shown in bold):

```
#ifdef __cplusplus
extern "C"
#endif
void Init_shapes() {
    VALUE mShapes;
    VALUE cShape, cCircle, cRectangle, cTriangle;
    mShapes = rb_define_module("Shapes");
    cShape = rb_define_class_under(mShapes, "Shape", rb_cObject);
    cCircle = rb_define_class_under(mShapes, "Circle", cShape);
    cRectangle = rb_define_class_under(mShapes, "Rectangle", cShape);
    cTriangle = rb_define_class_under(mShapes, "Triangle", cShape);
}
```

Here we've used the *rb_define_class_under()* function to define the four classes. This function takes three arguments; the first is the module under which to define the class, the second is the class name, and the third is the base class for this class. Since *Shape* is a top-level class, we pass *rb_cObject* as its base class; this is a predefined global variable corresponding to Ruby's *Object* class. For the other three classes, *Shape* is the base class and so we pass *cShape* as the third argument to *rb_define_class_under()*.

Next, we need to define some methods for these classes to make them useful. At a minimum, you'll probably want to define an *initialize* function for each class; Ruby calls this function whenever you create a new instance of that class (for example, with *Circle.new*). Let's assume that we'd also like each shape class to provide an *area* method that returns the shape's area. You can define instance methods for a class using the *rb_define_method()* function:

```
void rb_define_method(VALUE rubyClass,

                      const char * methodName,

                      VALUE(*)(…) cFunc,

                      int numArgs)
```

where *rubyClass* is a *VALUE* representing a module or class object, as might be returned from the *rb_define_class_under()* function; *methodName* is a string containing the method name; *cFunc* is the C function that implements this method; and *numArgs* is the number of arguments for the method. Let's say that *Circle#initialize* takes three arguments (*x*, *y*, and *radius*), *Rectangle#initialize* takes four arguments (*x*, *y*, *width*, and *height*) and *Triangle#initialize* takes six arguments (x_0, y_0, x_1, y_1, x_2, and y_2). The *area* method for each of these classes doesn't require any arguments. To register these methods for our classes, we'd further extend the initialization function as follows (again, with changes shown in bold):

```
#ifdef __cplusplus
extern "C"
#endif
void Init_shapes() {
    VALUE mShapes;
    VALUE cShape, cCircle, cRectangle, cTriangle;
    mShapes = rb_define_module("Shapes");
    cShape = rb_define_class_under(mShapes, "Shape", rb_cObject);
    cCircle = rb_define_class_under(mShapes, "Circle", cShape);
    rb_define_method(cCircle, "initialize", Circle_initialize, 3);
    rb_define_method(cCircle, "area", Circle_area, 0);
    cRectangle = rb_define_class_under(mShapes, "Rectangle", cShape);
    rb_define_method(cRectangle, "initialize", Rectangle_initialize, 4);
    rb_define_method(cRectangle, "area", Rectangle_area, 0);
```

```
    cTriangle = rb_define_class_under(mShapes, "Triangle", cShape);
    rb_define_method(cTriangle, "initialize", Triangle_initialize, 6);

    rb_define_method(cTriangle, "area", Triangle_area, 0);

}
```

The C functions that implement these instance methods (like *Rectangle_area*) are functions that you will need to write, but we'll save that for later. For now, it's sufficient to understand that we're telling Ruby that when a user of your *Shapes* module creates a *Rectangle* object and calls its *area* method, Ruby should hand that off to a C function named *Rectangle_area*.

Working with Datatype Conversions

A significant part of writing Ruby extensions in C involves conversions between Ruby and C datatypes. You'll use the *VALUE* type (defined in *ruby.h*) for all Ruby variable declarations; it more or less works like a pointer to a Ruby object. As you'll see in the following sections, the Ruby/C API includes a number of functions to create new Ruby objects (like strings and arrays); these functions always return a *VALUE*.

Working with Objects

Ruby is a highly object-oriented language, and most every "thing" in your Ruby programs is some kind of object. Ruby's *Object* class is the base class for all of these objects' classes, and Table 10.1 lists some of the functions that Ruby's C API provides for working with objects.

Table 10.1 Functions for Working with Objects

C Function/Macro	Description
void rb_obj_call_init (VALUE obj, int argc, VALUE *argv)	Calls the object's *initialize* method, passing the array of arguments, *argv*, with length *argc*.
VALUE rb_obj_is_instance_of (VALUE obj, VALUE klass)	Returns *Qtrue* (the C constant for Ruby's *true*) if *obj* is an instance of class *klass*.
VALUE rb_obj_is_kind_of (VALUE obj, VALUE klass)	Returns *Qtrue* is *obj* is an instance of class *klass* or one of its subclasses.
VALUE rb_obj_clone (VALUE obj)	Returns the result of calling the object's *clone* method.

Continued

Table 10.1 Continued

C Function/Macro	Description
VALUE rb_obj_dup (VALUE obj)	Returns the result of calling the object's *dup* method.
VALUE rb_any_to_s (VALUE obj)	Returns a string containing information about the object (the default *to_s* method from Ruby's *Kernel* module).
VALUE rb_obj_as_string (VALUE obj)	Returns a string representation of *obj* by first calling the object's *to_s* method or, if that fails, by calling *rb_any_to_s()* on *obj*.
VALUE rb_inspect (VALUE obj)	Returns the result of calling the object's *inspect* method.

Working with Numbers

The three numeric types used by Ruby are *Fixnum* (for integers that can be stored in all but the most significant bit of a system's *unsigned long* type), *Bignum* (for larger, arbitrary-length integers), and *Float* (for double-precision floating point values). To convert from Ruby numeric types into C numeric types you'll use the functions and macros shown in Table 10.2.

Table 10.2 Functions for Conversion from Ruby Numeric Types into C Numeric Types

C Function/Macro	Description
int NUM2INT (VALUE aNumeric)	Converts the input *Numeric* value to a C *int*. If you know that the input value is a *Fixnum*, use the faster *FIX2INT* macro.
int FIX2INT(VALUE aFixnum)	Converts the input *Fixnum* value to a C *int*.
unsigned int NUM2UINT (VALUE aNumeric)	Converts the input *Numeric* value to a C *unsigned int*. If you know that the input value is a *Fixnum*, use the faster *FIX2UINT* macro.
unsigned int FIX2UINT (VALUE aFixnum)	Converts the input *Fixnum* value to a C *unsigned int*.
long NUM2LONG (VALUE aNumeric)	Converts the input *Numeric* value to a C *long*. If you know that the input value is a *Fixnum*, use the faster *FIX2LONG* macro.

Continued

Table 10.2 Continued

C Function/Macro	Description
long FIX2LONG (VALUE aFixnum)	Converts the input *Fixnum* value to a C *long*.
unsigned long NUM2ULONG (VALUE aNumeric)	Converts the input *Numeric* value to a C *unsigned long*.
char NUM2CHR (VALUE aNumeric)	Converts the input *Numeric* value to a C *char*.
double NUM2DBL (VALUE aNumeric)	Converts the input *Numeric* value to a C *double*.

Similarly, to convert from C numeric types into Ruby numeric types, you'll use the functions and macros shown in Table 10.3.

Table 10.3 Functions for Conversion from C Numeric Types into Ruby Numeric Types

C Function/Macro	Descriptions
VALUE INT2NUM(int i) or VALUE INT2NUM(long l)	Converts the input *int* or *long* value into either a *Fixnum* or *Bignum* instance, depending on its size.
VALUE INT2FIX(int i) or VALUE INT2FIX(long l)	Converts the input *int* or *long* value into a *Fixnum*. If you're sure that the input value will "fit" into a *Fixnum*, this macro is a little faster than the *INT2NUM* macro.
VALUE CHR2FIX(char c)	Converts the input *char* value into a *Fixnum*.
VALUE rb_float_new(double f)	Converts the input *double* value into a *Float*.

Working with Strings

Ruby strings are not strictly identical to C strings. In C, a "string" is just an array of characters that is assumed to be terminated by a *NULL* character, and the length of a C string is implicit; the number of characters appearing before the *NULL* terminator is the string's length. Since Ruby strings can contain embedded *NULL* bytes (making them useful as general memory buffers), some additional information about the actual string length is stored.

To extract the contents of a Ruby string as a C string, use the *STR2CSTR* macro:

```
VALUE stringObj;

char *cstr;

cstr = STR2CSTR(stringObj);
```

Note that this macro returns a pointer to the actual string data stored by Ruby (and not a copy) so you should take care not to modify its contents unless you know what you're doing. Along those lines, since Ruby "owns" the memory pointed to by this string, you shouldn't attempt to *free()* it. Finally, if the Ruby string contains embedded *NULL* bytes, and if you're running Ruby in "verbose" mode (that is, with the *-w* command-line option), Ruby will warn you about this potential hazard. If you need to know the true length of a Ruby string (*NULL* bytes and all), you can use the alternate function *rb_str2cstr()*:

```
VALUE stringObj;

char *cstr;

int stringLength;

cstr = rb_str2cstr(stringObj, &stringLength);
```

As with the *STR2CSTR* macro, the *rb_str2cstr()* function returns a pointer to the actual string data stored by Ruby. It also modifies the value of its *stringLength* argument to hold the length of the string. Another slightly less safe (but faster) way to determine the string's length is to access the underlying C struct field directly using the *RSTRING* macro:

```
VALUE stringObj;

int stringLength;


stringLength = RSTRING(stringObj)->len;
```

To create a new string, use one of the functions listed in Table 10.4.

Table 10.4 Functions for Creating a New String

C Function	Description
VALUE rb_str_new (const char *str, long size)	Returns a new string whose contents are copied from the first *size* characters pointed to by *str*.
VALUE rb_str_new2 (const char *cstr)	Returns a new Ruby string whose contents are copied from the *NULL*-terminated C string *cstr*.

Table 10.5 lists other useful functions for working with strings.

Table 10.5 Functions for Working with Strings

C Function	Equivalent Ruby Statement	Description
VALUE rb_str_to_str (VALUE obj)	obj.to_str	Attempts to convert the original object to a string by calling its *to_str* method.
VALUE rb_str_dup (VALUE str)	String.new (str)	Returns a *new* string that is a duplicate of the original.
VALUE rb_str_plus (VALUE str1, VALUE str2)	str1 + str2.to_str	Returns a new string formed by concatenating the contents of *str1* and *str2*; neither of the original strings is modified. Note that if *str2* is not a string but is a string-like object that implements a *to_str* method, Ruby will first call that object's *to_str* method to get a string representation of *str2*,
VALUE rb_str_times (VALUE str, VALUE count)	str * count	Returns a new string which is formed by repeating the original string *count* times.
VALUE rb_str_substr (VALUE str, long start, long length)	str[start, length]	Returns a new string which is the substring of *str*, beginning at position *start* and with specified *length*.
VALUE rb_str_cat (VALUE str, const char *str, long size)	str += "another string"	Modifies the original string by adding the first *size* characters pointed to by *str* to the end of this string. Returns a reference to the modified string.
VALUE rb_str_cat2 (VALUE str, const char *cstr)		Same as *rb_str_cat()*, but assumes that *cstr* is a *NULL*- terminated C string.
VALUE rb_str_append (VALUE str1, VALUE str2)	str1 += str2.to_str	Modifies *str1* by appending *str2* to it. Note that if *str2* is not a string but is a string-like object that implements a *to_str* method, Ruby will first call that object's *to_str* method to get a string representation of *str2*,

Continued

Table 10.5 Continued

C Function	Equivalent Ruby Statement	Description
VALUE rb_str_concat (VALUE str1, VALUE str2)	str1 << str2	Modifies *str1* by concatenating it with *str2*. If *str2* is a *Fixnum*, it is interpreted as an ASCII character code; otherwise, the same rules used for *rb_str_append()* apply.
int rb_str_hash (VALUE str)	str.hash	Returns the hash code for *str*.
int rb_str_cmp (VALUE str1, VALUE str2)	str1 <=> str2	Compares the contents of the two strings and returns −1 if *str1* is lexicographically "less than" *str2*, 1 if *str1* is "greater than" *str2*, or 0 if they are equal.
VALUE rb_str_match (VALUE str, VALUE obj)	str =~ obj	Uses *obj* as a pattern to match against *str*. If *obj* is either a *Regexp* or *String* instance, *rb_str_match()* will return a *Fixnum* containing the match position or *Qnil* if no match is found. If *obj* is some other type that doesn't implement a =~ method, *rb_str_match()* will return *Qfalse*.
VALUE rb_str_split (VALUE str, const char *pattern)	str.split (pattern)	Returns a new array formed by splitting the input string at delimiters specified in the *pattern* string. If *pattern* is not a single character string (for example, a comma) it is evaluated as a regular expression.
VALUE rb_str_length (VALUE str)	str.length	Returns the length of *str*.
VALUE rb_str_empty (VALUE str)	str.empty?	Returns *Qtrue* if str is empty (its size = 0), otherwise it returns *Qfalse*.

Working with Arrays

In addition to the more basic datatypes like numbers and strings, you'll use Ruby's built-in *Array* and *Hash* classes in any significant program. To create a new array, use one of the functions listed in Table 10.6.

Table 10.6 Functions for Creating a New Array

C Function	Equivalent Ruby Statement	Description
VALUE rb_ary_new()	anArray = [] (or anArray = Array.new())	Returns a new empty array.
VALUE rb_ary_new2 (long size)	anArray = Array.new(size)	Returns a new array with *size* elements; each element is initialized to *Qnil* (Ruby's *nil*).
VALUE rb_ary_new3 (long size, VALUE arg1, VALUE arg2, ...)	anArray = [arg1, arg2, ...]	Returns a new array with *size* elements; each element is initialized with the corresponding argument passed into *rb_ary_new3()*.
VALUE rb_ary_new4 (long size, VALUE *values)	anArray = ["this," "that," "other"]	Returns a new array with *size* elements; each element is initialized with the corresponding element in the *values* array.

The primary difference between the first two functions (*rb_ary_new()* and *rb_ary_new2()*) has to do with runtime efficiency. In Ruby's internals, there is a distinction between an array's *length* and its *capacity*: An array's *length* is related to the index of the last array element currently in use, while an array's *capacity* is the amount of memory that has actually been allocated for that array. The first array creation function, *rb_ary_new()*, actually creates an array with the default capacity (currently, 16 elements). If you have some knowledge of the eventual size of an array, you can make your code more efficient by creating the array with *rb_ary_new2()*. This is true whether the number of elements is small or large; if the array size is less than Ruby's default capacity you will save yourself some potentially wasted memory, and if the array size is larger than the default capacity, you'll save yourself some time that would have been required to resize the array as you added new elements.

Table 10.7 lists some other useful functions for working with arrays.

Table 10.7 Functions for Working with Arrays

C Function	Equivalent Ruby Statement	Description
VALUE rb_ary_aref (int argc, VALUE *argv, VALUE array)	value = array[index] value = array[start, length] value = array[range]	This is the implementation of the *Array* class' *[]* method and accepts three different forms of inputs; here, *argv* is a C array of the input argument values and *argc* is the number of arguments in that array. If there's only one input argument, it's evaluated as either a *Fixnum* index into the array or a *Range* of indices. If there are two arguments, they are evaluated as *Fixnums* indicating the starting index and length of the subarray.
void rb_ary_store (VALUE array, long index, VALUE value)	array[index] = value	Stores *value* in the specified array slot (where *index* is zero-based).
VALUE rb_ary_entry (VALUE array, long index)	value = array[index]	Returns a reference to the specifiedarray element at position *index*.
VALUE rb_ary_push (VALUE array, VALUE value)	array.push(value)	Pushes *value* onto the end of *array* and returns a reference to it.
VALUE rb_ary_pop (VALUE array)	value = array.pop	Pops *value* off the end of *array* and returns a reference to it.
VALUE rb_ary_shift (VALUE array)	array.shift	Removes and returns the first element from *array*.
VALUE rb_ary_unshift (VALUE array, VALUE value)	array.unshift(value)	Pushes *value* onto the front of *array* and returns a reference to *value*.
VALUE rb_ary_each (VALUE array)	array.each	Calls *rb_yield()* on each element of the array in turn and returns a reference to the array as its result.
VALUE rb_ary_join (VALUE array, VALUE sep)	array.join(sep)	Returns a new string whose contents are formed by joining the array elements with the specified separator string *sep*.

Continued

Table 10.7 Continued

C Function	Equivalent Ruby Statement	Description
VALUE rb_ary_reverse (VALUE array)	array.reverse	Returns a reference to a new array whose elements are the same as those of *array*, in reverse order.
VALUE rb_ary_sort (VALUE array)	array.sort	Returns a reference to a new array whose elements are the same as those of *array*, in sorted order.
VALUE rb_ary_sort_ bang(VALUE array)	array.sort!	Performs an in-place sort of *array* and returns a reference to the array.
VALUE rb_ary_delete (VALUE array, VALUE value)	array.delete(value)	Deletes all occurrences of *value* from *array* and returns a reference to *value*.
VALUE rb_ary_delete_at (VALUE array, long index)	array.delete_at(index)	Deletes the *array* element at the specified *index*.
VALUE rb_ary_clear (VALUE array)	array.clear	Removes all elements from *array* and returns a reference to the array.
VALUE rb_ary_plus (VALUE array, VALUE other)	array + other	Creates a new array by concatenating the contents of *array* and *other*; returns a reference to the new array. Does not modify either of the original arrays.
VALUE rb_ary_concat (VALUE array, VALUE other)	array.concat(other)	Adds the contents of *other* onto the end of *array* and returns a reference to the array. Unlike *rb_ary_plus()*, this function does modify the first array.
VALUE rb_ary_includes (VALUE array, VALUE value)	array.include?(value)	Returns *Qtrue* or *Qfalse*, depending on whether *value* is found in *array*.
VALUE rb_ary_length (VALUE array)	array.length	Returns the length of the array as a *Fixnum*. An alternative method for determining the length of an array is to use *RARRAY(array)->len*.
VALUE rb_ary_empty_p (VALUE array)	array.empty?	Returns *Qtrue* if the array length is zero, *Qfalse* otherwise. An alternative is to check the array length directly with *RARRAY(array)->len*.

Working with Hashes

To create a new hash, you can call the C function *rb_hash_new()*:

```
VALUE aHash;
aHash = rb_hash_new();
```

This function returns a reference to a new (empty) hash; this is equivalent to the Ruby statement:

```
aHash = {}
```

To add new (*key, value*) pairs to the hash, use *rb_hash_aset()*, for example:

```
VALUE aHash, aKey, aValue;

aHash = rb_hash_new();
aKey = rb_str_new2("Oscar");
aValue = INT2NUM(6);
rb_hash_aset(aHash, aKey, aValue);
```

To retrieve previously stored values from the hash, use *rb_hash_aref()*:

```
int age;

aValue = rb_hash_aref(aHash, aKey);
age = NUM2INT(aValue); /* should return 6 */
```

Note that *rb_hash_aref()* returns *Qnil* if the specified key is not found in the hash. Don't forget that arguments to *rb_hash_aset()* and *rb_hash_aref()* must have type *VALUE*. So, for example, if your hash uses string keys, this means that you'll need to first convert your C strings into Ruby strings before passing them into these functions:

```
VALUE aStringKey, aValue;
aStringKey = rb_str_new2("Some Key");
aValue = rb_hash_aref(aHash, aStringKey);
```

Working with C/C++ Data Wrappers

The last datatype that we'll look at is one that's especially useful for C/C++ extension writers. Ruby's C API provides a special internal *Data* type that you can use to "wrap" a pointer to a block of C/C++ memory in what looks like a Ruby class instance to the Ruby interpreter. You've already seen that most arguments and return values for Ruby C API are of type *VALUE*, and so the first function (actually, a macro) associated with wrapping C datatypes serves that purpose:

```
VALUE Data_Wrap_Struct(VALUE class,
                           void (*mark_func)(void *),
                           void (*free_func)(void *),
                           void *ptr);
```

The *Data_Wrap_Struct()* macro takes a pointer to already-allocated memory, and so a typical sequence for its use in your extension code might look like:

```
CompoundShape *ptr;
VALUE obj;

ptr = CreateCompoundShape();
obj = Data_Wrap_Struct(cCompoundShape,
                           CompoundShape_mark,
                           CompoundShape_free,
                           ptr);
```

We'll discuss the meaning of the *mark_func* and *free_func* arguments shortly. An alternate form of this macro first allocates a new instance of your C struct and then performs the same actions as *Data_Wrap_Struct()* would have:

```
VALUE Data_Make_Struct(VALUE class,
                           type,
                           void (*mark_func)(void *),
                           void (*free_func)(void *),
                           void *ptr);
```

With *Data_Make_Struct()*, the memory is allocated using Ruby's *ALLOC* macro. This macro does a little more work on your behalf than would calling *malloc()* directly; if memory is limited it invokes Ruby's Garbage Collector to attempt to free up some memory before calling *malloc()*. Be sure to eventually free this memory using *free()*.

The flip side of these two macros is the case that you want to extract a C/C++ pointer from a *Data* object. For this, Ruby provides the *Data_Get_Struct()* macro:

```
void Data_Get_Struct(VALUE obj,
                         type,
                         type *ptr);
```

And your C extension code might use it thus:

```
VALUE CompoundShape_area(VALUE self) {
    CompoundShape *ptr;
    Data_Get_Struct(self, CompoundShape, ptr);
    ...
}
```

Now let's return to the *mark_func* and *free_func* arguments that we saw for *Data_Wrap_Struct()* and *Data_Make_Struct()*. The purpose of these functions is to ensure that your wrapped objects properly interact with Ruby's Garbage Collector. Specifically, we're concerned with two things:

- First, ensuring that all of the Ruby objects known by (owning a reference to) your *Data* object(s) are marked as in-use by the Garbage Collector; and,

- Second, that when your *Data* object is finally garbage-collected, any dynamically-allocated memory associated with the underlying C data structures is also freed.

As you might have guessed by now, Ruby can't handle either of these tasks without your help. Therefore, every time you use *Data_Wrap_Struct()* or *Data_Make_Struct()* to create a *Data* object, you can pass in pointers to C functions to handle the "mark" and "free" phases of the Garbage Collector. If the *Data* object doesn't hold any references to other Ruby objects, you can pass *NULL* for the *mark_func* argument. Similarly, if there's some reason not to free the memory associated with the *Data* object, you can pass *NULL* for the *free_func* argument.

As an example, let's consider a *CompoundShape* class (implemented as a C extension) whose member data includes an array of other *Shape* objects:

```
typedef struct CompoundShape {
    int nshapes;
    VALUE *shapes;
} CompoundShape;
```

A likely interface for this class will include one or more methods that return references to the shapes making up this *CompoundShape*. But a potential problem arises if your Ruby code gets hold of one of these references and later discards it:

```
cshape = CompoundShape.new(Circle.new(0.0, 0.0, 3.0),
                           Rectangle.new(0.5, 0.5, 4.0, 5.0))
totalArea = 0.0
cshape.each { |shape|
  totalArea += shape.area
}
```

The *each* iterator method for this *CompoundShape* class serves up references to its constituent *Shape* objects. On the first pass through the code block, *shape* will be assigned a reference to the *Circle* object we passed into *CompoundShape.new*. On the second pass, *shape* is assigned a reference to the *Rectangle* object. As far as the Ruby interpreter knows, there are no other outstanding references to the *Circle* that *shape* pointed to on the first pass; what's to stop the Garbage Collector from destroying that object?

This is the purpose for the "mark" function we've learned about. Since *CompoundShape* does in fact "know" about that *Circle* and *Rectangle*, it has the responsibility for informing the Ruby interpreter of that fact. You can do this by calling the *rb_gc_mark()* function in your "mark" function, passing in a *VALUE* that refers to the known object:

```
void CompoundShape_mark(void *ptr) {
    CompoundShape *cshape;
    int i;
    cshape = (CompoundShape *) ptr;
    for (i = 0; i < cshape->nshapes; i++)
        rb_gc_mark(cshape->shapes[i]);
}
```

The other issue to consider is what happens when a *CompoundShape* is itself garbage-collected. Ruby will take care of freeing the Ruby interpreter-side data structures associated with the *Data* object, but it can't automatically free the memory used by *CompoundShape*. There's no way for Ruby to know, for example, that there's an array of shapes to worry about, and this is why we'd also want to provide a "free" function:

```
void CompoundShape_free(void *ptr) {
    CompoundShape *cshape = (CompoundShape *) ptr;
    free((void *) cshape->shapes);
    free((void *) cshape);
}
```

At first glance, something might look wrong with this function. It's true that
we freed the *CompoundShape*'s *shapes* array, but what's going to happen to the
individual shapes that its elements pointed to? To be sure, the issues of object
ownership in Ruby are very tricky and require careful consideration. Your first
instinct might have been to write *CompoundShape_free()* like so:

```
void CompoundShape_free(void *ptr) {
    CompoundShape *cshape;
    int i;
    cshape = (CompoundShape *) ptr;
    for (i = 0; i < cshape->nshapes; i++) {
        Shape *s;
        Data_Get_Struct(cshape->shapes[i], Shape, s);
        free((void *) s); /* Don't do this! */
    }
    free((void *) cshape->shapes);
    free((void *) cshape);
}
```

After all, in the "mark" phase we took the trouble to loop over all the shapes
and mark them. Doesn't it make sense to do something parallel for the "free"
phase? Well, in this case the answer is no. We've already established that at least
some methods in *CompoundShape*'s interface return references to its constituent
shapes, such as:

```
thirdShape = cshape.getShape(2)
```

For argument's sake, let's assume that *thirdShape*'s scope is such that it "out-
lives" *cshape*. Since *thirdShape* still holds a reference to one of the shapes making
up a *CompoundShape*, we definitely don't want to destroy the C data backing up
that shape. As any experienced C programmer can testify, all kinds of very bad
things can happen when you try to use pointers to memory that's already been
freed.

This still begs the question: How is the data wrapped by the *Shape* for *thirdShape* ever going to be accounted for? But you already know the answer to that question, don't you? It's handled by the "free" function for that shape's *Data* object, for example:

```
void Rectangle_free(void *ptr) {
    free(ptr);
}
```

To properly associate this "free" function with the *Rectangle* instances that you create, you'd want to pass *Rectangle_free()* in as the third argument to *Data_Wrap_Struct()*, for example:

```
Rectangle *rect;
VALUE obj;

rect = CreateRectangle();
obj = Data_Wrap_Struct(cRectangle,
                       Rectangle_mark,
                       Rectangle_free,
                       rect);
```

When *thirdShape* finally goes out of scope, or is assigned a reference to some other object, the Ruby garbage collector should soon discover that there are no other references to that *Shape*; remember, we're assuming that this particular object has outlived the *CompoundShape* it was originally a part of. Since *Rectangle_free()* is registered as the "free" function for this *Rectangle*, the memory that was dynamically allocated from your C extension should get freed as well.

Implementing Methods

Now that we've seen how to work with some of Ruby's built-in datatypes, we can return to the *Shapes* module example and see how to actually implement the instance methods for the *Circle*, *Rectangle*, and *Triangle* classes. Recall that we registered both the *initialize* and *area* methods for each of these classes using the C function *rb_define_method()*, and two of the arguments passed to that function were a pointer to the C function that implements the Ruby method and the number of arguments expected by that Ruby method. We'll start with the easiest function, *Rectangle_area()*; it should calculate the area of the *Rectangle* instance and return the result as a *Float*:

```
VALUE Rectangle_area(VALUE self) {
    VALUE width, height;
    double doubleWidth, doubleHeight, doubleResult;

    width = rb_iv_get(self, "@width");
    height = rb_iv_get(self, "@height");
    doubleWidth = NUM2DBL(width);
    doubleHeight = NUM2DBL(height);
    doubleResult = doubleWidth*doubleHeight;
    return rb_float_new(doubleResult);
}
```

The first discrepancy you'll probably notice is that even though the corresponding Ruby instance method (*Rectangle#area*) doesn't take any arguments, this C function takes one. For any instance method, you should always write the corresponding C function assuming that the number of arguments will be one more than is required to call it from your Ruby code, and the very first argument passed will be a reference to the instance itself (Ruby's *self*). By convention, the C variable is usually named *self*, but that's up to you.

Since the rectangle's area is computed by multiplying its width by its height, the first step is to determine this rectangle's width and height. Let's assume that those two quantities are stored in the instance variables *@width* and *@height*. We can use the C API function *rb_iv_get()* to retrieve the current values of those instance variables:

```
width = rb_iv_get(self, "@width");
height = rb_iv_get(self, "@height");
```

The first important thing to note here is that *rb_iv_get()* returns a *VALUE*, which, as we said earlier, serves as a reference to some Ruby object. Because we're the extension writers, we can trust that the type of both these instance variables is *Float*, but in some cases you may want to test the types to be sure. The other important thing to note is that because these are instance variables we need to be sure to include the "@" sign in front of the variables' names; if we had instead written this:

```
width = rb_iv_get(self, "width");
```

the call would fail. Now that we've got the current rectangle width and height as *Float*s, we need to convert it to C *double*s so that we can multiply the two dimensions together:

```
doubleWidth = NUM2DBL(width);

doubleHeight = NUM2DBL(height);
```

The *NUM2DBL* macro takes a *VALUE* which should be a reference to some kind of *Numeric* object, and returns its value as a C *double*. In our case we expect the *VALUE* to be a reference to a *Float*, but this code would also work if the *VALUE* referred to a *Fixnum* or *Bignum*. The final steps of this function compute the result and return it as a *Float*:

```
doubleResult = doubleWidth*doubleHeight;

return rb_float_new(doubleResult);
```

Believe it or not, that's all there is to it (for this simple function, anyway). Most of Ruby's C API is similarly lean and straightforward, and you can usually write C extension code in a manner similar to writing the corresponding Ruby code. Next, let's take a look at implementation for the *Rectangle* class' *initialize* method:

```
VALUE Rectangle_initialize(VALUE self, VALUE x, VALUE y,
                           VALUE width, VALUE height) {
    rb_iv_set(self, "@x", x);
    rb_iv_set(self, "@y", y);
    rb_iv_set(self, "@width", width);
    rb_iv_set(self, "@height", height);
    return self;
}
```

You'll recall that earlier, when we registered this function with a call to *rb_define_method()*, we specified that the *Rectangle#initialize* method has four arguments (*x*, *y*, *width*, and *height*). But since all Ruby instance methods include a reference to the object instance as the first argument, this C function actually has five arguments. We use the *rb_iv_set()* C API function to initialize these instance variables' values.

The *area* and *initialize* methods for the other two classes (*Circle* and *Triangle*) would follow similar patterns to those shown for the *Rectangle* class. The purpose of this quick run-through was to introduce the basics of writing a C extension for Ruby and some of the C API functions you'll use. In the next section, we'll look at a more complex example for a C extension module.

An Example: K-D Trees

A *k-d tree* (or *k*-dimensional tree) is a spatial data structure for representing points in *k*-dimensional space; it is a kind of generalization of regular binary search trees useful for many applications. In this section we'll consider two implementations of a k-d tree for Ruby. The first implementation is written entirely in Ruby, requires less than 100 lines of Ruby code, and is fairly easy to understand. The second implementation is written in C, as a Ruby extension module.

For the purposes of this example, we'll keep the k-d tree class interface very simple: we'll have an *insert* method, to insert a new point into the tree, and a *find* method to search the tree for a specific point. Following the standard k-d tree algorithms, Figure 10.1 shows a pseudocode version of the procedure we'll use to insert a new point into the k-d tree, and Figure 10.2 shows the procedure to then find a point.

Figure 10.1 Pseudocode for the K-D Tree *insert* Algorithm

```
procedure insert(point)
  depth = 0
  if (no root node yet)
    create the root node and store this point
  else
    initialize current node to root node
    begin
      determine which point coordinates to use as keys for current depth
      compare the new point's key to the next point's key
      if (new point's key > next point's key)
        set current to the root of the right subtree
      else
        set current to the root of the left subtree
      end
      depth = depth + 1
    end while (current node is not nil)
```

Continued

Figure 10.1 Continued

```
    if (new point's key > next point's key)

      create a new node for the right subtree

    else

      create a new node for the left subtree

    end

  end

end
```

Figure 10.2 Pseudocode for the K-D Tree *find* Algorithm

```
procedure find(current, point)

  if (current node is nil)

    return nil (no match found)

  else if (point stored at current node == search point)

    return current node

  else if (key value for point > key value at current node)

    search the right subtree recursively

  else

    search the left subtree recursively

  end

end
```

Ruby Implementation of the K-D Tree

Figure 10.3 shows the driver program we'll use to demonstrate the k-d tree implementations.

Figure 10.3 Driver Program for K-D TREE Modules

```
require 'kdtree'


MAX_POINTS = 1024


# Generate a list of random points
```

Continued

Figure 10.3 Continued

```ruby
points = Array.new(MAX_POINTS).map! { [rand, rand, rand] }


# Construct an empty tree
kdTree = KDTree::KDTree.new


# Insert each of the points into this k-d tree
startTime = Time.now
points.each do |point|
  kdTree.insert(point)
end
insertTime = 1000.0 * (Time.now - startTime)
puts("Time to insert #{MAX_POINTS} points: #{insertTime} ms")


# Compute average lookup time
startTime = Time.now
points.each do |point|
  kdTree.find(point)
end
avgTime =  1000.0 * (Time.now - startTime) / MAX_POINTS
puts("Average lookup time: #{avgTime} ms")
```

It begins by requiring the *kdtree* feature:

```ruby
require 'kdtree'
```

Note that we didn't specify a ".*rb*" extension for the feature file name; this will allow us to later replace the original Ruby implementation of the *KDTree* module with a C extension module of the same name. Next, we define a constant *MAX_POINTS* to represent the number of points that will be inserted into the tree and then generate an array containing *MAX_POINTS* randomly located points:

```ruby
MAX_POINTS = 1024


# Generate a list of random points
points = Array.new(MAX_POINTS).map! { [rand, rand, rand] }
```

We're using Ruby arrays (of length 3) to store the three-dimensional point coordinates. The built-in *rand* function generates pseudo-random numbers, which is good enough for the purposes of this demonstration. For a real application, the point coordinates would probably be read from some external data source. After acquiring the point coordinates, we proceed to construct a new k-d tree instance and then insert each of the points into the tree:

```
# Construct an empty tree
kdTree = KDTree::KDTree.new


# Insert each of the points into this k-d tree
startTime = Time.now
points.each do |point|
  kdTree.insert(point)
end
insertTime = 1000.0 * (Time.now - startTime)
puts("Time to insert #{MAX_POINTS} points: #{insertTime} ms")
```

In order to compare the performance of the Ruby k-d tree implementation to that of the C implementation, we'll first measure the time required to insert all of the points into the tree. Ruby's standard library provides the *Time* class, which we make use of here; the *Time.now* singleton method returns a *Time* instance for the current system time (in seconds), and so we can compute the difference between system times before and after inserting the points. An even more significant measure of our k-d tree's performance is the average time required to find a point in the tree, and so we'll measure that next:

```
# Compute average lookup time
startTime = Time.now
points.each do |point|
  kdTree.find(point)
end
avgTime = 1000.0 * (Time.now - startTime) / MAX_POINTS
puts("Average lookup time: #{avgTime} ms")
```

Now we'll move on to the Ruby implementation of the k-d tree, shown in its entirety in Figure 10.4.

Figure 10.4 Ruby Implementation of the K-D Tree Module

```ruby
module KDTree
  class KDNode
    attr_reader :point
    attr_accessor :left, :right

    def initialize(point)
      @point, @left, @right = point, nil, nil
    end
  end

  class KDTree
    def initialize
      @root = nil
    end

    # Insert a new point into the tree
    def insert(point)
      depth = 0
      if @root.nil?
        @root = KDNode.new(point)
      else
        curNode = @root
        begin
          tmpNode = curNode
          discriminator = depth % point.length
          ordinate1 = point[discriminator]
          ordinate2 = tmpNode.point[discriminator]
          if ordinate1 > ordinate2
            curNode = tmpNode.right
          else
            curNode = tmpNode.left
          end
          depth += 1
        end while (curNode != nil)
```

Continued

Figure 10.4 Continued

```ruby
        if ordinate1 > ordinate2
          tmpNode.right = KDNode.new(point)
        else
          tmpNode.left = KDNode.new(point)
        end
      end
    end

  def distance(pt1, pt2)
    r2 = 0.0
    pt1.each_index { |i| r2 += (pt2[i] - pt1[i])**2 }
    Math.sqrt(r2)
  end

  def find2(root, depth, point, eps)
    d = depth % point.length
    if root.nil?
      nil
    elsif (distance(point, root.point) < eps)
      root
    elsif (point[d] > root.point[d])
      find2(root.right, depth+1, point, eps)
    else
      find2(root.left, depth+1, point, eps)
    end
  end

  def find(point, eps=1.0e-6)
    find2(@root, 0, point, eps)
  end
 end
end
```

For this implementation, we'll define two classes, *KDNode* and *KDTree*. The *KDNode* class describes a single node in the tree, and its definition is straightforward:

```
class KDNode
  attr_reader :point
  attr_accessor :left, :right

  def initialize(point)
    @point, @left, @right = point, nil, nil
  end
end
```

Here, *point* is the array of point coordinates and *left* and *right* are "pointers" to the left and right child nodes for this tree node. The *KDTree* class holds a reference to the root of the tree and provides methods for inserting a node into the tree (*insert*) and searching the tree for a point (*find*). The initialize method for our *KDTree* class just initializes the root node (an instance variable, which we're calling *@root*) to *nil*:

```
class KDTree
  def initialize
    @root = nil
  end
```

The *insert* method for *KDTree* more or less mirrors our previous pseudo-code description; its single input argument is an array (*point*) containing the point coordinates:

```
# Insert a new point into the tree
def insert(point)
  depth = 0
  if @root.nil?
    @root = KDNode.new(point)
  else
    curNode = @root
    begin
      tmpNode = curNode
      discriminator = depth % point.length
```

```
      ordinate1 = point[discriminator]
      ordinate2 = tmpNode.point[discriminator]
      if ordinate1 > ordinate2
        curNode = tmpNode.right
      else
        curNode = tmpNode.left
      end
      depth += 1
    end while (curNode != nil)


    if ordinate1 > ordinate2
      tmpNode.right = KDNode.new(point)
    else
      tmpNode.left = KDNode.new(point)
    end
  end
end
```

The last method we'll show for the Ruby implementation of *KDTree* is the *find* method. The public interface to this function takes a single input argument, an array containing the point coordinates. Under the hood, it uses two additional helper functions: *distance*, to compute the distance between two points, and *find2*, which calls itself recursively to search through the tree for the desired point:

```
# Compute the Euclidean distance between two points
def distance(pt1, pt2)
  r2 = 0.0
  pt1.each_index { |i| r2 += (pt2[i] - pt1[i])**2 }
  Math.sqrt(r2)
end


def find2(root, depth, point, eps)
  d = depth % point.length
  if root.nil?
```

```
      nil
    elsif (distance(point, root.point) < eps)
      root
    elsif (point[d] > root.point[d])
      find2(root.right, depth+1, point, eps)
    else
      find2(root.left, depth+1, point, eps)
    end
  end
end


def find(point, eps=1.0e-6)
  find2(@root, 0, point, eps)
end
```

Note that *find* (and *find2*) include an *eps* argument that specifies the tolerance used in comparing two points. It's rarely useful to compare floating-point values directly and so we instead compute the distance between the current point and the point we're searching for. If the distance between these two points is sufficiently small (less than *eps*) we assume that we've found a match.

C Implementation of the K-D Tree

Next, we'll take a look at a C implementation for the k-d tree (see Figure 10.5). Just like the Ruby implementation, we'll make use of data structures to represent both the tree itself and nodes in the tree. To simplify the implementation, however, we're going to make some assumptions about the tree data:

- The tree dimensionality (that is, the *k* value) is fixed at 3. A more general implementation of this C extension module could support arbitrary dimensionality, but we're trying to keep it simple here.

- The point coordinates are stored internally as C *double* arrays. For the Ruby implementation, the coordinates *could* be any arbitrary *Numeric* type.

- References to tree nodes that are returned by the tree's *find* method are only "borrowed" references, and they become invalid once the tree is garbage-collected.

Figure 10.5 C Implementation for the K-D Tree Module

```
/**
 * C implementation of k-d Tree for Ruby.
 */

#include <stdlib.h>
#include <math.h>

#include "ruby.h"

/* We're only interested in 3-D */
#define DIMENSIONS 3

/* A node in the K-D tree */
typedef struct KDNode {
    double point[DIMENSIONS];
    struct KDNode *left;
    struct KDNode *right;
} KDNode;

/* Each tree has a root node */
typedef struct KDTree {
    KDNode *root;
} KDTree;

static VALUE cKDNode;

/* Helper: returns a new node */
KDNode* new_node(double point[DIMENSIONS])
{
    KDNode *p;
    int i;
```

Continued

Figure 10.5 Continued

```
    p = (KDNode *) malloc(sizeof(KDNode));
    for (i = 0; i < DIMENSIONS; i++)
        p->point[i] = point[i];
    p->left = NULL;
    p->right = NULL;
}


/* Helper: Converts a Ruby array of Floats to C array of doubles */
void array2point(VALUE array, double point[DIMENSIONS])
{
    int i;
    for (i = 0; i < DIMENSIONS; i++)
        point[i] = NUM2DBL(rb_ary_entry(array, i));
}


/* Helper: Converts a C array of doubles to Ruby array of Floats */
VALUE point2array(double point[DIMENSIONS])
{
    int i;
    VALUE array;

    array = rb_ary_new2(DIMENSIONS);
    for (i = 0; i < DIMENSIONS; i++)
        rb_ary_store(array, i, rb_float_new(point[i]));

    return array;
}


/* Helper: Compute the distance between two points */
double distance(double pt1[DIMENSIONS], double pt2[DIMENSIONS])
{
    int i;
```

Continued

Figure 10.5 Continued

```
    double r2 = 0.0;
    for (i = 0; i < DIMENSIONS; i++)
        r2 += pow(pt2[i] - pt1[i], 2.0);
    return sqrt(r2);
}


/* Free this node */
void node_free(KDNode *node)
{
    if (node->left) {
      node_free(node->left);
      node->left = NULL;
    }
    if (node->right) {
      node_free(node->right);
      node->right = NULL;
    }
    free((void *) node);
}


/* Free the tree */
void tree_free(KDTree *tree)
{
    if (tree->root) {
      node_free(tree->root);
      tree->root = NULL;
    }
    free((void *) tree);
}


/* Create a new tree */
VALUE kdtree_new(VALUE class)
```

Continued

Figure 10.5 Continued

```
{
    KDTree *tree = (KDTree *) malloc(sizeof(KDTree));
    tree->root = NULL;
    return Data_Wrap_Struct(class, 0, tree_free, tree);
}


/* Insert a point into the tree */
VALUE kdtree_insert(VALUE self, VALUE array)
{
    KDTree *tree;
    KDNode *curNode, *prevNode;
    int depth, discriminator;
    double point[DIMENSIONS];

    /* Extract pointer to the KDTree */
    Data_Get_Struct(self, KDTree, tree);

    /* Convert the Ruby array into a C array */
    array2point(array, point);

    if (tree->root == NULL) {
        tree->root = new_node(point);
    } else {
        curNode = tree->root;
        depth = 0;
        do {
            prevNode = curNode;
            discriminator = depth % DIMENSIONS;
            if (point[discriminator] > prevNode->point[discriminator])
                curNode = prevNode->right;
            else
                curNode = prevNode->left;
```

Continued

Figure 10.5 Continued

```
            depth++;
        } while (curNode != NULL);


        if (point[discriminator] > prevNode->point[discriminator])
            prevNode->right = new_node(point);
        else
            prevNode->left  = new_node(point);

    }
    return Qnil;

}


#define EPS 1.0e-6

VALUE kdtree_find2(KDNode *root, int depth, double point[DIMENSIONS])
{
    int d = depth % DIMENSIONS;
    if (root == NULL)
        return Qnil;
    else if (distance(root->point, point) < EPS)
        return Data_Wrap_Struct(cKDNode, 0, 0, root);
    else if (point[d] > root->point[d])
        return kdtree_find2(root->right, depth + 1, point);
    else
        return kdtree_find2(root->left, depth + 1, point);
}


VALUE kdtree_find(VALUE self, VALUE arr)
{
    KDTree *tree;
    double point[DIMENSIONS];

    /* Extract pointer to the KDTree */
```

Continued

Figure 10.5 Continued

```
    Data_Get_Struct(self, KDTree, tree);


    /* Convert the Ruby array to a C array */
    array2point(arr, point);


    /* Recursively call kdtree_find2() */
    return kdtree_find2(tree->root, 0, point);
}


#ifdef __cplusplus
extern "C"
#endif
void Init_kdtree()
{
    VALUE mKDTree;
    VALUE cKDTree;


    mKDTree = rb_define_module("KDTree");
    cKDTree = rb_define_class_under(mKDTree, "KDTree", rb_cObject);
    rb_define_singleton_method(cKDTree, "new", kdtree_new, 0);
    rb_define_method(cKDTree, "insert", kdtree_insert, 1);
    rb_define_method(cKDTree, "find", kdtree_find, 1);
    cKDNode = rb_define_class_under(mKDTree, "KDNode", rb_cObject);
}
```

The code begins by including two standard C header files as well as the Ruby header file, "ruby.h":

```
#include <stdlib.h>
#include <math.h>


#include "ruby.h"
```

Next we'll define a constant *DIMENSIONS* that specifies the dimensionality of the tree, and the two C structs that represent a tree node (*KDNode*) and the tree itself (*KDTree*). We'll also declare a global (static) constant to hold the Ruby *Class* object for our *KDNode* class; we'll need that to create new *KDNode* instances later:

```
/* We're only interested in 3-D */
#define DIMENSIONS 3

/* A node in the K-D tree */
typedef struct KDNode {
    double point[DIMENSIONS];
    struct KDNode *left;
    struct KDNode *right;
} KDNode;

/* Each tree has a root node */
typedef struct KDTree {
    KDNode *root;
} KDTree;

static VALUE cKDNode;
```

Next we'll define a few helper functions that are used later in the extension module's implementation. These functions aren't called directly from Ruby, but they make the code more readable and easier to maintain. The first function is a "constructor" for *KDNode* instances that allocates memory for a new *KDNode* and initializes its members:

```
KDNode* new_node(double point[DIMENSIONS])
{
    KDNode *p;
    int i;

    p = (KDNode *) malloc(sizeof(KDNode));
    for (i = 0; i < DIMENSIONS; i++)
        p->point[i] = point[i];
```

```
    p->left = NULL;
    p->right = NULL;
}
```

The next pair of helper functions convert between Ruby arrays of *Floats* and C arrays of *doubles*:

```
void array2point(VALUE array, double point[DIMENSIONS])
{
    int i;
    for (i = 0; i < DIMENSIONS; i++)
        point[i] = NUM2DBL(rb_ary_entry(array, i));
}


VALUE point2array(double point[DIMENSIONS])
{
    int i;
    VALUE array;

    array = rb_ary_new2(DIMENSIONS);
    for (i = 0; i < DIMENSIONS; i++)
        rb_ary_store(array, i, rb_float_new(point[i]));

    return array;
}
```

The last helper just computes the distance between two points represented by C *double* arrays:

```
double distance(double pt1[DIMENSIONS], double pt2[DIMENSIONS])
{
    int i;
    double r2 = 0.0;
    for (i = 0; i < DIMENSIONS; i++)
        r2 += pow(pt2[i] - pt1[i], 2.0);
    return sqrt(r2);
}
```

Now, before getting to the core of the implementation, let's jump ahead and see the module initialization function. Since the feature name (the file name used in the *require* statement) is "kdtree," the initialization function's name should be *Init_kdtree()*. Its implementation follows:

```
#ifdef __cplusplus
extern "C"
#endif
void Init_kdtree()
{
    VALUE mKDTree;
    VALUE cKDTree;

    mKDTree = rb_define_module("KDTree");
    cKDTree = rb_define_class_under(mKDTree, "KDTree", rb_cObject);
    rb_define_singleton_method(cKDTree, "new", kdtree_new, 0);
    rb_define_method(cKDTree, "insert", kdtree_insert, 1);
    rb_define_method(cKDTree, "find", kdtree_find, 1);
    cKDNode = rb_define_class_under(mKDTree, "KDNode", rb_cObject);
}
```

From our experience with the previous *Shapes* module example, we can see that we're going to need to provide C implementations for three functions (*kdtree_new()*, *kdtree_insert()* and *kdtree_find()*). We'll start with the *kdtree_new()* function:

```
/* Create a new tree */
VALUE kdtree_new(VALUE class)
{
    KDTree *tree = (KDTree *) malloc(sizeof(KDTree));
    tree->root = NULL;
    return Data_Wrap_Struct(class, 0, tree_free, tree);
}
```

Because this is a singleton method, the first argument is a reference to the *KDTree* class object (which is itself an instance of the *Class* class). As discussed previously, we're using a Ruby *Data* object (created by *Data_Wrap_Struct*) that "wraps" around a C struct instance but looks like a Ruby *KDTree* instance to the Ruby interpreter.

This example illustrates the purpose of the third argument to *Data_Wrap_Struct*, the "free" function. When the Ruby *KDTree* instance is garbage-collected we need to make sure that the memory allocated for this tree (and all of the tree nodes under it) is properly released. Many programmers assume that Ruby will take care of this for them, but it's not as simple as it may seem. One problem is that Ruby doesn't know how the memory was originally allocated. For example, while memory for C extensions is typically allocated using *malloc()* and subsequently released with *free()*, objects in C++ extensions will typically use *operator new()* and *delete*. Another problem is that the object being freed may itself be responsible for other dynamically-allocated memory which it needs to free before it can be released. This is especially true in C++ classes, where such "cleanup" code is placed in the class destructor, but here we see an example of it in our *KDTree* extension module: Before calling *free()* on the *KDTree* pointer, we need to recursively traverse the tree and free the memory occupied by its child nodes:

```c
/* Free this node */
void node_free(KDNode *node)
{
    if (node->left) {
      node_free(node->left);
      node->left = NULL;
    }
    if (node->right) {
      node_free(node->right);
      node->right = NULL;
    }
    free((void *) node);
}


/* Free the tree */
void tree_free(KDTree *tree)
{
    if (tree->root) {
      node_free(tree->root);
```

```
    tree->root = NULL;
  }
  free((void *) tree);
}
```

The last two functions we'll examine implement the majority of the tree's functionality. What you'll discover, however, is that the code for these functions looks remarkably similar to the corresponding Ruby implementations in terms of structure. In fact, the only Ruby-specific code for these functions comes in around the "edges," as we convert function arguments from Ruby types into C types and then convert results back from C to Ruby. Let's start with the *kdtree_insert()* function:

```
/* Insert a point into the tree */
VALUE kdtree_insert(VALUE self, VALUE array)
{
    KDTree *tree;
    KDNode *curNode, *prevNode;
    int depth, discriminator;
    double point[DIMENSIONS];

    /* Extract pointer to the KDTree */
    Data_Get_Struct(self, KDTree, tree);

    /* Convert the Ruby array into a C array */
    array2point(array, point);

    if (tree->root == NULL) {
        tree->root = new_node(point);
    } else {
        curNode = tree->root;
        depth = 0;
        do {
            prevNode = curNode;
            discriminator = depth % DIMENSIONS;
            if (point[discriminator] > prevNode->point[discriminator])
```

```
                curNode = prevNode->right;
        else
                curNode = prevNode->left;
        depth++;
    } while (curNode != NULL);


    if (point[discriminator] > prevNode->point[discriminator])
        prevNode->right = new_node(point);
    else
        prevNode->left  = new_node(point);
  }

  return Qnil;

}
```

Take a moment to observe how little Ruby's C API "gets in the way" of writing this function. Since the Ruby interface to our *kdtree_insert()* function takes one argument (an array of *Floats*) we know that this C function will have two arguments. Since the *KDTree* instance (*self*) is just a wrapper around a C *KDTree* struct, we extract the C struct pointer using the *Data_Get_Struct* macro:

```
KDTree *tree;

Data_Get_Struct(self, KDTree, tree);
```

Since we want to work with the point coordinates as a C array of *doubles* instead of a Ruby array of *Floats*, we use our previously defined helper function *array2point()* to convert that data:

```
double point[DIMENSIONS];

array2point(array, point);
```

The bulk of this function, which actually searches the tree for the correct insertion point and so on, doesn't include any Ruby API calls. As we'll see later when we compare the runtimes for the Ruby and C implementations of the k-d tree, these factors allow you to take advantage of both C's speed and Ruby's ease of use. Finally, since all Ruby methods must have a return value, *kdtree_insert()* ends by returning *Qnil* (the C constant for Ruby's *nil*).

The last function is *kdtree_find()*, and as with the Ruby implementation, it actually uses recursive calls to a helper function, *kdtree_find2()*, to do the dirty work:

```c
#define EPS 1.0e-6

VALUE kdtree_find2(KDNode *root, int depth, double point[DIMENSIONS])
{
    int d = depth % DIMENSIONS;
    if (root == NULL)
        return Qnil;
    else if (distance(root->point, point) < EPS)
        return Data_Wrap_Struct(cKDNode, 0, 0, root);
    else if (point [d] > root->point[d])
        return kdtree_find2(root->right, depth + 1, point);
    else
        return kdtree_find2(root->left, depth + 1, point);
}


 VALUE kdtree_find(VALUE self, VALUE arr)
{
    KDTree *tree;
    double point[DIMENSIONS];

    /* Extract pointer to the KDTree */
    Data_Get_Struct(self, KDTree, tree);

    /* Convert the Ruby array to a C array */
    array2point(arr, point);

    /* Recursively call kdtree_find2() */
    return kdtree_find2(tree->root, 0, point);
}
```

Compiling the C Implementation of the K-D Tree

In order to use this C implementation of the k-d tree, we need to compile it into a shared library that can be loaded at runtime by the Ruby interpreter. Ruby's standard library provides several modules to facilitate this, and we'll cover those in more detail in the "Configuring Extensions with Mkmf" section later in this chapter. For now, just type:

```
ruby -r mkmf -e "create_makefile('kdtree')"
```

at the shell prompt. This instructs Ruby to first require the standard *mkmf* module and then execute the statement:

```
create_makefile('kdtree')
```

The result of this should be a Makefile that you can use to build the extension module. To do that, type:

```
make
```

Assuming that the extension builds properly, you should now have a shared library in the current directory with a file name like "kdtree.so".

Comparing the Results

It's all well and good to see the Ruby and C implementations of a k-d tree side by side, but there's still no compelling argument for choosing the C version over the Ruby version. After all, compared to the Ruby version, the C version requires more lines of code, will be harder to understand and maintain, and must be compiled into a system-dependent shared library. One of the principal reasons for moving extension modules to C code is for performance reasons, and this example demonstrates that point.

Table 10.8 shows the time required to insert *n* points into the tree, as well as the average lookup time, for both the Ruby and C implementations of our k-d tree. We can see that for small numbers of points the performance difference between the two implementations is negligible, but for larger point sets that the C implementation is much faster (remember, lower times indicate "faster" for this case).

Table 10.8 Runtime Comparison of Ruby and C Implementations

Number of Points	Insertion Time (Ruby) (ms)	Insertion Time (C) (ms)	Average Lookup Time (Ruby) (ms)	Average Lookup Time (C) (ms)
1,024	120	0	0.538	0.0195
2,048	240	10	0.743	0.0195
4,096	571	30	1.122	0.0195
8,192	1242	50	1.816	0.0258
16,384	2884	150	3.713	0.0262

Using SWIG

The Simplified Wrapper and Interface Generator (SWIG) was developed by David Beazley (see www.swig.org). It is a code generation tool intended to help you develop scripting language interfaces to C/C++ code. Although the release version of SWIG (version 1.1) doesn't provide any support for Ruby, the development version (currently at release 1.3.9) does, and that's the version we'll be describing in this section. It must also be pointed out that the SWIG documentation has not yet been updated to reflect changes in the development version, and as a result does not specifically discuss the Ruby language module for SWIG. Despite this discrepancy, most of the information presented in the SWIG 1.1 documentation is still relevant for the development version and will take you a long way in using SWIG to develop extensions for Ruby.

A Simple SWIG Example in C

At the risk of duplicating information you'll also find in the SWIG documentation, we'll briefly look at what's involved in writing a SWIG interface file and then running SWIG to generate C source code for a Ruby extension module. Let's suppose that we have a C library with functions for use with investment-tracking applications. One function provided by this library retrieves the current stock price for a given ticker symbol:

```
double get_current_stock_price(const char *ticker_symbol);
```

We'd like to be able to call this function from Ruby code:

```
def get_prices(symbols)
  prices = {}
  symbols.each { |symbol|
    prices[symbol] = get_current_stock_price(symbol)
  }
  prices
end
```

We certainly already have the skills to write a C extension module by hand that will accomplish this task. It's not difficult, but it is tedious to write a module initialization function that defines this method, write the C function that wraps this function call, converting the arguments and return values appropriately, etc. If nothing else, you'll probably forget the argument lists for some of Ruby's C API functions and have to track those down.

SWIG takes all of this (mostly mechanical) work off of your hands and lets you focus on developing a well-thought-out interface to a C code library. Your job is to write a SWIG interface file that describes the classes, constants, and functions for which you want to generate wrapper code. For the example at hand, we might write this SWIG interface file:

```
%module invest

%{
#include "invest.h"
%}


double get_current_stock_price(const char *ticker_symbol);
```

As you can see, SWIG interface files consist of SWIG directives interspersed with C-like declarations. The *%module* directive specifies the module name for this Ruby module. It's also the name that will be used as the feature name (for the module initialization function) unless you override this default with the *–feature* command line option to SWIG. The code between the "%{" and "%}" pair is code that should be copied verbatim into the generated C extension code, before any of the SWIG-generated function "wrappers." The last line (the function declaration) directs SWIG to generate a wrapper function for the *get_current_stock_price()* function.

By convention, SWIG interface filenames end with an ".i" extension. Assuming the above interface file is named "invest.i," we'd run SWIG on it as follows:

```
$ swig -ruby invest.i
```

The *–ruby* command line option instructs SWIG to generate Ruby wrapper code. In many cases (especially when you've planned ahead), the same SWIG interface files can be used to generate wrapper code for any of the programming languages supported by SWIG. On such a small interface file, SWIG will finish its work quickly and produce a new C file named *invest_wrap.c*. Given what we already know about writing Ruby extension modules, let's take a look at some of the code SWIG generated. First, the module initialization function:

```
#ifdef __cplusplus
extern "C"
#endif
```

```
void Init_invest(void) {
    int i;

    mInvest = rb_define_module("Invest");
    _mSWIG = rb_define_module_under(mInvest, "SWIG");

    for (i = 0; swig_types_initial[i]; i++) {
        swig_types[i] = SWIG_TypeRegister(swig_types_initial[i]);
        SWIG_define_class(swig_types[i]);
    }

    rb_define_module_function(mInvest, "get_current_stock_price",
                                _wrap_get_current_stock_price, 1);
}
```

There are a few unfamiliar lines in this function, mostly related to SWIG's runtime type-checking system, but we can pick out the important bits. There's a call to *rb_define_module()* to define the "Invest" module and assign it to a global variable, *mInvest*; and there's a call to *rb_define_module_function()*, to register the *get_current_stock_price* module method. Let's see how SWIG did with the wrapper function for *get_current_stock_price()*:

```
static VALUE
_wrap_get_current_stock_price(VALUE self, VALUE varg0) {
    char *arg0 ;
    double result ;
    VALUE vresult = Qnil;

    arg0 = STR2CSTR(varg0);
    result = (double )get_current_stock_price((char const *)arg0);
    vresult = rb_float_new(result);
    return vresult;
}
```

As with the module initialization function, we probably could have written shorter and more legible code if we'd done it "by hand." But consider all the work that SWIG has done for you in generating this wrapper code:

- It determined the number of arguments required to call the function (in this case, one).

- It recognized that the input to this function (the ticker symbol) was a C string, and that the Ruby interface would therefore expect a Ruby *String* as its input.

- It selected the appropriate type-conversion macro (*STR2CSTR*) to convert the Ruby *String* into a C string needed to call the C function.

- It recognized that the return value was a C *double*, and therefore Ruby code would be expecting a *Float* as the return value.

- It selected the appropriate type-conversion function (*rb_float_new()*) to convert the C function's return value from a *double* into a *Float*.

Using SWIG With C++

Now we'll look at a slightly more involved example, this time using SWIG to generate extension module code for a C++ class. Figure 10.6 shows the declaration of a simple C++ class we'll use for this example.

Figure 10.6 Declaration for the *Point* class

```
class Point
{
public:
    double x
    double y;


public:
    // Constructor
    Point(double xpos = 0.0, double ypos = 0.0);
};
```

Figure 10.7 shows the SWIG interface file that we'll use for this module. Note that it is almost identical to the original C++ header file.

Figure 10.7 SWIG Interface File for the *Point* Module

```
%module point

%{
#include "point.h"
%}

class Point
{
public:
  double x;
  double y;

public:
  Point(double xpos = 0.0, double ypos = 0.0);
};
```

To generate the wrapper code corresponding to this SWIG interface file, we need to run SWIG with the appropriate command-line arguments:

```
swig -c++ -ruby point.i
```

The *-c++* option for SWIG tells the SWIG parser that the interface file includes C++ (and not C) syntax. It also instructs SWIG to use C++ code in the wrapper code it generates. After processing the information in the interface file, SWIG will generate a new C++ source code file named "point_wrap.cxx" in the current working directory. You can next create a platform-dependent Makefile for this extension by typing:

```
ruby -r mkmf -e "create_makefile('point')"
```

and then compile the code into a dynamically-loadable Ruby extension by typing:

```
make
```

Now let's load this extension into Ruby and test it out. Start the interactive Ruby shell (*irb*) and at the *irb* prompt, type:

```
require 'point'
```

to load the extension into the Ruby interpreter. The shell should respond *true* to indicate that the extension was successfully loaded. Next, create a *Point* instance with coordinates (3, 4) by typing:

```
p1 = Point::Point.new(3, 4)
```

Note that since the *Point* belongs to the *Point*, we need to use the fully qualified class name *Point::Point*. We can already see that SWIG generated a *new* singleton method for the *Point* class based on the C++ constructor declaration from the interface file. We can also take advantage of the constructor's default argument values to create a *Point* instance with coordinates (0, 0) by simply typing:

```
p2 = Point::Point.new
```

Now let's create a third *Point* instance with a different set of coordinates:

```
p3 = Point::Point.new(5, 6)
```

SWIG automatically generates "get" and "set" accessor methods for all of the publicly accessible fields in a class or struct. We can use these accessor methods to get and set the points' x and y coordinates. For example, at the *irb* prompt we could now type:

```
"Point 1 coordinates: (#{p1.x}, #{p1.y})"
```

and Ruby should respond with:

```
"Point 1 coordinates: (3.0, 4.0)"
```

Well, we've suddenly run out of fun things to do with our *Point* class. One especially useful feature of SWIG is its ability to augment the scripting language interface to your C/C++ code using the *%addmethods* directive. One simple example would be adding a *to_s* instance method for our *Point* class. It's a standard Ruby idiom for classes to implement a *to_s* method to provide a string representation of their contents, but the default implementation isn't too informative. With our current *Point* class, the *to_s* method returns an uninspiring string like "#<Point::Point:0xa0a0bf0>".

Figure 10.8 shows a modified version of our previous SWIG interface file. Note that this version adds a new section, set off by the SWIG *%addmethods* directive.

Figure 10.8 Modified SWIG Interface File for the Point Module

```
%module point

%{
#include "point.h"
%}

class Point
{
public:
   double x;
   double y;

public:
   Point(double xpos = 0.0, double ypos = 0.0);

   %addmethods {
     const char *to_s() const {
       static char str[64];
       sprintf(str, "(%lg, %lg)", self->x, self->y);
       return str;
     }
   }
};
```

After rerunning SWIG and recompiling the extension module code as before, we can try out this new *to_s* method in the irb shell by typing:

```
p1.to_s
```

to which Ruby should respond "(3, 4)". It's important to note that we haven't modified the original C++ code for the *Point* class at all. Within the C++ code for your added methods, you can use the *self* parameter to refer to the current class instance (similar to the normal C++ *this* pointer). For example, in this added *to_s* method, we use *self->x* and *self->y* to refer to the current point's x and y coordinates.

With creative uses of the *%addmethods* directive (and other SWIG features we won't cover here) you can do a lot to improve the utility of your Ruby extensions' interfaces. As one last example, let's add an instance method that allows us to add two points together. Figure 10.9 shows the further modified version of our SWIG interface file.

Figure 10.9 Further Modified SWIG Interface File for the *Point* Module

```
%module point

%{
#include "point.h"
%}

class Point
{
public:
  double x;
  double y;

public:
  Point(double xpos = 0.0, double ypos = 0.0);

  %addmethods {
    const char *to_s() const {
      static char str[64];
      sprintf(str, "(%lg, %lg)", self->x, self->y);
      return str;
    }

    Point __add__(const Point& aPoint) const {
      return Point(self->x + aPoint.x, self->y + aPoint.y);
    }
  }
};
```

For this case, we're using a special "magic" method named *__add__*. When SWIG sees this method name it internally renames it to "+", the standard Ruby message for addition. When you once again rebuild the extension and test it out in *irb*, you should now be able to create new *Point* instances by adding points together. For example, try typing:

```
(p1 + p3).to_s
```

and you should see "(8, 10)", the string representation of the *Point* created when you add *p1* and *p3* together.

Choosing SWIG

For very small extension modules (that is, those that only expose a handful of functions) using SWIG may be overkill. But for modules with large numbers of functions, constants, and classes, maintaining the C source code for the extension may become more work than you'd like. It becomes especially significant if you're trying to maintain "wrapper" code for additional programming languages (such as Python and Perl); every time a new function is added to the interface, you'll end up modifying multiple source code files. SWIG is an ideal development tool for these kinds of situations.

This introduction just scratches the surface of what's possible with SWIG. In particular, SWIG is able to parse C++ class declarations in SWIG interface files and generate wrapper code for large C++ class hierarchies. A number of complex extension modules in the Ruby Application Archive (RAA) use SWIG in their development and can provide you further examples of how to design SWIG interface files for your C and C++ code libraries.

Embedding Ruby

When you make use of Ruby extension modules it is usually the case that Ruby is "on top;" that is to say, the controlling process for the application is the Ruby interpreter. Another valuable technique is to instead embed the Ruby interpreter into a C/C++ application as an extension language. As with C extension modules, code that embeds the Ruby interpreter needs to include the standard "ruby.h" header file. Your application's executable will also need to link against the Ruby library.

It turns out that the premiere example for embedding Ruby is Ruby itself. The command-line Ruby interpreter that you use to run your Ruby programs is itself little more than a "skeleton" main program that embeds the Ruby interpreter library, does a little bit of setup, and then starts running your program. If you take a look at the "main.c" file from the Ruby source code distribution, you'll see that, after cutting through various platform dependencies, the *main()* function consists entirely of four function calls:

```
#include "ruby.h"

int
main(argc, argv, envp)
    int argc;
    char **argv, **envp;
{
#if defined(NT)
    NtInitialize(&argc, &argv);
#endif
#if defined(__MACOS__) && defined(__MWERKS__)
    argc = ccommand(&argv);
#endif

    ruby_init();
    ruby_options(argc, argv);
    ruby_run();
    return 0;
}
```

These are, more or less, the contents of *main()* from the Ruby 1.6.4 source distribution. After some platform-specific initialization rituals for Windows NT and MacOS, the Ruby interpreter is initialized by a call to the *ruby_init()* function. It's only necessary to call this function once, but it must be done before you make any other calls into the Ruby library. This is followed up by a call to *ruby_options()*, which scans the command-line arguments array for Ruby-specific switches (like "-w" to turn on warning messages). The final call for this example is to *ruby_run()*, which begins parsing and running the current Ruby program.

The following example demonstrates how to embed Ruby into an existing application. Shown in the example and illustrated in Figure 10.10 is a GUI application in C++ created with the GUI-builder "fluid" from Fast Light Tool Kit (see www.fltk.org). Clicking the **OK** button (function *cb_Ok()*) invokes a Ruby method *getStockQuote* which calls a SOAP service to get the stock quote of the symbol entered in the input field. The stock quote is then displayed in the output field.

Again we initialize the Ruby interpreter with a call to the *ruby_init()* function, but then we call *ruby_init_loadpath()* instead of *ruby_options()* to setup Ruby's load path, so that *rb_require()* in the next line can find the required Ruby source file.

```
// file: stock.cxx
#include <FL/Fl.H>
#include <FL/Fl_Window.H>
#include <FL/Fl_Input.H>
#include <FL/Fl_Output.H>
#include <FL/Fl_Button.H>
#include <FL/Fl_Return_Button.H>
#include <stdlib.h>
#include "ruby.h"


Fl_Input  *symbol=(Fl_Input *)0;
Fl_Output *quote=(Fl_Output *)0;

static void cb_Ok(Fl_Return_Button*, void*)
{
  VALUE sym, res;
  sym = rb_str_new2(symbol->value());
  res = rb_funcall2(rb_eval_string("StockQuote.new"),
                    rb_intern("getStockQuote"), 1, &sym);

  quote->value(res == Qnil ? "n/a" : STR2CSTR(res));
}

static void cb_Exit(Fl_Button*, void*)
{
  exit(0);
}

Fl_Window* make_window()
{
  Fl_Window* w;
  { Fl_Window* o = new Fl_Window(190, 128, "Stock Quote");
    w = o;
    symbol = new Fl_Input(60, 10, 120, 25, "Symbol:");
    quote = new Fl_Output(60, 45, 120, 25, "Quote:");
```

```
     { Fl_Return_Button* o = new Fl_Return_Button(100, 95,
                                                  80, 25, "Ok");
       o->callback((Fl_Callback*)cb_Ok);
     }
     { Fl_Button* o = new Fl_Button(10, 95, 80, 25,"Exit");
       o->callback((Fl_Callback*)cb_Exit);
     }
     o->end();
   }
   return w;
}


int main(int argc, char **argv)
{
   ruby_init();
   ruby_init_loadpath();
   rb_require("./stock.rb");

   make_window()->show(argc, argv);
   return Fl::run();
}
```

The Ruby source code file uses SOAP4R (see Chapter 5) and is shown below:

```
# file: stock.rb
require "soap/driver"
class StockQuote < SOAP::Driver
   URL = "http://soaptest.activestate.com:8080/PerlEx/soap.plex"
   NS  = "http://activestate.com/"
   ACT = "urn:activestate"

   def initialize
     super(nil, nil, NS, URL, nil, ACT)
     addMethod('StockQuoteInCountry', 'Symbol', 'Country')
   end
```

```
    def getStockQuote(symbol)
      StockQuoteInCountry(symbol, 'US') + "$"
    rescue Exception => err
      STDERR.puts err.inspect
    end
end
```

Finally we need to compile the application. We do this with the following Makefile (note that you possibly have to change some library or header paths to get it to work):

```
TARGET = stock
OBJS = stock.o
LIBS = -rdynamic -L/usr/local/lib/ruby/1.6/i386-linux \
       -L/usr/X11R6/lib -lfltk -lX11 -lruby -lcrypt -lm
CFLAGS = -O2 -fpic -I/usr/local/lib/ruby/1.6/i386-linux \
         -I/usr/X11R6/include
CC = cc


${TARGET}: ${OBJS}
        ${CC} -o $@ ${OBJS} ${LIBS}


clean:
        rm ${OBJS} ${TARGET}


.cxx.o:
        ${CC} -c -o $@ ${CFLAGS} $<
```

Figure 10.10 C++ GUI Application Which Embeds Ruby to Invoke a SOAP Service

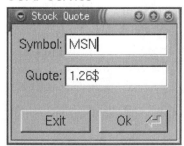

Configuring Extensions with Mkmf

After you've developed an extension module for Ruby, you may wish to distribute it to the Ruby community. One of the drawbacks of C extension modules, however, is that they exist as system-dependent shared libraries. The shared library required to use your extension module under the Linux operating system is going to be different from the shared library required under Windows. Thus, the standard practice is to just distribute your extension module as C source code, and let the end-user compile and install the shared library on his or her own system.

Of course, it's not that simple. Different versions of Ruby for different platforms are compiled using system-specific and compiler-specific settings. The Ruby library and header files may be installed under /usr/local on one user's Linux workstation, but under /home/ruby on another's; and you can't count on the user knowing where those files are in the first place. Because there are so many variables to consider when configuring the build and installation process for a C extension module, the standard Ruby library provides the *mkmf* (short for *make makefile*) module to help you do this.

Most C extension modules include a Ruby script, named extconf.rb by convention, that uses code from the *mkmf* module to detect system settings and automatically generate a Makefile for the shared library. You'll also want to write an extconf.rb for your extension modules as well, and it's not all that hard. The simplest extconf.rb script is only a few lines long:

```
require 'mkmf'
create_makefile('kdtree')
```

The *create_makefile* method is provided by the *mkmf* module, and it generates a Makefile that compiles all of the C source code files in the current directory, filling in the appropriate compiler settings, and links the resulting object files into a shared library. The string passed to *create_makefile* should be the feature name and thus the resulting shared library's file name, and the name used in your module's initialization function. For the two-line extconf.rb script shown above, *make* should end up building a shared library named "kdtree.so" and Ruby will expect to find an *Init_kdtree()* function somewhere in the mix.

For more complicated extension modules, the *mkmf* module provides a number of other methods to assist you in configuring the build. For example, if the extension module depends on the OpenGL library (named libGL.so on most Linux systems), you can use the *have_library* method to check for its presence:

```
if have_library("GL", "glBegin")
  # libGL.so was found; it will be added to the list
  # of libraries linked with this extension.
end
```

The *have_library* method depends on finding the library the standard library search path. If you need the option of searching specific directories (not necessarily on the standard library path), you might opt for the *find_library* method instead:

```
if find_library("GL", "glXCreateContext",
  "/usr/X11R6/lib", "/usr/openwin/lib", "/usr/local/lib")
  # libGL.so was found in either a standard library directory or
  # one of these three directories.
end
```

Here, the first two arguments are the same as those for *have_library*, but the remaining arguments are the names of non-standard directories in which to search. As with *have_library*, if the library is found and it exports the named function, it will be added to the list of libraries linked with the extension module's shared library.

A similar configuration issue is checking for the presence or absence of a function *somewhere* in the standard libraries. For example, some C libraries include a *strcasecmp()* function (for case-insensitive string comparisons) while others do not. In this case, you could use the *mkmf* module's *have_func* method:

```
if have_func("strcasecmp")
  # -DHAVE_STRCASECMP will be added to the
  # compiler flags in the Makefile
end
```

If your compiler requires function prototypes, and you know which header file contains the correct prototype, you can specify that header file name as the second argument to *have_func*:

```
if have_func("strcasecmp", "string.h")
  # as before
end
```

To check for the presence or absence of a specific header file, use the *have_header* method:

```
if have_header("png.h")
  # -DHAVE_PNG_H will be added to the compiler flags in the Makefile
end
```

Finally, your extconf.rb script can support command-line arguments of the form *--with-name-include=directory* and *--with-name-lib=directory* if you include a call to the *dir_config* method:

```
dir_config("foo")
```

This call in your extconf.rb script would result in a scan of the command-line arguments for the aforementioned options and modification of the include files and library path for the Makefile accordingly. For example, running the extconf.rb thus:

```
$ ruby extconf.rb --with-foo-include=/home/foo/include \
--with-fox-lib=/home/foo/lib
```

would cause */home/foo/include* to be added to the include files path, and */home/foo/lib* to be added to the library files path. In fact, for this particular case, you could shorten the command-line options to simply:

```
$ ruby extconf.rb --with-foo-dir=/home/foo
```

Although many Ruby extension modules consist of a single file, it is more likely that you'll want to distribute a package of files that includes source code for the extension module as well as supporting data files and scripts. Minero Aoki's setup.rb script provides one solution for distributing these kinds of Ruby packages. His system categorizes the files in a package into four basic groups: source code for C extension modules, pure Ruby code files, shared data files, and executable Ruby scripts.

To make use of the setup.rb script, you'll need to organize your extension module distribution into a specific directory structure; the details are provided in the documentation for setup.rb. Note that this system isn't a replacement for extconf.rb scripts and the *mkmf* module, but instead builds on them. In particular, each of the C extension modules in the package you're distributing will need to provide its own extconf.rb script.

For a link to the home page, and the latest version of setup.rb, check the RAA.

Summary

The ability to write Ruby extension modules in C or C++ truly provides application developers the best of both worlds: The rapid application development and quick turnaround of Ruby combined with the speed and universality of C/C++ creates opportunities for developing very powerful applications.

Ruby's C API offers a number of easy-to-understand functions for registering new classes, constants, and methods with the Ruby interpreter, as well as converting between C and Ruby datatypes. The API is so well-designed that you can typically write C code that looks similar to the corresponding Ruby code. A cookbook technique for developing new C/C++ extension modules was described in this chapter, along with several examples, and performance results for an advanced example.

SWIG is a must-have free software utility for Ruby extension module developers. While some consider SWIG to have a somewhat steep learning curve, you may find that the time you invest to learn SWIG will pay off in terms of maintenance and development costs, especially for larger extension modules.

It's an increasingly common need to enable end-users to customize applications using their own code "plug-ins". Microsoft made this feature somewhat popular by providing scripting capabilities for its Office applications suite, but they certainly weren't the first. Almost all the popular so-called "scripting" languages (including Ruby) provide lots of functionality for embedding in other applications as a scripting engine.

It's no fun to write a Ruby extension module that can't be used by a wide variety of people. At the same time, the wide variation in compilers and development environments and platforms makes it difficult for individual developers to come up with a consistent build and installation process. The Ruby standard library provides the useful *mkmf* module for this very purpose, and Ruby's developer has outlined the standard procedure for making use of this module's functionality: the extconf.rb script.

Solutions Fast Track

Writing C/C++ Extensions

☑ For various reasons, Ruby alone may not provide the speed or functionality required for your Ruby applications. When this is true, you can write extension modules in C or C++ that look like regular modules to the Ruby interpreter.

☑ Ruby's C API provides a wide variety of functions that assist extension writers in defining modules, classes, and constants, and converting back and forth between C and Ruby datatypes.

☑ It's a good development strategy to prototype new modules in pure Ruby. This approach allows you to work out practical interfaces, confirm that the basic algorithms are sound, and develop test cases. Once the Ruby implementation is solid, if performance is still an issue, you can consider moving the code to a C extension.

Using SWIG

☑ SWIG is an open-source, free software development tool that can greatly reduce the time required to develop Ruby interfaces to C and C++ code libraries.

☑ Although the code generated by SWIG is typically much longer and less readable than code you'd write by hand, it's worth the time saved.

Embedding Ruby

☑ Ruby makes a nice extension language for C or C++ applications that would benefit from end-user customization. Most users will appreciate the convenience of being able to extend the application's functionality by writing scripts in a high-level programming language like Ruby instead of a systems programming language like C.

Configuring Extensions with Mkmf

☑ Most Ruby extension modules intended for widespread use are distributed in source code form, for the user to compile and install locally on his or her workstation. By providing an extconf.rb script for your extension modules, you immediately lower the "acceptance" threshold since it facilitates a very familiar build and installation process.

☑ The standard Ruby library's *mkmf* module provides a number of useful methods for detecting system-specific resources (such as header files and libraries).

☑ For more complex Ruby code packages, third-party solutions like the setup.rb script can build on the *mkmf* module's functionality to provide an equally easy and familiar build and installation process.

Frequently Asked Questions

The following Frequently Asked Questions, answered by the authors of this book, are designed to both measure your understanding of the concepts presented in this chapter and to assist you with real-life implementation of these concepts. To have your questions about this chapter answered by the author, browse to **www.syngress.com/solutions** and click on the **"Ask the Author"** form.

Q: I've compiled a simple Ruby extension for use with the Microsoft Visual C++ build of Ruby, but the program crashes when I try to import and use the extension. I don't think I've made any programming errors, so what else could be the problem?

A: If you're using a Makefile generated by running an *extconf.rb* script (as described in this chapter), the correct compiler and linker options should have been written into that Makefile. If you have instead written your own Makefile, you may have omitted some important flags. First of all, be sure to define the NT and IMPORT symbols for the C preprocessor when compiling the extension source code; you can do this by passing the /DNT and /DIMPORT flags to the compiler. You'll also need to tell the compiler to compile your code to use the "multithreaded DLL" version of the C and C++ runtime libraries; you can do this by passing the /MD flag to the compiler.

Q: I'm getting some unusual compiler errors when trying to compile my C/C++ extension code. For example, when my extension code calls the Ruby function *rb_gc_mark()* the compiler stops with an error message that includes the text "too many arguments to function rb_gc_mark()." I am sure that I'm calling this function with the correct number of arguments, so what is wrong?

A: A large number of functions declared in the Ruby header files ("ruby.h" and others) use older, non-ANSI style C function declarations. If you're compiling your extension code with a C++ compiler, or a C compiler that doesn't allow non-ANSI declarations, you will definitely run into these kinds of errors. Matz has corrected these declarations in the Ruby 1.8 header files, but they will probably *not* be corrected for the Ruby 1.6 header files. There are two workarounds for dealing with this problem. The first is to study the documentation for your C/C++ compiler to see if it provides a command-line switch to support non-ANSI declarations. For example, versions 2.95 and earlier of GCC offered the *–fno-strict-prototype* option for this purpose. Another more drastic option is to actually patch your installation's Ruby header files to use ANSI C declarations for the offending function(s).

Index